German Order of Battle, 1944

German Order of Battle 1944

The Directory, Prepared by Allied Intelligence, of Regiments, Formations and Units of the German Armed Forces

Introduction by I. V. Hogg

Greenhill Books, London

Stackpole Books, Pennsylvania

This edition of *German Order of Battle, 1944*
first published 1994 by Greenhill Books, Lionel Leventhal Limited,
Park House, 1 Russell Gardens, London NW11 9NN
and
Stackpole Books, 5067 Ritter Road, Mechanicsburg, PA 17055, USA

British Library Cataloguing in Publication Data

German Order of Battle, 1944: Directory,
Prepared by Allied Intelligence, of
Regiments, Formations and Units of the
German Armed Forces. – New ed
940.54

ISBN 1–85367–170–3

Library of Congress Cataloging in Publication Data

German order of battle, 1944 : the directory / prepared by the Allied intelligence of regiments, formations and units of the German armed forces : introduction by I.V. Hogg.
p. cm.
Originally published : London : British War Office, 1944.
ISBN 1–85367–170–3 : $34.95
1. Germany—Armed Forces—Organization. 2. Germany—Armed Forces—History—World War, 1939–1945. 3. World War, 1939–1945—Germany.
UA710.G434 1994
950.54′1343—dc20 93-40525
CIP

Printed and bound in Great Britain by
Biddles of Guildford Ltd, Guildford, Surrey

Contents

Part J: German Forces in Action

Part K: Lists of Senior Officers

Part L: Tables of Formations and Units

Part M: Vocabulary and Abbreviations

Map: Germany—Wehrkreise

Introduction

Fifty years ago the Allied nations launched the greatest and most complex military operation ever seen (or ever likely to be seen – such a concentration of men and equipment would never survive today's technology), the invasion of the German occupied continent of Europe on the 6th of June 1944. This book delineates the German Army as it existed at that moment, and was the guide-book for the Allied planners.

Ever since warfare began, the question uppermost in a commander's mind has been that of the enemy's force: how large it is, how it is distributed, how the numbers are made up of cavalry, infantry, artillery, how it is fed and supplied. What the Duke of Wellington called 'Knowing what is over the other side of the hill'. Without such knowledge the commander is blind, basing his own actions purely upon guesswork. With such knowledge he can estimate what resistance he will find at any particular point, how long his enemy might be able to resist certain actions, and what manoeuvres his enemy might be expected to make.

In the earliest days it was a relatively simple problem, since the only real questions were how many troops the enemy had and where they were; warfare was a simple business of hand-to-hand fighting and numbers decided most of the action, tactical manoeuvre giving the more clever commander the decisive edge. Spies and outposts could provide much of this information, and once gathered it could be stored inside the commander's head. But as armies became more complex, so did the acquisition of information. The strength of the various arms, the number of guns and their size and performance, the quantity of ammunition, the amount and type of cavalry, the enemy's food supply, sources of water: all these and more had to be gathered and assessed, and gradually it all became too much for one brain to encompass, leading to the formation of staffs who could assess the information and present it to the commander in an assimilable form. By the nineteenth century most armies had 'intelligencers' whose task it was to acquire information, and it had become apparent by then that by the time battle was joined it was too late to start asking questions. This collection and assessment of information had to begin in peacetime so that a body of information upon all the armies likely to be future enemies was built up against the day of need.

Whatever their political masters may have thought, the British Army realised fairly quickly after 1934 that Germany was a likely enemy, and the collection of information on the rising Wehrmacht was put in hand. Open sources such as newspapers and magazines, less open sources such as holidaymakers in Germany who kept their eyes open, refugees and businessmen, and clandestine sources were all tapped and the individual details slowly fitted together until a coherent picture began to appear. Once war was joined, of course, other sources appeared. Captured prisoners, maps and documents yielded information, resistance forces within Europe reported what they saw and heard, aerial photography uncovered military activity, and, of course, the breaking of the Enigma code machine provided the sort of information which commanders throughout history had dreamed of.

The depth of detail revealed in this *Order of Battle* may surprise many people; but it would not be enough to know, for example, that the German infantry division contains thirty-six field howitzers, sixteen 15cm howitzers and eight 10cm guns. It is also necessary to know how these weapons are distributed and organised into units and sub-units, for only then will the counter-bombardment artillery know that it must locate three 10.5cm howitzer batteries, four troops of 15cm howitzers and two troops of 10cm guns, a total of nine different targets to be bombarded and neutralised before an attack begins. If the observation posts, aerial observers, photo interpreters and other sources have only located six artillery positions in the divisional area, then the attack will be surprised by three undetected groups of guns, possibly at a critical moment.

Similarly, the activities of support elements can provide information by inference: the sudden movement of airfield construction units to a particular area of the front could presage some strategic manoeuvre, whilst the movement of armoured repair facilities or engineer formations could signal the likely area of an attack. It was the movement of a German air signals unit to an obscure area of the Baltic which alerted the British to the testing of V2 missiles.

Similarly, details of individuals in the opposing force give valuable insight into the possible course of battle. Some commanders have tactical and strategic idiosyncracies which, when known, can often be used to gauge their likely reactions and future responses, and knowing who is in command of the opposing forces can give valuable insights into the likely course of a battle. And much the same goes for formations; one can often assess the likely worth of a unit by checking on its previous activities.

With all this in mind, it will by now be apparent that this volume represents years of work by hundreds of people, firstly to amass the information, then to assess and classify it, and finally to present it in a convenient form. This is one of a number of pamphlets and books produced by the British War Office which dealt with the German Army and its equipment and tactics. The *Order of Battle* is just that: the construction of the German Army from the lowest private to the Commander in Chief; other books dealt with equipment and operations, and most of them were periodically revised as and when sufficient new information had been acquired. This edition is of particular value, since, as already indicated, it represents the sum of Allied knowledge as it stood on the eve of the Invasion of Europe. There are gaps in the information; many of the ranks and personalities were to change before the war ended, many formations moved between commands, others were dissolved, and others formed, and as these changes were noted, so amendments were made. But this reprint has been made from the original edition, without the benefit of later amendment or hindsight, and with it the reader can see exactly what the Allied armies did or did not know about their adversaries in June 1944.

I.V. Hogg

PART A—THE GERMAN HIGH COMMAND

CONTENTS

A 2

(*a*) INTRODUCTION

Under the present German military system the basic principle is unity of command. Thus the Army, Navy and Air Force are regarded not as independent services but as branches of a single service, the Armed Forces (*die Wehrmacht*). The three Service ministries are subordinated to a single branch of the government known as the High Command of the Armed Forces (*das Oberkommando der Wehrmacht*), the head of which has a seat in the War Cabinet and represents the joint interests of the Armed Forces. This joint high command is responsible for the whole preparation of national defence in time of peace and for the general conduct of war; it appoints commanders for forces in the field wherever more than one of the three services is represented and, in general, sees to it that the activities of Army, Navy and Air Force are thoroughly co-ordinated.

Under the High Command of the Armed Forces (normally abbreviated *O.K.W.*), each service has its own high command: Army High Command (*Oberkommando des Heeres, O.K.H.*), Navy High Command (*Oberkommando der Kriegsmarine, O.K.M.*), and Air Force High Command (*Oberkommando der Luftwaffe, O.K.L.*); these are responsible for organising in detail, under the general direction of the O.K.W., the military, naval and air programmes and policies, and for carrying out the detailed study and development of the problems relating to their particular sphere of operations.

With this system it is a matter of course in a task force for units of one service to come under the immediate command of another, and all personnel may be transferred from one service to another (in the same or equivalent rank) whenever it is administratively convenient. In all cases, the O.K.W. alone decides what is most expedient in the national interest.

In time of war the O.K.W. as well as each of the service high commands is divided into two echelons. The advanced echelon (consisting of the C.-in-C., Chief of General Staff and the bulk of the General Staff itself) moves out to its war station, the location of which depends on the theatre of operations selected for main attention. The rear echelon, under a senior officer directly responsible to the C.-in-C., remains in Berlin to attend to all basic administrative matters, organisation, supply and training. This separation is made in order to relieve the advanced echelon of all non-operational concerns, thus leaving it free to concentrate on the operational control of the forces in the field.

(*b*) HIGH COMMAND OF THE ARMED FORCES (O.K.W.)

HITLER is the Supreme Commander of the Armed Forces (*Oberster Befehlshaber der Wehrmacht*). His deputy as such is Generalfeldmarschall Wilhelm KEITEL, Chief of the High Command of the Armed Forces (*Chef des Oberkommandos der Wehrmacht*), who is responsible for the smooth functioning of the High Command and for seeing that HITLER'S orders are carried out ; it is believed that he has comparatively little to do with the origination of policy.

In the O.K.W. the functions of a joint general staff are performed by what is known as the Armed Forces Operations Staff (*Wehrmachtführungsstab, W.F.St.*) ; the chief of this staff, Generaloberst Alfred JODL, is believed to be HITLER'S principal adviser on strategy and planning. Under JODL, the W.F.St. is divided into branches entrusted with special functions. The most important of these branches is the Joint Planning Staff, under Generalleutnant Walter WARLIMONT, which is responsible for all strategic and future plans. Another branch is solely concerned with inter-service communications, and maintains a special network of telephone, teleprinter and wireless links between Army, Navy and Air Force high commands and the principal subordinate headquarters.

The advanced echelon of the O.K.W., including the bulk of the Armed Forces Operations Staff, is stationed at HITLER'S headquarters in the field (known as the *Führerhauptquartier*), now probably near Rastenburg in East Prussia. The rear echelon in Berlin (in so far as it has not been evacuated to other towns less exposed to attack from the air) is divided into a number of branches or departments :—

(i) Joint intelligence (*Abwehr*), including both the collection of enemy intelligence and security (counter-intelligence), under Admiral CANARIS.

(ii) Public relations, including the issue of the regular joint communiques on the course of the war.

(iii) Military propaganda, including the control of the propaganda companies which accompany the forces in the field.

(iv) Welfare, including questions of pensions, bonuses, indemnities and rehabilitation.

(v) Prisoners of war, including relations with protecting powers and the International Red Cross.

(vi) Defence economics (*Wehrwirtschaft*), the over-all planning of production, the allocation of raw materials and the co-ordination of supply.

The personnel of the O.K.W. is drawn from all three services, but the Army naturally provides the largest element.

The name of a command, establishment or unit deriving from the O.K.W. is normally prefixed by *Wehrmacht-* or *Führungs-* to indicate its inter-service status. Thus, the commander in Holland, General der Flieger CHRISTIANSEN, has the title *Wehrmachtbefehlshaber*, and is directly responsible to the O.K.W., while General der Infanterie von FALKENHAUSEN, commanding in Belgium and Northern France, is *Militärbefehlshaber* and represents the Army only, coming immediately under Army Group West. Again, the special signals regiments which provide inter-service communications are called *Führungsnachrichtenregimenter*. The main branch in the rear echelon of the O.K.W. is known as the *Allgemeines Wehrmachtamt* (compare the corresponding branch in the rear echelon of the O.K.H., *Allgemeines Heeresamt*).

(*c*) HIGH COMMAND OF THE ARMY (O.K.H.)

Advanced Echelon O.K.H.

Since December, 1941, when von BRAUCHITSCH was dismissed as Commander in Chief of the Army (*Oberbefehlshaber des Heeres*) and HITLER took direct control of the Army, the advanced echelon of the O.K.H. has been virtually merged with that of the O.K.W. The functions of the two, however, have remained distinct, and there has been no personal union except at the top. KEITEL acts as HITLER'S deputy C.-in-C. in the latter's capacity as C. in C. Army as well as in his capacity as Supreme Commander of the Armed Forces.

The Army G.H.Q. includes the following :—

(1) The Commander in Chief of the Army, HITLER, with his deputy.

(2) The advanced echelon of the General Staff, under the Chief of Staff, General der Infanterie Kurt ZEITZLER, which is divided into two parts—one concerned with operations and intelligence, the other with administration and supply.

(*a*) *Generalquartiermeister* (abbreviated Gen Qu) is Deputy Chief of General Staff for all matters relating to the supply and administration of the armies in the field. He gives advice to the Commander in Chief and the Chief of Staff on all matters of supply, maintenance, and replacement of equipment, establishment and upkeep of transportation lines, and control of pay, rations and other administrative services. Since the beginning of the war the *Generalquartiermeister* has been General der Artillerie Eugen MÜLLER, a former O Qu III and Commandant of the Staff College (Kriegsakademie).

(*b*) *Oberquartiermeister*. The operations and intelligence part is divided into departments under Deputy Chiefs of General Staff, *Oberquartiermeister*, abbreviated O Qu.

O Qu I, the chief operations officer. This position is less important than one would suppose, since all important operational matters are handled by the Armed Forces Operations Staff under the O.K.W., to which the task force commanders are directly responsible.

O Qu II in charge of training within the Field Army (as distinct from training in the Replacement Training Army).

O Qu III in charge of organisation of the armies in the field, including the setting up of special staffs and definition of their functions.

O Qu IV in charge of operational intelligence.

O Qu V in charge of the historical section.

(3) Attached general officers of the various arms and services. These act as the principal advisers on the employment of troops of their respective arms and have authority down to the lowest echelons on various technical matters relating to these troops. They include the *General der Infanterie* (chief infantry officer), *General der Artillerie* (chief artillery officer), *Chef des Heeresnachrichtenwesens* (chief signals officer), *General der Pioniere* (chief engineer officer), *General der Nachschubtruppen* (chief supply troops officer), *General der Nebeltruppen* (chief chemical warfare officer), *Chef des Transportwesens* (chief transportation officer), and others.

(4) The forward echelon of the Army Personnel Branch.

(5) Liaison officers from the various bureaus in the Home Command.

(6) General Staff Corps. Army G.H.Q. is responsible for the operations of all army forces in the field, under the direction of the O.K.W. It exercises that control through Army Group or Army H.Q. not only by the normal chain of command, but also through the General Staff Corps.

The General Staff at G.H.Q. (with a rear echelon in Berlin) is drawn from the General Staff Corps, which consists of officers permanently transferred from their original arms of the service. This corps also supplies certain officers for the staffs of subordinate formations. The Chief of General Staff is the head of both the G.H.Q. General Staff and the whole corps of General Staff officers, so that such officers are responsible to him wherever they may be serving.

The number of General Staff Corps officers is strictly limited. An officer of the G.S.C. has authority over all other officers holding appointments on the same staff, even though some of them may be senior to him in rank. Thus, the staff of an army corps may be headed by a lieutenant-colonel, G.S.C., while the officers subordinated to him may include full colonels. The small number of G.S.C. officers at formation H.Q. may be shown best by some concrete instances. In November, 1941, there were only five at the H.Q. of ROMMEL'S Panzer Army of Africa ; the H.Q. of the subordinate Africa Corps included only two, and there were no more than five between the three German divisions of that corps.

Not only do G.S.C. officers look to the C.G.S. as the head of their corps, but they have the right, and in certain circumstances the duty, to report directly to him. In particular, the chief of staff of an army corps or any higher formation is in duty bound to report to the C.G.S. in writing any major difference of opinion between himself and his commander. In such a case the commander takes responsibility for the course of action decided upon, and the chief of staff complies to the best of his ability, but his opinion is on record at Army G.H.Q.

It follows that the C.G.S. at Army G.H.Q. is kept in very close touch with the whole course of the war. If he thinks it necessary, however, he may send a G.S.C. officer as special liaison officer to army group or army H.Q., to submit daily direct reports on the course of operations.

German commanders and chiefs of staff are expected to use their initiative. Individual responsibility for action is the German precept which officers of all ranks are required to observe. But by the system outlined above, Army G.H.Q. is enabled to keep in the closest touch with the course of operations, and so to direct them with full knowledge of the situation.

(*d*) **ARMY PERSONNEL BRANCH** (*Heerespersonalamt*)

This important bureau is independent of both the General Staff and the Home Command and comes directly under the Commander-in-Chief. Its chief, Generalleutnant Rudolf SCHMUNDT, is also the Chief Armed Forces Adjutant (*Chefadjutant der Wehrmacht*) to HITLER. The *Personalamt* (abbreviated PA or HPA) is responsible for the gazetting and promotion of all officers, and for all appointments except in the case of G.S.C. officers (whose appointments are made by the C.G.S. through the Central Department of the General Staff *Genstb.d.H./GZ*, which maintains one *Staffel* at Army G.H.Q.

and another in Berlin) though appointments of officers to various specialist posts are made on the nomination of the heads of the arms concerned.

(*e*) HOME COMMAND

All Army activities in the Home Command (*Heimatkriegsgebiet*) are controlled by a senior officer who was appointed for this purpose on mobilisation with the title Chief of Army Eqtiipment and Commander of the Replacement Training Army (*Chef der Heeresrüstung und Befehlshaber des Ersatzheeres*), abbreviated Ch H Rü u. BdE. This post has been held by Generaloberst Fritz FROMM since the beginning of the war ; his high rank indicates the importance of his position, and was achieved at the conclusion of the campaign in the West in 1940. It is his duty to administer the portion of the General Staff which remains behind in Berlin, to control all army units which are permanently or temporarily stationed in the Home Command and above all to supply the Field Army with all the equipment and trained personnel that it requires.

(1) General Army Branch (*Allgemeines Heeresamt*), abbreviated AHA. This includes separate sections to deal with draft-finding and supply, budgetary matters, the issuance of Army regulations, design of uniforms and insignia, and training. The latter function is supervised by the Chief of Training in the Replacement Training Army (*Chef des Ausbildungswesens im Ersatzheer*), General der Pioniere Walter KUNTZE, who is directly responsible to FROMM and operates through specialist directorates and the various inspectorates of arms and services (*Inspektion der Infanterie, Inspektion der Artillerie*, etc.) in the General Army Branch. The head of the AHA is General der Infanterie Friedrich OLBRICHT.

(2) Army Ordnance Branch (*Heeres Waffenamt*), abbreviated WaA. This office is responsible for the production and development of armaments and other equipment and for their storage in suitable depots for the use of the Field Army. It is divided into numerous sub-sections for the different categories of equipment (*Waffenrüstungsabteilungen* 1–10) and for their testing (*Waffenprüfungsabteilungen* 1–12). The Ordnance Branch is headed by General der Artillerie Emil LEEB.

(3) Army Administration Branch (*Heeresverwaltungsamt*). This branch includes sections concerned with the affairs of Armed Forces officials (*Wehrmachtbeamte*) and civilian employees of the Armed Forces, pay, rations, postal services, clothing, barracks and training grounds, and the administration of Army buildings, etc. It is headed by General der Artillerie OSTERKAMP.

The office formerly known as Chief of Mobile Troops (*Chef der Schnellen Truppen*) under FROMM'S command has been superseded by the *Generalinspekteur der Panzertruppen* responsible direct to HITLER. This position was created in March, 1943, for Generaloberst GUDERIAN, who was placed in complete control of the equipment, organisation, and training of tank, motorised, armoured infantry, armoured reconnaissance, anti-tank, and heavy assault gun units.

As will be seen in Part B below, the work of the rear echelon of the O.K.H. in Berlin is considerably lightened by the large degree of decentralisation to military district (*Wehrkreis*) H.Q.; policy is laid down, and plans are drawn up, in Berlin, but much of the detailed work is left to district H.Q.

As *Chef der Heeresrüstung*, FROMM is responsible for the provision and design of equipment of all kinds, both for the armies in the field and for all troops stationed within the area of the Home Command. As *Befehlshaber des Ersatzheeres* he is responsible for the training system described in Part B below, and in addition he commands such formations or units of the field army as may be sent to Germany to rest or re-form.

He is also partially responsible for certain areas outside Germany, in which training divisions are stationed or new units are being formed; but in such cases his responsibility is confined to equipping and training, and does not include operational control, which remains vested in the army group or army concerned.

PART B—THE BASIC STRUCTURE

CONTENTS

INTRODUCTION

Note.—The following equations are adopted throughout this description :—

Wehrkreis	Military District.
Wehrersatzbezirk	Area (sub-division of No. 1).
Wehrbezirk	Sub-Area (part of No. 2).
Division Nr. —	Depot Division (staff only).
Ersatz Regiment	Depot Regiment (staff only).
Ersatz (unit)	Depot Unit.
Ausbildungs Division ..	Training Division.
Ausbildungs Regiment ..	Training Regiment.
Ausbildungs (unit)	Training Unit.

The Germans aim at relieving commanders in the field of as much purely administrative work as possible, and at providing as regular as possible a flow of trained recruits and of supplies to the field army. The method which they have adopted is to separate the field army from the "Home Command" and to entrust the whole charge of training, draft-finding, supply and equipment to that command.

The German system is described in outline in the following paragraphs, *with special reference to the provision of recruits for the field army*. Such parts of the organisation as do not relate to that function are not referred to, but it may be noted that the provision of equipment (for example) is organised on similar lines.

(i) The District Organisation

Germany is divided into nineteen military districts. At the outbreak of war there were only fifteen, numbered I–XIII, XVII, XVIII ; two were added, XX, XXI after the Polish campaign, to include the Polish territory that had been held by Germany previous to the war of 1914–1918. In peace time, these districts contained the H.Q. and subordinate formations of the active Infantry Corps carrying the same Roman numeral (*e.g.*, II Infantry Corps has in peace time its H.Q. in Stettin, in II Military District). Two more districts, "Böhmen-Mähren," covering the Protectorate, and "General-Gouvernement," covering most of Poland not included in XX and XXI, have been added recently.

Before the war there were also four Motorised Corps—XIV, XV, XVI and XIX—(in effect, staffs to control the training of armoured and motorised formations) which had no corresponding military districts, but were served (as regards drafts and supplies) by the districts in which corps H.Q. or subordinate formations had their peace stations.

The commander of the Infantry Corps was also commander of the Military District; but because he was earmarked for taking his corps into the field, his chief concern in peace time was to maintain the fighting efficiency of the troops under his command. All administrative matters, therefore, were assigned to the charge of a Second-in-Command (*General z.b.V.*)—normally a general officer whose health or age renders him unsuited for further active service, while his seniority and experience qualify him for a post of great responsibility.

On mobilisation, the commander of the Infantry Corps departs with his corps to join the field army, and thereupon the Second-in-Command assumes direct command of the military district with the title of Deputy Corps Commander. The provision of trained drafts to all units of the field army mobilised in that district is one of his special concerns.

These units include the active units of the peace-time army which moved out with the active Infantry Corps and, in addition, all units formed on or after mobilisation in the military district in question. To illustrate this point: a military district which contained the peace stations of three divisions under one corps staff might mobilise as many as four corps staffs and twelve or fourteen divisions for the field army.

It may be noted that at present the average age of the Deputy Corps Commanders is about ten years above that of the known commanders of army corps in the field army.

(ii) Control of Replacement Training

The O.K.H. in Berlin retains close control over the whole system, but as much detail work as possible is decentralised. In general, policy is decided in Berlin, and the military districts are allowed a large measure of freedom to work out the plan decided upon.

All questions of supply, draft-finding and training are directed by the "Chief of Army Equipment and Commander of the Replacement Training Army," who is in effect both (*a*) head of the rear échelon of the High Command of the Army (the advanced échelon being at Army G.H.Q.), controlling all O.K.H. branches on behalf of the C.-in-C., and (*b*) specially concerned with the provisions of drafts and equipment for the field army.

Under him, training and draft-finding (including any reorganisation of formations temporarily withdrawn for that purpose from the field army) are looked after by the General Army Branch of the O.K.H., which issues such instructions as are necessary to the military districts.

The directives issued by the General Army Branch ensure uniformity of results; an additional assurance is provided by special staffs, under that branch, which keep close watch on any special programme (such as the conversion of infantry to motorised or armoured divisions), as well as by the Inspectors of the different arms, who supervise the training of units of those arms throughout Germany.

(iii) **Control of Man-power**

Within the military district the supervision of man-power (from civil life into the armed forces, within the armed forces and back to civil life) is entrusted to Inspectors of Recruiting (*Wehrersatzinspekteur*), each controlling an Area (*Wehrersatzbezirk*). For military districts the population of which is relatively small, one Area suffices, but others are sub-divided into two, three or (in one case) four Areas. The Inspector is a Major-General or Lieutenant-General, similar in his qualifications to the Deputy Corps Commander; he has the status and disciplinary authority of a divisional commander.*

Each Area is sub-divided into Sub-Areas (*Wehrbezirke*), which cover the area of a greater or lesser number of urban or rural local authorities, and are commanded by Lieut.-Colonels or Colonels, selected from the same category of officers whose suitability for active service in the field has ceased; they have the status of regiment commander (approximately that of a Brigadier).

As regards man-power, the duty of the Areas and Sub-Areas is to provide recruits to the depot units on such scale as may be

---

* He is not necessarily a soldier; some appointments of this type are given to senior officers of the German Navy and G.A.F., the man-power for which is provided by the same organisation.

called for by Berlin, and to select suitable officers and trained personnel to fill vacancies in the War Establishments of all units mobilised by the Military District concerned—in each case acting on instructions received from District H.Q.

An example will illustrate this point. When 33 Infantry Division was being transformed into 15 Panzer Division in XII Military District, during the autumn of 1940, its horses and the personnel which looked after them became spare, while the complete mechanisation of the units selected for conversion involved the need for many N.C.Os. with M.T. experience. Berlin laid down the use to be made of the bulk of the personnel and horses freed by the conversion (in this case the majority of the N.C.Os. and men concerned were transferred, with the horses, to IX Military District for incorporation in the newly formed 129 Infantry Division) ; but XII Military District disposed of the balance among its own units.

(iv) **Conscription System**

Universal compulsory military service has existed in Germany ever since the Napoleonic wars, with the exception of the period from 1918 to 1935. In March, 1935, conscription was reintroduced by law, with the period of active service fixed at one year ; this was extended to two years in August, 1936. The law provides that all males between the ages of 18 and 45 are subject to military service in peacetime ; in wartime these age limits may be extended and in addition all citizens of both sexes are liable to "service for the Fatherland."

Before the outbreak of war military service usually began at the age of 20. The first registration (*Musterung*), however, took place at the age of 18 and was accompanied by a preliminary medical examination and a classification according to degree of physical fitness as well as a provisional assignment to an arm or branch of the service (infantry, artillery, air force, navy, etc.). This procedure was carried out in small local registration areas (*Musterungsbezirke*) with the active collaboration of the district police and other local civil authorities. The recruits then awaited the next stage, their actual drafting (*Aushebung*), which involved a second physical examination, a definite assignment to an arm, and a decision regarding any request for deferment. If found fit (*tauglich*), they were then sent home pending their call to the colours (*Einberufung*) and their induction (*Einstellung*). Between their first registration and their induction the men ordinarily performed their required period of labour service (*Arbeitsdienst*).

All German men over 18 (except those considered totally unfit) are classified at any given time into the following categories :—

Aktiv Dienende—on active service.
Reserve I—fully trained, under 35 years of age.
Reserve II—partly trained, under 35.
Ersatzreserve I—untrained, not yet called up, under 35.
Ersatzreserve II—untrained, physically unfit, under 35.
Landwehr I—trained, between 35 and 45.
Landwehr II—untrained, between 35 and 45.
Landsturm I—trained, over 45.
Landsturm II—untrained, over 45.

In wartime the procedure for conscripting personnel for the German military forces is essentially the same as that outlined above for peacetime, except that it has been greatly accelerated and expanded. For example, the *Musterung* and *Aushebung* are now combined into a single operation. The usual age of induction has been lowered to 17, and older classes have also been called up. Members of the *Ersatzreserve II* and *Landwehr II* are subject to call, and occupational and other deferments are strictly limited.

The entire conscription system is organised under the General Army Branch (*AHA*), but its operation is highly decentralised through the corps areas, recruiting areas, and sub-areas down to the local recruiting districts (*Wehrmeldebezirke*). Navy and Air Force interests are represented by officers specially detailed to the Army recruiting organisation for this purpose.

(v) **Organisation of Replacement Training Army**

The basic principle is that every unit in the Field Army is affiliated for personnel replacement purposes with a specific unit of the Replacement Training Army located in its own original *Wehrkreis* and known as an *Ersatz* unit. The normal location of the *Ersatz* unit is the home station of the affiliated field unit, to which the soldiers expect ultimately to return for their discharge or for reassignment. For example, a soldier who is wounded and goes to a reserve hospital in the rear echelon will be sent, on leaving the hospital, to his affiliated *Ersatz* unit before being returned to the field.

Previous to the autumn of 1942, practically all training of recruits was done in Germany, although as early as autumn of 1939 certain depot units were transferred to Poland, in order to economise man-power by using recruits undergoing training to garrison an occupied territory, and this practice was extended to Denmark and Alsace-Lorraine from 1940 to 1942. Within the Military District, training was entrusted to Training Divisions, normally two to each Military District. At this time, however, a serious shortage in man-power and an increase of operational commitments necessitated the despatch of as many field-force divisions as possible from occupied countries where no operations were in progress, to the front line, and the garrisoning of the least dangerous areas of occupied countries by training formations and units.

In future, most training, except that of armoured and motorised troops, was to be done outside Germany, and this necessitated a drastic reorganisation of the Replacement Training Army. Over a period of about five months, beginning in September, 1942, the former Mobilisation and Training Divisions were reorganised in one of the two following ways :—

(*a*) Twenty were reorganised as purely *Training Divisions*, and moved into occupied countries.

(*b*) Nine were reorganised as *Depot Divisions*, and remained in Germany.

Both types have been added to since the original reorganisation.

Training Divisions, which are subordinated to Reserve Corps, also newly formed at the same time, have as their primary function the training of recruits, combined with a secondary role of maintaining order in occupied countries. They would also be used, as an extreme measure, as field-force divisions, in the event of the territory in which they are located becoming an operational zone. They have, therefore, been given a far greater cohesion of organisation and location than ever existed in the former Mobilisation and Training Divisions, by being organised broadly on the same lines as Field-Force Divisions. Their subordinate units are designated as "Training" Regiments and Units.

Depot Divisions, which are sub-divided into Depot Regiments, remain in Germany. They are no more than staffs, the term "Division" and "Regiment" merely indicating the status of their commanders. The Depot and equivalent Training Units, which appear to bear the same number, are very closely linked, and are apparently controlled by the same staff, since titles for "Ersatz- und Ausbildungsregimenter" (and "Bataillone"), *i.e.*, "Depot and Training Regiments" (and Battalions), are known for every arm of the service. This central staff (for example, on battalion level) will control :—

(*a*) The *Depot Battalion,* which will be located in the same town in Germany as the Depot and Training staff. This unit receives recruits drafted into the army, issues uniforms and personal papers, holds them for a short time until they are despatched to their Training units and holds the Convalescent Company. The Depot battalion stands in the same draft-finding and "record office" relation to the equivalent Training and Field Army units as the former Depot battalion did to the Field Army unit alone.

(*b*) The *Training Battalion,* which, except for those shown in (*c*) below, will generally be located outside Germany, and subordinated, for the purposes of training, administration, etc., to the Training regiment, Training division and Reserve corps.

(*c*) The *Training Battalion* inside Germany, *i.e.*, specialist troops, including certain types of engineers, whose size and number, and lack of adequate battalion commanders, has made it not worth while sending them to train outside Germany.

The commanders and subordinate officers of Depot divisions and units are drawn from the category of officers passed over for further service in the field.

It should be noted that the organisation of the Training Command, like most German systems, is not rigid, and affiliations may be changed if necessary. Thus, during the African campaign, III and XII Military Districts specialised in training troops for service in Africa, and a unit originally mobilised in another Military District had its affiliation transferred to a Depot unit in III or XII on its departure for Africa.

In the spring of 1943, the Germans extended the principle of combining training with garrison duties by sending motorised troops to train outside Germany, and now "Panzer" troops are doing the same thing.

Depot units are provided on a scale described in some detail in section (*a*).

(vi) **Summary**

It will be seen, therefore, that the German system involves decentralisation to Military Districts of a maximum of administrative detail, formations and units of the field army being administered by the appropriate Military Districts and not by the O.K.H. direct.

The provision of drafts and the training of recruits are arranged by the Military Districts ; the former through the Depot Divisions and Regiments, which are staffs only, having no function but to supervise the Depot units assigned to them ; the latter through the Reserve Corps, Reserve Divisions, and Training Regiments and units.

(*a*) DRAFT-FINDING

Introduction

The provision of trained drafts for divisions of the field army (in this context *Felddivisionen*) is organised through a system of depot staffs :—

Divisionen Nummer . . (*e.g.*, Div. Nr. 147) : Depot division—a staff responsible for collecting of recruits, issuing them with clothing, etc., drafting them to Training divisions and, if desirable, reassembling them on completion of training and forming drafts for the field army. The following staffs and units are subordinated :—

(i) *Infanterie-Ersatz-Regiment,* abbreviated Inf. Ers. Rgt. or J.E.R.—Infantry depot regiment—a staff controlling infantry depot units.

(ii) *Artillerie-Ersatz-Regiment,* abbreviated Art. Ers. Rgt. or A.E.R.—Artillery depot regiment, a staff controlling artillery depot units.

(iii) *Ersatz-Einheiten,* depot units, controlled, in the case of infantry by the depot regimental staffs (*see* following paragraphs)

Draft conducting and holding is the responsibility of the following formations and units :—

(i) *Marschbataillon z.b.V.*, abbreviated Marsch-Btl. z.b.V. : Draft-conducting battalion, a nucleus of officers and other ranks provided, as desired by the Training divisions or depot divisions, to conduct drafts to the zone of operations. Originally each such transfer unit was normally destined for a particular division and often carried the number of that division preceded by the roman numeral of the *Wehrkreis* are followed by a serial number. For example I/11/3 would be the third *Marschbataillon* raised in *Wehrkreis* I to replace personnel in 11 Division. Such battalions were usually attached to the rear echelon of the division in the field, and from there the personnel was filtered into the various divisional components as needed.

In many cases these units acquired a more permanent status as replacement pools for the divisions in the field and were renamed field reinforcement battalions (*Feldersatzbataillone*).

(ii) *Feldersatzbataillon,* abbreviated Feld-Ers.Btl.: First-line reinforcement battalion — a draft-holding battalion, stationed behind the line, which receives the drafts from the *Marschbataillon* and holds them until required by the division on whose establishment it is held. If casualties are heavy, and there is no period of waiting, the *Feldersatzbataillon* also becomes a draft-conducting battalion, and there were numerous cases in Tunisia and Sicily of *Feldersatzbataillone* and *Marschbataillone* being put into the line as fighting units.

(iii) *Feldausbildungs-Division,* abbreviated Fd. Ausb. Div.: Field training division—a staff responsible for administrating draft-holding units in the rear areas, and organising advanced training until they are required by the field army. Five—381, 382, 388, 390, 391—have been identified.

Notes on the main features of the system are given in the following paragraphs. English terms are used as far as possible, on the basis of the equations employed above.

(i) Depot Units : The Original Allotment

Every unit of the field army received drafts as necessary from a depot unit stationed in the military district in which it was raised; the depot unit carried the same number as the field army unit to which it supplied drafts. In general, the depot unit was one degree smaller than that in the field army (for each regiment a depot battalion or equivalent unit, and for each non-regimental battalion or equivalent unit a depot company); but there were two depot battalions for each regiment of the active (*i.e.*, peace-time standing) army, and a depot *battalion* in place of a *company* for each peace-time non-regimental battalion. This allotment of depot units may be made clearer by some concrete examples :—

Field Army units.	*Depot unit of peace-time*	*of newly-formed unit.*
26 Inf. Regt.	I/ and II/26 Inf.	
497 Inf. Regt.		497 Inf. Depot Bn.
19 Arty. Regt.	I/ and II/19 Arty.	
214 Arty. Regt.		214 Arty. Depot Bty.
14 A.Tk. Bn.	14 A.Tk. Depot Bn.	
157 Engineer Bn.		157 Engineer Depot Coy.

Specialist sub-units (such as infantry gun coys., infantry A.Tk. coys., mounted infantry platoons, etc.) were supplied with drafts on the basis of one depot sub-unit per division, carrying the divisional number, and serving the corresponding sub-units in each of its regiments: for example, in the case of 22 Inf. Div., 22 Inf. A.Tk. Depot Coy. provided drafts for the 14 (A.Tk.) Coys. of 16, 47 and 65 Inf. Regts.

All depot units serving the divisional infantry regiments were controlled by an infantry training regiment which carried the same number as the division: thus, 22 Inf. Training Regt. at Oldenburg controlled all depots units of 22 Inf. Div. Artillery training regiments were provided on a lower scale, one for each division of the peacetime army: thus, 22 Arty. Training Regt. controlled the training of drafts for 22 Inf. Div.

In general, at this stage, a depot unit of the same number served each unit of the field army, and the identification of either justified the assumption that the other existed; similarly, an infantry training regiment and an infantry division of the same number could be mutually inferred.*

(ii) **Subsequent Developments**

The above allotment has undergone substantial modifications, especially after completion of the maximum expansion programme (August 1939—January 1940), when the proportion of depot to field army units was reduced. Many of the original depot units were transferred bodily to the field army, receiving new numbers (161–164, 167–170, 181, 183, 196–198 and probably 199 Inf. Divs. were formed from such units); in consequence, there are now many infantry regiments without similarly numbered depot battalions, and one infantry training regiment will usually supply drafts to two or more divisions of the field army.

Again, in some cases infantry regiments of the field army have been disbanded or converted to Panzer Grenadier, but their original depot battalions still exist under numbers which now have no field-army counterpart; and a new series of infantry training regiments has recently been identified, carrying numbers in the series 601 and upwards, and so corresponding to no divisions of the field army.

The result of these changes has been to complicate the detailed study of the depot structure, but the following notes give a general picture of the system now in force.

---

* There were one or two exceptions: thus, 157 Inf. Training Regt. served 57 Inf. Div.

(iii) The Present Allotment

Panzer Divisions.—Drafts for the Panzer Grenadier regiments are controlled by a Panzer Grenadier depot regiment (*Panzer Grenadier Ersatz Regiment, Pz. Gren. E.R.*). As a result of the recent development in the Training Command and the decision to train Panzer troops outside Germany, war establishment titles have appeared for depot and training units of all types of unit (including artillery) found in a Panzer division, and Panzer divisions have been identified in occupied countries, leading to the conclusion that the former practice of training divisional units directly under normal training divisions or artillery training regiments has now stopped. There is still believed to be one Panzer Grenadier depot and training battalion for each pair of regiments, one armoured reconnaissance depot and training unit (*Panzer Aufklärungs Ersatz-und-Ausbildungs Abteilung*) for each pair of Panzer divisions, and also specialist depot and training companies under the training regiment. The following allotment of depot and training units to 5 and 11 Panzer Divisions of Wkr. VIII, though it may no longer be correct owing to the new organisation, is still valid for the purpose of giving an example of the working of the system as a whole :—

13 Pz. Gren. Depot and Training Bn. (serving 13 and 14 Pz. Gren. Regts. of 5 Pz. Div.),

110 Pz. Gren. Depot and Training Bn. (for 110 and 111 Pz. Gren. Regts. of 11 Pz. Div.),

55 Pz. Recce. Depot and Training Bn. (for 55 and 61 Pz. Recce. Bns.),

85 Sigs. Depot and Training Coy. and

85 Gun Depot and Training Coy. (for the specialist sub-units of 5 and 11 Pz. Gren. Bdes.).

Infantry Divisions.—One infantry training regiment may serve one or more field army divisions ; similarly, a depot and training unit is likely, in most cases, to provide drafts for two or more units of the field army.

In general, it is intended that depot and training units should be permanently affiliated to specific field army units (for example, a proportion of the officers of the depot or training unit will have seen service at the front with the field army unit, and convalescent soldiers are attached to a Convalescent Coy.—*Genesenden-Kompanie*—of the depot unit before returning to the field) but in times of stress the system becomes less rigid.

If very heavy casualties are sustained by forces in the field, the Training Command is called upon for larger drafts than can be provided without improvisation. In such cases, all the available men from each Wekrkreis are formed into draft-conducting battalions, which receive very high numbers (*e.g.*, 2021) or double numbers (*e.g.*, XIII/12—the twelfth battalion of a series provided by Wehrkreis XIII), and the men may be drafted from these battalions to whatever formation needs them most, even though its proper depot units are stationed in a different military district in Germany. In the last months of the North African campaign, when the demand for drafts far exceeded the supply, draft-conducting units were found bearing very low numbers preceded by "A" or "T" (*e.g.*, A3, T5), and these units were frequently put into the line exactly as they arrived, instead of being broken up and having their personnel allotted to different field army units.

Trained recruits arriving in small batches from the Home Command are sent to a *Frontsammelstelle* (Front Collecting Point), which distributes them to the formations or units where they are required.

(iv) **Recapitulation**

The essence of the German *Ersatz* system is the affiliation of every field unit with a specific *Ersatz* unit in its own *Wehrkreis*, to which its personnel will return in case of convalescence or discharge. Originally this *Ersatz* unit had the same number as the field unit, but this rule no longer applies generally.

A German recruit today is inducted into an *Ersatz* unit in the vicinity of his place of residence and is then sent almost at once to the training unit of the same number. This is likely to be part of a training division in occupied territory. After a period of training and occupational duties he will normally be sent, probably in a *Marschbataillon* with a large group of his fellows, to a field unit which is affiliated with his own original *Ersatz* unit, although he may go to almost any other field unit if circumstances so require.

A convalescent is sent back by the hospital to the affiliated *Ersatz* unit of his last field unit. There he is placed in a convalescent company to be restored to combat fitness. He is then despatched to the field, preferably to his own former unit otherwise probably to another unit affiliated with the *Ersatz* unit.

(b) MILITARY DISTRICTS (Wehrkreise)

A map showing the geographical divisions of Germany by *Wehrkreise* is appended to this volume.

In the following section are set out the essential facts concerning the military districts of Germany, *i.e.*, the commander, formations mobilised or maintained, geographical structure and basic training organisation. English terms are employed for convenience throughout, except in the case of area and sub-area H.Q., where place-names are given in their German form, since this will most commonly be encountered in documents. Where a more generally familiar form exists this follows in brackets and in italic type.

Wehrkreis I (H.Q. Königsberg)

East Prussia : Extended in March, 1939, to include the **Memel** area, in autumn 1939 the Zichenau (*Ciechanòw*) and **Sudauen** (*Suwalki*) areas, and in 1942 the Bialystok district.

Commander :—Gen. d. Art. Albert WODRIG (61).

C. of S. :—

Corps mobilised :—I and XXVI Inf.

Divisions mobilised :—24 Pz. (ex 1 Cav.) ; 1, 11, 21, 61, 161, 206, 217, 228 disbanded, 291, 311 disbanded, 340 Inf., 383 Inf. and 114 Jäg. (ex 714 Inf.).

Area H.Q. :—Königsberg: Genlt. RÜHLE v. LILIENSTERN (63).
Sub-areas :—Königsberg (Pr.) I–II, Tilsit, Gumbinnen, Treuburg, Bartenstein (Ostpr.), Braunsberg (Ostpr.).

Area H.Q. :—Allenstein.
Sub-areas :—Allenstein, Lötzen, Zichenau (*Ciechanòw*).

*Depot divisions :—
No. 401 Königsberg.
No. 461 Bialystok.

---

* From mid-1940 to mid-1941 most of the depot units from this military district were stationed in the Protectorate ; during that period Div. No. 141 was at Prag and Div. No. 151 at Budweis.

Depot regiments :—

(i) Infantry :— 1 Königsberg.
11 Allenstein.
21 Mohrungen.
61 Königsberg.
206 Gumbinnen.
217 Allenstein.
228 Lötzen.
607

(ii) Artillery :— 1 Insterburg.
11 Allenstein.

Training divisions :—141 Res.
151 Res.

Training areas :— Arys.
Stablack : Genmaj. DECKMANN (52).
Mielau.
Gilge (Engineers' Training Area).

Divisional staffs :—421 z.b.V., Zichenau.

Wehrkreis II (H.Q. Stettin)

Mecklenburg and Pomerania.

Commander :—Gen. d. Inf. Werner KIENITZ (59).

C. of S. :—

Corps mobilised :—II, LXV (L.E.) Inf., XXXVI Mtn. and LVII Pz.

Divisions mobilised :—12 Pz. (ex 2 Mot.) ; 12, 32, 75, 122, 162, 242, 258, 272 disbanded, 274, 292, 302, 328 Inf., 347 and 702 Inf. ; 207 "Sicherungs" (ex Inf.), 282 "Sicherungs."

Area H.Q. :—Köslin : Genlt. MOYSES (60).

Sub-areas :—Stolp, Köslin, Kolberg, Neustettin, Deutsch Krone, Woldenburg (Neum).

Area H.Q. :—Stettin : Genmaj. v. AMMON (61).

Sub-areas :—Stettin I–II, Swinemünde, Stargard (Pom.), Greifswald, Stralsund.

Area H.Q. :—Schwerin.

Sub-areas :—Schwerin (Meckl.), Rostock, Parchim, Neustrelitz.

Depot divisions :—No. 192 Rostock.

Depot regiments :—

(i) Panzer Grenadier :—Pz. Gren. 2, Stettin.

(ii) Infantry :—12.
32 Kolberg.
75 Neustrelitz.
207 Deutsch Krone.
258 Rostock.

(iii) Artillery :— 2 mot., Stettin.
12 Schwerin.
32 Kolberg.

Training divisions :—

Training areas :—GROSS-BORN : Genlt. THOFERN (59).
Hammerstein.
Wüstrow.
Altwarp.
Rattenhof-Havel (Combined Operations Training area).

Divisional staffs :—402 z.b.V. : Stettin.

Wehrkreis III (H.Q. Berlin)

Brandenburg and part of Neumark.

Commander :—Gen. d. Inf. Joachim v. KORTZFLEISCH (54).

C. of S. :—Genmaj. Heinrich ROTH.

Corps mobilised :—III Pz., XXVIII Inf., XXXIV (L.E.), LII Inf. and Africa Pz.

Divisions mobilised :—3, 8 (ex 3 Lt.), 21 (ex 5 Lt. Mot.), 26 Pz., 3 Pz. Gren. (ex Inf.), 90 Pz. Gren. (ex Lt. Afr.), 23, 50, 68, 76, 93, 123, 163, 208, 218, 257, 273 disbanded, 293, 333, 383, 719 Inf., 203 ? and 403 disbanded, " Sicherungs " Grossdeutschland Div.

Area H.Q. :—Berlin : Genlt. Karl v. THUNGEN (51).

Sub-areas : Berlin I–X.

Area H.Q. :—Frankfurt/Oder : Genlt. SATOW (56).

Sub-areas :—Frankfurt (Oder), Küstrin, Landsberg (Warthe), Crossen (Oder), Lübben (Spreewald), Cottbus.

Area H.Q. :—Potsdam : Genlt. Frhr. v. WILMOWSKY (63).

Sub-areas :—Potsdam I–II, Neuruppin, Eberswalde, Bernau b. Berlin (Berlin), Perleberg.

Depot division :—No. 433, Berlin.

Depot regiments :—

(i) Panzer Grenadier :—Pz. Gren. 83 Eberswalde.

(ii) Infantry :— 3 mot. Frankfurt/Oder.
23 Potsdam.
68 Guben.
76 Brandenburg.
208 Cottbus.
218 Spandau.
257 Landsberg/Warthe.
Ers. Brig. Grossdeutschland.

(iii) Artillery :— 3 mot. Frankfurt/Oder.
23 Potsdam.
168 Frankfurt/Oder.

Training divisions :—143 Res.
153 Res.
233 Res. Pz.

Training areas :—

Döberitz : Genmaj. v. GEYSO (52).
Jüterbog : Obst. v. MALLINCKRODT (51).
Wandern : Genmaj. OELSNER (55).
Zossen :
Grundlach-Zehrensdorf :
Rehagen-Klausdorf (Engineers' Training Area) :
Tiborlager über Schwiebus :
Berlin-Spandau (" Landwehr " Training Area) :

Divisional staffs :—Kdtr. Gross-Berlin.

Wehrkreis IV (H.Q. Dresden)

Saxony and part of Thuringia; extended in 1939 to include the northern frontier districts of Bohemia.

Commander :—Gen. d. Inf. Viktor von SCHWEDLER (59).

C. of S. :—

Corps mobilised :—IV, XXIX and XXXXIV Inf.

Divisions mobilised :—14 (ex 4 Inf.) and 18 Pz.; 14 (ex Inf.) and 164 (ex Inf.) Pz. Gren.; 104 (ex 704 Inf.) Jäg.; 24, 56, 87, 94, 134, 209 disbanded, 223, 255, 256, 294, 304, 336, 370, 384 Inf.

Area H.Q. :—Leipzig.

Sub-areas :—Leipzig I–III, Naumburg (Saale), Halle (Saale), Altenburg, Eisleben, Bitterfeld, Wittenberg, Grimma, Döbeln.

Area H.Q. :—Dresden : Genlt. PRAETORIUS (62).

Sub-areas :—Dresden I–III, Pirna, Bautzen, Zittau, Kamenz, Meissen, Grossenhain, Leitmeritz, Böhmisch-Leipa, Reichenberg.

Area H.Q. :—Chemnitz : Genlt. HENGEN (57).

Sub-areas :—Chemnitz I–II, Freiberg, Annaberg, Zwickau, Auerbach, Plauen, Glauchau, Teplitz-Schönau.

Depot division :—No. 464, Leipzig.

Depot regiments :—

(i) Panzer Grenadier :—Pz. Gren. 4, Dresden.

(ii) Infantry :—14 mot. Leipzig.
24 Chemnitz.
56 Dresden.
87 ?
209 ?
223 Bautzen.
255 Löbau.
256 Meissen.

(iii) Artillery :— 4 mot. Dresden.
24 mot. Chemnitz.

Training divisions :—154 Res.
174 Res.

Training areas :—Königsbrück.
Zeithain : Obst. MITSCHERLING.

Divisional staffs :—404 z.b.V. : Dresden.

Wehrkreis V (H.Q. Stuttgart)

Württemberg and part of Baden ; extended after the Battle of France to include the incorporated departments of Alsace.

Commander : Gen. d. Pz. Tr. Rudolf VEIEL (61).

C. of S. :—

Corps mobilised :—V and XXV Inf.

Divisions mobilised :—10 Pz. (destroyed in Tunisia), 23 Pz. ; 25 Pz. Gren. (ex Inf.) ; 5 (ex Inf.) and 101 Jäg. ; 35, 78, 125, 198, 205, 215, 260, 271 disbanded, 305, 323, 330, 335 and 715 Inf.

Area H.Q. :—Ulm.
Sub-areas :—Ulm, Tübingen, Ehingen, Ravensburg, Sigmaringen, Rottweil, Donaueschingen, Konstanz, Freiburg (Breisgau), Lörrach.

Area H.Q. :—Stuttgart : Genlt. Otto TSCHERNING (63).
Sub-areas : Gmünd, Hall, Heilbronn, Esslingen (Neckar), Ludwigsburg, Stuttgart I–II, Horb (Neckar), Calw, Karlsruhe, Pforzheim, Rastatt, Offenburg.

Area H.Q. :—Strassburg : Genlt. Erich VOLK (60).
Sub-areas :—Strassburg, Mülhausen, Tann, Kolmar, Schlettstadt, Zabern, Haguenau.

*Depot division :—No. 465 Stuttgart. Transferred to Epinal.

Depot regiments :—

(i) Panzer Grenadier :—86 Ludwigsburg.

(ii) Infantry :— 5 Konstanz.
25 mot. Stuttgart.
35 Ulm ?
78 Tübingen.
205 Ulm.
215 Heilbronn.
260 Luneville.

---

* From late 1939 to mid-1940 most of the depot units from this military district were stationed in the Protectorate ; during that period Div. No. 155 was at Prag and Div. No. 165 at Olmütz.

(iii) Artillery :— 5 Ulm. Kolmar.
25 mot. Ludwigsburg. Strassburg.
35 Karlsruhe.

Training divisions :—155 Res. Pz. Div.
165 Res.

Training areas :—Heuberg Baden : Genmaj. Franz SEUFFERT (52).
Münsingen :
Breisach (Engineers' Training Area) :—Obstlt. BUCHHOLZ.
Sennheim (Alsace) :

Divisional staffs :—405 z.b.V. : Stuttgart :

Wehrkreis VI (H.Q. Münster)

Westphalia and the Rhineland ; extended after the Battle of France to include the Eupen–Malmedy district of Belgium.

Commander : Gen. d. Inf. GLOKKE (60).

C. of S. :—

Corps mobilised :—VI and XXIII Inf., XXXIII (L.E.), LVI Pz.

Divisions mobilised : 6 (ex 1 Lt.), 16 (ex 16 Inf.) and 25 Pz. 16 Pz. Gren. ; 6, 26, 69, 86, 106, 126, 196, 199, 211, 227, 253, 254, 264, 306, 326, 329, 336, 371, 385 and 716 Inf.

Area H.Q. :—Münster : Genlt. v. dem KNESEBECK (67).

Sub-areas :—Münster (Westf.), Coesfeld, Paderborn, Bielefeld, Herford, Minden, Detmold, Lingen, Osnabrück, Recklinghausen, Gelsenkirchen.

Area H.Q. :—Dortmund :

Sub-areas : Arnsberg, Soest, Dortmund I–II, Iserlohn, Bochum, Herne, Hagen.

Area H.Q. :—Düsseldorf.

Sub-areas : Düsseldorf, Neuss, Krefeld, München-Gladbach, Wuppertal, Mettmann, Solingen, Essen I–II, Duisburg, Mörs, Oberhausen, Wesel.

Area H.Q. : Köln : Genlt. Frhr. ROEDER v. DIERSBURG (58).

Sub-areas : Köln I–III, Bonn, Siegburg, Aachen, Jülich, Düren, Monschau.

*Depot divisions :—No. 176 Bielefeld.
No. 526 Wuppertal.

---

*From late 1939 to late 1940, most of the depot units from this military district were stationed in Wehrkreis XX ; during that period Div. No. 156 was at Thorn and Div. No. 166 at Danzig.

Depot regiments :—

(i) Panzer Grenadier : Pz. Gren. 57, Wuppertal.

(ii) Infantry :— 6 Osnabrück.
16 mot. Rheine.
26 Düsseldorf.
69 Soest.
86 Herford.
211 Köln.
227 Düsseldorf.
253 Aachen.
254 Lingen.

(iii) Artillery :— 6 Münster.
26 Köln.

Training divisions :—156 Res.
166 Res.

Training areas :—Deilinghofen :
Elsenborn :
Meppen :
SENNELAGER : Obst. PAHL.
Wahn : Obst. BENCZEK.
Münster : Obst. BECKER

Divisional staffs : 406 z.b.V., Münster.

Wehrkreis VII (H.Q. Munich)

Southern Bavaria.

Commander : Gen. d. Inf. Karl KRIEBEL (56).

C. of S. :—Genlt. Johann KASPAR (70).

Corps mobilised : VII and XXVII Inf.

Divisions mobilised : 17 Pz. (ex 27 Inf.) ; 97 Jäg ; 1 Mtn. ; 4 Mtn. ; 7, 57, 88, 167, 212, 268, 277 disbanded, 337, 376, 387 and 707 Inf.

Area H.Q. : München : Genlt van GINKEL (62).

Sub-areas : München I–IV, Rosenheim, Traunstein, Weilheim, Augsburg, Kempten (Allgäu), Landshut, Pfarrkirchen, Ingolstadt.

Depot divisions :—No. 467 : München.

Depot regiments :—

(i) Panzer Grenadier :—Pz. Gren. 27. Augsburg.

(ii) Infantry :— 7 München.
157 München.
212 Ingolstadt.
268 München.

(iii) Mountain rifle : 100 Garmisch. 1 Füssen.

(iv) Artillery :— 7 München.
27 mot. Augsburg.
79 Mtn.

Training divisions :—147 Res.
157 Res.

Training areas :—Hohenfels :
Mittenwald :

Divisional staffs : 407 z.b.V. : München.

Wehrkreis VIII (H.Q. Breslau)

Silesia : extended in 1938 to include the Sudeten districts of Bohemia, in summer 1939 to include part of Moravia and in autumn 1939 to include part of South-West Poland.

Commander :—General d. Kav. Rudolf KOCH-ERPACH (58).

C. of S. :—

Corps mobilised :—VIII Inf., XXXV Inf., XXXVIII Inf. ?, XXXXI Pz.

Divisions mobilised :—5 and 11 Pz. ; 18 Pz. Gren. (ex Inf.) ; 8 and 28 Jäg (ex Inf.) ; 62, 81, 102, 168, 239 disbanded, 252, 298 (now possibly disbanded), 320, 332 and 708 Inf. ; 213 and 221 " Sicherungs " (ex Inf.).

Area H.Q. :—Breslau : Genlt. v. SCHAUROTH (58).

Sub-areas :—Breslau I–III, Oels, Brieg, Glatz, Waldenburg (Schles.), Schweidnitz, Mahrisch-Schönberg, Zwittau, Troppau, Wohlau, Jägerndorf.

Area H.Q. : Liegnitz : Genlt. Konrad SORSCHE (61).

Sub-areas :—Liegnitz, Glogau, Sagan, Görlitz, Bunzlau, Hirschberg (Riesengeb.), Trautenau.

Area H.Q. :—Kattowitz : Genlt. CARP (57).

Sub-areas : Kattowitz, Königshütte (Oberschles.), Loben, Rybnik, Teschen, Bielitz (Beskiden), Oppeln, Neisse, Neustadt (Oberschles.), Cosel, Gleiwitz.

*Depot division : No. 178, Liegnitz.

---

*From early 1942 until the reorganisation of the Training Command in September 1942, most of the depot units of this district were in Alsace-Lorraine. Div. No. 148 was at Metz (Wkr. XII) and Div. No. 158 at Strassburg (Wkr. V).

Depot regiments :—

(i) Panzer Grenadier : Pz. Gren. 85, Gleiwitz.

(ii) Infantry : 8 Neisse ? 18 (mot) Liegnitz ? 28 Mährisch-Schönberg ? 62 Görlitz. 213 Mährisch-Schönberg. 221 Breslau. 239 Gleiwitz. 252 Neisse.

(iii) Artillery : 8 116 Breslau ?

Training divisions :—148 Res.
158 Res.

Training areas :—Lamsdorf :
Neuhammer :
Hohenelbe :

Divisional staffs :—408 z.b.V. Breslau.
432 z.b.V. Neisse.

Wehrkreis IX (H.Q. Kassel)

Part of Thuringia and Hesse.

Commander : Gen. d. Inf. SCHELLERT (57).

C. of S. :—Genmaj. von NIDA.

Corps mobilised : IX Inf., XXXIX Pz.

Divisions mobilised :—1, 7 (ex 2 Lt.), 20, 27 (since disbanded) Pz. ; 29 Pz. Gren. ; 9, 15, 52, 82, 95, 129, 169, 214, 251, 299, 319, 339, 356, 377, 389, 709 Inf. ; 201 " Sicherungs " ?

Area H.Q. :—Kassel : Genlt. PINCKVOSS (58).

Sub-areas :—Kassel I-II, Korbach, Marburg (Lahn), Hersfeld, Siegen, Wetzlar, Fulda, Giessen.

Area H.Q. :—Frankfurt/Main : Genlt. DETMERING (57).

Sub-areas :—Frankfurt (Main) I-II, Offenbach (Main), Aschaffenburg, Friedberg, Hanau.

Area H.Q. :—Weimar.

Sub-areas :—Weimar, Sangerhausen, Gera, Rudolstadt, Mühlhausen (Thür.), Erfurt, Eisenach, Gotha, Meiningen.

Depot division :—No. 409 Kassel.

Depot regiments :—

(i) Panzer Grenadier :—Pz. Gren. 81, Meiningen.

(ii) Infantry :— 9 Siegen ? 15 Fulda. 29 mot. Erfurt. 52 Kassel. 214 Aschaffenburg. 251 Hanau.

(iii) Artillery :— 9. 44.
15 Kassel. 52.
29 mot. Erfurt.

Training divisions :—159 Res.
179 Res. (Pz.).
189 Res.

Training areas :—Ohrdruf.
Schwarzenborn.
Wildflecken : Genmaj. WALTER HOSSFELD (52).

Divisional staffs :—

Wehrkreis X (H.Q. Hamburg)

Schleswig-Holstein and part of Hanover; extended in 1940 to include part of Danish Slesvig.

Commander :—Gen. d. Inf. Walther RASCHICK (62).

C. of S. :—

Corps mobilised : X. Inf., XXXI (L.E.)? and XXXXVI Pz.

Divisions mobilised : 20 Pz. Gren. ; 22 LL Mot. (airborne motorised —ex Inf.), 30, 58, 83, 110, 121, 170, 225, 269, 270, 290, 710 Inf.; 416 Inf. ?

Area H.Q. :—Schleswig-Holstein (Hamburg) :—Genmaj. SCHAUWECKER (62).

Sub-areas :—Neumünster, Rendsburg, Schleswig, Kiel, Eutin, Lübeck.

Area H.Q. :—Hamburg.

Sub-areas :—Hamburg I-VI.

Area H.Q. :—Bremen.

Sub-areas :—Bremen I-II, Stade, Wesermünde, Oldenburg (Oldb.) I-II, Aurich, Nienburg (Weser), Lüneburg.

Depot divisions :—No. 180 Verden.
No. 190 Neumünster.

Depot regiments :—

(i) Infantry :—20 mot. Hamburg. 225 Itzehoe.
22 mot. Oldenburg. 269 Delmenhorst.
30 Ratzeburg.
58 Lüneburg ?

(ii) Artillery :—20 mot. Hamburg.
22 Bremen.
30 Lübeck.

Training divisions :—160 Res.

Training areas :—Munsterlager. (Obenst Becker) ?
Putlos.
Hamburg-Rahlstedt (Garrison Training Area).
Nienburg (" Landwehr " Training Area).

Divisional staff :—410 z.b.V., Hamburg : Genlt. POETTER (60).

Wehrkreis XI (H.Q. Hanover)

Brunswick, Anhalt and part of Hanover.

Commander :

C. of S. :

Corps mobilised :—XI Inf., XIV Pz., XXX Inf., XXXXIII Inf., LI Mtn.

Divisions mobilised :—13 (ex 13 Mot.) and 19 (ex 19 Inf.) Pz. ; 31, 71, 96, 111, 131, 181, 216, 265, 267, 295, 321 and 711 Inf.

Area H.Q. :—Hannover.

Sub-areas :—Hannover I-II, Braunschweig, Goslar, Hildesheim, Hameln, Göttingen, Celle.

Area H.Q. :—Magdeburg.

Sub-areas :—Stendal, Magdeburg I-II, Burg bei Magdeburg, Halberstadt, Dessau, Bernburg.

Depot divisions :—

Depot regiments :—

(i) **Panzer Grenadier** :—Pz. Gren. 13 Magdeburg.

(ii) **Infantry** :—31 Braunschweig. 267 Quedlinburg.
71 Hannover.
216 Hameln.

(iii) **Artillery** :—13 mot. Magdeburg.
19 Hannover.
31 Braunschweig.

Training divisions :—171 Res.
191 Res.

Training areas :—Altengrabow.
Bergen.
Hillersleben.
Salchau.
Raubkammer.
Fallingbostel.
Dessau-Rosslau (Engineers' Training Area).
Wolterdingen (" Landwehr " Training Area).

Divisional staffs :—411 z.b.V. Hannover.

Wehrkreis XII (H.Q. Wiesbaden)

Eifel, part of Hesse, the Palatinate and the Saar area ; extended after the Battle of France to comprise Lorraine (including the Nancy area), and the Grand Duchy of Luxembourg.

Commander :—Gen. d. Inf. WALTER SCHROTH (62).

C. of S. :—

Corps mobilised :—XII Inf., XXIV Pz., LIII Inf.

Divisions mobilised :—22 Pz. (since disbanded), 15 Pz. Gren. (ex 15 Pz., ex 33 Inf.), 36 Pz. Gren. ; 34, 65, 72, 79, 112, 132, 197, 246, 263, 282, 342, 712 Inf. ; 444 " Sicherungs."

Area H.Q. :—Koblenz : Genlt. v. BERG (62).

Sub-areas : Trier I-II, Koblenz, Neuwied, Kreuznach, Wiesbaden, Limburg, (Lahn), Mainz, Worms, Darmstadt, Luxemburg.

Area H.Q. :—Mannheim.

Sub-areas :—Saarlautern, Saarbrücken, St. Wendel, Zweibrücken, Kaiserslautern, Neustadt (Weinstrasse), Ludwigshafen (Rhein), Mannheim I-II, Heidelberg.

Area H.Q. :—Metz.

Sub-areas :—Metz, Diedenhofen (Thionville), St. Avold.

*Depot divisions :—No. 172 Mainz.
No. 462 Nancy.

Depot regiments :—

(i) Panzer Grenadier :—Pz. Gren. 12 Landau.

(ii) Infantry :—34 Heidelberg. 246 Trier.
36 mot. Wiesbaden. 263 Idar-Oberstein.
79 Koblenz. 342 Kaiserslautern.
112 Darmstadt. 572.

(iii) Artillery :—33 mot. Darmstadt. 263 Nancy.
34 Koblenz.

Training divisions :—182 Res.
391 Field Training.

Training areas :—Baumholder.
Bitsch.

Divisional staffs :—412 z.b.V Wiesbaden.

---

* From late 1939 to late 1940, most of the depot units from this military district were stationed in Wehrkreis XXI ; during that period Div. No. 172 was at Gnesen and Div. No. 182 at Litzmannstadt.

Wehrkreis XIII (H.Q. Nuremberg)

Northern Bavaria, extended in 1938 to include part of Western Bohemia.

Commander :—Gen. d. Inf. MAURIZ WIKTORIN (61).

C. of S. :—Genmaj. Paul VOIT (68).

Corps mobilised :—XIII Inf., XXXXV (L.E.) (?) (believed disbanded).

Divisions mobilised :—4 Pz., 7 Mtn., 10 Pz. Gren. (ex 10 Inf.), 17, 46, 73, 98, 113, 183, 231 disbanded, 296, 334, 343 and 713 Inf.

Area H.Q. :—Regensburg : Lt.-Gen. Bruno Edler v. KIESLING auf KIESLINGSTEIN (65).
Sub-areas :—Regensburg, Passau, Straubing, Weiden, Amberg.

Area H.Q. :—Nürnberg.
Sub-areas :—Nürnberg I-II, Fürth, Bamberg, Bad Kissingen, Würzburg, Ansbach, Coburg, Bayreuth, Bad Mergentheim, Tauberbischofsheim.

Area H.Q. :—Eger.
Sub-areas :—Kaaden, Karlsbad, Eger, Mies, Marktredwitz.

Depot divisions :—No. 473 Regensburg.

Depot regiments :—
(i) Panzer Grenadier : Pz. Gren. 84 Würzburg.
(ii) Infantry :—10 mot. Regensburg.
17 Nürnberg.
46 Bayreuth.
73 Nürnberg.
231 Coburg.
296 Regensburg ?
(iii) Artillery :—10 mot. Regensburg.
17 Nürnberg.

Training divisions : 173 Res.

Training areas :—Grafenwöhr : Genlt. HEBERLEIN (56).
Hammelburg : Obstlt. WITTE.

Divisional staffs :—413 z.b.V. Nürnberg.

Wehrkreis XVII (H.Q. Vienna)

Upper and Lower Austria ; extended in 1939 to include the southern districts of Bohemia and Moravia.

Commander :—Gen. d. Inf. Albrecht SCHUBERT (58).

C. of S. :—

Corps mobilised :—XVII Inf., LXXXII Inf. (ex XXXVII L.E.), XXXX Pz.

Divisions mobilised :—2 and 9 (ex 4 Lt.) Pz. ; 100 and 117 (ex 717 Inf.) Jäg. ; 44, 45, 137, 262, 297, 327, 331 Inf. (also administer 369 and 373 Croatian Inf.), 392.

Area H.Q. :—Linz : Genlt. RIEBESAM (56).
Sub-areas :—Wels, Ried i. Innkreis, Linz, Steyr, Krummau a.d. Moldau.

Area H.Q. :—Wien : Genlt. SCHWARZNECKER (60).
Sub-areas :—Melk, Zwettl, St. Pölten, Krems a.d. Donau, Znaim, Wiener-Neustadt, Baden, Nikolsburg, Wien I–IV.

Depot divisions :—No. 177 Wien.
No. 487 Linz.

Depot regiments :—
(i) Panzer Grenadier :—Pz. Gren. 82 Wien.
(ii) Infantry :—44 Wien.
45 Krummau.
130
131 Wien.
134 ?
262 Eggenburg.
462 Wien.
(iii) Mountain infantry :—Geb. Jäg. 130 Linz.
(iv) Artillery :—96 Wien.
98 Linz.

Training division : 187 Res.

Training areas :—Bruck a.d. Leitha.
Döllersheim : Genmaj. OFFENBÄCHER (54).

Divisional staffs : 417 z.b.V. Wien.

Wehrkreis XVIII (H.Q. Salzburg)

Styria, Carinthia, Tyrol ; extended in 1941 to include the northern districts of Slovenia.

Commander :—Gen. d. Inf. Friedrich MATERNA (59).

C. of S. :—

Corps mobilised :—XVIII and XIX (ex Norway) Mtn.

Divisions mobilised :—2, 3, 5, 6 and 8 Mtn. ; 118 Jäg. (ex 718 Inf.).

Area H.Q. :—Innsbruck : Lt.-Gen. Frhr. v. WALDENFELS (60).
Sub-areas :—Bregenz, Innsbruck, Salzburg.

Area H.Q. :—Graz : Genlt. GUNZELMANN (57).
Sub-areas : Spittal, Klagenfurt, Judenburg, Graz, Leitnitz, Fürstenfeld, Marburg (Maribor), Cilli (Celje), Krainburg (Kranj).

Depot regiments :—
(i) Mountain rifle :—136 Landeck.
137 Salzburg.
138 Leoben.
139 Villach.
(ii) Artillery :— 110.
111 Hall.
112 Kufstein.

Training division :—188 Res. Geb. Div.

Training areas :—Dachstein.
Seethaler Alpe.
Strass i. Steiermark.
Wattener Lizum.

Divisional staffs :—537 Frontier Guard : Innsbruck.
538 Frontier Guard : Klagenfurt.

Wehrkreis XX (H.Q. Danzig)

Formed after the Polish campaign, comprising the areas of Danzig Free State, the Polish Corridor, and the western part of East Prussia.

Commander :—Gen. d. Inf. Bodewin KEITEL (55).

C. of S. :—

Corps maintained :—XX Inf., XXXXVII Pz.

Divisions maintained :—60 Pz. Gren., 21 Inf.

Area H.Q. :—Danzig : Genlt. KURZ.

Sub-areas :—Danzig, Neustadt, Pr. Stargard, Marienwerder, Graudenz, Bromberg (Bydgoszcz), Thorn (Torun).

Depot division :—No. 152, Graudenz, Genlt. Boltze (64).
428, Graudenz.

Depot regiments :—Infantry : Pz. Gren. 60 Danzig.

Training areas : Thorn (Torun) : Genmaj. MELCHERT.
Gruppe :
Grossendorf.

Wehrkreis XXI (H.Q. Posen)

Formed after the Polish campaign, comprising Western Poland.

Commander : Gen. d. Art Walter PETZEL (61).

C. of S. :—

Corps maintained :—XXXXVIII Pz.

Divisions maintained :—

Area H.Q. :—Posen (Poznań).
Sub-areas :—Posen (Poznań), Lissa, Hohensalza, Leslau (Leszno), Kalisch (Kalisz), Litzmannstadt (Lodz).
Depot regiments :—Infantry : 50 Posen (Poznań).
Training areas :—Sieradsch (Sieratz).
Warthelager.
Divisional staffs :—429 z.b.V. Posen (Posnań).
430 z.b.V. Gnesen (Gniezno).
431 z.b.V. Litzmannstadt (Lodz).

Wehrkreis " General-Gouvernement " (H.Q. Cracow)

Formed late 1942 or early 1943. Comprises those parts of Poland not incorporated in " Wehrkreise " I, VIII, XX and XXI, and those parts in the extreme east that were not incorporated in the occupied territories of " Ostland " and Ukraine.
Commander :—Gen. d. Inf. Siegfried HAENICKE (66).
C. of S. :—Genmaj. Kurt HASELOFF (49).
Corps maintained :—
Divisions maintained :—
Area H.Q.—Krakau (Cracow).
Sub-areas :—Krakau, Warschau (Warsaw), Lemberg (Lwow).
Training areas :—Süd (South—H.Q. Demba) : Genmaj. Fritz SALITTER.
Mitte (Centre—H.Q. Radom) : Genmaj. von KUTZLEBEN.
Biedruska.
Galizien (Galicia—H.Q. Janow, near Lemberg). Genmaj. Helmut BESCH.
Pustkow, near Cracow.
Jablonna—Legionowo.

Wehrkreis Böhmen und Mähren (H.Q. Prague)

Formed late in 1942. Covers the whole of the Protectorate.
Commander :—Gen. d. Pz. Tr. Ferdinand SCHAAL (55).
C. of S. :—
Corps mobilised :—XXXXIX.
Divisions mobilised :—
Area H.Q. :—Prague : Genlt. von PRONDZYNSKI (63).
Sub-areas :—Prague, Budweis, Brünn, Olmütz.
Depot division :—No. 193, Pilsen.

Training area :—Wischau.
Milowitz, near Lissa.
Kammwald (formerly Brdy-Wald): Genmaj. THAMS (59).

Divisional staffs :—539 Frontier Guard, Prague: Genlt. Dr. SPEICH (60).
540 Frontier Guard, Brünn: Genlt. TARBUK v. SENSENHORST.

(c) THE ZONE OF OPERATIONS

In the zone of operations the place of the Wehrkreis organisation is to some extent taken by the L. of C. area command. Each Army Group disposes of a *Befehlshaber des Rückwärtigen Heeresgebiets,* with the status of a Corps Commander, and each army of a *Kommandant des Rückwärtigen Armeegebiets,* with the status of a Divisional Commander (Commander of Army Group L. of C. District, Commandant of Army L. of C. Area), whose main task is to supervise the administration of the L. of C., so that the Army Group or Army Commander can concentrate exclusively on the course of operations.

The commander of Army Group L. of C. District has, in addition, charge over " Sicherungs " formations and units—specially organised divisions and regiments formed to undertake " mopping-up " operations in the rear of the main battle area ; he is also in charge of such administrative H.Q.s as may be set up in the zone of operations assigned to him and of all supply units of the G.H.Q. pool and guard units stationed within that area.

His functions, therefore, correspond very closely with those of the static military commanders in occupied countries (*see* Part B below) ; it is known, for example, that the *Kommandant des Heeresgebiets Südfrankreich* (Commander of L. of C. Area, South France—*see* page B36), has the same status and powers as the Commanders of the military districts of " occupied " France. On the close of active operations he may, in fact, remain as military commander over the country or portion of a country which he has hitherto commanded as a L. of C. District.

The functions of the army L. of C. Area Commander, are less wide than those of the Army Group, L. of C. Commander, and his status compares more closely with that of the area, or military district commander within an occupied country ; for example, the Commander of L. of C. Area 560, formerly subordinated to 12 Army, remained in the Balkans after the Balkan campaign as *Befehlshaber Saloniki-Agäis* (Commander Salonica Aegean Islands—*see* page B39), his status therefore being equivalent to that of one of the Commanders of a military district in France, or in any other occupied territory that is so subdivided.

(*a*) ARMY ADMINISTRATION IN OCCUPIED COUNTRIES

General.—In the following pages the German occupied and satellite countries are set out in the order in which they were occupied by or became associated with Germany. Details are given regarding the military administration of, or German military relations with, each country. It should be understood that this administrative structure is distinct from the operational control of any German combat units stationed in the territory in question.

The administrative relations of the German Army with the different countries under German control vary widely according to German strategic needs as well as political, economic and psychological considerations. Several areas, for example, are extensively used for training and may be thought of as a projection of the German territorial organisation at home (*Wehrkreise*). The nomenclature of the German commands and the entire administrative organisation are in each case adapted to the special requirements and objectives.

The lower administrative headquarters and local military administration in several of the occupied areas are organised as follows :—

(1) *Oberfeldkommandantur* (administrative area headquarters). Headquarters of this type in the theatre of operations come under the commander of Army or Army Group Rear Area. In occupied territory outside the theatre of operations they come under the military commander in charge of the military administration of the country.

(2) *Subordinate administrative headquarters.*—These include :—

- (*a*) *Feldkommandantur* (administrative sub-area headquarters), normally commanded by a colonel or a *General-major.*
- (*b*) *Ortskommandantur* (town headquarters), major's command in a small town.
- (*c*) *Kreiskommandantur* (district headquarters), major's command in a rural district.
- (*d*) *Stadtkommandantur* (city headquarters), found in some cities : status varies with the size and importance of the city.

(*a*) AUSTRIA

Occupied in March 1938 and absorbed into the Reich as Wehrkreise XVII and XVIII (*q.v.*).

(*b*) **CZECHOSLOVAKIA**

First partitioned in September, 1938, when the Sudetenland was detached and incorporated in Wehrkreise IV, VIII, XIII and XVII (*q.v.*). Finally occupied in March, 1939, when the remaining territory was divided between the Protectorate (*Reichsprotektorat Böhmen Mähren*) and the protected Republic of Slovakia.

(i) **Protectorate** (H.Q., Prag)

The Protectorate became a Military District under the name of *Wehrkreis Böhmen Mähren* late in 1942. The office of *Wehrmachtsbevollmächtigter beim Reichsprotektor und Befehlshaber im Wehrkreis Böhmen-Mähren* (Armed Forces Plenipotentiary General on the Staff of the Reichs Protector and Commander in Wehrkreis Bohemia-Moravia).

(ii) **Slovakia** (H.Q., Pressburg (Bratislava))

This province is nominally an independent country with its own army and its own defence ministry (Minister of Defence and C.-in-C. : General CATLOS). It is, however, under complete German domination and the Germans not only have a military mission there but garrison and train their own troops in the territory.

German General with Slovak Defence Ministry and Head of Military Mission (*Deutscher General beim Slovakischen Verteidigungsministerium und Chef der Deutschen Heeresmission*) : — Genlt. SCHLIEPER (53).

C. of S. :—

Commandant of the Protected Area (*Kommandant der Schutzzone*) :—

Training Area :—Lower Carpathians (*Kleinkarpathen*), H.Q., Malacky :—Obstlt. von GROELING.

(*c*) **MEMEL DISTRICT**

Occupied in March, 1939, and incorporated in Wehrkreis I (*q.v.*).

(*d*) **POLAND**

Occupied after the campaign of September, 1939, the Northern and North-Eastern portions were incorporated into the Reich in Wehrkreis I, and the Western portions in Wehrkreis VIII and the newly formed Wehrkreise XX and XXI ; Central Poland was established as the General Government (*General-Gouvernement*), which became a Wehrkreis late in 1942. The administrative organisation originally set up when the General Government was officially an Occupied Territory has not lapsed, though the still distinct posts of Military Governor and Wehrkreis Commander at present appear to be held by the same man.

General Government (H.Q. : Krakau)

Commander (*Militärbefehlshaber*) :—Gen. d. Inf.von HAENICKE (66).

C. of S. :—Genmaj. Kurt HASELOFF (49).

Administrative H.Qs. (*Oberfeldkommandanturen, Feldkommandanturen, Ortskommandanturen*) :—

OFK	(365)	Lemberg (Lwow).	393	Piaseczno.
	372	Lublin.		Warsaw.
		Krakau.	FK 768	Minck Mazowiecki.
OK	II/354	Krakau area ?	I/604	Kielce
	I/411	Minsk Mazowiecki ?		

Those *Oberfeldkommandanturen* whose numbers are shown in brackets are at present known by the names of the towns in which they are located.

(*e*) DANZIG FREE STATE

Occupied in September, 1939, and incorporated subsequently in the newly formed Wehrkreis XX (*q.v.*).

(*f*) NORWAY

Occupied after a brief campaign in April, 1940, and subsequently allowed a degree of autonomy in internal affairs.

German civilian commissar : TERBOVEN.

German Forces in Norway (H.Q., Oslo)

Commander (*Wehrmachtbefehlshaber*) :—Genobst. Nikolaus von FALKENHORST (59), also commanding the Army of Norway.

C. of S. :—Genlt. Rudolf BAMLER (48).

G.S.O.1 :—Obstlt. von BUTTLAR.

Areas :—(i) *North* (H.Q., Alta) :—Gen. d. Art. Willi MOSER (56) (LXXI Corps Command).

Sub-areas :—Kirkenes, Alta, Narvik.

(ii) *Centre* (H.Q., Trondhjem) :—Gen. d. Kav. Erwin ENGELBRECHT (53) (XXXIII Corps Command).

Sub-areas :—Mo, Dombaas.

(iii) *South* (H.Q., Oslo) :—
(LXX Corps Command).

Sub-areas :—Bergen, Stavanger or Christiansand South, Oslo.

Note.—The administrative areas are Corps Commands, each having two or three sub-areas which are Divisional Commands ; these in turn are subdivided into three sectors, each under control of an infantry regiment. The commanders of areas and sub-areas are described as *Territorial-Befehlshaber*, and the commanders of sectors as *Abschnittskommandeure*.

(*g*) DENMARK

Occupied almost without resistance in April, 1940, and subsequently allowed a degree of autonomy in internal affairs.

German Troops in Denmark (H.Q., Copenhagen)

Commander (*Befehlshaber der Deutschen Truppen*) :—Gen. d. Inf. von HANNEKEN (54) (XXXI Corps Command).

C. of S. :—

Area H.Q. :—Copenhagen.

Sub-areas :—Jutland, Zeeland.

Training area :—Oxböl.

(*h*) HOLLAND

Occupied in May, 1940, but subsequently allowed a degree of autonomy in internal affairs.

German civilian commissar : SEYSS-INQUART.

German Forces in Holland (H.Q., Hilversum)

Commander (*Wehrmachtbefehlshaber*) :—Gen. d. Fl. (G.A.F.) Friedrich CHRISTIANSEN (65).

C. of S. :—

Commander of Troops in the Netherlands (*Befehlshaber der Truppen in den Niederlanden*) :—Gen. d. Inf. Hans REINHARD (55) (LXXXVIII Army Corps).

Administrative H.Q.s (*Feldkommandanturen, Ortskommandanturen*) :

FK	674 BREDA.	724 Utrecht.
OK :	Rotterdam.	Hague.

(*i*) LUXEMBURG

Occupied in May, 1940, and incorporated in Wehrkreis XII (*q.v.*).

(*j*) BELGIUM

Occupied in May, 1941 ; subsequently allowed a degree of autonomy in internal affairs, but for military administration purposes combined with the French Departments of Nord and Pas-de-Calais to form the unified command of *Belgien-Nordfrankreich.*

Belgium—North France (H.Q., Brussels)

Commander (*Militärbefehlshaber*) :—Gen. d. Inf. Alexander von FALKENHAUSEN (66).

C. of S. :—Obstlt. von HARBOU.

Administrative H.Qs. (*Oberfeldkommandanturen, Feldkommandanturen, Kreiskommandanturen, Ortskommandanturen*) :—

OFK	520 Mons.	670 Lille.
	570 Ghent.	672 Brussels.
	589 Liege.	
FK	178 Bruges.	611 Ghent.
	503 Courtrai.	681 Hasselt.
	520 Antwerp.	682 Namur.
	569 Lille.	683 Liege.
	598 Arlon.	718 Douai.
KK	510 Bruges.	687 Huy ?
	598 Wervicq.	694 Malines ?
	616 Charleroi.	703 Valenciennes ?
	633 Lille.	708 Alost ?
	636 Neufchateau ?	714 Dunkirk ?
	652 Courtrai ?	718 Douai.
	I/653 Bastogne.	772 Saint Omer.
	664 Albert.	913 Louvain.
	I/685 Tongres.	

OK II/630 Ghent.	853 Roulers.
I/644 Verviers.	914 Lille.
I/699 Tirlemont.	I/940 Liège.
I/702 Antwerp.	942 Namur.
759 Berck.	Brussels.

(*k*) **FRANCE**

Partially occupied after the capitulation of June, 1940 ; allowed a degree of local autonomy in local government throughout the occupied area, with the exception of Alsace Lorraine, which has since been incorporated in the Reich ; divided for the purposes of military administration into the areas " France " and " Northern France " (included in Belgium (q.v.)). " Unoccupied " France was occupied on 11 Nov., 1942 ; it has retained its autonomy in civil affairs under the government at Vichy, but for the purposes of military administration, the Commander of the Army Group L. of C. Area, South France, has the same status and powers as the Commanders of the Military Districts of " Occupied " France.

France (H.Q., Paris)

Commander (*Militärbefehlshaber*) :— Gen. d. Inf. Otto von STÜLPNAGEL (65).

C. of S. :—

Military Districts (*Militärverwaltungsbezirke*) :—

(i) A (H.Q., Paris), North France.
Commander :—
C. of S. :—

(ii) B (H.Q., Angers), North-West France.
Commander :—
C. of S. :—Obstlt. OELSNER-WOLLER.

(iii) C (H.Q., Dijon), North-East France.
Commander :—Genlt. Heinrich, Ritter von FÜCHTBAUER (64).
C. of S. :—

(iv) Bordeaux, South-West France.
Commander :—
C. of S. :—

(v) South France (*Kommandant des Heeresgebietes Südfrankreich*).

Commander :—Genlt. Heinrich NIEHOFF (60).

C. of S. :—

(vi) Greater Paris (*Kommandantur Gross-Paris*).

Commander :—Genlt. Freiherr von BOINEBURG-LENGSFELD (55).

C. of S. :—

Administrative H.Qs. (*Oberfeldkommandanturen, Feldkommandanturen, Kreiskommandanturen*) :—

OFK 592 Laon.

FK 505 La Roche-sur Yon.
515 Channel Islands.
517 Rouen.
529 Bordeaux.
531 Chalons-sur-Marne.
541 Biarritz.
545
549 Rennes.
560 Besancon.
563 Saint-Dizier.
580 Amiens.
588 Le Mans.
590 Bar-le-Duc.
595 Angers.
602 Laon.
622 Dijon.
638 Beauvais.
651 Niort.
677 Poitiers.
680 Melun.
684 Cherleville.
722 Saint-Lo.
723 Caen.
734 Paris area ?
746 Montdidier.
750 Vannes.
751 Chartrese.
752 Quimper ?
758 Marseille.
788 Tours.
801 Evreux.

KK 554 Belfort.
563 Dijon.
583 Cherbourg ?
612 Sedan.
623 Brest.
626 Abbeville.
637 Le Havre.
672 Verdun.
704 Marseille.
713 Boulogne ?
735 Lorient.
781 Fontainebleau.
800 Amiens.
892 Longevy.

Alsace Lorraine :—

FK 591 Nancy.
532 Epinal.

KK 593 Nancy.

(*l*) **ITALY**

Entered the war on 11 June, 1940, after which date German infiltration continued with growing intensity. After Marshal Badoglio's Government made a separate peace with the Allies in September, 1943, a puppet Republican Fascist Government was set up in German-occupied Italy, which is now entirely under German domination, under the nominal leadership of Mussolini.

Head of Military Mission and M.A. :—

C. of S. :—

(*m*) **ROUMANIA**

Under virtual German domination since October, 1940.

Head of Military Mission :—Gen. d. Kav. Erik HANSEN (55).

C. of S. :—

(*n*) **BULGARIA**

Passively associated with Germany since March, 1941. At war with the United States and Great Britain, but not with Russia.

Head of Military Mission :—

C. of S. :—

(*o*) **HUNGARY**

Allied with Germany since summer, 1940 ; since the autumn of that year German dominance has increased ; the Hungarians retain, however, a much greater degree of independence than the Roumanians.

Head of Military Mission :—

C. of S. :—

(*p*) **SOUTH-EAST**

A composite Occupied Territory, formed by Yugoslavia (less those parts annexed to Germany, ceded to Italy, Hungary or Bulgaria, or incorporated into the theoretically independent state of Croatia), Greece and the Greek Islands.

German Forces in the South-east (H.Q., Salonica)

Governor (*Wehrmachtbefehlshaber*) :—Generalfeldmarschall Maximilian Frhr. von WEICHS (63) (Army Group F).

C. of S. :—Genlt. Herm. FOERTSCH (49).

Military Districts :—

(i) Serbia–(approximately the Serbia of 1914) (H.Q., Belgrade).

Commander (*Kommandierender General und Befehlshaber in Serbien*) :—Gen. d. Inf. Hans Gustav FELBER (56).

C. of S. :—Oberst BODE.

(ii) Salonica Aegean (North Greece and the Aegean Islands) (H.Q., Salonica).

Commander (*Befehlshaber Saloniki Ägäis*) :—Genlt. Kurt PFLUGRADT (53).

C. of S. :—

(iii) South Greece (H.Q., Athens).

Commander (*Befehlshaber Südgriechenland*) :—Gen. d. Fl. (G.A.F.) SPEIDEL.

C. of S. :—

(iv) Fortress of Crete (H.Q., Heraklion)

Commander (*Kommandant der Festung Kreta*) :—Genlt. (G.A.F.) Bruno BRÄUER (51).

C. of S. :—Obst. Hans EHLERT.

Administrative H.Q.s :—(*Feldkommandanturen, Ortskommandanturen*) :—

FK 599 Belgrade.
606 Crete ?
808 Salonica.
809 Nish.
810 Greece.

OK I/856 Langadas (Greece).
I/866 Demotika (Greece).
I/825 Athens.
II/941 Crete ?
II/981 Crete ?

(*q*) YUGOSLAVIA

Occupied in May, 1941. Portions of the country ceded to Italy, Hungary and Bulgaria; part of Slovenia incorporated into Wehrkreis XVIII (*q.v.*); the rest divided into German, Italian and Slovenian spheres of influence.

Serbia

See under SOUTH-EAST.

Croatia (H.Q., Zagreb)

Formed into a theoretically independent kingdom under the Duke of Spoleto, who was deposed shortly after Italy made a separate peace.

German General Plenipotentiary in Croatia (*Deutscher Bevollmächtigter General in Kroatien*) :—Genlt. Dr. Edmund GLAISE von HORSTENAU (62).

C. of S. :—Obst. KAULBACH.

Administrative H.Q. (*Feldkommandantur*) :—
FK 735 Agram (Zagreb) :—Genmaj. Walter KOSSACK (61).

(*r*) **GREECE**

Occupied after the campaign of May, 1941. Portions ceded to Bulgaria; the rest divided into German and Italian spheres of influence. Since the Italian Armistice, the whole country has been administered by the Germans.

See under SOUTH-EAST.

(*s*) **FINLAND**

Allied to Germany since June, 1941; a German Army H.Q. controls German forces in North Finland; the German forces in South Finland come under the Finnish High Command, to which a German military mission is accredited.

Head of Military Mission :—Gen. d. Inf. Waldemar ERFURTH (65).

C. of S. :—Obstlt. HOLTER.

(*t*) **U.S.S.R.**

Attacked in June, 1941; the west of the country has been placed under German military administration and organised into the two *Reichskommissuriate* of *Ostland* and Ukraine.

Ostland (H.Q., Riga)

Governor (*Wehrmachtsbefehlshaber*) :—Gen. d. Kav. Walter BRAEMER. (61).

C. of S. :—

Military Districts (*Generalbezirke*) :—

(*a*) Esthonia (*Estland*), H.Q., Reval (Talinn).
Commander :—Gen. d. Inf. von BOTH (60).
C. of S. :—

(*b*) Latvia (*Lettland*), H.Q., Riga.
Commander :—Genlt. Dip. Ing. Frederich-Wilhelm JOHN.
C. of S. :—

(*c*) Lithuania (*Litauen*), H.Q., Kovno.
Commander :—Genmaj. JUST (54).
C. of S. :—

(*d*) White Russia (*Weiss Ruthenien*), H.Q., Minsk.
Commander :—
C. of S. :—

Administrative H.Q.s. (*Oberfeldkommandanturen, Feldkommandanturen, Ortskommandanturen*) :—

OFK 392 Minsk ?
FK 768 Minsk. 811 Zhitomir ?
OK I/257 Minsk ?

Ukraine

Comprised South-West Russia (less the Odessa area, which was ceded to Roumania), the Crimea and the Brest Litovsk–Rowno–Luck area of Poland. The recent Russian advances in this area make it unnecessary to give details of this Occupied Territory, which was administered by a Governor (*Wehrmachtsbefehlshaber*) and divided into six Military Districts (*Generalbezirke*).

PART C—IDENTIFICATIONS, NUMBERING, AND TYPES OF FORMATIONS AND UNITS

CONTENTS

(*a*) IDENTIFICATIONS

The interpretation and evaluation of any given information depends on a knowledge of German practice in the allocation of numbers to units and formations. In this section is a brief discussion of the various types of material which will furnish identifications. Paragraph (*b*) gives an outline of the overall numbering system for small units, and (*d*) contains detailed information on the numbering of specific units.

Identifications of German units and formations may be made from the following :—

(i) Identity Discs

These are normally issued by the depot unit which has received the soldier into the army and made out his paybook. Consequently they will seldom show the unit in which the man is actually serving unless he has lost his original disc and has been issued a replacement by his current unit. The issuing unit, however, will usually give an indication of the man's arm. Also, identity discs may record the existence of a previously unidentified unit, and a note should always be made of the entries upon them.

(ii) Shoulder Straps

The piping on the shoulder strap will show the arm of the service to which the soldier belongs (*e.g.*, white for infantry, red for artillery). If he is serving in a divisional unit, or in a non-divisional unit to which attention must not be drawn, he will display no numeral on the shoulder strap. If he does display a numeral, there are three possible explanations :—

(*a*) He belongs to a unit which is neither a divisional nor an organic corps unit. In general, there is no ban on the display of numerals whose number bears no permanent relation to a formation, although with individual cases a ban may be imposed.

(*b*) He is serving (*e.g.*, in a staff appointment) away from the formation to which his unit belongs.

(*c*) He is on leave in Germany.

(iii) **Paybooks**

Paybooks are one of the most satisfactory and frequent sources of order of battle information. The German paybook provides on page 4, paragraph C, several lines for the chronological entry of field units to which the owner of the book has been assigned during his military career. If the space is used up, further entries will be made on page 17, which is a continuation of page 4. The last entry of paragraph C on page 4 (or 17) will normally indicate the owner's present unit.

Caution must be exercised against wrong interpretations :—

(*a*) The unit at the bottom of page 2 is in most cases *not* the last unit but the unit which issued the paybook.

(*b*) The last entry on page 3 is the unit which has granted the owner his most recent promotion, but before accepting it as a current identification it should be checked for the date. The date is also valuable in establishing the dates of existence of units shown.

(*c*) The entry on page 15 is a security check on the paybook. It may or may not be the owner's unit—again the date should be checked.

(*d*) Carelessness or ignorance on the part of the company clerks often leads to erroneous interpretations of pages 4 and 17. The most common mistakes in entries are the crossing out of all entries, the omission of one or more units; or using the space on page 17 before the space on page 4 is exhausted. Consequently, every case must be examined carefully and compared, if possible, with other paybooks captured in the same sector.

(iv) **Markings on Vehicles**

Markings on vehicles fall into two distinct categories : tactical signs and symbols, and unit or formation emblems. The emblems usually identify organisations the size of divisions, while tactical signs and symbols identify units the size of battalions and regiments. No known standard method of identifying companies has been adopted. It is usually left to the various units to devise their own method.

In general, the tactical signs and symbols vary only slightly from those used on maps, and they usually show the arm of service and type of unit. In the case of G.H.Q. troops, the unit number is frequently (although not invariably) added. In the case of artillery, the signs will not normally indicate the calibre of guns, but will show whether they are horse-drawn, tractor-drawn, or on self-propelled mounts.

There is no short cut to interpreting the emblem of a division. In general, the emblems used by Panzer divisions are based on variations of simple geometrical patterns, while those used by infantry divisions are more representational in design and frequently bear some relation to the division's history, its character, or its nature.

For a full (but not exhaustive) list of tactical signs, *see* pages E 11, *et seq*.

Those relating to minor divisional units are reproduced below, pages C 13–15.

(v) **Documents**

All documents and orders state the issuing authority in the top left-hand corner, with the date in the top right-hand corner. The heading of the issuing authority gives the designation of the H.Q., staff, or unit, and the particular section concerned underneath, *e.g.*, Ia (operations), Ic (intelligence), etc. The degree of secrecy will usually give a preliminary indication of the importance of the document. It is indicated by the addition to the heading of the abbreviation *Geh.* (*Geheim*), for Confidential, or *g.Kdos.* (*Geheime Kommandosache*) for Secret documents, or it may be stamped (usually in full) at the top of the document. With the date may appear the abbreviation *Gef.St.* (*Gefechtsstand* = Battle H.Q.) or *O.U.* (*Ortsunterkunft* = local billets), the latter an indication that the unit is not in the front line. Documents and orders addressed to more than one recipient have a distribution list (*Verteiler*) in the bottom left-hand corner which often may be replaced by a fixed distribution list, *e.g.*, *Verteilungsplan* A, B, C, which might indicate distribution down to regiments, battalions or companies.

The following are the main categories of orders :—

(*a*) **Operationsbefehle** (operational orders).—These regulate the military operations of combat troops and also include orders for transport and L. of C. services. They are headed according to the issuing H.Q., *e.g.*, **Armeebefehl** (army order), **Regimentsbefehl** (regimental order), or according to the order of battle, *e.g.*

(*b*) **Vorhutbefehl** (order for advanced guard), **Vorpostenbefehl** (order for outpost), etc., or according to the arm, as, for example, an **Artilleriebefehl** (artillery order). The general remarks above on distribution, headings, and date apply.

(*c*) **Marschbefehle** (march orders).—These contain the order of battle according to arms, arranged in the following sequence : infantry, cavalry (horsed or mechanised), reconnaissance, artillery, Panzer troops, chemical and smoke troops, engineers, signals troops, supply services, special purpose units, G.A.F. troops and A.A. artillery

(*d*) **Besondere Anordnungen** (detailed administrative orders).—These supplement operational orders by giving detailed instructions to individual arms or to the supply services.

(*e*) **Tagesbefehle** (orders of the day).—These are concerned with such things as personnel matters, recognition of merit, etc.

(*f*) **Stabsbefehle** (H.Q. staff orders).—These regulate the internal workings of the various H.Q. staffs.

(vi) **Charts**

Prior to a major operation, G.Ops. in a German formation issues charts which show the composition and fire-power of the formation, including any attached G.H.Q. troops. Such charts form the most detailed and valuable aid to identification. Once their conventions are understood, they will give not only the identification of all units, but also full details of their sub-divisions and their allotment of guns, mortars and machine-guns ; details of strength in men, transport and tanks are not included, although these may be fairly accurately inferred from the organisation. For particulars of these charts and the symbols employed, *see German Military Symbols, January,* 1944.

(*b*) THE OVERALL GERMAN NUMBERING SYSTEM

Introduction

The overall system for the numbering of German units was originally designed to provide various series and blocks of numbers for all categories of units in the German Army, so arranged that the number of any unit would indicate, within certain limits of security, the status of the unit, *i.e.* whether it was divisional, corps, army, or independent, and in some cases, its affiliation.

This overall system was based on three main categories or groups, each of which contained numerous series of units. For convenience these are referred to here as categories A, B, and C.

Category A was designed for all organic divisional units as well as those G.H.Q. units which were intended to be attached to divisions, corps, and armies, with the important exception of infantry, artillery, Panzer, and C.W. units.

Category B was designed for infantry, artillery, Panzer, and C.W. units.

Category C was designed for those G.H.Q. units which were to be directly or indirectly under the control of the O.K.H. in Berlin and not under the Field Army or its subordinate armies, corps, and divisions.

Category A

(1) Units in this category received numbers from 1 to 700. This series was subdivided into three distinct blocks as follows :—

(*a*) 1–400 for organic divisional units. The number given such a unit was in most cases either the number of the division itself, 100 greater than the number of the division, or the same as the auxiliary unit number of the division.

(*b*) 401–500 for organic corps units. The last two digits correspond to the number of the corps ; thus Feldgen. Tr. 442 belonged organically to the XLII Corps and Brüko 404 to the IV Corps.

(*c*) 501–600 for organic army units. Here there was apparently no relationship between the number of the unit and the number of the army headquarters to which it belonged.

(*d*) 601–700 for attached army units. Here also the number of the unit did not correspond to that of the army to which it was attached.

Category B

(2) The numbers of infantry, artillery, Panzer, and C.W. units were taken from various blocks between 1 and 1000. Organic and G.H.Q. units are mixed throughout the numerical series. In the case of the artillery regiments in divisions, there is usually a close relationship between the regimental and divisional numbers, and there is usually a pattern for the assignment of infantry regiments to the divisions of any given wave. The numbers for C.W. units do not go above 150.

Category C

(3) Each type of unit in this category was numbered in a separate series from 1 up. Units in the zone of the interior* often took their numbers from the *Wehrkreis* ; other types may have been numbered on a pattern based on the *Wehrkreis* of origin. With many types of units in Category C only very low numbers will be found, and this often serves to distinguish them from the same types belonging to Category A. For example, units of the Secret Field Police which operate in Germany and in occupied countries are numbered below 200, while those belonging or attached to armies in the field have numbers above 500.

Variations and Exceptions

(4) While the system outlined above is still in general operation and can usually be relied on for identifications and affiliations, a number of minor variations have occurred in the course of the war due to various circumstances.

(*a*) Use of the 700, 800, and 900 series. When the fifteen divisions of the 15th wave, formed in the spring of 1941, were assigned numbers in the 700 series (702, 704, and 707–719), their minor components were all given the

*Home Command.

divisional number instead of a number from the series 1–400. (When four of the divisions were subsequently converted into light divisions in the 100 series their minor components likewise changed their numbers.) Since then the remaining numbers in the 700 series (720–800) as well as the 800 and 900 series have been drawn upon to a limited extent for the numbering of attached army units instead of the 600 series.

(*b*) Changes in status of units. When a unit hitherto attached to an army changes its status to that of an organic army unit, it does not necessarily change its number. Propaganda companies, for example, which were numbered in the 600 series because they were intended to be attached to armies, have actually been incorporated as organic army troops but have retained their original numbers instead of adopting new ones in the 500 series. The opposite policy has apparently been followed with the *Arkos*. These were originally numbered between 1 and 150 as part of the regular artillery series (Category B), but some have been found renumbered in the 400 series, indicating that they are now intended to be organic to corps (Category A).

(*c*) Change in the employment of units. When units belonging to Category C which are employed in the zone of the interior under *Wehrkreis* control or in occupied countries under the occupational authorities (*Oberfeldkommandanturen*, etc.) are transferred to the theatre of operations and attached to an army or subordinate field command, they may retain their previous numbering. For example, many *Landesschützen* battalions, formerly employed in Germany and consisting of low-grade personnel, have moved into the rear areas of the Russian front and have since operated under a Korück or directly under an army headquarters ; in some cases they have been renamed as *Sicherungs*, *Wach*, or *Baupionier* battalions, but without changing their numbers. Hence today there are some *Baupionier* units numbered above 500 (originally intended as army troops) and some below 500 (converted from *Landesschützen*) units).

(*d*) Possible future changes. As has been shown, the system here outlined is not a rigid one, and any form of violation of it may take place in the course of the extensive changes in the affiliations of German units which may be expected in the future.

(*c*) TYPES OF GERMAN DIVISIONS

It is extremely important to differentiate between the types of German divisions. Although the name by which a division is called will give a general indication of its nature, some of the names are slightly misleading and there are further sub-categories of the various types of divisions. (For details of their organisation, *see* Pocket Book of the German Army, September, 1943.)

(i) **Panzer-Divisionen** (Panzer Divisions)

Numbered in a separate series (at present 1–27); normally contain one tank regiment and two infantry (*Panzer-Grenadier*) regiments. Mark V or VI tanks (Panthers and Tigers) may be found in the tank regiments. The infantry, some of whom may be transported in armoured personnel carriers, has high automatic fire-power.

(ii) **Panzer-Grenadier-Divisionen** (Motorised Infantry Divisions)

Numbered in the main infantry series (1–400); contain two motorised Grenadier regiments and, in many cases, a tank battalion, which will normally carry the division number plus 100.

(iii) **Jäger-Divisionen** (Light Divisions)

Numbered in the main infantry series; contain two infantry (*Jäger*) regiments. Some may be organised similarly to mountain divisions.

(iv) **Gebirgs-Divisionen** (Mountain Divisions)

Numbered in a separate series (at present 1–8); contain two mountain-infantry (*Gebirgs-Jäger*) regiments. Weapons, equipment and organisation are designed primarily for mountain warfare, but these, particularly the artillery, may be modified when fighting in open terrain.

(v) **Waffen SS-Divisionen** (Armed SS Divisions)

These are distinguished in most cases by name and by number. At present there are 17, including Panzer, motorised, mountain, cavalry and infantry. For details of the large range of types in the SS category, *see* page 11.

These five types of divisions will normally form the spearhead of any German offensive.

(vi) **Infanterie-Divisionen** (Infantry Divisions)

These vary considerably in quality according to the tasks for which they were designed. The following are the main sub-categories. Within each sub-category there may be minor variations, as indicated in the divisional histories (pages D 51–D 114) :—

(*a*) Series 1–50. Active divisions which formed part of the peace-time standing army.

(*b*) Series 51–140 and 201–300, plus 14 divisions in the series 141–200. Divisions formed on or after mobilisation for service with the field army.

(*c*) Series 301–400. Divisions formed mainly in 1940, 1941 and 1942, primarily for the purpose of holding occupied territory. Many have been upgraded to first-line infantry divisions, however, and have seen extensive action on the Russian front.

(*d*) Series 701–720. "*Bodenständige*" divisions formed in 1941 for holding occupied territory ; some have been converted into light divisions and re-numbered in the corresponding positions of the 101–120 series.

(vii) **Sicherungs-Divisionen** (L. of C. Divisions)

Numbered in the gaps of the main infantry series or in the series 441–460, these are primarily divisional staffs controlling the equivalent of two brigade groups. The *Sicherungs* regiments are either old *Landwehr* regiments or former *Landesschützen* regimental staffs controlling re-named *Landesschützen* battalions. The divisions are normally assigned to L. of C. duties, which may include defence against saboteurs, raiding parties, etc.

(viii) **Divisions-Kommandos z.b.V.** (Special Duty Divisions)

Numbered in the series 401-450, these are divisional staffs which may be employed in Germany, the occupied territories, or the zone of the field army for control and administration of miscellaneous units such as *Wach* (guard) battalions, *Landesschützen* battalions and *Bau* (construction) battalions. Depending upon their function, they may be regarded as administrative or depôt commands. Some of those in Germany have taken over the functions of the depôt divisions, either with a change of name to Div.Nr. or without the change of name.

(ix) **Grenzwacht-Divisionen** (Frontier Guard Divisions)

Numbered in the series 501–550. They consist of divisional staffs controlling *Landesschützen* regimental staffs and battalions. For this reason they are sometimes reported as *Landesschützen* divisions. Divisional troops, apart from H.Q., probably consist of a signals company only.

(x) **Reserve-Divisionen** (Training Divisions)

Numbered in the series 140–200 plus 233. These are former depot divisions which were transferred outside Germany to carry out the dual role of training recruits and garrisoning occupied territory. In the latter role they would also be available as an emergency defensive combat unit in the event of military operations in their areas.

(xi) **Feldausbildungs-Divisionen** (Field Training Divisions)

Numbered in the series 381–391, five have been identified. These are the former field replacement units (*Feldersatz divisionen*) organised in 1942 in rear areas of Russia on a divisional basis, which later that year became field training divisions.

(xii) **Divisionen-Nr. . .** (Depot Divisions)

Numbered in the series 140–200 and 400–500. These are divisional staffs, of which there were formerly an average of two to each Wehrkreis. Since the constitution of training divisions, however, some Wehrkreise have only one. The function of the depot divisions is to receive recruits, process them, and send them to training units, which may be either in Germany and under control of the depot division, or outside Germany and under control of a training division.

(xiii) **Luftwaffe Feld-Divisionen** (G.A.F. Field Divisions)

Numbered in a separate series (1–22 at present), *see* page D 136 for details.

(*d*) TYPES OF DIVISIONAL UNITS

The identification of German divisions will be facilitated by a clear picture of the system on which their component units are numbered. The following paragraphs outline the general system, and in conjunction with the detailed lists of units in Part L, and the discussion of the overall numbering system on pages C 6 *et seq.*, they should provide such a picture. For details, history, and component units of any given division, *see* pages D 27 *et seq.*

(i) **Infantry Regiments**

Most infantry regiments, sub-divided into the types listed below, are allotted numbers from a single series. The only exceptions consist of groups of duplicate numbers occurring between

1 and 15, between 101 and 115, and several others beginning with 146. In all cases these involve one *Panzer-Grenadier* regiment in the pair. The allotment of regiments is not based on any one uniform system, although within a block of divisions formed at the same time the regiments may be given approximately consecutive numbers taken from one regimental block (*e.g.*, the infantry regiments of the 121–140 block of divisions carry numbers from 401–500). In general, the higher the number carried by the division, the less likely is it that the infantry regiments will be given random numbers. The following types of infantry regiments exist at present.

(*a*) *Grenadier-Regiment* (Standard Infantry Regiment) : There are normally three to an infantry division. The degree of mechanisation will vary, but primary means of transport is by foot and animal.

(*b*) *Grenadier-Regiment (mot)*. (Mechanised Infantry Regiment) : There are normally two to a *Panzer-Grenadier* (motorised) division. Organisation will show a greater degree of decentralisation of heavy weapons than in the case of the regular infantry division, and the fire-power will be greater. (Note, however, that regiments of 15, 90 and 164 *Panzer-Grenadier* divisions may still be referred to as *Panzer-Grenadier* regiments unofficially.)

(*c*) *Panzer-Grenadier-Regiment* (Infantry Regiment in an Armoured Formation) : Normally there are two to a Panzer Division. There are only two battalions instead of three, and part of the regiment may be transported in armoured personnel carriers. Fire-power is greater than in any other type of infantry.

(*d*) *Jäger-Regiment* (Infantry Regiment of a Light (*Jäger*) Division) : There are usually two to a light division. They may be organised on the lines of a mountain rifle regiment.

(*e*) *Gebirgs-Jäger-Regiment* (Mountain Rifle Regiment) : There are normally two to a mountain division. Battalions consist of five companies, including a M.G. company and a headquarters company. Weapons may include 12-cm. mortars, but normally no infantry gun company will be present.

(ii) **Other Basic Divisional Units**

Artillery, anti-tank, reconnaissance, engineer, and signals units are numbered on the following principles, according to the block of divisions concerned.

In general they carry the divisional number, but in the following cases the principle has been modified :—

(*a*) Divisions 97, 99–114, 117–118, most units *except* the artillery carry the divisional number : the number of the artillery regiment is a random one.

(*b*) Divisions 38, 39, 50–98 (excluding 90 and 97) : All units carry the divisional number plus 100.

(*c*) Divisions 161–164, 167–170, 181, 183, 196–198 : All units carry the divisional ancillary number (taken from the block 205–250).

(*d*) Divisions 44–46, Panzer Divisions and Mountain Divisions : There is no uniform system, although several of the units may carry the divisional ancillary number.

(iii) **Minor Divisional Units**

In addition to the infantry regiments and the other basic divisional units, each division contains a number of small units of various types, which are normally lumped together in staff tables as "services"; within each division these units all carry the divisional ancillary number, which is frequently, although not necessarily, the divisional number or the number carried by the basic divisional units given in (*b*) above. The list of ancillary numbers with their divisional equations, is given on pages L 104–L 106.

The following table shows the minor units which are included in this category :—

Unit.	*(In English.)*	*Conventional sign **
At Div. H.Q.		
Divisions-Kartenstelle (Div. K.St.).	Div. map-printing section (mot.).	
Other units, as grouped on formation charts.		
Nachschubdienste.	*Supply services.*	(a)*
Kommandeur der Divisions-Nachschubtruppen.	O.C. div. supplies.	D58
kleine Kraftwagenkolonne (kl. Kw. Kol.).	Lt. supply coln. (mech.).	le
Fahrkolonne (Fahrkol.).	H.T. coln.	

Unit.	*(In English.)*	*Conventional sign.**
Other units, as grouped on formation charts.		
Nachschubdienste.	*Supply services.*	
grosse Kw. Kol. (für Betriebsstoff).	Hy. supply coln. (mceh.) (for P.O.L.).	
kl. Kw. Kol. f. Betr. Stoff.	Lt. P.O.L. coln. (mech.).	
Werkstattkompanie (Wkst. Kp.).	Workshop coy. (mech.).	
Nachschubkompanie (Nsch. Kp.).	Supply coy. (mech.).	
Verwaltungsdienste.	*Administrative services.*	
Bäckereikompanie (Bäck. Kp.).	Bakery coy., field bakery (mech.).	 160 (b)*
Schlächtereikompanie (Schlächt. Kp.).	Butcher coy., fd. butchery (mech.).	
Verpflegungsamt (Vpfl. A.).	Rations office.	Vpfl.A
Sanitätsdienste.	*Medical services.*	
Sanitätskompanie (San. Kp.).	Medical coy. (mech.).	
Feldlazarett (Feldlaz.).	Field hospital (mech.).	
Krankenkraftwagenzug (Kr. Kw. Zug.).	Ambulance section (mech.).	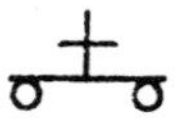
Veterinärdienste.	*Veterinary services.*	
Veterinärkompanie (Vet. Kp.).	Veterinary coy.	 or 

Unit.	*(In English.)*	*Conventional sign.**
Ordnungsdienste.	*Provost service.*	
Feldgendarmerietrupp (Feldgend. Tr.).	Military police detachment (mech.).	
Feldpostdienste.	*Field postal services.*	
Feldpostamt (F.P.A.).	Field post office (mech.).	
Feldersatz-Bataillon (Felders.-Btl.).	First line reinforcement battalion.	234 (c)*

* The basic sign O O distinguishes motorised (fully mechanised) units ; the addition of a numeral gives the unit identification, as in the following examples :—(*a*) O.C. 58 Div. Supplies (*i.e.*, 7 Pz. Div.) ; (*b*) 160 Bakery Coy. (mech.) (*i.e.*, 60 Mot. Div.) ; (*c*) 234 First Line Reinforcement Bn. (*i.e.*, 163 Inf. Div.).

(*e*) TYPES OF HIGHER FORMATIONS

Higher formations in the German Army fall into two categories, *regular* and *ad hoc*. Regular formations comprise army corps, armies and army groups ; and *ad hoc* formations, commonly called *Gruppen*, consist of whatever combination of combat and service units may be required for a particular operation.

(i) General Considerations

In any order of battle work involving these higher formations, several factors should be borne in mind.

In the German Army, corps, armies, and army groups are essentially staffs, and the allocation to them of lower formations and units depends primarily on current operational needs. Consequently both G.H.Q. units (with the exception of a small number of organic troops) and divisions, corps, etc., may be transferred from one higher formation to another as the situation requires. There is no permanent allocation of divisions to corps or corps to armies, nor is there any standard equation such as 2 divisions = 1 corps, or 2 corps = 1 army.

Distinction must be made between troops normally organic to a given formation, such as an infantry corps, and those normally attached to such a formation. Generally speaking, the organic troops of a corps are only those required to look after the needs of corps H.Q. and of the other organic corps troops. Attached to corps are combat troops (artillery, engineers, etc.), although there is a tendency to make a few combat troops organic.

The case of army is slightly different, for army has organic to it sufficient service troops to look after the needs both of the army headquarters and organic troops and of the subordinate formations. Normal attachments will be additional service troops.

It should be noted that as a rule G.H.Q. combat troops will be attached to corps and G.H.Q. service troops to army. There has been some tendency recently to attach a limited number of service units to corps, but this may have been because of the unusually long supply lines in Russia, and there is no indication that this has been accepted as a matter of principle.

Normal Attachments

(*a*) Normal attachments of service troops to army consist of :—

Nachschub units (*e.g.*, *Nachsch. Kol. Abt.*, *Kw. Trspt. Abt.*).

Instandsetzungs units (*e.g.*, *Kfz. Inst. Abt.*, *Werkstätte*).

Kraftfahr-Park units (*e.g.*, *A.K.P.*, *Pi.Pk.*).

Verwaltungs units (*e.g.*, *H. Betreuungs. Abt.*, *Verpfl. Ämte.*).

Feldzeug units (*e.g.*, *Mun. Verw. Kp.*, *Betr. St. Verw. Kp.*).

Sanitäts units (*e.g.*, *A. San. Abt.*, *Kr. Trspt. Abt.*).

Feldgendarmerie units (*e.g.*, *Feldgend. Tr.*, *Verk. Regl. Btl.*).

Veterinär units (*e.g.*, *A.Pf. Laz.*).

Nachrichten units (*e.g.*, *Fsp. Betr. Kp.*, *Fu. u. Wach. Kp.*).

Bau units (*e.g.*, *Str. Bau. Btl.*, *Br. Bau. Btl.*).

Also certain guard and defence units, such as *Fla*, *Flak* and *Wach*, will be attached for the protection of army installations.

(*b*) Normal attachments of combat troops to corps will consist of :—

Special infantry units (*e.g.*, *Jäg. Btl.*, *Fest. Btl.*).

Cavalry units (*e.g.*, *Kosaken* units).

Panzer units (*e.g.*, *Panzer-Flammenwerfer Abt.*).

Panzer-Jäger units (*e.g.*, *Pz. Jäg. Abt.*).

Artillerie units (*e.g.*, *Stu. Gesch. Abt.*, *Art. Abt.*).

Werfer units (*e.g.*, *Werf. Rgt.*, *Werf. Abt.*).

Pionier units (*e.g.*, *Brüko*, *Pi. Landungs-Kp.*).

(ii) Regular Formations

The different types of higher formations and their normal organic troops are listed below :—

(*a*) Army Corps.—Six types exist (for identifications *see* pp. D 9–26).

Armeekorps	Infantry Corps.
Panzerkorps	Panzer Corps.
Gebirgskorps	Mountain Corps.
Reservekorps	Reserve Corps.
Reserve Panzerkorps ..	Reserve Panzer Corps.
Höheres Kommando z.b.V.	Corps H.Q., lower establishment.

The first three types differ only in the measure of specialisation among their staffs and in minor differences of their war establishments. *Reservekorps* and *Reserve Panzerkorps* are designed to control the *Reserve* (training) divisions training in occupied territory. The last type is an infantry corps H.Q. with a lower establishment, designed to control the divisions in its area. Should it engage in active operations, however, it will be temporarily brought up to establishment to function as a normal infantry corps and will be called an *Armeekorps*.

(*b*) Corps troops.—Attached troops, such as artillery and engineers, may be allocated to corps as required, and will be shown under *Heerestruppen* as opposed to *Korpstruppen* on the chart produced by G.Ops. at corps H.Q. Organic troops are confined to the following types :—

Korps-Nachrichtenabteilung ..	Corps Signals Battalion.
Brückenkolonne	Bridging Column.
Kommandeur der Korps-Nachschubtruppen.	O.C. Corps Supplies.
Feldgendarmerie-Trupp ..	Military Police Detachment.
Feldpostamt	Field Post Office.
Sanitäts-Kompanie	Medical Company.
Kraftwagenwerkstatt	M.T. Workshop.
Veterinär-Kompanie	Veterinary Company.
Kartenstelle	Map Printing.

(*c*) Armies.—Two types exist, *Armee-Oberkommando A.O.K.* Army (H.Q.), and *Panzer-Armee-Oberkommando Pz. A.O.K.* Panzer Army (H.Q.). (For a list of identifications, *see* pp. D 4–9.)

These are more permanent command frameworks than army groups, and are not necessarily formed for a single campaign. Several of them have been disbanded during the course of the present war. It should be noted that the name Panzer Army may be slightly misleading, for there have been occasions on which a Panzer Army has had only a very few Panzer Divisions operating under it, no more in fact than one might expect to find in a normal army.

The two types carry numbers in a separate series, and it is probable that their war establishments differ to some extent. In addition to these two main categories, there is also an *A.O.K.-Norwegen*, which combines the military administration of Norway with control of the field force formations stationed there.

(*d*) Army troops.—G.H.Q. troops may be attached to armies according to the needs of current military operations. The organic army troops, however, will normally consist of the following types :—

Armee-Nachrichten-Regiment or *Abteilung.*	Army Signals Regiment or Army Signals Battalion.
Kommandeur der Armee-Nachschub-Truppen.	O.C. Army Supplies.
Kommandant des rückwärtigen Armeegebietes.	Army L. of C. Commander.
Feldgendarmerie-Abteilung ..	Military Police Battalion.
Geheime Feldpolizei	Field Security Police (Detachment).
Feldpostamt	Field Post Office.
Propagandakompanie	Propaganda Company.

These organic army troops will ordinarily carry numbers from the army block (501–600), allotted with no relationship to the army number or, in most cases, to the numbers of the other army troops. While they are considered as organic army troops they are not necessarily permanently assigned.

(*e*) Army groups.—The army groups *Heeresgruppen-Kommandos* are distinguished from one another by letters (*see* pp. D 3–4 for a list of identifications), but they are frequently known by the area or front to which they are for the time being assigned; as in the case of other higher formations the number of subordinate units they control is variable. Each army group has a special signal regiment (*Heeres-Nachrichten-Regiment*) and a *Befehlshaber des rückwärtigen Heeresgebiets* (G.O.C. army group rear area) (*see* pp. E 22, B 30).

(iii) " **Ad Hoc** " **Formations**

(*a*) *Gruppen*

A *Gruppe* is essentially a temporary *ad hoc* organisation, which may be anything from a platoon to an army group plus attached troops. The *Gruppe* is normally identified by its commander's name, such as *Kampfgruppe Schmidt*, and the best indication of its size is the rank of its commander, if that can be ascertained. This organisation is the most fluid in the entire Germany army, since it consists simply of a variety of troops temporarily grouped together for a specific mission. It is consequently one of the most difficult for the intelligence officer to cope with, and its order of battle must be carefully built up in detail and just as carefully watched, for its composition may change from day to day.

(*f*) TYPES OF NON-DIVISIONAL AND SMALL UNITS

In addition to divisional units and small units which are organic to divisions and higher formations, the non-organic small units must be considered apart. For their overall numbering system, *see* (*b*) above.

(i) **G.H.Q. Units** (*Heerestruppen*)*

G.H.Q. units are those units held in the G.H.Q. pool and allotted, or attached temporarily to army groups, armies, corps and divisions, for specific operations. The principal units, classified in German categories, are dealt with in Part E, Section (*a*). G.H.Q. units also include static units controlled by administrative headquarters in Germany and occupied countries; *see* (ii) below.

(ii) **O.K.H. Units**

O.K.H. units are those which come under direct or indirect control of the O.K.H. (War Office). Normally units of this type are not identified in field armies, but come under the control of static H.Q.s in occupied areas; *see* Part E, Section (*b*).

(iii) **G.A.F. Ground Units**

Air Force ground units include Flak units, parachute units, and other G.A.F. field units, ground combat troops, and services; *see* Part E, Section (*c*).

(iv) **Naval Artillery Units**

Non-organic Naval Artillery and Naval Flak units are discussed briefly in Part E, Section (*d*).

---

* It should be noted that, with the exception of the various types of infantry regiments, all units listed as organic may also be found as G.H.Q. troops.

PART D—DIVISIONS, DIVISIONAL UNITS AND HIGHER FORMATIONS

CONTENTS

INTRODUCTION

1. This Part consists of classified lists of German formations, from army groups down to divisions, with the names of their commanders (where known) and particulars of their composition, followed by brief notes on the campaigns in which they have taken part.

2. In the case of divisions, units, the number of which can be deduced with certainty, are included even although they may not yet have been identified ; the departure from the principle adopted in Section L is deliberate, in order to make this Part of greater utility to the reader who is not a specialist, and who wishes to see, at a glance, the composition of any particular German formation. The latter section will serve as an index to the various units which are given their affiliation only when established.

3. It should be noted that the ages shown in brackets after the names of commanders are those reached in 1944.

4. For the composition of formations higher than divisions and the allocation to them of units from the G.H.Q. pool, *see* Section L; classified lists of miscellaneous units, such as may be allotted to higher formations, are given in Part E below.

5. It must be emphasised that under the German system command is extremely fluid, and the Order of Battle of higher formations is liable to change from day to day during the course of active operations, in accordance with the needs of the immediate situation. Armies may be transferred from one army group to another, corps from army to army, divisions from corps to corps, and units of the G.H.Q. pool from one formation to another ; and there is no standard equation such as " 2 divisions = 1 corps " or " 2 corps = 1 army."

6. The divisions included in sections (*h*) to (*q*) and (*r*) below are those which are intended to operate as divisions ; divisional staffs whose function is the training or administration of depot units and low category troops in Germany itself or in occupied territory are shown in Part B above, under the military districts in which they are stationed. There is no fixed composition and no history of campaigning to be given in their case.

(*a*) ARMY GROUPS

(As constituted in January, 1944)

Army Group North (H. Gr. Nord)

Commander :—Genfeldm. Georg v. KÜCHLER (63).
C.G.S. :—Genlt. Eberhardt KINZEL (47).
G. Ops. :—

Army Group Centre (H. Gr. Mitte)

Commander :—Genfeldm. Günther v. KLUGE (62).
C.G.S. :—
G. Ops. :—

Army Group South (H. Gr. Süd)

Commander :—Genfeldm. Fritz Erich v. LEWINSKI gen. v. MANSTEIN (57).
C.G.S. :—Genlt. Theodor BUSSE (48).
G. Ops. :—

Army Group A (H. Gr. A)

Commander :—Genfeldm. Ewald v. KLEIST (63).
C.G.S. :—
G. Ops. :—

Army Group B (H. Gr. B)

Commander :—Genfeldm. Erwin ROMMEL (53).
C.G.S. :—Genlt. Alfrep GAUSE (48).
G. Ops. :—

Army Group West (H. Gr. D)

Commander :—Genfeldm. Gerd v. RUNDSTEDT (69).
C.G.S. :—Genlt. BLUMENTRITT (51).
G. Ops. :—

Army Group E (H. Gr. E)

Commander :—Genobst. (G.A.F.) Alexander LÖHR (59).
C.G.S. :—
G. Ops. :—

Army Group F (H. Gr. F)

Commander :—Genfeldm. Maximilian Frhr. v. WEICHS (63).
C.G.S. :—Genlt. Hermann FOERTSCH (49).
G. Ops. :—

(*b*) **ARMIES**

(For PANZER ARMIES *see* Section (*c*) below.)

1 Army (A.O.K.1)

Commander :—Genobst. Johannes BLASKOWITZ (61).
C.G.S. :—Genlt. Frhr. v. MAUCHENHEIM gen. BECHTOLSHEIM (50).
G. Ops. :—

Formed on mobilisation ; took part in the Western campaign, and has subsequently remained in France.

2 Army

Commander :—Gen. d. Pz.Tr. Josef HARPE (54).
C.G.S. :—Genlt. Gustav HARTENECK.
G. Ops. :—

Formed on mobilisation ; took part in the Polish, Western and Balkan campaigns, and in Russia since June, 1941.

3 Army

Formed on mobilisation ; took part, under v. KÜCHLER, in the Polish campaign ; disbanded late in 1939.

4 Army

Commander :—Genobst. Gotthard HEINRICI (57).
C.G.S. :—
G. Ops. :—

Formed on mobilisation ; took part in the Polish and Western campaigns, and in Russia since June, 1941.

5 Army

Formed on mobilisation for service in the West during the Polish campaign ; disbanded late in 1939.

6 Army

Commander :—Genobst. Karl HOLLIDT (53).

C.G.S. :—

G. Ops. :—

Formed early in 1940 ; took part, under v. REICHENAU, in the Western campaign ; in Russia since June, 1941. Destroyed at Stalingrad under PAULUS in January, 1943 ; reformed spring, 1943.

7 Army

Commander :—Genobst. Friedrich DOLLMANN (62).

C.G.S. :—Genlt. Friedrich SIXT (47).

G. Ops. :—

Formed on mobilisation ; took part in the Western campaign, and has subsequently remained in France.

8 Army

Commander :—Gen. d. Inf. Otto WÖHLER (50).

C.G.S. :—

G. Ops. :—

Formed on mobilisation ; took part, under BLASKOWITZ, in the Polish campaign ; not identified after 1939 and probably disbanded. Reformed in July, 1943, and since then in Russia.

9 Army

Commander :—Genobst. Walter MODEL (53).

C.G.S. :—Genlt. KREBS.

G. Ops. :—

Formed in spring, 1940 ; took part in the Western campaign, and in Russia since June, 1941.

10 Army

Commander :—Genobst. Heinrich von VIETINGHOFF gen. SCHEEL (57).

C.G.S. :—

G. Ops. :—

Formed on mobilisation ; took part, under von REICHENAU, in the Polish campaign ; not identified after 1939 and probably disbanded ; re-formed in August, 1943, and now operating in South Italy.

11 Army

Probably formed late in 1940 ; in Russia from June, 1941, until its disbandment probably early in 1943.

12 Army

Probably formed in Spring, 1940 ; took part in the Western and Balkan campaigns and remained in the Balkans ; upgraded to Army Group E, late 1942 or early 1943.

14 Army

Commander :—

C.G.S. :—

G. Ops.

Formed on mobilisation ; took part, under LIST, in the Polish campaign ; disbanded late in 1939. Re-formed in autumn, 1943.

15 Army

Commander :—Genobst. Hans v. SALMUTH (56).

C.G.S. :—

G. Ops. :—

Probably formed late in 1940 ; in France thereafter.

16 Army

Commander :—Genfeldm. Ernst BUSCH (59).
C.G.S. :—Genlt. Hans BOECKH-BEHRENS (48).
G. Ops. :—

Formed in spring, 1940 ; took part in the Western campaign and in Russia since June, 1941.

17 Army

Commander :—Genobst. Erwin JAENECKE (52).
C.G.S. :—
G. Ops. :—

Probably formed late in 1940 ; in Russia since June, 1941.

18 Army

Commander :—Genobst. Georg LINDEMANN (60).
C.G.S. :—Genmaj. SPETH.
G. Ops. :—

Formed in spring, 1940 ; took part in the Western campaign, and in Russia since June, 1941.

19 Army

Commander :—Gen. d. Inf. Georg von SODENSTERN (55).
C.G.S. :—Genmaj. Walter BOTSCH.
G. Ops. :—

Formed in the spring of 1943 in the South of France, where it still is.

20 Mountain Army

Commander :—Genobst. Eduard DIETL (54).
C.G.S. :—Genlt. Friedrich SCHULZ (47).
G. Ops. :—

Formed in winter, 1941/42, in North Finland, to control operations on the Murmansk front, as Army of Lapland (A.O.K. Lappland) ; name changed to 20 Mountain Army in summer, 1942.

Army of Norway (A.O.K. Norwegen)

Commander :—Genobst. Nikolaus von FALKENHORST (59).

C.G.S. :—Genlt. Rudolf BAMLER (48).

G. Ops. :—

Formed on mobilisation as XXI Inf. Corps, taking part as such in the Polish campaign ; as Gruppe XXI organised the conquest of Norway ; expanded to an army during summer, 1941, LXIII Corps (lower establishment) also being amalgamated into it ; until the formation of the Army of Lapland it was responsible for German operations in Finland as well as for the control of Norway.

(*c*) PANZER ARMIES

1 Panzer Army (Pz. A.O.K.1)

Commander :—

C.G.S. :—

G. Ops. :—

Formed on or shortly before mobilisation as XXII Inf. Corps, taking part as such in the Polish campaign ; fought in the west as Gruppe Kleist, in the Balkans as Panzergruppe 1, and towards the end of 1941 became 1 Panzer Army in Russia, where it still is.

2 Panzer Army

Commander :—Gen. d. Inf. Dr. Lothar RENDULIC (57).

C.G.S. :—

G. Ops. :—

As XIX Mot. Corps part (since May, 1939) of the peace-time standing army ; fought as such in the Polish campaign ; in the west as Gruppe Guderian, and in the early stages of the campaign in Russia as Panzergruppe 2, becoming 2 Panzer Army at the close of 1941. It is still in Russia.

3 Panzer Army

Commander :—Genobst. Georg-Hans REINHARDT (57).

C.G.S. :—

G. Ops. :—

As XV Mot. Corps part of the peace-time standing army ; fought as such in the Polish campaign, in the West as Gruppe Hoth, and in the early stages of the campaign in Russia as Panzergruppe 3, becoming 3 Panzer Army at the close of 1941. It is still in Russia.

4 Panzer Army

Commander :—Genobst. Hermann HOTH (60).

C.G.S. :—Genlt. RÖTTIGER.

G. Ops. :—

As XVI Mot. Corps part of the peace-time standing army ; fought as such in Poland and in the West, and as Panzergruppe 4 in the early months of the campaign in Russia, becoming 4 Panzer Army at the close of 1941. It is still in Russia.

5 Panzer Army

Formed late in 1942. Destroyed May, 1943, in Tunisia.

Panzer Army of Africa (Pz. A.O.K. Afrika)

Formed in June, 1941, as Panzergruppe Afrika, to control the Africa Corps and Italian formations in Cyrenaica, becoming a Panzer army at the close of 1941. Destroyed in Tunisia, May, 1943.

(*d*) INFANTRY CORPS

I Infantry Corps (I.A.K.)

Commander :—

C. of S. :—

Home station :—Königsberg (Wkr. I).

Part of the peace-time standing army.

Campaigns : Polish, Western, Russian.

II Infantry Corps

Commander :—Gen. d. Inf. Paul LAUX (56).

C. of S. :—Obst. SCHMIDT-RICHBERG.

Home Station :—Stettin (Wkr. II).
Part of the peace-time standing army.
Campaigns : Polish, Western, Russian.

III Infantry Corps—*see* III Pz. Corps (Section (*e*) below).

IV Infantry Corps

Commander :—

C. of S. :—

Home Station :—Dresden (Wkr. IV).
Part of the peace-time standing army.
Campaigns :—Polish, Western, Russian; destroyed at Stalingrad; re-formed summer, 1943; since then in Russia.

V Infantry Corps

Commander :—Gen. d. Inf. Wilhelm WETZEL (56).

C. of S. :—

Home Station :—Stuttgart (Wkr. V).
Part of the peace-time standing army.
Campaign :—Western, Russian.

VI Infantry Corps

Commander :—

C. of S. :—

Home Station :—Münster (Wkr. VI).
Part of the peace-time standing army.
Campaigns : Western, Russian.

VII Infantry Corps

Commander :—Gen. d. Art. Ernst-Ebenhard HELL (57).

C. of S. :—

Home Station :—Munich (Wkr. VII).
Part of the peace-time standing army.
Campaigns :—Polish, Western, Russian.

VIII Infantry Corps

Commander :—Gen. d. Pz. Tr. Erhard RAUS (55).

C. of S. :—

Home Station :—Breslau (Wkr. VIII).

Part of the peace-time standing army.

Campaigns :—Polish, Western, Russian ; destroyed at Stalingrad ; re-formed in South Russia.

IX Infantry Corps

Commander :—Gen. d. Inf. Hans SCHMIDT (66).

C. of S. :—

Home Station :—Kassel (Wkr. IX).

Part of the peace-time standing army.

Campaigns :—Western, Russian.

X Infantry Corps

Commander :—Gen. d. Art. Christian HANSEN (59).

C. of S.—

Home Station :—Hamburg (Wkr. X).

Part of the peace-time standing army.

Campaigns :—Polish, Western, Russian.

XI Infantry Corps

Commander :—

C. of S. :—

Home Station :—Hanover (Wkr. XI).

Part of the peace-time standing army.

Campaigns :—Polish, Western, Russian ; destroyed at Stalingrad ; re-formed summer, 1943 ; since in Russia.

XII Infantry Corps

Commander :—

C. of S. :—

Home Station :—Wiesbaden (Wkr. XII).

Part of the peace-time standing army.

Campaigns :—Western, Russian.

XIII Infantry Corps

Commander :—Gen. d. Inf. Erich JASCHKE (54).

C. of S. :—

Home Station :—Nuremburg (Wkr. XIII).
Part of the peace-time standing army.
Campaigns :—Polish, Western, Russian.

XIV Corps—*see* XIV Pz. Corps (Section (*e*) below).

XV Corps—*see* 3 Panzer Army (Section (*c*) above).

XVI Corps—*see* 4 Panzer Army (Section (*c*) above).

XVII Infantry Corps

Commander :—Gen. d. Art. Erich BRANDENBERGER (51).

C. of S.—

Home Station :—Vienna (Wkr. XVII).
Part of the peace-time standing army, since April, 1938.
Campaigns :—Polish, Western, Russian.

XVIII Corps—*see* XVIII Mtn. Corps (Section (*f*) below).

XIX Corps—*see* 2 Panzer Army (Section (*c*) above).

XX Infantry Corps

Commander :—Gen. d. Art. Rudolf Frhr. v. ROMAN (51).

C. of S.—

Home Station :—Danzig (Wkr. XX).
Formed shortly before mobilisation.
Campaigns :—Polish, Russian.

XXI Infantry Corps—*see* Army of Norway (Section (*b*) above).

XXII Infantry Corps—*see* 1 Panzer Army (Section (*c*) above).

XXIII Infantry Corps

Commander :—Gen. d. Inf. Karl HILPERT (56).

C. of S. :—

Home Station :—Bonn (Wkr. VI).
Part of the peace-time standing army (as " Eifel Frontier Corps").
Campaigns :—Western, Russian.

XXIV Infantry Corps—*see* XXIV Pz. Corps (Section (*e*) below).

XXV Infantry Corps

Commander :—Gen. d. Inf. Wilhelm FARMBACHER (56) ?

C. of S. :—

Home Station :—Baden-Baden (Wkr. V).

Part of the peace-time standing army (*as* " Upper Rhine Frontier Corps ").

Campaign :—Western.

XXVI Infantry Corps

Commander :—

C. of S.—

Home Station :—(Wkr. I).

Formed on mobilisation.

Campaigns :—Polish, Western, Russian.

XXVII Infantry Corps

Commander :—

C. of S. :—

Home Station :—(Wkr. VII).

Formed on mobilisation.

Campaigns :—Western, Russian.

XXVIII Infantry Corps

Commander :—Gen. d. Art. Herbert LOCH (58).

C. of S. :—

Home Station :—(Wkr. III).

Formed in early summer, 1940.

Campaign :—Russian.

XXIX Infantry Corps

Commander :—Gen. d. Inf. Hans v. OBSTFELDER (58).

C. of S.

Home Station :—(Wkr. IV).

Formed in early summer, 1940.

Campaign :—Russian.

XXX Infantry Corps

Commander :—Gen. d. Art. Maximilian FRETTER-PICO (53).
C. of S. :—
Home Station :—(Wkr. XI).
Formed on mobilisation.
Campaigns :—Polish, Western, Balkan, Russian.

XXXI–XXXIV Corps

See XXXI–XXXIV Corps (Lower Establishment) (Section (*g*) below).

XXXV Infantry Corps

Commander :—Gen. d. Art. Rudolf KAEMPFE (61).
C. of S. :—
Home Station :—(Wkr. VIII).
Probably formed shortly after mobilisation.
In Poland late in 1939 until June, 1941 ; thereafter operating as an Infantry Corps in Russia ; designation changed in May, 1942.

XXXVI, XXXVII Corps

See XXXVI and XXXVII Corps (Lower Establishment) (Section (*g*) below.)

XXXVIII Infantry Corps

Commander :—Gen. d. Inf. Kurt HERZOG (56).
C. of S. :—
Home Station :—(Wkr. VIII?).
Formed on mobilisation.
Campaigns :—Polish, Western, Russian.

XXXIX–XXXXI Corps

See XXXIX–XXXXI Pz. Corps (Section (*e*) below).

XXXXII Infantry Corps

Commander :—
C. of S. :—
Home Station :—(Wkr. III).
Formed on mobilisation.
Campaigns :—Polish, Western, Russian.

XXXXIII Infantry Corps

Commander :—Gen. d. Inf. Karl v. OVEN (56).

C. of S. :—Obst. Otto SCHULTZ ( ).

Home Station :—Hanover (Wkr. XI).
Formed in early summer of 1940.
Campaigns :—Western, Russian.

XXXXIV Infantry Corps

Commander :—Gen. d. Art. Maximilian ANGELIS (55).

C. of S. :—

Home Station :—Dresden (Wkr. IV).
Formed in early summer of 1940.
Campaigns : —Western, Russian.

XXXXV Corps

See XXXXV Corps (lower establishment) (Section (*g*) below).

XXXXVI–XXXXVIII Corps

See XXXXVI–XXXXVIII Pz. Corps (Section (*e*) below).

XXXXIX Corps

See XXXXIX Mtn. Corps (Section (*f*) below).

L Infantry Corps

Commander :—Gen. d. Inf. Philipp KLEFFEL (57).

C. of S. :—

Home Station :—(Wkr. V).
Formed late in 1940.
Campaigns :—Balkan, Russian.

LI Infantry Corps

Home Station :—(Wkr. XI).
Formed late in 1940.
Campaigns : Balkan, Russian ; destroyed at Stalingrad. *See* LI Mountain Corps (Section (*f*) below).

LII Infantry Corps

Commander :—

C. of S. :—

Home Station :—(Wkr. III).

Formed late in 1940.

Campaign :—Russian.

LIII Infantry Corps

Commander :—Gen. d. Inf. Erich CLÖSSNER (58).

C. of S. :—

Home Station :—(Wkr. XII).

Formed late in 1940.

Campaign : Russian.

LIV Infantry Corps

Commander :—Gen. d. Inf. Gustav HÖHNE (51).

C. of S. :—

Home Station :—

Formed as a corps (lower establishment) in 1940, and upgraded in the spring of 1941.

Campaign : Russian.

LV Infantry Corps

Commander :—Gen. d. Inf. Paul VOLCKERS (53) ?

C. of S. :—

Home Station :—

Probably formed in the spring of 1941.

Campaign : Russian.

LVI–LVII Corps

See LVI–LVII Pz. Corps (Section (*e*) below).

LVIII Infantry Corps

Not yet reported.

LIX Infantry Corps

Commander :—Gen. d. Inf. Kurt v.d. CHEVALLERIE (53).
C. of S. :—
Home Station :—
Probably formed in the Spring of 1941.
Campaign : Russian.

LX–LXVII Corps

See LX—LXVII Corps (lower establishment) (Section (*g*) below).

LXVIII Infantry Corps

Commander :—
C. of S. :—Genmaj. Heinz von GYLDENFELDT.
Home Station :—
Probably formed in summer of 1941.
Campaigns :

LXIX–LXXI Corps

See LXIX–LXXI Corps (lower establishment) (Section (*g*) below.)

LXXII–LXXV Corps

Not yet reported.

LXXVI Corps

See LXXVI Panzer Corps (Section (*e*) below).

LXXVII–LXXIX Corps

Not yet reported.

LXXX Infantry Corps

Commander :—
C. of S. :—
Home Station :—
Formed probably early summer, 1942, in France, where it has remained.

LXXXI Infantry Corps

Commander :—Gen. d. Pz. Tr. Adolf KUNTZEN (55).

C. of S. :—

Home Station :—

Formed early summer, 1942, by the upgrading of XXXII Corps (lower establishment) in France, where it has remained.

LXXXII Infantry Corps

Commander :—Gen. d. Art. SINNHUBER (57).

C. of S. :—Obst. von DITFURTH.

Home Station :—(Wkr. XVII).

Formed early summer, 1942, by upgrading XXXVII Corps (lower establishment) in France, where it has remained.

LXXXIII Infantry Corps

Commander :—

C. of S. :—

Home Station :—

Formed early summer, 1942, in France, where it has remained.

LXXXIV Infantry Corps

Commander :—Gen. d. Art. BEHLENDORFF (55).

C. of S. :—

Home Station :—

Formed early summer, 1942, by upgrading LX Corps (lower establishment) in France, where it has remained.

LXXXV Corps

Not yet reported.

LXXXVI Infantry Corps

Commander :—Gen. d. Inf. Bruno BIELER (56).

C. of S. :—

Home Station :—

Formed probably late 1942 in France, where it has remained.

LXXXVII Infantry Corps

Commander :—

C. of S. :—

Home Station :—

Formed probably late in 1942, in France.

LXXXVIII Infantry Corps

Commander :—Gen. d. Inf. Hans REINHARD (55).

C. of S. :—

Home Station :—

Formed summer, 1942, in Holland, where it has remained.

LXXXIX Infantry Corps

Commander :—Gen. d. Pz. Tr. Dr. Alfred Ritter von HUBICKI (53).

C. of S. :—

Home Station :—

Formed as " Schelde " Corps in summer, 1942, in Belgium, where it has remained. Renamed LXXXIX Corps in December, 1942, or January, 1943.

(*e*) PANZER CORPS

III Panzer Corps (III Pz. K.)

Commander :—Gen. d. Pz. Tr. Hermann BREITH (52).

C. of S. :—

Home Station :—Berlin (Wkr. III).

Part of peace-time standing army.

Campaigns : Polish and Western (as III Inf. Corps), Russian.

XIV Panzer Corps

Commander :—Gen. d. Inf. Hans HUBE (54).

C. of S. :—

Home Station :—Magdeburg (Wkr. XI).

Part of the peace-time standing army destroyed at Stalingrad ; re-formed summer, 1943.

Campaigns : Polish and Western (as XIV Mot. Corps), Balkan, Russian, Sicily, Italy.

XXIV Panzer Corps

Commander :—Gen. d. Pz. Tr. Walter NEHRING (52).

C. of S. :—

Home Station :—Kaiserslautern (Wkr. XII).

Part of the peace-time standing army (as "Saar-Palatinate Frontier Corps").

Campaigns : Polish and Western (as XXIV Inf. Corps), Russian.

XXXIX Panzer Corps

Commander :—Gen. d. Art. Robert MARTINEK (60).

C. of S. :—

Home Station :—(Wkr. IX).

Formed late in 1939.

Campaigns : Western, Russian.

XXXX Panzer Corps

Commander :—Gen. d. Art. Sigfrid HENRICI (56).

C. of S. :—Col. HESSE.

Home Station :—(Wkr. X).

Formed late in 1939.

Campaigns : Western, Balkan, Russian.

XXXXI Panzer Corps

Commander :—

C. of S. :—

Home Station :—

Formed late in 1939.

Campaigns : Western, Balkan, Russian.

XXXXVI Panzer Corps

Commander :—Genlt. Friedrich HOSSBACH (50).

C. of S. :—

Home Station :—(Wkr. X).

Formed in early summer, 1940 ; dissolved late 1940 ; re-formed early 1941.

Campaigns : Balkan, Russian.

XXXXVII Panzer Corps

Commander :—
C. of S. :—
Home Station :—Danzig (Wkr. XX).
Formed in early summer, 1940.
Campaign : Russian.

XXXXVIII Panzer Corps

Commander :—Gen. d. Pz. Tr. Otto v. KNOBELSDORFF (58).
C. of S. :—
Home Station :—Posen (Wkr. XXI).
Formed in early summer, 1940.
Campaign : Russian.

LVI Panzer Corps

Commander :—
C. of S. :—
Home Station :—(Wkr. VI).
Formed late in 1940.
Campaign : Russian.

LVII Panzer Corps

Commander :—Gen. d. Pz. Tr. Friedrich KIRCHNER (59).
C. of S. :—
Home Station :—(Wkr. II).
Formed late in 1940.
Campaign : Russian.

LXXVI Panzer Corps

Commander :—Gen. d. Inf. Traugott HERR (54).
C. of S. :—
Home Station :—
Formed summer, 1943, in Italy.
Campaigns : Italian.

Africa Panzer Corps (Pz. K. Afrika)

Formed (as the German Africa Corps) in the spring of 1941.
Campaigns : Libya and Egypt. Destroyed in Tunisia.

(*f*) MOUNTAIN CORPS

XV Mountain Corps (XV Geb. K.)

Commander :—Gen. d. Inf. Rudolph LÜTERS (61).
C. of S. :—
Home Station :—

XVIII Mountain Corps

Commander :—Gen. d. Inf. Franz BÖHME (59).
C. of S. :—
Home Station :—Salzburg (Wkr. XVIII).
Part of the peace-time standing army since April, 1938.
Campaigns : Polish, Western, Balkan, Finnish.

XIX Mountain Corps

Commander :—Genlt. Ritter v. HENGL.
C. of S. :—
Home Station :—(Wkr. XVIII).
Formed in summer, 1940, in North Norway, as Norway Mountain Corps. Renamed XIX Mountain Corps, summer, 1942.
Campaigns : Murmansk front.

XXI Mountain Corps

Commander :—Gen. d. Art. Paul BADER (59).
C. of S. :—
Home Station :—
Formed late summer, 1943.

XXII Mountain Corps

Commander :—Gen. d. Inf. Hubert LANZ (48).
C. of S. :—
Home Station :—
Formed late summer, 1943.

XXXVI Mountain Corps

Commander :—Gen. d. Inf. Karl WEISENBERGER (54).

C. of S. :—Obstlt. HÖLTER.

Home Station :—(Wkr. II).

Probably formed shortly after mobilisation.

In Norway from summer 1940, until June, 1941 ; thereafter operating as an infantry corps in North Finland ; converted into a mountain corps late 1941 or early 1942.

XXXXIX Mountain Corps

Commander :—Gen. d. Geb. Tr. Rudolf KONRAD (53).

C. of S. :—

Home Station :—Prague (Protectorate).

Formed early summer, 1940.

Campaigns : Balkan, Russian.

LI Mountain Corps

Commander :—Gen. d. Geb. Tr. Valentin FEURSTEIN (59).

C. of S. :—

Home Station :—(Wkr. XI).

Original LI Army Corps destroyed at Stalingrad (Section (*d*) above). LI Mountain Corps formed summer, 1943.

Norway Mountain Corps (Geb. K. Norwegen)

Formed in summer, 1940, in North Norway. Renamed XIX Mountain Corps.

(*g*) CORPS (LOWER ESTABLISHMENT)

XXXI Corps Command (Höh. Kdo. z.b.V. XXXI)

Commander.—Gen. d. Inf. v. HANNEKEN (54).

C. of S. :—

Home Station :—(Wkr. X ?).

Probably formed shortly after mobilisation.

In Denmark since April, 1940.

XXXII Corps Command

See LXXXI Infantry Corps (Section (*d*) above).

XXXIII Corps Command

Commander :—Gen. d. Kav. Erwin ENGELBRECHT (53).

C. of S.—

Home Station—(Wkr. VI).

Probably formed shortly after mobilisation.

In Norway since summer, 1940.

XXXIV Corps Command

Commander :—

C. of S. :—

Home Station : (Wkr. III).

Probably formed shortly after mobilisation ; continued existence uncertain.

In Poland from late 1939 until June, 1941 ; thereafter operating as an Infantry Corps in Russia.

XXXV Corps Command

See XXXV Infantry Corps (Section (*d*) above).

XXXVI Corps Command

See XXXVI Mountain Corps (Section (*f*) above).

XXXVII Corps Command

See LXXXII Infantry Corps (Section (*d*) above).

XXXXV Corps Command

Believed disbanded.

LX Corps Command

See LXXXIV Infantry Corps (Section (*d*) above).

LXI Reserve Corps (Gen. Kdo.Res.K.)

Commander :—Gen. d. Inf. Edgar THEISEN (55).

C. of S. :—

Home Station :—

Formed September, 1942, in Poland, where it has remained.

LXII Reserve Corps

Commander :—Gen. d. Inf. Ferdinand NEULING (59).

C. of S. :—

Home Station :—

Formed September, 1943, in Poland, where it has remained.

LXIII Corps Command

See Army of Norway (Section (*b*) above).

LXIV Reserve Corps

Commander :—

C. of S. :—

Home Station :—

Formerly LXIV Corps (Lower Establishment) : date of formation uncertain ; converted into a Reserve Corps in autumn, 1942, in France.

LXV Corps Command

Commander :—

C. of S. :—

Home Station :—(Wkr. II).

Probably formed early in 1941 : continued existence uncertain. In Yugoslavia since May, 1941.

LXVI Reserve Corps

Commander :—Gen. d. Inf. Baptist KNIESS (58).

C. of S. :—

Home Station :—

Formed in autumn, 1942, in France, where it has remained.

LXVII Reserve Corps

Commander :—

C. of S. :—

Home Station :—

Formerly LXVII Corps (Lower Establishment) : date of formation uncertain ; converted to a Reserve Corps probably in autumn, 1942, in France, where it has remained.

LXIX Reserve Corps

Commander :—Genlt. Erich DENECKE (52).

C. of S. :—

Home Station :—

Formed probably late in 1942 in the Balkans, where it has remained.

LXX Corps Command

Commander :—Gen. d. Art. Hermann TITTEL (55).

C. of S. :—

Home Station :—(Wkr. VI ?).

Formed in Norway in autumn, 1941.

In South Norway.

LXXI Corps Command

Commander :—Gen. d. Art. Willi MOSER (56).

C. of S. :—

Home Station :—

Formed in Norway in spring, 1942.

In North Norway.

(*h*) PANZER DIVISIONS

1 Panzer Division

Commander :—Genlt. Walter KRÜGER (54).

Composition :—Pz. Rgt. 1 ; Pz. Gr. Rgt. 1 ; Pz. Gr. Rgt. 113 ; Pz. Arty. Rgt. 73 ; Pz. Pi. Btl. 37 ; Pz. Jäg. Abt. 37 ; Pz. Aufkl. Abt. 1 ; Pz. Nachr. Abt. 37.

Auxiliary unit number :—81.

Home Station :—Weimar (Wkr. IX).

Active division. Personnel largely from Thüringen and Saxony. Fought well in Central Poland and throughout the operations of May–June, 1940. Continuously engaged in Russia, at first in the North and subsequently in the Centre. Transferred to France early in 1943. Sent to the Balkans, 1943, and returned to Russia in the late autumn.

2 Panzer Division

Commander :—Genlt. Vollrath LÜBBE (50).

Composition :—Pz. Rgt. 3 ; Pz. Gr. Rgt. 2 ; Pz. Gr. Rgt. 304 ; Pz. Arty. Rgt. 74 ; Pz. Pi. Btl. 38 ; Pz. Jäg. Abt. 38 ; Pz. Aufkl. Abt. 2 ; Pz. Nachr. Abt. 38.

Auxiliary unit number :—82.

Home Station :—Wien (Wkr. XVII).

Active division. Personnel largely Austrian. Fought in Southern Poland. Not so conspicuous as the other Panzer divisions during the operations in France. Fought in the Balkan campaign and has been engaged in Russia in the Central Sector since September, 1941. Took part in the Kursk offensive in summer 1943, and has latterly been defending the Middle Dnieper.

3 Panzer Division

Commander :—Genmaj. Fritz BAYERLEIN (55).

Composition :—Pz. Rgt. 6 ; Pz. Gr. Rgt. 3 ; Pz. Gr. Rgt. 394 ; Pz. Pi. Btl. 39 ; Pz. Jäg. Abt. — ; Pz. Aufkl. Abt. 3 ; Pz. Nachr. Abt. 39.

Auxiliary unit number :—83.

Home Station :—Berlin (Wkr. III).

Active division. Personnel mainly Prussian. Fought well in Poland and in Belgium and France. Continuously engaged in Russia since the outset of the campaign, first in the Central and subsequently in the Southern Sector. Suffered heavy losses in the Mozdok area at the end of 1942. Heavily engaged in the Kharkov area during summer 1943.

4 Panzer Division

Commander :—Genlt. Dietrich v. SAUCKEN (52).

Composition :—Pz. Rgt. 35 ; Pz. Gr. Rgt. 12; Pz. Gr. Rgt. 33; Pz. Arty. Rgt. 103 ; Pz. Pi. Btl. 79 ; Pz. Jäg. Abt. 49 ; Pz. Aufkl. Abt. 4 ; Pz. Nachr. Abt. 79.

Auxiliary unit number :—84.

Home Station :—Würzburg (Wkr. XIII).

Active division. Personnel largely Bavarian. Fought in Poland and in Belgium and France. Continuously engaged in the Russian campaign in the Central Sector. Took part in the Kursk offensive in summer, 1943, and subsequently fought on the Middle Dnieper.

5 Panzer Division

Commander :—Genmaj. Karl DECKER

Composition :—Pz. Rgt. 31 ; Pz. Gr. Rgt. 13; Pz. Gr. Rgt. 14; Pz. Arty. Rgt. 116 ; Pz. Pi. Btl. 89 ; Pz. Jäg. Abt. 53 ; Pz. Aufkl. Abt. 5 ; Pz. Nachr. Abt. 85 ?

Auxiliary unit number :—85.

Home Station :—Oppeln (Wkr. VIII).

Active division, formed late in 1938. Personnel mainly Silesian or Sudeten German. Inconspicuous in Poland, but prominent in the French campaign, where it shared with the 7th Panzer Division in the advance on Le Havre. Took part in the Balkan campaign, both in Yugoslavia and Greece, and has been continuously engaged in Russia in the Central Sector. Took part in the Kursk offensive in summer, 1943, where it apparently suffered heavy losses. Subsequently fought on the Middle Dnieper.

6 Panzer Division

Commander :—

Composition :—Pz. Rgt. 11 ; Pz. Gr. Rgt. 4 ; Pz. Gr. Rgt. 114 ; Pz. Arty. Rgt. 76 ; Pz. Pi. Btl. 57 ; Pz. Jäg. Abt. 41 ; Pz. Aufkl. Abt. 6 ; Pz. Nachr. Abt. 82.

Auxiliary unit number :—57.

Home Station :—Wuppertal (Wkr. VI).

Active division (formerly 1 Light Div.). Personnel mainly Westphalian. Fought hard in Poland and in France. Has been continuously engaged in the Russian campaign, first in the North and later in the Centre, where it apparently suffered serious losses. Transferred to France for rest and refit in May, 1942. In December, 1942, it returned to the Southern Sector of the Russian Front and was heavily engaged in the Byelgorod offensive of summer, 1943.

7 Panzer Division

Commander :—Genmaj. Hasso v. MANTEUFFEL (47).

Composition :—Pz. Rgt. 25 ; Pz. Gr. Rgt. 6 ; Pz. Gr. Rgt. 7 ; Pz. Arty. Rgt. 78 ; Pz. Pi. Btl. 58 ; Pz. Jäg. Abt. 42 ; Pz. Aufkl. Abt. 7 ; Pz. Nachr. Abt. 83.

Auxiliary unit number :—58.

Home Station :—Gera (Wkr. IX).

Active division (formerly 2 Light Div.). Personnel mainly Thuringian or Saxon. Fought in Poland and with outstanding dash in France, where it was mainly responsible for the successful advance to Le Havre. During these operations it was commanded by the then Genmaj. Rommel. Continuously engaged in Russia in the Central Sector where it appears to have sustained appreciable casualties. Transferred to France for rest and refit in May, 1942. Took part in the occupation of former unoccupied France. Returned to Russia, Southern Sector, in February, 1943. Engaged in Byelgorod offensive summer, 1943, and apparently suffered heavy losses in the retreat from Kiev, November 1943.

8 Panzer Division

Commander :—Obst. (?) FRÖHLICH.

Composition :—Pz. Rgt. 10 ; Pz. Gr. Rgt. 8 ; Pz. Gr. Rgt. 28 ; Pz. Arty. Rgt. 80 ; Pz. Pi. Btl. 59 ; Pz. Jäg. Abt. 43 ; Pz. Aufkl.Abt. 8 ; Pz. Nachr. Abt. 59.

Auxiliary unit number :—59.

Home Station :—Cottbus (Wkr. III).

Active division (formerly 3 Light Div.). Personnel mainly Prussian. Fought well in Poland and in France. In Yugoslavia during the Balkan campaign, but no evidence that it took any particular part in the operations. Continuously and heavily engaged on the Northern Russian front up to the end of 1941. Identified in the Central Sector in the autumn of 1942. Was transferred to the Southern Sector after the Orel offensive in summer, 1943. Apparently suffered heavy casualties in autumn, 1943, during the retreat from Kiev.

9 Panzer Division

Commander :—Genlt. Walter SCHELLER (52).

Composition :—Pz. Rgt. 33 ; Pz. Gr. Rgt. 10 ; Pz. Gr. Rgt. 11 ; Pz. Arty. Rgt. 102 ; Pz. Pi. Btl. 86 ; Pz. Jäg. Abt. 50 ; Pz. Aufkl. Abt. 9 ; Pz. Nachr. Abt. 81.

Auxiliary unit number :—60.

Home Station :—Wien (Wkr. XVII).

Active division (formerly 4 Light Div.). Personnel largely Austrian. Fought well in Poland. Continuously engaged throughout the operations in the West, covering a greater distance than any other Panzer division. Took part in the Balkan campaign, both in Yugoslavia and Greece. Continuously engaged in Russia during the advance through the Ukraine and during the offensive in the Southern Sector in 1942. Later transferred to the Central Sector, where it took part in the Kursk offensive of summer, 1943. It returned to the Southern Sector in the following autumn, where it has been heavily engaged.

10 Panzer Division

Commander :—

Composition :—Pz. Rgt. 7 ; Pz. Gr. Rgt. 69 ; Pz. Gr. Rgt. 86 ; Pz. Arty. Rgt. 90 ; Pz. Pi. Btl. 49 ; Pz. Jäg. Abt. 90 ; Pz. Aufkl. Abt. 10 ; Pz. Nachr. Abt. 90.

Auxiliary unit number :—90.

Home Station :—Stuttgart (Wkr. V).

Composite division, made up of active units from various parts of Germany. Fought well in Poland. Spearhead in the breakthrough at Sedan, taking only a minor part in subsequent operations. Heavily engaged in the Russian campaign in the Central Sector up to the end of 1941. Transferred to France for rest and refit in

May, 1942. Took part in the occupation of former unoccupied France. Transferred to Tunisia late in 1942, where it was destroyed in May, 1943. In view of its distinguished record it is likely that this division will eventually be re-formed, but its reconstitution has not yet been established.

11 Panzer Division

Commander :—Genmaj. Wend. v. WIETERSHEIM (44).

Composition :—Pz. Rgt. 15 ; Pz. Gr. Rgt. 110 ; Pz. Gr. Rgt. 111 ; Pz. Arty. Rgt. 119 ; Pz. Pi. Btl. 209 ; Pz. Jäg. Abt. — ; Pz. Aufkl. Abt. 11 ; Pz. Nachr. Abt. 341.

Auxiliary unit number :—61.

Home Station :—Görlitz (Wkr. VIII).

Formation completed after the French campaign during which the 11th Motorised Inf. Brig. fought and distinguished itself as an independent command. Took part in the Balkan campaign. Continuously engaged in Russia, first in the advance through the Ukraine and subsequently in the Central Sector. Transferred to the Southern Sector in the summer of 1942. It took part in the Byelgorod offensive of summer, 1943 and was subsequently heavily engaged in the Krivoi Rog area in the autumn of 1943.

12 Panzer Division

Commander :—

Composition :—Pz. Rgt. 29 ; Pz. Gr. Rgt. 5 ; Pz. Gr. Rgt. 25 ; Pz. Arty. Rgt. 2 ; Pz. Pi. Btl. 32 ; Pz. Jäg. Abt. 2 ; Pz. Aufkl. Abt. 12 ; Pz. Nachr. Abt. 2.

Auxiliary unit number :—2.

Home Station :—Stettin (Wkr. II).

Originally 2 Motorised Division, belonging to the peacetime army, with mainly Prussian personnel. As such saw little fighting in Poland, but was actively engaged in France. Reorganised as the 12 Panzer Division in the autumn of 1940. Was continuously engaged in Russia, first in the Centre and later in the North up to the end of 1941, when after sustaining considerable losses it was withdrawn to Estonia for rest and refit. Subsequently returned to the front in the Northern Sector. It was later transferred to the Central Sector and took part in the Kursk offensive of summer, 1943. Has since been heavily engaged in the Middle Dnieper.

13 Panzer Division

Commander :—Genmaj HAUSER.

Composition :—Pz. Rgt. 4 ; Pz. Gr. Rgt. 66 ; Pz. Gr. Rgt. 93 ; Pz. Arty. Rgt. 13 ; Pz. Pi. Btl. 4 ; Pz. Jäg. Abt. 13 ; Pz. Aufkl. Abt. 13 ; Pz. Nachr. Abt. 13.

Auxiliary unit number :—13.

Home Station :—Magdeburg (Wkr. XI).

Formed in the autumn of 1940 out of the former 13th Motorised Division, which had fought with great distinction in Poland and in France. Spent the winter of 1940–41 in Roumania. Continuously engaged on the Southern Russian front, where it took part in the encirclement of Kiev in 1941 and in the advance to Mozdok in 1942. Suffered heavy losses late in 1942. It took part in the retreat from the Caucasus in winter 1942 and remained in the Kuban until evacuated to the Lower Dnieper in autumn, 1943.

14 Panzer Division

Commander :—

Composition :—Pz. Rgt. 36 ; Pz. Gr. Rgt. 103 ; Pz. Gr. Rgt. 108 ; Pz. Arty. Rgt. 4 ; Pz. Pi. Btl. 13 ; Pz. Jäg. Abt. 4 ; Pz. Aufkl. Abt. 14 ; Pz. Nachr. Abt. 4.

Auxiliary unit number :—4.

Home Station :—Dresden (Wkr. IV).

Originally 4 Infantry Division, belonging to the peacetime army, with personnel from Saxony and Sudetenland. As such fought well in Poland and in the French campaign and was reorganised as 14 Panzer Division in the late summer of 1940. Fought in Yugoslavia in the Balkan campaign and was continuously engaged on the Southern Russian front, where it was finally encircled and virtually destroyed at Stalingrad. It was reformed in Brittany in summer 1943 and was transferred to the Southern Sector of the Russian front in October, 1943.

15 Panzer Division

See 15 Panzer Grenadier Division.

16 Panzer Division

Commander :—

Composition :—Pz. Rgt. 2 ; Pz. Gr. Rgt. 64 ; Pz. Gr. Rgt. 79 ; Pz. Arty. Rgt. 16 ; Pz. Pi. Btl. 16 ; Pz. Jäg. Abt. 16 ; Pz. Aufkl. Abt. 16 ; Pz. Nachr. Abt. 16.

Auxiliary unit number :—16.

Home Station :—Münster (Wkr. VI)

Originally 16 Infantry Division, belonging to the peacetime army, with personnel from Westphalia and some East Prussians. As such was on the Saar front for a period and later took part in the attack on Sedan in support of armoured formations. Reorganised as 16 Panzer Division in the late summer of 1940. First identified in action during the early weeks of the Russian campaign and then continuously engaged in the Southern sector. Virtually destroyed at Stalingrad. Re-formed in France, spring 1943. Moved to Italy June, 1943, where it has remained ever since.

17 Panzer Division

Commander :—Genmaj v. der MEDEN (48).

Composition :—Pz. Rgt. 39 ; Pz. Gr. Rgt. 40 ; Pz. Gr. Rgt. 63 ; Pz. Arty. Rgt. 27 ; Pz. Pi. Btl. 27 ; Pz. Jäg. Abt. 27 ; Pz. Aufkl. Abt. 17 ; Pz. Nachr. Abt. 27.

Auxiliary unit number :—27.

Home Station :—Augsburg (Wkr. VII).

Originally 27 Infantry Division, belonging to the peacetime army, with Bavarian personnel. As such fought and marched extremely well, both in Poland and in France. Reorganised as 17 Panzer Division in the autumn of 1940. First identified in action on the Central Russian front in late June 1941 and subsequently was continuously in action. Transferred to the Southern sector at the time of the Russian offensive in November, 1942, where it has been heavily engaged during the defensive operations of summer and autumn of 1943.

18 Panzer Division

Commander :—

Composition :—Pz. Rgt. 18 ; Pz. Gr. Rgt. 52 ; Pz. Gr. Rgt. 101 ; Pz. Arty. Rgt. 88 ; Pz. Pi. Btl. 98 ; Pz. Jäg. Abt. 88 ; Pz. Aufkl. Abt. 18 ; Pz. Nachr. Abt. 88.

Auxiliary unit number :—88.

Home Station :—(Wkr. IV).

Formed in the autumn of 1940. First identified in action on the Central Russian front in late June, 1941. Operated in the Southern sector in the summer of 1942 and subsequently transferred back to the Central sector. Believed still operating in Russia, autumn 1943:

19 Panzer Division

Commander :—Genlt. Gustav SCHMIDT (50).

Composition :—Pz. Rgt. 27 ; Pz. Gr. Rgt. 73 ; Pz. Gr. Rgt. 74 ; Pz. Arty. Rgt. 19 ; Pz. Pi. Btl. 19 ; Pz. Jäg. Abt. 19 ; Pz. Aufkl. Abt. 19 ; Pz. Nachr. Abt. 19.

Auxiliary unit number :—19.

Home Station :—Hannover (Wkr. XI).

Originally 19 Infantry Division, belonging to the peacetime army and recruited mainly in the Hannover area. As such fought well in Poland and against the British in Belgium. Not identified during the French campaign and was reorganised as 19 Panzer Division in the autumn of 1940. Took part in the initial attack on Russia, and has since operated in the Central sector. It was transferred to the Southern sector in spring 1943 and took part in the Byelgorod offensive in summer of that year where it apparently suffered very heavy casualties.

20 Panzer Division

Commander :—Genlt. Heinrich Frhr. v. LÜTTWITZ (48).

Composition :—Pz. Rgt. 21 ; Pz. Gr. Rgt. 59 ; Pz. Gr. Rgt. 112 ; Pz. Arty. Rgt. 92 ; Pz. Pi. Btl. 92 ; Pz. Jäg. Abt. 92 ; Pz. Aufkl. Abt. 20 ; Pz. Nachr. Abt. 92.

Auxiliary unit number :—92.

Home Station :—Gotha (Wkr. IX).

Formed in the autumn of 1940. First identified in action on the Central Russian front at the outset of the campaign, where it has been continuously engaged ever since. It took part in the Orel offensive in summer, 1943, and may now have transferred to the Southern sector.

21 Panzer Division

Commander :—

Composition :—Pz. Rgt. 5 ; Pz. Gr. Rgt. 192? ; Pz. Gr. Rgt. 492? ; Pz. Arty. Rgt. 155 ; Pz. Pi. Btl. 200 ; Pz. Jäg. Abt. 39 ; Pz. Aufkl. Abt. 21 ; Pz. Nachr. Abt. 200.

Auxiliary unit number :—200.

Home Station :—Berlin (Wkr. III).

At first known as 5 Light Division. Formed after the French campaign partly from units of 3 Panzer Division. Reorganised as a Panzer Division in Africa during the summer of 1941. Suffered heavy losses in the autumn of 1942. Entered Tunisia early in 1943, where it was destroyed in May, 1943. Re-formed in Normandy, France, in summer, 1943, and has remained in France ever since.

22 Panzer Division

Commander :—

Composition :—

Auxiliary unit number :—

Home Station :—(Wkr. XII).

Formed in France in October, 1940. Transferred to Russia (Southern sector) early in 1942 and thrown immediately into action, subsequently suffering heavy casualties both in the Crimea and at Stalingrad. It has since been disbanded.

23 Panzer Division

Commander :—Genlt. Nickolaus von VORMANN (49).

Composition :—Pz. Rgt. 201 ; Pz. Gr. Rgt. 126 ; Pz. Gr. Rgt. 128 ; Pz. Arty. Rgt. 128 ; Pz. Pi. Btl. 128 ; Pz. Jäg. Abt. 128 ; Pz. Aufkl. Abt. 23 ; Pz. Nachr. Abt. 128.

Auxiliary unit number :—128.

Home Station :—(Wkr. V).

Formed in France in October, 1940. Transferred to Russia in the spring of 1942 and identified in action in the Kharkov area. Later fought at Mozdok and then transferred to the Stalingrad area at the time of the Russian break through. It retreated from the Mius front in summer, 1943, and was heavily engaged in the Dnieper Bend in the following autumn.

24 Panzer Division

Commander :—Genlt. Reichsfrhr. von EDELSHEIM (47).

Composition :—Pz. Rgt. 24 ; Pz. Gr. Rgt. 21 ; Pz. Gr. Rgt. 26 ; Pz. Arty. Rgt. 89 ; Pz. Pi. Btl. 40 ; Pz. Jäg. Abt. 40 ; Pz. Aufkl. Abt. 24 ; Pz. Nachr. Abt. —.

Auxiliary unit number :—40.

Home Station :—(Wkr. I).

Formed in France in February, 1942, largely from the former 1st Cavalry Division, which had fought as a brigade in Poland and as a division in France and in the early stages of the Russian campaign. Transferred to the Southern Russian front in the summer of 1942 and virtually destroyed at Stalingrad. It later reformed in France and returned to the Southern sector of the Russian front in autumn, 1943.

25 Panzer Division

Commander :—Genlt. Adolf v. SCHELL (50).

Composition :—Pz. Rgt. 9 ; Pz. Gr. Rgt. 146 ; Pz. Gr. Rgt. 147 ; Pz. Arty. Rgt. 91 ; Pz. Pi. Btl. 75? ; Pz. Jäg. Abt. — ; Pz. Aufkl. Abt. 25 ; Pz. Nachr. Abt. 87?

Auxiliary unit number :—87?.

Home Station :—(Wkr. VI).

Reported forming in Norway early in 1942. It was transferred to Northern France in August, 1943, where it was probably brought up to establishment. It was sent to the Southern sector of the Russian front in October, 1943.

26 Panzer Division

Commander :—Genlt. Smilo Frhr. v. LÜTTWITZ (49).

Composition :—Pz. Rgt. 26 ; Pz. Gr. Rgt. 9 ; Pz. Gr. Rgt. 67 ; Pz. Arty. Rgt. 93 ; Pz. Pi. Btl. 93 ; Pz. Jäg. Abt. — ; Pz. Aufkl. Abt. 26 ; Pz. Nachr. Abt. 93.

Auxiliary unit number :—93.

Home Station :—Potsdam (Wkr. III).

Formed in France in autumn, 1942, from elements of 23 Infantry Division. Remained in France till June, 1943, when it was transferred to Italy.

27 Panzer Division

Commander :—

Composition :—

Auxiliary unit number :—

Home Station :—(Wkr. IX).

Formed in France during the summer and autumn of 1942. Operated on the Southern Russian front in winter, 1942–43 and is now believed to have been disbanded.

Panzer Division " Hermann Goering "

Commander :—Genlt. (Lw.) Paul CONRATH (48).

Composition :—Pz. Rgt. Hermann Goering ; Gr. Rgt. Hermann Goering 1 ; Gr. Rgt. Hermann Goering 2 ; Jäger Rgt. Hermann Goering ; Arty. Rgt. Hermann Goering ; Flak Rgt. Hermann Goering ; Pz. Pi. Btl. Hermann Goering ; Pz. Aufkl. Abt. Hermann Goering ; Nachr. Abt. Hermann Goering.

Auxiliary unit number :—All other units bear name " Hermann Goering."

Home Station :—

The " Hermann Goering " Brigade was formed in summer, 1942, from the " General Goering " Regiment and in January, 1943, was converted into a Panzer division. The greater part of it was sent to Tunisia, where it was virtually destroyed. In May and June, 1943, it was rapidly reformed from elements which had remained in South-West France, and sent to Sicily. It was heavily engaged in the Sicilian campaign and withdrew to the Italian mainland in August, where it has since been constantly in action.

Panzer Grenadier Division Grossdeutschland

Commander :—Genlt. Walter HOERNLEIN (51).

Deputy Commander :—Obst. Hyanzith Graf STRACHWITZ (50).

Composition :—Pz. Rgt. Grossdeutschland ; Gr. Rgt. Grossdeutschland ; Füs. Rgt. Grossdeutschland ; Arty. Rgt. Grossdeutschland ; Pi. Btl. Grossdeutschland ; Pz. Jäg. Abt. Grossdeutschland ; Pz. Aufkl. Abt. Grossdeutschland ; Nachr. Abt. Grossdeutschland.

Auxiliary unit number :—Grossdeutschland.

Home Station :—Berlin (Wkr. III).

Formed early in 1942 by the expansion of the former independent regiment of the same name, which had been operating in the Central sector in Russia. In peacetime this regiment was stationed in Berlin, its personnel being drawn from all over Germany. After a period of service in it, other ranks were normally promoted and posted to other units.

It was in action as a division in the Southern sector from June, 1942. Transferred to the Central sector in September, 1942, and back to the south at the time of the Russian offensive in winter, 1942, where it has been fairly heavily and continuously engaged. At the time of the German offensive in summer, 1943, it was transferred to the Orel area, but was hastily switched back to the Southern sector shortly after. Although it is known as Panzer Grenadier Division Grossdeutschland, it is rated as a full armoured division as it includes a tank regiment. This division is a *corps d'elite* and has the honour of providing the guard for the Führer's headquarters.

(*j*) MOTORISED DIVISIONS

2 Panzer Grenadier Division—*see* 12 Panzer Division.

3 Panzer Grenadier Division

Commander :—Genlt. Fritz GRÄSER (56).

Composition :—Pz. Abt. 103 ; Gr. Rgt. (mot.) 8 ; Gr. Rgt. (mot.) 29 ; Arty. Rgt. 3 ; Pi. Btl. 3 ; Pz. Jäg. Abt. 3 ; Pz. Aufkl. Abt. 103 ; Nachr. Abt. 3.

Auxiliary unit number :—3.

Home Station :—Frankfurt/Oder (Wkr. III).

Originally 3 Infantry Division, an active division mainly recruited in Prussia. As such it took part in the Polish and French campaigns without winning any special distinction. Motorised in the autumn of 1940. Fought in Russia from the beginning, at first in the centre and subsequently in the Southern sector, where it was virtually destroyed at Stalingrad. Reformed in south-west France in spring, 1943, and incorporated the bulk of 386 Panzer Grenadier Division. Transferred to Italy, June, 1943.

10 Panzer Grenadier Division

Commander :—Genlt. August SCHMIDT (51).

Composition :—Pz. Abt. 110 ? ; Gr. Rgt. (mot.) 20 ; Gr. Rgt. (mot.) 41 ; Arty. Rgt. 10 ; Pi. Btl. 10 ; Pz. Jäg. Abt. 10 ; Pz. Aufkl. Abt. 110 ; Nachr. Abt. 10.

Auxiliary unit number :—10.

Home Station :—Regensburg (Wkr. XIII).

Originally 10 Infantry Division, an active division with personnel from Northern Bavaria and Western Sudetenland. As such, it was actively engaged in Poland, less so in France. Motorised in the autumn of 1940. Fought in the Balkan campaign. Has operated in Russia in the Central sector from the beginning. It took part in the Kursk offensive in summer, 1943, and was subsequently transferred to the Southern sector.

13 Panzer Grenadier Division—*see* 13 Panzer Division.

14 Panzer Grenadier Division

Commander :—Genmaj. FLÖRKE.

Composition :—Pz. Abt. 114 ? ; Gr. Rgt. (mot.) 11 ; Gr. Rgt. (mot.) 53 ; Arty. Rgt. 14 ; Pi. Btl. 14 ; Pz. Jäg. Abt. 14 ; Pz. Aufkl. Abt. 114 ; Nachr. Abt. 14.

Auxiliary unit number : 14.

Home Station :—Leipzig (Wkr. IV).

As 14 Infantry Division, a Saxon division belonging to the peacetime army, it took part in the campaigns in Poland and France, without winning special distinction. Motorised in the autumn of 1940. Identified in the Russian campaign in the battle for Vitebsk. Since then, continuously in action in the Central sector. It appears to have sustained heavy casualties in autumn, 1943.

15 Panzer Grenadier Division

Commander :—Genmaj. Eberhardt RODT (49).

Composition :—Pz. Abt. 115 ; Pz. Gr. Rgt. 104 ; Pz. Gr. Rgt. 115 ? ; Pz. Gr. Rgt. 129 ; Arty. Rgt. 33 ; Pi. Btl. 33 ; Pz. Jäg. Abt. 33 ; Pz. Aufkl. Abt. 115 ? ; Nachr. Abt. 78.

Auxiliary unit number :—33.

Home Station :—Kaiserslautern (Wkr. XII).

Originally 33 Infantry Division, belonging to the peace-time army, with Bavarian personnel from the Palatinate. As such was on the Ardennes front in January, 1939, and fought well during the French campaign. Reorganised as 15 Panzer Division in the autumn of 1940. Transferred to Libya in the spring of 1941. Suffered heavy losses in the autumn of 1942. Entered Tunisia early in 1943 where it was virtually destroyed in May, 1943. In July, 1943, " Division Sizilien," an *ad hoc* division formed from miscellaneous units in Sicily after the fall of Tunisia was renamed 15 Panzer Grenadier Division. It incorporated elements of the former 15 Panzer Division and has been engaged in operations in Italy in autumn, 1943. Pz. Gren. Rgt. 115 has possibly been withdrawn to G.H.Q. pool.

16 Panzer Grenadier Division

Commander :—Genlt. Gerhard Graf v. SCHWERIN (45).

Composition :—Pz. Abt. 116 ; Gr. Rgt. (mot.) 60 ; Gr. Rgt. (mot.) 156 ; Arty. Rgt. 146 ; Pi. Btl. 146 ? ; Pz. Jäg. Abt. — ; Pz Aufkl. Abt. 116 ; Nachr. Abt. 228.

Auxiliary unit number :—66.

Home Station :—Rheine (Wkr. VI).

Formed in the late summer of 1940 from elements of 16 Infantry Division. An active division with personnel mainly Westphalian but partly Prussian. On the Saar front for a period and later took part in the attack on Sedan in support of Panzer units. Engaged in the Balkan campaign and later in the Ukraine. Has since remained in the Southern sector. It took part in the retreat from the Mius in summer, 1943, and has been engaged in the Zaporozhe area where it gained special distinction.

18 Panzer Grenadier Division

Commander :—Genmaj. Hans LEYSER (47).

Composition :—Pz. Abt. 118 ? ; Gr. Rgt. (mot.) 30 ; Gr. Rgt. (mot.) 51 ; Arty. Rgt. 18 ; Pi. Btl. 18 ; Pz. Jäg. Abt. 18 ; Pz. Aufkl. Abt. 118 ; Nachr. Abt. 18.

Auxiliary unit number :—18.

Home Station :—Liegnitz (Wkr. VIII).

Formerly 18 Infantry Division, an active division with Silesian personnel. As such, fought in Poland and in Northern France, winning distinction and sustaining considerable casualties. Motorised in the autumn of 1940. Fought in Russia from the beginning of the campaign, first in the Central and subsequently in the Northern sector. It appears to have transferred to the Central sector in autumn, 1943.

20 Panzer Grenadier Division

Commander :—

Composition :—Pz. Abt. 120 ? ; Gr. Rgt. (mot.) 76 ; Gr. Rgt. (mot.) 90 ; Arty. Rgt. 20 ; Pi. Btl. 20 ; Pz. Jäg. Abt. 20 ; Pz. Aufkl. Abt. 20 ; Nachr. Abt. 20.

Auxiliary unit number :—20.

Home Station :—Hamburg (Wkr. X).

Active division. Recruited mainly in Hamburg. Fought hard and well in Poland. In France it covered great distances but saw less action. Morale very high. First identified in Russia in the Minsk area and later in the Northern sector. Recently engaged at Velikie Luki (Central sector). It gained distinction on the Central sector in summer, 1943, and was later transferred to the Southern sector where it sustained very heavy losses in the retreat from Kiev in November, 1943.

22 Luftlande-Division (motorisiert)

Commander :—Genlt. Friedrich Wilhelm MÜLLER (47).

Composition :—Pz. Abt. 212 ? ; Gr. Rgt. (mot.) 16 ; Gr. Rgt. (mot.) 65 ; Arty. Rgt. 22 ; Pi. Btl. 22 ; Pz. Jäg. Abt. 22 ; Pz. Aufkl. Abt. 122 ; Nachr. Abt. 22.

Auxiliary unit number :—22.

Home Station :—Oldenburg (Wkr. X).

Active division. Personnel mainly from East Prussia and Oldenburg. Employed as air-borne division in Holland. Played a valuable part in the capture of Fortress Holland. Engaged continuously in Russia in the Southern sector. Transferred from the Crimea to Salonika thence to Crete in the late summer of 1942. Sent one regiment (Grenadier Regiment 47) to Tunisia at the end of 1942 where it was destroyed. The remaining two regiments stayed in Crete where the division was reorganised as a motorised division in spring, 1943.

25 Panzer Grenadier Division

Commander :—Genlt. Anton GRASSER (53).

Composition :—Pz. Abt. 125 ? ; Gr. Rgt. (mot.) 35 ; Gr. Rgt. (mot.) 119 ; Arty. Rgt. 25 ; Pi. Btl. 25 ; Pz. Jäg. Abt. 25 ; Pz. Aufkl. Abt. 125 ; Nachr. Abt. 25.

Auxiliary unit number :—25.

Home Station :—Ludwigsburg (Wkr. V).

Originally 25 Infantry Division, an active division recruited in Württemberg, which took little part in active operations. Motorised in the autumn of 1940. Has fought in the Central sector since the beginning of the Russian campaign. It took part in the Kursk offensive in summer, 1943, where it appears to have sustained heavy losses.

29 Panzer Grenadier Division

Commander :—Genmaj. FRIES (48).

Composition :—Pz. Abt. 129 ; Gr. Rgt. (mot.) 15 ; Gr. Rgt. (mot.) 71 ; Arty. Rgt. 29 ; Pi. Btl. 29 ; Pz. Jäg. Abt. 29 ; Pz. Aufkl. Abt. 129 ? ; Nachr. Abt. 29.

Auxiliary unit number :—29.

Home Station :—Erfurt (Wkr. IX).

Active division. Personnel largely Thuringian. Moved great distances and fought hard in Poland and France. Identified in the central sector in Russia in July, 1941. Transferred to the Southern sector in the summer of 1942 and virtually destroyed at Stalingrad. Reformed in south-west France in spring, 1943, incorporating the bulk of 345 Infantry Division. The greater part of the division took part in the Sicilian campaign, July, 1943, and has since been engaged in operations in Italy.

36 Panzer Grenadier Division

Commander :—

Composition :—Pz. Abt. 136 ? ; Gr. Rgt. (mot.) 87 ; Gr. Rgt. (mot.) 118 ; Arty Rgt. 36 ; Pi. Btl. 36 ; Pz. Jäg. Abt. 36 ; Pz. Aufkl. Abt. 136 ; Nachr. Abt. 36.

Auxiliary unit number :—36.
Home Station :—Wiesbaden (Wkr. XII).

As 36 Infantry Division (peace-time army: personnel mainly Bavarian from the Palatinate) it earned some distinction in France, but without a great deal of fighting. Motorised in the autumn of 1940. Entered Russia via the Baltic States and has since operated in the Central sector. It suffered heavy losses in the Rzhev area in summer, 1942, and again in summer, 1943, when taking part in the Kursk offensive.

60 Panzer Grenadier Division

Commander :—Gentl. Otto KOHLERMANN.

Composition :—Pz. Abt. 160 ? ; Füs. Rgt. Feldherrnhalle (120) ; Gr. Rgt. Feldherrnhalle (271) ; Arty. Rgt. 160 ; Pi. Btl. 160 ; Pz. Jäg. Abt. 160 ; Nachr. Abt. 160.

Auxiliary unit number :—160.

Home Station :—Danzig (Wkr. XX).

Originally 60 Infanterie Division formed at Danzig in August, 1939, and embodying the Danzig Heimwehr (S.A. Brigade Eberhadt). As such took part in the attack on the Hela peninsula in September, 1939, and in the French campaign. In the late summer of 1940 it provided a nucleus for the formation of 60 Motorised Division, which fought in Yugoslavia in April, 1941. Subsequently in the Southern sector in Russia. Virtually destroyed at Stalingrad. It was reformed as a Panzer Grenadier Division in the south of France in summer, 1943, and included 271 Mot. Infantry Regiment, previously belonging to 93 Infanterie Division in place of 92 Mot. Infanterie Regiment, which had been reconstituted in Croatia as an independent formation. The division assumed the name of Feldherrnhalle, previously borne by 271 Infanterie Regiment. It was still in France in autumn, 1943.

90 Panzer Grenadier Division

Commander :—Genlt. LUNGERSHAUSEN (48).

Composition :—Pz. Abt. 190 ; Pz. Gr. Rgt. 155 ; Pz. Gr. Rgt. 200 ; Pz. Gr. Rgt. 361 ; Arty. Rgt. 190 ; Pi. Btl. 190 ; Pz. Jäg. Abt. 190 ; Pz. Aufkl. Abt. — ; Nachr. Abt. 190.

Auxiliary unit number :—190.

Home Station :—(Wkr. III).

Formed as "Afrikâ-Division z.b.V." early in 1941. First identified in Africa during the autumn. Renamed "90 Light Division" in November, 1941. After being reorganised in March, 1942, played a prominent role in operations during June. Suffered heavy losses in Africa in the autumn of 1942. Renamed 90 Light Africa Division in the latter part of 1942. Entered Tunisia early in 1943 and was eventually destroyed in May, 1943. In June, 1943, Division Sardinien, an *ad hoc* division formed after the fall of Tunisia from miscellaneous units in Sardinia, was renamed 90 Panzer Grenadier Division. It withdrew to Corsica in autumn, 1943, and subsequently to North Italy.

164 Panzer Grenadier Division

Commander :—

Composition :—Pz. Abt. 164 ? ; Pz. Gr. Rgt. 125 ; Pz. Gr. Rgt. 382 ? Pz. Gr. Rgt. 433 ; Arty. Rgt. 220 ; Pi. Btl. 220 ; Pz. Jäg. Abt. 220 ; Pz. Aufkl. Abt. 164 ? ; Nachr. Abt. 220.

Auxiliary unit number :—220.

Home Station :—Leipzig (Wkr. IV).

Formed in January, 1940, as 164 Infantry Division. In reserve on the Western front ; first identified in action in Greece. Remained in the Aegean area after the Balkan campaign, based first at Salonika and, from early in 1942, on Crete. Transferred to the Panzer Army of Africa during the summer of 1942 and there classified as a light division. Renamed 164 Light Africa Division toward the end of the year. Entered Tunisia early in 1943, where it was destroyed in summer 1943. Re-identified in Brittany where it was re-forming in autumn, 1943, as a Panzer Grenadier Division. Pz. Gren. Rgt. 382 is now possibly a G.H.Q. unit.

386 Panzer Grenadier Division

Commander :—

Composition :—Pz. Gr. Rgt. 149 ; Pz. Gr. Rgt. 153.

Auxiliary unit number :—

Home station :—

Formed in October, 1942. First identified in March, 1943, in south-western France, where the bulk of its personnel was shortly thereafter incorporated into the re-forming 3 Panzer Grenadier Division ; in effect, Pz. Gr. Rgt. 149 was converted into the 8th, and Pz. Gr. Rgt. 153 into the 29th Pz. Gr. Rgts. Its continued existence as a division is doubtful, although it may be re-forming.

(*k*) LIGHT DIVISIONS

5 Jäger Division

Commander :—Genlt. Helmuth THUMM (49).

Composition :—Jäg. Rgt. 56 ; Jäg. Rgt. 75 ; Arty. Rgt. 5 ; Pi. Btl. 5 ; Pz. Jäg. Abt. 5 ; Aufkl. Abt. (mot.) 5 ; Nachr. Abt. 5.

Auxiliary unit number :—5.

Home station :—Konstanz (Wkr. V.).

Active division (as 5 Infantry Division). Recruited in Baden and Württemberg. Not actively engaged before the French campaign, where it played a minor rôle. Identified in Russia during the summer of 1941. After suffering heavy casualties in the Vyazma sector, withdrawn to France during December for rest and conversion to a light division. Returned to Russia, Northern sector, in February, 1942. It has remained in the Northern sector probably in the Staraya Russa area, ever since.

8 Jäger Division

Commander :—

Composition :—Jäg. Rgt. 28 ; Jäg. Rgt. 38 ; Arty. Rgt. 8 ; Pi. Btl. 8 ; Pz. Jäg. Abt. 8 ; Aufkl. Abt. 8 ; Nachr. Abt. 8.

Auxiliary unit number :—8.

Home Station :—Neisse (Wkr. VIII).

Active division (as 8 Infantry Division). Personnel from Silesia. Fought well in Poland and in France. Took part in the Russian campaign as an infantry division from the beginning. After suffering heavy casualties, withdrawn to France in December, 1941, for rest and conversion to a light division. Returned to Russia, Northern sector, in the early spring of 1942. It appears to have remained in the Northern sector ever since.

28 Jäger Division

Commander :—

Composition :—Jäg. Rgt. 49 ; Jäg. Rgt. 83 ; Arty. Rgt. 28 ; Pi. Btl. 28 ; Pz. Jäg. Abt. 28 ; Aufkl. Abt. 28 ; Nachr. Abt. 28.

Auxiliary unit number :—28.

Home Station :—Breslau (Wkr. VIII).

Active division (as 28 Infantry Division). Personnel Silesian, with some German Poles. Actively engaged in the Polish campaign and in operations in the West. First identified in Russia during the late summer of 1941 in the Central sector. Withdrawn to France in November for rest and conversion to a light division. Returned to Russia at the end of the winter and took part in operations in the Kerch sector during May, 1942. Transferred to the Northern sector in the late summer of 1942. It has remained in that area ever since.

90 Leichte Afrika Division—*see* 90 Panzer Grenadier Division.

97 Jäger Division

Commander :—Genlt. Ludwig Müller (52).

Composition :—Jäg. Rgt. 204 ; Jäg. Rgt. 207 ; Arty. Rgt. 81 ; Pi. Btl. 97 ; Pz. Jäg. Abt. 97 ; Aufkl. Abt. 97 ; Nachr. Abt. 97.

Auxiliary unit number :—97.

Home Station :—(Wkr. VII).

Formed in December, 1940. First identified in action on the Southern Russian front during the summer of 1941, where it has remained. It took part in the advance into the Caucasus in summer 1942 and later retreated to the Kuban, where it remained until evacuated to the Lower Dnieper area in autumn, 1943.

99 Jäger Division—*see* 7 Gebirgsdivision.

100 Jäger Division

Commander :—Genmaj. Willibald UTZ.

Composition :—Jäg. Rgt. 54 ; Jäg. Rgt. 227 ; Arty. Rgt. 83 ; Pi. Btl. 100 ; Pz. Jäg. Abt. 100 ; Aufkl. Abt. 100 ; Nachr. Abt. 100.

Auxiliary unit number :—100.

Home Station :—(Wkr. XVII).

Formed in December, 1940. First identified in action during the summer of 1941 on the Southern Russian front. The 369 Reinforced Infantry Regiment (Croatian) was attached to it until late in 1942. The division was virtually destroyed at Stalingrad. Reformed in the Belgrade area in May, 1943, and transferred in the summer of that year to Albania.

101 Jäger Division

Commander :—Genlt. Emil VOGEL (50).

Composition :—Jäg. Rgt. 228 ; Jäg. Rgt. 229 ; Arty. Rgt. 85 ; Pi. Btl. 101 ; Pz. Jäg. Abt. 101 ; Aufkl. Abt. 101 ; Nachr. Abt. 101.

Auxiliary unit number :—101.

Home Station :—(Wkr. V).

Formed in December, 1940. First identified in action on the Southern Russian front during the summer of 1941, where it has remained. It took part in the advance into the Caucasus in summer, 1942, and later retreated to the Kuban where it remained until evacuated to the Lower Dnieper area in autumn, 1943.

104 Jäger Division

Commander :—Genmaj. Hartwig v. LUDWIGER (49).

Composition :—Jäg. Rgt. 724 ; Jäg. Rgt. 734 ; Arty. Rgt. 654 ; Pi. Btl. 104 ; Pz. Jäg. Abt. — ; Aufkl. Abt. — ; Nachr. Abt. 104.

Auxiliary unit number :—104.

Home Station :—(Wkr. IV).

Formed in April, 1941, as 704 Infantry Division. Known to have been in Yugoslavia between September, 1941, and April, 1943, where it was converted into a Jäger Division and renumbered. In June, 1943, it moved to South Greece where it has since been engaged in occupational duties.

114 Jäger Division

Commander :—Genlt. Karl EGLSEER.

Composition :—Jäg. Rgt. 721 ; Jäg. Rgt. 741 ; Arty. Rgt. 661 ; Pi. Btl. 114 ; Pz. Jäg. Abt. — ; Aufkl. Abt. — ; Nachr. Abt. 114.

Auxiliary unit number :—114.

Home Station :—(Wkr. I).

Formed in April, 1941, as 714 Infantry Division. Engaged in mopping-up duties in Yugoslavia from November, 1941, to April, 1943, when it was converted into a Jäger Division and renumbered. It has remained in Yugoslavia ever since.

117 Jäger Division

Commander :—Genmaj. von LE SUIRE (48).
Composition :—Jäg. Rgt. 737 ; Jäg. Rgt. 749 ; Arty. Rgt. 670 ; Pi. Btl. 117 ; Pz. Jäg. Abt. —; Aufkl. Abt. — ; Nachr. Abt. 117.
Auxiliary unit number :—117.
Home Station :—(Wkr. XVII).

Formed in April, 1941, as 717 Infantry Division. Engaged in mopping-up operations in Yugoslavia from November, 1941, to April, 1943, when it was converted into a Jäger Division and renumbered. In May, 1943, it moved to Greece and has since been engaged in occupational duties in the Peloponnese.

118 Jäger Division

Commander :—Genmaj. Josef KÜBLER.
Composition :—Jäg. Rgt. 738 ; Jäg. Rgt. 750 ; Arty. Rgt. 668 ; Pi. Btl. 118 ; Pz. Jäg. Abt. — ; Aufkl. Abt. — ; Nachr. Abt. 118.
Auxiliary unit number :—118.
Home Station :—(Wkr. XVIII).

Formed in April, 1941, as 718 Infantry Division. Stationed in Yugoslavia since the summer of 1941. In April, 1943, it was converted to a Jäger Division and renumbered.

164 Leichte Afrika Division—*see* 164 Panzer Grenadier Division.

(*m*) MOUNTAIN DIVISIONS

1 Gebirgsdivision

Commander :—Genmaj. Walter STETTNER, Ritter v. GRABENHOFEN (52).
Composition :—Geb. Jäg. Rgt. 98 ; Geb. Jäg. Rgt. 99 ; Geb. Arty. Rgt. 79 ; Geb. Pi. Btl. 54 ; Geb. Pz. Jäg. Abt. 44 ; Aufkl. Abt. 54 ; Geb. Nachr. Abt. 54.
Auxiliary unit number :—54.
Home Station :—Garmisch (Wkr. VII).

Active division. Personnel mainly Bavarian, with some Austrians. Fought with great distinction in Southern Poland. Less prominent during the French campaign. Played a minor rôle in the Yugoslavian campaign of 1941. In July, 1941, it was in action on the Southern Russian front and in 1942 was in the Caucasus. In March, 1943, it was transferred to North Greece and in the summer of 1943 to the Greco-Albanian frontier.

2 Gebirgsdivision

Commander :—Obst. DEGEN. ?

Composition :—Geb. Jäg. Rgt. 136 ; Geb. Jäg. Rgt. 137 ; Geb. Arty. Rgt. 111 ; Geb. Pi. Btl. 82 ; Geb. Pz. Jäg. Abt. 47 ; Aufkl. Abt. 67 ; Geb. Nachr. Abt. 67.

Auxiliary unit number :—67.

Home Station :—Innsbruck (Wkr. XVIII).

Active division. Personnel Austrians from the Tyrol. Fought well in Southern Poland and during the Norwegian campaign. Part of the Mountain Corps in Northern Norway (later expanded to the Lapland Army) at the opening of the Russian campaign. After suffering casualties in operations on the Murmansk front was withdrawn to Northern Norway and held in reserve during the winter of 1941–42. Since then operating in Northern Finland.

3 Gebirgsdivision

Commander :—Genmaj. WITTMANN (49).

Composition :—Geb. Jäg. Rgt. 139 ; Geb. Jäg. Rgt. 144 ; Geb. Arty. Rgt. 112 ; Geb. Pi. Btl. 83 ; Geb. Pz. Jäg. Abt. 48 ; Aufkl. Abt. 68 ; Geb. Nachr. Abt. 68.

Auxiliary unit number :—68.

Home Station :—Graz. (Wkr. XVIII).

Active division. Personnel Austrian. Fought with distinction in Southern Poland and in Norway. Part of the Mountain Corps (later expanded to the Lapland Army) at the opening of the Russian campaign. Probably partly in Norway and partly in Finland during the winter of 1941–42. Transported from Norway to the Baltic states in the autumn of 1942. Transferred to the Southern Sector early in 1943. It took part in the retreat from the Mius in summer, 1943, and earned distinction in the Zaporozhe area in autumn, 1943.

4 Gebirgsdivision

Commander :—

Composition :—Geb. Jäg. Rgt. 13 ; Geb. Jäg. Rgt. 91 ; Geb. Arty. Rgt. 94 ; Geb. Pi. Btl. 94 ; Geb. Pz. Jäg. Abt. 94 ; Aufkl. Abt. 94 ; Geb. Nachr. Abt. 94.

Auxiliary unit number :—94.

Home Station :—(Wkr. VII).

Formed in autumn of 1940. Personnel mainly South Germans. First identified during the Balkan campaign where it played a minor role. Has operated in the Southern sector in Russia since the beginning of the campaign. It took part in the advance to the Caucasus in summer, 1942, and was later withdrawn to the Kuban in winter of that year and evacuated to the Crimea in autumn, 1943.

5 Gebirgsdivision

Commander :—Genlt. Julius RINGEL (55).

Composition :—Geb. Jäg. Rgt. 85 ; Geb. Jäg. Rgt. 100 ; Geb. Arty. Rgt. 95 ; Geb. Pi. Btl. 95 ; Geb. Pz. Jäg. Abt. 95 ; Aufkl. Abt. 95 ; Geb. Nachr. Abt. 95.

Auxiliary unit number :—95.

Home Station :—Salzburg (Wkr. XVIII).

Formed in the autumn of 1940. Personnel mainly Bavarian, with some Austrians. First identified in Greece, where it fought well during the Balkan campaign. Subsequently took part in the air-borne attack on Crete. Remained in the Aegean area during 1941. Transferred to the Leningrad front early in 1942, and to Italy late in 1943.

6 Gebirgsdivision

Commander :—Genlt. Christian PHILIPP.

Composition :—Geb. Jäg. Rgt. 141 ; Geb. Jäg. Rgt. 143 ; Geb. Arty. Rgt. 118 ; Geb. Pi. Btl. 91 ; Geb. Pz. Jäg. Abt. 55 ; Aufkl. Abt. 112 ; Geb. Nachr. Abt. 91.

Auxiliary unit number :—91.

Home Station :—Klagenfurt ? (Wkr. XVIII).

Formed in winter, 1939–40. Took part in the later stages of the French campaign. In Greece it played a leading part in the advance on Salonika. Elements took part in the attack on Crete. Transferred in the late summer of 1941 from Greece to Finland, where it has since operated as part of the Twentieth (Lapland) Army on the North Finnish front.

7 Gebirgsdivision

Commander :— Genlt. KRAKAU (50).

Composition :—Geb. Jäg. Rgt. 206 ; Geb. Jäg. Rgt. 218 ; Geb. Arty. Rgt. 82 ; Geb. Pi. Btl. 99 ; Geb. Pz. Jäg. Abt. 99 ; Aufkl. Abt. 99 ; Geb. Nachr. Abt. 99.

Auxiliary unit number :—99.

Home Station :—(Wkr. XIII).

Formed during the winter of 1941–42, mainly by conversion of the former 99 Light Division (formed in December, 1940), which had operated for a time on the Southern Russian front. First in action in Finland in the late spring of 1942, where it has since remained.

8 Gebirgsdivision

Commander :—

Composition :—Geb. Jäg. Rgt. 138? ; Geb. Jäg. Rgt. 142? ; Geb. Arty. Rgt. ?

Auxiliary unit number :—

Home Station :—(Wkr. XVIII).

Probably formed late in 1942. Present location believed to be in Germany.

(*n*) CAVALRY DIVISIONS

There is no German Cavalry Division, but one has been formed of Cossacks (*see* Part H).

(*o*) INFANTRY DIVISIONS

1 Infanterie Division

Commander :—Genlt. Martin GRASE (53).

Composition :—Gren. Regts. 1, 22, 43 ; Art. Regt. 1 ; Pi. Btl. 1 ; Pz. Jäg. Abt. 1 ; Aufkl. Abt. 1 ; Nachr. Abt. 1.

Auxiliary unit number :—1.

Home Station :—Insterburg (Wkr. 1).

Active division. Personnel partly East Prussian, partly from the Rhineland. Fought well in Poland, less actively engaged in France. Engaged on the Northern Russian front since June, 1941. It appears to have gained particular distinction during fighting south of Lake Ladoga in summer, 1943.

2 Infanterie Division—*see* 12 Panzer Division.

3 Infanterie Division—*see* 3 Panzer Grenadier.

4 Infanterie Division—*see* 14 Panzer Division.

5 Infanterie Division—*see* 5 Jäger Division.

6 Infanterie Division

Commander :—Genlt. Horst GROSSMAN (53).

Composition :—Gren. Regts. 18, 37, 58 ; Art. Regt. 6 ; Pi. Btl. 6 ; Pz. Jäg. Abt. 6 ; Aufkl. Abt. 6 ; Nachr. Abt. 6.

Auxiliary unit number :—6.

Home Station :—Bielefeld (Wkr. VI).

Active division. Personnel from Westphalia and, in part, East Prussia. Fought with distinction throughout the French campaign. Engaged in Russia, Central sector, since the beginning of the campaign. It took part with distinction in the Kursk offensive in summer, 1943, and has latterly been defending the Middle Dnieper.

7 Infanterie Division

Commander :—Genlt. Fritz v. RAPPARD

Composition :—Gren. Regts. 19, 61, 62 ; Art. Regt. 7 ; Pi. Btl. 7 ; Pz. Jäg. Abt. 7 ; Aufkl. Abt. 7 ; Nachr. Abt. 7.

Auxiliary unit number :—7.

Home Station :—München (Wkr. VII).

Active division. Personnel Bavarian. Heavily engaged in Southern Poland. Fought against the British in Belgium, but took no part in the French campaign. A good fighting division. Continuously engaged in Russia, Central sector, since the beginning of the campaign. (638 Infantry Regiment, composed of French volunteers, is believed to have operated under its command.) It took part in the Kursk offensive in summer, 1943, and has latterly taken part in the defence of the Middle Dnieper.

8 Infanterie Division—*see* 8 Jäger Division.

9 Infanterie Division

Commander :—Genlt. Frhr. v. SCHLEINITZ (54).

Composition :—Gren. Regts. 36, 57, 116 ; Art. Regt. 9 ; Pi. Btl. 9 ; Pz. Jäg. Abt. 9 ; Aufkl. Abt. 9 ; Nachr. Abt. 9.

Auxiliary unit number :—9.

Home Station :—Giessen (Wkr. IX).

Active division. Personnel from Hessen-Nassau. On the Saar front for a time. Fought well in France. Engaged in Russia, on the Southern front, since the beginning of the campaign. It was in the Caucasus in summer, 1942, and later withdrew to the Kuban where it remained until evacuated to Lower Dnieper area in autumn, 1943.

10 Infanterie Division—*see* 10 Panzer Grenadier Division.

11 Infanterie Division

Commander :—Genlt. Karl BURDACH (50).

Composition :—Gren. Regts. 2, 23, 44 ; Art. Regt. 11 ; Pi. Btl. 11 ; Pz. Jäg. Abt. 11 ; Aufkl. Abt. 11 ; Nachr. Abt. 11.

Auxiliary unit number :—11.

Home Station :—Allenstein (Wkr. I).

Active division. Personnel from East Prussia and from the Rhineland. Fought well in Poland. Not identified during the French campaign. Engaged in Russia from the beginning of the campaign in the Northern sector, but now possibly in the Centre. It gained distinction in fighting south of Lake Ladoga in summer, 1943.

12 Infanterie Division

Commander :—Genlt. Kurt Frhr. v. LÜTZOW (52).

Composition :—Gren. Regts. 27, 48, 89 ; Art. Regt. 12 ; Pi. Btl. 12 ; Pz. Jäg. Abt. 12 ; Aufkl. Abt. 12 ; Nachr. Abt. 12.

Auxiliary unit number :—12.

Home Station :—Schwerin (Wkr. II).

Active division. Personnel mainly Prussian. Fought with distinction in Poland and in France. Identified in Russia on the Northern sector, but so far has played an inconspicuous part.

13 Infanterie Division—*see* 13 Panzer Division.

14 Infanterie Division—*see* 14 Panzer Grenadier Division.

15 Infanterie Division

Commander :—Genlt. Erich BUSCHENHAGEN (52).

Composition :—Gren. Rgts. 81, 88, 106 ; Art. Rgt. 15 ; Pi. Btl. 15 ; Pz. Jäg. Abt. 15 ; Aufkl. Abt. 15 ; Nachr. Abt. 15.

Auxiliary unit number :—15.

Home Station :—Kassel (Wkr. IX).

Active division. Recruited partly in the Frankfurt area and partly in Austria. On the Saar front for some months and later in the Luxemburg area. Engaged on the central Russian front until April, 1942, when it was transferred to France. Returned to the southern Russian front in March, 1943. It appears to have suffered heavy losses in the Dniepropetrovsk area in autumn, 1943.

16 Infanterie Division—*see* 16 Panzer Division and 16 Panzer Grenadier Division.

17 Infanterie Division

Commander :—

Composition :—Gren. Rgts. 21, 55, 95 ; Art. Rgt. 17 ; Pi. Btl. 17 ; Pz. Jäg. Abt. 17 ; Aufkl. Abt. 17 ; Nachr. Abt. 17.

Auxiliary unit number :—17.

Home Station :—Nürnberg (Wkr. XIII).

Active division. Personnel Bavarian. Distinguished alike in Poland and in France. A good fighting division. Engaged in Russia from the beginning of the campaign in the central sector. Transferred to France in the summer of 1942 and returned to Russia in February, 1943. It has been operating on the southern sector and suffered severe losses during the encirclement of Taganrog in summer, 1943. It later gained distinction in the defence of the Lower Dnieper.

18 Infanterie Division—*see* 18 Panzer Grenadier Division.

19 Infanterie Division—*see* 19 Panzer Division.

20 Infanterie Division—*see* 20 Panzer Grenadier Division.

21 Infanterie Division

Commander :—Genlt. Gerhard MATZKY (51).

Composition :—Gren. Rgts. 3, 24, 45 ; Art. Rgt. 21 ; Pi. Btl. 21 ; Pz. Jäg. Abt. 21 ; Aufkl. Abt. 21 ; Nachr. Abt. 21.

Auxiliary unit number :—21.

Home Station :—Elbing (Wkr. XX).

Active division. Personnel from East Prussia and from the Rhineland. Fought well in Poland. Played an inconspicuous part in the French campaign. Engaged in Russia in the northern sector since the beginning of the campaign.

22 Infanterie Division—*see* 22 LL Div. (mot.) under Pz. Gren. Div.

23 Infanterie Division

Commander :—

Composition :—Gren. Rgts. 68, -- ; Art. Rgt. 23 ; Pi. Btl. 23 ; Pz. Jäg. Abt. 23 ; Aufkl. Abt. 23 ? ; Nachr. Abt. 23 ?

Auxiliary unit number :—23.

Home Station :—Potsdam (Wkr. III).

Active division. Personnel mainly from Greater Berlin. Heavily engaged in Poland, less so in France. Fighting value obscure, but morale likely to be high. Engaged continuously in Russia, in the central sector, where it appears to have suffered appreciable losses. It was transferred to France in spring, 1942, where the bulk of it was used in the formation of 26 Pz. Div. At this time a new 23 Infantry Division was formed in Berlin and went to Russia, northern sector, in winter, 1942–1943.

24 Infanterie Division

Commander :—Genlt. Hans v. TETTAU (56).

Composition :—Gren. Rgts. 31, 32, 102 ; Art. Rgt. 24 ; Pi. Btl. 24 ; Pz. Jäg. Abt. 24 ; Aufkl. Abt. 24 ; Nachr. Abt. 24.

Auxiliary unit number :—24.

Home Station :—Chemnitz (Wkr. IV).

Active division. Personnel, Saxon. Morale and fighting value very high, to judge by the Polish campaign. Less prominent during the French campaign. Engaged in Russia from the beginning of the campaign, on the Southern front and in the Crimea. It was transferred to the Northern sector in winter, 1942–1943, where it has remained ever since.

25 Infanterie Division—*see* 25 Panzer Grenadier Division.

26 Infanterie Division

Commander :—Genlt. Friedrich HOCHBAUM (50).

Composition :—Gren. Rgts. 39, 77, 78 ; Art. Rgt. 26 ; Pi. Btl. 26 ; Pz. Jäg. Abt. 26 ; Afkl. Abt. 26 ; Nachr. Abt. 26.

Auxiliary unit number :—26.

Home Station :—Koln (Wkr. VI).

Active division. Personnel mainly from the Rhineland, with drafts from East Prussia. Took a minor part in the Battle of France. Continuously engaged in Russia, in the Central sector, since beginning of campaign. It took part in the Kursk offensive in summer, 1943, sustaining heavy losses.

27 Infanterie Division—*see* 17 Panzer Division.

28 Infanterie Division—*see* 28 Jäger Division.

29 Infanterie Division—*see* 29 Panzer Grenadier Division.

30 Infanterie Division

Commander :—Genlt. Emil v. WICKEDE (51).

Composition :—Gren. Rgts. 6, 26, 46 ; Art. Regt. 30 ; Pi. Btl. 30 ; Pz. Jäg. Abt. 30 ; Aufkl. Abt. 30 ; Nachr. Abt. 30.

Auxiliary unit number :—30.

Home Station :—Lübeck (Wkr. X).

Active division. Recruited mainly in Schleswig-Holstein. Earned special distinction in Northern Poland. Fought in Belgium, but took no part (so far as is known) in the French campaign. Engaged in Russia in the Northern sector, since the beginning of the campaign. It was possibly transferred to the Central sector in autumn, 1943.

31 Infanterie Division

Commander :—

Composition :—Gren. Rgts. 12, 17, 82 ; Art. Rgt. 31 ; Pi. Btl. 31 ; Pz.-Jäg. Abt. 31 ; Aufkl. Abt. 31 ; Nachr. Abt. 31.

Auxiliary unit number :—31.

Home Station :—Braunschweig (Wkr. XI).

Active division. Recruited mainly in the Braunschweig area. Took little part in the Polish campaign, but fought hard in Belgium and throughout the French campaign. Continuously engaged in Russia in the Central sector since the beginning of the campaign. It gained distinction in the Kursk offensive in summer, 1943, and later took part in the defence of the Middle Dneiper.

32 Infanterie Division

Commander :—Genlt. Wilhelm WEGENER (49).

Composition :—Gren. Rgts. 4, 94, 96 ; Art. Rgt. 32 ; Pi. Btl. 21 ; Pz. Jäg. Abt. 32 ; Aufkl. Abt. 32 ; Nachr. Abt. 32.

Auxiliary unit number :—32.

Home Station :—Köslin (Wkr. II).

Active division. Personnel Prussian and Pomeranian. Fought well in Poland and in France. A good attacking division. Engaged in Russia, Northern sector, since the beginning of the campaign.

33 Infanterie Division—*see* 15 Panzer Grenadier Division.

34 Infanterie Division

Commander :—Genmaj. FÜRSTENBERG.

Composition :—Gren. Rgts. 80, 107, 253 ; Art. Rgt. 34 ; Pi. Btl. 34 ; Pz. Jäg. Abt. 34 ; Aufkl. Abt. 34 ; Nachr. Abt. 34.

Auxiliary unit number :—34.

Home Station :—Heidelberg (Wkr. XII).

Active division. Personnel mainly from the Rhineland. On the Saar front for some months and later took part in the French campaign, without winning special distinction. Continuously engaged in Russia, Central sector, since the beginning of the campaign. It was transferred to the Southern sector in August, 1943, and earned special distinction in fighting in the Kharkov area.

35 Infanterie Division

Commander :—Genlt. Ludwig MERKER (50).

Composition :—Gren. Rgts. 34, 109, 111 ; Art. Rgt. 35 ; Pi. Btl. 35 ; Pz. Jäg. Abt. 35 ; Aufkl. Abt. 35 ; Nachr. Abt. 35.

Auxiliary unit number :—35.

Home Station :—Karlsruhe (Wkr. V).

Active division. Personnel from Baden and Württemberg. Fought against the B.E.F. in Belgium, otherwise saw little active fighting prior to the Russian campaign. Continuously engaged in Russia, in Central sector, where it has suffered considerable casualties.

36 Infanterie Division—*see* 36 Panzer Grenadier Division.

38 Infanterie Division

Commander :—Genlt. EBERHARDT (51).

Composition :—Gren. Rgts. 108, 112 ; Art. Rgt. 138 ; Pi. Btl. 138 ; Schnelle. Abt. 138 ; Nachr. Abt. —.

Auxiliary unit number :—138.

Home Station :—

Formed in Brittany in summer, 1942. First identified in Russia, Southern sector, in April, 1943. It appears to include many Poles and other non-German nationals and contains only two infantry regiments.

39 Infanterie Division

Commander :—

Composition :—Gren. Rgts. 113, 114 ; Art. Rgt. 139 ; Pi. Btl. 139 ; Schnelle Abt. 139 ; Nachr. Abt. —.

Auxiliary unit number :—139.

Home Station :—

Formed in summer, 1942, and identified in Holland in the Flushing area in autumn, 1942. It was transferred to the Southern sector, Russian front, in March, 1943. It contains many Austrians, Poles and other non-German nationals, and consists of only two infantry regiments.

44 Infanterie Division

Commander :—Genlt. Dr. Friedrich FRANEK (53).

Composition :—Gren. Rgts. 131, 132, 134 ; Art. Rgt. 96 ; Pi. Btl. 80 ; Pz. Jäg. Abt. 46 ; Aufkl. Abt. 44 ; Nachr. Abt. 64.

Auxiliary unit number :—44.

Home Station :—Wien (Wkr. XVII).

Active division. Personnel mainly Austrian. Sustained heavy casualties in Poland. Saw little fighting but marched great distances in France. Morale less high than that of the other Austrian active divisions. Engaged in Russia on the Southern front from the beginning of the campaign. Virtually destroyed at Stalingrad. Was re-formed in France in April, 1943, and in June, 1943, was honoured with the title of "Reichsgrenadier Division Hoch and Deutschmeister." In August, 1943, it was transferred to North Italy and in October, 1943, moved to Slovenia.

45 Infanterie Division

Commander :—Genmaj. Hans Frhr. v. FALKENSTEIN (51).

Composition :—Gren. Rgts. 130, 133, 135 ; Art. Rgt. 98 ; Pi. Btl. 81 ; Pz. Jäg. Abt. 45 ; Aufkl. Abt. 45 ; Nachr. Abt. 65.

Auxiliary unit number :—45.

Home Station :—Linz (Wkr. XVII).

Active division. Personnel mainly Austrian. Fought well in south Poland and in the Battle of France. Continuously engaged in Russia, in the Central sector, where it appears to have sustained considerable casualties. It was possibly transferred to the Southern sector but returned to the Central sector in spring, 1943, and appears to have taken part in the Kursk offensive in summer of that year.

46 Infanterie Division

Commander :—Genmaj. Kurt RÖPKE (48).

Composition :—Gren. Rgts. 42, 72, 97 ; Art. Regt. 114 ; Pi. Btl. 88 ; Pz. Jäg. Abt. 52 ; Aufkl. Abt. 46 ; Nachr. Abt. 76.

Auxiliary unit number :—46.

Home Station :—Karlsbad (Wkr. XIII).

Active division, formed at the close of 1938. Personnel Bavarian, partly Sudeten German. Saw comparatively little active fighting before the Russian campaign where it has been engaged on the Southern front, in the Crimea, and in the Caucasus. It also fought on the Donetz front and took part in the Byelgorod offensive in the summer of 1943, gaining particular distinction.

50 Infanterie Division

Commander :—

Composition :—Gren. Rgts. 121, 122, 123 ; Art. Regt. 150 ; Pi. Btl. 150 ; Pz. Jäg. Abt. 150 ; Aufkl. Abt. 150 ; Nachr. Abt. 150 ?

Auxiliary unit number :—150.

Home Station :—(Wkr. III).

Active division as "Grenzkommando Küstrin" (Küstrin Frontier Command). Personnel Prussian. Had little fighting to do in Poland, but took an active part in the French campaign. Continuously engaged on the Southern Russian front, in the Crimea, and later in the Caucasus. It withdrew to the Kuban in winter, 1942–1943, and later was evacuated to the lower Dnieper area in autumn, 1943.

52 Infanterie Division

Commander :—

Composition :—Gren. Rgts. 163, 181, 205 ; Art. Rgt. 152 ; Pi. Btl. 152 ; Pz. Jäg. Abt. 152 ; Aufkl. Abt. 152 ; Nachr. Abt. 152.

Auxiliary unit number :—152.

Home Station :—Kassel (Wkr. X).

Formed on mobilisation from reservists. Personnel mainly from Hessen. On the Saar front for some months. Some units fought in France, but the division may have been sent to Norway. Engaged in Russia, in the Central sector, from the beginning of the campaign.

56 Infanterie Division

Commander :—Genlt. Otto LÜDECKE (50).

Composition :—Gren. Rgts. 171, 192, 234 ; Art. Rgt. 156 ; Pi. Btl. 156 ; Pz. Jäg. Abt. 156 ; Aufkl. Abt. 156 ; Nachr. Abt. 156.

Auxiliary unit number :—156.

Home Station :—Dresden (Wkr. IV).

Formed on mobilisation from reservists. Personnel Saxon. Took part in the Polish campaign. Fought well against the British in Belgium. Identified in the Central Sector of the Russian front in

November, 1941, where it has since remained. Took part in the Kursk offensive in summer, 1943, and appears to have suffered very heavy casualties.

57 Infanterie Division

Commander :—

Composition :—Gren. Rgts. 179, 199, 217 ; Art. Rgt. 157 ; Pi. Btl. 157 ; Pz. Jäg. Abt. 157 ; Aufkl. Abt. 157 ; Nachr. Abt. 157.

Auxiliary unit number :—157.

Home Station :—Bad Reichenhall (Wkr. VII).

Formed on mobilisation from reservists. Personnel mainly Bavarian. Distinguished itself in Southern Poland and in the operations on the lower Somme. A good fighting division. Continuously engaged in Russia on the Southern front since the beginning of the campaign. It has been constantly in action and has suffered appreciable losses.

58 Infanterie Division

Commander :

Composition :—Gren. Rgts. 154, 209, 220 ; Art. Rgt. 158 ; Pi. Btl. 158 ; Pz. Jäg. Abt. 158 ; Aufkl. Abt. 158 ; Nachr. Abt. 158.

Auxiliary unit number :—158.

Home Station :—Rendsburg ? (Wkr. X).

Formed on mobilisation from reservists. Personnel from Northern Germany. On the Saar front in April, 1940. Identified in the Northern sector of the Russian front in December, 1941, but little evidence that it has seen much action. It was possibly transferred to the Central sector in autumn, 1943.

60 Infanterie Division—*see* 60 Pz.G. Division.

61 Infanterie Division

Commander :—Genlt. Günther KRAPPE (51).

Composition :—Gren. Rgts. 151, 162, 176 ; Art. Rgt. 161 ; Pi. Btl. 161 ; Pz. Jäg. Abt. 161 ; Aufkl. Abt. 161 ; Nachr. Abt. 161.

Auxiliary unit number :—161.

Home Station :—Königsberg (Wkr. I).

Formed on mobilisation from reservists. Personnel mainly from East Prussia. Fought well against the British in Belgium. Identified on the Northern sector of the Russian front but little evidence that it has seen much action.

62 Infanterie Division

Commander :—

Composition :—Gren. Rgts. 164, 183, 190 ; Art. Rgt. 162, Pi. Btl. 162 ; Pz. Jäg. Abt. 162 ; Aufkl. Abt. 162, Nachr. Abt. 162.

Auxiliary unit number :—162.

Home Station :—Glatz (Wkr. VIII).

Formed on mobilisation from Silesian reservists personnel. Fought well in Poland and in Flanders. Identified on the Southern Russian front and suffered casualties on withdrawal from Stalingrad. It has since been constantly engaged on the Southern sector.

65 Infanterie Division

Commander :—Genlt. Dr. Phil. Georg PFEIFFER (54).

Composition :—Gren. Rgts. 145, 146 ; Art. Rgt. 165 ; Pi. Btl. 165 ; Schnelle Abt. 165 ; Nachr. Abt. 165.

Auxiliary unit number :—165.

Home Station :—(Wkr. XII).

Formed in the summer of 1942. First identified in Holland, in the Flushing area, late in 1942, where it remained until August, 1943, when it was transferred to north Italy. In Oct. 1943, it, was moved to the Italian theatre of operations.

68 Infanterie Division

Commander :—Obst. Paul SCHEUERPFLUG (48).

Composition :—Gren Rgts. 169, 188, 196 ; Art. Rgt. 168 ; Pi. Batl. 168 ; Pz. Jäg Abt. 168 ; Aufkl. Abt. 168 ; Nachr. Abt. 168.

Auxiliary unit number :—168.

Home Station :—Guben (Wkr. III).

Formed on mobilisation from reservists. Took part in the operations in France without earning special distinction. Engaged since the beginning of the Russian campaign in the Southern sector. Suffered heavy losses in autumn, 1943 during the retreat from Kiev.

69 Infanterie Division

Commander :—Genlt. Bruno ORTNER.

Composition :—Gren Rgts. 159, 193*, 236 ; Art. Rgt. 169 ; Pi. Batl. 169 ; Schnelle Abt. 169 ; Nachr. Abt. 169.

Auxiliary unit number :—169.

Home Station :—Soest (Wkr. VI).

Formed on mobilisation and recruited mainly from reservists from the Ruhr area. Fought well against weak Norwegian forces. Remained in Norway on occupational and defence duties until early in 1943, when it was transferred to the Central sector in Russia. It was sent to the Northern sector in the spring of 1943 and may have returned to the Central sector in autumn, 1943. It does not appear to have seen much fighting.

71 Infanterie Division

Commander :—Genmaj. RAAPKE (46).

Composition :—Gren. Rgt. 191, 194, 211 ; Art. Rgt. 171 ; Pi. Batl. 171 ; Pz. Jäg. Abt. 171 ; Aufkl. Abt. 171 ; Nachr. Abt. 171.

Auxiliary unit number :—171.

Home Station :—Hildesheim (Wkr. XI).

Formed on mobilisation and recruited mainly from reservists from the Hannover area. On the Saar front for a period. Fought with distinction in the Sedan area and in the advance on Verdun. Fought in Russia in the Southern sector for the first four months of the campaign, then returned to France and left again for the Eastern front during April, 1942. Virtually destroyed at Stalingrad. Reformed in Denmark in April, 1943, and transferred to Slovenia in August, 1943, where it remains.

---

* Gren. Rgt. 193 possibly detached and is under 210 Inf. (Coastal) Div. in Norway.

72 Infanterie Division

Commander :—Obst. Dr. HOHN.

Composition :—Gren. Rgts. 105, 124, 266 ; Art. Rgt. 172 ; Pi. Batl. 72 ; Pz. Jäg. 172 ? ; Aufkl. Abt. 172 ? Nachr. Abt. 172 ?

Auxiliary unit number :—172.

Home Station :—(Wkr. XII).

Formed on mobilisation in Wkr. IX and XII, incorporating two active infantry regiments and one reserve. Mainly Rhinelander and Bavarians. Originally known as "Grenzkommando Trier" (Trier Frontier Command). On the Saar front for many months. Not an aggressive division during the early part of the war. Took part in the Balkan campaign and was continuously engaged in Russia on the Southern front and in the Crimea. Transferred to the Central sector in the autumn of 1942. It took part in the Kursk offensive in summer, 1943, and was later transferred to the Southern sector.

73 Infanterie Division

Commander :—Genlt. Rudolf v. BÜNAU (54).

Composition :—Gren. Rgts. 170, 186, 213 ; Art. Rgt. 173 ; Pi. Batl. 173 ; Pz. Jäg. Abt. 173 ; Aufkl. Abt. 173 ; Nachr. Abt. 173.

Auxiliary unit number :—173.

Home Station :—Würzburg (Wkr. XIII).

Formed on mobilisation from Bavarian reservists. Saw little fighting in Poland, less on the Saar front, and was not distinguished during the campaign in France. Took part in the Balkan campaign and has been continuously engaged on the Southern Russian front, in the Crimea, and later in the Caucasus. It withdrew to the Kuban in winter, 1942–1943, and was evacuated to the Lower Dnieper area in autumn, 1943.

75 Infanterie Division

Commander :—Genlt. Erich DIESTEL.

Composition :—Gren. Rgts. 172, 202, 222 ; Art. Rgt. 175 ; Pi. Batl. 175 ; Pz. Jäg. Abt. 175 ; Aufkl. Abt. 175 ; Nachr. Abt. 175.

Auxiliary unit number :—175.

Home Station :—Neustrelitz Wkr. (II).

Formed on mobilisation from reservists. Personnel Prussian, mainly from Schwerin area. On the Saar front for several months and in France in June, 1940. Identified in the Southern sector of the Russian front where it has been continuously engaged. It sustained heavy losses in the retreat from Kiev in autumn, 1943.

76 Infanterie Division

Commander :—Genmaj. Erich ABRAHAM (49).

Composition :—Gren. Rgts. 178, 203, 230 ; Art. Rgt. 176 ; Pi. Batl. 176 ; Pz. Jäg. Abt. 176 ; Aufkl. Abt. 176 ; Nachr. Abt. 176.

Auxiliary unit number :—176.

Home Station :—Berlin (Wkr. III).

Formed on mobilisation from Prussian reservists. Fought well in France. Engaged in Russia in the Southern sector from the beginning of the campaign. Virtually destroyed at Stalingrad. It re-formed in Brittany in spring, 1943, and was sent to North Italy in the following summer. In autumn, 1943, it was transferred to the Southern sector of the Russian front.

78 Infanterie Division

Commander :—

Composition :—Gren. Rgts. 195, 215, 238* ; Art. Rgt. 178 ; Pi. Batl. 178 ; Pz. Jäg. Abt. 178 ; Aufkl. Abt. 178 ; Nachr. Abt. 178.

Auxiliary unit number :—178.

Home Station :—Ulm (Wkr. V).

Formed on mobilisation from reservists. Personnel mainly from Württemberg. Took part in the French campaign where its fighting value was indeterminate. Continuously engaged since the beginning of the Russian campaign in the Central sector. It took part in the Kursk offensive in summer, 1943, where it gained distinction. It is usually referred to as "78 Sturm Div."

---

* Gren. Regt. 238 possibly disbanded, but probably replaced by Gren. Regt. 14.

79 Infanterie Division

Commander :—Genlt. SCHERBENING (53).

Composition :—Gren. Rgts. 208, 212, 226 ; Art. Rgt. 179 ; Pi. Batl. 179 ; Pz. Jäg. Abt. 179 ; Aufkl. Abt. 179 ; Nachr. Abt. 179.

Auxiliary Unit Number :—179.

Home Station :—Koblenz (Wkr. XII).

Formed on mobilisation from reservists. Personnel mainly from the Rhineland. On the Saar front for a period, but took little part in active operations. Identified on the Southern sector of the Russian front. Virtually destroyed at Stalingrad. It reformed on the Southern Russian front in spring 1943 and was identified in action in the Kuban in the early summer. In autumn 1943, it was transferred to the Lower Dnieper area. Fighting quality of this division appears to be low.

81 Infanterie Division

Commander :—

Composition :—Gren. Rgts. 161, 174, 189 ; Art. Rgt. 181 ; Pi. Batl. 181 ; Pz. Jäg. Abt. 181 ; Aufkl. Abt. — ; Nachr. Abt. 181.

Auxiliary unit number :—181.

Home Station :— (Wkr. VIII).

Formed on mobilisation from reservists. Took part in the French campaign without winning special distinction. Apparently arrived on the Northern sector of the Russian front from France in January, 1942, and has remained there.

82 Infanterie Division

Commander :—

Composition :—Gren. Rgts. 158, 166, 168 ; Art. Rgt. 182 ; Pi. Batl. 182 ; Schnelle Abt. 182 ; Nachr. Abt. 182.

Auxiliary unit number :—182.

Home Station :—Frankfurt/Main ? (Wkr. IX).

Formed on mobilisation from reservists. Not identified during the French campaign. Identified in Holland late in 1941 but left for Russia in May, 1942, where it has since operated on the Southern sector. It apparently transferred to the Central sector in summer, 1943, where it took part in the Kursk offensive, and returned to the Southern sector in the autumn. It suffered severe losses in the retreat from Kiev in Nov., 1943.

83 Infanterie Division

Commander :—Genlt. Theodore SCHERER (55).

Composition :—Gren. Rgts. 251, 257, 277 ; Art. Rgt. 183 ; Pi. Batl. 183 ; Schnelle Abt. 183 ; Nachr. Abt. 183.

Auxiliary unit number :—183.

Home Station :—Hamburg (Wkr. X).

Formed on mobilisation from reservists. Took part in the Polish and French campaigns without winning special distinction. Left France for Russia early in 1942 and has fought on the Central sector since April, 1942. It has been operating near the boundary between the Northern and Central sectors, and may now be in the Northern sector.

86 Infanterie Division

Commander :—Genlt. Helmuth WEIDLING (52).

Composition :—Gren. Rgts. 167, 184, 216 ; Art. Rgt. 186 ; Pi. Btl. 186 ; Pz. Jäg. Abt. 186 ; Aufkl. Abt. 186 ; Nachr. Abt. 186.

Auxiliary unit number :—186.

Home Station :— (Wkr. VI).

Formed on mobilisation from reservists. Personnel mainly Westphalian. On the Saar front for two months. Took part in the French campaign. Continuously engaged in Russia, in the Central sector, since the beginning of the campaign. It took part in the Kursk offensive in summer, 1943, where it gained distinction.

87 Infanterie Division

Commander :—

Composition :—Gren. Rgts. 173, 185, 187 ; Art. Rgt. 187 ; Pi. Btl. 187 ; Schnelle Abt. 187 ; Nachr. Abt. 187.

Auxiliary unit number :—187.

Home Station :— (Wkr. IV).

Formed in Wkr. IV and Wkr. IX from Reservists on mobilisation. Personnel mainly from Saxony (Wkr. IV) and Thüringen. First in action during French campaign, when it fought well. Continuously engaged in Russia, in the Central sector, since the beginning of the campaign.

88 Infanterie Division

Commander :—Genlt. Friedrich GOLLWITZER (55).

Composition :—Gren. Rgts. 245, 246, 248 ; Art. Rgt. 188 ; Pi. Btl. 188 ; Pz. Jäg. Abt. 188 ; Aufkl. Abt. ; Nachr. Abt. 188.

Auxiliary unit number :—188.

Home Station :—(Wkr. VII).

Formed in autumn, 1939 from reservists. Played an inconspicuous part in the French campaign. Left France for Russia early in 1942, and has fought on the Southern front. It apparently suffered heavy losses in the retreat from Kiev in autumn, 1943.

93 Infanterie Division

Commander :—Genlt. Otto TIEMANN (56).

Composition :—Gren. Rgts. 270, 272 ; Art. Rgt. 193 ; Pi. Btl. 193 ; Pz. Jäg. Abt. 193 ; Aufkl. Abt. 193 ; Nachr. Abt. 193.

Auxiliary unit number :—193.

Home Station :—Berlin (Wkr. III).

Formed in September, 1939, from Prussian reservists. On the Saar front for several months without distinguishing itself. It was identified in the Northern sector of the Russian front in summer, 1941. In summer, 1943, it was transferred to Poland, where I.R. 271 (Feldherrnhalle Rgt.) was withdrawn and became part of the new 60 Pz. Gren. Div. then re-forming in France. The division later returned to the Northern sector of the Russian front.

94 Infanterie Division

Commander :—Genlt. STEINMETZ.

Composition :—Gren. Rgts. 267, 274, 276 ; Art. Rgt. 194 ; Pi. Btl. 194 ; Schnelle Abt. 194 ; Nachr. Abt. 194.

Auxiliary unit number :—194.

Home Station :—(Wkr. IV).

Formed in September, 1939. Personnel mainly Saxon or Sudeten German reservists. Took some part in the French campaign. Engaged in Russia in the Southern sector where it was virtually destroyed at Stalingrad. It is believed to have re-formed in Brittany where it was identified in July, 1943. It was transferred to North Italy in August, 1943, and was reported in action in Southern Italy in October, 1943.

95 Infanterie Division

Commander :—

Composition :—Gren. Rgts. 278, 279, 280 ; Art. Rgt. 195 ; Pi. Btl. 195 ; Pz. Jäg. Abt. 195 ; Aufkl. Abt. 195 ; Nachr. Abt. —.

Auxiliary unit number :—195.

Home Station :—(Wkr. IX).

Formed in September, 1939. Personnel mainly Westphalian and partly Thuringian reservists. Showed initiative and dash on the Saar front. Not identified during the French campaign. Continuously engaged in Russia, on the Southern front, until it was transferred to the Central sector, probably late in 1942. It was apparently defeated at Bryansk in late summer, 1943.

96 Infanterie Division

Commander :—

Composition :—Gren. Rgts. 283, 284, 287 ; Art. Rgt. 196 ; Pi. Btl. 196 ; Schnelle Abt. 196 ; Nachr. Abt. 196.

Auxiliary unit number :—196.

Home Station :—(Wkr. XI).

Formed in September, 1939, mainly from reservists. Took part in the French campaign. Engaged in Russia in the Northern sector.

98 Infanterie Division

Commander :—Genlt. Martin GAREIS (53).

Composition :—Gren. Rgts. 282, 289, 290 ; Art. Rgt. 198 ; Pi. Btl. 198 ; Schnelle Abt. 198 ; Nachr. Abt. 198.

Auxiliary unit number, 198.

Home Station :—(Wkr. XIII).

Formed in September, 1939. Personnel mainly Bavarian reservists. Fought well in the French campaign. Identified in the Central sector of the Russian front in November, 1941. It was transferred to the Kuban in summer, 1943, and later gained distinction in defence of the Crimea.

102 Infanterie Division

Commander :—Obst. von BERCKEN.

Composition :—Gren. Rgts. 232, 233, 235* ; Art. Rgt. 104 ; Pi. Btl. 102 ; Pz. Jäg. Abt. 102 ; Aufkl. Abt. 102 ; Nachr. Abt. 102.

Auxiliary unit number :—102.

Home Station :—(Wkr. VIII).

Formed in December, 1940. First identified in action on Central Russian front in August, 1941. Constantly engaged until February, 1942, when it may have been withdrawn to Germany to rest. Returned to the Central front in mid April, 1942, and in summer, 1943, took part in the Kursk offensive.

106 Infanterie Division

Commander :—Genlt. Werner FORST (52).

Composition :—Gren. Rgts. 239, 240, 241 ; Art. Rgt. 107 ; Pi. Btl. 106 ; Pz. Jäg. Abt. 106 ; Aufkl. Abt. 106 ; Nachr. Abt. 106.

Auxiliary unit number :—106.

Home Station :—(Wkr. VI).

Formed in December, 1940. First identified in action on the Central Russian front in August, 1941. Fought in the Central sector throughout the winter, sustaining heavy casualties, particularly in the latter half of January, 1942. Subsequently returned to France for rest and refit. It was transferred to Russia in spring, 1943, where it has been heavily engaged in the Southern sector.

---

* Gren. Rgt. 235 possibly disbanded, but may be replaced by an unknown regt.

110 Infanterie Division

Commander :—Genlt. SEYFFARDT (50).

Composition :—Gren. Rgts. 252, 254, 255 ; Art. Rgt. 120 ; Pi. Btl. 110 ; Pz. Jäg. Abt. 110 ; Aufkl. Abt. 110 ; Nachr. Abt. 110.

Auxiliary unit number :—110.

Home Station :—Oldenburg (Wkr. X).

Formed in December, 1940. First identified in action on the Russian front in August, 1941, where it has been heavily engaged in the Central sector.

111 Infanterie Division

Commander :—Genlt. Hermann RECKNAGEL (52).

Composition :—Gren. Rgts. 50, 70, 117 ; Art. Rgt. 117 ? ; Pi. Btl. 111 ; Pz. Jäg. Abt. 111 ; Aufkl. Abt. 117 ; Nachr. Abt. 111.

Auxiliary unit number :—111.

Home Station :—(Wkr. XI).

Formed in December, 1940. Has been in action in Russia in the Southern sector, where it took part in the fighting for Mozdok. It withdrew to the Kuban in winter, 1942–1943, and was transferred to the Mius front in the following summer, sustaining heavy losses at Taganrog. It later gained distinction in the defence of the Lower Dnieper.

112 Infanterie Division

Commander :—

Composition :—Gren. Rgts. 110, 256, 258 ; Art. Rgt. 86 ; Pi. Btl. 112 ; Pz. Jäg. Abt. 112 ; Aufkl. Abt. 120 ; Nachr. Abt. 112.

Auxiliary unit number :—112.

Home Station :—Darmstadt (Wkr. XII).

Formed in December, 1940. Engaged on the Russian front, Central sector, since August, 1941. It took part in the Kursk offensive in summer, 1943, sustaining heavy losses and was later transferred to the Southern sector.

113 Infanterie Division

Commander :—

Composition :—Gren. Rgts. 260, 261, 268 ; Art. Rgt. 87 ; Pi. Btl. 113 ; Pz. Jäg. Abt. 113 ; Aufkl. Abt. 113 ; Nachr. Abt. 113.

Auxiliary unit number :—113.

Home Station :—(Wkr. XIII).

Formed in December, 1940. Was in the Balkans on occupational duties during November and December, 1941. Later transferred to the Southern sector of the Russian front, where it was virtually destroyed at Stalingrad. It was re-formed in Brittany in spring, 1943, and returned to Russia, Central sector in summer, 1943.

121 Infanterie Division

Commander :—

Composition :—Gren. Rgts. 405, 407, 408 ; Art. Rgt. 121 ; Pi. Btl. 121 ; Pz. Jäg. Abt. 121 ; Aufkl. Abt. 121 ; Nachr. Abt. 121.

Auxiliary unit number :—121.

Home Station :—(Wkr. X).

Formed in Wehrkreis X in October, 1940. In action in the Northern sector since the outset of the Russian campaign. It appears to include many non-German nationals.

122 Infanterie Division

Commander :—

Composition :—Gren. Rgts. 409, 411, 414 ; Art. Rgt. 122 ; Pi. Btl. 122 ; Pz. Jäg. Abt. 122 ; Aufkl. Abt. 122 ; Nachr. Abt. 122.

Auxiliary unit number :—122.

Home Station :—(Wkr. II).

Formed in October, 1940. In action on the Northern Russian front since the outset of the campaign. It appears to have been transferred to the Central sector in autumn, 1943.

123 Infanterie Division

Commander :—Genlt. Erwin RAUCH (55).

Composition :—Gren. Rgts. 415, 416, 418 ; Art. Rgt. 123 ; Pi. Btl. 123 ; Pz. Jäg. Abt. 123 ; Aufkl. Abt. 123 ; Nachr. Abt. 123.

Auxiliary unit number :—123.

Home Station :—(Wkr. III).

Formed in October, 1940. In action on the Northern Russian front, where it appears to have been fairly heavily engaged. It may have been transferred to the Southern sector in autumn, 1943.

125 Infanterie Division

Commander :—

Composition :—Gren. Rgts. 419 420, 421 ; Art. Rgt. 125 ; Pi. Btl. 125 ; Pz. Jäg. Abt. 125 ; Aufkl. Abt. 125 ; Nachr. Abt. 125.

Auxiliary unit number :—125.

Home Station :—(Wkr. V).

Formed in October, 1940. Continuously engaged on the Southern Russian front in the Crimea and in the Caucasus since July, 1941. It withdrew to the Kuban in winter, 1942–1943, where it gained distinction. It was evacuated to the Dnieper Bend area in autumn, 1943.

126 Infanterie Division

Commander :—Genlt. Arthur HOPPE (49).

Composition :—Gren. Rgts. 422, 424, 426 ; Art. Rgt. 126 ; Pi. Btl. 126; Pz. Jäg. Abt. 126; Aufkl. Abt. 126; Nachr. Abt. 126.

Auxiliary unit number :—126.

Home Station :—(Wkr. VI).

Formed in October, 1940. In action on the Northern Russian front since the outset of the campaign, where it appears to have been fairly continuously engaged.

129 Infanterie Division

Commander :—Genlt. Albert PRAUN (50).

Composition :—Gren. Rgts. 427, 428, 430 ; Art. Rgt. 129 ; Pi. Btl. 129 ; Pz. Jäg. Abt. 129 ; Aufkl. Abt. 129 ; Nachr. Abt. 129.

Auxiliary unit number :—129.

Home Station :—Fulda (Wkr. IX).

Formed in October, 1940, and has been continuously engaged on the Central Russian front since the beginning of the campaign.

131 Infanterie Division

Commander :—Genlt. Heinrich MEYER-BUERDORF (56).

Composition :—Gren. Rgts. 431, 432, 434 ; Art. Rgt. 131 ; Pi. Btl. 131 ; Pz. Jäg. Abt. 131 ; Aufkl. Abt. 131 ; Nachr. Abt. 131.

Auxiliary unit number :—131.

Home Station :—(Wkr. XI).

Formed in October, 1940. Has fought on the Central Russian front since August, 1941. It took part in the Moscow offensive in November, 1941, sustaining very heavy losses.

132 Infanterie Division

Commander :—

Composition :—Gren. Rgts. 436, 437, 438 ; Art. Rgt. 132 ; Pi. Btl. 132 ; Pz. Jäg. Abt. 132 ; Aufkl. Abt. 132 ; Nachr. Abt. 132 (or Schn. Abt. 132 instead of Pz. Jäg. Abt. and Aufkl. Abt.).

Auxiliary unit number :—132.

Home Station :—(Wkr. XII).

Formed in Wehrkreis VII in October, 1940. Subsequently transferred to Wehrkreis XII. Engaged on the Southern Russian front and in the Crimea from July, 1941, where it sustained heavy losses. It was transferred to the Northern sector in autumn, 1942, where it has remained.

134 Infanterie Division

Commander :—Genlt. Dipl. Ing. Hans SCHLEMMER (51).

Composition :—Gren. Rgts. 439, 445, 446 ; Art. Rgt. 134 ; Pi. Btl. 134 ; Pz. Jäg. Abt. 134 ; Aufkl. Abt. 134 ; Nachr. Abt. 134.

Auxiliary unit number :—134.

Home Station :—(Wkr. IV).

Formed in Wehrkreis XIII in October, 1940. Subsequently transferred to Wehrkreis IV. Continuously and heavily engaged on the Central Russian front since the beginning of the campaign. It suffered defeat at Bryansk in summer, 1943, but later gained distinction in the defence of Gomel.

137 Infanterie Division

Commander :—

Composition :—Gren. Rgts. 447, 448, 449 ; Art. Rgt. 137 ; Pi. Btl. 137 ; Pz. Jäg. Abt. 137 ; Aufkl. Abt. 137 ; Nachr. Abt. 137.

Auxiliary unit number :—137.

Home Station :—(Wkr. XVII).

Formed in October, 1940. Identified on the Central Russian front in August, 1941, where it appears to have been fairly heavily engaged. It took part in the Kursk offensive in summer, 1943.

161 Infanterie Division

Commander :—Genlt. Heinrich RECKE (54).

Composition :—Gren. Rgts. 336, 364, 371 ; Art. Rgt. 241 ; Pi. Btl. 241 ; Schn. Abt. 241 ; Nachr. Abt. 241.

Auxiliary unit number :—241.

Home Station :—(Wkr. I).

Formed in January, 1940. Continuously engaged on the Central Russian front where it suffered heavy losses. It may have been withdrawn from Russia for rest and refit during the winter, 1942–1943. It was again identified on the Southern Russian front in spring, 1943, where it has been constantly in action.

162 Infanterie Division

Commander :—Genmaj. Prof. Dr. Ritter v. NIEDERMAYER (59).

Composition :—Gren. Rgts. 303, 314, 329 ; Art. Rgt. 236 ; Pi. Btl. 236 ; Pz. Jäg. Abt. 236 ; Aufkl. Abt. —— ; Nachr. Abt. 236.

Auxiliary unit number :—236.

Home Station :—Rostock (Wkr. II).

Formed in January, 1940. Continuously engaged on Central Russian front from the beginning of the campaign until the late summer of 1942, when it was transferred to the Southern sector. At this time it was known to contain a number of Turanian Bns. It is therefore possible that it is identical with the Turanian infantry Division, a war establishment for which is known to exist.

163 Infanterie Division

Commander :—Genmaj. Karl RÜBEL (49).

Composition :—Gren. Rgts. 307, 310, 324 ; Art. Rgt. 234 ; Pi. Btl. 234 ; Schn. Abt. 234 ; Nachr. Abt. 234.

Auxiliary unit number :—234.

Home Station :—Berlin (Wkr. III).

Formed in January, 1940. Personnel mainly Prussian. Fought well in the Gudbransdal during the Norwegian campaign. Transferred to Finland at the beginning of the Russian campaign, where it took an active part in the fighting in 1942. It has remained in Finland ever since.

164 Infanterie Division *see* 164 Panzer Grenadier Division.

167 Infanterie Division

Commander :—Genlt. Wolf TRIERENBERG (53).

Composition :—Gren. Rgts. 315, 331, 339 ; Art. Rgt. 238 ; Pi. Btl. 238 ; Pz. Jäg. Abt. 238 ; Aufkl. Abt. 238 ; Nachr. Abt. 238.

Auxiliary unit number :—238.

Home Station :—(Wkr. VII).

Formed in January, 1940. Personnel Bavarian. First in action during the French campaign. Continuously engaged on the Central Russian front from the beginning of the campaign. Transferred to Holland in the summer of 1942. Returned to the Southern Russian front early in 1943. It took part in the Byelgorod offensive in summer, 1943, sustaining heavy losses.

168 Infanterie Division

Commander :—

Composition :—Gren. Rgts. 417, 429, 442 ; Art. Rgt. 248 ; Pi. Btl. 248 ; Pz. Jäg. Abt. 248 ; Aufkl. Abt. 248, Nachr. Abt. 248.

Auxiliary unit number : 248.

Home Station :—(Wkr. VIII).

Formed in January, 1940. Identified on the Southern Russian front in July, 1941, where it has been continuously engaged. It took part in the Byelgorod offensive in summer, 1943, where it suffered heavy losses.

169 Infanterie Division

Commander :—Genmaj. RADZIEJ.

Composition : Gren. Rgts. 378, 379, 392 ; Art. Rgt. 230 ; Pi. Btl. 230 ; Pz. Jäg. Abt. 230 ; Aufkl. Abt. —— ; Nachr. Abt. 230.

Auxiliary unit number : 230.

Home Station :—(Wkr. IX).

Formed in January, 1940. First in action during the French campaign. Apparently arrived in Finland from Norway during the early stages of the Russian campaign and was in action on the Kandalaksha front in 1942. It has remained in Finland ever since.

170 Infanterie Division

Commander : Genlt. Erwin SANDER (52).

Composition :—Gren. Rgt. 391, 399, 401 ; Art. Rgt. 240 ; Pi. Btl. 240 ; Pz. Jäg. Abt. 240 ; Aufkl. Abt. 240 ; Nachr. Abt. 240.

Auxiliary unit number :—240.

Home Station :—Bremen (Wkr. X).

Formed in January, 1940. Fairly continuously engaged on the Southern Russian front and in the Crimea from the beginning of the campaign. Transferred to the Northern sector in the late summer of 1942, where it has remained.

181 Infanterie Division

Commander :—Genlt. BAYER (57).

Composition : Gren. Rgts. 334, 349, 359 ; Art. Rgt. 222 ; Pi. Btl. 222 ; Pz. Jäg. Abt. 222 ; Aufkl. Abt. 222 ; Nachr. Abt. 222.

Auxiliary unit number :—222.

Home Station :— (Wkr. XI).

Employed in Norway (Trondheim–Dombaas area) from April, 1940, until October, 1943, when elements of it were reported on the Russian front, while the main body of the Division appears to have been transferred to Yugoslavia.

183 Infanterie Division

Commander :—Genlt. DETTLING (53).

Composition : Gren. Rgts. 330, 343, 351 ; Art. Rgt. 219 ; Pi. Btl. 219 ; Pz. Jäg. Abt. 219 ; Aufkl. Abt. 219 ; Nachr. Abt. 219.

Auxiliary unit number :—219.

Home Station :— (Wkr. XIII.)

Formed in January, 1940. Identified on Central Russian front late in 1941, where it was fairly constantly in action. It was transferred to the Southern sector in autumn, 1943, where it gained distinction in the fighting in the Kiev area but suffered heavy losses.

196 Infanterie Division

Commander :—

Composition :—Gren. Rgts. 340, 345, 362 ; Art. Rgt. 233 ; Pi. Btl. 233 ; Pz. Jäg. Abt. 233 ; Aufkl. Abt. 233 ; Nachr. Abt. 233.

Auxiliary unit number :—233.

Home Station : Bielefeld ? (Wkr. VI).

Formed early in 1940. Fought well during the Norwegian campaign and stayed on as a garrison division in Central Norway.

197 Infanterie Division

Commander : Genlt. Ehrenfried BOEGE (50).

Composition : Gren. Rgts. 321, 332, 347 ; Art. Rgt. 229 ; Pi. Btl. 229 ; Pz. Jäg. Abt. 229 ; Aufkl. Abt. 229 ; Nachr. Abt. 229.

Auxiliary unit number :—229.

Home Station :—Speyer (Wkr. XII).

Formed early in 1940. Identified on the Central Russian front in August, 1941, where it has since remained. It has apparently suffered heavy losses.

198 Infanterie Division

Commander :—

Composition : Gren. Rgts. 305, 308, 326 ; Art. Rgt. 235 ; Pi. Btl. 235 ; Pz. Jäg. Abt. 235 ; Aufkl. Abt. 235 ; Nachr. Abt. 235.

Auxiliary unit number : 235.

Home Station :— (Wkr. V.).

Formed early in 1940. Has been in Russia continuously since the beginning of the campaign. Took part in the invasion of the Crimea, and in operations in the Caucasus.

199 Infanterie Division

Commander :—

Composition : Gren. Rgts. 341, 357, 410 ; Art. Rgt. 199 ; Pi. Btl. 199 ; Schn. Abt. 199 ; Nachr. Abt. 199.

Auxiliary unit number :—199.

Home Station :—Düsseldorf (Wkr. VI).

Formed on mobilisation. In Southern Norway from the end of 1940 until the middle of May, 1941, when it was moved to Northern Norway. During the latter half of 1941 it may have been for a time in Finland, but did not do any fighting. Since December, 1941, in Norway (Tromsö area).

205 Infanterie Division

Commander :—

Composition :—Gren. Rgts. 335, 353, 358 ; Art. Rgt. 205 ; Pi. Btl. 205 ; Schn. Abt. 205 ; Nachr. Abt. 205.

Auxiliary unit number : 205.

Home station :—Ulm (Wkr. V).

Formed on mobilisation with a high proportion of Landwehr personnel, from Baden and Württemberg. Identified in France in August, 1941, and left for Russia early in 1942. Subsequently in action in the Central sector. It may possibly have been transferred to the Northern sector in autumn, 1943. Personnel now more uniformly distributed in age groups.

206 Infanterie Division

Commander :—Genlt. Alfons HITTER.

Composition :—Gren. Rgts. 301, 312, 413 ; Art. Rgt. 206 ; Pi. Btl. 206 ; Schn. Abt. 206 ; Nachr. Abt. 206.

Auxiliary unit number : 206.

Home station :—Gumbinnen (Wkr. I).

Formed on mobilisation. Personnel mainly East Prussian, of the Landwehr age group. Fairly continuously engaged on the Central Russian front since the beginning of the campaign. Personnel now of normal age groups.

207 Infanterie Division—*see* 207 Sicherungs Division

208 Infanterie Division

Commander : Genmaj. Karl v. SCHLIEBEN (50).

Composition :—Gren. Rgts. 309, 337, 338 ; Art. Rgt. 208 ; Pi. Btl. 208 ; Schn. Abt. 208 ; Nachr. Abt. 208.

Auxiliary unit number : 208.

Home station : Cottbuss (Wkr. IV).

Formed on mobilisation. Personnel Prussian, originally mainly Landwehr. Identified in France in April, 1941, and was transferred to Russia, probably in December, where it has been continuously engaged in the Central Sector since January, 1942. It took part in the Kursk offensive in summer, 1943, and sustained very heavy losses. It was transferred to the Southern sector in the following autumn. Personnel age groups now normal.

209 Infanterie Division

Landwehr division formed on mobilisation in Wehrkreis IV with Saxon personnel. Disbanded after the French campaign in the summer of 1940.

210 Infanterie Division

Commander :—Genlt. Karl WINTERGERST (52).

Composition :—Gren. Rgt. 193 ? ; Art. Rgt. 210.

Auxiliary unit number :—

Home Station :—

Identified in Northern Finland late in 1942. Probably a coastal defence division consisting of a divisional staff controlling fortress bns. and coastal batteries.

211 Infanterie Division

Commander :—

Composition :—Gren. Rgts. 306 ; 317, 365 ; Art. Rgt. 211 ; Pi. Btl. 211 ; Pz. Jäg. Abt. 211 ; Aufkl. Abt. 211 ; Nachr. Abt. 211.

Auxiliary unit number :—211.

Home Station :—Köln (Wkr. VI).

Formed on mobilisation. Personnel mainly from the Köln area and of the Landwehr age group. In South-western France during most of 1941. It was transferred to Russia at the beginning of 1942, where it has been continuously engaged on the Central front. It took part in the Kursk offensive, where it sustained very heavy losses. Personnel now normal.

212 Infanterie Division

Commander :—

Composition :—Gren. Rgts. 316, 320, 423 ; Art. Rgt. 212 ; Pi. Btl. 212 ; Schn. Abt.—; Nachr. Abt. 212.

Auxiliary unit number : 212.

Home Station :—München (Wkr. VII).

Formed on mobilisation with personnel mainly from Southern Bavaria and of the Landwehr age group. On the Saar front for a time, later in France. Left France for Russia late in 1941, where it was identified in the Central sector and subsequently in the Northern sector, where it has remained, but has seen little action.

213 Infanterie Division.—*See* 213 Sicherungs Division.

214 Infanterie Division

Commander :—Genlt. Max HORN (56).

Composition :—Gren. Rgts. 355, 367 ; Art. Rgt. 214 ; Pi. Btl. 214 ; Schn. Abt. 214 ; Nachr. Abt. 214.

Auxiliary unit number :—214.

Home Station :—Hanau (Wkr. IX).

Formed on mobilisation with personnel from the Frankfurt area. On the Saar front until December, 1939. In Southern Norway from May, 1940. Since December, 1941, 388 Infantry Regiment has been detached for service in Northern Finland, and may now be under the control of the new 210 Infantry Division.

215 Infanterie Division

Commander :—Genlt. FRANKEWITZ.

Composition :—Gren. Rgts. 380, 390, 435 ; Art. Rgt. 215 ; Pi. Btl. 215 ; Pz. Jäg. Abt. 215 ; Aufkl. Abt. 215 ; Nachr. Abt. 215.

Auxiliary unit number :—215.

Home Station :—Heilbronn (Wkr. V).

Formed on mobilisation. Personnel mainly Landwehr from Baden and Württemberg. On the Saar front in May, 1940. In Central France during the summer of 1941, but left for Russia late in that year and has been identified subsequently in the Northern sector. Personnel age groups now normal.

216 Infanterie Division

Commander :—Genlt. GIMMLER (54).

Composition :—Gren. Rgts. 348, 396, 398 ; Art. Rgt. 216 ; Pi. Btl. 216 ; Pz. Jäg. Abt. 216 ; Aufkl. Abt. 216 ; Nachr. Abt. 216.

Auxiliary unit number :—216.

Home Station :—Hameln (Wkr. XI).

Formed on mobilisation. Personnel mainly Landwehr from the Hannover area. Fought in Holland and Belgium. Apparently arrived on the Central Russian front from France early in January, 1942, where it has since remained. Personnel now normal.

217 Infanterie Division

Commander :—Genlt. POPPE (51).

Composition :—Gren. Rgts. 311, 346, 389 ; Art. Rgt. 217 ; Pi. Btl. 217 ; Pz. Jäg. Abt. 217 ; Aufkl. Abt. 217 ; Nachr. Abt. 217.

Auxiliary unit number :—217.

Home Station :—Allenstein (Wkr. I).

Formed on mobilisation. Personnel mainly East Prussian of the Landwehr age group. Fought in Poland and in Flanders. Identified on the Northern Russian front in July, 1941, where it has been employed on coastal defence duties. It was transferred to the Southern sector in autumn, 1943, where it gained distinction in the Kiev area but suffered heavy losses. Personnel now normal.

218 Infanterie Division

Commander :—

Composition :—Gren. Rgts. 323, 386, 397 ; Art. Rgt. 218 ; Pi. Btl. 218 ; Schn. Abt. 218 ; Nachr. Abt. 218.

Auxiliary unit number :—218.

Home Station :—Spandau (Wkr. III).

Formed on mobilisation. Personnel mainly of the Landwehr age group. Distinguished itself both in Poland and France, but has been reorganised since those campaigns with younger men. In Denmark from May, 1941, till January, 1942, when it left for the Eastern front and has since fought in the Northern sector.

221 Infanterie Division—*see* 221 Sicherungs Division.

223 Infanterie Division

Commander :—

Composition :—Gren. Rgts. 344, 385, 425 ; Art. Rgt. 223 ; Pi. Btl. 223 ; Schn. Abt. 223 ; Nachr. Abt. 223.

Auxiliary unit number :—223.

Home Station :—Dresden (Wkr. IV).

Formed on mobilisation. Personnel Saxon, mainly Landwehr. No evidence for active operations prior to the Russian campaign. Identified in South-western France in May, 1941, where it remained until transferred to Russia at the end of the year. Subsequently fought in the Northern sector. It was transferred to the Southern sector in the summer of 1943, where it has been heavily engaged. Personnel now normal.

225 Infanterie Division

Commander :—

Composition :—Gren. Rgts. 333, 376, 377 ; Art. Rgt. 225 ; Pi. Btl. 225 ; Schn. Abt. 225 ; Nachr. Abt. 225.

Auxiliary unit number :—225.

Home Station :—Hamburg (Wkr. X).

Formed in the greater Hamburg district on mobilisation. Personnel mainly of Landwehr age groups. Arrived on the Northern Russian front from France in January, 1942, and has since remained there. Personnel now normal.

227 Infanterie Division

Commander :—

Composition :—Gren. Rgts. 328, 366, 412 ; Art. Rgt. 227 ; Pi. Btl. 227 ; Pz. Jäg. Abt. 227 ; Aufkl. Abt. 227 ; Nachr. Abt. 227.

Home Station :—Düsseldorf (Wkr. VI).

Formed on mobilisation. Personnel mainly of the Landwehr age group. Took part in active operations in Belgium. In North-eastern France in the latter part of 1941. Transferred to the Northern Russian front in April, 1942, where it has since remained. Personnel now normal.

228 Infanterie Division

Commander :—

Composition :—

Auxiliary unit number :—

Home Station :—(Wkr. I).

Landwehr division formed in Wehrkreis I on mobilisation. Distinguished itself in Northern Poland ; later in action in Holland and Belgium. Disbanded in the late summer of 1940.

230 Infanterie Division

Commander :—Genmaj. MENKEL.

Composition :—

Auxiliary unit number :—

Home Station :—

Probably formed in the summer of 1942 as a coastal defence division in Northern Norway consisting of a divisional staff controlling fortress btns. and coastal batteries.

231 Infanterie Division

Landwehr division formed in Wehrkreis XIII on mobilisation. No evidence of any active operations. Disbanded in the late summer of 1940.

239 Infanterie Division

Formed on mobilisation. No evidence of any active operations prior to the Russian campaign. In the Protectorate during the winter of 1940–1941. Engaged in the Southern sector at the beginning of the Russian campaign. Disbanded late in 1941.

240 Infanterie Division

Commander :—

Composition :—

Auxiliary unit number :—

Home Station :—

Coastal Division formed in summer of 1942.

242 Infanterie Division

Commander :—

Composition :—Gren. Rgts. , , 917 ; Art. Rgt. 242.

Auxiliary unit number :—

Home Station :— (Wkr. II).

Formed in Belgium in summer, 1943, from various depot units.

246 Infanterie Division

Commander :—

Composition :—Gren. Rgts. 352, 404, 689 ; Art. Rgt. 246 ; Pi. Btl. 246 ; Schn. Abt. 246 ; Nachr. Abt. 246.

Auxiliary unit number :—246.

Home Station :—Trier (Treves) (Wkr. XII).

Formed on mobilisation. On the Saar front for a time. In South-western France from August, 1941, until January, 1942, when it left for Russia. Has since operated in the Central sector.

250 Infanterie Division (Blue Division)

Commander :—Gen. d. Divisions Emilio ESTEBAN INFANTES (52).

Composition :—

Auxiliary unit number :—

Home Station :—

Formed in August, 1941, from Spanish volunteers, at Grafenwöhr (Wehrkreis XIII). Originally destined for the Southern Russian front, it was eventually sent to the Northern sector, late in 1941 and suffered considerable casualties. Disbanded in autumn of 1943.

251 Infanterie Division

Commander :—Genmaj. Maximilian FELZMANN (50).

Composition :—Gren. Rgts. 451, 459, 471 ; Art. Rgt. 251 ; Pi. Btl. 251 ; Pz. Jäg. Abt. 251 ; Aufkl. Abt. 251 ; Nachr. Abt. 251.

Auxiliary unit number :—251.

Home Station :—Frankfurt/Main (Wkr. IX).

Formed on mobilisation from men already serving in Ergänzungs units in Hessen and Thüringen. First identified on the Central Russian front in July, 1941, where it has been fairly heavily and continuously engaged. It took part in the Kursk offensive in summer, 1943, and has since gained distinction in defensive fighting.

252 Infanterie Division

Commander :—

Composition :—Gren. Rgts. 452, 461, 472 ; Art. Rgt. 252 ; Pi. Btl. 252 ; Pz. Jäg. Abt. 252 ; Aufkl. Abt. 252 ; Nachr. Abt. 252.

Auxiliary unit number :—252.

Home Station :—Neisse (Wkr. VIII).

Formed on mobilisation from Silesians already serving in Ergänzungs units. On the Saar front for several months. Later distinguished itself in the attack on the Maginot line. Morale high. Continuously and heavily engaged on the Central Russian front since the beginning of the campaign.

253 Infanterie Division

Commander :—Genlt. Fritz. BECKER (52).

Composition :—Gren. Rgts. 453, 464, 473 ; Art. Rgt. 253 ; Pi. Btl. 253 ; Pz. Jäg. Abt. 253 ; Aufkl. Abt. 253 ; Nachr. Abt. 253.

Auxiliary unit number : 253.

Home Station :—Aachen (Wkr. VI).

Formed on mobilisation from men already serving in Westphalian Ergänzungs units. Took part in the French campaign. First identified on the Northern Russian front in July, 1941, but subsequently transferred to the Central sector, where it has fought with distinction.

254 Infanterie Division

Commander :—

Composition :—Gren. Rgts. 454, 474, 484 ; Art. Rgt. 254 ; Pi. Btl. 254 ; Pz. Jäg. Abt. 254 ; Aufkl. Abt. 254 ; Nachr. Abt. 254.

Auxiliary unit number :—254.

Home Station :—Dortmund (Wkr. VI).

Formed on mobilisation from men already serving in Westphalian Ergänzungs units. Took part in active operations in Holland, Belgium and Northern France. Identified on the Northern Russian front in July, 1941, where it has since remained.

255 Infanterie Division

Commander :—

Composition :—Gren. Rgts. 455, 465, 475 ; Art. Rgt. 255 ; Pi. Btl. 255 ; Pz. Jäg. Abt. 255 ; Aufkl. Abt. 255 ; Nachr. Abt. 255.

Auxiliary unit number :—255.

Home Station :—Löbau (Wkr. IV).

Formed on mobilisation from men already serving in Saxon Ergänzungs units. Also contains a proportion of Sudeten Germans. Took an inconspicuous part in the French campaign. Identified on the Central Russian front in August, 1941. It was subsequently transferred to the Southern front in spring, 1943, where it has been fairly continuously engaged.

256 Infanterie Division

Commander :—Genlt. Paul DANHAUSER (51).

Composition :—Gren. Rgts. 456, 476, 481 ; Art. Rgt. 256 ; Pi. Btl. 256; Pz. Jäg. Abt. 256 ; Aufkl. Abt. 256 ; Nachr. Abt. 256 ?

Auxiliary unit number :—256.

Home Station :—Meissen ? (Wkr. IV).

Formed in Wehrkreis IV and XIII on mobilisation from men already serving in Ergänzungs units. Personnel Saxon, Bavarian and Sudeten German. Fought in Holland and Belgium. Continuously engaged in Russia, Central sector, since the beginning of the campaign. It appears to have suffered heavy losses.

257 Infanterie Division

Commander :—Genlt. PÜCHLER.

Composition :—Gren. Rgts. 457, 466, 477 ; Art. Rgt. 257 ; Pi. Btl. 257 ; Pz. Jäg. Abt. 257 ; Aufkl. Abt. 257 ; Nachr. Abt. 257.

Auxiliary unit number :—257.

Home Station :—Frankfurt/Oder (Wkr. III).

Formed on mobilisation from men already serving in Ergänzungs units. Personnel Prussian. On the Saar front for a time. Identified on the Southern Russian front in July, 1941, where it was continuously and heavily engaged. It was transferred to France in autumn, 1942, for rest and refit and returned to the Southern sector of the Russian front in April, 1943, where it has remained.

258 Infanterie Division

Commander :—Genlt. Hans HÖCKER (50).

Composition :—Gren. Rgts. 458, 478, 479 ; Art. Rgt. 258 ; Pi. Batl. 258 ; Pz. Jäg. Abt. 258 ; Aufkl. Abt. 258 ; Nachr. Abt. 258.

Auxiliary unit number :—258.

Home Station :—Rostock (Wkr. II).

Formed in Wehrkreis II and III on mobilisation from men already serving in Ergänzungs units. Personnel Prussian. On the Saar front for some months and took part in the attack on the Maginot line. Continuously engaged on the Central Russian front from the beginning of the campaign until it was transferred in late summer, 1943, to the Southern sector, where it has remained.

260 Infanterie Division

Commander :—Obst. Alexander CONRADY (40).

Composition :—Gren. Rgts. 460, 470, 480 ; Art. Rgt. 260 ; Pi. Btl. 260 ; Pz. Jäg. Abt. 260 ; Aufkl. Abt. 260 ; Nachr. Abt. 260.

Auxiliary unit number :—260.

Home Station :—Karlsruhe (Wkr. V.).

Formed on mobilisation from men already serving in Ergänzungs units in Baden and Württemberg. No evidence of active operations prior to the Russian campaign. Continuously and heavily engaged on the Central front until transferred to France in the summer of 1942. Subsequently returned to Russia, Central sector, in winter, 1942, where it fought with distinction during summer, 1943.

262 Infanterie Division

Commander :—

Composition : Gren. Rgts. 462, 482, 486 ; Art. Rgt. 262 ; Pi. Btl. 262 ; Pz. Jäg. Abt. 262 ; Aufkl. Abt. 262 ; Nachr. Abt. 262.

Auxiliary unit number :—262.

Home Station :—Wien (Wkr. XVII).

Formed on mobilisation from men already serving in Ergänzungs units in Austria. On the Saar front for several months. Identified on the Central Russian front in September, 1941, where it has since remained. It took part in the Kursk offensive in summer, 1943, sustaining heavy losses.

263 Infanterie Division

Commander :

Composition : Gren. Rgts. 463, 483, 485 ; Art. Rgt. 263 ; Pi. Btl. 263 ; Pz. Jäg. Abt. 263 ; Aufkl. Abt. 263 ; Nachr. Abt. 263.

Auxiliary unit number : 263.

Home Station :—Idar-Oberstein (Wkr. XII).

Formed on mobilisation from men already serving in Ergänzungs units. Personnel mainly Bavarians from the Palatinate. Fought with distinction during the French campaign. Identified on the Central Russian front in July, 1941, where it has since remained.

264 Infanterie Division

Commander :—Genmaj. Wilhelm METGER.

Composition :—Gren. Rgts. 891, 892, 893 ; Art. Rgt. 264 ; Pi. Btl. 264 ; Pz. Jäg. Abt. 264 ; Aufkl. Abt. — ; Nachr. Abt. — .

Auxiliary unit number : 264.

Home Station :—(Wkr. VI).

Was formed in summer, 1943, in Belgium, and was transferred to Croatia in October, 1943.

265 Infanterie Division

Commander :—Genlt. Wilhelm RUSSWURM (65).

Composition :—Gren. Rgt. 894, 895, 896 ; Art. Rgt. — ; Pi. Btl. — ; Pz. Jäg. Abt. — ; Aufkl. Abt. — ; Nachr. Abt. —

Auxiliary unit number :—

Home Station :— (Wkr. XI).

Formed in Wkr. XI early in 1943. Identified in Brittany in September, 1943.

267 Infanterie Division

Commander :—

Composition :—Gren. Rgts. 467, 487, 497* ; Art. Rgt. 267 ; Pi. Btl. 267 ; Pz. Jäg. Abt. 267 ; Aufkl. Abt. 267 ; Nachr. Abt. 267.

Auxiliary unit number :—267.

Home Station : Hannover ? (Wkr. XI).

Formed on mobilisation from men already serving in Ergänzungs units in the Hannover–Braunschweig area. Identified on the Central Russian front in July, 1941, where it has been fairly continuously engaged.

268 Infanterie Division

Commander :—Genlt. Heinz GREINER (49).

Composition :—Gren. Rgts. 468, 488, 499 ; Art. Rgt. 268 ; Pi. Batl. 268 ; Schnelle Abt. 268 ; Nachr. Abt. 268.

Auxiliary unit number :—268.

Home Station :—München (Wkr. VII).

Formed in Wehrkreis VII and XVII on mobilisation from men already serving in Ergänzungs units. On the Saar front for several months. Continuously engaged since the beginning of the Russian campaign on the Central front. It fought with distinction during summer, 1943, and suffered heavy losses.

269 Infanterie Division

Commander :—Genlt. Kurt BADINSKI (49).

Composition :—Gren. Rgts. 469, 489, 490 ; Art. Rgt. 269 ; Pi. Batl. 269 ; Schnelle Abt. 269 ; Nachr. Abt. 269.

Auxiliary unit number :—269.

Home Station :—Delmenhorst (Wkr. X).

Formed on mobilisation from men already serving in Ergänzungs units. Personnel North German. Fought in Northern France. Transferred to Denmark in the late summer of 1940, where it remained until May, 1941. Engaged in Russia, Northern sector, until early in 1943, when it was transferred to Norway.

---

* Gren. Rgt. 497 possibly disbanded.

270 Infanterie Division

Commander :—Genlt. Ralf SODAN (64).

Composition :—

Auxiliary unit number :—

Home Station :— (Wkr. X).

Probably formed in the summer of 1942 as a coastal defence division in Central Norway. It is believed to consist of a divisional staff with fortress bns. and coastal defence batteries under its control.

271 Infanterie Division

Formed in Wkr. V and disbanded in the summer of 1940.

272 Infanterie Division

Formed and disbanded in the summer of 1940.

273 Infanterie Division

Formed in Wkr. III and disbanded in the summer of 1940.

274 Infanterie Division

Commander :—

Composition :—

Auxiliary unit number :—

Home Station :— (Wkr. II).

Formed in the summer of 1943 and transferred in early autumn, 1943, to Norway.

276 Infanterie Division

Formed and disbanded in the summer of 1940.

277 Infanterie Division

Formed and disbanded in the summer of 1940.

280 Infanterie Division

Commander :—Genlt. v. BEEREN (53).

Composition :—Gren. Rgts. 223 ? 224 ?

Auxiliary unit number :—

Home Station :—

Probably formed in the summer of 1942 as a coastal defence division in Southern Norway. It is believed to consist of a divisional staff with fortress bns. and coastal batteries under its control.

282 Infanterie Division

Commander :—Genmaj KOHLER.

Composition :—Gren. Rgts. 848, 849, 850 ; Art. Rgt. 282.

Auxiliary unit number :—282.

Home Station :— (Wkr. XII).

Formed in France 1942–1943. Identified on the Southern Russian front in April, 1943, where it has since remained and has been continuously engaged.

290 Infanterie Division

Commander :—Genlt. HEINRICHS (52).

Composition :—Gren. Rgts. 501, 502, 503 ; Art. Rgt. 290 ; Pi. Btl. 290 ; Schnelle Abt. 290 ; Nachr. Abt. —

Auxiliary unit number :—290.

Home Station :— (Wkr. X).

Formed in March/April, 1940, from newly-trained personnel. First in action in June, 1940, during the French campaign. Continuously engaged on the Northern Russian front since July, 1941.

291 Infanterie Division

Commander :—Genlt. Werner GOERITZ (52).

Composition :—Gren. Rgts. 504, 505, 506 ; Art. Rgt. 291 ; Pi. Btl. 291 ; Schnelle Abt. 291 ; Nachr. Abt. 291.

Auxiliary unit number :—291.

Home Station :—Insterburg (Wkr. I).

Formed in March/April, 1940, from newly-trained Prussian personnel. First in action during the French campaign, but did little fighting. Identified on the Northern Russian front in July, 1941, where it remained until it was transferred to the Southern sector in late summer, 1943, where it has seen heavy fighting.

292 Infanterie Division

Commander :—Genmaj. JOHN.

Composition :—Gren. Rgts. 507, 508, 509 ; Art. Rgt. 292 ; Pi. Batl. 292 ; Pz. Jäg. Abt. 292 ; Aufkl. Abt. — ; Nachr. Abt. 292.

Auxiliary unit number :—292.

Home Station :— (Wkr. II).

Formed in March/April, 1940, from newly trained Prussian personnel. Experience in the French campaign similar to that of 291 Division. Identified on the Central Russian front in August, 1941, where it has remained ever since. It took part in the Kursk offensive of summer, 1943.

293 Infanterie Division

Commander :—Genmaj. Karl ARNDT.

Composition :—Gren. Rgts. 510, 511, 512 ; Art. Rgt. 293 ; Pi. Batl. 293 ; Pz. Jäg. Abt. 293 ; Aufkl. Abt. 293 ; Nachr. Abt. 293.

Auxiliary unit number :—293.

Home Station :— (Wkr. III).

Formed in March/April, 1940, from newly trained Prussian personnel. Experience in the French campaign similar to that of 291 Division. Identified on the Central Russian front in July, 1941. It took part in the Kursk offensive in summer, 1943, suffering very heavy losses. It was apparently transferred to the Southern sector in autumn, 1943.

294 Infanterie Division

Commander :—Genlt. Johannes BLOCK (50).

Composition :—Gren. Rgts. 513, 514, 515 ; Art. Rgt. 294 ; Pi. Batl. 294 ; Pz. Jäg. Abt. 294 ; Aufkl. Abt. 294 ; Nachr. Abt. 294.

Auxiliary unit number :—294.

Home Station :— (Wkr. IV).

Formed in March/April, 1940, from newly trained Saxon personnel. First identified in action during the Balkan campaign and has fought on the Russian front, Southern sector, since September, 1941. Suffered heavy losses on withdrawal from Stalingrad, and later during the encirclement of Taganrog.

295 Infanterie Division

Commander :—

Composition :—Gren. Rgts. 516, 517, 518 ; Art. Rgt. 295 ; Pi. Batl. 295 ; Pz. Jäg. Abt. 295 ; [Aufkl. Abt. — ; Nachr. Abt. 295.

Auxiliary unit number :—295.

Home Station :— (Wkr. XI).

Formed in March/April, 1940, from newly trained personnel. Not identified in action prior to the Russian campaign, where it was continuously engaged on the Southern front from July, 1941. Virtually destroyed at Stalingrad.

296 Infanterie Division

Commander :—Genlt. Antur KULLMER (48).

Composition :—Gren. Rgts. 519, 520, 521 ; Art. Rgt. 296 ; Pi. Batl. 296 ; Pz. Jäg. Abt. 296 ; Aufkl. Abt. 296 ; Nachr. Abt. 296.

Auxiliary unit number :—296.

Home Station :—Nürnberg ? (Wkr. XIII).

Formed in March/April, 1940, from newly trained men from Northern Bayern and Western Sudetenland. Not identified in action prior to the Russian campaign, where it has operated in the Central sector.

297 Infanterie Division

Commander :—

Composition :—Gren. Rgts. 522, 523, 524 ; Art. Rgt. 297 ; Pi. Batl. 297 ; Pz. Jäg. Abt. 297 ; Aufkl. Abt. 297 ; Nachr. Abt. 297.

Auxiliary unit number :—297.

Home Station :—Wien (Wkr. XVII).

Formed in March/April, 1940, from newly trained Austrian personnel. Not identified in action prior to the Russian campaign where it operated in the Southern sector from July, 1941. Virtually destroyed at Stalingrad. Reformed in summer, 1943, in the Belgrade area and transferred to Albania in September, 1943.

298 Infanterie Division

Commander :—Genlt. SZELINSKI (53).

Composition :—Gren. Rgts. 525, 526, 527 ; Art. Rgt. 298 ; Pi. Batl. 298 ; Pz. Jäg. Abt. 298 ; Aufkl. Abt. 298 ; Nachr. Abt. 298.

Auxiliary unit number :—298.

Home Station :— (Wkr. VIII).

Formed in March/April, 1940, from newly trained Silesian personnel. Not identified in action prior to the Russian campaign, where it has operated with the Southern Group since July, 1941. Now possibly disbanded.

299 Infanterie Division

Commander :—Genlt. Graf. v. ORIOLA.

Composition :—Gren. Rgts. 528, 529, 530 ; Art. Rgt. 299 ; Pi. Batl. 299 ; Pz. Jäg. Abt. 299 ; Aufkl. Abt. 299 ; Nachr. Abt. —.

Auxiliary unit number :—299.

Home Station :—Weimar (Wkr. IX).

Formed in March/April, 1940, from newly trained men from Hessen and Thüringen. First in action during the French campaign in June, 1940. Continuously engaged in Russia, on the Southern front and later in the Central sector. It gained distinction in fighting during summer, 1943.

302 Infanterie Division

Commander :—

Composition :—Gren. Rgts. 570, 571, 572 ; Art. Rgt. 302 ; Pi. Batl. 302 ; Schnelle Abt. 302 ; Nachr. Abt. 302.

Auxiliary unit number :—302.

Home Station :—Schwerin (Wkr. II).

Formed late in 1940, but not reliably identified until early in 1942 in Northern France, where it remained until it was transferred to the Russian front, Southern sector, early in 1943.

304 Infanterie Division

Commander :—Genlt. Heinrich KRAMPF (56).

Composition :—Gren. Rgts. 573, 574, 575 ; Art. Rgt. 304 ; Pi. Btl. 304 ; Pz. Jäg. Abt. 304 ; Aufkl. Abt. ; Nachr. Abt. 304.

Auxiliary unit number :—304.

Home Station :— (Wkr. IV).

Formed late in 1940. From April, 1942, in Belgium. Transferred to the Southern sector in Russia early in 1943, where it has been constantly engaged, suffering heavy losses at Taganrog.

305 Infanterie Division

Commander :—Genmaj. Bruno HAUCK.

Composition :—Gren. Rgts. 576, 577, 578 ; Art. Rgt. 305 ; Pi. Btl. 305 ; Pz. Jäg. Abt. ; Aufkl. Abt. 305 ; Nachr. Abt. 305.

Auxiliary unit number :—305.

Home Station :—Konstanz (Wkr. V).

Formed late in 1940. In Western France from the end of 1941 until the beginning of May, 1942, when it left for the Russian front, Southern sector. Virtually destroyed at Stalingrad. Reformed in France in May, 1943. In August, 1943, it was transferred to Italy where it has since been in action.

306 Infanterie Division

Commander :—

Composition :—Gren. Rgts. 579, 580, 581 ; Art. Rgt. 306 ; Pi. Btl. 306 ; Schnelle Abt. 306 ; Nachr. Abt. 306.

Auxiliary unit number :—306.

Home Station :—(Wkr. VI).

Formed late in 1940. In Belgium from late 1941. Transferred to the Russian front, Southern sector, in December, 1942, where it has been constantly engaged, sustaining heavy losses at Taganrog.

307 Infanterie Division—Probably disbanded in 1940.

310 Infanterie Division—Probably disbanded in 1940.

311 Infanterie Division

Commander :—

Composition :—

Auxiliary unit number :—

Home Station :— (Wkr. I).

Classification uncertain. Stationed in Poland during 1940. No recent evidence for location and continued existence. Possibly disbanded.

317 Infanterie Division—Probably disbanded in 1940.

319 Infanterie Division

Commander :—Genlt. Erich MÜLLER (55).

Composition :—Gren. Rgts. 582, 583, 584 ; Art. Rgt. 319 ; Pi. Btl. 319 ; Nachr. Abt. ; Schnelle Abt. 319.

Auxiliary unit number :—319.

Home Station :— (Wkr. IX).

Formed late in 1940. In Brittany from August, 1941, where it holds a coastal sector, including the Channel Islands.

320 Infanterie Division

Commander :—Genmaj. Georg. POSTEL (48).

Composition :—Gren. Rgts. 585, 586, 587; Art. Rgt. 320 ; Pi. Btl. 320 ; Pz. Jäg. Abt. 320 ; Aufkl. Abt. — ; Nachr. Abt. 320.

Auxiliary unit number : 320.

Home Station : (Wkr. VIII).

Formed late in 1940. Moved early in January, 1942, from Belgium to Brittany. Transferred early in April to North-eastern France and to the Southern sector in Russia early in 1943, where it has been continuously and heavily engaged.

321 Infanterie Division

Commander :—

Composition :—Gren. Rgts. 588, 589, 590 ; Art. Rgt. 321 ; Pi. Btl. 321 ; Pz. Jäg. Abt. — ; Aufkl. Abt. — ; Nachr. Abt. 321.

Auxiliary unit number :—321.

Home Station :—(Wkr. XI).

Formed late in 1940. In North-eastern France from the end of 1941 until it was transferred to the Central sector in Russia early in 1943, where it has remained.

323 Infanterie Division

Commander :—Genlt. Johann BERGEN (53).

Composition :—Gren. Rgts. 591, 592, 593 ; Art. Rgt. 323 ; Pi. Btl. 323 ; Nachr. Abt. 323 ; Schnelle Abt. 323.

Auxiliary unit number :—323.

Home station :— (Wkr. V).

Formed late in 1940. In North-western France, from the end of 1941 until early in May, 1942, when it left for Russia, Southern sector. It fought with distinction in the retreat from Kiev, sustaining heavy losses.

326 Infanterie Division

Commander :—Genlt. Viktor V. DRABICH-WAECHTER (53).

Composition :—Gren. Rgts. 751, 752, 753 ; Art. Rgt. 326 ; Pi. Btl. 326 ; Pz. Jäg. Abt. 326 ; Aufkl. Abt. ; Nachr. Abt. 326.

Auxiliary unit number :—326.

Home Station :— (Wkr. VI).

Probably formed late in 1942. In former unoccupied France, where it held a Mediterranean coastal sector. It is a static (bodenständige) division.

327 Infanterie Division

Commander :—

Composition :—Gren. Rgts. 595, 596, 597 ; Art. Rgt. 327 ; Pi. Btl. 327 ; Pz. Jäg. Abt. 327 ; Aufkl. Abt. — ; Nachr. Abt. 327.

Auxiliary unit number :—327.

Home Station :— (Wkr. XVII).

Formed late in 1940. In Eastern France in the latter half of 1941 and in South-western France from January, 1942. Took part in the occupation of former unoccupied France and transferred to Russia, Southern sector, early in 1943. It suffered heavy losses in the retreat from Kiev.

328 Infanterie Division

Commander :—Genlt. Joachim v. TRESCKOW (50).

Composition :—Gren. Rgts. 547, 548, 549 ; Art. Rgt. 328 ; Pi. Btl. 328 ; Pz. Jäg. Abt. — ; Aufkl. Abt. 328 ; Nachr. Kp. 328.

Auxiliary unit number :—328.

Home Station :— (Wkr. IX).

Formed late in 1941. First identified in March, 1942, in the Central sector in Russia. Transferred to former unoccupied France in November, 1942, and back to Russia, Southern sector, in summer, 1943, where it has since remained.

329 Infanterie Division

Commander :—

Composition :—Gren. Rgts. 551 ?, 552 ?, 553 ; Art. Rgt. 329 ; Pi. Btl. 329 ; Schnelle Abt. 329 ; Nachr. Abt. 329.

Auxiliary unit number :—329.

Home Station :— (Wkr. VI).

Formed late in 1941. First identified in May, 1942, in the Northern sector of the Russian front, where it has since remained.

330 Infanterie Division

Commander :—

Composition :—Gren. Rgts. 554, 555, 556 ; Art. Rgt. 330 ; Pi. Btl. 330 ? ; Pz. Jäg. Abt. — ; Aufkl. Abt. 330 ; Nachr. Abt. 330.

Auxiliary unit number :—330.

Home Station :— (Wkr. V).

Formed late in 1941. First identified in February, 1942, and has subsequently been in action on the Central Russian front.

331 Infanterie Division

Commander :—Genmaj. Karl RHEIN (50).

Composition :—Gren. Rgts. 557, 558, 559 ; Art. Rgt. 331 ; Pi. Btl. 331 ; Pz. Jäg. Abt. 331 ; Aufkl. Abt. 331 ?; Nachr. Abt. 331.

Auxiliary unit number :—331.

Home Station :— (Wkr. XVII).

Formed late in 1941. First identified in February, 1942, and has operated on the Central Russian front. It was transferred to the Northern sector in autumn, 1943.

332 Infanterie Division

Commander :—

Composition :—Gren. Rgts. 676, 677, 678 ; Art. Rgt. 332 ; Pi. Btl. 332 ; Pz. Jäg. Abt. 332 ; Aufkl. Abt. ; Nachr. Kp. 332.

Auxiliary unit number :—332.

Home Station :— (Wkr. VIII).

Formed in January, 1941. In Normandy from August, 1941, to spring, 1943, when it was transferred to the Southern Russian front, where it has since been in action.

333 Infanterie Division

Commander :—

Composition :—Gren. Rgts. 679, 680, 681 ; Art. Rgt. 333 ; Pi. Btl. 333 ; Schnelle Abt. 333 ; Nachr. Kp. 333.

Auxiliary unit number :—333.

Home Station :—Berlin (Wkr. III).

Formed in January, 1941. Moved in May, 1941, from Wehrkreis III to South-western France. Transferred to Brittany in March, 1942, and to Russia, Southern sector, early in 1943. It appears to include many Poles.

334 Infanterie Division

Commander :—

Composition :—Gren. Rgts. 754, 755, 756 ; Art. Rgt. 334 ; Pi. Btl. 334 ; Schnelle Abt. 334 ; Nachr. Abt. 334.

Auxiliary unit number :—334.

Home Station :— (Wkr. XIII).

Formed in the autumn of 1942. Sent to Tunisia in December, 1942, where it was virtually destroyed in May, 1943. It was re-formed in South-west France in July and August, 1943.

335 Infanterie Division

Commander :—Genlt. CASPER (51).

Composition :—Gren. Rgts. 682, 683, 684 ; Art. Rgt. 335 ; Pi. Btl. 335 ; Pz. Jäg. Abt. 335 ; Auflk. Abt. — ; Nachr. Kp. 335.

Auxiliary unit number :—335.

Home Station :—(Wkr. V).

Formed in January, 1941. First identified in Northern France in October, 1941. Moved to Brittany in February, 1942. Took part in the occupation of former unoccupied France. Transferred to Russia, Southern sector, early in 1943, where it has been fairly constantly in action. It appears to include a large proportion of Poles.

336 Infanterie Division

Commander :—Genlt. Walter LUCHT (62).

Composition :—Gren. Rgts. 685, 686, 687 ; Art. Rgt. 336 ; Pi. Btl. 336 ; Pz. Jäg. Abt. 336 ; Aufkl. Abt. — ; Nachr. Abt. 336.

Auxiliary unit number :—336.

Home Station :—Rheine (Wkr. VI).

Formed in January, 1941, with cadres from 256 Infanterie Division and moved to Normandy. Transferred at the end of March, 1942, to Brittany. Left for the Eastern front at the end of May, 1942, where it has operated in the Southern sector. It sustained heavy losses during the encirclement of Taganrog.

337 Infanterie Division

Commander :—Genlt. Otto SCHÜNEMANN (53).

Composition :—Gren. Rgts. 313, 688, 690 ; Art. Rgt. 337 ; Pi. Btl. 337 ; Pz. Jäg. Abt. 337 ; Aufkl. Abt. — ; Nachr. Kp. 337.

Auxiliary unit number :—337.

Home Station :— (Wkr. VII).

Formed in January, 1941. In Central France from August, 1941, until late in 1942, when it was transferred to the Central sector in Russia, where it has remained.

338 Infanterie Division

Commander :—Genlt. FLOTTMANN (55).

Composition :—Gren. Rgts. 757, 758, 759 ; Art. Rgt. 338 ; Pi. Batl. 338 ; Pz. Jäg. Abt. 338 ; Aufkl. Abt. — ; Nachr. Abt. 338.

Auxiliary unit number :—338.

Home Station :—

Probably formed in France early in 1943.

339 Infanterie Division

Commander :—

Composition :—Gren. Rgts. 691, 692, 693 ; Art. Abt. 339 ; Pi. Batl. 339 ; Nachr. Kp. 339 ; Schnelle Abt. 339

Auxiliary unit number :—339.

Home Station :—Jena (Wkr. IX).

Formed in January, 1941. In Central France until it left for the Russian front at the end of 1941. Has subsequently been in action in the Central sector. It transferred to the Southern sector in autumn, 1943, where it has since remained.

340 Infanterie Division

Commander :—Genlt. BUTZE (53).

Composition :—Gren. Rgts. 694, 695, 696 ; Art. Rgt. 340 ; Pi. Batl. 340 ; Pz. Jäg. Abt. 340 ; Aufkl. Abt. — ; Nachr. Abt. 340.

Auxiliary unit number :—340.

Home Station :— (Wkr. I).

Formed in January, 1941, but first identified in April, 1942, in North-eastern France. Left in May, 1942, for the Eastern front, where it has operated in the Southern sector. It suffered heavy losses in the retreat from Kiev.

341 Infanterie Division (Probably disbanded in 1940)

342 Infanterie Division

Commander :—

Composition :—Gren. Rgts. 697, 698, 699 ; Art. Rgt. 342 ; Pi. Batl. 342 ; Pz. Jäg. Abt. 342 ; Aufkl. Abt. 342 ; Nachr. Abt. 342.

Auxiliary unit number :—342.

Home Station :—Kaiserslautern (Wkr. XII).

Formed in January, 1940. Engaged in mopping-up operations in Yugoslavia from late 1941 until February, 1942, when it was transferred to the Central sector of the Russian front where it has remained.

343 Infanterie Division

Commander :—

Composition :—Gren. Rgts. 851, 852, 853 ; Art. Rgt. — ; Pi. Batl. 343 ; Pz. Jäg. Abt. — ; Aufkl. Abt. — ; Nachr. Abt. — .

Auxiliary unit number :—343.

Home Station :— (Wkr. XIII).

Formed late in 1942 and identified in Brittany in April, 1943. It is a static (bodenständige) division.

344 Infanterie Division

Commander :—

Composition :—Gren. Rgts. 854, 855, 856 ; Art. Rgt. 344 ; Pi. Batl. — ; Pz. Jäg. Abt. — ; Aufkl. Abt. — ; Nachr. Abt. —.

Auxiliary unit number :—344.

Home Station :—

Probably formed late in 1942. Identified in France in the Bordeaux area. In autumn, 1943, it was holding the coastal sector from Arcachon to Hendaye. A static (bodenständige) division.

345 Infanterie Division

Commander :—

Composition :—Gren. Rgt. —.

Auxiliary unit number :—

Home Station :—

Probably formed late in 1942. Was in Southern France until spring, 1943, when the bulk of it was incorporated in 29 Panzer Grenadier Division. Its continued existence as a division is uncertain.

346 Infanterie Division

Commander :—

Composition :—Gren. Rgts. 858, —, —.

Auxiliary unit number :—

Home Station :—

Probably formed in autumn, 1942. Since early in 1943 it has occupied a coastal sector in North-west France.

347 Infanterie Division

Commander :—

Composition :—Gren. Rgts. 861, —, —.

Auxiliary unit number :—347 ?

Home Station :— (Wkr. II).

Probably formed in 1942. In Holland since March, 1943. A static (bodenständige) division.

348 Infanterie Division

Commander :—

Composition :—Gren. Rgts. 863, 864, 865 ?

Auxiliary unit number :—

Home Station :—

Formed late in 1942. Held Dieppe sector from October, 1942, and is probably still in same area.

351 Infanterie Division (Probably disbanded in 1940)

355 Infanterie Division

Commander :—

Composition :—Gren. Rgts. 866, 867, 868.

Auxiliary unit number :—

Home Station :—

Formed in Eastern France in winter, 1942–1943. Identified on the Southern Russian front in August, 1943, where it has remained.

356 Infanterie Division

Commander :—Genlt. FAULENBACH (52).

Composition :—Gren. Rgts. 869, 870, 871 ; Art. Rgt. 356.

Auxiliary unit number :—356.

Home Station :— (Wkr. IX).

Formed in France in summer, 1943. Elements of it are reported to have been in Corsica. The division moved to North Italy in October, 1943.

358 Infanterie Division

Landwehr division formed in Wkr. III late in 1939 and disbanded after the French campaign.

365 Infanterie Division

Landwehr division formed late in 1939. Now Oberfeldkommandantur 365.

369 Infanterie Division

Commander :—Genmaj. Fritz NEIDHOLDT (54).

Composition :—Gren. Rgts. 369, 370 ; Art. Rgt. 369 ; Art. Rgt. — ; Pi. Btl. — ; Pz. Jäg. Abt. — ; Aufkl. Abt. — ; Nachr. Abt. —

Auxiliary unit number :—369.

Home Station :—Stockerau (Wkr. XVII).

Formed in the latter part of 1942 by the expansion of 369 Infanterie Regiment, consisting of Croatians, which formerly operated under 100 Jäger Division. Now in Croatia.

370 Infanterie Division

Commander :—

Composition :—Gren. Rgts. 666, 667, 668 ; Art. Rgt. 370 ; Pi. Btl. 370 ; Pz. Jäg. Abt. 370 ; Aufkl. Abt. — ; Nachr. Abt. 370.

Auxiliary unit number :—370.

Home Station :— (Wkr. VIII).

Completed formation in France in May, 1942, and then transferred to the Southern Russian front, where it operated in the Caucasus in winter, 1942–1943. It was evacuated to the Lower Dnieper area in autumn, 1943.

371 Infanterie Division

Commander :—Genlt. Johannes NIEHOFF.

Composition :—Gren. Rgts. 669, 670, 671 ; Art. Rgt. 371 ; Pi. Btl. 371 ; Pz. Jäg. Abt. 371 ; Aufkl. Abt. — ; Nachr. Abt. —.

Auxiliary unit number :—371.

Home Station :— (Wkr. VI).

Completed formation in France in May, 1942, and then transferred to the Russian front, where it operated in the Southern sector. Virtually destroyed at Stalingrad. Reformed in France in April and May, 1943, and transferred to Italy in autumn, 1943.

372 Infanterie Division

Landwehr division formed late in 1939. Now Oberfeldkommandantur 372.

373 Infanterie Division

Commander :—Genlt. Emil ZELLNER.

Composition :—Gren. Rgts. 383, 384 ; Art. Rgt. 373 ; Pi. Btl. 373 ; Pz. Jäg. Abt. 373 ; Aufkl. Abt. — ; Nachr. Abt. —.

Auxiliary unit number :—373.

Home Station :— (Wkr. XVII).

Formed early in 1943 in Croatia.

376 Infanterie Division

Commander :—

Composition :—Gren. Rgts. 672, 673, 767 ; Art. Rgt. 376 ; Pi. Btl. — ; Pz. Jäg. Abt. 376 ; Aufkl. Abt. — ; Nachr. Abt. —.

Auxiliary unit number :—376.

Home Station :— (Wkr. VII).

Completed formation in France in May, 1942; then transferred to the Russian front, where it operated in the Southern sector. Virtually destroyed at Stalingrad. Reformed in Holland during summer, 1943, and returned to the Southern Russian front in autumn, 1943.

377 Infanterie Division

Commander :—Genmaj. Erich BAESSLER (52).

Composition :—Gren. Rgts. 768, 769, 770 ; Art. Rgt. 377 ; Pi. Btl. 377 ; Pz. Jäg. Abt. 377 ; Aufkl. Abt. 377 ; Nachr. Abt. 377.

Auxiliary unit number :—377.

Home Station :— (Wkr. IX).

Completed formation in France in May, 1942; then transferred to the Russian front, where it has operated in the Southern sector.

379 Infanterie Division

(Formed after mobilisation. Now Oberfeldkommandantur 379.)

380 Infantry Division—Probably disbanded in 1940.

383 Infanterie Division

Commander :—

Composition :—Gren. Rgts. 531, 532, 533 ; Art. Rgt. 383 ; Pi. Btl. 383 ; Nachr. Abt. 383 ; Schnelle Abt. 383.

Auxiliary unit number :—383.

Home Station :— (Wkr. III).

Formed in winter, 1941–1942 in East Prussia. Continually and heavily engaged in the Southern sector of the Russian front since June, 1942.

384 Infanterie Division

Commander :—

Composition :—Gren. Rgts. 534, 535, 536 ; Art. Rgt. 384 ; Pi. Btl. — ; Pz. Jäg. Abt. 384 ; Aufkl. Abt. — ; Nachr. Abt. 384.

Auxiliary unit number :—384.

Home Station :—(Wkr. IV).

Formed in winter, 1941–1942. In action on the Southern Russian front from May, 1942. Virtually destroyed at Stalingrad. Partially reformed in South Russia early in 1943 and transferred to France in spring of that year for completion and training. It returned to the Southern sector of the Russian front in autumn, 1943.

385 Infanterie Division

Commander :—

Composition :—Gren. Rgts. 537, 538, 539 ; Art. Rgt. 385 ; Pi. Btl. 385 ; Pz. Jäg. Abt. 385 ; Nachr. Abt. 385 ; Aufkl. Abt.

Auxiliary unit number :—385.

Home Station :—

Formed in winter of 1941–1942. In action on the Central Russian front from May, 1942 ; later transferred to the Southern sector. Now possibly disbanded.

386 Infanterie Division

Formed late in 1939 in Wehrkreis VI. Disbanded after the French campaign.

387 Infanterie Division

Commander :—

Composition :—Gren. Rgts. 541, 542, 543 ; Art. Rgt. 387 ; Pi. Btl. 387 ; Pz. Jäg. Abt. 387 ; Aufkl. Abt. — ; Nachr. Abt. 387.

Auxiliary unit number :—387.

Home station :— (Wkr. VII).

Formed in the winter of 1941–1942. On the Southern Russian front from May, 1942, where it has been constantly in action.

389 Infanterie Division

Commander :—Genmaj. FORSTER (52).

Composition :—Gren. Rgts. 544, 545, 546 ; Art. Rgt. 389 ; Pi. Btl. — ; Pz. Jäg. Abt. 389 ; Aufkl. Abt. — ; Nachr. Abt. —.

Auxiliary unit number :—389.

Home Station :—(Wkr. IX).

Formed in the winter, 1941–1942. In action on the Southern Russian front from May, 1942. Virtually destroyed at Stalingrad. Reformed in Brittany during summer, 1943, and returned to the Southern sector of the Russian front in autumn, 1943.

393 Infanterie Division

Formed late in 1939 in Wkr. X. Now Oberfeldkommandantur 393.

395 Infanterie Division

Formed after mobilisation and disbanded late in 1940. Now Oberfeldkommandantur 395.

399 Infanterie Division

Formed after mobilisation in Wkr. I and disbanded in 1940. Now Oberfeldkommandantur 399.

416 Infanterie Division

Commander :—Genlt. PFLIEGER (54).

Composition :—Gren. Rgts. 930, 931.

Auxiliary unit number :—466 ?

Home Station :—(Wkr. X).

Previously 416 Division z.b.V. In Denmark, stationed in the Silkeborg area.

554 Infanterie Division

Formed in Wehrkreis V early in 1940 and disbanded after the French campaign.

555 Infanterie Division

Formed in Wehrkreis VI in 1940 and disbanded after the French campaign.

556 Infanterie Division

Formed in Wehrkreis XII in 1940 and disbanded after the French campaign.

557 Infanterie Division

Formed in Wehrkreis IV in 1940 and disbanded after the French campaign.

702 Infanterie Division

Commander :—Genmaj. Otto SCHMIDT (52).

Composition :—Gren. Rgts. 722, 742 ; Art. Rgt. 662 ; Nachr. Abt. 702.

Auxiliary unit number :—702.

Home Station :—(Wkr. II).

Formed in April, 1941, and sent to Southern Norway in May, 1941. Moved at the end of June, 1941, to Northern Norway.

704 Infanterie Division—*see* 104 Jäger Division.

707 Infanterie Division

Commander :—

Composition : Gren. Rgts. 727, 747 ; Art. Rgt. 657 ; Pi. Abt. 707 ; Nachr. Abt. 707.

Auxiliary unit number :—707.

Home Station :—(Wkr. VII).

Formed in April, 1941. Identified on the Central Russian front in October, 1941, where it was employed on rear area duties. It is believed that it was in action in the Bryansk area in summer, 1943.

708 Infanterie Division

Commander :—Genlt. Hermann WILCK (59).

Composition :—Gren. Rgts. 728, 748 ; Art. Rgt. — ; Pi. Abt. 708 ; Nachr. Abt. 708.

Auxiliary unit number :—708.

Home Station :—(Wkr. VIII).

Formed in April, 1941. Probably in Central France in November, 1941 ; from December, 1941, in South-western France.

709 Infanterie Division

Commander :—

Composition :—Gren. Rgts. 729, 739 ; Art. Rgt. — ; Pi. Abt. 709 ; Nachr. Abt. 709.

Auxiliary unit number :—709.

Home Station :—(Wkr. IX).

Formed in April, 1941. In Brittany from November, 1941, to early 1943, when it moved to the Cherbourg Peninsula.

710 Infanterie Division

Commander :—Genlt. PETSCH (56).

Composition :—Gren. Rgts. 730, 740 ; Art. Rgt. — ; Pi. Abt. 710 ; Nachr. Abt. 710.

Auxiliary unit number :—710.

Home Station :—(Wkr. X).

Formed in April, 1941. In Southern Norway since June, 1941.

711 Infanterie Division

Commander :—Genmaj DEUTSCH (52).

Composition :—Gren. Rgts. 731, 744 ; Art. Rgt. 651? ; Pi. Abt. 711 ; Nachr. Abt. 711.

Auxiliary unit number :—711.

Home Station :—(Wkr. XI).

Formed in April, 1941. From August to December, 1941, in North-eastern France. In Normandy since January, 1942.

712 Infanterie Division

Commander :—Genlt. Friedrich-Wilhelm NEUMANN (64).

Composition :—Gren. Rgts. 732, 745 ; Art. Rgt. 652 ; Pi. Abt. 712 ; Nachr. Abt. 712.

Auxiliary unit number :—712.

Home Station :—(Wkr. XII).

Formed in April, 1941. Was in France early in 1942, but subsequently moved to Belgium. Since June, 1942, it has held a coastal sector in the Bruges area.

713 Infanterie Division

Commander :—

Composition :—Gren. Rgts. 733, 746 ; Art. Rgt. 653? ; Pi. Abt. 713 ; Nachr. Abt. 713.

Auxiliary unit number :—713.

Home Station :—(Wkr. XIII).

Formed in April, 1941. One of its regiments was in Crete in September, 1943, where it has remained. Gren. Rgt. 746 is now under "Festungsbrigade Kreta." The continued existence of the division as such is uncertain.

714 Infanterie Division—*see* 114 Jaeger Division.

715 Infanterie Division

Commander :—Genlt. Kurt HOFFMANN (53).

Composition :—Gren. Rgts. 725, 735 ; Art. Rgt. — ; Pi. Abt. 715 ; Nachr. Abt. 715.

Auxiliary unit number :—715.

Home Station :—(Wkr. V.).

Formed in April, 1941. In Southwestern France from August, 1941, to June, 1942, when it moved to the Cannes-Nice coastal sector.

716 Infanterie Division

Commander :—

Composition :—Gren. Rgts. 726, 736 ; Art. Rgt. 656 ; Pi. Abt. 716 ; Nachr. Abt. 716.

Auxiliary unit number :—716.

Home Station :—(Wkr. VI).

Formed in April, 1941, and identified in February, 1942, in Brittany. In Normandy since 1942.

717 Infanterie Division—*see* 117 Jäger Division.

718 Infanterie Division—*see* 118 Jäger Division.

719 Infanterie Division

Commander :—Genlt. Erich HOCKER (61).

Composition :—Gren. Rgts. 723, 743 ; Art. Rgt. 663 ; Pi. Abt. 719 ; Nachr. Abt. 719.

Auxiliary unit number :—719.

Home station :—(Wkr. III).

Formed in April, 1941. Has been in Brabant, Holland, since late 1942.

999 Afrika Division

Commander :—

Composition :—

Auxiliary unit number :—

Home Station :—

Afrika Brigade 999 was formed in Antwerp in October, 1942, and in March, 1943, was converted to Afrika Division 999. Two of its regiments were transferred to Tunisia in March, 1943, where they were virtually destroyed. Since May, 1943, it appears to have ceased to exist as a division and to consist merely of a regimental HQ for the control of fortress bns. in Greece. Its original supporting arms and services have been incorporated in Assault Div. Rhodes.

Assault Division, Rhodes

Commander : Genlt. Ulrich KLEEMANN (52).

Composition :—

Auxiliary unit number :—

Home Station :—

Formed in Rhodes in early summer, 1943, from the former Assault Brigade, Rhodes. Its infantry component appears to have been formed largely from Grenadier Regiment 440 of 164 Jäger Division and from elements of 22 Panzer Grenadier Division. Its supporting arms and services were largely produced by 999 Division. It has so far only been employed for the garrisoning of the island of Rhodes.

(p) "SICHERUNGS" DIVISIONS

201 Sicherungs Division

Commander :—Genlt. Alfred JACOBI (58).
Composition :—
Auxiliary unit number :—
Home Station :—(Wkr. IX ?).

Expanded from 201 Sicherungs Brigade during the summer of 1942. Employed in the rear area of the Northern sector in Russia on L. of C. In autumn, 1943, it may have moved to the forward area.

203 Sicherungs Division

Commander :—
Composition :—
Auxiliary unit number :—
Home Station :— (Wkr. III ?).

Expanded from 203 Sicherungs Brigade during the summer of 1942. Employed in the rear area of the Central sector in Russia on L. of C. duties. It was identified in the front line in autumn, 1943, in the Kiev area.

207 Sicherungs Division

Commander :—Genmaj. Paul HOFFMANN.
Composition :—
Auxiliary unit number :—
Home Station :—Stargard (Wkr. II).

Formed on mobilisation as 207 Infanterie Division with Prussian personnel from Pomerania. Fought with distinction in Poland. Converted in the winter of 1940–1941, when it lost one infantry regiment and its artillery staff. Employed in rear area duties on the Northern Russian front since the outset of the campaign.

213 Sicherungs Division

Commander :—
Composition :—
Auxiliary unit number :—
Home Station :—Glogau (Wkr. VIII).

Formed on mobilisation as 213 Infanterie Division in the Breslau area. Converted in the winter of 1940–1941, when it lost one infantry regiment and its artillery staff. No evidence for its part in active operations prior to the Russian campaign, where it appears to have been employed on rear area duties in the Southern sector. It was identified in the front line, Kiev area, in autumn, 1943, where it appears to have been fairly heavily engaged. At one time Cossack units were apparently subordinated to the division. It is believed that these were withdrawn in summer, 1943, and incorporated into a Cossack Division.

221 Sicherungs Division

Commander :—Genlt. LENDLE (52).

Composition :—

Auxiliary unit number :—

Home Station :—Breslau (Wkr. VIII).

Formed on mobilisation as 221 Infanterie Division with Silesian personnel. Saw active fighting in Poland. Converted in the winter of 1940–1941, when it lost one infantry regiment and its artillery staff. Employed first on the Central Russian front and subsequently in the south. It was identified in the front line in autumn, 1943, in the Kiev area.

281 Sicherungs Division

Commander :—Genmaj. v. STOCKHAUSEN (54).

Composition :—

Auxiliary unit number :—

Home Station :—(Wkr. II).

Probably formed in the summer of 1942. On rear area duties in the Northern sector in Russia. In autumn, 1943, it may have been moved to the forward area.

284 Sicherungs Division

Commander :—

Composition :—

Auxiliary unit number :—

Home Station :—

Date of formation uncertain. On rear area duties in the Northern sector in Russia since early in 1943.

285 Sicherungs Division

Commander :— Genlt. Gustav ADOLPH - AUFFENBERG-KOMAROW.

Composition :—

Auxiliary unit number :—

Home Station :—

Date of formation uncertain. On rear area duties in the Northern Sector in Russia since early in 1942.

286 Sicherungs Division

Commander :—Genlt. RICHERT (52).

Composition :—

Auxiliary unit number :—

Home Station :—

Date of formation uncertain. In the rear area of the Central sector since the autumn of 1942.

403 Sicherungs Division

Commander :—

Composition :—

Auxiliary unit number :—

Home Station :—Berlin (Wkr. III).

Formed in the spring of 1940 as a z.b.V. divisional staff. Given security functions during the Russian campaign and employed in the rear area of the Central sector from November, 1941, later moving to the south. It is believed that personnel from this division was used to re-form 79 and 384 Infanterie Divisions early in 1943, and the division as such has possibly been disbanded.

442 Sicherungs Division

Commander :—

Composition :—

Auxiliary unit number :—

Home Station :—

Formed early in 1940. In Russia in the rear area of the Central sector.

444 Sicherungs Division

Commander :—Genlt. AULEB (57).

Composition :—

Auxiliary unit number :—

Home Station :—(Wkr. XII)

Formed early in 1940. In the rear area of the Southern sector in Russia since the autumn of 1941.

454 Sicherungs Division

Commander :—

Composition :—

Auxiliary unit number :—

Home Station :—

Date of formation uncertain. In the rear area of the Southern sector in Russia since the autumn of 1941.

455 Sicherungs Division

Commander :—

Composition :—

Home Station :—

Date of formation uncertain. In the rear area of the Southern sector in Russia from the autumn of 1941. Believed disbanded.

(*q*) RESERVE DIVISIONS

141 Reserve Division

Commander :—

Composition :—Res. Gren. Rgts. 1, 11, 61.

Auxiliary unit number :—

Home Station :—Insterburg (Wkr. I).

Originally a draft-finding divisional staff. Believed to have been formed into a Reserve Division late in 1942. Located in Poland in autumn, 1943.

143 Reserve Division

Commander :—Genlt. Paul STOEWER (55).

Composition :—Res. Gren. Rgts. 68?, 76?, 208?.

Auxiliary unit number :—

Home Station :—Frankfurt/Oder (Wkr. III).

Originally a draft-finding divisional staff. Believed to have been formed into a Reserve Division in late autumn, 1942, and sent to Poland in December, 1942. May have been used on L. of C. duties in Poland for Army Group Centre in Russia.

148 Reserve Division

Commander :—Genlt. Hermann BOETTCHER (58).

Composition :—Res. Gren. Rgts. 8?, 239?, 252?

Auxiliary unit number :—

Home Station :—(Wkr. VIII).

Originally a training division from Wkr. VIII, but later transferred to Wkr. XII. At the end of 1942 it was formed into a reserve division and was stationed at Toulouse early in 1943. In October, 1943, it was transferred to a coastal sector on the Italian Riviera.

151 Reserve Division

Commander :—

Composition :—Res. Gren. Rgts. 21, 217, 228.

Auxiliary unit number :—

Home Station :—Allenstein (Wkr. I).

Originally a draft-finding divisional staff. Probably converted into a Reserve Division in autumn, 1942. It was possibly in Poland in spring, 1943, but its present location is unknown.

153 Reserve Division

Commander :—Genlt. de l'Homme de COURBIERE (57).

Composition :—Res. Gren. Rgts. : 23?, 218?, 257?

Auxiliary unit number :—

Home Station :—Potsdam (Wkr. III).

Identified in the Crimea in December, 1942, where it remained until transferred to the mainland in autumn, 1943.

154 Reserve Division

Commander :—Genlt. Dr. Friedrich ALTRICHTER (53).
Composition :—Res. Gren. Rgts. 56, 223, 255.
Auxiliary unit number :—
Home Station :—Dresden (Wkr. IV).

Originally a draft-finding divisional staff. Probably converted into a Reserve Division late in 1942. Believed to have been in Poland in spring, 1943, where it is probably still located.

155 Reserve Panzer Division

Commander :—
Composition :—Res. Gren. Rgts. (Mot.) 25 ? ; Res. Pz. Gren. Rgt. 86 ?, Res. Pz. Abt. 7 ? ; Res. Pz. Abt. 18 ?.
Auxiliary unit number :—
Home Station :—Ulm (Wkr. V).

As Division Nummer 155 (mot) was a draft-finding divisional staff until September, 1943, when it was transferred to France as a Reserve Panzer Division.

156 Reserve Division

Commander :—
Composition :—Res. Gren. Rgts. 6, 227?, 254.
Auxiliary unit number :—
Home Station :—Köln (Wkr. VI).

Was stationed in Belgium in the Spa area at the end of 1942. In spring, 1943, it appears to have been sent to Poland, but was re-identified in the Boulogne–Calais region in September, 1943.

157 Reserve Division

Commander :—Genlt. Karl PFLAUM (54).
Composition :—Res. Geb. Rgt. 1 ; Res. Gren. Rgts. 7, 157. ; Res. Art. Abt. 7 ? ; Res. Geb. Art. Abt. 79 ? ; Res. Pi. Btl. 7 ?.
Auxiliary unit number :—
Home Station :—München (Wkr. VII).

First moved into France in autumn, 1942, and took part in the occupation of Vichy France. Has been stationed in the Grenoble area since the Italian evacuation of South-east France.

158 Reserve Division

Commander :—Genlt. Ernst HÆCKEL (54).

Composition :—Res. Gren. Rgts. 62?, 213?, 221?.

Auxiliary unit number :—

Home Station :— (Wkr. VIII).

First appeared as a Reserve Division in France in November, 1942, where it took part in the advance to the Mediterranean coast. In March, 1943, it was transferred to a coastal sector in the Vendee, where it remains.

159 Reserve Division

Commander :—Genlt. Hermann MEYER-RABINGEN (55).

Composition :—Res. Gren. Rgts. 9, 15, 251.

Auxiliary unit number :—

Home Station :—Frankfurt/Main (Wkr. IX).

First appeared as a Reserve Division in France in November, 1942, when it took part in the advance into Vichy France. Since then it has occupied an area in the interior around Clermont-Ferrand.

160 Reserve Division

Commander :—Genlt. Horst. Frhr. v. UCKERMANN (52).

Composition :—Res. Gren. Rgts. 30, 58, 225.

Auxiliary unit number :—

Home Station :— (Wkr. X).

First identified in the Copenhagen area in 1940. Moved to Jutland at the beginning of 1943.

165 Reserve Division

Commander :—Genlt. Sigmund Frhr. v. SCHACKY AUF SCHÖNFELD (58).

Composition :—Res. Gren. Rgts. 205, 215?, 260.

Auxiliary unit number :—

Home Station :—Stuttgart (Wkr. V.).

Stationed at Epinal, France, since its arrival there early in 1942. It was a training and draft-finding division until September, 1943, when it became a Reserve Division.

166 Reserve Division

Commander :—Genmaj. Dipl. Ing. Helmut CASTORF (54).

Composition :—Res. Gren. Regts. :—26?, 69, 86.

Auxiliary unit number :—

Home Station :—Bielefeld (Wkr. VI).

Originally a draft-finding divisional staff and training division. Transferred to Copenhagen, probably as a reserve division, early in 1943.

171 Reserve Division

Commander :—Genlt. Friedrich FÜRST (54).

Composition :—Res. Gren. Rgts. 71, 31 ?, 216 ?

Auxiliary unit number :—

Home Station :—Hannover (Wkr. XI).

As a training and draft-finding division it occupied the Dijon area from 1942 until spring, 1943, when it was transferred to Belgium as a Reserve Division, and held the Dixmude coastal sector.

173 Reserve Division

Commander :—

Composition :—Res. Gren. Rgts. 17, 73.

Auxiliary unit number :—

Home Station :—Nürnberg (Wkr. XIII).

First mentioned in March, 1940, as a Division Nummer. In July, 1943, it moved from Würzburg to the Belgrade area and was upgraded to a Reserve Division. It has fulfilled the normal functions of a Reserve Division and also taken part in anti-partisan activities.

174 Reserve Division

Commander :—

Composition :—Res. Gren. Rgts. 24 ?, 209 ?, 256 ?.

Auxiliary unit number :—

Home Station :—Leipzig (Wkr. IV).

Originally a draft-finding divisional staff. Probably converted into a Reserve Division in 1942 and sent to Poland, where it is believed to be still located.

179 Reserve Panzer Division

Commander :—

Composition :—Res. Gren. Rgts. (mot.) 29; Res. Pz. Gren. Rgt. 81; Res. Pz. Abt. 1?.

Auxiliary unit number :—

Home Station :—Weimar (Wkr. IX).

A draft-finding divisional staff until September, 1943, when it was transferred to France as a Panzer Reserve Division.

182 Reserve Division

Commander :—Genmaj. Paul LETTOW (53).

Composition :—Res. Gren. Rgts. 34, 79, 112.

Auxiliary unit number :—

Home Station :—Nancy (Wkr. XII).

Formed early in 1940 (?), as a training and draft-finding division, from depôt units of Wkr. XII. Transferred to East France early in 1942, and converted into a Reserve Division in autumn, 1942.

187 Reserve Division

Commander :—Genlt. Josef BRAUNER.

Composition :—Res. Gren. Rgts. 45, 130, 462; Res. Pz. Jäg. Abt. 48?.

Auxiliary unit number :—

Home Station :—Linz (Wkr. XVII).

First mentioned in April, 1940. Moved to Zagreb, Croatia, in October, 1942, where it has fulfilled the normal functions of a Reserve Division and also taken part in anti-partisan warfare.

188 Reserve Gebirgs Division

Commander :—Genlt. Wilhelm v. HÖSSLIN (66).

Composition :—Res. Geb. Jäg. Rgt. 136 ?, 137 ?, 138 ?, 139 ?

Auxiliary Unit Number :—

Home Station :—Salzburg (Wkr. XVIII).

Originally a training and draft-finding division.

189 Reserve Division

Commander :—Genmaj Bogislav Graf v. SCHWERIN (48).

Composition :—Res. Gren. Rgt. 28, 52, 214 ; Res. Art. Rgt. 28.

Auxiliary unit number :—

Home Station :—Kassel (Wkr. IX).

Moved into East France in Oct., 1942. Subsequently took part in the occupation of Vichy France and was stationed in the Bouches du Rhône area. Later moved to the interior with its H.Q. at Chatelguyon.

191 Reserve Division

Commander :—

Composition :—Res. Gren. Rgt. (mot.) 20 ; Res. Pz. Gren. Rgt. 13 ; Res. Gren. Rgt. 267.

Auxiliary unit number :—

Home Station :—Braunschweig (Wkr. XI).

First appeared as a Reserve Division in Belgium in 1942. It was transferred to Southern France early in 1943, but since March, 1943, it has been holding a coastal sector in Northern France.

233 Reserve Panzer Division

Commander :—Genlt. Heinrich WOSCH (54).

Composition :—Res. Gren. Rgt. (mot.) 3? ; Res. Pz. Gren. Rgt. 83? ; Res. Art. Rgt. (mot.) 3? ; Res. Pz. Abt. 5? ; Res. Pi. Btl. 68 ?

Auxiliary unit number :—

Home Station :—Frankfurt/Oder? (Wkr. III).

Was formerly Division Nummer 233 and served as a training division for Panzer and motorised troops in Wkr. III. In September, 1943, it was transferred to Denmark and up-graded to a Reserve Panzer Division.

(r) FIELD TRAINING DIVISIONS

Feldausbildungs Division 381

Commander :—Genmaj. Helmut EISENSTÜCK (50).

Composition :—Gren. Feld. Ausb. Rgt. ? 616.

Home Station :—

First identified on the Southern Russian front in January, 1943 where it is believed to have remained.

Feldausbildungs Division 382

Commander :—Genmaj. HOHLER.

Composition :—Gren. Feld. Ausb. Rgt. 617, 618, 619.

Home Station :—

First identified in Russia in January, 1943, and it is believed that it has been operating in the Southern sector.

Feldausbildungs Division 388

Commander :—

Home Station :—

First identified in Russia in May, 1943, where it has been operating in the Northern sector.

Feldausbildungs Division 390

Commander :—

Home Station :—

First identified in Russia in May, 1943, where it has possibly been operating in the Central sector.

Feldausbildungs Division 391

Commander :—Genlt. Albrecht Barron DIGEON v. MONTETON (52).

Composition :—Gren. Feld. Ausb. Rgts. 718, 719, 720.

Home Station :—Koblenz (Wkr. XII).

First identified in Russia in March, 1943, where it has been operating in the Central sector.

(*s*) FRONTIER GUARD DIVISIONS

537 Grenzwacht Division

Commander :—

Home Station :—Innsbruck (Wkr. XVIII).

A Frontier guard division.

538 Grenzwacht Division

Commander :—

Home Station :—Klagenfurt (Wkr. XVIII).

A Frontier guard division.

539 Grenzwacht Division

Commander :—Genlt. Dr. Richard SPEICH (60).

Home Station :—Prague (Prot.).

A Frontier guard division.

540 Grenzwacht Division

Commander :—Genlt. Karl TARBUK v. SENSENHORST.

Home Station :—Brünn (Prot.).

A Frontier guard division.

(*t*) DEPOT DIVISIONS

Division Nummer 147

Commander :—Genlt. Otto MATTERSTOCK (55).

Home Station :—Augsburg (Wkr. VII).

A draft-finding divisional staff.

Division Nummer 152

Commander :—Genlt. Arthur BOLTZE (66).

Home Station :—Graudenz (Wkr. XX).

A draft-finding divisional staff.

Division Nummer 172

Commander :—

Home Station :—Mainz (Wkr. XII).

A draft-finding divisional staff.

Division Nummer 176

Commander :—

Home Station :—Bielefeld (Wkr. VI).

A draft-finding divisional staff.

Division Nummer 177

Commander :—

Home Station :—Wien (Wkr. XVII).

A draft-finding divisional staff.

Division Nummer 178

Commander :—

Home Station :—Liegnitz (Wkr. VIII).

A draft-finding divisional staff.

Division Nummer 180

Commander :—

Home Station :—Verden (Wkr. X).

A draft-finding divisional staff.

Division Nummer 190

Commander :—

Home Station :—Neumünster (Wkr. X).

A draft-finding divisional staff.

Division Nummer 192

Commander :—

Home Station :—Rostock (Wkr. II).

A draft-finding divisional staff.

Division Nummer 193

Commander :—
Home Station :—Pilsen ? (Wkr. Böhmen-Mähren).

A draft-finding divisional staff. Now believed to be stationed at Pilsen (Protectorate).

Division Nummer 401

Commander :—
Composition :—
Home Station :—Königsberg (Wkr. I).

A draft-finding divisional staff.

Division Nummer 409

Commander :—Genmaj. Hans EHRENBERG (55).
Home Station :—Kassel (Wkr. IX).

A draft-finding divisional staff.

Division Nummer 433

Commander :—
Home Station :—Berlin (Wkr. III).

A draft-finding divisional staff.

Division Nummer 461

Commander :—Genlt. Hans Erich NOLTE (62).
Home Station :—Bialystok (Wkr. I).

A draft-finding divisional staff.

Division Nummer 462

Commander :—
Home Station :—Nancy (Wkr. XII).

A draft-finding divisional staff in the Nancy area, France, since early 1943. When 182 Reserve Division was up-graded to its present status, this divisional staff was set up to carry out the functions hitherto carried out by 182.

Division Nummer 464

Commander :—

Home Station :—Leipzig (Wkr. IV).

A draft-finding divisional staff.

Division Nummer 465

Commander :—

Home Station :—Stuttgart (Wkr. V).

A draft-finding divisional staff in the Epinal area, France, since early 1943. When 165 Reserve Division was up-graded to its present status, this divisional staff was set up to carry out the functions hitherto performed by 165.

Division Nummer 467

Commander :—Genlt. Karl GRAF ?

Home Station :—München (Wkr. VII).

A draft-finding divisional staff.

Division Nummer 473

Commander :—

Home Station :—Regensburg (Wkr. XIII).

A draft-finding divisional staff.

Division Nummer 487

Commander :—

Home Station :—Wien (Wkr. XVII).

A draft-finding divisional staff.

Division Nummer 526 *

Commander :—Genlt. Albin NAKE.
Home Station :—Wuppertal (Wkr. VI).

Formerly a frontier guard division. Now believed to be a draft-finding divisional staff. Elements controlled by it may be located in Belgium.

(*u*) SPECIAL DIVISIONAL STAFFS

Division Kommando z.b.V. 402

Commander :—
Composition :—
Home Station :—Stettin (Wkr. II).

An administrative divisional staff.

Division Kommando z.b.V. 404

Commander :—
Composition :—
Home Station :—Dresden (Wkr. IV).

An administrative divisional staff.

Division Kommando z.b.V. 405

Commander :—
Composition :—
Home Station :—Stuttgart (Wkr. V).

An administrative divisional staff.

Division Kommando z.b.V. 406

Commander :—
Composition :—
Home Station :—Münster (Wkr. VI).

An administrative divisional staff.

Division Kommando z.b.V. 407

Commander :—

Composition :—

Home Station :—München (Wkr. VII).

An administrative divisional staff.

Division Kommando z.b.V. 408

Commander :—

Composition :—

Home Station :—Breslau (Wkr. VIII).

An administrative divisional staff.

Division Kommando z.b.V. 410

Commander :—

Composition :—

Home Station :—Hamburg (Wkr. X).

An administrative divisional staff.

Division Kommando z.b.V. 411

Commander :—

Composition :—

Home Station :—Hannover (Wkr. XI).

An administrative divisional staff.

Division Kommando z.b.V. 412

Commander :—

Composition :—

Home Station : Wiesbaden (Wkr. XII).

An administrative divisional staff.

Division Kommando z.b.V. 413

Commander :—

Composition :—

Home Station :—Nürnberg (Wkr. XIII).

An administrative divisional staff.

Division Kommando z.b.V. 417

Commander :—

Composition :—

Home Station :—Vienna (Wkr. XVII).

An administrative divisional staff.

Division Kommando z.b.V. 421

Commander :—

Composition :—

Home Station :— (Wkr. I).

An administrative divisional staff.

Division Kommando z.b.V. 428

Commander :—

Composition :—

Home Station :—Graudenz (Grudziadz) (Wkr. XX).

An administrative divisional staff.

Division Kommando z.b.V. 429

Commander :—

Composition :—

Home Station :—Posen (Poznań) (Wkr. XXI).

An administrative divisional staff.

Division Kommando z.b.V. 430

Commander :—

Composition :—

Home Station :—Gnesen (Gniezno) (Wkr. XXI).

An administrative divisional staff.

Division Kommando z.b.V. 431

Commander :—

Composition :—

Home Station :—Litzmannstadt (Lodz) (Wkr. XXI).

An administrative divisional staff.

Division Kommando z.b.V. 432

Commander :—

Composition :—

Home Station :—Kattowitz (Katowice) (Wkr. VIII).

An administrative divisional staff.

(*v*) BRIGADES

The German infantry regiment corresponds approximately to the British infantry brigade; the German *Brigade* is intermediate between the regiment and the division, and normally controls two regiments. The following types have been noted :—

(i) *Lehrbrigade 900.* A staff controlling the two infantry demonstration regiments (*Grenadier-Lehr-Regiment 900* and *Panzer-Gren.-Lehr-Rgt. 901*) on such occasions as both regiments are required to serve together in the field; in that case, the brigade will also dispose of supply services under *Kommandeur der Divisions-Nachschubtruppen 900.*

(ii) Panzer brigades. In peace time and in the first year of the war each Panzer division contained two tank regiments, controlled by a brigade staff which sometimes but not invariably carried the divisional number (thus, *Pz. Brig. 4* was in *10 Pz. Div.*) ; the reduction to one tank regiment per division made these staffs unnecessary, and most of them were either disbanded or used as nuclei for new divisional staffs (thus, *Pz. Brig. 3* from *3* Pz. *Div.* provided the staff for *5.le.Div.* (*mot.*), out of which *21.Pz.Div.* developed). But some Panzer brigade staffs were retained to control tank units of the G.H.Q. pool, and others were formed for the same purpose ; those known to exist in 1943 are *Panzer-Brigaden 18* and *100* (the latter permanently stationed in France, and responsible for forming and training new tank units).

(iii) Motor brigades in Panzer divisions (*Schützen-Brigaden*). Until the end of 1942, each Panzer division normally disposed of a brigade staff, carrying the divisional number, responsible for the tactical control of the two infantry (*Schützen-*, later *Panzer-Grenadier-*) regiments and the motor cycle battalion (*Kradschützen-Bataillon*, now *Panzer-Aufklärungs-Abteilung*). This type of brigade has now been abolished.

(iv) Mobile brigades (*Schnelle Brigaden*). This is a new type of staff, which is believed to control a number of mobile battalions (*Schnelle Abteilungen*) of the G.H.Q. pool. *Schn. Brig. 20* and *30* have been identified, both under command of Army Group West.

(v) Cavalry brigades (*Kavallerie-Brigaden*). The former 1 Cavalry Division, before its conversion to 24 Panzer Division, contained two cavalry brigades, each of two regiments ; it is believed that 1 Cossack Division has a similar composition, but that there are now no other cavalry brigades in the German Army (*see*, however, Part F below for S.S. cavalry brigades).

(vi) Infantry brigades. Apart from S.S. infantry brigades (Part F below), there are the following types :—

(*a*) *Sicherungs-Brigade* (L. of C. Brigade). *Sich. Brig. 202* is known. *Sich. Brigaden 201* and *203* have been converted to divisions, retaining the same numbers. Compare (*c*) below.

(*b*) *Festungs-Brigade* (Fortress Brigade). The German forces in Crete were formerly controlled, under 164 Infantry Division, by two fortress brigades ; *Fest. Brig. 1*, now known as *Fest. Brig. Kreta,* remains on the island, but *Fest. Brig. 2* has been withdrawn and may have been dissolved.

(*c*) *Ersatz-Brigade* (Depôt Brigade). During 1941 and the first half of 1942, a number of infantry training regiments, carrying numbers from 601 upwards, were stationed in Poland and on the L. of C. in Russia ; these regiments were at the disposal of G.H.Q. Field Armies (and not part of the Training Command), and were administered by *Ersatz-Brigaden* 201–204. During 1942 these brigade staffs were reorganised for L. of C. duties (*see* (*a*) above) or dissolved. It should be noted that the training and depôt units of the Grossdeutschland and Hermann Goering Divisions are each under an *Ersatz-Brigade,* which carries the name of the division (but these brigades control all arms, and not merely infantry).

(vii) Armoured artillery brigade (*gepanzerte Artillerie-Brigade*). Army Group West disposed, until recently, of one brigade of two armoured artillery regiments ; the brigade (which may have been dissolved) carried the number 1, and the regiments are numbered 1 and 2.

(viii) Motor transport brigades. Special brigade staffs may be found controlling the M.T. regiments and battalions of the G.H.Q. pool (e.g., *Wirtschafts-Kraftwagen-Transport-Brigade z.b.V.*1).

(ix) Finally, reference may be made to the staffs which are of brigade status and display the brigade flag, though they are not specifically described as brigades :—

(*a*) Artillery commanders (*Artillerie-, Küstenartillerie-, Festungsartillerie-Kommandeur*).

(*b*) Senior signals officers (*Heeresgruppen-, Armee-* or *Panzerarmee-, höherer Wehrmacht-Nachrichtenführer* ; *Kommandeur der Führungsnachrichtentruppen*).

(*c*) Senior engineer officers (*Befehlshaber der Eisenbahntruppen, Festungspionierkommandeur, Kommandeur eines Oberbaustabes*).

For Flak brigades *see* p. E 54.

(*w*) G.A.F. FIELD DIVISIONS

In the autumn of 1942 surplus personnel of G.A.F. ground staffs, Flak units, and Fliegerregimenter (G.A.F. recruit depôts) were transferred to a new type of ground-fighting unit, the G.A.F. Felddivision. This "combing-out" process, presumably made necessary by man-power difficulties in Germany, produced some twenty field divisions with the requisite replacement and training units.

The G.A.F. Felddivision includes two Jägerregimenter, each of three Abteilungen, plus divisional units. Strength was originally intended to be 10,000 all ranks. The Jägerregimenter are numbered in numerical sequence beginning with the first division, *e.g.*, Luftwaffefelddivision 11 has Jägerregimenter 21 and 22. In other words, the number of the second Jägerregiment equals the divisional number multiplied by two a d that of the first Jägerregiment equals the divisional number mult.plied by two minus one.

Some G.A.F. Felddivisionen have been used in front-line fighting while others have been assigned such static duties as airfield defence, coastal defence, line of communications duties, etc.

(*x*) G.A.F. ANTI-AIRCRAFT FORMATIONS—(*See* Part E, Sec. (c))

(i) FLAK KORPS

I. Flak Korps

Commander :—

Operated in France in 1940 and in Russia 1941–43, at first on the Central and later on the Southern front.

II. Flak Korps

Commander :—

Operated in France in 1940 and in Russia 1941–43, at first on the Southern and later on the Central front.

(ii) FLAKDIVISIONEN

1. Flak Division

Commander :—

H.Q. :—Berlin.

2. Flak Division (mot.)

Commander :—

Transferred from the Paris area to Russia (Northern front) early in 1942.

3. Flak Division

Commander :—

H.Q. :—Hamburg.

4. Flak Division

Commander :—

H.Q. :—Düsseldorf.

5. Flak Division

Commander :—

Operated in Western Germany late in 1941 (H.Q.; Frankfurt a/M.) and during 1942 (H.Q. :—Darmstadt). Transferred to South-east Europe late in 1943.

6. Flak Division (mot.)

Commander :—

Operated in Western Europe (probably Belgium and Northern France) in 1941 and early 1942. Transferred to Russia (Northern front) later in 1942.

7. Flak Division

Commander :—Generalleutnant Dipl. Ing. Heinrich Burchard.

H.Q. :—Cologne.

8. Flak Division

Commander :—Generalleutnant Wagner.

H.Q. :—Bremen.

9. Flak Division (mot.)

Commander :—Generalleutnant Wolfgang PICKERT (47).

Transferred from the Paris area to Russia (Central front) early in 1942 and to the Crimea in 1943.

10. Flak Division (mot.)

Commander :—Generalleutnant Johann SEIFERT.

Controlled all Flak in Roumania and Bulgaria in 1941 ; in Russia (Southern front) since early in 1942.

11. Flak Division (mot.)

Commander :—Generalleutnant Helmuth RICHTER (52).

H.Q. :—Avignon.

Operated in Northern France (Rennes-Paris area) late in 1941 until autumn, 1942, when it was transferred to Southern France.

12. Flak Division (mot.)

Commander :—Generalleutnant Rudolf EIBENSTEIN (50).

Operating in Russia (Central front) since late in 1941.

13. Flak Division

Commander :—Generalleutnant SPIESS (52).

H.Q. :—Caen.

14. Flak Division

Commander :—

H.Q. :—Leipzig.

15. Flak Division (mot.)

Commander :—

Believed to have been formed in Roumania by expansion of III Flak Brigade late in 1941 ; transferred to Russia (Southern front) early in 1942.

16. Flak Division

Commander :—

H.Q. :—Lille.

17. Flak Division (mot.)

Commander :—

Transferred from Germany to Russia (Southern front) early in 1942.

18. Flak Division (mot.)

Commander :—Generalmajor Heinrich XXXVII Prinz von REUSS.

Operating on the Central front in Russia since early in 1942.

19. Flak Division (mot.)

Commander :—

Operated in North Africa in 1942 and early in 1943. Re-formed and operating in Greeçe since late 1943.

20. Flak Division (mot.)

Commander :—

Operated in North Africa in 1942 and early in 1943. Believed to have been re-formed for operations in South-eastern Europe late in 1943.

21. Flak Division

Commander :—

Believed to be operating in South-western Germany.

22. Flak Division

Commander :—

Believed to be operating in Western Germany

PART E—NON-DIVISIONAL AND OTHER SMALL UNITS

CONTENTS

(i) INTRODUCTION

In (*a*) the principal units of the *Heerestruppen* (units employed in the field army) are detailed as far as possible according to the German classification (*e.g.*, under *Infanterie* or *Landesschützen Einheiten*, E 8 and E 38). The only deliberate departure from that system has been to place the various types of park at the end of the sections which they serve (*e.g.*, *Heergeräte-Park* at the end of section on Cavalry, instead of in a single group among the administrative units (E 37) to which they are formally assigned).

In (*b*) units which come under direct or indirect control of *O.K.H.* (War Office) are discussed. Normally units of this type will not be identified in field armies, but will come under control of static H.Q.s in occupied areas.

(*c*) Deals with G.A.F. Flak units primarily; a brief summary of other Air Force units is also given here.

(*d*) Naval Artillery and Naval Flak units are discussed briefly.

For divisional and corps troops reference should be made to Part C.

(a) HEERESTRUPPEN

(ii) INDEX TO HEERESTRUPPEN

(j) Transport Units

(k) Nachschub Units

(l) Medical Units

(iii) DISCUSSION

(*a*) Formations of Higher Level

(i) *Kommandeur des Rückwärtigen Armee-Gebiets* (Army Rear Area Commander) : are numbered in series 501–600, one to each army. They organise and control army rear areas and will normally have some Landesschützen and Wach units subordinate to them.

(ii) *Kommandeur der Kraftfahrparktruppen* (O.C. of M.T. Equipment Park Troops) : One O.C. of Motor Transport Troops is normally assigned to each army ; to control all repair and equipment parks and transport troops in army areas. These units are numbered from 801– (twelve identified). Most of the units listed under transport troops, page E 24, of this part come under control of a H.Q. of this type.

(*b*) Units which Defy Classification

(i) *Lehr-Regiment BRANDENBURG z.b.V.* 800 (Brandenburg Special Purpose Demonstration Unit) : This special unit was formed on the outbreak of the war as Bau-Lehr-Bataillon 800, it was later expanded to a regiment and was recently upgraded to divisional status. Its home station is at Brandenburg (Wehrkreis III), where its recruits are trained, but detachments from it may be met with wherever German forces are operating.

Its primary function is sabotage (whether by companies, platoons or individuals). Its personnel contains a high proportion of Germans who have lived abroad and speak foreign languages fluently, and different companies of the regiment specialise in preparation for operating in specific countries. Its members often operate in civilian clothes, in some cases dropping by parachute in enemy-occupied countries. Though they hold military rank the unit is under direct control of the intelligence branch of the Defence Ministry (*OKW/Abwehr*) as regards its policy and organisation.

(ii) *Propaganda-Kompanie :* These units are provided with drafts from the propaganda depot battalion at Potsdam (Wkr. III). Propaganda companies include number 501 and at least 25 numbers selected from the series 601–700 : these companies are normally allotted to armies. In addition, there are unnumbered battalions and companies. (*Frankreich,* allotted to G.O.C., Occupied France ; *Belgien,* under G.O.C., Belgium and Northern France ; the personnel (*Schützen*) are mainly journalists, press photographers or film cameramen in civil life, and their main function is front-line reporting; they are a separate arm of the German Armed Forces and wear light grey as distinguishing colour.

(*c*) **Infantry**

White piping, the distinguishing colour of the infantry arm, is also worn by *Landesschützen* units, *Fla* units (but not *Heeres-Flak*, *see* page E 16), and certain administrative units (*see* page E 37). For divisional infantry, reference should be made to Part C; the following paragraphs detail various miscellaneous infantry units which may be met with.

(i) *Infanterie-Lehr-Regiment* (Infantry Demonstration Regiment): Numbers 900 and 901 identified. These regiments form *Lehr-Brigade* 900, which is normally stationed at the Infantry School at Döberitz (Wkr. III), providing demonstrations of tactics and carrying out experiments with new infantry weapons; but it is possible that one or both regiments, or the *Lehr-Brigade* may be found, in whole or part, on active field service.

(ii) *Führerbegleitbataillon* (Führer's Escort Bn.): This unit was formed after the Polish campaign from picked personnel, to serve as Hitler's escort in the field; it is fully motorised and consists of headquarters, four companies, and a supply column.

1. *Wach* (guard).
2. *Panzerjäger* (anti-tank).
3. *Schwere Sicherungs* (heavy protective).
4. *Fla* (A.A.)
5. *Kw. Kolonne* (supply column).

(iii) *Sonderverband* 287 (Special Unit 287): This unit was a pocket-size division which was formed in early 1942 and disbanded in the summer of 1943. Parts of this unit may still be identified as *Heerestruppen.*

(iv) *Sonderverband* 288 (Special Unit 288): A small self-contained group originally consisting of H.Q. and eight companies. It was formed in the summer of 1941, served with the Africa Panzer Army, was later known as *Panzer-Grenadier-Regiment Afrika* and destroyed in Tunisia, May, 1943.

(v) *Wachbataillon* (Guard Battalion): Guard battalions will be found serving with armies in the field. Two series exist, 1–500 and 501–800. The units of the latter series provide guards for army parks, depots, etc.

The units of series 1–500 were originally *Baubataillone* (Construction Battalions) which were renamed. For example, *Wachbataillon* (B) was previously a *Baubataillon*, as the B indicates. Battalions of this series, although originally designed only for duty in Germany and the occupied countries, will frequently be found with the field army.

(vi) *Festungsregiment* (Fortress Regiment) : Several identified in the series 921–930 ; they are regimental staffs controlling *Festungsbataillone.*

(vii) *Festungsbataillon* (Fortress Battalion) : This is an independent unit for construction and defence of field fortifications. Two series exist : 601–700 (22 battalions identified), and 901–1000 (13 battalions identified). These units consist largely of *Landesschützen* and other personnel of low fighting value.

(viii) *Sicherungsregiment* (L. of C. Regiment) : In addition to a number of down-graded infantry divisions, commanders of army groups L. of C. groups have at their disposal, in some cases, these special regiments. Units of this type are numbered in a separate series, 16 is the highest number so far noted. Identification of a Radfahr Sicherungs Regiment (Cyclist L. of C. Regiment) has recently been made.

(ix) *Sicherungsbataillon* (L. of C. Battalion) : Some sixty *Landesschützen* battalions were renamed *Sicherungs* battalions numbered between 200 and 1000. Most of these battalions are now subordinate to *Sicherungs* divisions, *Korücks*, *OFK's*, etc. Some may, however, be regarded as independent L. of C. and guard units.

(x) *Maschinengewehr-Bataillon* (M.G. Battalion) : M.G. battalions have been incorporated in the forms of companies and platoons to a greater or lesser extent in infantry divisions, some, however, still exist as independent units, carrying numbers between 1 and 66.

(xi) *Fla Bataillon* (A.A. Battalion) : Two series existed ; 22–66 and 601–620. Also No. 501 identified. Units of the 22–66 series have probably all been dissolved ; there are, however, several battalions still existing in the 601–620 series and No. 501. Personnel in such a unit wear white infantry piping with the addition of the Gothic letter *Fl* on the shoulder straps. The closer co-operation of G.A.F. *Flak* units with army, which has recently been brought about will probably permit the incorporation of the remaining *Fla* units into divisions. Those numbered in the low series consisted of six companies, equipped with 2 cm. (0·79-in.) or 3·7 cm. (1·75-in.)

guns which operated separately ; those numbered above 500 consist of three or four companies and normally operate as battalions (*see* page E 54 for operational employment).

(xii) *Jägerbataillon* (Raiding Battalion) (previously known as *Jagdkommando*) : During the winter of 1941–42 a number of units of this type were formed to serve on the Russian front ; they are numbered at random in a separate series, 1–100 and 201–300. Some twenty battalions have been identified. Units of this type are for the disposal of army and are used in anti-sabotage activities or on special raiding missions.

(xiii) *Granatwerferbataillon* (Rocket Projector Battalion) : May be found allotted to corps on special missions. They are numbered in an independent series of 1 upwards (several have been identified).

(xiv) *Bewährungsbataillon* (Rehabilitation battalion) are also referred to as Infanterie-Bataillon z.b.V. Numbers 500 and 540 have been identified. Army may dispose of such a battalion for special duties. Personnel serving in such units are political enemies of the German regime, or characters otherwise undesirable, given a chance for rehabilitation under most adverse conditions. A man serving in a unit of this type can redeem his character by good behaviour and exceptional service.

(xv) *Feldsonderbataillon* (Special Field Battalion) : This is a penal battalion, to which soldiers guilty of severe offences may be posted ; it was formed in the winter 1941–42 and sent to the area of the Army Group North, where it was used in clearing minefields, removing duds and the exhumation and reburial of corpses. Personnel in a special battalion wear the army field grey uniform without any insignia or identifications.

(xvi) *Heeres Infanterie-Geschütz-Kompanie* (Army Infantry Gun Coy.) : Most of the infantry gun companies in the 701– series have been disbanded ; some may still exist. They are most commonly found attached to infantry of a Panzer division ; they are equipped with 15 cm. guns mounted on Pz.Kw.II chassis. Several of these units have been renumbered and have become an organic part of the 13th company of *Panzer Grenadier* Regiments.

(xvii) *Infanterie Park* (Infantry Equipment Park) : Each army disposed of one of these equipment parks carrying a number selected from the series 501–600, recently, however, most of these parks along with artillery parks (*see* page E17) have been combined under the O.C. of Equipment Parks in *Heergeräteparks* (*see* page E 12).

It should be noted that the infantry of the *Panzer* divisions are classified as *Panzertruppen.*

The following figures show the tactical signs for infantry units :—

(both are found with tactical signs of other arms).

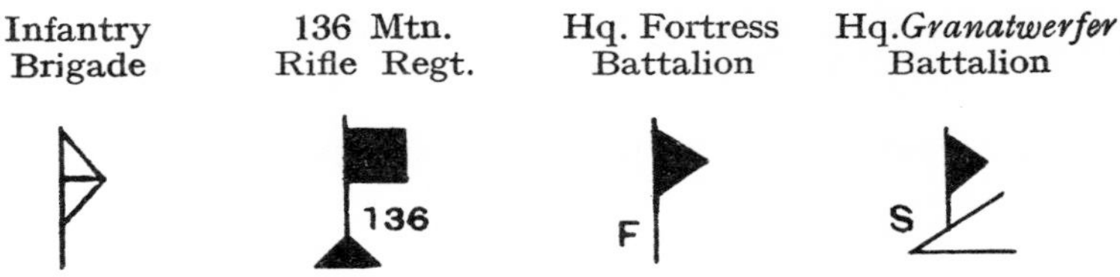

(*d*) **Cavalry** (*the Cavalry arm now falls under infantry for administration*).

Yellow piping is the distinguishing colour for cavalry (including horsed and partly horsed cavalry regiments) ; it is also worn, in place of pink, by units of 24 Panzer Division (formed by conversion of the former 1st Cavalry Division). It is also worn by reconnaissance units which receive their drafts from the cavalry depot units (with the exception of the *Panzer* reconnaissance units of *Panzer* and *Panzer Grenadier* Divisions ; which wear copper-brown). The following types of unit may be met with, apart from the divisional reconnaissance units:

(i) *Aufklärungs und Kavallerie Lehr Abteilung* (Recce. and Cavalry Demonstration Unit) : Stationed at the Recce. and Cavalry School at Hannover (Wkr. XI), but potentially available for service in the field.

(ii) *Aufklärungs-Abteilung* (Recce. Battalion) (previously known as *Radfahr-Abteilung*) : There are some numbered in the 401 series in the G.H.Q. pool, which may be found operating in the spearhead of the attack. The cyclist battalion includes a motor cycle company, so that some motor-cyclists may still be seen wearing the yellow piping. Most of the units found in the 401 series have been disbanded ; some may, however, still be found in the original series.

(iii) *Heergeräte-Park* (*Armee-Geräte-Park*) (H.T. Equipment Park) : There is one such equipment park on the strength of each army. Recently the *Heergeräte-Parke* have taken over the responsibility of serving infantry and artillery formations, previously served by Infantry and Artillery Parks (*see* p. E 17). Officers wear the colour of their arm and other ranks light blue piping with the arabic numeral of the park. *Heergeräte-Parke* and *Armee-Geräte-Parke* 463 and 501—(some twelve have been identified). *Armee-Geräte-Parke* serving *Panzer* armies will be identified as *Panzer-Armee-Geräte-Parke*.

(iv) *Reiter Regiment* (Cavalry Regiment) : A new W.E. for Cavalry Regiments exists. (For Cossack Cavalry Regiments, *see* Part H.)

The following figure shows the tactical signs for cavalry units :—

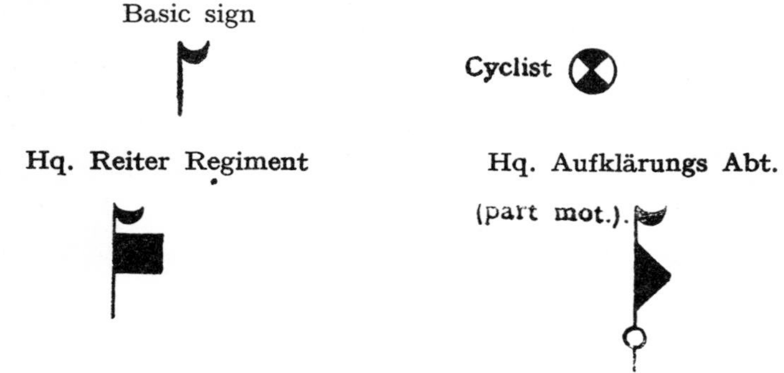

(*e*) **Armoured Troops**

Tank units and anti-tank battalions wear pink piping, the latter with the addition of the letter " P " on the shoulder-strap ; Panzer Grenadiers wear grass green, and Panzer reconnaissance units and motor-cycle battalions copper-brown. For divisional units *see* Part C ; the following types may also be met with.

(i) *Panzer-Lehr-Regiment* (Tank Demonstration Regiment) : This demonstration regiment, stationed at the Tank School at Wünsdorf (Wkr. III), consists of I and II Tank and III Anti-Tank Bns. ; like other demonstration units, it is potentially available for service in the field.

(ii) *Non-divisional Tank Units :* The G.H.Q. pool includes some independent tank battalions, which may be found under corps supporting infantry divisions. A number of independent tank battalions exist in series 501 upwards; some of these, however, have been disbanded or have been incorporated in divisions in part or whole.

(iii) *Panzerabteilung* (*Flammenwerfer*) (Tank Battalion (Flame Thrower)) : The G.H.Q. pool also includes a number of independent flame-thrower tank battalions (series 100 upwards), which will normally be found employed under corps in the spearhead of the attack. (For *Panzer Werfer Abteilung, see* E 18.)

(iv) *Panzerjäger-Abteilung* (Anti-Tank Battalion) : Among the G.H.Q. anti-tank battalions (*see* tables, Part L) several are classified as heavy. Independent *Pz. Jäger Bataillone* will normally operate in army areas with the primary mission of defending Army H.Q.; they may, however, occasionally operate under corps command on offensive missions. Weapons of these units are self-propelled. Numbers 501 upwards (some 25 identified) exist.

(v) *Other Independent Panzer Troops : Schnelle Abteilungen* (Mobile Units) 602, 608 and 621, which have been identified (their composition is not known at present) are allotted to C.-in-C., West, as anti-invasion units. There are also tank formations held in readiness in France with the primary mission of repelling invasion, when it takes place (*see* D 134 for Mobile Brigades 20 and 30).

The following figures show the tactical signs for units in this category :—

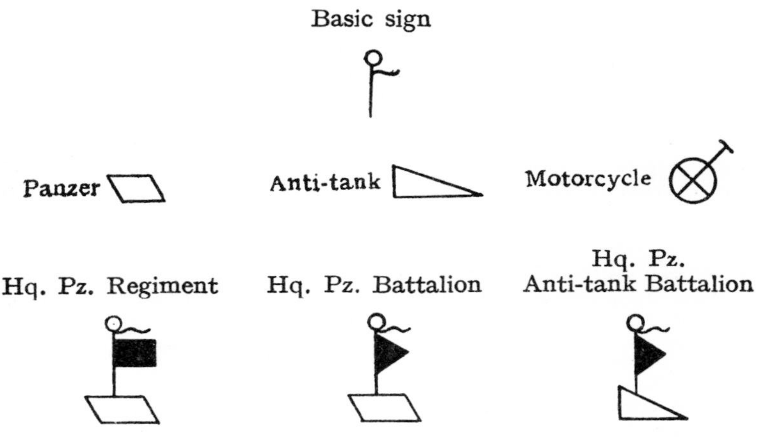

(*f*) ARTILLERY

Red is the colour of the artillery arm, including assault artillery and *Heeres-Flak Abteilungen*; artillery survey units and survey and mapping units are distinguished, in addition, by the gothic letters "*B*" or "*V*" as the case may be. For lists of identified artillery and artillery survey units, *see* Part L. Employment of G.H.Q. artillery and special artillery units is discussed below.

In the German Army all artillery, apart from the divisional allotment, belongs to the G.H.Q. pool (*Heerestruppen*). From this pool units are allotted to army groups or armies according to the needs of the moment; they may be sub-allotted, for shorter or longer periods, to divisions or as corps troops (in both cases normally being placed under the immediate control of special artillery commanders and staffs, also provided from the G.H.Q. pool).

With the exception of artillery commanders and staffs and artillery survey units, all types of artillery carry numbers allotted from a single series (for a list of identifications, *see* Part L).

The following brief notes will indicate the possible variations in composition and allocation of artillery.

ARTILLERY COMMANDS

There are no exact equivalents, in the German Army, to the C.R.A., C.C.R.A., B.R.A. or M.G.R.A. When the divisional artillery regiment is not reinforced from the G.H.Q. pool, its commander is known as *Artillerie-Führer* (*Arfü*), and in effect acts as C.R.A.; but whenever G.H.Q. artillery units are attached to the division—in effect, whenever it is attacking—the *Arfü* is subordinated to an artillery commander (*Artillerie Kommandeur*, abbreviated *Arko*), whose small special staff is supplemented in action by the larger staff of the regimental H.Q. The *Arko* may equally be assigned to command an allotment of artillery to corps; in this case a G.H.Q. artillery regimental staff and an artillery survey unit are regularly included in the allotments. The following grades in the chain of artillery command have been distinguished:—

(i) *At G.H.Q.*—The artillery general at G.H.Q. (*O.K.H./Gen.d.Art.*) is the principal adviser on the employment of artillery, and units from the G.H.Q. pool are probably allotted to army groups and armies on his recommendations.

(ii) *At Army Group and Army H.Q.*—The artillery general at army group or army H.Q. (*Stoart*, or, in a coastal sector, *General der Küstenartillerie*) advises the commander of the formation on all artillery matters and recommends the sub-allotment of G.H.Q. artillery units to lower formations.

(iii) *Within Army Group and Army.*—It is thought that each army group disposes of one senior artillery commander (*Höherer Artillerie-Kommandeur*, abbreviated *Höh. Arko*) and staff, available to exercise command over G.H.Q. artillery units operating in an area larger than that of a single army corps. He is normally a lieutenant-general and he has the status of a divisional commander.

(iv) *Under Corps.*—An *Arko* and staff act as the equivalent of C.C.R.A. whenever necessary, but a corps which is not in action may merely have a relatively junior artillery staff officer (*Stoart*) at corps H.Q.

(v) *Under Division.*—An *Arko* and staff act as the equivalent of C.R.A. when assigned to a division in action.

The *Höh. Arkos* carry numbers in the block 301 and upwards ; the *Arkos* carry numbers in two blocks 1–44 and 101 upwards ; recently several *Arkos* have been identified renumbered to the corps block of numbers 401–500 ; this may indicate an intention to make *Arkos* a permanent part of corps H.Q. (*e.g.*, 451, *Arko* of the *LI Armee Korps*).

NON-DIVISIONAL ARTILLERY UNITS

(i) *Abteilungen and Batterien :* These include field, medium, heavy and super-heavy units, and may be horsed, mechanised (tractor drawn or on self-propelled mountings), railway or fixed artillery. The numbers allotted to them have no necessary connection with their particular category, though certain groups of C.D. artillery *Batterien* which are equipped with weapons of the same type carry adjacent numbers (*e.g.*, 996–998, C.D. *Batterien* equipped with French 15·5 cm. guns). The mechanised *II Abteilung* of the peace time medium regiment invariably consists of three four-gun *Batterien*, but many of the *Abteilungen* formed on or after mobilisation may have three-gun *Batterien*, and heavy or super-heavy *Batterien* may include two guns only or even one.

(ii) *Artillerie Regimentsstab* (Artillery Regimental Staff) : These include staffs of the peace time divisional medium regiments (Nos. 37–72, 97, 99 and 115 ; it is not known if the whole series was ever filled), and special staffs formed on or about mobilisation (carrying numbers above 500); most of the latter are independent staffs, with no *Abteilungen* carrying the same number. Apart from C.D. staffs, all G.H.Q. artillery regimental staffs are fully motorised.

(iii) *Artillerie Abteilungsstab* (Artillery Abteilung Staff): There are a number of independent *Abteilung* staffs, whose function is to administer and control independent G.H.Q. medium, heavy or super-heavy *Batterien.*

(iv) *Sturmgeschütz Abteilung* (Assault Gun *Abteilung*): Assault gun *Abteilungen* are numbered in the main artillery series (20 identified); with numbers ranging from 177 to 667 (*see* Artillery tables, page L 38). *Batterien* of the *Abteilung* may operate independently as *Sturmgeschütz Batterien.*

(v) *Heeresflakabteilung* (Army *Flak Abteilung*): These belong to the artillery arm. Numbered in G.A.F. Flak series 271 upwards, highest number identified is 315. Personnel in such units wear red piping. Normally an *Abteilung* is organic to the artillery regiment of Panzer divisions. *Heeresflakabteilungen* are usually "mixed," comprising two heavy *Batterien* equipped with 8·8-cm. (3·46-in.) guns and one light *Batterie* equipped with 2-cm. (0·79-in.) guns, and are fully motorised (*see* page E 54 for operational employment).

(vi) *Beobachtungs-Abteilung* (Observation Bn.): They are numbered in series 1 upwards (*see* tables, page L 103). Their normal allotment is to corps, where they come under direct control of an *Arko. Panzer Beobachtungs Batterien* (numbered originally from 320 upwards) have probably all been incorporated in artillery regiments of Panzer divisions and probably carry the divisional auxiliary numbers, *e.g., Panzer Beobachtungs Batterie* 326, renumbered *Pz. Beobachtungs Battr.* 33, now found in A.R. 33.

(vii) *Vermessungs-und Karten-Abteilung* (Survey and Mapping Unit): Two series exist, 501–600, units on the strength of an army H.Q., and 601–700, units which may be allocated to army groups or armies wherever needed. (Twenty of these survey and mapping units have been identified.)

(viii) *Velocitäts-Mess-Zug* (Calibration Platoon): Numbered in series 701 and upwards (some five identified).

(ix) *Astronomischer Mess-Zug* (Astronomical Survey Section): Numbered in series from 720 upwards.

(x) *Wetter-Peilzug* (Meteorological Section): Numbered from 501–600.

(xi) *Armee-Kartenstelle* (Army Map Depot) (previously known as *Armee-Karten Lager*): Carry numbers from 501 upwards.

(xii) *Artillerie-Park* (Artillery Equipment Park): One of these units was normally allotted to each army; recently Artillery Parks and Infantry Parks were combined under *Heergeräte Park* (*see* E 12).

(xiii) *Artillerie-Lehr-Regimenter* (Artillery Demonstration Regiments): There are three of these demonstration regiments, all stationed at the School of Artillery at Jüterbog (Wkr. III): No. 1 is horse-drawn, No. 2 motorised (including an assault gun *Batterie*) and No. 3 consists of artillery survey and mapping, rangefinding and balloon *Batterien*. Portions of one or more of these regiments may be found serving in the field from time to time.

(xiv) *Heeresküsten Artillerie* (Coast Artillery): C.D. *Regimenter*, *Abteilungen* and *Batterien* are numbered in the main artillery series (*see* tables of artillery, page L 38). Coastal Artillery is organised in coastal defence sectors and may be commanded by an army or navy artillery H.Q. in a particular sector. G.A.F. *Flak* units in C.D. sectors are normally subordinated to a local H.Q. responsible for the defence of a certain sector. *Flak* is here used in dual-purpose rôle, for air and coastal defence.

Note.—A division responsible for the defence of certain coastal sectors controls C.D. units in its area.

The following figure shows the tactical signs for artillery units:—

Basic sign: ı|ı

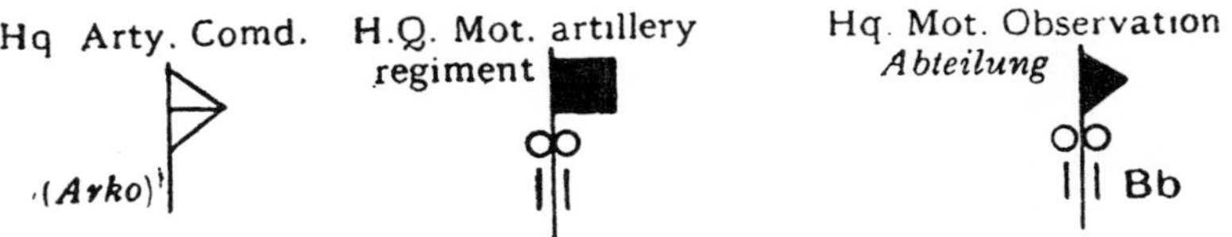

(*g*) PROJECTOR UNITS (C.W.)

(Previously known as Smoke Units)

Projector Troops wear maroon piping; they include the following types of unit, all belonging to the G.H.Q. pool. Reference to *Nebel* units instead of *Werfer* units is often made, the tactical unit is normally referred to as *Werfer* (projector), whereas a staff will normally be called a *Nebelwerfer Stab* (smoke-projector staff).

(i) *Werfer-Lehr-Regiment* (Projector Demonstration Regiment): Numbers 1 and 2 Projector Demonstration Regiment have been identified. They are liable to service in the field in whole or in part. No. 1 is located at Celle (Wkr. XI), No. 2 at Bremen (Wkr. X).

(ii) *Regimentsstab der Nebeltruppen* or *Werfer-Regiment z.b.V.*: Regimental staffs to control projector *Abteilungen* in action; numbered in series 1 upwards.

(iii) *Werfer-Regiment* (Projector Regiment): Regiments of H.Q. and three *Abteilungen* (numbered I–III); series 41 and upwards exists (ten identified).

(iv) *Schweres Werfer-Regiment* (Heavy Projector Regiment): Three heavy projector regiments numbered from 1 upwards have been identified.

(v) *Werfer-Abteilung* (Projector *Abteilung*): Independent *Abteilungen*, which in action will be controlled by projector regimental staffs; series 1 upwards exists.

(vi) *Panzer Werfer Abteilung* (Armoured Projector *Abteilung*): Newly formed armoured projector *Abteilungen* have recently been identified; they are numbered from 50 on upwards.

(vii) *Werfer Batterie* (Projector *Batterie*): Some independent *Batterien*, numbered above 100, have been identified. They are equipped with six-barrelled projectors.

(viii) *Gebirgs-Werfer-Abteilung* (Mountain Projector *Abteilung*): A war establishment for mountain projector *Abteilungen* exists, but no identifications have been made as yet.

(ix) *Entgiftungs-Abteilung* (Decontamination Bn.) are also equipped for service as contaminator *Abteilungen*; series 101 and upwards (five identified to date).

(x) *Strassenentgiftungs-Abteilung* (Road Decontamination Bn.): Road decontamination *Abteilungen* existed, but have not been identified again since the Balkan campaign.

(xi) *Gasschutz-Gerätepark* (Anti-Gas Equipment Park): Numbered in series 501 upwards (also 463 for *Armee Norwegen*); the normal allotment is one to each army. Officers wear the colour of their arm, other ranks pale blue, in each case the arabic number of the park.

Types 1–10 are fully motorised.

The following figure shows the tactical signs for projector units :—

Basic sign :—

Hq. Motorised projector regiment

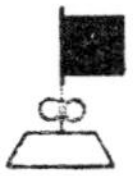

Hq. Motorised projector *Abteilung*

(*h*) ENGINEERS

The engineer arm includes combat engineers, technical troops, construction units. The distinguishing colour is black. There are additional construction units, however, which are not classed as engineers by the Germans which wear brown. For these units *see* E 39.

(i) *Pionier-Lehr-Bataillon* (Engineer Demonstration Bn.) : Nos. 1 and 2 are stationed at No. 1 Engineer School (*Pionier Schule* 1) at Dessau-Rosslau (Wkr. XI) ; there is also a *Pionier-Lehr-Bataillon z.b.V.* (*Special Engineer Demonstration Bn.*) at Offenbach-on-Main (Wkr. IX), which specialises in tunnelling and similar activities. These units may also be found serving in the field.

(ii) *Pionier-Lehr-Bataillon für schweren Brückenbau* (Engineer Heavy Bridging Demonstration Battalion) : Located at Speyer-on-Rhein (Wkr. XII). This unit is liable to service in the field.

(iii) *Pionier-Regiment z.b.V. or Pionier-Regimentsstab* (*Engineer Regimental Staff*) : Some twenty have been identified, carrying numbers selected from the series 501–700, such staffs are used to control engineer battalions, bridging columns and, if need be, construction units in the area of an army, and may occasionally come under command of a corps.

(iv) *Pionier Bataillon* (Engineer Battalion) : The divisional engineer battalion may on occasions be transferred to the G.H.Q. pool and employed as corps or army troops, if the division itself is serving in a quiet sector ; its identification, therefore, does not invariably imply the presence of the division. Engineer units, which were always part of *Heerestruppen*, are numbered from 501 upwards. There is also a series from 41–53, which were corps *Pionier* battalions before the outbreak of war and were subsequently detached from corps formations and became *Heerestruppen.*

(v) *Pionier-Bataillon z.b.V.* (Engineer Bn. Staff) : Nos. 300 and 750 have been identified ; these consist of staffs controlling independent companies of platoons.

(vi) *Pionier-Landungs Bataillon* (Engineer Landing Bn.) : A new war establishment for engineer landing battalions exists ; there have been no identifications of this type unit. A *Pionier-Landungs-Regiment* also exists, of which two have been identified.

(vii) *Pionier-Landungsbootkompanie* (Engineer Landing Craft Company) : Numbered in series 771 upwards (several identified). These units are equipped with M.L.C.s.

(viii) *Sturmbootkommando* (Assault Boat Detachment) : Six have been identified. Each detachment has three large platoons and may be either partly or fully motorised. Although the personnel is primarily trained for landing operations, they may also be employed as sappers. These units are numbered from 901 on upwards.

(ix) *Brückenkolonne or Brüko* (Bridging Column) : In addition to the bridging columns which form part of the divisional and G.H.Q. engineer battalions, there are two series of independent bridging columns in the G.H.Q. pool. One series carrying numbers in the range 401–450. These are corps bridging columns, consisting each of two columns (*e.g.*, 1/403, 2/403). In some cases these columns have been detached from corps and now operate independently as *Heerestruppen* the other series, in range 601–700, consisting of single columns which were the original G.H.Q. bridging columns. All are fully motorised.

(x) *Brückenbau-Bataillon* (Bridge Building Battalion) : Numbered in two series. Those originally designed to serve armies in the field were numbered in the 501–800 series. These battalions are reckoned in all respects as engineers ; the lower series (1–500) were bridge-building battalions originally at disposal of O.K.H. for employment in occupied countries. The personnel in the latter type unit normally consists of *Landesschützen* and other old personnel.

(xi) *Strassenbau-Bataillon* (Road Construction Battalion) : Numbered in 501–700 series (shared with the field army bridge-building battalions) : about 30 have been identified, including seven *Radfahr-* (Cyclist) battalions (in series 501–510, intended to accompany spearhead formations) : they may be qualified as *leichte* or *schwere* (*i.e.*, light or heavy), but it is not known how the two varieties differ from each other.

(xii) *Eisenbahn-Baubataillon* (Railway Construction Battalion) : Their function is to provide less specialised labour than that of the construction units described on page E41. Several in series above 501 have been identified. There are also some Railway construction battalions numbered below 501. Here, as in the foregoing paragraph, the personnel in the lower numbered ones is apt to be older.

(xiii) *Feldwasserstrassenräum Abteilung* (Waterways Clearing Bn.) : Several have been identified engaged in clearing and maintaining waterways which are essential for military transport.

(xiv) *Schneeräum Regiment and Abteilung* (Snow Removal Regiment and Bn.): Several numbered in series 501 upwards. These units are employed as construction troops in the summer.

(xv) *Pionier-Park* (Engineer Equipment Park): One to each army, allotted numbers in the series 501–; officers wear the colour of their arm, other ranks light blue, in each case with the arabic number of the park.

(xvi) *Pionier-Parkkompanie* (Engineer Park Company): Two companies are included in each engineer park, likewise numbered in series 501 upwards, carrying the number of their park.

(xvii) *Pionier-Maschinenzug* (Engineer Machine Platoon): One is included in each engineer park and carries the number of the park. Engineer Machine Platoons may also appear independently under engineer battalion staffs "z.b.v." (*see* (v) above).

(xviii) *Festungs Pionier Park* (Fortress Engineer Equipment Park) numbered from 501 upwards. They are allotted to those armies which control fortified areas (seven have been identified).

(xix) The following figure shows the tactical signs for engineer units:—

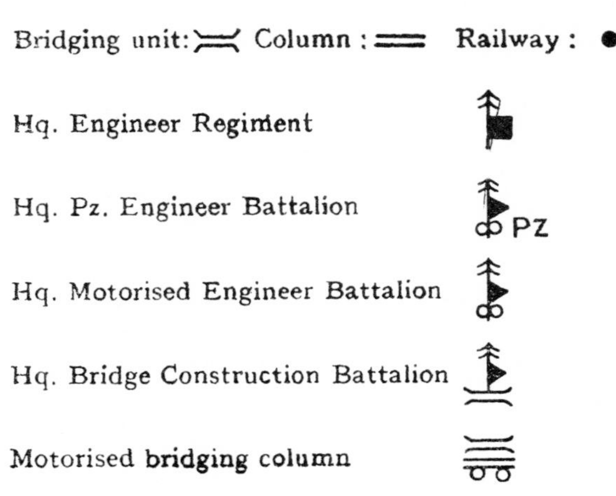

(*i*) SIGNALS TROOPS

Lemon-yellow is the distinguishing colour of signals; it should not be confused with yellow of the cavalry piping. For a listing of the main types of Signals units *see* tables, page L 62. The following types of unit may be met with: Army, corps and divisional units are excluded.

(i) *Nachrichten-Lehr-Regiment* (Signals Demonstration Regiment): Stationed at the Army Signals School at Halle (*Wkr.* IV), this signals demonstration regiment (like other demonstration units) is potentially available for service in the field.

(ii) *Nachrichten-Regimentsstab z.b.V.* (Special Signals Regimental Staff): several numbered in series 501 upwards identified; these staffs control independent signals companies.

(iii) *Nachrichtenführer z.b.V.* and *Nachrichten-Abteilungsstab z.b.V.* (Special Signals (Bn.) Staff): formed to control independent signals companies in the field. Mainly numbered from 601 upwards.

(iv) *Führungsnachrichten-Regiment* (Operational Signals Regiment): Nos. 40 and 601, in the main signals unit series (tables Part L, section *k*) have this classification; their function is to provide and maintain the highest grade signals network between G.H.Q. Army and army group and army H.Q. Recently the war establishment of these units was reduced to that of army signals regiments.

(v) *Heeres-Nachrichten-Regiment* (G.H.Q. Signals Regiment): Carrying numbers selected from the 501–700, provide and maintain signals networks of lesser importance or are allotted to army groups as army group signals regiment.

(vi) *Eisenbahn-Nachrichten-Abteilung* (Railway Signals Bn.): There are several railway signals battalions numbered in the main signal unit series (*see* tables Part L). Four are numbered upwards in the 303 series; several others carry numbers in the 501–600 block. Although these units are primarily responsible for setting up and maintaining railway communications, they may supplement army L. of C. signals channels.

(vii) Independent signals companies, etc. The following are the principal types of independent signals companies and platoons which may be met with :—

Fernsprech-Baukompanie (Telephone Construction Company).
Fernschreibkompanie (Teleprint Company).
Horchkompanie (Intercept Company).
Funküberwachungskompanie (W.T. Company).
Nachrichten Fern-Aufklärungs Komp. (Distant Signals Recce. Coy.).
Nachrichten Nah-Auflärungs Komp. (Local Signals Recce. Coy.).
Eisenbahn-Funkkompanie (Railway Signals Company).
All these are numbered in the series 601 upwards.
Fernsprech Betriebskompanie (Telephone Operating Company). Numbered in series 901 upwards.

(viii) *Nachrichtenhelferinnen Abteilung* (Signals Female Assistant Bn.) : are at disposal of *O.K.H.* (numbered from 1 upwards). A unit of this type may be employed in the zone of operation ; it will then be called a *Nachrichtenhelferinneneinsatz Abteilung*, or *Nachrichtenhelferinnen Abteilung (E)*, the "E" denoting that it is employed under field armies. There are also *Nachrichtenhelferinnen Trupps* numbered in the same series.

(ix) *Armee-Nachrichten-Park* (Army Signals Equipment Park) : One to each army, carrying numbers in the 501 upwards series ; officers wear the colour of their arm, other ranks light blue, in each case with the arabic number of the park.

The following figure shows the tactical signs for signals units :—

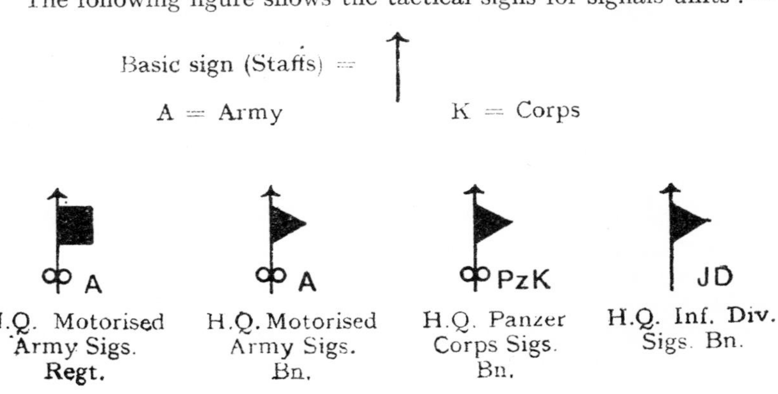

(*j*) TRANSPORT TROOPS

The distinguishing colour of transport (including supply) units is light blue ; the following list includes the main types of unit belonging to this category, with the exception of divisional and corps units (*see* Part C).

(i) Transport Units

(i) *Kraftwagentransport-Regiment* (M.T. Regiment) : The primary purpose of these regiments is to lift non-motorised fighting units ; they may also be used, however, for the transport of supplies. Units identified are numbered from 340 up (26 regiments identified).

(ii) *Kraftwagentransport-Abteilung* (M.T. Bn.) : Independent battalions, similar in function to the foregoing units ; numbered in series 340–1000, with *Kraftwagentransport-Regimenter* (fifty-nine units identified). There also exists a small series of these M.T. battalions above 1000. Examples identified are 1020 *z.b.V.*, 1021, 1022, 1023, 1024 *z.b.V.*

(iii) *Kraftwagentransport-Kompanie* (M.T. Company) : Independent companies, similar in function to the units mentioned in foregoing paragraph ; examples identified are 945 *z.b.V.*, 974, 1155, 1156, 1157, and 1203 *z.b.V.*

(iv) *Kraftfahrzeuginstandsetzungs-Abteilung* (M.T. Repair Bn.) : Numbers have been identified in the series 501–600 (twenty-five units identified). Some of these M.T. repair units have been expanded to regiments (*e.g. Kraftfahrzeuginstandsetzungsregiment* 548).

(v) *Kraftfahrzeug-Abschleppzug* (M.T. Recovery Platoon) : Some newly formed independent units numbered in the series 720–800 are equipped with 6 to 8-ton salvage trucks. They operate in conjunction with the foregoing unit.

(vi) *Panzerinstandsetzungsabteilung* (Tank Repair Bn.) : Numbered in the series 501–600 with *Kraftfahrzeuginstandsetzungsabteilungen.* Each tank repair unit has several repair companies and one or two *Panzer Bergezüge* (Tank Salvage Platoons).

(vii) *Panzer Bergezug* (Tank Salvage Platoon) : These units normally operate in conjunction with repair units and M.T. equipment parks.

(viii) *Werkstattkompanie* (*mot.*) (Motorized Workshop Company) : Six have been identified numbered in the series 501–600.

(ix) *Werkstatt Kompanie* (Workshop Company): Several units identified numbered in the 501–600 series.

(x) *Pz. Werkstatt Kompanie* (Pz. Workshop Company): Numbered in the same series as the foregoing; they are normally found operating with *Panzer* Corps.

(xi) *Armee- und Heeres-Kraftfahr-Park* (Army and G.H.Q. M.T. Park): Numbered in the series 501–600 and 601–700; some of the more recently formed parks are numbered in the 700–900 block. *A.K.P.* and *H.K.P.* are somewhat similar in organisation. A *H.K.P.* will become an *A.K.P.* when assigned to an army. Organisation of a park is as follows:—

3 *Werkstattzüge* (Workshop Platoons).
1 *Nachschub Kompanie fur Betriebsstoff* (P.O.L. Supply Coy.) (formerly known as *Parkkompanie*).
1 *Nachschubgruppe* (Supply Section), consisting of several *Nachschubstaffeln.*
1 *Instandsetzungsgruppe* (Repair Section).
1 *Ersatzteilgruppe* (Spare Parts Section).
Leitung und Versorgung (Administration and Rations).

In the occupied countries a park is responsible for the repair of M.T. as well as the upkeep of lines of transportation in its area. A park under command of an army has similar responsibilities in the army area.

(*H.K.P.* is also an abbreviation for *Heimat-Kraftfahr-Park* (M.T. Park in Germany). These are easily distinguishable in that they carry the Roman numeral of the *Wehrkreis* in which they operate.)

(xii) *Kraftfahrpark Eisenbahn* (M.T. Park on Rails): Numbering not known but it is probable that they fall in the 501 upwards series. These units are similar in organisation to M.T. parks referred to in foregoing paragraph, but are not motorised.

(xiii) *Reifen Staffel or Lager* (Tire Section or Depot): May be subordinate to M.T. parks or repair shops.

(*k*) SUPPLY UNITS

It should be noted that several indentifications have been made of divisional supply officers with numbers outside the divisional blocks (1–400 and 700–710) *e.g. Kdr. d. Div. Nachschubtruppen* 466 and 724. The identification of an O.C. of divisional supply troops may not always mean the presence of a division, but may only identify the supply staff of a special formation (*e.g., Kdr. d. Div. Nachschubtruppen* 900 of the *Lehr Brigade* 900, *see* page E 8).

(i) *Heeres-Nachschubtruppen-Schule* (Army SupplyTroops School): This school is located at Hannover (*Wkr.* XI). It was previously known as *Fahrtruppen Schule.*

(ii) *Nachschub-Bataillon* (Supply Battalion): Two series exist, namely 1–200 (half a dozen identified) which are non-motorised, and 501–700 (twenty-six identified) which are fully motorised. The *Nachschub-Bataillone* in the 501–700 block are found serving as army troops. Series 1–200 is discussed on page E46 under *O.K.H.* units. These may, however, occasionally be found serving as army troops.

(iii) *Nachschubstab z.b.V.* (Special Supply Staff): When employed as loading or unloading staffs at a seaport they are described as *Verladestab* or *Entladestab*. Numbers between 1 and 1000 may occur. Numbers will, however, fall in gaps left by divisional auxiliary numbers. In some cases supply staffs of disbanded divisions operate independently. It has been noticed that *Nachschubstäbe z.b.V.* not numbered in the Army or G.H.Q. series have in several instances become the nuclei of the supply organisations of new divisions.

(iv) *Nachschub-Kolonnenabteilung* (Supply Column Battalion): Fifty have been noted carrying numbers between 501 and 950. Their component columns are distinguished by an arabic number preceding that of the battalion (*e.g.* 8/*N.K.A.*529). A supply column battalion consists of eight columns numbered 1 to 8; the ninth column is a *Werkstattzug*. Some supply column battalions are horse-drawn and some have M.T.; they are assigned to armies as required and no standard allotment can be given.

(v) *Nachschubkolonnenabteilung z.b.V* (Supply Column Bn. Staff): Special staffs formed to control and administer independent supply columns of the G.H.Q. pool; they are numbered in series with the foregoing (a dozen have been identified).

(vi) Independent supply columns: these include the following types:

Grosse Kraftwagenkolonne—capacity 60 tons (Heavy M.T. Column).

Kleine Kraftwagenkolonne—capacity 30 tons (Light M.T. Column).

Betriebsstoff-Kolonne (*grosse Kraftwagen-Kolonne fur Betriebsstoff, kleine Kraftwagen-Kolonne fur Betriebsstoff* (Heavy and Light P.O.L. Column)).

Kesselwagen-kolonne fur Betriebsstoff (P.O.L. Tank Column).

Filterkolonne (Filter Column).

Fahrkolonne (Horse-drawn Column).

These are numbered between 501 and 999 and take those numbers not occupied by *Nachschubkolonnenabteilungen* (*see* (iv) above).

(vii) *Nachschub-Kompanie z.b.V.* (Special Supply Company) : Several in the series 600–700 have been identified. These companies operate independently and are not to be confused with independent G.H.Q. supply columns. Some recent identifications of special supply companies, have revealed numbers above 1,000, *e.g.*, Nachschubkompanie z.b.V. 1326. These are believed to consist mainly of foreigners and P.W.s which have agreed to fight on Germany's side.

The following figure shows the principal tactical signs for transport (including supply) troops :—

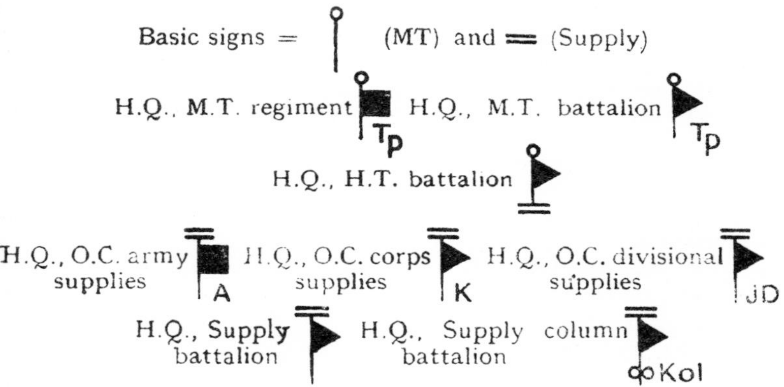

(*l*) SANITÄTS-EINHEITEN

Dark blue is the distinguishing colour for medical units. The following varieties may be met with, in addition to divisional medical units (for which see Army Medical Unit).

(i) *Armee Sanitäts-Abteilung :* These are staffs, normally controlling *Feldlazarette.* The staffs and their units are in some cases fully and in others partly motorised. They carry numbers allotted at random from the series 501–700, and, as their numbering indicates, are found attached to armies. An army medical staff will normally control from four to six *Feldlazarette.* For example, *Armee Sanitäts-Abteilung* 572 controlled *Feldlazarette* 1./572, 2./572, 3./572, etc. 2./ will normally be a *Sanitäts Kompanie* which sets up *Krankensammelstellen* in the area of its *Sanitäts Abteilung.* A *Kranken Transport Abteilung* normally operates with a *Sanitäts Abteilung* and carries its number.

In the chain evacuation the various sections of an army Medical Staff sets up to the rear of divisional medical stations.

(ii) *Kriegslazarett-Abteilung :* (War Hospital Unit). Carrying numbers in the 501–700 series. Normally these staffs will control from four to six hospitals (*Kriegslazarette*), *e.g.*, *Kriegslazarett-Abteilung* 541 is the controlling staff for 1./541, 2./541, 3./541, etc. Two of the hospitals under a hospital staff will normally be *Leichtkranken Kriegslazarette*, the others will be regular *Kriegslazarette*. In addition to controlling from four to six hospitals, a *Kriegslazarett-Abteilung* will have attached to it a *Kranken Transport Abteilung* often of the same number. In the chain of evacuation the *Kriegslazarett-Abteilung*, with its various sections, will normally be to the rear of the *Armee-Sanitäts-Abteilungen*.

(iii) *Kriegslazarett Abteilung* (*R*) (War Hospital Bn.) (Reserve) (previously known as *Reserve-Kriegslazarett Abteilung*) *:* Numbered in series 601–700. These units were intended to form the link in the chain of evacuation between the *Kriegslazarett Abteilung* (*see* (ii) above) and Germany. In 1941, however, the *Reserve Kriegslazarette* were attached to armies and moved into Russia under the new name of *Kriegslazarett Abteilung* (*R*) and there performed the same functions as the *Kriegslazarett Abteilung*. The vacancy in the evacuation system was then filled by forming the *Kriegslazarette* in the block 901–960 (*see* (iv) below).

(iv) *Kriegslazarett* (War Hospital) : These units are numbered in series 901–960. They are newly formed hospitals which take the place of the old *Reserve Kriegslazarette* and set up main hospitals in large towns well to the rear of the fighting area, along the lines of evacuation.

(v) *Armee-Feldlazarett* (Army Field Hospital) : Units of this type carry the number of the army medical staffs preceded by 1, 2, 3, or 4 (*e.g.*, 3/542) ; the prefix *Armee-* will often be dropped but the type can be recognised by its double numbering (*see Armee Sanitäts Abteilung* above).

(vi) *Leichtkranken-Kriegslazarett* (War Hospital for Minor Cases) : Some are motorised and others are not. Although identifications will be made of *Leichtkranken Kriegslazarette*, these only represent one section of a *Kriegslazarett Abteilung*, as mentioned in (ii) above).

(vii) *Krankentransport -Abteilung* (Ambulance Bn.) : Numbered in the series 501–700 and allotted to armies. These will normally be attached to a *Kriegslazarett-Abteilung* or an *Armee Sanitäts-Abteilung* (*see* above).

(viii) *Leichtkranken-Zug* (Ambulance Section for Minor Cases) Falls in same series as the *Krankentransport-Abteilung*.

(ix) *Truppenentgiftungskompanie* (Personnel Decontamination Coy.) : Numbered in series 601–700 (ten have been identified). In spite of the similarity of titles these are definitely medical units and not smoke troops like decontamination and road-contamination battalions.

(x) *Kranken-Kraftwagenzug* (Mechanised Ambulance Section) : Numbered in series 501–800 ; they are an organic part of *Armee-Sanitats-Abteilungen.* Some independent ambulance sections have been identified.

(xi) *Lazarett-Zug* (Hospital Train) : Numbered in the series 501–800. Some new identifications have been made of Hospital Trains numbered above 1,000.

(xii) *Armee-Sanitätspark* (Army Medical Stores Park) : Numbered in series 501–600. Both officers and other ranks wear dark blue with the arabic number of the park.

The following figure shows the tactical signs for medical units :

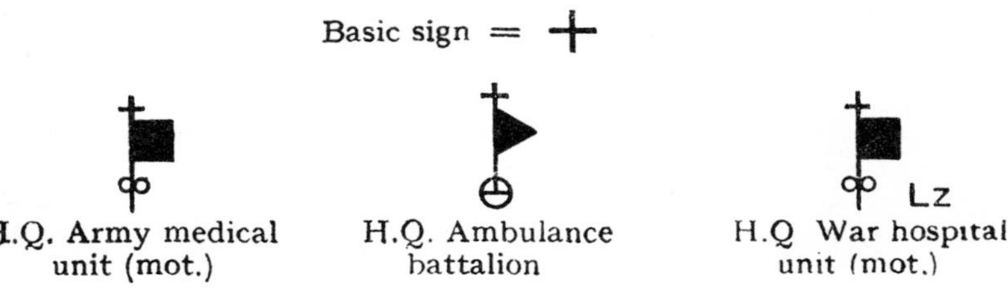

(m) VETERINARY UNITS

Carmine is the distinguishing colour of veterinary units. For divisional units *see* Part D. The following GHQ veterinary units may be met with :

(i) *Armee-Pferdelazarett* (Army Horse Hospital) : Numbered in the series 501–600. Two are numbered in the 600–700 block.

(ii) *Pferde-Transportkolonne (mot.)* (Motorised Horse Transport Column) : Numbered in the same series.

Veterinär-Kompanie (Veterinary Company) : One or more normally attached to an army ; numbered from 501 up.

(iii) *Armee-Pferdepark* (Army Horse Park) : Numbered in the series 501–600 ; also 689.

(iv) *Armee-Veterinärpark* (Army Veterinary Stores Park): Numbering and allocation as for *Armee-Pferdepark*. The personnel of both types, officers as well as other ranks, wear carmine piping with the arabic number of the park.

The following figure shows the tactical signs for veterinary units:

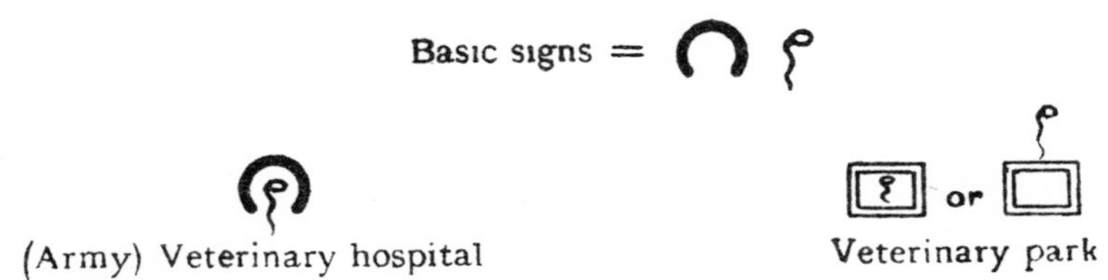

(*n*) MILITARY POLICE UNITS

Military police units wear yellow piping and carry no number. They wear, however, on the left upper arm the Nazi eagle and swastika surrounded by an oak-wreath, and on the lower arm a brown band inscribed with the word "*Feldgendarmerie*" in silver.

(i) *Feldgendarmerie-Abteilung* (M.P. Unit): One is allotted to each Army or Panzer Army: the following units of this type have been identified: 501, 520, 521, 531, 541, 551, 571, 582, 591, 614, 682, 683, 690, 693, 697.

(ii) *Feldgendarmerie-Trupp* (M.P. Detachment): Detachments of the military police allocated to the military administration of an occupied country carry the number of the *Kommandantur* to which they are attached, or, for example, appear as follows: *Feldgendarmerie-Trupp* 659 *der Feldkommandantur* 602.

(iii) *Verkehrsregelung-Bataillon* (Traffic Control Unit): Eight units of this type, carrying numbers in series 751–760, have been identified to date; a battalion or company may be allocated for as long as necessary to an Army on the move.

(iv) *Geheime Feldpolizei* (Secret Field Police): *Gruppen* of the G.F.P. may be assigned impartially to army or G.A.F. formations; there is normally one *Gruppe* at the disposal of each Army, and one or more attached to the military administration of each occupied country. Series 501–800. Recently some identifications have been made in the series 1–100, these are controlled by *O.K.H.*

The following figure shows the tactical sign for military police units :—

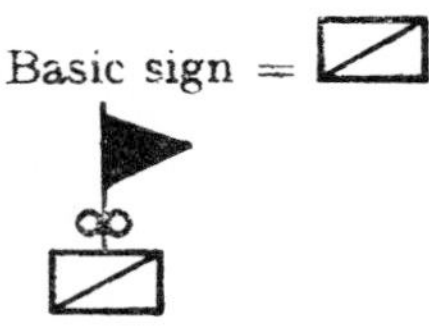

Military police battalion (mot.)

(o) ADMINISTRATIVE UNITS

This category includes a variety of units, and no single distinguishing colour can be specified to it. For particulars of corps and divisional units *see* Part C ; in the following list units have been grouped for convenience approximately according to their functions and to their place in the German war establishment list.

Administration of Supplies

Units in this group are largely staffed by officials, who wear dark green piping ; officers will wear the colour of their original arm of the service (*e.g.*, white or red).

(i) *Hauptverbindestab* and *Verbindestab* (Main Liaison and Liaison staff) : Numbered from 501 upwards, they are found operating in army areas, mainly in the west, where their primary mission consists of exploiting occupied areas, providing billets for army use, etc. They operate in close liaison with static H.Q., such as *Feldkommandanturen* and in some instances a liaison staff has been identified carrying the same number as a *Feldkommandantur*.

(ii) *Bäckerei-Kompanie*, *Gross-Bäckerei-Kompanie* (Bakery Company, Large Bakery Company) : *Bäckerei-Kompanien* are allotted random numbers in the series 501–700. *Gross-Bäckerei-Kompanien* are of more recent formation, and are numbered in the series 801 upwards.

(iii) *Schlächterei-Einheiten* (Butchery Coy.) : These vary in size, *Schlächterei-Abteilungen*, *Schlächterei-Kompanien*, and *Schlächterei-Züge* having been identified. These are all numbered concurrently in series 501–600 and 601–700. The companies are normally allotted to Armies, whereas battalions are found in large military establishments.

(iv) *Zugwach-Abteilung* (Railway Guard Bn. or Company) : Numbered in series 501–600 ; they guard and check army personnel and perform police duties along the lines of communication in army areas. One is normally allotted to an army. The duties of a unit of this type is similar to the work performed by the *Streifendienst* (Patrol Service) of the *O.K.H.* which operates in Germany and occupied areas.

(v) *Armee-Verpflegungsamt* and *Heeres-Verpflegungsamt* (Army and G.H.Q. Ration Office) : There are several of these available for each Army or army group in the field, carrying numbers selected from the series 501–800.

(vi) *Feldpostamt* (Field Post Office) : Army and G.H.Q. field post offices carry numbers selected from the series 501 and upwards ; in addition to its proper number, each post office (including corps and divisional offices) uses, for all open correspondence, a *Kenn-Nummer* (Code number) selected at random from the series 1–999 : thus, K.943 might be the code number for 571 Army F.P.O. It is therefore necessary to exercise particular care in studying identifications of F.P.O.s.

(vii) *Armee-Briefstelle* (Army Letter Office) : Numbered in the same series as series (vi) above, these are branches of the Army F.P.O. for the collection and delivery of the field post.

(viii) *Armee-Bekleidungsamt* (Army Clothing Office) : Numbering as for series (v) above.

(*p*) ADMINISTRATION OF ORDNANCE STORES, ETC.

Officers wear the colour of their original arm ; other ranks wear light blue piping. All except serial 3 are distinguished by Latin "FZ" on shoulder straps.

(i) *Munitions-Verwaltungskompanie* (Munition Administration Coy.) : Series 501 and upwards.

(ii) *Betriebsstoff-Verwaltungskompanie* (P.O.L. Administration Coy.) : Series 971–980.

(iii) *Feldwerkstatt* (Field Workshop (Ordnance)). Normally one of these is allotted to each Army or Panzer Army ; they carry numbers allotted arbitrarily, in the series 501–700. Those numbered in series 1–200 are under O.K.H. control (these units are ordnance workshops).

(iv) *Heeres-Feldzeug-Park* (G.H.Q. Ordnance Park). A new war establishment for this unit exists, probably numbered in series 601–700.

PART E—MISCELLANEOUS UNITS

(*b*) O.K.H. UNITS

(i) INDEX TO PART E (*b*)

(ii) DISCUSSION

(*a*) ADMINISTRATIVE UNITS

Other ranks belonging to units of the following types wear white piping, with the Latin letter " K," followed by the Arabic number of their unit.

(i) *Oberfeldkommandantur* (Higher Field H.Q. of Divisional status) : H.Q.s of this type in the zone of operations come under Army L. of C. Commander, or G.O.C., Army Group L. of C. District (*see* Part B) ; in occupied territory outside the zone of operations they come under the general in command of the military administration and in such cases they are distinguished by the addition of the letter (V)—for *Verwaltung*—to their title. Numbers 365, 372, 379 and 393 were formed in Poland from the staffs of divisions disbanded in 1940, etc., and continue to carry the same numbers ; all other identified instances carry numbers in the series 501 and upwards, and are Army L. of C. Commands renamed. (For identifications, *see* divisional tables, Part L).

(ii) *Subordinate H.Q.s :* The following H.Q.s carry numbers in the same series, in which the lowest number yet identified is 178 and the highest 928 ; according to their special description or the rank of the officer in command their relative importance may be elucidated, but there is no system discoverable in the allocation of numbers to them :—

Feldkommandantur (Field H.Q.) : Approximately equivalent to an area command (*see* Part B) ; the term may also be used, loosely, to describe one of the following types.

Ortskommandantur : Town Major's command in a small town.

Stadtkommandantur : Town Major's command in a city or large town.

Kreiskommandantur : Town Major's command in a rural district.

About 400 examples in all have been identified to date, the majority of which carry numbers above 500.

Note.—A *Feldgendarmerietrupp* carrying the number of the O.F.K. (or giving other indication of its subordination) is normally found with a higher field H.Q. Administrative H.Q. of the above type may also control certain *Landesschützen* personnel for police and guard duty.

(*b*) Local Defence Units

Local defence units wear white piping with the Latin "L," followed by an arabic number in the case of *Landesschützen* regimental staffs and battalions; various other types of unit fall under the same heading in the German classification, although they are not specifically described as *Landesschützen* and lack the distinguishing "L."

(i) *Landesschützen-Regiment* (*Landesschützen* Regt. Staff): This is a regimental H.Q. controlling a varying number of battalions. Some are qualified "*z.b.V.*" and have special war establishments. In the case of two-figure numbers, the first, and in the case of three-figure numbers, the first two figures give the *Wehrkreis* of origin (*e.g.*, *Lds. Schtz.* Regt. 115 comes from *Wkr.* XI).

(ii) *Landesschützen-Bataillon* (*Landesschützen* Bn.): Battalions vary in strength from two to six companies; some are qualified "*z.b.V.*" and have special war establishments. *Landesschützen* Battalions may be employed in guard duties at P.W. camps, war factories and vulnerable points in Germany or the occupied countries, on the L. of C. they may be used to guard dumps, parks, etc. Some 400 battalions have been identified, numbered according to the *Wehrkreis* of origin as follows:—

Wkr.		*Series.*	*Wkr.*		*Series.*
I	..	201–250	IX	..	601–650
II	..	251–300	X	..	651–700
III	..	301–350	XI	..	701–750
IV	..	351–400	XII	..	751–800
V	..	401–450	XIII	..	801–850
VI	..	451–500	XVII	..	851–900
VII	..	501–550	XVIII	..	901–950
VIII	..	551–600	Various	..	951–1001

The G.A.F. also disposes of *Landesschützen* units; these, however, may be distinguished from Army *Landesschützen*, since they wear double numbers, roman for the *Luftgau* of origin and arabic for the particular unit.

(iii) *Stromsicherungs-Regiment* (River Guard Regiment): Several of these units have been identified carrying the Roman numeral of the *Wehrkreis* in which they operate. They are controlling staffs of River Guard Battalions. Normally these units are found along the large rivers of Germany and occupied areas.

(iv) *Stromsicherungs-Bataillon* (River Guard Battalion): Several *Landesschützen* Battalions have been renamed River Guard Battalions. They are numbered in the main *Landesschützen* series (200–1000).

Some of these units have been known to operate independently; others are under control of River Guard Regiments as mentioned in the foregoing paragraph.

(v) *Transport-Begleit-Regiment* (Transport Escort Regiment) (Railway Transport): These units are regimental staffs controlling *Transport Begleit Battaillone.* They operate from main railway junctions, such as Wien, Breslau, Königbserg, Posen, etc. *Transport Begleit Regiments* do not carry numbers but the names of cities used as their bases, *e.g. Transport Begleit Regiment Wien.*

(vi) *Transport-Begleit-Bataillon* (Transport Escort Battalion) (Railway Transport): Between 40 and 50 *Landesschützen* Battalions have been renamed *Transport Begleit Bataillone.* These units operate from main railway centres guarding supply and hospital trains in occupied countries, subordinate to transport Escort Regiment, as mentioned in the foregoing paragraph. They are numbered in the main *Landesschützen* series (200–1000).

(vii) *Grenzwacht* (Frontier Guard): In peace time the main units stationed in the frontier districts were reinforced by a frontier guard organisation, with the following chain of command :—

Grenzschutz-Abschnittskommando (Sector Command=Regt. H.Q.)
Grenzwacht-Unterabschnitt (Sub-sector=Bn. H.Q.).
Grenzwacht-Kompanie (Frontier Guard Coy.).

Each sector disposed of a signals coy., one of more fixed batteries and other units. On mobilisation the sector commands were renamed regiments and numbered on similar principles to the *Landesschützen* Regiments (*see* (i) above); it is probable that they have since been renamed *Landesschützen* regiments (*e.g.*, 122 *Lds. Schtz. Rgt.* is probably the former 122 Frontier Guard Regiment, from *Wkr.* XII, renamed).

(viii) Some *Landesschützen* Regiments have been reported to wear light green piping, the colour of mountain rifle (*Gebirgs-Jäger*) and rifle (*Jäger*) units; the reason for this is unknown.

(ix) The tactical signs for *Landesschützen* units are the same as those for comparable infantry units, with the addition of the letter "L."

(*c*) CONSTRUCTION UNITS

Light brown is the distinguishing colour of construction units, but railway construction battalions wear black piping, as do bridge-building battalions (with the possible exception of those carrying numbers below 501) and fortress construction battalions. For the employment of construction units in the field, *see* page E 19.

The following types may be met with :—

(i) *Oberbaustab* (Higher Construction Staff) : Equivalent in status to the staff of the *Arko*, or to a Brigade staff (in the German sense). They are numbered in the series 1–36.

(ii) *Kommandeur der Bautruppen* (O.C. Construction Troops) : Equivalent in status to the artillery regimental commander. It should be noted that engineer and construction units are often employed interchangeably under whichever staff is most conveniently placed to control them ; and units of the state labour service (*R.A.D.*) or of the G.A.F. construction troops may also be found under the same control. These staffs are numbered at random from 1–108, about twenty-five having been identified.

(iii) *Baubataillon* (Construction Bn.) : Series 1–500 (about 100 identified, of which the majority carry numbers below 300), excluding bridge-building, fortress and railway construction battalions which are numbered concurrently. A number of these, although originally controlled by O.K.H., have been identified in the zone of operations attached to Army (*see* page E 20).

(iv) *Festungsbau-Bataillon Fest. Bau-Btl.* (Fortress Construction Bn.) : Some fifteen have been identified, carrying numbers between inclusive 19 and 242. They operate under the direction of fortress engineer staffs (*see* (xiii) below).

(v) *Marine-Baubataillon, Mar. Bau-Btl.* (Naval Construction Bn.) : Nos. 311, 312, 313 and 323 in the main series are described thus ; they are presumably intended to carry out construction work for the German Navy, though their personnel are provided by the Army.

(vi) *Technisches-Bataillon* (Technical Battalion) : These battalions, supplied with drafts by the Technical Depot Battalion at Pirna (*Wkr.* IV), are intended for such specialised functions as the production and treatment of mineral oil, for coal-mining and the like ; they are numbered in series 1–50 (15 battalions have been identified to date).

(vii) *Landesbau-Bataillon* (Agricultural Bn.) : A series 1–10 has recently been identified ; they do construction of a very general type.

(viii) *Kriegsgefangene-Bau-und Arbeits-Bataillon* (P.W. Construction and Labour Bn.) : Numbered in series 1–250 (50 identified) ; the German cadre personnel acts as guards to P.W. employed within Germany or on the L. of C.

(ix) *Kriegsgefangene-Arbeitskommando* (P.W. Labour Unit): Numbered at random from 250 to 5000 (fifteen identified). German cadre personnel act as guards to P.W. employed within Germany.

(x) *Kriegsgefangene-Hafenarbeiter-Abteilung* (P.W. Dock Labourer Bn.): Numbered concurrently with P.W. construction battalions.

(xi) *Heeresbaudienststelle* and *Grosse Heeresbaudienststelle* (Army Works Office and Main Army Works Office): Numbered in series 1–150; these units lay plans for construction but do not take part in the actual construction, they are classified as *Verwaltungstruppen* (Administrative Troops) but are listed here, since they will often be found with construction troops.

Fortress Engineers

Fortress engineers wear the letter "Fp" or "F" on their shoulder straps (gothic "Fp" if the unit existed in peace time, Latin "F" if it was formed on or after mobilisation); the following units and staffs may be identified:—

(xii) *Festungspionier-Kommandeur* (Fortress Engineer Commander): Gothic "Fp" followed by the Roman number of a *Wehrkreis*; in effect, regimental commander and H.Q. for fortress engineer units in the military district concerned.

(xiii) *Festungspionier-Stab* (Fortress Engineer Staff): Gothic "Fp" or Latin "F" followed by an arabic number in series 1–50; a regimental staff, normally controlling two sector groups.

(xiv) *Festungspionier-Abschnittsgruppe* (Fortress Engineer Sector Group): Numbers I or II followed by the arabic number of the controlling staff (*e.g., Fest. Pi. Abschn. Gr.* II/21); equivalent in status to a battalion staff.

Railway Engineers

Railway engineers wear black piping with the letter "E" (Gothic if the unit existed in peace time, otherwise Latin) on the shoulder strap; they are not always easy to distinguish from *Eisenbahntruppen* (Railway Troops), for which *see* (*d*) below. The following types of unit may be met with:—

(xv) *Eisenbahnpionier-Regiment* (Railway Engineer Regt.): Ten exist (numbered 1–13); each consists of H.Q. and two battalions, each of four companies, numbered consecutively (*e.g., 7/Eisb. Pi. Rgt.* 3 = 3 Coy. 2 Bn. 3 Railway Engineer Regt.); in common with the independent companies listed below, they receive drafts from five railway engineer depot battalions (Nos. 1–5).

(xvi) *Eisenbahnpionierstab z.b.V.* (Special Railway Engineer Staff) : Nos. 7 and 8 identified.

(xvii) *Eisenbahn (Pionier)-Baukompanie* (Railway (Engineer) Construction Coy.) ; Numbered in series 101–200, these are specialist companies, the function of which may be defined by a further title : *e.g., Eisb. Pfeilerbaukp.* (Rly. Pier Construction Coy. ; in others the special title replaces *Bau., e.g., Eisb. Fernsprechkompanie* (Rly. Telephone (Construction) Coy.). By contrast, the *Eisenbahn-Baubataillon* (Railway Construction Battalion) belongs to the category of construction troops (*see* (*c*) above).

(xviii) *Eisenbahnpionier-Park* (Rly. Engineer Equipment Park) : Nos. 402, 403 and 408 have been identified , in addition there is a *Heimat-Eisenbahn-Pionier-Park* at Rehagen-Klausdorf (Wkr. III), where the railway engineer school is situated.

(*d*) RAILWAY UNITS

(i) Operating staffs : The following railway operating staffs, numbered concurrently in series 1 and upwards, have been identified :—

Feldeisb. Kommando (Fd. Railway Command).
Feldeisb. Betriebsabteilung (Fd. Railway Operating Unit).
Feldeisb. Maschinenabteilung (Fd. Rly. Machinery Bn.).
Feldeisb. Werkstättenabteilung (Fd. Rly. Workshop Bn.).

The departments are believed to be sub-divisions of the directorates which carry the same number.

(ii) Operating units : Two series of operating units have been identified as follows :—

Eisenbahnbetriebskompanie (Rly. Operating Coy.).—Series 200 and upwards.
Feldbahnkompanie (Fd. Rly. Coy.).—Series 301 and upwards.

It is possible that some of the independent companies noted under section (xvii) above may come under control of railway operating staffs on occasion, although their personnel are railway engineers and wear black piping accordingly.

(iii) *Feldeisenbahn-Nachschublager* (Field Railway Supply Depot): A new war establishment for a unit of this type exists ; no identifications have been made as yet.

(iv) *Transport-Kommandantur* (Transport Office) : These H.Q.s are located in the major railway junctions in Germany and occupied countries. They are responsible for the smooth functioning of the supply system and the upkeep of military order and discipline in the areas assigned to them. Normally a guard company or battalion will be attached to a transport office.

(v) *Bahnhofs-Kommandanturen I or II* (Railway Station Command I or II) : Numbered at random in independent series from 1 upwards. Railway station commands are subordinated to transport offices ; they are responsible for military order and discipline and the smooth functioning of the military supply system at their respective railway stations. Normally a guard unit is attached to a H.Q. of this type. Railway Station Commands I and II have the same responsibilities and only differ in size, II being a larger H.Q. than I.

(*e*) ARMOURED RAILWAY UNITS

(i) *Eisenbahn-Panzer-Einheiten* (Railway Armoured Units) : *Eisenbahn-Panzerzüge* (Railway Armoured Trains) are numbered in the series 1–66 ; twenty have been identified to date. The personnel wear pink piping with the letter " E " on the shoulder strap.

(ii) *Streckenschutzzug* (Railway Guard Train) : Numbered in series with railway armoured trains. These units guard railway communications in occupied countries.

(*f*) SIGNALS TROOPS

The following units are controlled by *O.K.H.* (for signals units normally found under Army, *see* page E22).

(i) *Kommandeur der Nachrichtentruppen* (O.C. Signals) : A Roman number with yellow piping denotes the staff of O.C. Signals in a particular *Wehrkreis* ; he has the status of a regimental commander, and controls both training and army communications within his district ; officers of the same title may also be found in the field.

(ii) *Feldnachrichtenkommandantur* (Field Signals Command) : A static signals H.Q. for a sector of occupied territory or in back areas of the zone of operations. The personnel wear yellow piping and a Latin " K " followed by the Arabic number of the unit (series 1–60).

(iii) *Festungsnachrichten-Kommandantur—Stelle* (Fortress Signals Command, Station) : The command carries the same number as the *Festungs-Pionier-Stab* to which it is attached. These units may carry an Arabic or Roman numeral between 1 and 25.

(iv) *Feldschaltabteilung z.b.V.* (Special Signals Relay Unit) : Numbered from 1 upwards. They are located in occupied countries.

(v) *Fernkabel-Bau-Abteilung* (Long Distance Telegraph Construction Bn.) : No. 1 identified.

(vi) *Sonder-Funk-Überwachungs-Stelle* (Special Signals Control Station) : Numbered from 1 upwards. Several have been identified in occupied countries.

(vii) *Feste Nachrichtenstelle* (Static Signals Station) : Numbered from 1 upwards. About 20 have been identified in occupied countries.

(viii) *Horchstelle* (Listening Station) : Sometimes identified as *Feste Horchstelle* (Static Listening Station) : Numbered from 1 upwards. Normally found in occupied countries.

(ix) *Funk-Kompanie* (*O.K.H.*) (W.T. Coy.) : Numbered from 1 upwards. None have yet been identified, but the war establishment is known to exist.

(x) *Nachrichten-Fern-Aufklärungs-Kompanie* (Long Range Signals Recce. Coy.) : and *Nachrichten-Nah-Aufklärungs-Kompanie* (Short range Signals Recce. Coy.) : numbered from 1 upwards. There are units of the same type for the use of armies, numbered from 501 upwards (*see* page E22).

(xi) *Funkeinsatztrupp* (Signals Demolition Platoon) : Several have been identified, numbered at random in the series 1 upwards. These units are employed in the demolition of civilian signals establishments in occupied countries in the event of German withdrawal.

(xii) *Nachrichtenhelferinnenabteilung* (Signals Female Assistant Unit) : As yet Nos. 51 and 52 are the only examples of this type of unit to be identified ; they administer the women telephone operators over a wide area, such as Occupied France.

(xiii) *Nachrichtenhelferinnentrupp* (Signals Female Assistant Operational Unit) : Several of these units have been identified numbered between 50 and 200. Units of this type may be found along the main channel of communications in army rear areas or in occupied countries. When under control of an army, they will generally appear as *Nachrichtenhelferinnenabteilung* (*E*) the " E " (*Einsatz*) indicating that the unit is for employment in the operational area.

(*g*) ORDNANCE UNITS

(*See* page E32 for ordnance units found under Army Command.)

(i) *Feldzeugkommando* (Ordnance H.Q.) : One or two in each ***Wehrkreis*** in Germany (the Gothic letters " FZ " followed by a Roman numeral give the identification) and some in occupied countries (*e.g.*, Belgium and Northern France) ; the officer appointed to this post has the status of a brigade commander. In the zone of operations there is no comparable post.

(ii) *Panzer-Feldzeugkommando* (*Panzer* Ordnance Stores H.Q.) : A new war establishment for this unit exists. (No identifications to date).

(iii) *Oberfeldzeugstab* (Higher Ordnance Staff) : Series 1 and upwards ; the commander has the status of a regimental commander.

(iv) *Feldzeugstab* (Ordnance Staff) : Series 1–50 (a dozen identified) ; equivalent in status to Bn. H.Q.

(v) *Feldzeugbataillon* (Ordnance Bn.) : Series 1–50 (half a dozen identified).

(vi) *Feldwerkstatt* (Ordnance Workshop) : Numbered 1–200. They are normally found in occupied countries. For those numbered from 501 upwards *see* page E32.

(*h*) SUPPLY, TRANSPORT AND REPAIR UNITS

For those numbered above 501 *see* page E24–25.

(i) *Heeres-Kraftfahr-Bezirk* (H.K.B.) (Military M.T. Area) : Carry Roman numerals from I upwards. Those above 100 carry arabic numerals.

(ii) *Wirtschaft* (*Strassen*) *Transport Brigade z.b.V.* (Agricultural and Industrial M.T. Staff) : Numbered from 1 upwards. These are special staffs which normally control from four to six M.T. Bns. A M.T. Bn. under control of a special staff of this type will be called a *Wirtschafts Transport Abteilung z.b.V.*

(iii) *Wirtschafts-Transport Bereich- und Bezirk* (Agricultural and Industrial M.T. area) : Numbered from 340 upwards. A M.T. regiment or battalion, as discussed in (i) on page E24 when responsible for transportation in an assigned area (*Bereich* for *Regiment* and *Bezirk* for *Abteilung*), will appear as *Wirtschafts-Transport-Bereich* or *Bezirk*. Army M.T. units (above 501) will normally come under control of *O.K.H.*, when they are responsible for transportation of agricultural and industrial products. A great number of these units were employed in Russia for the exploitation of the occupied areas.

(iv) *Kraftwagentransport-Regiment* and *Abteilung* (M.T. Regt. and Bn.) : Those numbered from 340 to 400 are normally controlled by *O.K.H.* For those above 501 *see* page E24.

(v) *Nachschub-Bataillon* (Supply Bn.): Those numbered in series 1–200 are normally controlled by *O.K.H.*, but may occasionally be found serving under Armies. The personnel used in these battalions is of low quality, and P.W.s will often be employed in them. Several *Bau-Bataillone* have been found renamed *Nachschub-Bataillone* in the 1–200 block.

(For *Nachschub-Bataillone* in the series 501–700 *see* page E 26).

(vi) *Gebirgsträger-Bataillone* (Mountain Carrier Bns.): Numbered from 50 upwards; four have been identified. P.W.s are employed in these units; German officers and N.C.O.s form the cadre.

(vii) *Kraftfahrzeuginstandsetzungskompanie* (Kfz. Inst. Kp.) (M.T. Repair Coy.): These are independent coys., numbered in series 101–200. Twenty-five have been identified operating in occupied areas.

(viii) *Werkstatt* (Workshop): A component unit of a M.T. Park. As mentioned on page E 25 the workshop of an H.K.B. may set up repair stations in occupied areas and carry numbers in the O.K.H. series 1 upwards. These units are not to be confused with *Werkstattkompanien* as described on page E 25.

(ix) *Zentral-Ersatzteillager, Z.E.L.* (Central Spare Parts Depot): Series 1–400. *O.K.H. Ersatzteillager* operate independently in occupied areas. (M.T. Parks normally have a spare parts section, *see* page E 25).

(x) *Panzer-Ersatzteillager* (Tank Spare Parts Depot): operate in conjunction with army repair shops and M.T. Parks.

(*i*) WELFARE UNITS

(i) *Heeres-Betreuungsabteilung* (Army Welfare Bn.): Series 1–6 identified. A battalion consists of as many as 5–7 coys., which operate independently in a large area which is normally assigned to the Bn. Coys may be subdivided again into platoons and operate independently.

(ii) *Eisenbahn-Küchenwagen-Abteilung* (Railway Kitchen Car Unit): Nos. 1 to 4 have been identified.

(*j*) ADMINISTRATION OF P.W. CAMPS

The following types of P.W. camp staff have been identified; personnel wear the colour of their original arm. It should be noted that a P.W. camp located in a *Wehrkreis* carries (and in all open correspondence uses) the roman number of the *Wehrkreis* followed by a letter of the alphabet (*e.g.*, *Stalag* XXI A).

(i) *Frontstalag* (Forward P.W. Camp) : Twenty-five identified, numbered from 1 upwards.

(ii) *Dulag* (P.W. Transit Camp) : twenty identified numbered from 1 upwards.

(iii) *Oflag* (Camp for Officer P.W.) : Carry roman number of the *Wehrkreis* in which they are located, followed by a letter of the alphabet (*e.g.*, *Oflag* XI d).

(iv) *Stalag* (Camp for O.R. P.W.) : Carry roman number of the *Wehrkreis* in which they are located and a letter of the alphabet (*e.g. Stalag* XI c). Eighty have been identified. Two or more *Landesschützen* coys. normally guard a *Stalag*.

(*k*) MISCELLANEOUS O.K.H. UNITS

(i) *Feldstrafgefängnis Abteilung* (Field Penal Unit) : Numbered from 1 upwards. Several have been identified, mainly in Army rear areas on the Russian front.

(ii) *Filmtrupp* (Film Section) : Numbered from 1 upwards. Several have been identified.

(iii) *Abwehr* (Intelligence) : These units are numbered from 1 upwards, and as the numbering indicates are controlled by *O.K.H.*, their duties vary from field Security work to counter espionage.

(iv) *Streifendienst* (Patrol service) : Numbered from 1 upwards according to the subordination, *e.g. Streifendienst* 1/III, subordinate to a *Wehrkreis* H.Q. of Wkr. III. Their task consists of policing main lines of communication in Germany and occupied countries, and enforcing military order particularly in *Wehrkreise*.

(v) *Geheime Feldpolizei Gruppe* (Secret Field Police Group) : Those numbered above 501 are for employment in field armies and have already been discussed on page E 30. O.K.H. also controls several of these units carrying numbers from 1 on upwards (eight have been identified in the low series).

E 48

PART E—MISCELLANEOUS UNITS

(*c*) FLAK AND OTHER AIR FORCE GROUND UNITS

(i) ANTI-AIRCRAFT ARTILLERY

German A.A. Artillery (*Flak artillerie or Flak*) is, in the main, part of the G.A.F.; there are also Army A.A. units (*Heeresflak and Fla*) and Naval A.A. units (*Marineflak*). The primary function of the G.A.F. and Naval Flak artillery is the static defence of Germany and occupied territories; in field operations, however, G.A.F. Flak units are so closely associated with the army that a survey of their organisation and operational employment, together with that of the Army Flak units, is essential in a conspectus of the German forces in the field.

(*a*) System of Numbering

(i) *G.A.F. Flak.*—German Flak is organised into *Korps, Divisionen, Brigaden, Regimenter, Abteilungen and Batterien.* Of these, *Korps, Brigaden* and *Abteilungen* (other than independent *Abteilungen, i.e.* those which do not form part of a Regiment) are denoted by roman numerals, while *Divisionen, Regimenter,* independent *Abteilungen* and *Batterien* are denoted by arabic numerals.

Formations identified include two *Korps* (I and II), *Divisionen* falling between numbers 1 and 22 and *Brigaden* between I and XXII.

The main series of units carry numbers in the range 1–999; in some cases, one number in this series is carried by two or more units of different types. Numbers from 1,000 upwards are confined to separate *Batterien.* The following are the principal groups in the entire series :—

Nos. 1–70 : *Regimenter* consisting of Staff (H.Q.) I and II (mixed gun) *Abteilungen* each of three heavy and two light *Batterien* III (searchlight) *Abteilung* of three or four searchlight *Batterien* and an *Ersatzabteilung.* The numbers 80 and 90 seem also to have been intended for this group, although in fact never formed as *Regimenter.*

Nos. 71–99 : Light *Abteilungen* each of three or four light Batterien. There are also light *Ersatzabteilungen* and independent regimental staffs (*i.e.* without correspondingly numbered subordinate *Abteilungen*) carrying numbers in this series.

The above two groups together constitute the so-called " active " series. Most of the units existed in peacetime. The *Abteilungen* (other than *Ersatzabteilungen*) are fully motorised as are the regimental staffs other than those in the group 71–79 which are of later formation and may be motorised or non-motorised. With some exceptions the numbers in the active series are allotted on the basis of the *Luftgau** or origin.

The *final digit* is the key figure and indicates the *Luftgau* as follows : key figure 1 (*Luftgau* I), 2 (III), 3 (IV), 4 (VI), 5 (VII), 6 (XI), 7 (VIII), 8 (XVII) and 9 (XII/XIII). Numbers whose final digit is 0 are allotted by the first digit. Examples, 25 and 50 *Regimenter* (key figure 5) originate in *Luftgau VII*, 74 light *Abteilung* (key figure 4) in *Luftgau VI*.

Nos. 100–999 : Units formed on or after mobilisation are allotted numbers in this group ; they include *Regimenter*, independent regimental staffs and independent *Abteilungen*, which may be heavy (four heavy *Batterien*), mixed, light, searchlight or *Ersatz*.

Regimenter in this group are rarely complete. They are often restricted to a single mixed *Abteilung* (I), a second mixed *Abteilung* (II) being occasionally found and very rarely a searchlight *Abteilung* (III). All their *Abteilungen* are fully motorised. Such *Regimenter* seldom have staffs or *Ersatzabteilungen*. The independent regimental staffs may be motorised or non-motorised. The independent *Abteilungen* are generally non-motorised. The term "reserve" prefixed to independent *Abteilungen* in this group indicated that they had a non-motorised war establishment and did not mean that the units in question were necessarily formed immediately on mobilisation ; this term is now apparently being abandoned in favour of the suffixes (V) (*verlegefähhig, i.e.* mobile) and (O) (*ortsfest, i.e.* static), which denote non-motorised units with trailer-mounted and static equipment respectively.

The allocation of numbers bears a close relation to that in the active series which subsequent developments, however, have done much to weaken. The mobilisation scheme provided for expansion by the creation of independent (reserve) *Abteilungen* by the *Regimenter* and light *Abteilungen* of the active series. The units so

*The G.A.F. district corresponding in function to the Wehrkreis. L.G. I/II=Wkr. I, II, XX, XXI and part of the General Gouvernement ; L.G. III/IV=Wkr. III, IV and portions of Wkr. II, VIII, IX and XI ; L.G. VI=Wkr. VI and parts of Wkr. IX ; L.G. VII=Wkr. V, VII, portions of Wkr. XVIII and Eastern France ; L.G. VIII=Wkr. VIII and a large portion of the General Gouvernement ; L.G. XI=Wkr. X and parts of Wkr. II, VI and XI ; L.G. XII/XIII=Wkr. XII, XIII and portions of Wkr. IX ; L.G. XVII=Wkr. XVII and parts of Wkr. XVIII and the Protectorate. According to the latest information, *Luftgaue* III, IV, I and II are now referred to in official documents as *Luftgau* III/IV and *Luftgau* I/II. This represents another step in the economy of administration begun by amalgamation of *Luftgaue* XII and XIII.

formed were given numbers consisting of the number of the parent unit plus a third (final) digit ; thus 33 *Regiment* might form 331 *Abteilung* and 76 light *Abteilung* might form 761 light *Abteilung*. Of the *Abteilungen* formed by the *Regimenter, i.e.*, the range 100–709, 800–809 and 900–909, those with final digits 1–7 were intended to be mixed and those with final digits 8, 9 and 0 searchlight. The *Abteilungen* formed by the active light *Abteilungen* were all light, *i.e.*, the range 710–999, but excepting the ranges 800–809 and 900–909. The key figure, showing the *Luftgau* of origin as in the active series, was thus the *second* digit, except where this was 0, when it was the *first* digit.

Independent regimental staffs were formed on a different system and have no apparent connection with the series of active units. It is possible that the *final* digit is the key figure and indicates the *Luftgau* of origin. These staffs are in no way related to similarly numbered independent *Abteilungen.*

Example : 135 regimental staff originates in *Luftgau* VII (key figure 5), (but
135 Abteilung originates in *Luftgau* IV (key figure 3)).

The regimental staffs are mostly in the ranges 100–200 and 650–659.

Balloon barrage *Abteilungen* and railway *Flak* units of all types are found with numbers between 100 and 999. Both categories of unit are believed to constitute parallel series and no special system of numbering has yet been discerned.

Nos. 1,000 upwards : These are given to separate (*z.b.V.*, *i.e.*, special) *Batterien*, which may be heavy, light or searchlight, and appear to be all non-motorised. In many cases they have been found to be former component *Batterien* of identified *Abteilungen* renumbered.

Example : 4 *Batterie* 750 light *Abteilung* renumbered 2021 light *Batterie*.

No special system in the allocation of numbers is yet discernible, but it appears probable that all *Batterien* having the same first two digits are of the same type.

Examples : Heavy—first two digits 13, 14, 15, 16, 37.
Light—first two digits 20, 38, 92.
Searchlight—first two digits 25, 77.

Future policy regarding the development of this series is uncertain and its wide range and the few identifications render it unsuitable for inclusion in the scheme of this book, from which it is therefore omitted.

The orderly expansion of the series—in particular the formation of independent *Abteilungen,* which began tentatively as far back as the 1938 mobilisation for the SUDETENLAND occupation—was complicated almost from the start by a number of confusing factors, such as the uneven and incomplete development of the active series and the changes of designation consequent on the conversion of non-motorised units into motorised units and vice versa (*see* Note (1)). Nevertheless, the key figure system is still a fair guide to the *Luftgau* of origin and the numerotation still gives a reasonable indication of the types of unit. In regard to the latter the following general principles apply with few exceptions :—

Abteilungen in the series 71 – 99 and *Abteilungen* numbered as components of *Regimenter* are motorised. All other *Abteilungen* are non-motorised, unless described as (mot).

Abteilungen in the ranges 71–99, 710–799, 810–899 and 910–999 are light.

Abteilungen numbered as I and II, *Abteilungen* of *Regimenter,* are mixed and III *Abteilungen* are searchlight (*see* Note (2)).

Independent *Abteilungen* in the ranges 100–599, 700–709, 800–809, 900–909, are heavy or mixed when their final digit is 1–7 and usually searchlight when their final digit is 8, 9 or 0.

The range 600–699 is irregular and contains heavy, mixed, light and searchlight *Abteilungen* ; there are also independent regimental staffs in the range 650–659.

Units numbered over 1,000 are separate *Batterien. Batterien* with the same first two digits are of the same type, as stated above.

---

(1) Light *Abteilungen* on motorisation merely dropped the prefix "reserve" and added the suffix (mot) to their designation. Mixed and searchlight *Abteilungen* were more usually renumbered as regimental *Abteilungen.*

(*Example :* 251 (mixed) reserve *Abteilung* renumbered II *Abteilung,* 25 *Regiment*) ; 241 (mixed) reserve *Abteilung* renumbered I *Abteilung,* 241 *Regiment.*)

(2) A large number of non-motorised mixed *Abteilungen* have been converted to non-motorised heavy *Abteilungen* and their former light *Batterien* regrouped in newly formed light *Abteilungen* without regard to the key figure system.

(*Example :* 462 (mixed) reserve *Abteilung* became 462 heavy *Abteilung* and its light *Batterien* were regrouped in 750 light *Abteilung.*)

If a heavy *Abteilung* is to be motorised it is first converted back to mixed establishment.

(ii) *Heeresflakabteilung* (*Army Flak Abteilung*) (*see* Page E 16).

(iii) *Fla-Battalion* (A.A.Bn.).—Series 22–66 existed. Some, if not all, of the battalions in this series have been incorporated in divisions.

They consisted of six companies, equipped with 2-cm. (0·79-in.) or 3·7-cm. (1·45-in.) guns, which operated separately.

Nos. 601–620, also No. 501. Some *Fla*-Battalions in this series are still in existence ; the tendency, however, has been to incorporate *Fla* in divisions.

(iv) *Naval Flak* (*Marineflak*) (*see* Page E 60).

(*b*) Operational Employment of G.A.F. and Army Flak in the Field

(i) *G.A.F. Flak*.—The tactical unit is the *Abteilung* and not the Regiment ; in action *Abteilungen* (whether regimental or independent), rarely operate under a regimental staff of the same number. *Flak* forces serving with the armies in the field are as far as possible fully motorised and may include units equipped for cross-country operations.

Command is exercised through the chain *Korps-Division-Regiment-Abteilung*. On fronts where there is no Corps the Division is normally the highest formation. The Brigade, which is, as a rule, a static formation, is exceptionally found on some fronts either interposed in the chain between Division and Regiment or as the highest formation. There is no fixed allotment of units to higher formations, but the following "normal" scale, which is a fair average of the wide variations encountered in practice, is quoted in a German document :—

To *Flakkorps* : Three *Flakdivisionen*.

To *Flakdivision* : Three *Regimenter*.

(To *Flakbrigade* : No "normal" allotment, this formation being usually restricted to static defence).

To *Flakregiment* : Three *Abteilungen* (two mixed and one light).

In general, the *Flakkorps* is responsible for the area of a *Heeresgruppe* and the *Flak* division for the area of an *Armee* (or, where there is no *Flakkorps*, a *Heeresgruppe*) ; the *Flakbrigade*, when it occurs, is usually at *Armee* level, while the *Flak* regiment may be found at *Armee*, *Armeskorps* or *Division* level, *Armee Korps* being the most usual. The *Flakabteilung* is normally attached to a *Division*, preference generally being given to armoured motorised divisions.

G.A.F. *Flak* formations and units operating with the army are subordinated operationally to the army formation concerned and administratively to the G.A.F. air fleet (*Luftflotte*) through the normal *Flak* chain of command. Rear areas are given *Flak* protection by units subordinated for all purposes to the G.A.F. ground organisation (*Luftgaustab*) ; advanced airfield defence may also be entrusted to such units or, if the situation requires, to units subordinated to the *Flak* formations.

The main function of *Flak* in the field is the defence of the zone of the armies ; in practice this is not confined to the protection of troop columns and concentrations, supply dumps and L. of C. On the contrary, motorised *Flak* units regularly operate in the spearhead of the attack, being employed not only to provide protection against air attack, but also for engaging land targets (tanks, pillboxes, strongpoints, etc.). In defensive fighting and retreat such units frequently constitute the backbone of defence against advancing AFVs and may also find employment in a field artillery role to engage troop concentrations or to harass the bringing forward of men and supplies. For all these purposes reliance continues to be placed chiefly on the 8·8-cm. (3·46-in.) gun, with which the heavy troop is normally equipped.

(ii) *Army Flak. Heeresflakabteilungen.*—All these units hitherto formed part of the G.H.Q. pool, but a *Heeresflakabteilung* is now included in the WE artillery complement of armoured and motorised divisions (*see* (i) (*b*) (i) above). Their employment is almost invariably with these divisions in the dual-purpose (AA and ground) role and does not differ materially from that of motorised G.A.F. *Flak* units in the same role.

Fla-Bataillone.—Some of these units still exist ; they form part of the G.H.Q. pool and are allotted to divisions according to tactical requirements, being subordinated direct to the Commander of the division with which they are operating. (*Fla* companies included in A/Tk Bns. and tank regts. form integral parts of these units and are numbered accordingly). Their employment is highly flexible, the battalion being frequently split up and employed in company or section strength for the protection of divisional H.Q.s, Panzer Grenadiers, recce groups, supply units, etc. Although their primary role is that of *Flak* protection against low-flying aircraft, they are also employed in a ground role to support artillery, tank and anti-tank units.

(c) Conventional Signs

In November, 1942, the tactical signs for units of the (G.A.F.) A.A. Artillery were revised, the basic symbol for the anti-aircraft gun was modified as follows :—

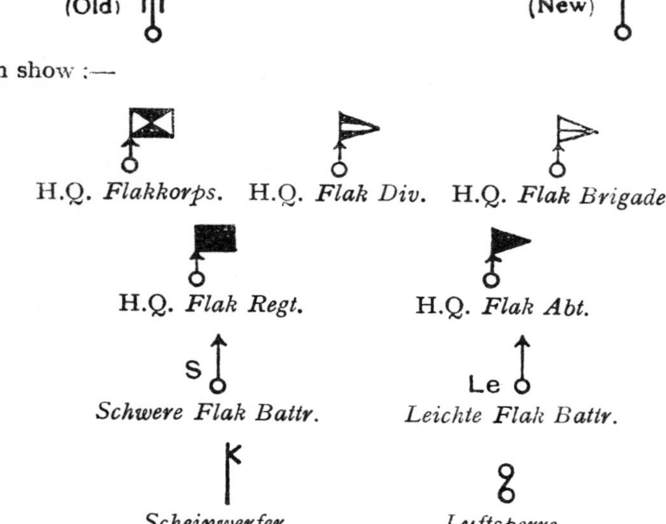

(ii) OTHER G.A.F. UNITS

The following are the principal types of unit likely to be found co-operating with army formations in fighting on land.

(*a*) Parachute troops (*Fallschirmjäger*). For details *see* "Pocket Book of the German Army."

(i) The establishment of a parachute division is believed to be —

H.Q.
Signals battalion.
Signals operating company.
Three parachute rifle regiments.
Parachute artillery regiment.
Parachute engineer battalion.
Parachute anti-tank battalion.
Services.

(ii) 1. Parachute Division is believed to include :—

Parachute Rifle Regiment 1, 3 and 4.
Parachute Artillery Regiment 1.
Parachute Engineer Bn. 1.
Signals Bn. 1.

(iii) 2. Parachute Division is believed to include Parachute Rifle Regiment 6, 7 and 5 (or 2).

(iv) Corps troops are believed to include a parachute engineer battalion, parachute M.G. battalion, parachute A.A. battalion, medical unit, field hospital and services.

(*b*) In addition, G.A.F. construction, supply, transport and repair units may be met with, these can readily be distinguished because, like G.A.F. *Landesschützen* units (*see* page E 38), they carry double numbers, arabic for the particular unit and roman for *Luftgau* (G.A.F. administrative district) in which it was formed.

G.A.F. supply and repair units have often been found serving army units as well as *Luftwaffe* units, and under abnormal conditions, a G.A.F. supply or repair unit may be absorbed by an army unit, *e.g.*, *Nachschubkolonnen Abteilung* 673 absorbed one or more *Lw. Transport Kolonnen* during the latter stages of the African campaign.

Basic Parachute symbol 

Parachute Division Headquarters. 

G.A.F. Supply Company. 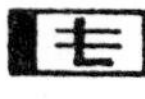

E 58

PART E—MISCELLANEOUS UNITS

(*d*) NAVAL ARTILLERY AND NAVAL FLAK

(*d*) NAVAL ARTILLERY AND NAVAL FLAK

Personnel in naval artillery and naval *Flak* units wear the German navy shore service uniform, which is field-grey in colour and very similar to the field-grey uniform worn by the personnel of the German Army.

The three main differences between the uniform of naval troops and that of army troops are the following :—

The *Hoheitsabzeichen* (National Service Badge), in shape identical to that worn by army personnel, is gold (silver for army).

The buttons on the service uniform are gold (silver for army).

The gorget-patch differs in colour from that of the army.

Badges indicating the various branches of the naval service are worn on the upper left sleeve.

The badge if naval artillery is a winged and flaming shell on an oval patch. Naval *Flak* personnel wear a badge identical to that of artillery with the letter "F" added.

(i) *Marineflak-Einheiten* (Naval *Flak* Units).

These are generally mixed, but may contain more *Batterien* than G.A.F. mixed *Abteilungen*, and have no fixed organisation.

They have arabic numbers and form part of the series of naval artillery *Abteilungen* ; the *Flakabteilungen* are found in the series 100–999, in which the numbers above 700 appear to be exclusively *Flak*, while the remainder are irregularly allotted to *Flak* and coastal artillery *Abteilungen*,

Identifications include one naval *Flakbrigade* (IV) and three regiments (20, 22 and 24), which are probably staffs. Naval Depot *Abteilungen* do not appear to exist, recruits being presumably trained in artillery depot *Abteilungen*.

(ii) *Marine Küsten Artillerie Einheiten* (Naval Artillery Units).

Abteilungen and *Batterien* are numbered concurrently with army artillery units. Nos. 122, 202, 205, 256, 260, 286, 501–513, 604, 605, 611, 616, 621, 622, 623, 640, 683 and 689 have been identified.

Naval artillery may come under navy or army command.

E 61

Basic sign Naval Artillery :

Naval. *Flak Batterie* :

Heavy Naval Artillery *Batterie* (flat trajectory in position) : 

Heavy Naval Artillery *Batterie* (high trajectory in position) : 

PART F—ARMED SS (WAFFEN SS) FORMATIONS AND UNITS

CONTENTS

Note.—The alphabetical list of senior SS officers is included with the officers of the Army and the G A.F. in Part K.

ARMED SS (WAFFEN SS) FORMATIONS AND UNITS

(*a*) IDENTIFICATION

Deathshead badge on cap; black collar patches and shoulder straps; piping of the SS arm of the service (which differs from those of the army in some respects); SS symbol on right collar patch*; national emblem (*Hoheitsabzeichen*) on left upper sleeve; narrow armband (*Bindel*) on left lower sleeve with name of division or regiment.

The following SS formations and units in effect form part of the German field army although they are in principle raised, equipped and maintained by the SS organisation. Although SS formations correspond in general to their army equivalents, variations in organisation are common.

(*b*) SS CORPS

A number of SS Corps have been identified numbered from I to V. SS corps signals and supply units exist and it is probable that combatant corps troops may also be found. It is not yet clear what system of numbering is used for these SS corps troops. Arabic numbers corresponding to the Roman number of the Corps would certainly involve risk of confusion with SS divisional units of the same number. It is possible therefore that some distinctive series of numbering may be adopted for corps troops.

The following are believed to exist :—

I.—SS Panzer Corps.
II.—SS Panzer Corps.
III.—SS (Germanic) Panzer Corps.
IV.—SS (Germanic ?) Panzer Corps.
V.—SS Mountain Corps.

Note.—The title Germanic indicates that the corps has been formed from or is designed to control Germanic (*i.e.*, non-native German) units and formations.

---

* Except in the case of :—

(*a*) Officers of the rank of Colonel (*Standartenführer*) and above who wear badges of rank on both collar patches.

(*b*) Certain divisions (*e.g.*, SS Pz. Div. Totenkopf) which wear a divisional badge in place of the SS flash.

(*c*) SS Polizei Division which wears a green collar patch similar to that used in the army.

(c) SS DIVISIONS

In addition to their names, SS divisions now bear numbers, which are used as ancillary numbers by all divisional units other than the infantry regiments. The infantry regiments have until recently been numbered internally within each division, but an overall numbering system has now been introduced ; thus, PGR 1 and 2 of *4.SS Polizei Pz. Gren. Div.* have been renumbered PGR 7 and 8 in the single regimental series, which is believed to be as shown in the following tables :—

(i) SS Panzer Divisions (*SS Panzerdivisionen*)

Division	Infantry regiments		Ancillary number
1. Leibstandarte SS Adolf Hitler (L SS AH).	PGR 1	PGR 2	1
2. Das Reich	PGR 3	PGR 4	2
3. Totenkopf	PGR 5	PGR 6*	3
5. Wiking	PGR 9	PGR 10	5
9. Hohenstaufen	PGR 19	PGR 20	9
10. Frundsberg	PGR 21	PGR 22	10
12. Hitler Jugend	PGR 25	PGR 26	12

* SS Pz. Div. Totenkopf formerly had 3 Totenkopf Regts., of which the 3 Regt. was named Theodor EICKE. It is highly probable that one of these may have been converted to a M.C. Regt. There is no evidence at the moment upon which to decide which Regt., if any, has been reorganised in this manner.

(ii) SS Motorised Divisions (*SS Panzergrenadierdivisionen*)

Division	Infantry regiments		Ancillary number
4. Polizei	PGR 7	PGR 8	4
11. Nordland	PGR 23	PGR 24	11
16. Reichsführer SS	PGR 35	PGR 36	16
17. Götz von Berlichingen ..	PGR 37	PGR 38	17
? Nederland	PGR 47	PGR 48	?

(iii) **SS Mountain Divisions** (*SS Gebirgsdivisionen*)

Division	Mountain inf. regts.	Ancillary number
6. Nord	GJR 11 GJR 12	6
7. Prinz Eugen	GJR 13 GJR 14	7
13. Kroatien	GJR 27 GJR 28	13

(iv) **SS Cavalry Division** (*SS Kavalleriedivision*)

Division	Cavalry regiments	Ancillary number
8. Kavallerie	RR 15 RR 16 RR 17 RR 18	8

(v) **SS Infantry Divisions** (*SS Schützen-* or *Grenadierdivisionen*)

Division	Infantry regiments	Ancillary number
14. Galizien	(G or S) R 29(G or S) R 30 (G or S) R 31	14
15. Lettische	GR 32 GR 33 GR 34	15

Further SS divisions are believed to be forming, but particulars are not yet available.

(*d*) INDEPENDENT SS BRIGADES

Several independent SS brigades have been identified ; some of them have certainly been used in the formation of new divisions, so that the following list probably includes some which no longer exist in that form :—

(i) 1.SS Inf. Brig. (mot.).
(ii) 2.SS Inf. Brig. (mot.)—personnel largely Latvian.
(iii) SS Estnische Freiwillige Brig.—Estonian.
(iv) SS Sturmbrig. Langemarck—*see* (*f*) below.
(v) SS Sturmbrig. Wallonia—*see* (*f*) below.

(e) SS INFANTRY AND CAVALRY REGIMENTS

In the first part of the war a number of SS Totenkopf infantry regiments were identified. Most of these are believed to have been disbanded, whilst a few have been incorporated in existing formations and re-numbered.

Full details of the new regimental series (cf. (c) above) are not yet available, but the following index, as far as it goes, is believed to be accurate :—

Type*	No.	In Div.	Type	No.	In Div.
PGR	1	1. L SS AH	(G or S) R	31	14. Galizien
PGR	2	1. L SS AH	GR	32	15. Lettische
PGR	3	2. Das Reich	GR	33	15. Lettische
PGR	4	2. Das Reich	GR	34	15. Lettische
PGR	5	3. Totenkopf	PGR	35	16. Reichsführer SS
PGR	6	3. Totenkopf	PGR	36	16. Reichsführer SS
PGR	7	4. Polizei	PGR	37	17. Götz v. Berlichingen
PGR	8	4. Polizei	PGR	38	17. Götz v. Berlichingen
PGR	9	5. Wiking		..	
PGR	10	5. Wiking		..	
GJR	11	6. Nord		..	
GJR	12	6. Nord		..	
GJR	13	7. Prinz Eugen		..	
GJR	14	7. Prinz Eugen		..	
RR	15	8. Kavallerie		..	
RR	16	8. Kavallerie		..	
RR	17	8. Kavallerie	PGR	47	— Nederland
RR	18	8. Kavallerie	PGR	48	— Nederland
PGR	19	9. Hohenstaufen		..	
PGR	20	9. Hohenstaufen		..	
PGR	21	10. Frundsberg		..	
PGR	22	10. Frundsberg		..	
PGR	23	11. Nordland		..	
PGR	24	11. Nordland		..	
PGR	25	12. Hitlerjugend		..	
PGR	26	12. Hitlerjugend		..	
GJR	27	13. Kroatien		..	
GJR	28	13. Kroatien		..	
(G or S) R	29	14. Galizien		..	
(G or S) R	30	14. Galizien		..	

* PGR—*Panzergrenadier-Regiment.* GR—*Grenadier-Regiment.*
GJR—*Gebirgsjäger-Regiment.* RR—*Reiter-* or *Kavallerie-Regiment.*
SR—*Schützen-Regiment.*

(f) INDEPENDENT SS LEGIONS

Since 1940 a number of national units have been recruited by the SS from various parts of occupied Europe. These were generally styled Legions. It is believed that all the original Legions have now been reorganised into more regular formations or units, but the term Legion may still be employed to cover the various organisations used to raise and maintain them. The following table gives a list of identified SS Legions, together with details of known reorganisation :—

SS Legion	Reorganised as	In
Freikorps Danmark	PGR Danmark	11. Nordland Div.
Estnische	*Estnische Freiw. Brig.	Independent
Flandern	Sturmbrig. Langemarck	Independent
Lettische	†15 Lettische Div.	—
Litauische	(Existence doubtful)	—
Nederland	Nederland Div.	—
Norwegen	PGR Norge	11. Nordland Div.
Wallonia	Sturmbrig. Wallonia	Independent

* An Estonian bn. (" Narva ") is incorporated in 5. Wiking Div.
† Latvian units are also incorporated in 2. SS Inf. Brig.

(*g*) FORMATION HISTORIES

(i) SS CORPS

(I) **SS Panzer Corps**

Commander :—SS Oberstgruppenführer and Genobst. of the Waffen SS Sepp DIETRICH (51).

Formed summer of 1943.

(II) **SS Panzer Corps**

Commander :—SS Obergruppenführer and General of the Waffen SS Paul HAUSSER (63).

Formed in the summer of 1942. Took part in operations round Kharkov and Byelgorod in the first part of 1943. Subsequently moved to northern Italy.

(III) **SS (Germanic) Panzer Corps**

Commander :—SS Gruppenführer and Genlt. of the Waffen SS Felix STEINER (47).

Formed in the spring of 1943. Operating in Yugoslavia autumn 1943.

IV. **SS (Germanic ?) Panzer Corps**

Commander :—

Believed forming in the West in 1943.

V. **SS Mountain Corps**

Commander :—Obergruppenführer and General of the Waffen SS Arthur PHLEPS (62).

Formed summer 1943. Operating in Yugoslavia in winter 1943–44.

(ii) **SS DIVISIONS**

1. **Leibstandarte SS Adolf Hitler (LSSAH)**

Commander :—SS Oberführer and Obst. of the Waffen SS Theodor WISCH (36).

Composition :—Two Pz. Gren. Regts., Pz. Regt., Arty. Regt., Assault Gun Abt., Recce. Unit, A.Tk. Bn., Flak Abt., Eng. Bn., Sigs. Bn.

Ancillary number :—1.

Depot :—Berlin-Lichterfelde.

Formed in 1933 as a bodyguard regiment for the Führer. Took part in Polish and Western campaigns ; expanded into a division by spring of 1941, and was subsequently engaged in the Balkan and Russian campaigns. Withdrawn to France summer 1942 to reorganise as a Pz. Gren. Div. Sent to Russia and took part in operations round Kharkov and Byelgorod. Moved to Italy autumn 1943 but returned to Russia for the German counter-offensive in the Kiev sector.

2. **SS Pz. Div. Das Reich**

Commander :—SS Gruppenführer and Genlt. of the Waffen SS Walter KRÜGER (53).

Composition :—Pz. Gren. Regt. Deutschland, Pz. Gren. Regt. Der Führer, M.C. Regt. Langemarck, Pz. Regt., Arty. Regt., Assault Gun Abt., Recce. Unit, A.Tk. Bn., Flak Abt., Eng. Bn., Sigs. Bn.

Ancillary number :—2.

Depots :—Pz. Gren. Regt. Deutschland, Prague.
Pz. Gren. Regt. Der Führer, ? Stettin.

Formed by spring 1941 from the former SS Verfügungs Division. Took part in the Balkan and Russian campaigns. Withdrawn to France to reorganise as a Pz. Gren. Div. in summer 1942. Sent to Russia and took part in fighting in the Kharkov area in spring 1943. Has been continuously engaged since then in the southern sector.

3. **SS Pz. Div. Totenkopf**

Commander :—SS Brigadeführer and Genmaj. of the Waffen SS Hermann PRIESS (42).

Composition :—Three SS Totenkopf Pz. Gren. Regts. (one named Theodor EICKE)*, Pz. Regt., Arty. Regt., Assault Gun Abt., Recce. Unit, A.Tk. Bn., Flak Abt., Eng. Bn., Sigs. Bn.

Ancillary number :—3.

Depot :—Berlin-Oranienburg.

Formed in 1939 mainly from concentration camp guard units and fought in the western campaign. Was among the divisions encircled near Staraya Russa in January, 1942, and distinguished itself in the defence of Demyansk. Withdrawn to France autumn, 1942, to reorganise as a Pz. Gren. Div. Sent to Russia early 1943 and took part in fighting in the Donetz area, where the divisional commander Theodor EICKE was killed in action. Has since been continuously engaged in the southern sector.

4. **SS Polizei Pz. Gren. Div.**

Commander :—

Composition :—Pol. Pz. Gren. Regts. 7 and 8, Arty. Regt., Recce. Unit, A.Tk. Bn., Flak Abt., Eng. Bn., Sigs. Bn.

Ancillary number :—4.

Depot :—

Formed in autumn, 1939, by drafts from police units in all parts of Germany. Took part in the Western campaign, and since 1941 has been engaged on the Leningrad front. Became a motorised division in autumn, 1942. Bulk of division moved to Greece in autumn, 1943, when a measure of reorganisation took place.

---

* One Totenkopf regiment was probably converted to M.C. Regt

5. SS Pz. Div. Wiking

Commander :—SS. Gruppenführer and Genlt. of the Waffen SS Herbert GILLE (46).

Composition :—Pz. Gren. Regt. Germania, Pz. Gren. Regt. Westland, Pz. Regt., Arty. Regt., Assault Gun Abt., Recce. Unit, A.Tk. Bn., Flak Abt., Eng. Bn., Sigs. Bn.

Ancillary number :—5.

Depots :—Pz. Gren. Regt. Germania, Arnheim (Holland).
Pz. Gren. Regt. Westland, Klagenfurt.

Formed in spring 1941 from a regiment of the SS Verfügungs Division and from Scandinavian and Flemish volunteers. The Scandinavian regiment Nordland was apparently withdrawn in 1943. The division now includes the Estonian Bn. Narva. The division took part in the Russian campaign of 1941 in the Rostov area. In 1942 reorganised as a Pz. Gren. Div. and fought in the Caucasus, and in the German counter-attacks between the Don and Dnieper in spring 1943. Has since been continuously engaged in the southern sector.

6. SS Geb. Div. Nord

Commander :—SS Gruppenführer and Genlt. of the Waffen SS Matthias KLEINHEISTERKAMP (50).

Composition :—SS Mtn. Rifle Regt. Reinhardt HEYDRICH*, Mtn. Rifle Regt., Mtn. Arty. Regt., Assault Gun Abt., Recce. Unit, A.Tk. Bn., Flak Abt., Mountain Eng. Bn., Sigs. Bn.

Ancillary number :—6.

Depots :—Trautenau.
Wehlau.

Formed in the summer of 1941 and continuously stationed since then in Finland, fighting on the Murmansk and Salla sectors. Is believed to include a Norwegian ski battalion.

7. SS Freiw. Geb. Div. Prinz Eugen

Commander :—SS Brigadeführer and Genmaj. of the Waffen SS Carl Ritter von OBERKAMP (50).

Composition :—Two SS Geb. Jg. Regts., Tk. Sqn., Arty. Regt., Recce. Unit, Cyclist Bn., A.Tk.Bn., Flak Abt., Mtn. Eng. Bn., Sigs. Bn.

---

* Formerly SS Mtn. Regt. 6.

Ancillary number :—7.

Depot :—Pancevo (near Belgrade).

Formed in spring of 1942 and includes large numbers of racial Germans from Hungary and Roumania. Since autumn, 1942, has been engaged in anti-guerilla warfare in Yugoslavia.

8. **SS Kavallerie Division (SS Cavalry Division)**

Commander :—SS Brigadeführer and Genmaj. of the Waffen SS Hermann FEGELEIN (37).

Composition :—Four Cavalry Regts., Arty. Regt., Recce. Unit, A.Tk. Bn., Flak Abt., Eng. Bn., Sigs. Bn.

Ancillary number :—8.

Depot :—Warsaw.

Formed in summer of 1942 by expansion of the SS Cavalry Brigade. Mainly composed of racial Germans from Hungary. In action on the central sector in Russia from autumn, 1942, often in anti-guerilla warfare. Moved to southern sector in autumn, 1943, where it is believed to have suffered heavy casualties.

9. **SS Pz. Div. Hohenstaufen**

Commander :—SS Gruppenführer and Genlt. of the Waffen SS Willi BITTRICH (49).

Composition :—Two Pz. Gren. Regts., M.C. Regt., Pz. Regt., Arty, Regt., Assault Gun Bty., A.Tk. Bn., A.A. Bty., Eng. Bn., Sigs. Bn.

Ancillary number :—9.

Depot :—

Forming in the West since early 1943.

10. **SS Pz. Div. Frundsberg**

Commander :—

Composition :—Two Pz. Gren. Regts., M.C. Bn., Pz. Regt., Arty. Regt., A.Tk. Bn., A.A. Bty., Eng. Bn., Sigs. Bn.

Ancillary number :—10.

Depot :—

Forming in the West since early 1943.

11. **SS Pz. Gren. Div. Nordland**

Commander :—SS Brigadeführer and Genmaj. of the Waffen SS Fritz von SCHOLZ (47).
Composition :—SS Pz. Gren. Regt. Norge, SS Pz. Gren. Regt. Danmark, Pz. Bn.
Ancilliary number :—11.
Depot :—

Formed in Germany summer 1943 from SS Pz. Gren. Regt. Nordland and Scandinavian SS Legions. Operating in Yugoslavia late autumn 1943.

12. **SS Pz. Div. Hitler Jugend**

Commander :—SS Oberführer and Obst. of the Waffen SS Fritz WITT (35).
Composition :—
Ancillary number :—12.
Depot :—

Forming autumn 1943 in Belgium from cadres largely supplied by Leibstandarte SS Adolf Hitler.

13. **SS Freiw. BH* Geb. Div. Kroatien (SS Volunteer BH Mtn. Div. Croatia)**

Commander :—SS Brigadeführer and Genmaj. of the Waffen SS SAUBERZWEIG.
Composition :—
Ancillary number :—13.
Depot :—

Formed in spring, 1943, from Moslem and Catholic subjects of the Kingdom of Croatia. Organisation believed similar to that of SS Geb. Div. Prinz Eugen.

14. **SS Schützen Div. Galizien**

Commander :—
Composition :—
Ancillary number :—14.
Depot :—

Formed in Poland in summer, 1943, from Polish and Ukranian volunteers.

---

* BH may stand for Bosanka-Hrvatska (Bosnian-Croatian), or Bosnia-Herzegovina.

15. **SS Lettische Freiw. Division (SS Latvian Volunteer Div.)**

Commander :—SS Brigadeführer and Genmaj. of the Waffen SS Carl-Friedrich Graf von PÜCKLER-BURGHAUSS.

Composition :—

Ancillary number :—15.

Depot :—? Riga.

Formed in Latvia in 1943 from Lettish volunteers. Believed to be in the northern sector of the Russian front in autumn, 1943.

16. **SS Pz. Gren. Div. Reichsführer SS**

Commander :—

Composition :—Two SS Pz. Gren. Regts., Arty. Regt.

Ancillary number :—16.

Depot :—

Forming winter 1943–1944 in North Italy by expansion of the former SS Assault Brigade of the same name.

17. **SS. Pz. Gren. Div. Götz von Berlichingen**

Commander :—

Composition :—

Ancillary number :—? 17.

Depot :—

Forming in France, winter, 1943–1944.

? SS Pz. Gren. Div. Nederland

Commander :—

Composition :—

Ancillary number :—?

Depot :—

Formed 1943 probably by expansion of the former SS Legion Nederland. Although publicised as a division at formation, was only at brigade strength when first identified operating in Yugoslavia in late autumn, 1943.

PART G—SEMI-MILITARY AND AUXILIARY ORGANISATIONS

CONTENTS

INTRODUCTION

In this Part a brief survey is given of such semi-military organisations as are likely to be found co-operating closely with the German army in the field, although organised, equipped and, if need be, maintained independently.

The following abbreviations, which will frequently be met with in documents relating to the SS, police and other semi-military organisations, are employed in sections (*a*) to (*d*) below :—

Abbreviation	*Signification*	*In English*
Abs.	Abschnitt	(SS) administrative area.
B.d.O.	Befehlshaber der Ordnungspolizei.	G.O.C. Uniformed Police.
B.d.Sipo u.d. SD	Befehlshaber der Sicherheitspolizei und des Sicherheitsdienstes.	G.O.C. Security Police and (SS) Security Service.
C.d.S.	Chef der Sicherheitspolizei ..	Head of the Security Police.
d.G.	der Gendarmerie	Of the Gendarmerie.
Gen.Govt. ..	General Gouvernement ..	General-Government (in Poland).
Gestapo ..	Geheime Staatspolizei ..	Secret State Police.
HA	Hauptamt	Central Office.
H.SS Pf. ..	Höherer SS und Polizeiführer.	Senior SS and Police Commander.
I.d.O.	Inspekteur der Ordnungspolizei.	Inspector of Uniformed Police.
I.D.Sipo u.d. SD	Inspekteur der Sicherheitspolizei und des Sicherheitsdienstes.	Inspector of Security Police and Security Service.
K.d.G. ..	Kommandeur der Gendarmerie.	O.C. Gendarmerie.
K.d.O. ..	Kommandeur der Ordnungspolizei.	O.C. Uniformed Police.
K.d.Schupo ..	Kommandeur der Schutzpolizei.	O.C. Municipal Police.
K.d.Sipo u.d. SD	Kommandeur der Sicherheitspolizei und des Sicherheitsdienstes.	O.C. Security Police and Security Service.

Abbreviation	*Signification*	*In English*
Kripo	Kriminalpolizei	Criminal Police.
LS Pol. ..	Luftschutzpolizei	A.R.P. Police.
N.S.K.K. ..	National Sozialistisches Kraftfahrkorps.	Nazi Party M.T. Corps.
Oa.	Oberabschnitt	(SS) administrative district.
Orpo	Ordnungspolizei	Uniformed Police.
O.T.	Organisation Todt	Todt Construction Organisation.
RAD	Reichsarbeitsdienst ..	National Labour Service.
Rf. SS	Reichsführer SS	State SS Leader.
RSHA	Reichssicherheitshauptamt	Central Security Police H.Q.
Schupo ..	Schutzpolizei	Municipal Police.
SD	Sicherheitsdienst	(SS) Security Service.
SHD	Sicherheits- und Hilfsdienst	A.R.P. Emergency Service.
Sipo	Sicherheitspolizei	Security Police.
SS Pf.	SS und Polizeiführer ..	O.C. SS and Police.
SS Psf... ..	SS und Polizeistandortführer	O C. SS and Police Garrison.
Teno	Technische Nothilfe ..	Technical Emergency Corps.
Vomi	Volksdeutsche Mittelstelle ..	Bureau for repatriation of German ethnic groups.
Wkr.	Wehrkreis	(Army) administrative district.
z.b.V.	zu besonderer Verwendung	For special employment.

(*a*) THE SS AND POLICE ORGANISATION

The German Police have been transformed by the National Socialist regime from an uncoordinated federal system into a single body within the Reich Ministry of the Interior. It is under the direct control of HIMMLER whose official title is *Reichsführer SS und Chef der Deutschen Polizei im Reichsministerium des Innern.* Thus HIMMLER, who is also Minister of the Interior, coordinates the security forces of both State and Party and is virtually dictator of the Home Front. The fusion of Police and SS is reflected in many administrative directions and in the double rank titles carried by officers belonging to these bodies (*e.g., SS Standartenführer* and *Oberst der Schutzpolizei*).

(i) **The SS** (Schutzstaffel)

2. The SS is the *corps d'elite* of the National Socialist Party. Originally formed as protective squads for political meetings and bodyguards for the leaders of the party, it has been considerably expanded and is now widely employed, both for internal security duties in Germany and German occupied territories, and in permanently embodied military formations.

HITLER is the supreme Head of the SS ; under him, HIMMLER is the executive chief of the organisation, with H.Q. in Berlin. This H.Q. is in effect a complete Ministry, with branches and departments comparable to most of those maintained by the three service ministries for the recruiting, training, equipment, administration and control of the SS organisation.

For administrative purposes, much of the work is decentralised to district H.Q. (*SS Oberabschnitte,* abbreviated SS Oa.) ; the administrative districts correspond very closely, topographically, to the *Wehrkreise*—but they are known by names and not by numbers.

The SS districts are normally sub-divided into either two or three areas (*Abschnitte*), which carry roman numbers ; the following table shows this topographical organisation in detail :—

SS District (*component areas*)	*H.Q.*	*Corresponding Wehrkreis*
Alpenland (XXXV, XXXVI) ..	Salzburg ..	XVIII
Donau (VIII, XXXI)	Vienna ..	XVII
Elbe (II, XVIII, XXXVII) ..	Dresden ..	IV
Fulda-Werra (XXVII, XXX) ..	Arolsen ..	IX
Main (IX, XXVIII, XXXVIII) ..	Nürnberg ..	XIII
Mitte (IV, XVI)	Brunswick ..	XI
Nordost (VII, XXII, XXXIV) ..	Königsberg ..	I
Nordsee (XIV, XV, XX)	Hamburg ..	X
Ostsee (XIII, XXXIII)	Stettin.. ..	II
Rhein* (XI, XXXIV)	Wiesbaden ..	XII

* Includes former Oa WESTMARK and sometimes styled Oa RHEIN-WESTMARK.

SS District (*component areas*)	*H.Q.*	*Corresponding Wehrkreis*
Spree (III, XII, XXIII)	Berlin	III
Süd (I, XXXII)	Munich ..	VII
Südost (VI, XXI, XXIV)	Breslau ..	VIII
Südwest (X, XIX, XXIX, XXXXV)	Stuttgart ..	V
Warthe (XXXXII, XXXXIII) ..	Posen	XXI
Weichsel (XXVI, XXXX, XXXXI)	Danzig ..	XX
West (V, XVII, XXV)	Düsseldorf ..	VI

In addition to the above there are two foreign OA :—

	H.Q.	*Area*
Nord	Oslo	Norway
Nordwest	Hague ..	Holland
Ostland	Riga	Latvia
and one Abschnitt in the Protectorate of		
Bohemia/Moravia (XXXIX) ..	Prague ..	—

Each district is commanded by a senior SS officer, who is also HIMMLER'S immediate representative at the H.Q. of the corresponding Wehrkreis ; in the latter capacity he is described as *Höherer SS und Polizeiführer* (abbreviated H.SSPf., *i.e.*, Senior SS and Police Commander) in the Wehrkreis concerned.

In the case of SS and police units stationed in occupied countries a Senior SS and Police Commander and staff assumes control, co-operating closely with the military administration but closely controlled by the SS H.Q. in Berlin ; within an occupied country an area may be assigned, if this is thought necessary, to an SS and Police Commander, whose sphere of command corresponds in status to the *Abschnitt* in Germany.

In certain areas outside Germany where there is a number of SS depot in training units permanently stationed, *e.g.*, Holland, the Protectorate of Bohemia and Moravia, a regional commander of the Waffen SS (*Befehlshaber der Waffen SS*) has been appointed. Although presumably subordinate to the senior SS and police commander patrolling his area, the *Befehlshaber der Waffen SS* is likely in such cases to have the real responsibility for the local administration of the Waffen SS.

The units of the SS fall into two distinct categories, namely *Allgemeine* SS (Ordinary SS) and *Waffen-SS* (Armed SS). The former consists of part-time volunteers (with a permanent administrative staff) employed for general security purposes within Germany, and need not, therefore, be considered here: the *Waffen-SS* is mentioned among the semi-military services in section (*b*) below, but is dealt with in full in Part F.

(ii) **Police** (Polizei)

The Police is divided into two main branches, as follows :—

Ordnungspolizei, Orpo : uniformed constabulary, including the municipal *Schutzpolizei* (Schupo), rural *Gendarmerie*, river and fire-fighting police and A.R.P. police (LSPol.). The barrack police battalions (Section (*b*) below) are drawn from this branch, the head of which is *General der Polizei SS Obergruppenführer* WÜNNENBERG.

Sicherheitspolizei, Sipo : Security police, comprising the Secret State Police (*Geheime Staatspolizei*—Gestapo) and the Criminal Police (*Kriminalpolizei*—Kripo). The Secret State Police have as their special task the liquidation and prevention of all activity inimical to the regime ; the force works in close touch with the Secret Field Police (Part D, Section (*o*) 4 above), the personnel of which is largely drawn from the Security Police.

The Police in general and the security police in particular are closely related to the Security Service of the SS (*Sicherheitsdienst des Reichsführers SS*, abbreviated SD Rf.SS) ; this was originally the intelligence branch of the SS, but since 1936 it has been directly connected with the security police through the appointment as head of both services (*Chef der Sicherheitspolizei und des SD*) of Reinhard HEYDRICH. Following the assassination of HEYDRICH the post of C.d.S. was filled by *General der Polizei SS Obergruppenführer* KALTENBRUNNER.

Each branch of the Police is administered from a central office (*Hauptamt* or HA) in Berlin, *i.e.*, the *Hauptamt* Orpo and the *Reichssicherheitshauptamt* (RSHA). At regional and local levels the existing federal authorities exercise ex-officio police functions, but all Police and SS activity in the regions is co-ordinated by a Senior SS and Police Commander (para. 6 above). In addition to being the direct personal representative of HIMMLER this office also assists the Gauleiter, in the latter's capacity of *Reichsverteidigungskommissar* (*i.e.*, regional defence commissioner) in regulating civil security measures.

Below the Senior SS and Police Commander, command is exercised by *Inspekteure* and *Befehlshaber* (posts which may be held independently or concurrently)—Inspectors and Commanders—qualified by *d.O.* or *d.Sipo u.d.SD*, according to their branch of the service.

The extent to which German police units operate in occupied countries depends on the extent to which the local national police service is thought strong and reliable enough to maintain law and order and to co-operate with the German military and civil authorities; the basic pattern followed in the majority of the occupied countries is that established in the Reich, namely, an H.SS Pf. with subordinate B.d.O. and B.d.Sipo und SD, with at lower levels, K.d.O. and K.d.Sipo und SD.

Apart from normal administrative personnel, the H.SS Pf may also employ regiments, battalions and lesser formations of uniformed police drawn from the German municipal barrack police (*Kasernierte* units of the Orpo—*see* Section (*b*) below; and mobile security police detachments (*Einsatzkommandos der Sipo u.d. SD*). Although the latter are mainly concerned with political and economic counter-intelligence they are also concerned in tasks which normally fall within the province of the Military Security Service (*Abwehr*) and the G.F.P.

(*b*) SEMI-MILITARY SERVICES

In the following list brief particulars are given of the principal semi-military services which may be met with in the zone of the armies; in each case a note has been added on the uniform and distinguishing badges.

Waffen-SS (Armed SS): This is a fully militarised and permanently embodied force organised in corps, divisions and a number of independent brigades and regiments. It is in principle raised, administered and maintained by the SS organisation but its operational control comes under the competent *Wehrmacht* authorities. Non-divisional units are normally employed for "mopping up" purposes on the L. of C., coming under the operational control, in some cases, of the Army Group L. of C. Commander; they may also, however, be employed on occasions in the front line, subordinated to the nearest convenient Army formation. (See Part F).

> *Uniform*: Field grey as in the Army, but the national emblem is worn on the upper left sleeve instead of on the right breast; the cap badge is a skull and crossbones and the SS sign is worn on the right-hand side of the steel helmet and on the collar facings.

Police battalions: These may be either fully or partly motorised; the battalion is approximately 550 strong and consists of H.Q. and four companies ; it is equipped with rifles, machine guns, anti tank guns and armoured cars. Police battalions are normally used for internal security or " mopping up " duties, but they may, if necessary, be employed in the line under Army command. Whilst tactically they remain independent units, for administrative purposes they are grouped into police regiments of three battalion strength and numbered in series 1–50 (about 35 identified).

Uniform : Field grey with dark-brown collar and cuffs and white metal buttons. The police version of the national emblem—the eagle and swastika enclosed in and resting on a wreath of oak leaves—is worn on the left sleeve and on the cap, shako or steel helmet.

**National Sozialistisches Kraftfahrkorps,* N.S.K.K. (Nazi Party M.T. Corps) : The functions of this organisation are varied. It provides pre-military training for the armoured and motorised units of the Army ; undertakes traffic control as an auxiliary police corps ; and supplements the transport services of the armed forces. For this last purpose there exists an N.S.K.K. Transport Brigade called SPEER (the Reich Minister for Armaments and Munitions) divided into regiments attached to the Army and Air Force.

In addition the N.S.K.K. is responsible for the transport arrangements for the organisation TODT (*see* below) and a *Transportgruppe TODT* has been established to meet the requirements of the O.T.

Uniform : Brown shirt and black breeches. The national emblem is mounted on a wheel enclosing a swastika, and is worn on the cap or black crash-helmet; white arabic numerals preceded by the letter " M " on the right-hand collar patch give the number of the battalion. In the case of the SPEER regiments the letters SP are carried on the right-hand collar patch. Personnel employed in TODT transport wear a white brassard on the left arm inscribed " Org. Todt " over the national emblem.

**Organisation Todt,* O.T. (Todt Construction Organisation) : This was first formed by the late Dr. TODT, for the construction of the *Autobahn* system, and was subsequently expanded to build the western defences known in this country as the Siegfried Line and in Germany as the *Westwall.* It is now employed to assist army engineer units in road building, railway repairs, bridge construction, etc., in the wake of advancing troops, and for longer term in occupied territory, *e.g.*, restoring and expanding communications, preparing sites for aerodromes, building fortifications, clearing harbours of wreckage. It is organised in battalions and labour gangs composed of hired foreign labour with a nucleus of skilled German personnel.

O.T. guard detachments (*Schutzkommandos*) also exist. Their normal armament is believed to consist of rifle, M.P. and L.M.G. The M.T. is provided by the N.S.K.K. mainly, but in part by local contractors.

Uniform : In principle, only the German members of the organisation wear uniform—a khaki-coloured tunic, open at the neck, and breeches ; on the left sleeve is a red brassard with a black swastika set in white circle and, immediately above, the inscription "Org. Todt" in black letters on white. This inscription may alternatively be worn on a separate brassard above the left cuff. Foreign workers normally wear civilian clothes with a red or white brassard inscribed "Org. Todt" on the left arm. Those employed in the West may, in addition, carry their nationol colours in a shield on the brassard.

**Reichsarbeitsdienst*, R.A.D. (State Labour Service) : All German men who are physically fit are required in peace time to perform six months' service in the R.A.D. before beginning their military service. They are organised in companies under a cadre of permanent officers and N.C.O.s, and such companies are available in considerable numbers for service on the L. of C. and in occupied countries, where they provide additional manual labour for the O.T.

Uniform : Brownish-grey tunic with dark-brown collar. Standard white fatigue dress may also be worn. On the left sleeve the R.A.D. emblem (a spade head containing the arabic number of the unit) and, beneath it, a red brassard with a black swastika set in a white circle.

**Technische Nothilfe*, Teno *or* T.N. (Technical Emergency Corps) : An auxiliary police, the Teno is used in the zone of the armies or in occupied territory for such tasks as the restoration of essential services, the demolition of damaged buildings, the removal of unexploded bombs, or the reconstruction of installations of all kinds ; in Germany it plays an important part in A.R.P. work.

Uniform : When serving in the field, field grey, with a narrow armband immediately above the left cuff with the inscription "Technische Nothilfe" in white ; the police version of the national emblem is now worn on the upper arm in place of the standard *Hoheitsabzeichen*. In addition, Teno officers may be found wearing the SS flash on their collar patches in combination with the Teno emblem—a cog wheel ; the latter may also be carried immediately above the left cuff.

---

* Personnel of these services are equipped, wherever it is thought necessary, with rifles and in some cases with M.G.s for protective purposes or guard duty.

(c) PARTY ORGANISATIONS

Certain uniformed organisations of the Party, in addition to those described above, may also be considered as potential auxiliary units to the military forces and are likely to be encountered performing important functions in the occupied countries. The following are the principal organisations of this type :—

(i) NSDAP, *the National-Socialist Party as such.*—It is organised regionally down to the smallest local units, and its officials, known as *politische Leiter,* keep close control of the activities of all German civilians at home and abroad.

(ii) *Sturmabteilungen,* SA (*storm troops*).—These are organised on a pattern similar to that of the *SS* and are now used for a great variety of purposes on the home front, including the pre-military training of men over 18 who for some reason have not yet been called to the colours. The great majority of *SA* men, and particularly of *SA* officers, are now serving in the Army as regular soldiers. The 60th Motorised Division is officially stated to consist of volunteers from the *SA* and has been given the honorary designation of *Panzer-Grenadier-Division "Feldherrnhalle."*

The present chief (*Stabschef*) of the *SA* is Wilhelm SCHEPMANN.

(iii) *Nationalsozialistisches Fliergerkorps,* NSFK (*Nazi Party Aviation Corps*).—This organisation performs an important function in training personnel for the Air Force and particularly in developing the use of gliders. Until recently it was headed by General der Flieger Friedrich CHRISTIANSEN ; its present chief, with the title *Korpsführer,* is Generaloberst Alfred KELLER.

(iv) *Hitler-Jugend,* HJ (*Hitler Youth Organisation*).—All German youths up to their 17th birthday belong to this organisation, which is in charge of their thorough pre-military training and indoctrination. This has recently been greatly expanded in the so-called military fitness camps (*Wehrertüchtigungslager*). The *HJ* is headed by *Reichsjugendführer* Arthur AXMANN.

PART H—FOREIGN LEGIONS AND UNITS

FOREIGN LEGIONS AND UNITS

The Germans started enlisting foreigners into the army (as opposed to the S.S.) early in 1942. These units, which have chiefly German officers and some German N.C.O.s, are mainly drawn from more or less disaffected minority nationalities in Russia, and many of the personnel in them are released prisoners-of-war. They are employed normally on L. of C. duties, and have little fighting value.

The following list excludes all foreign units of the S.S. (Part F) and all Belgian, French and Croatian divisions or units, which are numbered in the main German divisional or regimental series (Part L) and concentrates only on legions and units of East European nationality. It is arranged alphabetically, and shows the types of unit that are known to exist, and gives identifications where known.

(*a*) *Armenians*
Armenian Legion.
Armenian Infantry Battalion 808.
Armenian Infantry Battalion 809.

(*b*) *Azerbaijanians*
Azerbaijanian Legion.
Azerbaijanian Infantry Battalion 804.
Azerbaijanian Infantry Battalion 805.

(*c*) *Cossacks*
Cossack Construction Battalion.
Cossack "Century" (three are believed to exist).
Cossack Battalion 403 (cf. 403 Sich. Div.).

1 Cossack Division

Commander :—
Composition :—
Auxiliary unit number :—
Home Station :—

Formed in Poland in summer, 1943. Said to be composed of Cossacks from the Don, Kuban and Terek districts. Some of the troops in this Division may have previously performed L. of C. duties in Russia. The majority of officers are stated to be Cossacks, but some German officers are attached to the division, which is commanded by a German general. In autumn, 1943, it was operating in Croatia.

Cossack Construction Battalion.
Cossack "Century" (three are believed to exist).
Cossack Battalion 403 (cf. 403 Sich. Div.).

(*d*) *Esthonians*

Esthonian Battalion (38 believed to exist).
Esthonian Engineer Battalion (two believed to exist).
Esthonian Jäger Battalion (two believed to exist).

(*e*) *Georgians*

Georgian Legion.
Georgian Infantry Battalion 795.
Georgian Infantry Battalion 796.

(*f*) *Krim Tartars*

Tartar Legion.

(*g*) *Lithuanians*

Lithuanian Construction Battalion 4.

(*h*) *North Caucasians*

North Caucasian Legion.
North Caucasian Infantry Battalion 800.
North Caucasian Infantry Battalion 801.
North Caucasian Infantry Battalion 802.

(*i*) *Turcomans* (Turkestan)

Turcoman Infantry Division (*see* 162 Inf. Div., Part D).
Turcoman Legion.
Turcoman Construction Battalion.
Turcoman Infantry Battalion 450.
Turcoman Infantry Battalion 452.
Turcoman Guard Battalion 720.
Turcoman Infantry Battalion 781.
Turcoman Infantry Battalion 782.
Turcoman Infantry Battalion 783.
Turcoman Infantry Battalion 784.
Turcoman Infantry Battalion 785.
Turcoman Infantry Battalion 787.
Turcoman Supply Battalion.

(*j*) *Ukranians*

Ukranian "Century" 151.
Ukranian Supply Column 551.

(*k*) *Volga-Tartars*

Volga-Tartar Legion.

J 1

PART J—GERMAN FORCES IN ACTION

J 2

PART J.—GERMAN FORCES IN ACTION

The previous parts of this book have described in some detail the structure of the German Army and the basic organisation of its various elements. The present section is designed to explain briefly how these elements are combined in action in task forces and battle groups ; it is rare that they will be found in a pure state, when in action.

Like the Army, the German Navy and Air Force are composed of many different types of units for the various purposes which these branches of the service have to fulfil. The Navy includes coastal artillery units, naval A.A. artillery, naval air units, in addition to the various types of formations of fighting ships. The German Air Force has, in addition to its flying units, its various types of A.A. guns, aircraft warning service organisations, civilian A.R.P. organisations, signals, engineers, balloon barrage, and administrative units.

The O.K.W. considers all these types of units in all three services as a pool. Various units and formations may be withdrawn from this pool and formed into task forces, which then function as battle groups for specific operations. The factors considered in the selection of a combat team are :—

(*a*) Task.
(*b*) Commander's appreciation.
(*c*) Availability of units.

The commander will be selected from one of the three services, normally from the one which predominates in the task force or whose interests are paramount. He will be of a rank commensurate with the size of the force and the importance of its task.

Since tasks and circumstances may vary almost without limit, every German task force or battle group encountered is likely to be composed differently from any other. Standard German organisations, especially from the division (inclusive) upwards, should be regarded merely as frameworks, with a minimum of establishment fighting and supply units ; task forces and battle groups will be formed around these frameworks. Thus it is impossible, in the majority of cases, to determine the composition of the larger German formations at any particular time except by experience, *i.e.*, intelligence results, patrolling reports and results of fighting.

The standard German formations are given on establishment the minimum of fighting units necessary to act independently and a maximum number of fighting units is kept in the various types of G.H.Q. pool.

Consequently, when a German formation is engaged in battle it will almost invariably be reinforced by units from the G.H.Q. pools. When the amount of reinforcements is large, additional commanders with adequate staffs will also be attached. These G.H.Q. reinforcements have a decisive influence on the strength of the standard organisations, *e.g.*, the division. The German system as thus outlined is both rigid and flexible. It is rigid in the sense that all the units in the pool which holds any one arm are as nearly alike in composition and equipment as possible; it is flexible because the number of combining units from the various pools is utilised to obtain any sort of battle group which may be required for a given purpose.

Battle groups for a particular task are tactically independent and self-contained organisations; co-operation with other units and formations is arranged in advance; the battle group is not normally required to depend on any other units than those it contains to carry out its task. The battle group will be given a modicum of supply services to enable it to supply itself in the most urgent cases, but the elements of which it is composed may well continue administrative subordination to their parent unit or depot.

It is hardly necessary to point out that this arrangement of organisation for battle is economical and enables commanders to concentrate their striking force at the most crucial points without changing basic dispositions. The method is also deceptive to the enemy in that it is difficult for the latter to estimate the German strength in such a situation—though this may well be unintentional.

The German administrative organisation for supply and casualties is arranged in a similar fashion to that of the fighting organisations; the principle followed, however, is that the administrative plan is always subordinate to the tactical plan and must under all circumstances adapt itself to the latter; this, despite great efficiency on the part of the German administrative services, must be considered unsatisfactory and has contributed not inconsiderably to the Germans suffering from local shortages and bottlenecks. Like the tactical organisation, the administrative organisation is likely to be different in practically all situations.

One of the outstanding characteristics of the German military system is unity of command. All units engaged on a single task are under one commander, who is responsible for the execution of the task. As a corollary, two or more forces are never given the same task at the same time. Units from the Air Force, the Navy and the Army serve together under a commander chosen from one of the three. In basic training, likewise, great emphasis is placed on inter-service co-operation and on co-operation amongst the arms of the same service. Service rivalry is discouraged. The three services are all combined under the O.K.W. which would be similar in this country to an inter-service command serving under a combined War Office–Admiralty–Air Ministry.

To sum up, it should always be borne in mind, when appreciating the employment of German forces in any situation that there is a marked predilection in the German Army for the combination of the services, of all the arms and of any number of units for any specific task into one task force or battle group under one single commander.

PART K

LISTS OF SENIOR OFFICERS

CONTENTS

K 2

INTRODUCTION

In this part are included lists of senior officers of the German Army, given alphabetically within each rank down to and including Generalmajors ; and of senior officers of the G.A.F., whose titles of rank are indistinguishable from those of Army Officers, except in the case of full generals.

Lists of senior officers of the S.S. and Police are also given, in sections (*f*) and (*g*), below. It has not proved practicable to include a consolidated alphabetical index of all the officers mentioned, and it has been found necessary to exclude colonels from the present edition ; it is hoped that a list of colonels and a consolidated index may be issued subsequently.

The classified lists are preceded by a series of brief notes on German surnames, titles and ranks, which are liable to provide stumbling-blocks for all except specialists in their study.

(i) German Surnames

The most confusing form of German surname is that in which a person has two surnames, of which he habitually uses only one, since there is no rule of thumb to indicate which of the two names is generally used. For example, Field-Marshal von Lewinski genannt von Manstein (literally, von Lewinski *styled* von Manstein) is customarily known as von Manstein, and he is listed among the field-marshals under the letter M. By contrast Generalleutnant von Hartlieb genannt Walsporn is normally known as von Hartlieb, and he is therefore listed under the letter H.

In some cases of double surnames, where the term *genannt* is not employed, the *von* (equivalent to *de* in French surnames) is customarily transposed ; for example, General Geyr von Schweppenburg, formerly German M.A. in London, is normally referred to as von Geyr. In general, where two surnames are connected by *und* (and), the first of the two is used : thus Generalleutnant von Rothkirch und Panthen is usually described as von Rothkirch ; hyphenated names are often but not invariably used in full.

Christian names are seldom if ever used in signatures ; officers sign orders with name and rank only. It is therefore difficult, at times, to discover an officer's christian name or initials (neither of which are shown in any official document, except in his original gazetting or when two men of the same name and rank require distinguishing from each other), so that in a few cases in the following lists there is a possibility of confusion between officers having the same surname.

Academic degrees such as Dr. or Dr.Ing., in contrast to christian names, are regularly shown in front of the surname both in official documents and in signatures, and are therefore included in the following lists.

(ii) **German Titles**

Persons with hereditary titles are more frequently found in Germany than in Great Britain, because German titles do not pass only from eldest son to eldest son, or to the nearest male blood relation (as in the United Kingdom), but from the father to all his sons, who in their turn transmit them to their sons (except in certain princely families in which the title *Fürst* is borne solely by the head of the family. It is consequently only possible to find British equivalents for the heads of German titled families; the British counterparts of other titled members of such families bear either a courtesy title or no title at all. The titles most commonly met with are listed below.

Graf (Count): corresponding approximately to Earl. As with other titles, it is usually followed by *von*, though in referring to a Count the prefix is often omitted; thus Generalleutnant Graf von Sponeck is normally described as Graf Sponeck.

Freiherr, abbreviated *Frhr.* (Baron): corresponding approximately to the lowest degree of the British peerage. The title *Baron*, which also occurs, is of non-German origin. In conversation a *Freiherr* is generally referred to as *Baron*, the prefix *von* being omitted; thus, General-Oberst Frhr. v. Weichs is liable to be described as Baron Weichs.

Ritter (Knight): corresponding in some cases to Baronet and in others to Knight. A Ritter whose title is hereditary usually owns a *Rittergut* or Knight's estate and takes his name from it; in other cases the title is derived from a grant made to an officer for heroism in action or for distinguished service to the state; in Bavaria, until 1919, the Military Order of Max Joseph carried with it a patent of Knighthood which was not hereditary—hence the title of Field-Marshal Ritter von Leeb whose son, killed in action in Poland in 1939, was Lieutenant Leeb.

Edler (Noble): approximately equivalent to Baronet. The titles Ritter and Edler are, in most cases, of Bavarian or Austrian origin.

The prefix *von* corresponds most closely to the English suffix Esquire (in the strict sense), denoting the right to bear arms.

(iii) German Military Ranks

In the following table, the approximate English equivalent is given for each German rank. It should be noted, however, that the appointments held by officers of any given rank may vary widely in status, and no appointment carries or presupposes specific rank: for example :—

A *Generalmajor* may command an infantry regiment, a division or, on occasions, an army corps.

An infantry regiment may be commanded by a *Generalmajor*, an *Oberst*, an *Oberstleutnant* or, on occasions, a *Major*.

A " First General Staff Officer " (Ia) may be a *Hauptmann*, *Major*, *Oberstleutnant* or *Oberst*.

Abbreviation	*In full*	*In English*
Genfeldm., Gen.Feldm...	Generalfeldmarschall	Field-Marshal.
Genobst., Gen. Obst. ..	Generaloberst.. ..	*None* (Colonel-General).
Gen. (d. Inf., d.Geb.Tr., d.Kav., d.Pz.Tr., d.Art., d.Pion., d.Na.Tr.; d.Flieg., d.Flak, d.Luftna.Tr.).	General (der Infanterie—Gebirgstruppen—Kavallerie—Panzertruppen—Artillerie—Pioniere — Nachrichtentruppen; der Flieger — Flakartillerie — Luftnachrichtentruppen).	General (Infantry, Mountain Troops, Cavalry, Panzer Troops, Artillery, Engineers, Signal Troops; Air, A.A. Artillery, Air Signal Troops.
Genlt., Gen.Lt.	Generalleutnant ..	Lt.-General.
Genmaj., Gen.Maj. ..	Generalmajor ..	Maj.-General.
None	*None*	Brigadier.
Obst.	Oberst	Colonel.
Oberstlt., Obst.Lt. ..	Oberstleutnant ..	Lt.-Colonel.
Maj.	Major	Major.
Hptm.	Hauptmann	Captain.
Rittm.	Rittmeister	Captain (Cavalry).
Oblt., Ob.Lt.	Oberleutnant ..	Lieutenant.
Lt., Ltn.	Leutnant	Second-Lieutenant.
Fhj	Fahnenjunker ..	*None* (Candidate for Regular Commission).

In the German Army acting or temporary rank is not granted—hence the variety in ranks to be found among officers holding similar appointments; but two qualifications of rank occur:—

1. *Ernennung* (approximately the equivalent of brevet rank): An Oberstleutnant may be *ernannt* Oberst, or an Oberst *ernannt* Generalmajor, in order to obtain the higher rank sooner than his seniority in the lower rank would permit (promotion is normally strictly according to seniority up to and including the rank of Genlt.); such officers receive the pay of the higher rank, but do not obtain a specific seniority (*Rangdienstalter*, abbreviated R.D.A.) until their substantive promotion.
2. *Charakterisierung* (honorary rank): An officer may be *charakterisiert* to a higher rank (*e.g.*, to Major to Oberstleutnant); such officers do not receive the pay of the higher rank until their substantive promotion, but they obtain a specific seniority in a separate *charakterisiert* list; the qualification is regularly shown in titles of rank: *e.g.*, char. Oberst.

Officers are borne on separate lists, according to their status, as follows:—

Regular officers on the active list.—An *aktiv* officer is distinguished by the title of his rank without qualification: *e.g.*, Oberst.

Regular officers on the re-employed list.—During the period of maximum expansion of the German Army (1934–1939), large numbers of additional officers were required, in particular to hold administrative appointments; to meet this special requirement, an *Ergänzungs* list was formed, to which ex-officers were gazetted after undergoing suitable courses. An *Ergänzungs* officer is distinguished by the addition of (Erg.) or (E) to the title of his rank: *e.g.*, Oberst (Erg.). Officers on this list take precedence immediately after those holding the same rank on the active list.

Reserve officers.—Retired officers from the active or *Ergänzungs* list may be transferred to the reserve list, to which suitable candidates may be commissioned direct. Commissions on this list correspond to some extent, in peace time, to commissions in the Territorial Army. A reserve officer takes precedence immediately below *Ergänzungs* officers of the same rank, and is distinguished by the addition of *der Reserve*, *d.Res.* or *d.R.* to the title of his rank: *e.g.*, Oberst d.R.

Landwehr officers.—Reserve officers may be downgraded, because of age or relative unfitness, to the Landwehr list. Such officers are distinguished by the addition of *der Landwehr*, *d.Landw.* or *d.L.* to the title of rank: *e.g.*, Major d.L.

Over-age officers.—Officers who have passed the age-limit for their rank and list, but remain fit and willing to serve, are transferred to the *zu Verfugung* (i.e., available) list and are distinguished by the addition of *z.V.* to the title or rank : *e.g.*, Maj.d.R.z.V.

Unemployable retired officers.—Retired officers who are no longer fit or suitable for employment are described as *ausser Dienst* or *a.D.* : *e.g.*, Oberst a.D.

Regular officers on the emergency list.—For the duration of the war, emergency commissions (*auf Kriegsdauer*, abbreviated *a.K.*) are granted to suitable candidates ; such commissions rank immediately below those on the *aktiv* list.

(iv) **Officers of the Army Medical and Veterinary Services**

The names of officers of the Army Medical and Veterinary Services are not included in the following lists. The ranks in these services of the German Army, with the appointments normally held, are as follows :—

Medical Officers	*Ranking as*	*Normal Appointment*
Generaloberstabsarzt.	General	Chief of the Inspectorate of Army Medical Services.
Generalstabsarzt	Generalleutnant ..	Chief M.O. of army group or army.
Generalarzt ..	Generalmajor ..	Chief M.O. of corps or Wehrkreis.
Oberstarzt ..	Oberst	Chief M.O. of division.
Oberfeldarzt ..	Oberstleutnant ..	Chief M.O. of regiment, station, hospital or medical battalion.
Oberstabsarzt ..	Major	Senior M.O. of battalion, oi O.C. of a medical company.
Stabsarzt	Hauptmann ..	On the establishment of hospital, medical unit, etc., or attached to a combatant unit.
Oberarzt	Oberleutnant ..	
Assistenzarzt ..	Leutnant ..	
Feldunterarzt ..	—	

Veterinary Officers	*Ranking as*	*Normal appointment*
Generaloberstabsveterinär.	General	Chief of the Inspectorate of Army Veterinary Services.
Generalstabsveterinär.	Generalleutnant ..	Chief V.O. of army group or army.
Generalveterinär	Generalmajor ..	Chief V.O. of corps or Wehrkreis,
Oberstveterinär ..	Oberst	Chief V.O. of division, O.C. veterinary hospital.
Oberfeldveterinär	Oberstleutnant ..	
Oberstabsveterinär	Major	Senior M.O. of battalion or regt., O.C. a veterinary company.
Stabsveterinär ..	Hauptmann ..	On the establishment of veterinary unit or attached to a unit.
Oberveterinär ..	Oberleutnant ..	
Veterinär	Leutnant ..	

(v) Some Common Abbreviations

The following list contains the commonest abbreviations of name, style and appointment; it should be used in conjunction with the list of abbreviations of ranks (given above) and with the list of Order of Battle abbreviations in Part M.

Abbreviation	*Signification*	*In English*
Abt.Chef ..	Abteilungschef	Head of a section.
a.D.	ausser Dienst	*See* Introduction.
AHA	Allgemeines Heeresamt	General Army Branch, War Office.
a.K.	auf Kriegsdauer	*See* Introduction.
Bfh.	Befehlshaber	Army commander, commander.
char.	charakterisiert	*See* Introduction.
Ch. (d. Genstb.) ..	Chef (des Generalstabes)	Chief (of General Staff).
Ch H Rü u. BdE	Chef der Heeresrüstung und Befehlshaber des Ersatzheeres.	Head of Army Equipment and Commander of the Training Army (*i.e., War Office*).*
d.B.	des Beurlaubtenstandes	Holding a reserve or a Landwehr commission.
d.G.	des Generalstabes ..	Of the General Staff.
d.L., d.R. ..	der Landwehr, der Reserve.	*See* Introduction.
Dipl.	Diplomierter	Certificated.
Dr.	Doktor	Doctor (of any branch of learning).
Erg., E	Ergänzungs	*See* Introduction.
ern.	ernannt	*See* Introduction.
Frhr.	Freiherr	Baron.
Fü.	Führer	O.C., acting commander.
gen.	genannt	*See* Introduction.
Gen.Qu	Generalquartiermeister ..	Q.M.G.
Genstb.d.H. ..	Generalstab des Heeres ..	General Staff, Army.
höh.	höherer	Senior.
Ia	(*pronounced "einss ah"*)	*See* Introduction.
i.G.	im Generalstabe ..	In the General Staff.
Ing.	Ingenieur	Technical engineer.
Insp., Inspiz. ..	Inspekteur, Inspizient ..	Inspector.
Kdr.	Kommandeur	O.C., commander.
Kdt.	Kommandant	O.C., commandant.
Kom.Gen. ..	KommandierenderGeneral	Corps commander.
Landw., L. ..	Landwehr	"Landwehr" (*see* Introduction).
Leit.	Leiter	O.C., head.

* *See* Part A.

Abbreviation	*Signification*	*In English*
Lw.	Luftwaffe	"Luftwaffe," G.A.F.
Ob.Bfh.	Oberbefehlshaber	Army group commander.
Ob.d.H.	Oberbefehlshaber des Heeres.	C.-in-C., Army.
Offz.	Offizier	Officer.
O.K.H.	Oberkommando des Heeres.	Army G.H.Q., War Ministry.
O.K.W.	Oberkommando der Wehrmacht.	Armed Forces G.H.Q., Defence Ministry.
OQu	Oberquartiermeister	D.C.G.S., A.Q.M.G.
PA	Heeres-Personalamt	Army Personnel Branch.
R.D.A.	Rangdienstalter	*See* Introduction.
Res., R	Reserve	Reserve (*see* Introduction).
R.L.M.u.Ob.d.L.	Reichsluftfahrtminister und Oberbefehlshaber der Luftwaffe.	Air Minister and C.-in-C., Air Force.
Rü	Rüstungs-	Equipment, armament.
stv.	stellvertretender	Deputy.
Uffz.	Unteroffizier	N.C.O.
v.	von	*See* Introduction.
(V)	(Verwaltung)	Administration.
WaA	Heeres-Waffenamt	Army Ordnance Branch.
WeWi	Wehrwirtschaft	Military Economics.
z.b.V.	zu besonderer Verwendung	For special employment.
z.V.	zu Verfügung	*See* Introduction.

(*a*) **Rank : GENERALFELDMARSCHALL (Field Marshal)**

Name (*age*)	*Appointment* (*date*)	*Seniority*	*Arm*
BOCK, Fedor v. (64)	Retired	19. 7.40	Inf.
BRAUCHITSCH, Walther v. (63)	Retired	19. 7.40	Art.
BUSCH, Ernst (59)	16 Army	1. 2.43	Inf.
KEITEL, Wilhelm (62)	Chief of O.K.W.	19. 7.40	Art.
KLEIST, Ewald v. (63)	H. Gru. A	1. 2.43	Kav.
KLUGE, Günther v. (62)	H. Gru. Mitte	19. 7.40	Art.
KÜCHLER, Georg. v. (63)	H. Gru. Nord	30. 6.42	Art.
LEEB, Wilhelm Ritter v. (68)	Retired	19. 7.40	Art.
LIST, Wilhelm (64)	Retired	19. 7.40	Inf.
MANSTEIN, Fritz Erich v. LEWINSKI gen. v. (57).	H. Gru. Süd	1. 7.42	Inf.
PAULUS, Friedrich (54)	Prisoner of War	31. 1.43	Pz. Tr.
ROMMEL, Erwin (53)	Insp. Gen. of Defence	22. 6.42	Pz. Tr.
RUNDSTEDT, Gerd v. (69)	H. Gru. West	19. 7.40	Inf.
WEICHS, Maximilian Frhr. v. (63)	H. Gru. F	1. 2.43	Kav.
WITZLEBEN, Erwin v. (63)	Retired	19. 7.40	Inf.

(*b*) **Rank : GENERALOBERST (Colonel-General)**

Name (age)	Appointment (date)	Seniority	Arm
ARNIM, Jürgen v. (55)	Prisoner of War	3.12.42	Pz. Tr.
BLASKOWITZ, Johannes (61)	1 Army	1.10.39	Inf.
DIETL, Eduard (54)	20 Mtn. Army	1. 6.42	Geb. Tr.
DOLLMANN, Friedrich (62)	7 Army	19. 7.40	Art.
FALKENHORST, Nikolaus v. (59)	Army of Norway, C.O.G. Norway	19. 7.40	Inf.
FROMM, Fritz (56)	Ch.H. Rü u. Bde.	19. 7.40	Art.
GUDERIAN, Heinz (56)	Insp. d. Pz. Waffe	19. 7.40	Pz. Tr.

Rank : Generaloberst (*Colonel-General*)—*continued*

Name (*age*)	*Appointment* (*date*)	*Seniority*	*Arm*
HALDER, Franz (60)	Retired	19. 7.40	Art.
HEINRICI, Gotthard (57)	4 Army	1. 1.43	Inf.
HEITZ, Walter (66)	Prisoner of War	31. 1.43	Art.
HOEPNER, Erich (58)	Retired	19. 7.40	Kav.
HOLLIDT, Karl (53)	6 Army	1. 9.43	Inf.
HOTH, Hermann (60)	4 Pz. Army	1. 7.40	Inf.
JAENECKE, Erwin (52)	17 Army	30. 1.44	Pio.
JODL, Alfred (54)	C. of S. O.K.W.	30. 1.44	Art.
LINDEMANN, Georg (60)	18 Army	1. 7.42	Kav.
MACKENSEN, Eberhard v. (55)	..	6. 7.43	Kav.
MODEL, Walter (53)	9 Army	1. 2.42	Pz. Tr.
REINHARDT, Georg-Hans (57)	3 Pz. Army	1. 1.42	Pz. Tr.
RUOFF, Richard (59)	Retired	1. 4.42	Inf.
SALMUTH, Hans v. (56)	15 Army	1. 1.43	Inf.
SCHMIDT, Rudolf (58)	..	1. 3.42	Pz.Tr.
STRAUSS, Adolf (65)	Retired	19. 7.40	Inf.
VIETINGHOFF gen. SCHEEL, Heinrich v. (57).	10 Army	1. 9.43	Pz. Tr.
WEISS, Walter (54)	..	30. 1.44	Inf.
ZEITZLER, Kurt (49)	C. of S. O.K.H.	30. 1.44	Inf.

(*c*) **Rank : GENERAL (d. Inf., Kav., etc.)**

ALLMENDINGER, Karl (52)	..	1. 4.43	Inf.
ANGELIS, Maximilian (55)	XXXXIV A.K.	1. 3.42	Art.
BADER, Paul (59)	XXI Geb. K.	1. 7.41	Art.
BARCKHAUSEN, Franz (62)	Wi. Rü. Stab Frankreich	1. 7.43	Art.
BEHLENDORFF (55)	LXXXIV A.K.	1.10.41	Art.
BIELER, Bruno (56)	LXXXVI A.K.	1.10.41	Inf.
BOCK; Max (62)	Retired	1.12.40	Inf.
BÖCKMANN, Herbert v. (57)	..	1. 4.42	Inf.
BÖHME, Franz (59)	XVIII Geb. K.	1. 8.40	Inf.
BOETTICHER, Friedrich v. (63)	..	1. 4.40	Art.
BOTH, Kuno v. (60)	G.O.C. Estonia	1. 6.40	Inf.
BRAEMER, Walter (61)	Cdr. Ostland	1. 9.42	Kav.
BRAND, Fritz (56)	..	1. 8.40	Art.
BRANDENBERGER, Erich (52)	XVII A.K.	1. 8.43	Art.
BRANDT, Georg (68)	Retired	1. 8.41	Kav.
BREITH, Hermann (52)	III Pz. K.	1. 3.43	Pz. Tr.
BRENNECKE, Kurt (52)	..	1. 2.42	Inf.
CHEVALLERIE, Kurt v. der (53)	LIX A.K.	1. 3.42	Inf.
CLÖSSNER, Erich (58)	LIII A.K.	1. 1.42	Inf.
COCHENHAUSEN, Friedrich v. (65)	Retired	1.12.40	Art.
CRAMER, Hans (48)	Prisoner of War	1. 5.43	Pz.Tr.
CRÜWELL, Ludwig (52)	Prisoner of War	1.12.41	Pz. Tr.
DALWIGK zu LICHTENFELS Franz Frhr. v. (67).	..	1.12.40	Inf.
DEHNER, Ernst (55)	LXXXII A.K. (?)	1.12.42	Inf.
DOSTLER, Anton (53)	..	1. 8.43	Inf.
EBERBACH, Heinrich Hans (49)	..	1. 8.43	Pz. Tr.
EBERT, Karl (65)	..	..	Art.
ENDRES, Theodor (48)	..	..	Art.
ENGELBRECHT, Erwin (53)	Höh. Kdo. z.b.V.XXXIII	1. 9.42	Kav.
ERFURTH, Waldemar (65)	Mil. Mission Finland	1. 4.40	Inf.
FAHRMBACHER, Wilhelm (56)	XXV A.K. (?)	1.11.40	Art.
FALKENHAUSEN, Alexander v. (66)	G.O.C., Belgium and N. France	..	Inf.
FEHN, Gustav (52)	..	1.11.42	Pz. Tr.
FELBER, Hans (56)	Cdr. Serbia	1. 8.40	Inf.
FELLGIEBEL, Erich (57)	Inspector-General, Sigs.	1. 8.40	Na. Tr.
FEURSTEIN, Valentin (59)	LI Geb. K.	1. 9.41	Geb.Tr.
FISCHER v. WEIKERSTHAL, Walter (54).	..	1.12.41	Inf.
FÖRSTER, Otto (59)	..	1. 4.38	Pion.
FÖRSTER, Sigismund v. (57)	..	1. 5.43	Inf.

Rank : General (*d. Inf., Kav., etc.*)—*continued*

Name (*age*)	*Appointment* (*date*)	*Seniority*	*Arm*
FRETTER-PICO, Maximilian (53)	XXX A.K.	1. 6.42	Art.
FREDERICI, Erich (59)	..	1. 4.39	Inf.
FRIESSNER, Johannes (52)	An Army Corps	1. 4.43	Inf.
GALLENCAMP, Curt (55)	..	1. 4.42	Art.
GEIB, Theodor (59)	Feldzeugmeister, O.K.H.	1.12.41	Art.
GERCKE, Rudolf (58)	H. Transport Chef, O.K.H.	1. 4.42	Inf.
GEYR v. SCHWEPPENBURG, Leo Frhr. (58).	General d. Pz. Tr. West	1. 4.40	Pz. Tr.
GIENANTH, Frhr. v. (68)	..	1. 4.36	Kav.
GLOKKE, Gerhard (60)	Wkr. VI	1.12.40	Inf.
GOLLNICK, Hans (52)	..	1.10.43	Inf.
GREIFF, Kurt v. (65)	..	27. 8.39	Inf.
GRÜN, Otto (62)	Inspector of Artillery	..	Art.
HAENICKE, Siegfried (66)	General-Gouvernement	..	Inf.
HANNEKEN v. (54)	Höh. Kdo. z.b.V. XXXI and G.O.C., Denmark.	1.12.41	Inf.
HANSEN, Christian (59)	X A.K.	1. 6.40	Art.
HANSEN, Erik (55)	Mil. Mission Rumania	1. 8.40	Kav.
HARPE, Josef (54)	XXXXI Pz. K.	1. 6.42	Pz. Tr.
HARTMANN, Otto (60)	..	1. 4.40	Art.
HAUFFE (52)	..	..	Inf.
HELL, Ernst (57)	VII A.K.	1. 3.42	Art.
HENRICI, Sigfrid (56)	XXXX Pz.K.	1. 1.43	Pz. Tr.
HERR, Traugott (54)	LXXVI Pz. K.	1. 9.43	Pz. Tr.
HERZOG, Kurt (56)	XXXVIII A.K.	1. 7.42	Art.
HILPERT, Karl (56)	XXIII A.K.	1. 9.42	Inf.
HÖHNE, Gustav (51)	LIV A.K.	1. 5.43	Inf.
HUBE, Hans (54)	XIV Pz. K.	1.10.42	Pz. Tr.
HUBICKI, Dr. Alfred (53)	LXXXIX A.K.	1.10.42	Pz. Tr.
JACOB, Alfred (61)	Insp. d. Pion. u. Fest.	1. 6.40	Pion.
JASCHKE, Erich (54)	XIII A.K.	..	Inf.
JORDAN, Hans (52)	..	1. 1.43	Inf.
KAEMPFE, Rudolf (61)	XXXV A.K.	1. 7.41	Art.
KEINER, Walter (54)	..	1. 1.43	Art.
KEITEL, Bodewin (55)	Wkr. XX	1. 4.41	Inf.
KEMPF, Werner (58)	..	1. 4.41	Pz. Tr.
KIENITZ, Werner (59)	Wkr. II	1. 4.38	Inf.
KIRCHNER, Friedrich (59)	LVII Pz. K.	1. 2.42	Pz. Tr.
KLEFFEL, Philipp (57)	L A.K.	1. 3.42	Inf.
KNIESS, Baptist (63)	LXVI Res. K.	1.12.42	Inf.
KNOBELSDORFF, Otto v. (58)	XXXXVIII Pz. K.	1. 8.42	Pz. Tr.
KOCH-ERPACH, Rudolf (58)	Wkr. VIII	1.12.40	Kav.
KÖSTRING, Ernst (68)		1. 9.40	Kav.
KONRAD, Rudolf (53)	XXXXIX Geb. K.	1. 3.42	Geb. Tr.
KORTZFLEISCH, Joachim v. (54)	G.G. Wkr. III	1. 8.40	Inf.
KRIEBEL, Karl (56)	Wkr. VII	1. 4.43	Inf.
KRUSE, Hermann	..	..	Art.
KÜBLER, Ludwig (55)	..	1. 8.40	Pz. Tr.
KÜHN, Friedrich (55)	Insp. d. Verkehrs-Tr. O.K.W.	1. 4.43	Pz. Tr.
KUNTZE, Walter (61)	Chef. d. Ausb. Wesens i. Ers. H.	1. 3.38	Pion.
KUNTZEN, Adolf (55)	LXXXI A.K.	1. 4.41	Pz. Tr.
LANZ, Hubert (48)	XXII Geb. K.	28. 1.43	Geb. Tr.
LAUX, Paul (57)	II A.K.	1.12.42	Inf.
LEEB, Emil (63)	H. Waffenamt	1. 4.39	Art.
LEMELSEN, Joachim (56)	..	1. 8.40	Pz. Tr.
LEYSER, v. (56)	..	1.12.42	Inf.
LICHEL, Walter (59)	..	1.12.42	Inf.
LOCH, Herbert (58)	XXVIII A.K.	1.10.41	Art.
LÜDKE, Erich (62)	..	1.12.40	Inf.
LÜTERS, Rudolf (61)	15 Geb. K.	1. 1.43	Inf.
MARCKS, Erich (53)	..	1.10.42	Art.
MARTINEK, Robert (60)	XXXIX Pz. K.	1. 1.43	Art.
MATERNA, Friedrich (59)	Wkr. XVIII	1.11.40	Inf.
MATTENKLOTT, Franz (60)	XXXXII A.K.	1.10.41	Inf.

Rank: General (*d. Inf., Kav., etc.*)—*continued*

Name (age)	*Appointment (date)*	*Seniority*	*Arm*
METZ, Hermann (66)	..	41	Inf.
MIETH (56)	An Army Corps	1.5.43	Inf.
MITTELBERGER, Hilmar Ritter v. (66)	..	..	Inf.z.V.
MOSER, Willi (57)	Höh. Kdo. LXXI	1.12.42	Art.
MÜLLER, Eugen (53)	Generalquartiermeister, O.K.H.	1. 6.42	Art.
NAGY, Emmerich (62)	..	1. 8.42	Inf.
NEHRING, Walter (52)	XXIV Pz. K.	1. 7.42	Pz. Tr.
NEULING, Ferdinand (59)	LXII Res. K.	1.10.42	Inf.
NIEBELSCHÜTZ, Gunther v. (62)	An Oberfeldkdtr.	38	Inf.
OBSTFELDER, Hans v. (58)	XXIX A.K.	1. 7.40	Inf.
OLBRICHT, Friedrich (56)	Chef. d.A.H.A., O.K.H.	1. 6.40	Inf.
OSSWALD, Erwin (62)	..	1.12.40	Inf.
OSTERKAMP (52)	H. Verw. Amt. O.K.H.	1. 6.43	Inf.
OTT, Eugen (54)	..	1.10.41	Inf.
OTTENBACHER, Otto (56)	..	42	Inf.
OTTO, Paul (63)	..	1.12.40	Inf.
OVEN, Karl v. (56)	XXXXIII A.K.	1. 4.43	Inf.
PETZEL, Walter (61)	Wkr. XXI	1.10.39	Art.
PFEFFER, Max	Prisoner of War	22. 1.43	Art.
RABENAU, Dr. phil.h.c. Friedrich v.(60)	..	1. 9.40	Art.
RASCHICK, Walther (62)	Wkr. X	1. 4.39	Inf.
RAUS, Erhard (55)	VIII A.K.	1. 5.43	Pz. Tr.
REINECKE, Hermann (56)	Amt. Allg. WM. Angelegenheiten, O.K.W.	1. 6.42	Inf.
REINHARD, Hans (55)	LXXXVIII A.K.	1.11.40	Inf.
RENDULIC, Dr. Lothar (57)	2 Pz. Army	1.12.42	Inf.
RINTELEN, Enno v. (53)	..	1. 7.42	Inf.
ROESE, Franz v. (66)	Heeres-Museum	1. 2.42	Inf.
ROETTIG, Otto (54)	..	1. 8.43	Inf.
ROMAN, Rudolf Frhr. v. (51)	XX A.K.	1.11.42	Art.
ROQUES, Franz v. (65)	Ruckw. Arm. Geb. Süd	1. 7.42	Inf.
SACHS (58)	..	1.10.42	Pion.
SCHAAL, Ferdinand (55)	G.O.C. Protectorate	1.10.41	Pz. Tr.
SCHALLER-KALIDE, Hubert (62)	..	1.12.40	Inf.
SCHELLERT (57)	Wkr. IX	1. 7.43	Inf.
SCHMIDT, Hans (66)	IX A.K.	1. 2.42	Inf.
SCHNECKENBURGER, Wilhelm (53)	..	1. 5.43	Inf.
SCHÖRNER, Ferdinand (52)	..	1. 6.42	Geb.Tr.
SCHROTH, Walther (62)	Wkr. XII	1. 2.38	Inf.
SCHUBERT, Albrecht (58)	Wkr. XVII	1. 6.40	Inf.
SCHWANDER, Maximilian (63)	..	1.12.40	Inf.
SCHWEDLER, Viktor v. (59)	Wkr. IV	1. 2.38	Inf.
SEYDLITZ-KURZBACH, Walter v. (56)	Prisoner of War	1. 6.42	Art.
SINNHUBER (57)	..	1. 9.43	Art.
SODENSTERN, Georg v. (55)	19 Army	1. 8.40	Inf.
SPONHEIMER, Otto (58)	..	1. 8.43	Inf.
STAPF, Otto (54)	Insp. d. Wirtsch. Stab Ost	1.10.42	Inf.
STEMMERMANN, Wilhelm (54)	..	1.12.42	Art.
STEPPUHN, Albrecht (67)	..	1.12.40	Inf.
STRAUBE, Erich (57)	..	1. 6.42	Inf.
STRECCIUS, Alfred (65)	..	..	Inf.
STRECKER	Prisoner of War	1. 4.42	Inf.
STÜLPNAGEL, Heinrich (58)	..	1. 4.39	Inf.
STÜLPNAGEL, Joachim (64)	Retired	31.12.31	Inf.
STÜLPNAGEL, Otto (65)	G.O.C., Occupied France	1. 1.32	Inf.
THEISEN, Edgar (55)	LXI Res. K.	1.10.42	Art.
THOMA, Wilhelm Ritter v. (53)	Prisoner of War	1.11.42	Pz. Tr.
THOMAS, Georg (54)	Wehrwirtsch. u. Rüst, Amt OKW.	1. 8.40	Inf.
TIPPELSKIRCH, Kurt (53)	An Army Corps	27. 8.42	Inf.
TITTEL, Hermann (55)	Höh. Kdo. LXX	1. 9.43	Art.
TOUSSAINT, Rudolf (53)	..	14. 9.43	Inf.
ULEX, Wilhelm (64)	..	1.10.36	Art.
UNRUH, Walter Rudolf v. (66)	Mobzn. of Manpower	1. 7.42	Inf.

Rank : General (*d. Inf., Kav., etc.*)—*continued*

Name (*age*)	*Appointment* (*date*)	*Seniority*	*Arm*
UNRUH, Walter Willy v. (69)	..	..	..
VAERST, Gustav v. (50)	Prisoner of War	1. 3.43	Pz. Tr.
VEIEL, Rudolf (61)	Wkr. V	1. 4.42	Pz. Tr.
VIEROW, Erwin (54)	..	1. 1.41	Inf.
VÖLCKERS, Paul (53)	LV A.K. (?)	1. 9.43	Inf.
VOGL, Oskar (63)	Head of Armistice Commission	41	Art.
VOLLARD-BOCKELBERG, v. (70)	..	1.10.33	Art.
WÄGER, Alfred (61)	..	1.11.38	Inf.
WAGNER, Eduard (50)	..	1. 8.43	Art.
WANDEL (54)	Prisoner of War	1. 1.43	Art.
WEISENBERGER, Karl (54)	XXXVI A.K.	1. 4.41	Inf.
WETZEL, Wilhelm (56)	V A.K.	1. 3.42	Inf.
WEYER, Peter (65)	..	1.12.40	Art.
WIESE, Friedrich (52)	11 Pz. Div.	1.10.43	Inf.
WIETERSHEIM, Gustav v. (60)	Wkr. XIII	1. 2.38	Inf.
WIKTORIN, Mauriz (61)	..	1.11.40	Inf.
WITTHÖFT (57)	..	1. 3.42	Inf.
WÖDRIG, Albert (61)	Wkr. I	1.10.39	Art.
WÖHLER, Otto (50)	8 Army	1. 6.43	Inf.
ZANGEN, Gustav v. (52)	..	1. 6.43	Inf.

(*d*) **Rank : GENERALLEUTNANT (Lt.-General)**

Name (*age*)	*Appointment* (*date*)	*Seniority*	*Arm*
ADAM, Wilhelm (66)	Insp. d.Fahrtr.	..	Fahr Tr.
ADOLPH-AUFFENBERG-KOMAROW, Gustav.	Sich Div. 285	1. 9.43	Inf.
AGRICOLA, Kurt (54)	Rückw. Arm. Geb.	..	Inf.
ALDRIAN, Eduard	..	1. 6.43	..
ALTRICHTER, Dr. Friedrich (53)	154 Res. Div.	1. 4.43	Inf.
ALTROCK, Wilhelm v. (54)	O.F.K. 372 Lublin	1. 4.43	Inf.
ANDREAS (59)	O.F.K. 242	1. 4.41	Inf.
ANGERN, Günther (51)	..	1.12.42	Kav.
ANSAT, Johann (52)	..	1. 8.42	Art.
APELL v. (58)	..	1. 6.38	Inf.
APELL, Wilhelm v. (51)	..	1. 4.43	Inf.
AULEB (57)	Sich. Div. 444	1.12.40	Inf.
BADINSKI, Kurt (49)	269 Inf. Div.	1. 3.43	Inf.
BAIER, Albrecht (50)	..	1. 1.43	Art.
BALCK, Hermann (51)	..	1. 1.43	Kav.
BALTZER (57)	..	1.10.39	Inf.
BAMLER, Rudolf (48)	C.G.S. Army of Norway	1. 4.43	Art.
BASSE, Hans v. (55)	..	1. 4.42	Inf.
BAYER (57)	181 Inf. Div.	1.10.40	Inf.
BECHTOLSHEIM, Anton Frhr. v. MAUCHENHEIM gen. (50)	C.G.S. 1 Army	1. 6.43	Art.
BECKER, Fritz (52)	253 Inf. Div.	1. 4.43	Inf.
BECKMANN, Alfred (67)	..	1. 4.43	Inf.
BEEREN v. (53)	280 Inf. Div.	1. 5.43	Inf.
BEHR v. (54)	..	1.11.42	Inf.
BEHSCHNITT, Walter (59)	..	1. 9.40	Inf.
BERG, Ludwig v. (62)	Coblenz, Wkr. XII	1.11.40	Art.
BERGEN, Johann (53)	323 Inf. Div.	1.10.43	Inf.
BERLIN (54)	Art. Schule Jüterbog, Wkr. III	1. 3.42	Art.
BERNARD, Kurt (57)	..	1.10.39	Pz. Tr.
BERNHARD, Friedrich Gustav (54)	..	1. 8.42	Na. Tr.
BERTRAM, Georg (59)	Cdt. Lille	1. 8.39	Kav.
BEUKEMANN, Helmuth (50)	An Inf. Div.	1. 5.43	Inf.
BEUTTEL (57)	O.F. K. 365 Lemburg	1. 3.41	Inf.
BEYER, Dr. Franz (54)	..	1. 1.43	Inf.
BIELFELD (55)	Stadtkdt. Posen	1. 2.42	Inf.
BLOCK Johannes (50)	294 Inf. Div.	1. 1.43	Inf.
BLÜMM, Oskar (60)	..	1. 3.40	Inf.
BLUMENTRITT (51)	C.G.S. H. Gru. West	1.12.42	Inf

Rank : Generalleutnant (*Lt.-General*)—*continued*

Name (age)	*Appointment (date)*	*Seniority*	*Arm*
BOCK v. WÜLFINGEN, Ferdinand (61)	..	1. 4.38	Art.
BOECKH-BEHRENS (48)	C.G.S. 16 Army	1. 9.43	Inf.
BOEGE, Ehrenfried (50)	197 Inf. Div.	1. 1.43	Inf.
BOEHM-BEZING, Dieter v. (64)	..	1. 4.35	Kav.
BOETTCHER, Hermann (58)	148 Res. Div.	1.11.39	Inf.
BÖTTCHER, Karl (54)	..	1. 3.42	Art.
BÖHNSTEDT, Wilhelm (54)	..	1. 4.42	Inf.
BOINEBURG-LENGSFELD, Wilhelm, Frhr. v. (55).	Cdt. Paris	1.12.42	Kav.
BOLTENSTERN, Walter v. (53)	Cdt. Weimar	1. 8.42	Inf.
BOLTZE, Arthur (66)	Div. Nr. 152	.	Art.
BORDIHN (55)	..	1.11.42	Pion.
BOROWIETZ, Willibald (51)	Prisoner of War	1. 5.43	Pz. Tr.
BOYSEN, Wolf (60)	..	1. 9.42	Inf.
BRABÄNDER (53)	..	1. 1.43	Inf.
BRAND, Albrecht (56)	Befest. Ostpreussen	1.10.39	Art.
BRAUNER, Josef	187 Res. Div.	1. 3.41	Inf.
BREITH, Friedrich (52)	Art. Schule 1	1. 4.43	Art.
BREMER (57)	..	1.10.38	Art.
BRODOWSKI, Fritz v. (58)	..	1. 2.41	Kav.
BROICH, Frhr. v. (58)	Prisoner of War	1. 5.43	Kav.
BÜCHS (58)	Staff of Wkr. VI	1.10.39	Inf. ?
BÜLOWIUS, Karl (53)	Prisoner of War	1. 4.43	Pion.
BÜNAU, Rudolf v. (54)	73 Inf. Div.	1. 9.42	Inf.
BUHLE, Walter (50)	Chef. d.Org.Abt.O.K.H.	1. 4.42	Inf.
BURCKHARDT (53)	..	1. 3.42	Na. Tr.
BURDACH, Karl (50)	11 Inf. Div.	1.11.42	Art.
BUSCHENHAGEN, Erich (52)	15 Inf. Div.	1. 5.43	Inf.
BUSCHMANN (55)	..	1.11.41	Art.
BUSSE, Theodor (48)	C.G.S. H. Gru. Süd	1.9.43	Inf. ?
BUTZE (53)	340 Inf. Div.	1. 1.43	Inf.
CANTZLER, Oskar (54)	Gen. d. Pion. b.d.H. Gru. Süd	1. 8.42	Pion.
CARP, Georg (57)	Kattowitz, Wkr VIII	1. 6.41	Art.
CASPER (51)	335 Inf. Div.	1. 7.43	Inf. ?
CHEVALLERIE, Helmuth v. der (48)	..	1. 5.43	..
CHILL, Kurt	122 Inf. Div.	1. 6.43	..
CHOLTITZ, Dietrich v. (50)	..	1. 2.43	..
COURBIERE, Rene de l'HOMME de (57)	153 Res. Div.	1. 6.40	Inf.
DANHAUSER, Paul (51)	256 Inf. Div.	1. 3.43	Inf.
DANIELS, Alexander Edler v. (53)	Prisoner of War	1.12.42	Inf.
DEBOI, Heinrich (51)	Prisoner of War	1.12.42	Inf.
DEHMEL (56)	..	1. 6.41	Pion.
DEMOLL (62)	..	1. 6.43	Art.
DENECKE, Erich (52)	LXIX Res. K.	1.12.39	Inf.
DENNERLEIN, Max (59)	..	1. 3.40	Pion.
DETMERING (57)	Frankfurt a/m, Wkr IX	1. 6.41	Inf.
DETTLING (53)	183 Inf. Div.	1. 1.43	Inf.
DIESTEL, Erich	75 Inf. Div.	1. 8.43	..
DIGEON v. MONTETON, Baron Albrecht (52).	Feldausb. Div. 391	1. 6.43	Kav.
DIHM, Friedrich (64)	An Inf. Div.	1.10.42	Art.
DIPPOLD, Benignus (55)	..	1.10.41	Inf.
DIRINGSHOFEN v.	Div. Nr. z.b.V. 401	1. 3.43	Kav.
DITTMAR, Kurt (54)	Public Relations	1. 4.42	Pion.
DOEHLA, Heinrich (63)	..	..	Inf.
DRABICH-WAECHTER, Viktor v. (53)	326 Inf. Div.	1. 8.42	Inf.
DROGAND (61)	Inspector of Welfare, O.K.W.	1. 7.41	Inf.
DÜVERT, Walther (52)	..	1. 1.43	Art.
EBERHARDT (51)	38 Inf. Div.	1. 2.41	Kav.
EBERLÉ, René (53)	..	1. 9.43	Pion.
ECKSTEIN (54)	..	1. 6.42	Pion.
EDELMANN, Karl (53)	O.K.H. (AHA/AG)	1.10.43	Inf.
EDELSHEIM, Maximilian Reichsfreiherr v. (47).	24 Pz. Div.	43?	Inf. ?

Rank : Generalleutnant (*Lt.-General*)—*continued*

Name (*age*)	*Appointment* (*date*)	*Seniority*	*Arm*
EGLSEER, Karl	114 Lt. Div.	1. 2.43	Geb.Tr.
ELFELDT, Otto	..	1. 7.43	Art.
ERDMANNSDORF, Werner v. (53)	..	1. 1.43	Inf.
ESEBECK, Hans-Karl Frhr. v. (52)	..	1.12.42	Kav.
FABER de FAUR Moritz v. (58)	Kdt. Innsbruck, Wkr. XVIII	1. 4.39	Kav.
FAECKENSTEDT, Ernst Felix (48)	..	1. 9.43	Kav.
FAULENBACH (52)	356 Inf. Div.	1. 1.43	Inf.
FELDT, Kurt (55)	..	1. 2.42	Inf.
FETT, Albert (70)	..	..	Kav.
FICHTNER, Sebastian	..	1. 8.43	Pz. Tr.
FISCHER, Herbert (62)	..	1. 1.36	Inf.
FISCHER, Herman (50)	..	1. 4.43	Inf.
FISCHER, Kurt (67)	..	..	Inf.
FOERTSCH, Herman (49)	C.G.S. Army Gp. F.	1. 1.43	Inf.
FOLTTMANN (55)	338 Inf. Div.	1. 2.41	Inf.
FORST, Werner (52)	106 Inf. Div.	1. 1.43	Art.
FORTNER, Johann (60)	..	1.11.42	Inf.
FRANEK, Dr. Friedrich (53)	44 Inf. Div.	1. 4.43	Inf.
FRANKEWITZ	..	1. 7.43	Art.
FREMEREY, Max (55)	Kdt. Hannover	1. 6.43	Kav.
FRIEBE, Helmuth	..	1. 9.43	Inf.
FRIEDRICH, Rudolf (53)	..	1. 4.42	Art.
FÜCHTBAUER, Heinrich, Ritter v. (64)	Mil. Distr. N.E. France ?	..	Inf.
FÜRST, Friedrich (54)	171 Res. Div.	1.10.42	Inf.
FUNCK, Hans Frhr. v. (49)	..	1. 9.42	Kav.
GABLENZ, Eccard Frhr. v. (53)	..	1. 8.40	Inf.
GAREIS, Martin (53)	98 Inf. Div.	1. 1.43	Inf.
GAUSE, Alfred (48)	C.G.S. Army Gp. B.	1. 4.43	Pion.
GERHARDT, Paul (63)	..	1. 2.41	Inf.
GERKE, Ernst (54)	..	1. 1.43	Na. Tr.
GILBERT, Martin (55)	..	1. 1.42	Inf.
GILSA, Werher Frhr. v.u.zu (55)	..	1.10.42	Inf.
GIMBORN, Hermann v. (64)	..	..	Inf.
GIMMLER (54)	216 Inf. Div.	1. 4.43	Na. Tr.
GINKEL, Oskar von (62)	Munich, Wkr. VII	..	Art.
GLAISE-HORSTENAU Dr. h.c. Edmund v. (62).	Mil. Plenipotentiary in Croatia	1. 8.42	..
GOERITZ, Werner (52)	291 Inf. Div.	1. 1.43	Inf.
GOESCHEN (55)	..	1. 8.43	Kav.
GOETTKE (60)	..	1.11.41	Art.
GOLLWITZER, Friedrich (55)	88 Inf. Div.	1.10.41	Inf.
GRÄSER, Fritz Hubert (56)	3 Pz. Gren Div.	1. 3.43	Inf.
GRAF, Karl (61)	467 Div. Nr. ?	1. 2.41	Inf.
GRAFFEN, Karl v.(51)	An Inf. Div.	1. 1.43	Art.
GRASE, Martin (53)	1 Inf. Div.	1. 1.43	Inf.
GRASSER, Anton (53)	25 Pz. Gren. Div.	1. 1.43	Inf.
GREIFFENBERG, Hans v. (51)	M.A. Budapest	1. 4.42	Inf.
GREINER, Heinz (49)	268 Inf. Div.	1. 1.43	Inf.
GRIMMEISS	Army General at G.A.F. H.Q.	1. 4.43	Art.
GROSCHOPF (62)	..	1. 7.42	Art.
GROSSMANN (53)	6 Inf. Div.	1. 1.43	Inf.
GROTE, Waldemar Frhr. (66)	..	1.11.39	Kav.
GÜMBEL, Karl (56)	..	1. 1.43	Inf.
GULLMANN, Otto (54)	..	1. 1.43	Art.
GUNZELMANN, Emil (57)	Graz 2, Wkr. XVIII	1.10.41	Inf.
HAARDE (55)	..	1.10.41	Pz. Tr.
HAASE Conrad (56)	..	1. 1.42	Inf.
HABENICHT (53)	..	1. 6.43	Inf.
HACCIUS, Ernst (47)	..	1. 1.43	Inf.
HAECKEL, Ernst (54)	158 Res. Div.	1.10.42	Inf.
HAHM, Walter (50)	..	1. 1.43	Inf.
HAMMER, Ernst (61)	An Inf. Div.	1.11.40	Inf.
HAMMERSTEIN-EQUORD, Gunther Frhr. v. (67)	O.F.K. 672 Brussels	1.10.33	Inf.

Rank : Generalleutnant (*Lt.-General*)—*continued*

Name (*age*)	*Appointment* (*date*)	*Seniority*	*Arm*
HARTENECK, Gustav	C.G.S. 2 Army	1. 4.43	Kav.
HARTLIEB gen. WALSPORN, Maximilian v. (61).	..	1. 4.39	Pz. Tr.
HARTMANN, Walter (51)	An Inf. Div.	1. 2.43	Art.
HASE, Paul v. (59)	Cdt. Berlin	1. 4.40	Inf.
HASSE, Ulrich (49)	..	1. 1.43	Inf.
HEBERLEIN, Hans (56)	T.R.G. Area, Grafenwöhr	1. 4.41	Inf.
HEIM, Ferdinand (49)	..	1.11.42	Art.
HEINECCIUS v. (62)	..	1. 2.41	Inf.
HEINEMANN, Erich (63)	..	..	Art.
HEINRICHS (52)	290 Inf. Div.	1. 2.43	Inf.
HELD, Karl (62)	..	..	Inf.
HELLMICH, Heinz (52)	Inspector of Eastern Legions	1. 9.41	Inf.
HEMMERICH, Gerlach (62)	..	1.12.41	Inf.
HENGEN, Fritz (57)	Chemnitz, Wkr. IV	1. 2.41	Art.
HENGL, Ritter v.	XIX Geb. K.	1. 1.43	Inf.
HENRICI, Dr. Waldemar (66)	..	..	..
HERRLEIN, Friedrich (54)	Infantry General at G.H.Q.	1. 9.42	Inf.
HEUNERT (56)	Staff of 20 Army	1.10.40	Kav.
HEUSINGER (49)	O.K.H. (Ops.)	1. 1.43	Inf.
HINDENBURG, Oskar v. (59)	..	..	Kav.
HINGHOFER, Dr. Walter	..	1. 7.41	Inf.
HITTER, Alfons	206 Inf. Div.	1. 3.43	Art.
HOCHBAUM, Friedrich (50)	26 Inf. Div.	1. 1.43	Inf.
HÖBERTH, Eugen v.	..	..	Kav.
HÖCKER, Hans Kurt (50)	258 Inf. Div.	1.11.42	Inf.
HÖCKER, Erich (61)	719 Inf. Div.	1. 1.43	Inf.
HOEGNER, Herman (59)	..	1. 2.41	..
HOERNLEIN, Walter (51)	Pz. Gren. Div. Gross Deutschland	1. 1.43	Inf.
HÖSSLIN, Wilhelm v. (66)	188 Res. Mtn. Div.	..	Inf.
HOFFMANN, Kurt (53)	715 Inf. Div.	1. 7.43	Inf.
HOFFMANN, Erich	..	1. 9.43	Inf.
HOFFMANN, Rudolf (48)	..	1. 4.43	Inf.
HOPFF, Herman (68)	..	..	Pion.
HOPPE, Arthur (49)	126 Inf. Div.	1. 6.43	Inf.
HORN, Max (56)	214 Inf. Div.	1.10.41	Inf.
HOSSBACH, Friedrich (50)	XXXXVI Pz. K.	1. 3.43	Inf.
HÜHNER, Werner (50)	An Inf. Div.	1. 1.43	Inf.
HUFFMANN, Helmuth (53)	An Inf. Div.	1. 8.43	..
JACOBI, Alfred (58)	Sich. Div. 201	1. 3.43	Inf.
JAHN (52)	..	1.11.40	Art.
JODL, Ferdinand	..	1. 9.43	Art.
JOHN, Dipl. Ing. Friedrich-Wilhelm	Cdt. Latvia	1. 5.43	Inf.
JUPPE, Hans (52)	..	1. 8.42	Na. Tr.
KARL, Franz (56)	..	1. 3.41	Inf.
KARST, Friedrich (51)	..	1. 4.43	Inf.
KASPAR, Johann (70)	Chief of Staff, Wkr. VII	1. 8.42	Kav.
KAUFFMANN (53)	..	1. 4.41	Inf.
KEMPSKI, Hans v. (59)	..	1. 2.41	Inf.
KERN, Emil (52)	..	1.10.41	Pion.
KERSTEN	..	1.10.42	Na. Tr.
KESSEL, Hans (53)	..	1.11.42	Inf.
KIEFFER, Friedrich Ritter v. (64)	Cdt. Munich	1. 6.42	Inf.
KIESLING auf KIESLINGSTEIN, Bruno Edler v. (65).	Regensburg, Wkr. XIII	1.11.41	Inf.
KINZEL, Eberhardt (47)	C.G.S. Army Group North	1. 9.43	Inf.
KIRCHHEIM, Heinrich (62)	..	1. 7.42	Inf.
KLEEMANN, Ulrich (52)	Assault Div. Rhodes	1. 5.43	Kav.
KLEIST v. (57)	O.F.K. 225, Warsaw	1. 4.41	Kav.
KLINGBEIL, Erich (63)	Insp. of H. Bautruppen	..	Pion.
KLUGE, Wolfgang v. (52)	An Inf. Div.	1. 4.43	Art.
KLUTMANN (64)	..	1. 4.42	Kav.
KNESEBECK, v. dem (67)	Münster, Wkr. VI	1. 2.41	Kav.
KOBUS	..	1. 7.42	Inf.

Rank : Generalleutnant (*Lt.-General*)—*continued*

Name (*age*)	*Appointment* (*date*)	*Seniority*	*Arm*
KOCH, Helmuth (63)		1.11.42	Art.
KÖCHLING, Friedrich (51)	An Inf. Div.	1. 1.43	Inf.
KOEHLER, Carl-Erich (50)	O.K.H.	1. 6.43	Kav.
KÖRNER, Willy (66)	WE Insp. Mannheim, Wkr. XII	1.11.39	Inf.
KOHL, Otto (56)	Army Transp., France	1. 9.41	Inf.
KOHLERMANN, Otto	60 Pz. Gren. Div.	1. 7.43	..
KOREUBER (54)		1. 1.43	Pz. Tr.
KRAISS, Dietrich (55)	An Inf. Div.	1.10.42	Inf.
KRAKAU, August (50)	7 Mtn. Div.	1. 6.43	Inf.
KRAMPF, Heinrich (56)	304 Inf. Div.	1.12.41	Inf.
KRAPPE, Günther (51)	61st Inf. Div.	1.12.43	Kav.
KRATZERT, Hans (61)		1. 1.38	Art.
KRAUSE, Walter (54)	An Inf. Div.	1. 9.43	Inf.
KREBS	C.G.S. 9 Army	1. 4.43	Inf.
KRENZKI, Kurt v. (57)		..	Inf.
KREYSING, Hans (54)		1. 7.42	Inf.
KRISCHER, Friedrich (53)		1.12.41	Art.
KRÜGER Walter (54)	1 Pz. Div.	1.10.42	Kav.
KUBENA, Johann (62)		..	Art.
KÜHLENTHAL, Erich (64)		1.10.33	Art.
KÜHLWEIN (51)		1. 1.43	Inf.
KÜHNE, Fritz (61)		1. 4.36	Inf.
KULLMER (48)	296 Inf. Div.	1. 9.43	Inf.
KUROWSKI, Eberhard v. (49)		1. 6.43	Inf.
KURZ	Danzig, Wkr. XX	1. 3.42	Inf.
LAHODE, Kurt (55)		1. 7.42	Inf.
LANDGRAF, Franz (56)		1. 9.42	Pz. Tr.
LANG, Viktor (52)		1. 1.43	Inf.
LASCH (51)		1. 4.43	..
LECHNER, Adolf (60)		1. 3.42	Art.
LEHMANN, Joseph (56)	O.F.K. 398	1. 6.41	Inf.
LEISTER (56)		1. 1.41	Art.
LENDLE (52)	Sich. Div. 221	1. 6.43	Pz. Tr.
LENSKI, Arno v. (51)	Prisoner of War	1. 1.43	Pz. Tr.
LEYEN, Ludwig v. der (58)		1. 6.38	Inf.
LEYKAUF, Hans (59)	Rü. Insp. VIII	1. 2.41	Inf.
LIEB (54)		1. 6.43	Inf.
LIEBER, Hans (62)	H. Archiv Zweigstelle Prague	..	Art.
LINDEMANN, Fritz (52)		1. 1.43	Art.
LINDIG, Max (56)	O.K.H.	1.12.42	Art.
LINN, Philip	AHA (In T)	1. 1.42	Inf.
LOEPER v. (56)		1. 9.40	Inf.
LOHMANN, Hans (62)	Rü. Insp. XII	1. 2.41	Art.
LUCHT, Walter (62)	336 Inf. Div.	1.11.42	Art.
LÜBBE, Vollrath (50)	2 Pz. Div.	1. 4.43	Inf.
LÜDECKE, Otto (50)	56 Inf. Div.	1.10.43	Pion.
LÜTTWITZ, Heinrich Frhr. v. (48)	20 Pz. Div.	1. 6.43	Pz. Tr.
LÜTTWITZ, Smilo Frhr. v. (49)	26 Pz. Div.	1.10.43	Kav.
LÜTZOW, Kurt-Jürgen Frhr. v. (52)	12 Inf. Div.	1. 1.43	Inf.
LUNGERHAUSEN, Karl Hans (48)	90 Pz. Gren Div.	1. 9.43	Kav.
MACHOLZ (54)	An. Inf. Div.	1. 6.42	Inf.
MADERHOLZ, Karl (59)		1.10.41	Inf.
MAJEWSKI, v. (54)		1.12.42	Pion.
MANTELL (63)		1.10.42	Art.
MATTERSTOCK, Otto (55)	Div. Nr. 147	1.11.42	Inf.
MATZKY, Gerhard (51)	21 Inf. Div.	1. 4.43	Inf.
MAYER, Dr.-Ing., Johannes (48)	An Inf. Div.	1. 2.43	Inf.
MEDEM (51)	Chef. d. Nebel Tr. Army Group Centre.	1. 9.43	Pion.
MEHNERT, Karl 56)	Cdt. Dresden	1.11.40	Na. Tr.
MEISE, Dr. Wilhelm 53)		1. 9.42	Pion.
MEISSNER, Robert (56)		1.10.42	Inf.
MELZER, Karl		1.10.43	Inf.
MENGE, v.		1. 1.43	

Rank : Generalleutnant (*Lt.-General*)—*continued*

Name (*age*)	*Appointment* (*date*)	*Seniority*	*Arm*
MERKER, Ludwig (50)	35 Inf. Div.	1. 4.43	Inf.
MEYER-BUERDORF, Heinrich (56)	131 Inf. Div.	1. 9.41	Art.
MEYER-RABINGEN, Hermann (55)..	159 Res. Div.	1.11.41	Inf.
MIKULICZ, Adalbert	.. ..	1. 2.43	Inf.
MITTERMAIER, Wilhelm (54) ..	.. ..	1.12.42	Inf.
MOLO, Louis Ritter v. (63)	Kdt. Stuttgart	1. 7.42	Inf.
MOYSES, Karl (60)	Wkr. II (Köslin)	1. 2.41	Pion.
MÜHLMANN, Max (55)	.. ..	1. 9.41	Art.
MÜLLER, Erich (55)	319 Inf. Div.	1. 6.42	Kav.
MÜLLER, Ferdinand (62)	.. ..	..	Pion.
MÜLLER, Friedrich-Wilhelm (47) ..	22 L.L. Div. (mot.)	1. 4.43	..
MÜLLER, Ludwig (52)	97 Lt. Div.	1. 7.43	Inf.
MÜLLER, Vincenz (49)	.. ..	1. 3.43	Pion.
MÜLLER-GEBHARD, Philipp-Alfred (55)	.. ..	1. 1.42	Inf.
NAKE, Albin	526 Div. Nr.	1. 7.43	Inf.
NAUMANN (54)	.. ..	1. 4.42	Pz. Tr.
NEUBRONN v. EISENBURG, Alexander Frhr. v. (61).	Liaison Officer with French War Ministry.	1.12.42	Inf.
NEUMANN, Friedrich-Wilhelm (64) ..	712 Inf. Div.	1. 2.42	Inf.
NEUMANN-NEURODE, Karl-Ulrich (64)	.. ..	..	Inf.
NIEHOFF, Heinrich (60)	Cdt. H. Gebiet Süd Frankreich	1. 2.38	Inf.
NIEHOFF, Johannes	371 Inf. Div.	..	Inf.
NOELDECHEN, Ferdinand (49) ..	An Inf. Div.	1. 5.43	Art.
NOLTE, Hans Erich (62)	Div. Nr. 461	1.10.42	Kav.
OBERHÄUSSER, Eugen (55)	C.S.O. H. Gru. Mitt.	1.11.42	Na. Tr.
OBERNITZ, Justin v. (60)	.. ..	1. 6.40	Kav.
OCHSNER, Hermann (52)	Insp. d. Nebel Tr.	1. 6.43	Nbl.Tr.
OESTERREICH, v. (62)	Rear Area, P.W. Camps ..	1. 7.43	Inf.
ONDARZA, Herbert v. (66)	Höh Arko. 305	1.11.42	Art.
OPPENLÄNDER, Kurt (52)	.. ..	1. 8.43	Inf.
ORIOLA, Graf v.	299 Inf. Div.	1.11.43 ?	Art.
ORTNER, Bruno	69 Inf. Div.	1.10.42	Inf.
PELLENGAHR, Richard (61) ..	.. ..	1. 6.40	Art.
PELTZ, Joachim (60)	.. ..	1. 4.41	Inf.
PESCHEL	.. ..	1. 6.43	Inf.
PETSCH (56)	710 Inf. Div.	1.11.42	Inf.
PFEIFFER, Dr. phil. Georg (54) ..	65 Inf. Div.	1. 6.42	Art.
PFLAUM, Karl (54)	157 Res. Div.	1.10.43	Inf.
PFLIEGER (54)	416 Inf. Div.	1.10.42	Art.
PFLUGBEIL, Johann (62)	388 Feldausb. Div.	1.10.39	Inf.
PFLUGRADT, Kurt (53)	Befehlshaber Salonika-Aegean	1. 4.42	Inf.
PHILIPP, Christian	6 Mtn. Div.	1. 1.43	Geb.Tr.
PHILIPPS, Dipl. Ing.	.. ..	1.10.43	Pz. Tr.
PILZ	.. ..	1. 2.42	Inf.
PINCKVOSS (58)	Kassel, Wkr. IX	1. 2.41	Inf.
PLOTHO, Wolfgang Edler Herr u. Frhr. v. (65).	.. ..	..	Inf.
POETTER, Adolf (60)	410 Div. z.b.V.	..	Inf.
POPPE (51)	217 Inf. Div.	1. 1.43	Inf.
POSTEL, Georg (48)	320 Inf. Div.	1.12.43 ?	Art.
PRAETORIUS, Robert (62)	Dresden, Wkr. IV	1. 2.38	Art.
PRAGER, Karl (56)	Admin. Post. in Wkr. IX ..	1. 2.42	Art.
PRAUN, Albert (50)	129 Inf. Div.	1. 2.43	Inf.
PRIESS	.. ..	1. 7.43	Inf.
PRONDZYNSKI, v. (63)	Prague, Protectorate ..	1. 4.42	Art.
PÜCHLER	257 Inf. Div.	1. 4.43	Inf.
PUTTKAMER, Alfred v. (59)	.. ..	1. 8.39	Kf. Tr.
RAITHEL (49)	.. ..	1. 5.43	Art.
RAPPARD, Fritz Georg v.	7 Inf. Div.	1. 5.43	Inf.
RATHKE	.. ..	1.10.42	Art.
RAUCH, Erwin (55)	123 Inf. Div.	1.11.42	Inf.
RAVENSTEIN, Johann v. (55) ..	Prisoner of War	1.10.43	Inf.
RECKE, Heinrich (54)	161 Inf. Div.	1. 6.42	Inf.
RECKNAGEL, Hermann (52)	111 Inf. Div.	1. 3.43	Inf.

Rank : Generalleutnant (*Lt.-General*)—*continued*

Name (*age*)	*Appointment* (*date*)	*Seniority*	*Arm*
REICHE, v. (59)	..	1. 4.38	Kav.
REICHERT, Joseph (53)	..	1. 9.43	Inf.
RENZ, Maximilian (61)	..	31.10.38	Kav
REYMANN, Hellmuth	..	1. 4.43	Inf.
RICHERT (52)	Sich. Div. 286	1. 3.43	Inf.
RICHTER, Werner (51)	..	1. 3.43	Inf.
RICHTER (55)	..	1.10.39	Inf.
RIEBESAM, Ludwig (56)	Linz, Wkr. XVII	1. 6.41	Inf.
RINGEL, Julius (55)	5 Mtn. Div.	1.12.42	Geb.Tr.
RISSE, Walter	..	1. 6.43	Inf.
RODENBURG, Karl (50)	Prisoner of War	1.12.42	Inf.
ROEDER v. DIERSBURG, Kurt Frhr. (58).	Cologne, Wkr. VI	1. 2.41	Art.
RÖRICHT	..	1. 4.43	Inf.
RÖTTIGER	C.G.S. 4 Pz. Army	1. 9.43	Pz. Tr.
ROHDE, Hans (51)	M.A. Ankara	1. 1.43	Inf.
ROSENBUSCH (54)	Insp. d. Landesbefest. Nord	1. 4.42	Pion.
ROSSI, Franz	A Div.	1. 9.43	Art.
ROSSUM (54)	..	1.12.42	Inf.
ROTHKIRCH u. PANTHEN, Friedrich-Wilhelm v. (60).	..	1. 8.40	Kav.
ROTHKIRCH u. TRACH, Edwin, Graf v. (56).	..	1. 3.42	Kav.
RÜDIGER, Dr. Ing.	..	1. 6.43	Art.
RÜHLE v. LILIENSTERN, Alexander (63).	Wrk. I, Königsberg	1. 2.42	Inf.
RUPP (51)	..	1. 1.43	Inf.
RUPPRECHT, Wilhelm (54)	..	1.11.42	Inf.
RUSSWURM, Josef (56)	General d. Nachr. Tr. Ersatzheer	1. 9.40	Na. Tr.
RUSSWURM, Wilhelm (56)	265 Inf. Div.	1. 9.40	Na. Tr.
SANDER, Erwin (52)	170 Inf. Div.	1. 1.43	Art.
SANNE (54)	Prisoner of War	1. 4.42	Inf.
SATOW (56)	Frankfurt a/O, Wkr. III	1.11.41	Kav.
SAUCKEN, Dietrich v. (52)	4 Pz. Div.	1. 4.43	Kav.
SAUER, Otto Ritter v. (68)	..	..	Inf.
SCHACKY auf SCHÖNFELD, Sigmund Frhr. v. (58).	165 Res. Div.	1. 8.40	Inf.
SCHAEFER Hans (52)	Kdt. Kassel	1. 1.43	Inf.
SCHAEFER (57)	..	..	..
SCHAEWEN, Dr. v. (57)	..	1. 2.41	Pion.
SCHARTOW (54)	429 Div. z.b.V.	1. 3.43	Inf.
SCHAUM (53)	..	1.10.43	Pion.
SCHAUMBURG, Ernst (64)	..	1. 2.38	Inf.
SCHAUROTH, Athos v. (58)	Breslau, Wkr. VIII	1. 4.38	Inf.
SCHEDE, Wolfgang (56)	..	1. 7.40	Inf.
SCHEELE, Hans Karl v. (52)	An Armee Korps	1. 1.43	Inf.
SCHELL, Adolf v. (50)	25 Pz. Div.	1. 4.42	.
SCHELLER, Walter (52)	9 Pz. Div.	1. 1.43	Inf.
SCHERBENING (53)	79 Inf. Div.	1. 9.43	Inf.
SCHERER, Theodor (55)	83 Inf. Div.	1.11.42	Inf.
SCHIMPF (57)	..	1.12.40	Pion.
SCHINDLER, Maximilian (64)	Rü. Insp. in Gen. Govt.	1. 2.34	Inf.
SCHIRMER, Georg (54)	..	1. 1.43	Inf.
SCHLEINITZ, Siegmund Frhr. v. (54)	9 Inf. Div.	1. 9.42	Inf.
SCHLEMMER, Ernst (55)	..	1.12.42	..
SCHLEMMER, Dipl. Ing. Hans (51)	134 Inf. Div.	1. 1.43	Art.
SCHLENTHER, Eugen (66)	..	1. 3.38	Inf.
SCHLIEPER (53)	Head of Mil. Mission to Slovakia	1.11.41	Art.
SCHLÖMER, Helmut (51)	Prisoner of War	1.12.42	Inf.
SCHMETZER, Rudolf (60)	Insp. of Western Fortifications	1. 2.41	Pion
SCHMID-DANKWARD, Walter (57)	..	1.12.40	Art.
SCHMIDT, Arthur (49)	P.W., Russia	17.1.43	Inf.
SCHMIDT, August (51)	10 Pz. Gr. Div.	1. 1.43	Inf.
SCHMIDT, Curt (54)	..	1.12.42	Inf.

Rank : Generalleutnant (*Lt.-General*)—*continued*

Name (age)	*Appointment (date)*	*Seniority*	*Arm*
SCHMIDT, Gustav (50)	19 Pz. Div.	1. 1.43	Inf.
SCHMIDT-LOGAN, Wolfgang (60)	..	..	Art.
SCHMITT, Artur	Prisoner of War	1. 1.43	Inf.
SCHMUNDT, Rudolf (56)	Chef d. H.P.A., O.K.H.	1. 4.43	Inf
SCHNEIDER, Dipl. Ing. Erich (50) (?)	..	1. 7.43	..
SCHNEIDER, Ernst (61)	Fest. Pion. Kdr. XVII	1. 7.42	Pion.
SCHÖNHÄRL, Hans (66)	..	1.12.40	Inf.
SCHÖNHERR, Otto (54)	..	1. 9.43	Inf.
SCHOPPER, Erich (52)	An Inf. Div.	1. 2.43	Art.
SCHRADER, Rudolf (55)	C.S.O. Army Gr. West	1. 7.42	Na.Tr.
SCHREIBER (67)	Cdt. Hannover, Wkr. XI	..	Inf.
SCHROECK (55)	..	1. 6.41	Inf.
SCHUBERT, Rudolf (55)	C.S.O. Greece	1. 4.43	Na.Tr.
SCHÜNEMANN, Otto (53)	337 Inf. Div.	1. 5.43	Inf.
SCHULZ, Friedrich (47)	C.G.S. 20 Army	1. 7.43	..
SCHWARZENECKER (60)	Vienna, Wkr. XVII	1. 3.38	Inf.
SCHWERIN, Gerhard Graf v. (45)	16 Pz. Gren. Div.	1. 6.43	
SCHWERIN, Richard v. (49)	..	1.12.42	Inf.
SCOTTI, Friedrich v. (55)	Höh. Art. Kdo. of an Army	1. 2.41	Art.
SEEGER (53)	..	1. 9.43	Inf.
SEIFERT, Ernst (60)	..	1. 8.38	Inf.
SELLE, v.	Art. Kdr. 113	1. 1.42	Art.
SENGER u. ETTERLIN, Fridolin v. (53)	..	1. 5.43	Kav.
SEYFFARDT (50)	110 Inf. Div.	1. 1.43	Inf.
SIEBERT, Friedrich (56)	..	1. 4.41	Inf.
SIELER (49)	..	1. 7.43	Inf.
SINTZENICH, Rudolf (55)	..	1.12.41	Inf.
SINZINGER, Adolf (53)	..	1. 1.43	Inf.
SIRY, Max (53)	..	1. 1.43	Art.
SIXT, Friedrich (47)	C.G.S. 7 Army	1. 6.43	Art.
SIXT v. ARMIN, Hans Heinrich (55)	Prisoner of War	1. 3.40	Inf.
SODAN, Ralf (64)	270 Inf. Div.	1.12.42	Kav.
SOMMERFELD, Hans v. (58)	..	1. 9.41	Inf.
SORSCHE, Konrad (61)	Liegnitz, Wkr. VIII	1. 3.38	Art
SPANG, Karl (58)	..	1. 4.40	Art.
SPECHT, Karl-Wilhelm (51)	Cdt. Inf. School Döberitz	1. 8.43	Inf.
SPEEMANN, Kurt (67)	A rückw. Armeegeb.	..	..
SPEICH, Dr. Richard (60)	Grenzwach Div. 539	..	Pion.
SPONECK, Hans Graf v. (56)	..	1. 2.40	Inf.
SPONECK, Graf v. (48)	Prisoner of War	1. 5.43	..
STAHL, Friedrich (54)	..	1. 9.42	Pz. Tr.
STEINBAUER, Gerhard (55)	..	1.10.42	Art.
STEINMETZ	94 Inf. Div.	1.12.43 (?)	Art.
STENGEL, Hans (64)	..	1. 4.41	Kav.
STEPHAN, Friedrich (52)	..	1. 1.43	Inf.
STEPHANUS (63)	..	..	Inf.
STEVER (56)	..	1. 6.41	Kav.
STIELER v. HEYDEKAMPF (63)	Rü. Insp. III	1. 2.41	Inf.
STIMMEL (58)	..	1. 6.41	Inf.
STOEWER, Paul (55)	143 Res. Div.	1. 2.42	Inf.
STRACK, Heinrich (57)	..	1. 9.41	Inf.
STREICH, Hans (53)	..	1.10.43	Pz. Tr.
STUD (55)	Rü. u. Beschaffs. amt France	1. 2.40	Art.
STÜMPFL, Heinrich (60)	Cdt. Vienna, Wkr. XVII	1. 6.40	Inf.
STUMPFELD v. (58)	..	1. 4.43	Art.
STUMPFF, Horst (57)	..	1. 2.41	Pz. Tr.
SZELINSKI (53)	298 Inf. Div.	1. 1.43	Inf.
TARBUK v. SENSENHORST, Karl	Grenzwach Div. 540	..	Inf.
TETTAU, Hans v. (56)	24 Inf. Div.	1. 3.42	Inf.
THOFERN, Wilhelm (59)	Tr. Üb. Pl. Grossborn	1. 9.42	Inf.
THOMA, Heinrich (53)	..	1. 9.43	Inf.
THOMAS, Wilhelm (51)	Ord. School	1. 7.43	Inf.
THOMASCHKI, Siegfried (50)	..	1. 1.43	Art.
THON, Friedrich (66)	Insp. d. Nachr. Tr.	..	Na.Tr.

Rank : Generalleutnant (*Lt.-General*)—*continued*

Name (age)	*Appointment (date)*	*Seniority*	*Arm*
THÜNGEN, Karl Frhr. v. (51)	Berlin, Wkr. III	1. 1.43	Pz. Tr.
THUMM, Helmuth (49)	5 Lt. Div.	1. 9.43	Inf.
TIEDEMANN, Karl (56)	..	1.11.39	Inf.
TIEMANN, Otto (56)	93 Inf. Div.	1.10.39	Pion.
TRAUT, Hans (49)	An Inf. Div.	1. 1.43	Inf.
TRESCKOW, Joachim v. (50)	328 Inf. Div.	1. 3.43	Inf.
TRIERENBERG, Wolf (53)	167 Inf. Div.	1.11.42	Inf.
TROTHA, V.	In France	—	Inf.
TSCHERNING, Otto (63)	Stuttgart, Wkr. V	1. 4.36	Art.
UCKERMANN, Horst Frhr. v. (52)	160 Res. Div.	1. 9.43	Inf.
USINGER	..	1. 7.43	Art.
UTHMANN, Bruno v. (53)	M.A. Stockholm	1. 9.41	Inf.
VEITH, Richard (54)	General z.b.V. Army Group North	1. 8.42	Inf.
VOGEL, Emil (50)	101 Lt. Div.	1. 4.43	Inf.
VOLCKAMER v. KIRCHENSITTENBACH, Friedrich Jobst.	..	1. 9.43	Inf.
VOLK, Erich (60)	Strassburg, Wkr. V	1. 2.41	Kav.
VORMANN, Nikolaus v. (49)	23 Pz. Div.	1. 7.43	Inf.
WACHTER, Friedrich Karl v. (55)	Chef. d. Ag. P4, O.K.H.	1. 4.42	Inf.
WAEGER, Kurt	Armaments Office in Min. for War Pr.	1. 1.43	Art.
WAGNER, August (60)	..	1. 8.40	Pz. Tr.
WAGNER, Eduard (50)	..	1. 4.42	Art.
WALDENFELS, Wilhelm Frhr. v. (60)	Innsbruck, Wkr. XVIII	1. 2.41	Inf.
WANGER, Rudolf (56)	..	1. 2.42	Inf.
WARLIMONT, Walter (50)	Head of Ops. Section O.K.W.	1. 4.42	Art.
WEGENER, Wilhelm (49)	32 Inf. Div.	1. 2.43	Inf.
WEIDINGER, Wilhelm (54)	Insp. d. Flak. Art., O.K.H.	1.10.43	Art.
WEIDLING, Helmuth (52)	86 Inf. Div.	1. 1.43	Art.
WEINGART, Erich (57)	..	1. 8.40	Fahr.Tr.
WESSEL, Walter (52)	..	1. 1.43	Inf.
WESSELY, Marian	..	..	Inf.
WESTHOVEN, Franz (50)	..	1. 5.43	Kav.
WICKEDE, Emil v. (51)	30 Inf. Div.	1. 1.43	Inf.
WILCK, Hermann (59)	708 Inf. Div.	42	Inf.
WILL, Otto (53)	Insp. d. Eisb. Pion., O.K.H.	1.12.42	Pion.
WILLICH, Fritz (62)	..	..	Inf.
WILMOWSKY, Friedrich Frhr. v. (63)	Insp. Potsdam, Wkr. III	1. 8.35	Kav.
WINDECK (55)	..	1. 4.42	Inf.
WINTER, Paul (49)	..	1. 6.43	Art.
WINTERFELD, v.	Cdt. Befest. Saarpfalz u. Eiffel	1. 1.42	..
WINTERGERST, Karl (52)	210 Inf. Div.	1. 4.43	Art.
WINTZER, Heinz (54)	Chef. d. Wirtschaft Stab, Norway	1.10.41	Art.
WITTKE, Walter (56)	General z.b.V. Army Group South	1. 8.41	Inf.
WOLFF, Ludwig (51)	Insp. d. Erz. u. Bildungswesens	1.12.42	Inf.
WOLFF	..	1. 1.43	Inf.
WOLFSBERGER, Franz	..	1.10.43	Kav.
WOLLMANN (54)	..	1. 6.40	Pion.
WOSCH, Heinrich (54)	233 Res. Pz. Div.	1. 1.43	Inf.
WOYTASCH, Kurt (63)	..	1. 8.41	Inf.
WREDE, Theodor Frhr. v. (56)	..	2. 3.41	Kav.
WUTHMANN, Rolf	..	1. 3.43	Art.
ZEHLER, Albert (56)	..	1.12.41	Art.
ZELLNER, Emil	373 Inf. Div.	1. 4.43	Inf.
ZICKWOLFF, Friedrich (55)	..	1.10.41	Inf.
ZIEGLER, Heinz (50)	..	3.12.42	Art.
ZIMMERMANN, Georg (65)	Mil. Plen., North Italy	..	Inf.
ZÜLOW, Alexander v. (54)	..	1.10.41	Inf.
ZUKERTORT, Johannes (59)	Art. Cmdr. H. Gru. West	1. 2.41	Art.
ZWENGAUER, Karl (62)	General z.b.V. b.Insp.d.Art.	1. 2.41	Art.

(e) Rank : GENERALMAJOR (Major-General)

Name (age)	*Appointment (date)*	*Seniority*	*Arm*
ABRAHAM, Erich (49)	76 Inf. Div.	1. 6.43	Inf.
ABT (52)	..	1. 4.42	Na. Tr.
ADLHOCH	..	1.11.42	Inf.
ADOLPH, Ernst (67)	..	..	Inf.
ALBERTI, Konrad v.	..	1. 4.43	..
AMMON, Carl v. (61)	Stettin, Wkr. II	1. 4.40	Kav.
ARNDT, Karl	293 Inf. Div.	1. 4.43	Inf.
ARNDT (52)	..	1. 8.43	Inf.
ARNIM, Friedemund v. (51)	Cdt. Amiens	1.11.42	Kav.
ARNOLD, Karl (54)	..	1. 6.41	Inf.
ARNOLD, Wilhelm	..	1.10.43	Na. Tr.
ASCHEBERG, Percy Baron v. (62)	..	1. 6.42	Na. Tr.
ASCHENBRANDT, Heinrich (59)	Cdt. Rakvere, Esthonia	1.12.41	Art.
AUER, Franz (65)	..	..	Art.
BAARTH, Jürgon (53)	O.F.K. 595 Angers	1. 4.42	Kav.
BACHER, Hermann	..	1.12.42	Pion.
BADE, Hans Albert	..	1. 4.43	..
BAESSLER, Erich (52)	377 Inf. Div.	1. 1.42	Inf.
BAESSLER, Hans (51)	A Pz. Div.	1. 2.42	Pz. Tr.
BALTZER, Martin (53)	..	1. 4.41	Na. Tr.
BAMBERG, Dr. (55)	Cdt. Riga	1. 2.41	Inf.
BARENDS (63)	..	1. 6.41	Inf.
BARTENWERFER, Gustav (62)	..	1. 2.42	Inf.
BARTON, Gottfried	..	1. 2.42	Kav.
BASSE, Max v. (59)	Staff Wkr. XII	1. 4.42	Inf.
BAUER, Franz	..	..	Inf.
BAUMGARTNER, Richard (61)	..	1.12.39	Pion.
BAYERLEIN, Fritz (55)	3 Pz. Div.	. 3.43	Pz. Tr.
BAZING (51)	Armee Pion. Führer 20 Mtn.Army	1.11.42	Pion.
BECHER (51)	Cdt. Königsberg, Wkr. I	1. 4.43	Inf.
BECHT, Dipl. Wirtsch. Ernst (49)	O.K.W. (W. Rü.)	1. 4.42	Art.
BECHTOLSHEIM, Gustav Frhr. v. MAUCHENHEIM gen. (55).	..	1. 8.41	Inf.
BECKÉ	Rü. Insp. XVIII	1.12.42	Inf.
BECKER, Carl (49)	An Inf. Div.	1. 4.43	Inf.
BECKER, Franz (52)	..	1. 8.42	Inf.
BEHRENS, Wilhelm (53)	..	1. 1.42	Inf.
BEININGER	..	1. 8.41	..
BEISSWÄNGER, Hugo (48)	..	1. 6.43	Art.
BEISSWÄNGER, Walter	O.K.H. (Wa. Prüf.)	1. 4.43	Art.
BENICKE, Dr. Fritz	..	1. 7.43	Pion.
BERG, Kurt v. (58)	..	1. 3.38	Art.
BERKA (63)	..	1. 3.41	Inf.
BERTHOLD	..	..	Inf.
BESCH, Helmut	T.Ü.P., Galicia	1.11.42	Inf.
BESSEL, Hans	..	1. 4.43	Pion.
BESSEL, v.	..	1. 6.41	Inf.
BIERINGER	Supply Off., Italy	1. 7.43	Kf. Tr.
BIERMANN (71)	Staff General b.d. Pion. u. Fest., O.K.H.	1. 4.41	Pion.
BILHARZ, Eugen (56)	..	1. 2.41	Inf.
BISLE, Artur (56)	Cdt. Tallinn, O.F.K. 545	1. 4.43	Inf.
BLOCK, Lothar v. (52)	..	1. 2.42	Inf.
BLÜCHER, Johann-Albrecht v. (52)	..	1. 8.42	Kav.
BOCK, Franz Karl v. (68)	Cdt. Nancy, O.F.K. 591	..	Inf.
BODENHAUSEN, Erpo Frhr. v.	..	1. 5.43	Pz. Tr.
BOEHRINGER, Gustav (52)	..	1. 2.42	Pion.
BÖMERS, Hans (50)	..	1. 4.42	Art.
BOER, John de (47)	..	1.10.43	Art.
BOESSER (65)	..	1. 4.42	Art.
BÖTTGER, Karl (53)	..	1. 4.41	Inf.
BOGEN, v.	..	1. 2.43	Inf.
BOIE, Sigurd	Cdt. Biarritz, O.F.K. 541	1.12.42	Inf.

Rank : Generalmajor (*Major-General*)—*continued*

Name (*age*)	*Appointment* (*date*)	*Seniority*	*Arm*
BORCHERS (62)		1.12.42	Pion.
BORK, Max		1. 4.43	..
BOROWSKI (62)		1. 4.41	Art.
BOTSCH, Walter	C.G.S. 19 Army	1. 9.43	Inf.
BRAUMÜLLER, Hans (61)		1. 6.41	Art.
BRAUN		1. 8.42	Na. Tr.
BRAUN, Julius		1. 4.43	Art.
BRAUSE		1. 8.42	Art.
BREHMER Walter		1. 3.43	Kav.
BRENKEN (63)		1. 6.42	Kav.
BRIESEN, v.	Cdt. Prague	1.10.42	Inf.
BRUNNER		..	..
BRUNS (53)	T.Ü.P. Harskamp	1. 4.42	Inf.
BRUNS, Walter	Cdt. Ghent	1. 4.42	Inf.
BÜGGENMANN		1. 4.42	..
BÜLOW, Cord v. (52)		1. 2.42	Kav.
BURGDORF, Wilhelm (49)	Deputy Chief Army Personnel Branch, O.K.H.	1.10.42	..
BUSICH, Rudolf	707 Inf. Div.	1. 5.42	Pion.
BUTTLAR, Edgar v.		1.10.43	Na. Tr.
CABANIS, Horst (Hans) (52)	Staff Wkr. III	1. 1.43	Kav.
CASTORF, Dipl. Ing. Helmut (54)	166 Res. Div.	1. 2.42	Inf.
CHALES DE BEAULIEU		1. 6.43	Pz. Tr.
CLAER, Bernhard v. (56)	Cdt. Liege	1. 4.42	Inf.
CONRADI, Siegfried (56)		1. 1.40	Art.
CRAMOLINI (63)		1. 6.41	Kav.
CRATO (62)		1. 6.42	Art.
CUNO, Kurt (48)		1. 7.43	Pz. Tr.
CZETTRITZ u. NEUHAUS, Conrad v.		1. 2.43	Kav.
DAHLMANN (54)		1. 7.40	Inf.
DANNEHL		1. 2.43	Inf.
DASER, Wilhelm (60)		1. 7.42	Inf.
DAUBER, Julius		1. 7.42	..
DECKER, Karl	5 Pz. Div.	1.12.43 ?	Pz. Tr.
DECKMANN (52)	Stablack Tng. Area., Wkr. I	1. 9.42	Inf.
DEDEK, Emil		1. 7.42	Pion.
DEGENER (51)		1.11.42	Kav.
DEINDL, Otto (54)		1. 2.42	Pz. Tr.
DEININGER (62)		1. 8.41	Inf.
DERMAGEN		1. 4.42	Inf.
DEITEN, Gustav v.		1.11.41	..
DEUTSCH (52)	711 Inf. Div.	1. 7.42	Inf.
DEWALD, Fritz		1.10.43	Inf.
DEYHLE, Willy	Ob. Qu., 18 Army	..	..
DICKMANN (63)		1. 6.42	Inf.
DINTER, Georg		1. 2.43	Pion.
DITTMEYER		1. 5.43	Pz. Tr.
DÖHREN, v. (58)		1. 7.41	Inf.
DÖPPING		1. 7.43	Inf.
DOHNASCHLOBITTEN, Heinrich Burggraf u. Graf z. (62)		1. 6.42	Kav.
DONAT, Dipl. Ing. Hans v. (53)		1.11.41	Pion.
DORNBERGER, Dr. Ing. h. c.		1. 6.43	Neb. Tr.
DREBBER, Moritz v. (52)	Prisoner of War 1.2.43	1. 1.43	Inf.
DRECKMANN, Dipl. Ing. Paul		1.10.43	Inf.
DREES (60)		1. 7.41	Art.
DRESCHER		1. 6.43	Art.
DRESSLER Rudolf (61)	In Stuttgart	1. 1.43	Art.
DROBNIG (56)		1. 7.41	Art.
DYBILASZ, Dipl. Ing.		1. 8.42	Pion.
EBELLING, Curt (52)	Art. Schiessschule Thorn, Wkr. XX.	1. 4.42	Art.
EBELING, Fritz (56)		1. 6.41	Inf.
EBERDING		1. 8.43	Inf.

Rank : Generalmajor (*Major-General*)—*continued*

Name (*age*)	*Appointment* (*date*)	*Seniority*	*Arm*
EBERHARDT, Kurt	..	..	..
ECKARDT, Eduard	..	1. 4.41	Art.
ECKHARDT, Hans-Heinrich (48)	..	1.10.43	Inf.
EHRENBERG, Hans (55)	Div. Nr. 409	1. 8.40	Inf.
EHRIG, Richard (61)	Staff Wkr. IV	1. 6.41	Inf.
EISENBACH	..	1.10.43	Inf.
EISENHART-ROTHE, Hans Georg v. (54).	..	1. 4.42	Kav.
EISENSTÜCK, Helmut (50)	Feldausb. Div. 381	1. 9.42	Inf.
ELSTER, Botho (50)	Cdt. Marseilles	1. 3.43	Art.
ELVERFELDT, Frhr. v.	..	1. 9.43	..
ENGELHARDT, Alfred (51)	..	1.11.42	Inf.
ERDMANN, Kurt	Rü. Insp. VI	1.1.43	Art.
ERDMANNSDORFF, Gottfried v. (51)	..	1.12.42	Inf.
ERTEL, Theodor (70)	..	1.9.41	Art.
ERXLEBEN	..	1.10.43	Na. Tr.
ESTORFF, v.	..	..	..
FABRICE, Ebernard v. (52)	Adm. Mainz.	1.3.42	Inf.
FALKENSTEIN, Erich Frhr. v. (64)	..	1.4.41	Inf.
FALKENSTEIN, Hans Frhr. v. (51)	45 Inf. Div.	1.5.43	Inf.
FANGOHR, Joachim	..	1.2.43	Inf.
FEHN, Franz (61)	Cdt. Augsburg, Wkr. VII	1.6.41	Kav.
FELBERT, Paul v.	..	1.10.43	Inf.
FELZMANN, Maxmilian (50)	251 Inf. Div.	1.6.43	Art.
FIEDLER, Erich (60)	..	1.7.42	Pion.
FISCHER, Karl (52)	..	1.4.42	Art.
FISCHER, Theodor	..	1.8.42	Inf.
FITZLAFF	..	1.1.43	Art.
FLÖRKE	14 Pz. Gren. Div.	1.6.43	Inf.
FORSTER, Paul Herbert (52)	389 Inf. Div.	1.7.42	Art.
FRETTER-PICO, Otto	..	1.3.43	Pz. Tr.
FREYE (66)	..	1.7.42	Pion.
FREYTAG, Walter (52)	Cdt. Besancon	1.8.42	Inf.
FRIEDRICHS, Walter (60)	..	1.10.37	Inf.
FRIEMEL, Georg (53)	Prisoner of War	1.2.41	Inf.
FRIES (48)	29 Pz. Gren. Div.	1.6.43	Inf.
FUCHS, Willi v.	..	1.7.42	Inf.
FUCIK, Karl	..	1.7.41	Inf.
FÜRSTENBERG	34 Inf. Div.	1.9.41	Inf.
GALL (53)	France	1.1.43	Inf.
GALLWITZ, Werner v.	..	1.10.43	Art.
GEBAUER, Artur	Cdt. Graz, Wkr. XVIII	1.6.42	Inf.
GEIS, Hermann (66)	..	..	Inf.
GEMPP, Fritz (70)	O.K.W. (Ausl. Abw.)	..	Inf.
GENEE, Paul (64)	..	1.2.42	Inf.
GERBER, Alexander	..	1.9.42	Inf.
GERLACH, Erwin	Stab. 1 Armee	1.6.43	Art.
GERMAR, v. (66)	W.B.K. Stolp, Wkr. II	1.3.41	Inf.
GEROCK	..	1.3.43	Art.
GERSDORF, Gero v. (51)	..	1.1.43	Kav.
GESCHWANDTNER (53)	..	1.10.42	Art.
GEYSO, Eckhard v. (52)	Döberitz Tng. Area	1.10.42	Inf.
GIEHRACH (62)	..	1.8.41	Art.
GIHR	..	1.10.43	Inf.
GLODOWSKI, Erich (64)	W.B.K. Essen, Wkr. VI	1.4.41	Inf.
GOECKEL, Hans v. (55)	..	1.2.41	Inf.
GOELDEL, v. (54)	..	1.2.41	Inf.
GOTHSCHE, Reinhold	O.K.H. (Amtsgruppe K)	1.10.43	..
GRACHEGG, Gustav (62)	..	..	Inf.
GRAEVENITZ, Hans v. (50)	O.K.W. (W. Vers.)	1.2.42	Inf.
GRASSMANN, Kuno	..	1.3.43	Art.
GRAU, Josef (55)	..	..	Inf.
GROBHOLZ, Dr. (51)	..	1.10.42	Kf. Tr
GRODDECK, Karl Albrecht v. (52)	..	1.8.42	Inf.

Rank : Generalmajor (*Major-General*)—*continued*

Name (*age*)	*Appointment* (*date*)	*Seniority*	*Arm*
GROSSE, Dr. Walther	..	1.4.43	Pion.
GRÜNER, Erich	..	1.9.43	Inf.
GÜNDELL, Walther v. (52)	O.K.H. (H. Qu.)	1.12.41	Inf.
GUHR (71)	..	..	Inf.
GURRAN	..	1.10.43	Inf.
GUTKNECHT (56)	..	1.7.42	Inf.
GYLDENFELDT, Heinz v.	G.C.S. LXVIII A.K.	1.7.43	Art.
HAACK	..	1.4.43	Art.
HAECKL, Ferdinand	..	..	..
HAGL, August (56)	..	1.12.40	Inf.
HAHN, Johannes (54)	Cdt. Lyons	1. 4.43	..
HAMANN, Adolf	..	1. 6.42	Inf.
HANSTEIN, Hans v.	O.K.H. (W)	1. 8.42	Inf.
HARTMANN, Martin (59)	Staff of an Army in East	1. 4.43	Inf.
HARTMANN, Wilhelm Dipl. Ing.	O.K.W. (W)	1. 8.42	Art.
HARTTMANN, Herman (59)	..	1. 4.43	Inf.
HASELMAYR	..	..	..
HASELOFF, Kurt (49)	C.G.S. General Government	1. 1.43	Inf.
HAUCK, Bruno	..	1. 6.43	Art.
HAUENSCHILD, Bruno Ritter v. (50)	..	1. 4.42	Pz. Tr.
HAUGER, Dipl. Wirtsch.	Rü. Insp. Oberrhein	1. 8.42	Inf.
HAUGK, Siegfried (58)	..	1. 6.43	..
HAUSER	13 Pz. Div.	..	Inf.
HAUSER, Wolfgang	..	1.12.42	Art.
HAVERKAMP, Wilhelm (53)	General z.b.V. b. Mil. Bfh. General Government.	1. 8.41	Inf.
HEDERICH, Hans (65)	Retired	1. 4.41	Art.
HEDERICH, Willy (64)	..	1. 2.42	Art.
HEIDRICH, Fritz	..	1. 8.43	Art.
HEINZ, v.	..	..	Inf.
HEISTERMANN v. ZIEHLBERG, Gustav	..	1. 8.43	Inf.
HELLWIG, Georg	..	1. 6.42	Pion.
HELWIG, Hans	..	1.10.43	Inf.
HENKE, Gerhard (66)	..	1. 2.43	Inf.
HENRICI, Dipl. Ing. Hans (48)	O.K.H. (Wa Z)	1. 7.43	Art.
HENRICI, Rudolf (52)	..	1. 8.42	Art.
HERFURTH, Otto (51)	..	1.10.43	Inf .
HERNEKAMP, Dipl. Ing. Karl (49)	Rü. Insp. Prague	1. 6.42	Art.
HERRMANN, Hans	W.B.K. Tilsit, Wkr. XX	..	..
HERRMANN, Paul	..	1.10.42	Pion.
HESSELBARTH (52)	..	1. 4.43	Inf.
HEYDENREICH, Dipl. Ing.	..	1. 4.43	Art.
HEYGENDORFF, Ralph v.	..	1. 6.43	..
HEYL, Friedrich (63)	..	1.10.41	Art.
HEYNE, Hans-Walter (60)	..	1. 6.43	Art.
HIEPE, Hellmuth (53)	..	1. 2.42	Art.
HILDEBRANDT, Hans Georg	..	1. 3.43	Pz. Tr.
HILDEMANN (52)	Staff 16 Army	1.11.41	Pion.
HILLERT, Dipl. Ing. Walter	Rü. Insp. IX	1. 1.42	Inf.
HINTZE (66)	..	1. 7.42	Art.
HITZFELD (46)	..	1. 4.43	Inf.
HOCHBAUM, Hans (66)	..	..	Inf.
HÖRAUF, Franz Ritter v. (66)	..	..	Inf.
HÖRMANN, Dr. Maximilian (53)	..	1. 4.42	Na. Tr.
HÖSSLIN, Hubert v.	Staff of Wkr. XII	1. 9.43	..
HOFERT, Johannes (59)	..	..	Art.
HOFFMANN, Dr. Heinrich	..	1.12.42	Inf.
HOFFMAN, Max (52)	..	1. 1.42	Na. Tr.
HOFFMANN, Paul	Sich. Div. 207	1. 6.41	Inf.
HOFFMANN, Paul	Sich. Div. 207	1. 6.42	Art.
HOFFMEISTER, Edmund	An Inf. Div.	1. 9.43	Inf.
HOFMANN, Friedrich	O. K. H.	1.11.42	..
HOFMAN, Helmut Frhr. v. (52)	..	1. 6.42	Inf.

Rank : Generalmajor (*Major-General*)—*continued*

Name (*age*)	*Appointment* (*date*)	*Seniority*	*Arm*
HOLZHAUSEN (52)	Fz. Dienst Lundenburg Wkr. XVII.	1. 9.42	Art.
HORN, Hans-Joachim v.	M.A. Helsinki	1. 4.43	Cav.
HORSTIG gen. d'AUBIGNY v. EZ GELBRUNNER, Dr. Ing. Ritter v. (50).	.. ..	1. 3.42	Art.
HOSSFELD, Walter (52)	Trg. Area Wildflecken	1. 8.42	Inf.
HOTZY, Dr. Otto	.. ..	1. 4.42	Inf.
HUBER, Werner..	.. ..	..	..
HÜBNER, Kurt (53)	.. ..	1. 4.42	Kav.
HÜHNLEIN, F. (70)	.. ..	..	Inf.
HÜLSEN Heinrich Hermann v. (49) ..	Prisoner of War..	1. 5.43	..
HÜNERMANN, Dipl. Ing. Rudolf (50)	O. K. W. (W Amt)	1. 4.42	Art.
IHSSEN Hugo (57	Fz. Kdo. III	1.10.40	Art.
ILGEN, Max	.. ..	1. 2.43	Art.
JACOBI	Feld Kdtr. Rennes (549) ..	1.12.41	Pz. Tr
JACOBSEN, Heinrich	.. ..	1. 2.43	Inf.
JAEHN	.. ..	1. 1.43	..
JAIS, Max	Cdt. Klagenfurt XVIII ..	1.10.42	Inf.
JAKOWITZ (54)	.. ..	..	Inf.
JANSEN (63)	Rü. Insp. Ostland	1.11.41	Na. Tr.
JANSSEN Adolf-Wilhelm (67).. ..	.. ..	..	Kav.
JANUSZ, Johann (62)	.. ..	..	Art.
JATZOW, Hermann (64)	.. ..	1.10.41	Inf.
JAUER (48)	.. ..	1. 4.43	Art.
JESSER, Kurt (54)	.. ..	1.12.42	Pz. Tr.
JÖRLING..	.. ..	1. 2.42	Inf.
JOHNS	292 Inf. Div	..	Inf. ?
JOLASSE, Erwin (52)	.. ..	1.10.43	Inf.
JORDAN, Gerhard (49)..	.. ..	1. 4.42	Pion.
JOST, Walter (48)	.. ..	1. 4.43	Inf.
JUST, Emil (54)	G. O. C. Lithuania	1.10.42	Art.
KALDRACK, Otto (64)	.. ..	..	Inf.
KALM, Otto v. (54)	.. ..	1. 2.41	Art.
KAMPFHENKEL	.. ..	1. 4.43	Art.
KANITZ, Hans Graf v. (51)	Gas School, Celle, Wkr. XI ..	1.12.42	Neb. Tr.
KARL	.. ..	1. 9.42	Inf.
KATTNER, Heinz (48)	Cdt. Toulon	1.10.43	Inf.
KEIL, Rudolf	Insp. Transport, East	1. 7.42	Pz. Tr.
KEIM (62)	.. ..	..	Inf.
KELTSCH, Eduard	.. ..	1.11.42	Art.
KEPER	.. ..	1. 3.43	Kav.
KESSEL, Paul v.	.. ..	1.11.42	Pz. Tr.
KIRCHBACH, Harry v.	.. ..	1. 7.42	Inf.
KIRCHENPAUER v. KIRCHDORFF	Staff, Wkr. IV	1. 1.43	Inf.
KISTNER	.. ..	1. 4.43	Art.
KITTEL, Heinrich (52)	.. ..	1. 4.42	Inf.
KLEINSCHROTH, Dipl. Ing.	.. ..	1.10.43	..
KLEIST (58)	.. ..	27. 8.39	Art.
KLEMM, Kuno	.. ..	1.10.43	Inf.
KLEPP, Dr. Ernst	.. ..	1. 4.42	Inf.
KLISZCZ, Ing. Otto	Fest. Pion. Kdr. IV	1. 9.41	Pion.
KLÜG	.. ..	1. 9.43	Inf.
KNOERZER, Hans (56)	Cdt. Bordeaux, O.F.K. 529 ..	1. 7.42	Inf.
KOCH, Dipl. Ing. Walter (53)	O.K.H. (Wa Prüff.)	1. 4.42	Art.
KÖNIGSDORFER, Josef (69)	.. ..	..	Pion.
KOHL, Gustav (57)	.. ..	1. 2.41	Inf.
KOHLER..	282 Inf. Div.	1. 6.43	Inf.
KOHNKE..	.. ..	1.12.42	Art.
KOLL	.. ..	1. 8.43	..
KOPP, Arthur (58)	.. ..	1. 2.43	Art.
KORFES, Dr. Otto (55)..	Prisoner of War..	1. 1.43	..
KORTE, Heinz (52)	.. ..	1. 4.42	Art.
KORTÜM, Dr.	.. ..	1. 4.43	Art.
KOSSACK, Walter (61)	Cdt. Agram, F.K. 735	1. 6.42	Art.

Rank : Generalmajor (*Major-General*)—*continued*

Name (*age*)	*Appointment* (*date*)	*Seniority*	*Arm*
KRÄTZER, Franz	..	1. 6.42	Inf.
KRAUSE, Fritz (49)	Prisoner of War	1. 7.42	Art.
KRAUSE, Johannes	..	1. 2.43	Art.
KREBS, v. Detwitz gen. V.	..	1. 8.41	Inf.
KRECH, Franz (54)	..	1. 4.42	Inf.
KREIPE	..	1. 9.43	Inf.
KRETSCHMER, Alfred	M.A. Tokio	1. 7.42	Inf.
KRIEBEL, Ritter v. Friedrich (63)	..	1. 2.41	Inf.
KRIEGER, Hans (52)	..	1. 6.42	Inf.
KROPFF, v. (57)	..	1. 3.39	Inf.
KROSICK, Ernst Anton v.	..	1. 9.43	..
KRUMMEL, Adolf	..	1.12.42	Pion.
KÜBLER, Josef	118 Jäg. Div.	1. 1.43	Inf.
KÜHNE, Gerhard	..	1. 9.43	..
KÜPPER, Hans (51)	..	1.11.42	Kav.
KUMMER, v.	..	1. 9.41	..
KUNZE, Friedrich (64)	..	1. 4.41	Art.
KURNATOWSKI, v. (64)	F. Kdtr. 505	1. 2.42	Inf.
KURZ, Karl Ritter v. (71)	..	..	..
KUSSIN, Friedrich	Railway Eng. School	1. 4.43	Pion.
KUTZLEBEN, v.	T.U.P. Radom, General Government.	..	..
LATTMANN, Martin	Prisoner of War	1. 1.43	Art.
LECHNER, Heinrich (71)	Fortress Bde. 2, Kreta	1. 7.41	Inf.
LEDEBUR, Frhr. v. (64)	..	..	Inf.
LEEB, Leopold	..	1. 9.42	..
LEHMANN, Hans-Albrecht	..	1. 9.43	Na. Tr
LEMKE, Herbert (55)	Prisoner of War	1. 8.41	Inf.
LEOPRECHTING, Waldemar Frhr. v. (64).	..	1. 7.42	Na. Tr.
LE SUIRE v. (48)	117 Jäg. Div.	1. 5.43	Inf.
LETTOW, Paul (53)	182 Res. Div.	1. 4.42	Inf.
LEUZE, Walter (53)	..	1. 4.42	Kav.
LEYERS, Dr. Ing.	Rü. u. Beschaff Stab Italy	1. 1.43	Krf. Tr.
LEYSER Hans Georg (47)	18 Pz. Gren. Div.	1.11.42	Inf.
LEYTHÄUSER, Hermann (60)	..	1. 4.40	Kav.
LICHT (53)	..	1. 2.42	Inf.
LIEBENSTEIN, Kurt Frhr. v. (45)	Prisoner of War	1. 7.43	..
LIEGMANN, Wilhelm (55)	..	1. 6.41	Inf.
LINDE, v. der (53)	..	1. 3.42	Kav.
LINDEMANN, Wilhelm (71)	..	..	Inf.
LINDENAU (63)	Staff G.O.C. Ostland	1. 8.41	Inf.
LINDNER, Kurt	..	1. 4.43	Inf.
LINKENBACH (55)	..	1. 8.41	Kav.
LINNARZ	Head of Army Personnel Office, O.K.H.	1. 1.43	Krf. Tr.
LIPPE, v. der	..	..	Kav.
LOCHAU, Axel v. der (61)	..	1. 7.41	Inf.
LOEHNING, Paul (55)	..	1. 4.40	Inf.
LOEWENICH, v.	..	1. 4.43	Kav.
LONTSCHAR, Adalbert	Cdt. Belgrade F.K. (599)	1. 7.41	Inf.
LORENZ, Hans (63)	..	1. 4.41	Inf.
LUDWIGER, Hartwig v. (49)	104 Jäg. Div.	1. 5.43	Inf.
LÜER, Hilmar (60)	..	1. 8.41	Inf.
LÜTKENHAUS	Cdt. Mannheim, Wkr. XII	1. 3.43	Inf.
LUTZ, Ernst Frhr. v. (60)	..	1. 7.42	Inf.
LUZ, Helwig (52)	Casualty Dept. O.K.H.	1. 4.42	Kav.
MAERCKER	..	..	Inf.
MAGNUS	Prisoner of War	1.10.42	Inf.
MAHLMANN, Paul	..	1. 1.43	Inf.
MAISEL, Ernst (48)	..	1. 6.43	Inf.
MANKEL	230 Inf. Div.	..	..
MANN, Edler v. TIECHLER, Ferdinand Ritter v. (53).	Cdt. Bucharest	1. 4.42	Inf.
MANTEUFFEL, v. Hasso Eccard v. (47)	7 Pz. Div.	1. 5.43	Cav.

Rank : Generalmajor (*Major-General*)—*continued*

Name (*age*)	*Appointment* (*date*)	*Seniority*	*Arm*
MARCINKIEWICZ, August		1.12.41	Pion.
MARKGRAF, Emil		1. 9.41	Inf.
MARLOW	Fz. Kdo. XXI	1.10.43	Art.
MARNITZ, Dipl. Ing. Viktor v.		1. 9.43	Pion.
MARSEILLE Joachim		..	..
MARSEILLE, Siegfried (56)		1. 7.41	Inf.
MAYER, Siegfried v.		1. 4.43	Inf.
MEDEN, Karl Friedrich v. d. (48)	17th Pz. Div.	1.10.43	Kav.
MEINHOLD (54)		1. 4.42	Inf.
MEISSNER, Hans (60)		1. 4.41	Na. Ta.
MEISSNER, Dipl. Ing. Felix		1.10.43	Na. Tr.
MELCHERT	Thorn, Wkr. XX	1. 2.43	Inf.
MELTZER, Karl		1.10.43	Art.
MELTZER, Rudolf (53)		1. 4.42	Na. Tr.
MENKEL	230 Inf. Div.	1.10.42	Inf.
MENNY, Erwin (51)		1.11.42	Pz. Tr.
METGER, Wilhelm	264 Inf. Div.	1. 7.43	Art.
METSCHER, Karl		1. 6.42	Art.
METZ, Eduard (53)		1. 8.42	Art.
METZ		1. 1.43	Art.
MEYER, Carl Ludwig		1. 4.42	Art.
MEYER, Fritz (51)	Oberbaustab, VII Army Corps	1. 4.43	Pion.
MEYER, Heinrich		..	Pz. Tr.
MICHELMANN, Axel		..	Inf.
MICKL, Johann (51)		1. 3.43	Inf.
MIERZINSKY (64)	FeldKdtr. 245	1. 2.42	Inf.
MILISCH, Leopold (72)		1. 7.42	Inf.
MORITZ, Georg (52)	FeldKdtr. Pärnu	1.12.41	Kav.
MOST (59)		..	Inf.
MÜLLER, Angelo (52)		1. 4.42	Art.
MÜLLER, Dipl. Ing. Gerhard (48)		1. 4.43	Art.
MÜLLER, Hans Ludwig		1.12.42	Na. Tr.
MÜLLER-DERICHSWEILER		1. 9.43	Inf.
MUHL (52)		1.10.42	Art.
MYLO, Walther (64)		1. 1.42	Inf.
NAGEL, Frederich Wilhelm (55)	Insp. d. Wirtschaftsinsp. Süd	1. 4.42	Inf.
NEIDHOLDT, Fritz (54)	369 Inf. Div.	1.10.42	Inf.
NEINDORFF, v.		1.12.42	Inf.
NEUMAYR Franz (54)	Cdt. Sofia	1. 4.42	Inf.
NEWIGER, Albert (55)		1. 1.43	Kav.
NEYMANN		1. 2.42	Inf.
NICKELMANN (51)		1. 2.43	Inf.
NIDA, v.	C. of S., Wkr. IX	1. 6.43	..
NIEBECKER, Georg (67)		..	Pion.
NIEDENFÜHR, Günther (55)		..	Kav.
NIEDERMAYER, Prof. Dr. Ritter v. (59).	162 Inf. Div.	1. 9.42	Art.
NIEMANN		1.10.43	Neb. Tr.
NOACK, Rudolf (63)		1. 9.43	Inf.
NOSTITZ-WALLWITZ, Gerhard v. (59)		1.12.41	Inf.
ÖLLER		1.10.43	Inf.
OELSNER (55)	Trg. Area, Vandern	1. 2.41	Inf.
OFFENBÄCHER, Konrad (54)	T.Ü.P. Dollersheim Wkr. XVII	1. 6.41	Inf.
OHNACKER, W. (52)		1. 4.42	Inf.
OLBERG, v.		1. 2.42	Inf.
OSTER, Hans (56)		1.12.42	Inf.
OTTO (57)		1. 8.38	Pion.
PACHMAYR (61)		1. 9.41	Art.
PANNWITZ, Helmuth v. (46)	1st Kossack Div.	1. 6.43	Kav.
PAUER, Ernst		1. 9.41	Art.
PAWEL		1. 9.42	Inf.
PECHMANN, Albrecht Frhr. v. (64)		1. 9.41	Art.
PEMSEL, Max		1. 9.43	Inf.
PETERSEN, Matthias	Cdt. Kaiserslautern, Wkr. XII	1. 2.42	Inf.

Rank : Generalmajor (*Major-General*)—*continued*

Name (*age*)	*Appointment* (*date*)	*Seniority*	*Arm*
PETERSEN, Wilhelm (52)		1. 4.42	Pion.
PFEIFER, Helmut (50)		1. 9.43	Inf.
PFETTEN		1.11.42	Kav.
PFUHLSTEIN, Alexander v. (45)		1. 7.43	Inf.
PHILIPP, Ernst	Art. School, Wkr. III	1. 5.42	Art.
PIEKENBROCK, Hans	An Inf. Div.	1. 4.43	Kav.
PLAMBÖCK (64)		1. 4.41	Art.
PLAMMER		..	Inf.
PLEHWE, v.	FeldKdtr. Saare Maa	1.10.43	Kav.
PLEWIG, Willy (64)		1. 4.41	Inf.
PLOETZ, Egon v. (66)	W.B.K. Rostock, Wkr. II	1. 8.42	Kav.
POEL, Gerhard (58)		1. 7.41	Kav.
POHL, v. (70)		..	Art.
POTEN, Ernst		1. 7.42	Geb. Art.
PRESSENTIN, Richard v. (70)	Landesschütz. Rgt. z.b.V. 26	1. 7.42	Art.
PREUSSER, Arnold (67)		..	..
PRIEM, v. (61)		1. 1.42	Inf.
PRINNER		1. 3.43	Art.
PRITTWITZ u. GAFFRON, Max. v. (68)	Cdt. Lwow, Gen. Gouvernment	1. 9.41	Inf.
PRÜGEL, Dr. Karl (67)		1. 1.42	Na. Tr.
PRÜTER		1. 1.43	Inf.
PUTTKAMER, v. (63)		..	Inf.
RAAB, Matthias		1. 4.42	Art.
RAAPKE (46)	71 Inf. Div.	1. 6.43	Art.
RABE v. PAPPENHEIM, Fritz Karl		1. 8.43	Kav.
RABSILBER, Friedrich (65)		1. 4.41	Inf.
RADZIEJ	169 Inf. Div.	1. 9.43	Inf.
RAESFELD, Werner v. (52)	Transportbezirk Essen, Wkr. VI	1. 6.42	Inf.
RÄSSLER, Rudolf (59)		1. 6.42	Kav.
RAITZ v. FRENTZ, Maximilian Frhr. (64)		1. 6.41	Art.
RANFT, Albert (45)		1. 8.43	Inf.
REIBNITZ, Leo v. (55)		1. 4.42	Inf.
REICHER, Franz		..	Inf.
REIN		1. 9.43	Na. Tr
REINHARDT, Fritz (54)		1. 4.41	Inf.
REISS, Ritter v.	O.F.K. 750 Vannes	..	..
REMLINGER		1.12.42	Kav.
REXILIUS		1. 2.43	Inf.
RHEIN, Karl (50)	331 Inf. Div.	1. 5.43	Inf.
RICHTER, Gerhard		1. 8.42	Inf.
RICHTER, Wilhelm		1. 3.43	Inf.
RIEDEL (52)		1. 8.42	Art.
RIEGER, Leopold (54)		1. 6.41	Art.
RIEMHOFER, Gottfried (51)		1.10.42	Kfr. Tr.
RINCK v. BALDENSTEIN Frhr. v. Werner (65).		1. 3.43	Inf.
RINGE, Hans		1. 3.43	Kav.
RITTER, Rene	Retired	1. 4.42	Inf.
RITTWEGER, Ernst (58)	Cdt. Karlsruhe, Wkr. V	1. 2.42	Inf.
RODEN, Emmo v.		1. 4.43	Inf.
RODEWALD (58)		..	Fahr. Tr.
RODT, Eberhard (49)	15 Pz. Gren. Div.	1. 3.43	Kav.
RÖMER, Martin v.	Fldkdtr. 579	1. 1.43	Inf.
RÖPKE, Kurt (48)	46 Inf. Div.	1. 8.43	Inf.
ROESINGER, Otto (54)		1. 4.42	Pion.
RÖSLER, Eberhard (54)		1. 4.42	Inf.
RONICKE, Martin		1. 3.43	Inf.
RORICH (52)		1. 9.43	Inf.
ROSKE, Dipl. Ing. Fritz	Prisoner of War	1. 1.43	..
ROST, v.		1. 3.43	Art.
ROTH, Hans (60)	Cdt. Cologne, Wkr. VI	1. 8.42	Inf.
ROTH, Heinrich	C. of S. Wkr. III	1. 6.43	Inf.
ROTHE, Erich	Oberbaustab 10, Minsk	1. 7.42	Pion.
RÜBEL, Karl (49)	163 Inf. Div.	1. 3.43	In

Rank : Generalmajor (*Major-General*)—*continued*

Name (*age*)	*Appointment* (*date*)	*Seniority*	*Arm*
RÜDT v. COLLENBERG, Frhr. Ludwig	Rü. Insp. A	1. 4.41	Art.
RÜGAMER, Ferdinand	H. Abn. Insp. XVII	1. 7.41	Art.
RÜGGENMANN, Alfons (52)	Rü. Insp. I	1. 4.42	Fahr. Tr.
RÜHLE v. LILIENSTERN, Kurt (62)	..	1. 7.42	Art.
RUFF (49)	..	1.12.42	Art.
RUNGE, Wilhelm (54)	..	1. 6.41	Pion.
RUPPERT, Hans-Eberhard (52)	..	1. 6.42	Fahr. Tr.
RUVILLE, v.	..	1. 7.42	Inf.
SAGERER	..	1. 8.41	Inf.
SALENGRE-DRABBE, Hans de (50)	..	1. 5.43	Inf.
SALITTER, Fritz (62)	T.U.P. Deba, Gvt. Gen.	1. 4.41	Art.
SATTLER	..	1.10.43	Inf.
SAUVANT (53)	..	1. 3.42	Inf.
SCHACK, Friedrich August	..	1. 7.43	Inf.
SCHACKE (63)	..	1. 3.43	Inf.
SCHADE (61)	..	1. 8.41	Inf.
SCHAEFER, Dr. Gotthold	Cdt. Lille	1. 4.43	..
SCHAUWECKER (62)	Hamburg, Wkr. X	..	Na. Tr.
SCHEFOLD (57)	..	..	Art.
SCHELLER (67)	..	1. 6.42	Art.
SCHELLMANN (66)	..	1. 4.41	Inf.
SCHELLWITZ, v.	..	1. 1.43	Inf.
SCHERFF, Walter	O.K.W. (7 Abt.)	1. 9.43	Inf.
SCHICKFUS u. NEUDORF, Erich v. (64).	..	1. 2.32	Inf.
SCHILLING, Otto (55)	..	1.12.42	Inf.
SCHINDKE, Wilhelm (51)	..	1. 1.43	Kav.
SCHITTNIG	..	1. 4.43	Inf.
SCHLIEBEN, Dietrich v.	..	1. 1.43	Kav.
SCHLIEBEN, Karl Wilhelm v. (50)	208 Inf. Div.	1. 6.43	Kav.
SCHLÜTER, Robert	..	1. 3.43	Art.
SCHMETTOW, Graf v. (52)	G.O.C. Channel Islands	1. 4.42	Kav.
SCHMIDT, Hans	..	1. 4.43	Pion.
SCHMIDT, Dipl. Ing. Johannes	..	1.10.43	Inf.
SCHMIDT, Otto	..	1.10.41	Inf.
SCHMIDT, Otto (52)	702 Inf. Div.	1. 1.42	Inf.
SCHMIDT, Ulrich	..	1.10.43	Inf.
SCHMIDT-KOLBOW (64)	..	..	Art.
SCHMIDT, v. Luisingen	..	..	Inf.
SCHNARRENBERGER, Ernst (51)	Prisoner of War	1.11.42	Inf.
SCHNEIDEMESSER, Gustav v. (52)	O.K.H. (P4)	1. 6.42	Inf.
SCHNEIDER, Otto	..	1.12.41	Na. Tr.
SCHÖNFELDER, Fritz (53)	..	1. 4.41	Pion.
SCHOLZ, Erich	..	1. 8.42	Art.
SCHREIBER, Alfred (52)	..	1. 6.42	Inf.
SCHRÖDER, Fritz	..	1.10.43	..
SCHROETER, v. (53)	Cdt. Breslau, Wke. VIII	1. 1.42	Kav.
SCHROETTER, Dipl. Ing. (51)	..	1. 4.42	Inf.
SCHUBERTH (53)	Cdt. Toulouse	1. 7.42	Krf. Tr.
SCHUCKMANN, Eberhard v.	..	1. 8.43	Inf.
SCHÜTZ, Max v.	O.K.H.	1. 7.42	Inf.
SCHULENBURG, Winfried v. d. (62)	General z.b.V. f. Kriegsgefangenenwesen.	..	Kav.
SCHULER, Rüdiger v. (53)	..	1. 9.41	Inf.
SCHULZ, Otto	..	..	Inf.
SCHUNCK, Theodor (55)	..	1. 6.41	Art.
SCHUSTER, Friedrich (63)	..	1. 1.42	Inf.
SCHUSTER-WOLDAN	..	1. 9.43	Art.
SCHWALBE, Eugen Felix (52)	..	1.10.42	Inf.
SCHWARTZ (52)	..	1. 8.41	Kav.
SCHWERIN, Bogislav Graf v. (48)	189 Res. Div.	1.10.43	Inf.
SCULTETUS, Bruno (62)	..	1.12.41	Inf.
SCULTETUS, Herbert (66)	..	1.12.41	Inf.
SEEBOHM	..	1. 4.43	Inf.

Rank: Generalmajor (*Major-General*)—*continued*

Name (*age*)	*Appointment* (*date*)	*Seniority*	*Arm*
SEELIG, Oskar	..	1.10.43	Pion.
SEHMSDORF, Hans (54)	..	1. 2.41	Inf.
SENSFUSS, Franz (51)	..	1.10.42	Pion.
SERINI	..	1. 4.43	Inf.
SEUFFERT, Franz (52)	Trg. Area, Heuberg	1.12.40	Inf.
SICHART, Werner v. (63)	W.B.K. Kiel, Wkr. X	1. 9.41	Inf.
SIECKENIUS (48)	..	1. 6.43	Pz. Tr.
SIEGLIN, Kurt (60)	O.F.K., Ukraine	..	Inf.
SIEVERS, Karl	..	1.10.43	Inf.
SOHN (62)	..	1. 9.41	Art.
SOUCHAY, Stephen (58)	..	1. 8.42	Inf.
SPALCKE, Dr.	M.A. Bucharest	..	Inf.
SPEIDEL, Dr. Hans	..	1. 1.43	Inf.
SPENGLER (53)	..	1. 3.43	Inf.
SPETH	C.G.S. 18 Army	1. 1.43	Art.
STAHR, Wolfgang (53)	H. Waffenm. Schule II	1. 4.42	Inf.
STAMM (66)	..	1. 7.42	Inf.
STAMMER (53)	..	1.11.42	Inf.
STEGMANN (49)	..	1. 8.43	Inf.
STEIGLEHNER, Wilhelm (62)	..	1. 8.42	Art.
STEIN, Johann v. (53)	..	1. 7.42	Inf.
STEINBACH, Paul (55)	Fz. Kdo. XX	1.10.41	Art.
STENZEL, Richard	..	1. 4.42	Art.
STETTNER, Walter, Ritter v. GRABENHOFEN (52).	1 Mtn. Div.	1. 3.43	Inf.
STEUDTNER (66)	Retired (?)	..	Art.
STILLFRIED v. RATTONITZ, Waldemar Graf v. (67)	Ch. d. H. u. Bde	..	Inf.
STOCKHAUSEN, v. (54)	Sich. Div. 281	1. 4.42	Inf.
STOCKHAUSEN, v. (72) Dipl. Ing.	..	1. 9.41	Inf.
STOLBERG-STOLBERG, Christoph Graf zu (56).	..	1. 9.43	Inf.
STRACK, Karl (53)	..	1. 2.42	Inf.
STUBENRAUCH, Wilhelm (59)	F Kdtr. 686	1. 6.41	Kav.
STÜLPNAGEL, Siegfried v. (53)	Cdt. Stettin II	1. 6.42	Inf.
STUMM, Berthold (52)	..	1. 6.42	Inf.
STURM, Hans (60)	..	1. 2.43	Art.
STURT, Gerhard	..	1.10.43	Inf.
SUSCHNIGG, Gustav	..	1. 2.43	Geb.
TAEGLICHSBECK	..	1. 2.43	Inf.
TANN-RATHSAMHAUSEN, Eberhard Reichsfrhr. v. u. zu der (59).	..	1. 7.42	..
TARBUK, Johann	..	1. 8.41	Inf.
TESCHNER, Georg (71)	..	..	Inf.
THADDEN, v.	..	1. 4.43	Inf.
THÄTER, Maximilian (66)	..	1.12.41	Inf.
THAMS (59)	Trg. Area, Kammwald	1. 3.41	Inf.
THEISS, Rudolf (59)	..	1. 9.41	Pz. Tr.
THIELE, Fritz	O.K.W. (Insp. 7)	1.10.42	Na. Tr.
THIELMANN	..	1. 4.43	Pion.
THOENISSEN	Chef d. St. Beschaff. St. Frankreich.	1. 8.42	Art.
THOHOLTE	..	16. 2.43	Art.
THOMAS, Alfred (59)	..	1.12.42	Inf. ?
THOMAS, Kurt	..	1. 4.43	Inf.
THOMAS (56)	..	1.11.40	Pion.
TRAUCH, Rudolf (52)	O.K.H. (Insp. 8)	1.10.41	Fahrtr.
TRÖGER, Hans	..	1. 1.43	Kav.
TSCHAMMER u. OSTEN, Eckhart v. (56)	..	1.12.40	Inf.
TSCHUDI-JACOBSEN, Rudolf ? v .(52)	..	1. 2.43	Inf.
UBL, Bruno	..	1. 7.42	Inf.
ULRICH	Prisoner of War	..	..
UNRUH, Walter Willi Herm. v.	..	..	..

Rank : Generalmajor (*Major-General*)—*continued*

Name (age)	*Appointment (date)*	*Seniority*	*Arm*
USEDOM v.	..	1. 1.43	Cav.
UTZ, Wilibald	100 Lt. Div.	1. 7.43	Inf.
VASSOLL (60)	..	1. 6.42	Art.
VATERRODT (54)	Cdt. Strassburg, Wkr. V	1. 3.41	Inf.
VERSOCK, Kurt (49)	..	1. 5.43	Inf.
VIEBAHN, Hans Albert v. (55)	..	1. 7.42	Inf.
VIEROW, Dipl. Ing. (51)	..	1.10.42	Pion.
VOIGT, Adolf (52)	Cdt. Graudenz, Wkr. XX	1. 7.42	Kav.
VOIT, Paul (68)	C. of S. Wkr. XIII	1. 4.38	Inf.
VOSS, Erich	Cdt. P.W. Camps IX	1. 6.42	Na. Tr.
WAGNER, Gustav	..	1.10.43	Inf.
WAGNER, Paul	..	1. 1.43	Inf.
WAHLE, Carl (51)	Cdt. Hamburg, Wkr. X	1. 7.42	Inf.
WALLNER, Otto (62)	Staff, Wkr. VII	1.11.41	Kav
WALTER, Helmuth (53)	..	1. 7.43	Inf.
WARNICKE (62)	W.B.K. Danzig, Wkr. XX	1. 8.41	Kav.
WARTENBERG, Bodo v. (51)	..	1. 1.43	Inf.
WEBER, Friedrich (45)	..	1. 1.43	..
WEBERN, v. (51)	..	1.10.42	Art.
WECKMANN	Cdt. Kriegsacademie	1. 4.42	Inf.
WEDEL, Hasso v. (56)	O.K.W. (W Pr.)	1. 9.43	Inf.
WEDEL, Hermann v. (51)	Kdr. d. Osttruppen, 18 Army	1. 6.43	Pz. Tr.
WEDELSTÄDT, Friedrich Wilhelm v. (57).	..	..	Inf.
WEHRIG	..	1.10.43	..
WEIDEMANN	O.K.W.	1. 9.43	Inf.
WEINKNECHT	..	1.10.43	Kav.
WEISS, Wilhelm (58)	..	1.10.41	Inf.
WENCK, Walter (44)	..	1. 2.43	Art.
WENING, Ernst (57)	..	1. 6.41	Inf.
WENNINGER	..	1.10.43	Inf.
WERTHERN, Georg Thilo Frhr. v. (52)	..	1. 6.42	Art.
WESTPHAL, Siegfried (42)	..	1. 3.43	Kav.
WESTRAM	C. of S. to Kesselring	..	Art.
WICKEDE, v.	..	..	..
WIETERSHEIM, v. (44)	11 Pz. Div.	..	Kav.
WILKE, Carl	..	1. 9.43	Inf.
WILKE, Kurt (54)	..	1.12.42	Pz. Tr.
WINDISCH, Alois	..	1. 9.43	Inf.
WINDISCH, Josef	..	1. 7.43	..
WINKLER, Hermann (56)	Feld Kdtr. Nikolaiev	1. 7.41	Inf.
WINKLER, Max	..	1.10.43	Inf.
WINTER, August	Staff of Army, Gp. F	1. 8.43	Na. Tr.
WIRTZ, Richard (53)	..	1. 4.42	Pion.
WISSELINCK, Ernst (52)	..	1. 3.43	Inf.
WITTMANN (49)	3 Mtn. Div.	1. 6.43	Art.
WITZLEBEN, Hermann v. (52)	..	1. 6.42	Kav.
WÖSSNER	..	1.10.43	Art.
WOLF	..	1. 3.43	..
WOLPERT, Johann (55)	In Luxemburg	1. 9.41	Inf.
WUERST	..	1. 2.43	Pion.
WULFFEN, Gustav Adolf (66)	Cdt. Potsdam, Wkr. III	..	Inf.
WULZ (51)	..	1.11.42	Art.
WUTHENOW	..	1. 4.43	Kav.
XYLANDER, Rudolf Ritter und Edler v. (72)	In O.K.W.	1. 7.42	Art.
ZAPFEL, Alexander (62)	..	..	Art.
ZAHN, Alois (54)	We Insp. Stuttgart, Wkr. V	1. 8.41	Inf.
ZANTHIER, v. (53)	..	1.10.41	Kav.
ZEDNICEK, Franz	..	1. 4.42	Pion.
ZEISS, Walter (52)	Feldzg. Kdo. VII	1. 7.42	Art.
ZEITZ, Erich (57)	..	1. 2.41	Pz. Tr.
ZELTMANN	..	1. 1.43	..
ZIEGENRÜCKER (59)	..	1. 2.43	Pion.

Rank : Generalmajor (*Major-General*)—*continued*

Name (*age*)	*Appointment* (*date*)	*Seniority*	*Arm*
ZIMMER Richard	..	1. 6.43	Pion.
ZIMMERMANN, Karl	..	..	..
ZUCKERTORT, Karl (54)	..	1. 3.40	Pz. Tr.
ZUNEHMER	..	..	Inf.
ZUTAVERN (51)	..	1. 6.42	Art.
ZWADE	O.K.H. (Ch. H. Rü. u. Bde)	1.10.43	Inf.

Notes

1. Two lists of officers follow: SS and Police. In many cases the same personalities will appear in both lists, since it is normal for all senior Police officers to hold SS rank. On the other hand, not all SS officers hold Police rank, even when performing primarily police functions.

2. In the case of such double rank, it does not follow, however, that possession of SS rank of a certain grade automatically implies possession of Police rank of equal grade (or vice-versa). Examples will be found in which a given rank in one service is held in conjunction with a higher (or lower) rank in the other.

3. Ages given are as on 1 January, 1944.

(*f*) SENIOR SS OFFICERS

Name (*age*).	*Appointment.*
(i) Rank : Reichsführer SS	
HIMMLER, Heinrich (43) ..	Head of the SS and German Police.
(ii) Rank : SS Oberstgruppenführer = Generaloberst	
*DALUEGE, Kurt (46)	Present appointment not known.
†DIETRICH, Josef ("Sepp") (51)	Comd. I SS Pz. Corps.
(iii) Rank : SS Obergruppenführer = General	
ALPERS, Friedrich (42) ..	Staff of Rf. SS.
*v.d. BACH-ZELEWSKI, Erich (44).	In charge of all anti-guerilla activity
†BERGER, Gottlob (47) ..	Head of SS Central Office.
*Frhr. v. EBERSTEIN, Karl (49)	H.SS Pf. Wkr. VII and Chief of SS Oa. Süd.
*FRANK, Karl-Hermann (45) ..	H.SS Pf. Wkr. Protectorate and State Secretary for Bohemia and Moravia.
†Dr. Med. GENZKEN, Karl (58)	Head of Medical Dept. in SS Ops. H.Q.

* = also holds Police rank.
† = also holds Waffen-SS rank.

Rank : SS Obergruppenführer *(General)—continued*

Name (age).	*Appointment.*
†HAUSSER, Paul (63)	Comd. II SS Pz. Corps.
*HILDEBRANDT, Richard (46)	Head of SS Race and Settlement Dept.
*†HOFMANN, Otto (47) ..	H.SS Pf. Wkr. V and Chief of SS Oa. Südwest.
*JECKEIN, Friedrich (48) ..	H.SS Pf. Ostland.
†JUETTNER, Hans (49) ..	Head of SS Ops. H.Q.
*Dr. KALTENBRUNNER, Ernst (40).	Head of the Security Police and the Security Service of the SS.
†KNAPP	SS Ops. H.Q. Inspector of MT tps.
*KOPPE, Wilhelm (47)	H.SS Pf. Wkr. Gen. Govt. and Under-Secretary for Security in the Gen. Govt.
*KRÜGER, Friedrich Wilhelm (49).	Present appointment not known.
*LORENZ, Werner (52)	Head of Vomi.
*MAZUW, Emil (43)	H.SS Pf. Wkr. II and Chief of SS Oa. Ostsee.
*v. PFEFFER-WILDENBRUCH, Karl (55).	Head of Colonial Police Dept.
†PHLEPS, Arthur (62)	Comd. V SS. Mtn. Corps.
†POHL, Oswald (51)	Head of SS Economic and Administrative Dept.
*PRÜTZMANN, Hans (42) ..	H.SS Pf. Ukraine.
*QUERNER, Rudolf (50) ..	H.SS Pf. Wkr. XVII and Chief of SS Oa. Donau.
*RAUTER, Hanns (48)	H.SS Pf. Holland, Chief of SS Oa. Nordwest and General Commissioner for Security in Holland.
*REDIESS, Wilhelm (43) ..	H.SS Pf. Norway and Chief of SS Oa. Nord.
†SACHS, Ernst (63)	Head of Communications on Staff of Rf. SS and Chief of German Police.
SCHAUB, Julius (45)	Personal Adjutant to Hitler.
*SCHMAUSER, Heinrich (53) ..	H.SS Pf. Wkr. VIII and Chief of SS Oa. Südost.
*Erbprinz v. WALDECK und PYRMONT, Josias (47).	H.SS Pf. Wkr. IX and Chief of SS Oa. Fulda-Werra.
†WOLFF, Karl (43)	Chief of Personal Staff Rf. and H.SS Pf. Italy.
*v. WOYRSCH, Udo (48) ..	H.SS Pf. Wkr. IV and Chief of SS Oa. Elbe.
*†WÜNNENBERG, Alfred (52)	Head of the Uniformed Police.

* = also holds Police rank.
† = also holds Waffen-SS rank.

(iv) **Rank: Gruppenführer** (*Generalleutnant*)

Name (*age*).	*Appointment.*
*v ALVENSLEBEN-SCHOCHWITZ, Ludolf (42).	H.SS Pf. Black Sea.
†BANGERSKI, Rudolf	Inspector-General of the Latvian SS Volunteer Legion.
†BITTRICH, Willi (49)	Comd. SS Pz. Div. Hohenstaufen.
BRACHT, Werner (55).. ..	Uniformed Police H.Q.
BREITHAUPT, Franz (63) ..	Head of SS Legal Dept.
†DEMELHUBER, Karl (47) ..	Comd. Waffen SS, Holland.
*EBRECHT, Georg (48) ..	Chief of SS Abs. XXVI (Zoppot-Danzig).
†Prof. Dr. GEBHARDT, Karl (46)	Head of SS Medical Corps.
†GILLE, Herbert (46)	Comd. SS Pz. Div. Wiking.
†GLÜCKS, Richard (54) ..	Head of the Concentration Camp Section in the SS Economic and Administrative Dept. and Chief of Staff of the SS Deathshead Units.
*†v. GOTTBERG, Curt (47) ..	General Commissioner White Russia.
†GRAWITZ, Ernst-Robert (44)	Chief SS and Police Medical Officer.
GREIFELT, Ulrich (47) ..	Head of the Office of the Reich Commissioner for the Consolidation of Germanism (Himmler).
*GUTENBERGER	H.SS Pf. Wkr. VI and Chief of SS Oa. West.
*HALTERMANN, Hans (45) ..	Present appointment not known.
*HANSEN	SS Ops. H.Q. ; Inspector of Artillery.
HELLWIG	Present appointment not known.
HENNICKE, Paul (60) ..	Present appointment not known.
v. HERFF, Maximilian ..	Head of SS Personnel Main Office.
*HÖFLE, Hermann	H.SS Pf. Wkr. XI and Chief of SS Oa. Mitte.
JUERS, Heinrich (46) ..	Head of Recruiting Section in SS Central Office.
JUNGCLAUS, Richard (38) ..	Representative of Rf. SS in Belgium.
*KAMMERHOFER, Konstantin (44).	Representative of Rf. SS with Comd. German tps. in Croatia.
*KAUL, Curt (53)	Present appontment not known.
*KATZMANN, Fritz (37) ..	H.SS Pf. Wkr. XX.
*KEPPLER, Georg (49) ..	Comd. Waffen SS Bohemia and Moravia.

---

* = also holds Police rank.
† = also holds Waffen-SS rank.

Rank : Gruppenführer (*Generalleutnant*)—*continued*

Name (*age*).	*Appointment.*
†KLEINHEISTERKAMP, Matthias (50).	Comd. SS Mtn. Div., Nord.
KNOBLAUCH, Kurt (58) ..	SS Ops. H.Q.
*KORSEMANN	H.SS Pf. Central Sector and White Russia.
†KRÜGER, Walter (53)	Comd. SS Pz. Div., Reich.
*Dr. MARTIN, Benno (50) ..	H.SS Pf. Wkr. XIII and Chief of SS Oa., Main.
*†MEYSSNER, August (57) ..	H.SS Pf., Serbia.
MÜLLER, Heinrich (48) ..	Head of Section IV (Gestapo) Security Police H.Q.
NEBE, Arthur (49)	Head of Section V (Kripo) Security Police H.Q.
*OBERG, Karl Albrecht (46) ..	H.SS Pf., France.
*PANCKE, Günter (44) ..	Representative of Rf. SS in Denmark.
PETRI, Leo (67)	Head of Allgemeine SS Dept. in SS Ops. H.Q.
RÖSENER, Erwin (41) ..	H.SS Pf. Wkr. XVIII and Chief of SS Oa., Alpenland.
†STEINER, Felix (47)	Comd. III SS Germanic Pz. Corps.
*STRECKENBACH, Bruno (41)	Security Police H.Q.
*STROOP, Josef (48)	H.SS Pf. Wkr. XII and Chief of SS Oa., Rhein-Westmark.
*Dr. THOMAS	B.d. Sipo u.d. SD, Ukraine.
*WAPPENHANS, Waldemar (50)	Present appointment not known.
*Dr. WENDLER, Richard (45)	Governor of District, Lublin.
ZIMMERMANN, Paul (48) ..	Stab Rf. SS.

Rank : SS Brigadeführer (*Generalmajor*)

BLUMENREUTER, Carl (62) ..	SS Ops. H.Q. Medical Dept.
*Dr. BÖTTCHER	SS Pf. Radom.
CREUTZ, Rudolf (47)	SS Central Office.
†Dr. DERMIETZEL, Friedrich Karl (44).	Chief Medical Officer II SS Pz. Corps.
*DÖRING, Hans (42)	Present appointment not known.
†FEGELEIN, Hermann (37) ..	Comd. SS Cavalry Div.
*Prof. Dr. GERLOFF, Helmuth (49).	Head of SS and Police Technical Academy.
GIESECKE, Gustav (62) ..	SS Race and Settlement Dept.

---

* = also holds Police rank.
† = also holds Waffen SS rank.

Rank : SS Brigadeführer *(Generalmajor)—continued*

Name (age).	*Appointment.*
†GOEDICKE, Bruno (64) ..	SS Garrison Comd., Vienna.
†HAERTEL	Head of SS Welfare.
†HANSEN	Present appointment not known.
*HARM, Hermann (49)	SS Pf., Kovno
Dr. HARSTER, Wilhelm (39) ..	B.d. Sipo u.d. SD, Italy.
HELLWIG, Otto (45)	SS Pf., Bialystok.
HOFFMEYER	Vomi representative, South Russia.
*Dr. HUBER, Franz Josef (41) ..	I.D. Sipo u.d. SD Wkr. XVII.
†Dr. Ing. KAMMLER	SS Economic and Administrative Dept.
KANSTEIN, Paul (44)	Present appointment not known.
KELS, Hans (44)	Chief of SS Abs. XXXV (Graz).
†KLINGEMANN, Gottfried (59)	Comd. 2 SS Inf. Bde.
*KUTSCHERA, Franz (39) ..	SS Pf. Mogilev.
MEYER, Fritz (43)	Chief of SS Abs. XV (Hamburg).
*MÖRSCHEL, Johann	C. of S. SS Oa., Nordsee.
†v. OBERKAMP, Carl (50) ..	Comd. SS Mtn. Div. Prinz Eugen.
†v. OPLÄNDER, Walther (37) ..	Chief of SS Abs. XXXIX (Prague).
†PRIESS, Hermann (42) ..	Comd. SS Pz. Div., Totenkopf.
†Graf v. PÜCKLER-BURGHAUSS, Carl-Friedrich.	Comd. SS. Latvian Div.
*REINEFARTH, Heinz (40) ..	Inspector- General of Administration in Bohemia and Moravia.
†SAUBERZWEIG	Comd. SS Croatian Mtn. Div.
SCHÄFER, Karl	Present appointment not known.
*†SCHIMANA	H. SS Pf., Greece.
†v. SCHOLZ, Fritz (47)	Comd. SS Pz. Gren. Div., Nordland.
*Dr. SCHRÖDER, Walther (41)	SS Pf., Latvia.
SCHULZ, Erwin (43)	Security Police H.Q.
†SCHWEDLER, Hans (65) ..	Present appointment not known.
†SIMON, Max. (44)	Present appointment not known.
STARCK, Wilhelm (52) ..	Chief of SS Abs. XXXII (Augsburg) and Police President, Augsburg.
†STAUDINGER, Walter (45) ..	Present appointment not known.
*STOLLE, Gustav (44)	Present appointment not known.
TENSFELD, Willy (47) ..	Present appointment not known.
*THIER, Theobald (46)	Present appointment not known.
v. TREUENFELD	Comd. Waffen SS Ukraine.
†VAHL, Herbert Ernst (47) ..	Present appointment not known.

---

* = also holds Police rank.
† = also holds Waffen-SS rank.

Rank : SS Brigadeführer (*Generalmajor*)—*continued*

Name (age).	*Appointment.*
VOGLER	SS Garrison Comd. Munich.
VOSS, Bernhard (51)	Comd. SS Depot Debica (Poland).
Frhr. v. WÄCHTER, Otto (42)	Governor of District Galicia.
†WAGNER, Jürgen (42) ..	Present appointment not known.
WEBER, Christian (60) ..	Inspector of SS Riding Schools.
WEISS	SS Pf. Nikolayev.
*WILLICH, Hellmut (48) ..	I.d. Sipo u.d. SD Wkr. XX.
†WISCH, Theodor (36)	Comd. SS Pz. Div. Leibstandarte Adolf Hitler.
*WYSOCKI	SS Pf. Lithuania.
*ZENNER, Carl (44)	SS Pf. Minsk.
ZIMMERMANN	SS Economic and Administrative Dept.

* = also holds Police rank.
† = also holds Waffen-SS rank.

(*g*) SENIOR POLICE OFFICERS

(i) **Rank :** Colonel-General **(Generaloberst der Polizei)**

*DALUEGE, Kurt (46)	Present appointment not known.

(ii) **Rank :** General **(General der Polizei)**

*v.d. BACH-ZELEWSKI, Erich (44).	In charge of all anti-guerilla activity.
*Frhr. v. EBERSTEIN, Karl (49)	H.SS Pf. Wkr. VII and Chief of SS Oa. Süd.
*FRANK, Karl-Hermann (45) ..	H.SS Pf. Wkr. Protectorate and State Secretary for Bohemia and Moravia.
*†HOFMANN, Otto (47) ..	H.SS Pf. Wkr. V and Chief of SS Oa. Südwest.
*JECKELN, Friedrich (48) ..	H.SS Pf. Ostland.
*KOPPE, Wilhelm (47)	H.SS Pf. Wkr. Gen. Govt. and Under-Secretary for Security in the Gen. Govt.
*KRÜGER, Friedrich-Wilhelm (49).	Present appointment not known.
*MAZUW, Emil (43)	H.SS Pf. Wkr. II and Chief of SS Oa. Ostsee.
*v. PFEFFER-WILDENBRUCH, Karl (55).	Head of Colonial Police Dept.
*PRÜTZMANN, Hans (42) ..	H.SS Pf. Ukraine.

* = also holds SS rank.
† = also holds Waffen-SS rank.

Rank : General **(General der Polizei)**—*continued*

Name (*age*).	*Appointment.*
*REDIESS, Wilhelm (43) ..	H.SS Pf. Norway and Chief of SS Oa. Nord.
*SCHMAUSER, Heinrich (53) ..	H.SS Pf. Wkr. VIII and Chief of SS Oa. Südost.
*Erbprinz v. WALDECK und PYRMONT, Josias (47).	H.SS Pf. Wkr. IX and Chief of SS Oa. Fulda-Werra.
*v. WOYRSCH, Udo (48) ..	H.SS Pf. Wkr. IV and Chief of SS Oa. Elbe.
*†WÜNNENBERG, Alfred (52)	Head of the Uniformed Police.

(iii) **Rank :** Lt.-General **(Generalleutnant der Polizei)**

*v. ALVENSLEBEN-SCHOCHWITZ, Ludolf (42).	H.SS Pf. Black Sea.
*BECKER, Herbert	B.d.O. Gen. Govt.
*v. BOMHARD, Adolf (52) ..	B.d.O Ukraine.
*GLOBOCNIK, Odilo (39) ..	B.d.O. Adriatic Coastal Zone.
*GUTENBERGER	H.SS Pf. Wkr. VI and Chief of SS Oa. West.
*HALTERMANN, Hans (45) ..	Present appointment not known.
*HÖFLE, Hermann	H.SS Pf. Wkr. XI and Chief of SS Oa. Mitte.
HÖRING	B.d.O. Norway.
*JEDICKE, Georg	B.d.O. Ostland.
*Dr. KALTENBRUNNER, Ernst (40).	Head of the Security Police and the Security Service of the SS.
*KAMMERHOFER, Konstantin (44).	Representative of Rf. SS with Comd. German tps. in Croatia.
*v. KAMPTZ, Jürgen (52) ..	B.d.O. Italy.
*KAUL, Curt (53)	Present appointment not known.
KLINGER	K.d Schupo Berlin.
*KORSEMANN	H.SS Pf. Central Sector and White Russia.
*Dr. LANKENAU	B.d.O. Holland.
*Dr. MARTIN, Benno (50) ..	H.SS Pf. Wkr. XIII and Chief of SS Oa. Main.
Dr. Ing. MEYER	Inspector-General of Fire-Fighting Services.
*†MEYSSNER, August (57) ..	H.SS Pf. Serbia.

* = also holds SS rank.

† = also holds Waffen-SS rank.

Rank : *Lt.-General* **(Generalleutnant der Polizei)**—*continued*

Name (age).	*Appointment.*
*v. ÖLHAFEN, Otto (57) ..	I.d.O. Wkr. VII.
*PANCKE, Günter (44) ..	Representative of Rf. SS in Denmark.
*QUERNER, Rudolf (50) ..	H.SS Pf. Wkr. XVII and Chief of SS Oa. Donau.
*RAUTER, Hans (48)	H.SS Pf. Holland, Chief of SS Oa. Nordwest and General Commissioner for Security in Holland.
*RETZLAFF, Dr.	B.d.O. Wkr. X.
RIEGE, Paul (55)	Present appointment not known.
*RÖSENER, Erwin (41) ..	H.SS Pf. Wkr. XVIII and Chief of SS Oa, Alpenland.
*SCHREYER, Georg (58) ..	Inspector-General of Municipal Police.
*SCHUMANN	Present appointment not known.
*STRECKENBACH, Bruno (41)	Security Police H.Q.
*THOMAS, Dr.	B.d. Sipo u.d. SD Ukraine.
*WINKELMANN (49)	Uniformed Police H.Q.

(iv) **Rank :** Maj.-General **(Generalmajor der Polizei)**

*BADER, Dr. Kurt (44) ..	I.d.O. Wkr. XVII.
*BRENNER, Karl Heinrich (48)	Present appointment not known.
*DÖRING, Hans (42)	Present appointment not known.
*DUNCKERN, Anton (38) ..	Present appointment not known.
v. FALKOWSKI	B.d.O. Wkr. XX.
*GERLOFF, Prof. Dr. Helmuth (49).	Head of SS and Police Technical Academy.
GÖHRUM, Kurt	B.d.O. Wkr. VI.
*†v. GOTTBERG, Curt (47) ..	General Commissioner, White Russia.
*GROLMANN, Wilhelm ..	Police President, Leipzig.
*GRÜNWALD, Hans-Dietrich ..	Uniformed Police H.Q.
*HARM, Hermann (49)	SS Pf. Kovno.
v. HEIMBURG	B.d.O. Denmark.
HILLE	B.d.O. Wkr. XII.
*HITZEGRAD, Ernst (54) ..	B.d.O. Bohemia and Moravia.
*HOFFMANN, Karl (41) ..	I.d.O. Wkr. IX.
*HUBER, Dr. Franz Josef (41) ..	I.d. Sipo u.d. SD Wkr. XVII.
*KATZMANN, Fritz (37) ..	H.SS Pf. Wkr. XX.
*KNOFE	Present appointment not known.

* = also holds SS rank.
† = also holds Waffen SS rank.

Rank : *Major-General* **(Generalmajor der Polizei)**—*continued*

Name (*age*).	*Appointment.*
*KRUMHAAR	Inspector of German Water Police.
KUSCHOW	Police President, Nuremberg-Fürth.
*KUTSCHERA, Franz (39) ..	SS Pf. Mogliev.
*LIESSEM	I.d.O. Wkr. VIII.
*MASCUS, Hellmuth (52) ..	B.d.O. Wkr. XII.
MAY	B.d.O. Serbia.
MONTUA	Police President, Posen.
*MÜLLER	B.d.O. Wkr. I.
*OBERG, Karl-Albrecht (46) ..	H.SS Pf. France.
POHLMEYER	K.d.O. Vienna.
RAUNER, Adolf (63)	Bavarian State Ministry of the Interior, Police Dept.
*REINEFARTH, Heinz (40) ..	Inspector-General of Administration in Bohemia and Moravia.
*RITZER, Konrad	B.d.O. Wkr. II.
RUMPF	Inspector - General of Fire-Fighting Services in Town and Country.
*SCHEER	Present appointment not known.
*†SCHIMANA	H.SS Pf., Greece.
*SCHMELCHER, Willi (49) ..	Head of Teno.
SCHNELL	Head of Dept. for Voluntary Fire-Fighting Services, Uniformed Police H.Q.
*SCHRÖDER, Walther (41) ..	SS. Pf., Latvia.
*SCHROERS	Police President, Bremen.
SIEBERT	Deputy Head of Teno.
*STROOP, Josef (48)	H.SS Pf. Wkr. XII and Chief of SS. Oa Rhein-Westmark.
*THIER, Theobald (46) ..	Present appointment not known.
*WAPPENHANS, Waldemar (50)	Present appointment not known.
*WENDLER, Dr. Richard (45)	Governor of District Lublin.
*WILL, Paul	Present appointment not known.
*WILLICH, Hellmut (48) ..	I.d. Sipo u.d. SD Wkr. XX.
*WINKLER	B.d.O. Wkr. V.
*WYSOCKI	SS Pf., Lithuania.
*ZENNER, Carl (44)	SS Pf., Minsk.

---

* = also holds SS rank.
† = also holds Waffen SS rank.

(*h*) SENIOR G.A.F. OFFICERS

Name (age)	*Command or Appointment*	*Seniority*
Rank : Reichsmarschall (Marshal of the Reich)		
GÖRING, Hermann (51)	C.-in-C., Air Force	19. 7.40
Rank : Generalfeldmarschall (Field-Marshal)		
KESSELRING, Albert (59)	C.-in-C., South	19. 7.40
MILCH, Erhard (52)	Inspector-General G.A.F.	19. 7.40
Dipl. Ing. Frhr. v. RICHTHOFEN (49)	Luftflotte 2	16. 2.43
SPERRLE, Hugo (59)	Luftflotte 3	19. 7.40
Rank : Generaloberst (Colonel-General)		
GREIM, Robert Ritter v. (52)	Fliegerkorps V	16. 2.43
KELLER, Alfred (62)	Head of N.S.F.K.	19. 7.40
LÖHR, Alexander (59)	H. Gruppe E	9. 5.41
LOERZER, Bruno (53)	..	16. 2.43
RÜDEL, Gunther (61)	Chief of Air Defence	17.11.42
STÜMPFF, Hans-Jürgen (55)	Luftflotte 5	19. 7.40
WEISE, Hubert (58)	C.-in-C., Flak	19. 7.40
Rank : General der Flieger, der Flakartillerie or der Luftnachrichtentruppen (General)		
ANDRAE, Waldemar (54)	..	1. 7.41
BIENECK, Hellmuth (57)	Luftgau II	1. 7.41
BODENSCHATZ, Karl (54)	C.-of-S. to GÖRING	1. 7.41
BOGATSCH, Rudolf (53)	..	1. 7.41
CHRISTIANSEN, Friedrich (65)	G.O.C., Holland	1. 1.39
COELER, Joachim (53)	..	1. 1.42
DANCKELMANN (56)	..	1. 4.41
DESSLOCH, Otto (55)	Luftflotte 4	1. 1.42
DOERSTLING, Egon (55)	R.L.M. Supply Depot	1. 6.42
DRANSFELD, Eduard (61)	..	1.10.40
FELMY, Helmuth (59)	..	1. 2.38
FIEBIG, Martin (53)	Lw. K.D.O. Südost	30. 1.43
FISCHER, Veit	..	1. 6.42
FÖRSTER, Hellmuth (55)	..	1. 5.41
FRÖHLICH, Stefan (45)	Luftgau XVII	1. 7.43
GEISSLER, Hans (53)	..	19. 7.40
GOSSRAU, Karl Siegfried (63)	R.L.M.	1. 9.41
HARMJANZ, Willi (53)	Luftgau, Norway	1. 9.42
HAUBOLD, Alfred (56)	Luftgau III/IV (Flak)	1.10.41
HEILINGBRUNNER, Friedrich (53)	(Flak)	1. 7.42
HIRSCHAUER, Friedrich (61)	President Air Defence League	1. 8.39
HOFFMAN (53)	A Flak Div.	1.12.42
KAMMHUBER, Josef (48)	Fliegerkorps XII	30. 1.43
KASTNER-KIRDORF, Gustav (63)	..	1. 7.41
KITZINGER, Karl (59)	G.O.C., Ukraine	1.10.39
KLEPKE, Waldemar (62)	..	1. 1.39
KORTEN, Günther (46)	C.G.S., Air Force	31. 1.43
KÜHL, Leonhard (59)	R.L.M.	1. 4.39
MAHNCKE, Alfred (56)	Luftgau Süd	1. 9.43
MARTINI, Hermann (53)	Director of Sigs.	20. 9.41
MAYER, Wilhelm (58)	Luftgau S.E.	1. 2.41
MOHR, Max	Liaison Officer, French Air Force	1. 4.41
ODEBRECHT	G.A.F., Field Corps III	1.12.42
PETERSEN (53)	..	1.11.42
PFLUGBEIL, Kurt (54)	Fliegerkorps IV	1. 2.42
POHL, Erich Ritter v.	..	1. 3.42
PUTZIER (53)	..	1. 7.42

Rank : General der Flieger, der Flakartillerie or der Luftnachrichtentruppen (General)—*continued*

Name (age)	*Command or Appointment*	*Seniority*
QUADE, Erich (61)	Public Relations	1. 9.40
RENZ, v. (53)	(Flak)	31. 1.43
RITTER, Hans (51)	Liaison with Navy	1. 4.42
RUGGERA, Kamillo	(Flak) Luftgau II	1.12.40
SCHLEMM		30. 1.43
SCHMIDT, August (55)	(Flak) Luftgau VI	1. 7.41
SCHMIDT, Hugo		1. 4.41
SCHUBERT, Dr. (56)		1. 7.42
SCHULZ (55)		1.12.42
SCHWEICKHARD, Karl (62)		1. 6.38
SEIDEL, Hans-Georg v. (53)	Q.M.G., G.A.F.	1. 1.42
SIBURG, Hans (50)	Luftgau, Holland	1. 4.42
SOMME, Walter (57)	Luftgau VIII	1. 6.42
SPEIDEL, Wilhelm	G.O.C., S. Greece	1. 1.42
STUDENT, Kurt (54)	Fliegerkorps XI	30. 5.40
VIERLING, Albert (57)	Luftgaustab z.b.V. 4	1. 6.42
WABER, Bernhard	Luftgau Kiev	1. 3.42
WEISSMANN, Dr. Eugon (53)	Luftgau XII and XIII	1. 6.42
WENNINGER, Ralph (54)		1.11.40
WIMMER, Wilhelm (55)	Luftgau Belgium and N. France	1.10.39
WITZENDORF, Bodo v. (67)	R.L.M.	1. 2.39
WOLFF Ludwig (58)	Luftgau XI	1. 2.41
ZANDER, Konrad (61)	Fliegerführer Crimea	1. 4.38
ZENETTI, Emil (61)	Luftgau VII	1. 2.41

Rank : Generalleutnant (Lieut.-General)

Name (age)	Command or Appointment	Seniority
ANGERSTEIN (53)	Fliegerkorps I	1. 4.43
v. ARNAUD de la PERRIERE		1. 1.41
AXTHELM, Walter v. (51)	Inspector-General Flak	1.10.42
BARLEN, Karl (53)	G.O.C., Defence Zone Slovakia	1. 4.41
BAUR de BETAZ (60)	(Admin.)	1. 8.43
BECKER, Hermann		1.11.42
BECKER, Wilhelm, Dipl.Ing.	Sigs.	1. 7.43
BEHRENDT, Hans (52)		1.10.43
BOENICKE, Walter		1.9. 43
BRÄUER, Bruno (51)	G.O.C., Crete	1.10.42
BRUCH, Herman (62)		1.11.40
BRUNNER, Josef		1.10.43
BÜLOW, Hilmer Frhr. v. (60)	Director of Mil Science Dept. G.A.F.	1. 4.41
BÜLOWIUS, Alfred (51)	Fliegerkorps II	1. 3.43
BUFFA, Ernst (52)	A Flak Div.	1. 2.43
BURCHARD, Heinrich, Dipl.Ing.	7 Flak Div.	1. 8.42
CABANIS, Ernst (53)	R.L.M.	1. 5.43
CARLSEN	Luftzeuggr. XI	1.10.40
CONRAD, Gerhard, Dipl. Ing.	Staff, Fliegerkorps XI	1. 4.43
CONRATH, Paul (48)	Hermann Göring Div.	1. 9.43
CRANZ (55)	Fliegerausb. Kdo., Prague	1.11.40
CZECH	Naval Air Service	1. 4.43
DEINHARDT		1. 1.42
DÖRFFLER (54)	Field Equipment Group	1. 4.43
DÖRING, Kurt v.	Jagddivision 1	1.11.41
DRUM, Karl (55)	11 G.A.F. Field Div.	1. 1.43
EGAN-KRIEGER, Jeno v. (59)		1.12.42
EIBENSTEIN, Rudolf (50)	Flak Div. 12	1. 8.43
FAHNERT, Friedrich (65)	Head of Amtsgruppe W.N.V. (O.K.W.)	1. 4.40
FEYERABEND, Walter (53)	(Flak)	1. 4.41
FINK, Dipl. Ing.	Insp. d. Kampfflieger	1.10.42
FRANSSEN	Rü. Insp., Belgium	1. 8.42
FRANTZ, Gotthard	Prisoner of War	1. 4.48
FRANTZ, Walter	C.S.O., A.O.C. in C. Centre	1. 6.43
FRIEDENSBURG, Walter		1.12.41

Rank : Generalleutnant (Lieut.-General)—*continued*

Name (age)	*Command or Appointment*	*Seniority*
GAUTIER, Theophil	Rü. Insp. XVII	1. 4.42
GERSTENBERG, Alfred (51)	Head of Airforce in Rumania	1. 9.43
GROSCH, Walter (53)	Chief Q.M., Luftflotte 5	1. 6.43
HAEHNELT, Wilhelm (69)	R.L.M.	1.12.40
HANESSE (63)	Head of G.A.F. Liaison Staff, Paris	1. 4.42
HEIDRICH, Richard (48)	1 Para Div.	1. 7.43
HERMANN	..	1.11.40
HILGERS, Dipl. Ing.	..	1. 4.43
HEYKING, Rüdiger v.	6 G.A.F. Field Div.	1. 7.43
HOFMANN, Hans	C. of S., Luftflotte 4	1. 6.43
KARLEWSKI	..	
KEIPER	G.A.F. Mission to Slovakia	1. 1.43
KESSLER (53)	Fliegerführer Atlantik	1. 4.41
KETTEMBEIL, Karl (54)	Air Attaché, Ankara	1. 6.43
KETTNER (51)	..	1.10.43
KIEFFER, Maximilian (53)	..	1. 6.42
KNAUSS, Dr. (52)	Luftgauakademie, Gatow	1. 8.42
KOLB, Alexander (55)	Air Defence Command, Stettin	1.11.40
KRAHMER, Eckart (52)	Air Attaché, Madrid	1.10.43
KROCKER, Viktor (55)	..	1.12.41
KRUEGER, Ernst	..	1. 6.43
KÜHNE, Otto	C.S.O., Luftflotte 5	1. 6.42
LACKNER, Walter (53)	Fliegerdivision 10	1.12.42
LANGEMEYER, Otto (59)	Quartermaster's Staff, Luftflotte 4	1. 4.42
LAULE (53)	..	1. 9.43
LECH	..	1.11.40
LENTZSCH, Johannes (60)	(Flak)	1. 3.38
LINDNER	Aviation Ordnance	1. 8.41
LORENZ, Walter	Supplies, Norway	1. 2.43
MACKENSEN v. ASTFELD, Hans-Georg (58).	..	1. 4.41
MÄLZER, Dipl. Ing. Kurt	Commandant of Rome (?)	1.10.43
MANN, Ritter v. TIECHLER, Hermann Edler v. (55)	A. Luftgaustab	1.11.40
MEISTER	Operational Staff Ia Op. 1	1. 3.43
MENSCHING (56)	..	1. 4.43
MERTITSCH (51)	..	1.10.42
MOLL (57)	With Luftflotte 4 (sea-plane expert)	1. 4.42
MOOYER	Technical Training Dept., R.L.M.	1. 4.41
MÜLLER, Ernst	Luftzeuggruppe XI	1. 1.42
MUSSHOF (58)	..	1.11.40
NIEHOFF, Heinrich (62)	Possibly transferred to Army	1. 2.38
NUBER	..	1. 9.43
OSTERKAMP, Theodor (52)	..	1. 8.42
PISTORIUS	Fliegerregiment 11	1. 7.43
RAMCKE, Hermann (56)	2 Para. Div.	21.12.42
RANTZAU, Heine v.	..	1. 6.43
REIMANN, Richard (52)	A Flak Div.	1. 3.43
RICHTER, Hellmuth (52)	Flak Div. 11	1. 8.41
RÖMER, Erwin v. (56)	..	1. 4.41
ROQUES, Karl v.	Retired	1.10.38
RUDLOFF, Werner v.	Personal Dept., R.L.M.	1. 8.43
RÜDT v. COLLENBERG, Kurt Frhr. (62)	Insp. of Arm., Paris and N.W. France	1. 7.42
SATTLER, Ottfried (57)	..	1. 1.40
SCHEURLEN	..	1.11.42
SCHIMPF, Richard, Dipl. Ing.	C. of. S. Luftgau VIII	1. 8.43
SCHLEICH, Ritter v. (56)	..	1. 9.43
SCHMIDT, Kurt (56)	..	1. 1.40
SCHUBERT	..	1.11.42
SCHULTHEISS, Pavel (51)	..	1. 1.43
SCHULTZE, Rudolf	..	1. 9.43
SCHWABEDISSEN, Walter	..	1. 3.42
SCHWUB, Albert (57)	..	1.10.40

Rank : Generalleutnant (Lieut.-General)—*continued*

Name (age)	*Command or Appointment*	*Seniority*
SEIFERT, Johann	Flak Div. 10	1. 6.42
SOMMER, Johannes (57)	..	1. 3.40
SPANG, Willibad (57)	15 G.A.F. Field Div.	1. 1.42
SPIESS, Theodore (53)	Flak Div. 13	1. 8.41
SPRUNER v. MERTZ, Hermann (60)	Staff of Luftgau VII	1. 4.43
STEUDEMANN, Kurt (54)	(Flak), R.L.M.	1. 1.41
STUBENRAUCH, Wilhelm v. (59)	(Flak)	1. 6.42
STURM, Alfred (56)	..	1. 8.43
SUREN, Walter (56)	..	1. 4.41
TIPPELSKIRCH, v.	..	1. 4.43
TRIENDL, Theodor (55)	..	1. 4.43
WAGNER	Flak Div. 8	1.11.42
WALZ, Franz (59)	..	1. 4.41
WEESE	..	1. 4.43
WEIGAND, Dipl. Volksw. Wolfgang (59)	Insp. Armaments, H. Gruppe Mitte	1.11.40
WITTING (53)	..	1. 2.41
WÜHLISCH, Heinz-Helmut v. (52)	..	1. 4.42
ZIEGLER, Dr. Günther	..	1. 2.43
ZOCH, Philipp (52)	..	1. 4.42

Rank : Generalmajor (Major-General)

Name (age)	Command or Appointment	Seniority
ADAMETZ	..	1. 2.41
ANTON	(Flak)	1. 2.43
ARNIM, Hans v.	..	1.11.42
ASCHENBRENNER, Heinrich	C.S.O., A.O.C. in C. South	1. 8.42
BAIER, Eberhard	..	1. 4.42
BANSE	..	1. 4.42
BARENTHIN	St. of Flieg. Korps XI (?)	1. 9.43
BASSENGE, Dipl. Ing. Gerhard	Prisoner of War	1. 5.43?
BERTHOLD	Admin.)	1. 7.41
BERTRAM (53)	(Flak)	1. 6.39
BIEDERMANN, Wolf. Frhr. v. (52)	A G.A.F. Field Div.	1. 4.41
BIWER (50)	..	1. 9.41
BOENIGK, Oskar Frhr. v. (51)	..	1. 2.41
BOETTGE	G.A.F. Recruit Depot 31	1.10.41
BONATZ, Ernst (51)	Personnel Abt. R.L.M.	1. 8.41
BRAKERT	..	1. 4.43
BRANDT	..	1. 1.43
BUCHHOLZ	Air Transport, Medit.	1.12.41
CARGANIGO (57)	..	1.12.41
CHAULIN-EGERSBERG, v.	(Flak)	1.12.41
CRIEGERN	..	1. 4.43
DAHLMANN, Dr. Hermann	R.L.M.	1.12.41
DEICHMANN, Paul	C.G.S. Luftflotte 2	1. 9.42
DEWALL, Job v. (64)	..	1.11.40
DOMMENGET	..	1. 8.43
DRECHSEL, Ernst	..	1. 2.42
ERDMANN, Dipl. Ing. Wolfgang	General Staff, Q.M.G. 2 (organisation)	1. 3.43
ERDMANN	..	1. 4.43
EXSZ (50)	Armistice Commission, Aix-en-Provence	1. 4.42
FALKENHAYN, Erich v. (54)	(Admin.)	1.11.41
FALKOWSKI, v.	..	1.11.41
FINK, Johannes	..	1. 6.43
FREYBERG-EISENBERG-ALLMENDINGEN, Egloff Frhr. v. (51).	(Flak) in Avignon	1. 4.39
FROMMHERZ	..	1. 4.43
FUCHS	..	1. 9.43
FÜTTERER, Cuno	Air Attaché, Budapest	1.11.41
FUNCKE, Heinz	Flying Training Regt.	1.10.41
GALLAND, Adolf (32)	Insp. d. Jagdflieger	19.11.42
GANDERT, Hans Eberhardt (52)	R.L.M.	1.12.39

Rank : Generalmajor (Major-General)—*continued*

Name (age)	*Command or Appointment*	*Seniority*
GNAMM, Dr.	Luftgau XVII	1. 6.43
GOLTZ	Sea Rescue Service	1. 4.41
GOSEWISCH	..	1.10.43
GRONAU, Wolfgang v. (51)	Air Attaché, Tokyo	
HACHENBÜRG, v. (56)	(Admin.)	1.11.40
HAENSCHEKE (50)	..	1. 2.42
HAMEL	Air Works Inspectorate, R.L.M.	1. 4.43
HANTELMANN (52)	An Airdrome Reg. Com. in France	1. 2.42
HARLINGHAUSEN, Martin (42)	..	
HARTING	..	1.11.40
HARTOG (52)	H.Q. Staff of Luftgau, Belgium – N. France.	1. 4.41
HASSE (66)	(Admin.)	1.11.41
HEIDENREICH	..	1.10.43
HEMPEL, Fritz (55)	..	1. 2.43
HERHOTH v. ROHDEN	..	1.10.43
HERWARTH v. BITTENFELD, Eberhard (56).	An Airfield Regional Comd.	1. 4.40
HESSE, Max	..	1. 4.41
HEYDE, v. der	..	1.10.42
HEYDENREICH, Leopold	R.L.M.	1. 4.42
HINKELBEIN (66)	(Admin.)	1. 9.41
HINTZ	Flak Arty School, Rerik	1. 4.43
HIPPEL, Walter v.	A Flak Div.	1. 4.43
HOEFERT, Johannes (61)	..	1. 4.41
HOHNE, Otto	..	
HOLLE, Alexander (46)	..	1. 2.43
HOMBURG, Erich (68)	General Staff, G.A.F.	1.11.40
HORNUNG, Ferdinand (53)	..	1. 9.42
HÜCKEL (52)	..	1. 9.41
HUTH, Joachim	..	1. 4.43
JAKOBY	(Sigs)	1. 2.43
JENNY	..	1. 9.43
JUNCK, Werner	Jagddivision 3	1. 4.43
KAHL, Siegfried	Luftgau Kommando VIII	1. 8.43
KATHMANN, Dipl. Ing.	..	1. 4.42
KLEIN, Hans (53)	A.O.C.-in-C., Fighters	27. 8.39
KLEIN, Dipl. Ing.	..	1. 2.41
KLEINRATH, Kurt	Chief of Dept., Q.M.G. 6., R.L.M.	1. 3.43
KÖCHY, Karl (49)	Prisoner of War	1.11.41
KOLLER, Karl (46)	C. of S., Luftflotte 3	1. 3.43
KORTE, Hans	..	1. 7.43
KRAPP	(Admin.)	1. 4.41
KRAUSS, Dipl. Ing.	..	1. 8.43
KREIPE	R.L.M.	1. 3.43
KRESSMANN, Erich	(Flak)	1. 2.42
KRIEGBAUM (52)	A Cadet School	1.12.39
KRÜGER, Otto (51)	..	1. 5.41
KRUEGER	..	1.11.41
KRUG, Michael	..	1. 1.43
KUDERNA	..	1. 9.43
KUEN	Luftgau Westfrankreich	1. 4.42
KUTZLEBEN, v. (58)	Possibly Trsfd. to Army	1. 1.38
LICHTENBERGER, Hermann	(Flak)	1. 2.43
LÖDERER	..	1. 9.43
LOHMANN (51)	Field Div. 14	1. 2.42
LONGIN, Anton	..	1. 8.43
LORENZ, Heinrich (52)	..	1. 2.42
LUCZNY, Alfons (50)	(Flak)	1. 2.43
MAASS	Staff of Luftgau VII	1. 8.41
MAIER-NIKOLAUS	..	1.10.43
MASSOW, v.	..	1. 4.43
MASSOW Albrecht v. (58)	Equipment Group in Luftgau VIII	1. 1.41

Rank : Generalmajor (Major-General)—*continued*

Name (age)	*Command or Appointment*	*Seniority*
MEINDL, Eugen (52)	Fliegerkorps XIII	1. 1.41
MENSCH (57)	Staff Luftflotte 5	1.11.40
MENTZEL	Recce. School, Braunschweig-Broitzem	1. 6.41
MENZEL, Georg-Adolf (57)	Air Defence Command 7	1.10.39
METZNER	..	1. 4.42
MORZIK	..	1.10.43
MÜLLER, Gottlob	In Italy	1.11.41
MUGGENTHALER, Hermann (52)	(Admin.)	1. 7.41
MUHR, Eduard	..	1. 7.43
NEUFFER	Prisoner of War	1.12.41
NIELSEN	C. of S. Luftflotte 5	1. 3.43
NITZSCHE, Martin	L.G.N. Regt. 3	1. 1.41
NORDT	..	1. 4.41
NOWACK, Franz	R.L.M.	1. 9.41
OLBRICH	..	1. 4.42
ORTNER-WEIGAND, Bruno	..	1. 9.41
OVERDYCK	(Sigs.)	1. 8.43
PAWELKE	..	1.10.43
PELTZ, Dietrich	Fl. Korps IX (?)	1.12.43
PETRAUSCHKE	..	1. 7.43
PFEIFFER	Inspector of Clothing and Rations	1. 7.42
PICKERT, Wolfgang 47)	9 Flak Div.	1.10.42
PLOCH, Dipl. Ing. August (49)	R.L.M.	1. 8.40
PLOCHER, Hermann	C. of S. a Luftgruppe	1. 3.43
POETSCH (52)	..	1. 8.41
PRELLBERG	Flak. Brigade VII	1. 8.42
PREU	Luftgaustab S.E.	1. 2.43
PRINZ	..	1. 9.43
PUESCHEL, Konrad (62)	(Admin.)	1. 8.43
PULTAR, Josef	Fliegerausb. Regt. 43	1. 7.40
PUNZERT, Josef	Fliegerregiment 23	1. 3.43
RAITHEL, Dipl. Ing. Hans (47)	..	1. 4.42
RAUCH, Hans	..	1. 6.42
REINSHAGEN	Flying School, Hildesheim	1. 7.43
REUSS, Heinrich XXXVII Prinz v.	Flak Div. 18	1. 2.43
RIBENSTEIN	..	1. 8.41
RIECKHOFF, Herbert	C. of S. Luftflotte 1	1. 3.43
RIEKE, Georg	R.L.M.	1. 9.41
RIESCH, Dipl. Ing.	Airfield Reg. Command, Werl	1.11.41
RIVA, Erich	..	1. 9.42
RÖMER	..	1.10.43
ROESCH (57)	Rü. Insp. VII	1.12.41
ROTH, Ernst August (46)	Fliegerführer Lofoten	1. 8.42
RÜTER, Wolfgang (52)	..	1.12.39
SATTLER, Alfred (49)	(Sigs.)	1.12.41
SCHALLER	Flak. Div. I	1.10.43
SCHAUER, Ludwig (56)	..	1. 4.39
SCHILFFARTH, Ludwig (51)	..	1. 2.42
SCHMID, Josef	..	1. 3.43
SCHÖBEL, Otto	..	1.10.41
SCHÖRGI, Hugo	..	1.11.42
SCHROEDER, Severin	..	1. 4.41
SCHROTH	..	1. 8.41
SCHÜTZE (63)	..	1.11.41
SCHÜTZEK	..	1.10.43
SCHULTZE-RHONHOF (54)	C.S.O. Luftgau XVII	1. 4.41
SEIBT	Staff C.-in-C., South	1. 4.43
SEIDEMANN, Hans (42)	..	1. 8.42
SELDNER, Eduard (54)	..	19. 7.40
SEYWALD, Heinz	Bomber School, Thorn	1.11.41
SIESS, Gustav (49)	..	1.11.40
SOELDNER (54)	..	1. 4.42
SONNENBURG (53)	..	1. 6.41

Rank : Generalmajor (Major-General)—*continued*

Name (age)	*Command or Appointment*	*Seniority*
SPERLING (51)		1. 4.41
STAHEL, Reiner (52)	Special Staff C.-in-C., South	21. 1.43
STAHL		1. 1.43
STARKE, Friedrich		1. 6.41
STEIN	Insp. of Motor Transport	1.11.40
STEINKOPF		1.11.40
STEPHAN		1.10.43
STUTZER (56)	Judge Advocate General's Dept.	1.12.40
TESCHNER		1.11.40
THYM, Heinrich		1.11.40
TIPPELSKIRCH, v.		1.11.40
TSCHOELTSCH, Ehrenfried (51)		1.11.41
UNGER (53)		1. 6.41
VEITH (54)	(Flak)	1. 2.43
VODEPP		1. 2.43
VOELK		1.10.43
VOIGT-RUSCHEWEYH		1.10.43
VOLKMANN, Dietrich	Staff of C.-in-C., Air Force	1. 7.43
VORWALD, Dipl. Ing. Wolfgang	R.L.M.	1. 3.43
WADEHN		1. 9.43
WALLAND, Eugen		1.11.41
WALLNER, Otto (62)		1.11.41
WANGANHEIM, Edgar Frhr. v. (54)		1.11.40
WEECH, v.	Sigs. Luftgau Norway	1. 8.43
WEIL		1.10.43
WEINER		1.10.43
WICHARD	Staff Airfield Reg. Comd., Warsaw	1. 1.43
WIELAND		1.10.43
WILCK	Ru. Insp. Ukraine	1.11.40
WILKE, Gustav (46)	R.L.M.	1. 4.43
WITZENDORFF, Gotthard v. (52)		1. 2.43
ZECH	R.L.M.	1. 4.42
ZIERVOGEL		1. 1.43

PART L—TABLES OF FORMATIONS AND UNITS

CONTENTS

(*a*) ARMIES, PANZER ARMIES AND MOUNTAIN ARMIES

(*Armee-Oberkommando* = A.O.K., *Panzer-Armeeoberkommando* = Pz. A.O.K. and *Gebirgs-Armeeoberkommando* = Geb. A.O.K.)

A.O.K.	Wkr.	Army Troops.*							See Page
		A.N.R.	K.d.N.	r.Ag.	F.G.A.	G.F.P.	F.P.A.	P.K.	
1	IX	596	579		591	590	591		D 4
Pz. 1		Pz. 1	Pz. 1				422	691	D 8
2	XIII?	563?		550?					D 4
Pz. 2	XVII	Pz. 2	Pz. 2	532?			419		D 8
3(§)									D 4
Pz. 3	IX	Pz. 3	Pz. 3		551			697?	D 9
4	VI	589		580		721?	580	689	D 4
Pz. 4	III	Pz. 4	Pz. 4					694	D 9
5(§)									D 5
Pz. 5(‡)									D 9
6	IV	549		585?			540?	637	D 5
7	V	531†	551		690?			649?	D 5
8									D 5
9		520?					583?	583?	D 5
10		512?			498	741			D 6
11(‖)									D 6
(12		*Upgra*	*ded to H*	*eeresgru*	*ppe E.*)				D 6
..									
14									D 6
15		509†				625?		698	D 6
16	I?	501?				616?			D 7
17		596?					550	666?	D 7
18			516						D 7
19		445?	445?						D 7
20(¶)		550		525			537		D 7
Norwegen	XXI	463†	463			629	463		D 8
Pz. Afrika (‡)									D 9

* Combatant units, such as artillery, may be allotted to an army for the period of an operation, but are reckoned as pool troops (*see* Part E).

† Bn. only.

(‡) Destroyed in Tunisia.

(§) Formed and disbanded in 1939.

(‖) Disbanded late 1942.

(¶) Formerly A.O.K. Lapland.

(*b*) ARMY CORPS, RESERVE CORPS AND CORPS (LOWER ESTABLISHMENT)

(*Generalkommando* = Gen. Kdo. and *Höheres Kommando zu besonderer Verwendung* = Höh. Kdo. (z.b.V.); the different types of Army Corps are distinguished from one another as follows :—

Armeekorps	..	A.K.	..	Infantry Corps.
Panzerkorps	..	Pz.K.	..	Panzer Corps.
Gebirgskorps	..	Geb.K.	..	Mountain Corps.
Reservekorps	..	Res.K.	..	Reserve Corps.

No.	Type.	Wkr.	Corps troops.*		Home Station.	*See* page
			Nachr. Abt.	Services		
I	A.K.	I	41	401	Königsberg	D 9
II	A.K.	II	42	402	Stettin	D 10
III	Pz.K.	III	Pz. 43	403	Berlin	D 19
IV	A.K.	IV	44	404	Dresden	D 10
V	A.K.	V	45	405	Stuttgart	D 10
VI	A.K.	VI	46	406	Münster	D 10
VII	A.K.	VII	47	407	München	D 10
(*VIII*(†)	*A.K.*	*VIII*)				D 11
IX	A.K.	IX	49	409	Kassel	D 11
X	A.K.	X	50	410	Hamburg	D 11
XI	A.K.	XI	51	411	Hannover	D 11
XII	A.K.	XII	52	412	Wiesbaden	D 11
XIII	A.K.	XIII	53	413	Nürnberg	D 12
XIV	Pz.K.	XI	Pz. 60	414	Magdeburg	D 19
(*XV*	*Now up*	*graded to*	*3 Panzer A*	*rmy*)		D 9
XV	Geb.K.					D 22
(*XVI*	*Now up*	*graded to*	*4 Panzer A*	*rmy*)		D 9
XVII	A.K.	XVII	66	417	Wien	D 12
XVIII	Geb.K.	XVIII	Geb. 70	418	Salzburg	D 22
(*XIX*	*Now up*	*graded to*	*2 Panzer A*	*rmy*)		D 8
XIX	Geb.K.	XVIII				D 22
XX	A.K.	XX	420	420	Danzig	D 12
(*XXI*	*Now up*	*graded to*	*A.O.K. No*	*rwegen*)		D 8
XXI	Geb.K.					D 22
(*XXII*	*Now up*	*graded to*	*1 Panzer A*	*rmy*)		D 8
XXII	Geb.K.					D 22
XXIII	A.K.	VI	423	423?	Bonn	D 12

* Combatant units, such as artillery, may be allotted to a corps for the period of an operation, but are reckoned as pool troops (*see* Part E).

(†) Destroyed at Stalingrad.

(b) Army Corps, Reserve Corps and Corps (Lower Establishment)—*contd.*

No.	Type.	Wkr.	Corps troops.*		Home Station.	*See* page
			Nachr. Abt.	Services.		
XXIV	Pz.K.	XII	Pz. 424	424	Kaiserslautern.	D 20
XXV	A.K.	V	425	425?	Baden-Baden.	D 13
XXVI	A.K.	I	426	426		D 13
XXVII	A.K.	VII	427	427		D 13
XXVIII	A.K.	III	428	428		D 13
XXIX	A.K.	IV	429	429		D 13
XXX	A.K.	XI	430	430		D 14
XXXI	Höh. Kdo.	X?	431	431		D 14
(*XXXII*	*Höh. Kdo.*	*Reorganised as LXXXI A.K.*)				D 14
XXXIII	Höh Kdo.	VI	433	433		D 14
XXXIV (†)	Höh Kdo.	III	434	434?		D 14
XXXV	A.K.	VIII	435	435		D 14
XXXVI	Geb.K.	II	436	436		D 23
(*XXXVII*	*Höh Kdo.*	*Reorganised as LXXXII A.K.*)				D 14
XXXVIII	A.K.	VIII?	438?	438?		D 14
XXXIX	Pz.K.	IX	Pz. 439	439		D 20
XXXX	Pz.K.	XVII	Pz. 440	440		D 20
XXXXI	Pz.K.	VIII	Pz. 441	441?		D 20
XXXXII	A.K.	III	442	442		D 14
XXXXIII	A.K.	XI	443	443	Hannover	D 15
XXXXIV	A.K.	IV	444	444	Dresden	D 15
(*XXXXV*(‡))						D 15
XXXXVI	Pz.K.	X	Pz. 446	446		D 20
XXXXVII	Pz.K.	XX	Pz. 447	447	Danzig	D 21
XXXXVIII	Pz.K.	XXI	Pz. 448	448	Posen	D 21
XXXXIX	Geb.K.	Prot.	Geb. 449	449	Prag	D 23
L	A.K.	V		450		D 15
LI	Geb.K.	XI	451	451		D 15
LII	A.K.	III	452	452		D 16
LIII	A.K.	XII	453	453		D 16
LIV	A.K.		454	454		D 16
LV	A.K.		455	455		D 16

* Combatant units, such as artillery, are allotted to corps for the period of an operation, but are reckoned as pool troops (*see* Part E).

(†) Continued existence uncertain. (‡) Believed disbanded.

(*b*) Army Corps, Reserve Corps and Corps (Lower Establishment)—*contd.*

No.	Type.	Wkr.	Corps Troops.*		Home Station.	*See* page
			Nachr. Abt.	Services.		
LVI	Pz.K.	VI	Pz. 456	456		D 21
LVII	Pz.K.	II	Pz. 457	457		D 21
...						
LIX	A.K.		459	459		D 17
(*LX*	*Höh. Kdo.*	*Reorgan*	*ised as LX*	*XXIIII*	*A.K.*)	D 17
LXI	Res.K.					D 25
LXII	Res.K.					D 25
(*LXIII*	*Absorbe*	*d by A.O.*	*K. Norwege*	*n*)		D 8
LXIV	Res.K.		464?			D 25
LXV	Höh. Kdo.	II		465?		D 25
LXVI	Res.K.					D 25
LXVII	Res.K.			467?		D 26
LXVIII	A.K.		468	488		D 17
LXIX	Res.K.			469?		D 26
LXX	Höh. Kdo.	VI?	480			D 26
LXXI	Höh. Kdo.					D 26
...						
...						
...						
...						
LXXVI	Pz.K.					D 21
...						
...						
...						
LXXX	A.K.			480		D 17
LXXXI	A.K.		432?			D 18
LXXXII	A.K.	XVII	437?	437?		D 18
LXXXIII	A.K.					D 18
LXXXIV	A.K.		460?	460?		D 18
...						
LXXXVI	A.K.					D 18
LXXXVII	A.K.					D 19
LXXXVIII	A.K.					D 19
LXXXIX	A.K.					D 19
(*XC*(†)						
(*Norwegen*	*Geb.K.*	*Rename*	*d XIX Geb.*	*K.*)		D 22
(*Afrika* (†)						

* Combatant units, such as artillery, are allotted to a corps for the period of an operation, but are reckoned as pool troops (*see* Part E).

(†) Destroyed in Tunisia.

(c) PANZER DIVISIONS (Panzer-Divisionen = Pz.D.)

Div.	Wkr.	Component Units.									Home Stations.	See Page.
		Pz. R.	Pz.G.R.	Pz.G.R.	Pz.A.R.	Pz. Pi.Btl.	Pz. Jäg.Abt.	Pz.A.A.	Pz.N.A.	Services.		
1	IX	1	1	113	73	37	37	1	37	81	Weimar	D 27
2	XVII	3	2	304	74	38	38	2	38	82	Wien (Vienna)	D 27
3	III	6	3	394	75	39		3	39	83	Berlin	D 27
4	XIII	35	12	33	103	79	49	4	79	84	Würzburg	D 28
5	VIII	31	13	14	116	89	53	5	85?	85	Oppeln	D 28
6	VI	11	4	114	76	57	41	6	82	57	Wuppertal	D 29
7	IX	25	6	7	78	58	42	7	83	58	Gera	D 29
8	III	10	8	28	80	59	43	8	59	59	Cottbus	D 29
9	XVII	33	10	11	102	86	50	9	81	60	Wien	D 30
*10	V	7	69	86	90	49	90	10	90	90	Stuttgart	D 30
11	VIII	15	110	111	119	209		11	341	61	Görlitz	D 31
12	II	29	5	25	2	32	2	12	2	2	Stettin	D 31
13	XI	4	66	93	13	4	13	13	13	13	Magdeburg	D 32
14	IV	36	103	108	4	13	4	14	4	4	Dresden	D 32
15	XII	Reformed as 15 Pz. Gren. Div.										D 39
16	VI	2	64	79	16	16	16	16	16	16	Münster	D 33
17	VII	39	40	63	27	27	27	17	27	27	Augsburg	D 33
18	IV	18	52	101	88	98	88	18	88	88		D 33
19	XI	27	73	74	19	19	19	19	19	19	Hannover	D 34
20	IX	21	59	112	92	92	92	20	92	92	Gotha	D 34
21	III	5	192?	492?	155	200	39	21	200	200	Berlin	D 35
22	V	Believed Disbanded.										D 35
23	V	201	126	128	128	128	128	23	128	128		D 35
24	I	24	21	26	89	40	40	24		40		D 36
25	VI	9	146	147	91	75?		25	87?	87?		D 36
26	III	26	9	67	93	93	90	26	93	93	Potsdam	D 36
27	IX	Believed Disbanded.										D 37

* Destroyed in Tunisia ; reconstruction not yet established.

Div.	*Pz. R.*	*Pz G.R.*	*Pz. G.R.*	*Pz. G.R.*	*Pz. A.R.*	*Services Other Units.*
Gross Deutschland.	Gross Deutschland.	Gren. Regt. Gross Deutschland.	Fus. Regt. Gross Deutschland.		Gross Deutschland.	Gross Deutschland.
Hermann Goering.	Hermann Goering.	Gren. Regt. Hermann Goering 1.	Gren. Regt. Hermann Goering 2.	Jäger Regt. Hermann Goering.	Hermann Goering.	Hermann Goering.

(*d*) MOUNTAIN DIVISIONS

(Gebirgs-Divisionen = Geb.D.)

Div.	Wkr.	Component Units.								Home Stations.	*See* Page.
		Geb. J.R.	Geb. J.R.	Geb. A.R.	Pz. Pi.Btl.	Pz. Jäg.Abt.	Pz.A.A.	Pz.N.A.	Services.		
1	VII	98	99	79	54	44	54	54	54	Garmisch	D 48
2	XVIII ..	136	137	111	82	47	67	67	67	Innsbruck	D 49
3	XVIII ..	139	144	112	83	48	68	68	68	Graz	D 49
4	VII	13	91	94	94	94	94	94	94		D 49
5	XVIII ..	85	100	95	95	95	95	95	95	Salzburg	D 50
6	XVIII ..	141	143	118	91	55	112	91	91	Klagenfurt ?	D 50
7	XIII	206	218	82	99	99	99	99	99		D 50
8	XVIII ..	138?	142?								D 51
...											
...											

(e) MOTORISED DIVISIONS

(Panzergrenadier Divisionen)

Pz. Gr. Div.	Wkr.	Component Units.										Home Station.	See Page.
		Pz.Abt.	G.R. (mot).	G.R. (mot).	G.R. (mot).	A.R.	Pi.Btl.	Pz. Jäg.Abt.	Pz.A.A.	N.A.	Services.		
3	III	**103**	**8**	29	—	3	3	3	103	3	3	Frankfurt/Oder	D 38
10	XIII	110?	**20**	41	—	10	10	10	110	10	10	Regensburg	D 39
14	IV	114?	**11**	53	—	14	14	14	114	14	14	Leipzig	D 39
15	XII	**115**	Pz.104	Pz.115§	Pz.129	33	33	33	115?	78	33	Kaiserslautern	D 39
16	VI	**116**	60	156	—	146	146?		116	228	66	Rheine	D 40
18	VIII	118?	30	51	—	18	18	18	118	18	18	Liegnitz	D 40
20	X	120?	76	90	—	20	20	20	120	20	20	Hamburg	D 41
22 LL (mot)	X	212?	16	65	—	22	22	22	122	22	22	Oldenburg	D 41
25	V	125?	35	119	—	25	25	25	125	25	25	Ludwigsburg	D 42
29	IX	129	15	71	—	29	29	29	129	29	29	Erfurt	D 42
36	XII	136?	87	118	—	36	36	36	136	36	36	Wiesbaden	D 42
*60	XX	160?	†120	‡271	—	160	160	160	160	160	160	Danzig	D 43
90	III	190	Pz.155	Pz.200	Pz.361	190	190	190		190	190		D 43
164	IV	164?	Pz.125	Pz.382§	Pz.433	220	220	220	164?	220	220	Leipzig	D 44
**386			149	153									D 44

* Called " Panzergrenadierdivision Feldherrnhalle."
† Called " Füsilierregiment Feldherrnhalle."
‡ Called " Grenadierregiment Feldherrnhalle."
§ Possibly withdrawn permanently to G.H.Q. troops.
** Div. disb.; Rgts. absorbed by Pz. Gr. Div. 3.

(*f*) DIVISIONS NUMBERED IN THE MAIN INFANTRY SERIES

(Infanterie-Divisionen = J.D., Jäger Divisionen = Jäg.Div.)

Div.	Wkr.	Component Units.									Home Stations.	*See* Page.
		G.R.	G.R.	G.R.	A.R.	Pi.Btl.	Pz. Jäg.Abt.	A.A.	N.A.	Services.		
1 Inf.	I	1	†22	43	1	1	1	1	1	1	Insterburg	D 51
(2 Mot.	II	Convert	ed to 12	Pz. Div.)								
3 Mot.	(*See* 3 Pz. Gr	en. Div.).										
(4 Inf.	IV	Convert	ed to 14	Pz. Div.)								
5 Jäg.	V	56	75	—	5	5	5	*5	5	5	Konstanz	D 45
6 Inf.	VI	18	37	58	6	6	6	6	6	6	Bielefeld	D 52
7 Inf.	VII	19	61	62.	7	7	7	7	7	7	München	D 52
8 Jäg.	VIII	28	38	—	8	8	8	8	8	8	Neisse	D 45
9 Inf.	IX	36	57	116	9	9	9	9	9	9	Giessen	D 52
10 Mot.	(*See* 10 Pz.	Gren. Di	v.).									
11 Inf.	I	2	23	44	11	11	11	11	11	11	Allenstein	D 53
12 Inf.	II	27	48	89	12	12	12	12	12	12	Schwerin	D 53
13 Mot.	XI	Convert	ed to 13	Pz. Div.)								
14 Mot.	(*See* 14 Pz. G	ren. Div.	).									
15 Inf.	IX	81	88	106	15	15	15	15	15	15	Kassel	D 54
16 Mot.	(*See* 16 Pz. G	ren. Div.	and 16th	Pz. Div.)								
17 Inf.	XIII	21	55	95	17	17	17	17	17	17	Nürnberg (Nuremburg).	D 54
18 Mot.	(*See* 18 Pz. G	ren. Div.	).									
(19 Inf.	XI	Convert	ed to 19	Pz. Div.)								
20 Mot.	(*See* 20 Pz. G	ren. Div.	).									
21 Inf.	XX	3	24	45	21	21	21	21	21	21	Elbing	D 55
22 LL(mt.)	(*See under* Pz	. Gren. D	iv.).									
23 Inf.	III		†68	149?	23	23	23	23	23	23	Potsdam	D 55
24 Inf.	IV	31	32	102	24	24	24	24	24	24	Chemnitz	D 55
25 Mot.	(*See* 25 Pz. G	ren. Div.	).									
26 Inf.	VI	39	77	78	26	26	26	26	26	26	Köln (Cologne)	D 56
(27 Inf.	VII	Convert	ed to 17	Pz. Div.)								
28 Jäg.	VIII	49	83	—	28	28	28	28	28	28	Breslau	D 45
29 Mot.	(*See* 29 Pz. G	ren. Div.	).									

*Aufkl. Abt. (Mot.).

† Füsilier Regiment.

(*f*) DIVISIONS NUMBERED IN THE MAIN INFANTRY SERIES—*continued*

Div.	Wkr.	Component Units.									Home Stations.	*See* Page.
		G.R.	G.R.	G.R.	A.R.	Pi.Btl.	Pz. Jäg.Abt.	A.A.	N.A.	Services.		
30 Inf.	X	6	26	46	30	30	30	30	30	30	Lübeck	D 56
31 Inf.	XI	12	17	82	31	31	31	31	31	31	Braunschweig (Brunswick).	D 57
32 Inf.	II	4	94	96	32	2	32	32	32	32	Köslin	D 57
(33 Inf.	XII	Convert	ed to 15	Pz. Div.	(now 15	Pz. Gren	Div.).)					
34 Inf.	XII	80	107	253	34	34	34	34	34	34	Heidelberg	D 57
35 Inf.	V	34	109	111	35	35	35	35	35	35	Karlsruhe	D 58
36 Mot.	(*See* 36 Pz. G	ren. Div.	)									
. .												
38 Inf.		108	112	—	138	138	†138			138		D 58
39 Inf.		113	114	—	139	139	†139			139		D 58
. .												
. .												
. .												
. .												
‡44 Inf.	XVII	131	132	134	96	80	46	44	64	44	Wien (Vienna)	D 58
45 Inf.	XVII	130	133	135	98	81	45	45	65	45	Linz	D 59
46 Inf.	XIII	42	72	97	114	88	52	46	76	46	Karlsbad	D 59
. .												
. .												
. .												
50 Inf.	XXI	121	122	123	150	150	150	150	150	150	Posen	D 60
. .												
52 Inf.	X	163	181	205	152	152	152	152	152	152	Kassel	D 60
. .												
. .												
. .												
56 Inf.	IV	171	192	234	156	156	156	156	156	156	Dresden	D 60
57 Inf.	VII	179	199	217	157	157	157	157	157	157	Bad Reichenhall	D 61
58 Inf.	X	154	209	220	158	158	158	158	158	158	Rendsburg (?)	D 61
. .												
60 Mot.	(*See* 60 Pz.	Gr. Div.)										
61 Inf.	I	151	162	176	161	161	161	161	161	161	Königsberg	D 61
62 Inf.	VIII	164	183	190	162	162	162	162	162	162	Glatz	D 62
. .												

65 Inf.	XII	145	146?	—	165	165		†165		165	165		D 62
..													
68 Inf.	III	169	188	196	168	168	168		168	168	168	Guben	D 62
69 Inf.	VI	159	193	236	169	169		†169		169	169	Soest	D 63
71 Inf.	XI	191	194	211	171	171	171		171	171	171	Hildesheim	D 63
72 Inf.	XII	105	124	266	172	72	172?		172	172?	172		D 64
73 Inf.	XIII	170	186	213	173	173	173		173	173	173	Würzburg	D 64
75 Inf.	II	172	202	222	175	175	175		175	175	175	Neustrelitz	D 64
76 Inf.	III	178	203	*230	176	176	176		176	176	176	Berlin	D 65
78 Inf.	V	195	215		178	178	178		178	178	178	Ulm	D 65
79 Inf.	XII	208	212	226	179	179	179		179	179	179	Koblenz (Coblence)	D 66
81 Inf.	VIII	161	174	189	181	181	181			181	181		D 66
82 Inf.	IX	158	166	168	182	182		†182		182	182	Frankfurt/Main (?)	D 66
83 Inf.	X	251	257	277	183	183		†183		183	183	Hamburg	D 67
..													
86 Inf.	VI	167	184	214	186	186	186		186	186	186		D 67
87 Inf.	IV	173	185	187	187	187		†187		187	187		D 67
88 Inf.	VII	245	246	248	188	188	188			188	188		D 68
90 Lt.		(Now 90	Pz. Gren.	Div.)									
..													
93 Inf.	III	270	272		193	193	193		193	193	193	Berlin	D 68
94 Inf.	IV	267	274	276	194	194		†194		194	194		D 68
95 Inf.	IX	278	279	280	195	195	195		195		195		D 69
96 Inf.	XI	283	284	287	196	196		†196		196	196		D 69
97 Jäg.	VII	204	207	—	81	97	97		97	97	97		D 46
98 Inf.	XIII	282	289	290	198	198		†198		198	198		D 69
(99 Lt.	XIII	Convert	ed to 7 M	tn. Div.).									
100 Jäg.	XVII	54	227	—	83	100	100		100	100	100		D 46

† Schnelle Abt.
‡ Also called " Reichsgrenadier division Hoch-und Deutschmeister."
* Füsilier Regiment.

(*f*) DIVISIONS NUMBERED IN THE MAIN INFANTRY SERIES—*continued*

Div.	Wkr.	Component Units.									Home Stations.	*See* Page.
		G.R.	G.R.	G.R.	A.R.	Pi.Btl.	Pz. Jäg.Abt.	A.A.	N.A.	Services.		
101 Jäg.	V	228	229	—	85	101	101	101	101	101		D 46
102 Inf.	VIII	232	233	*235	104	102	102		102	102		D 70
..												
104 Jäg.	IV	724	734	—	654	104			104	104		D 47
..												
106 Inf.	VI	239	240	241	107	106	106	106	106	106		D 70
..												
..												
..												
110 Inf.	X	252	254	255	120	110	110	110	110	110	Oldenburg	D 71
111 Inf.	XI	50	70	117	117?	111	111	117	111	111		D 71
112 Inf.	XII	110	256	258	86	112	112	120	112	112	Darmstadt	D 71
113 Inf.	XIII	260	261	268	87	113	113	113	113	113		D 72
114 Jäg.	I	721	741	—	661	114			114	114		D 47
..												
..												
117 Jäg.	XVII	737	749	—	670	117			117	117		D 47
118 Jäg.	XVIII	738	750	—	668	118			118	118		D 48
..												
..												
121 Inf.	X	405	407	408	121	121	121	121	121	121		D 72
122 Inf.	II	409	411	414?	122	122	122	122	122	122		D 72
123 Inf.	III	415	416	418	123	123	123	123	123	123		D 73
..												
125 Inf.	V	419	420?	421	125	125	125	125	125	125		D 73
126 Inf.	VI	422	424	426	126	126	126	126	126	126		D 73
..												
..												
129 Inf.	IX	427	428	430	129	129	129	129	129	129	Fulda	D 74
..												
131 Inf.	XI	431	432	434	131	131	131	131	131	131		D 74
132 Inf.	XII	436	437	438	132	132	†132	†132	132	132		D 74
..												
134 Inf.	IV	439	445	446	134	134	134	134	134	134		D 75
..												

137 Inf.	XVII	447	448	449	137	137	137	137	137	137		D 75
..												
..												
..												
141 Res.	I	‡1	‡11	‡61							Insterburg	D 118
..												
143 Res.	III	‡68?	‡76?	*208?							Frankfurt/Oder	D 119
..												
..												
..												
147††	VII	Depot units only.									Augsburg	D 126
148 Res.	VIII	‡8?	‡252?	‡239?							Metz	D 119
..												
..												
151 Res.	I	‡21	‡217	‡228							Allenstein	D 119
152††	XX	Depot units only.									Graudenz	D 126
153 Res.	III	‡23?	‡218?	‡257?							Potsdam	D 119
154 Res.	IV	‡56	‡223	‡255							Dresden	D 120
155 Res. Pz.**	V	‡25? (mot.).	‡86? (Pz. Gr.).								Ulm	D 120
156 Res.	VI	‡6	‡227?	‡254							Köln	D 120
157 Res.	VII	‡7	‡157	‖1	‡7? Geb.‡79?	‡7	‡7?				München	D 120
158 Res.	VIII	‡62?	213?	221?							Strassburg	D 121
159 Res.	IX	‡9	15	251							Frankfurt/Main	D 121
160 Res.	X	‡30	58	225								D 121
161 Inf.	I	336	364	371	241	241		§241		241		D 75
162 Inf.	II	303	314	329?	236	236	236		236	236	Rostock	D 76
163 Inf.	III	307	310	324	234	234		§234		234	Berlin	D 76
164	(*See* 164 Pz. Gren. Div.).											
165 Res.	V	‡205	‡215?	‡260							Stuttgart	D 121
166 Res.	VI	‡26?	‡69	‡86							Bielefeld	D 122
167 Inf.	VII	315	331	339	238	238	238	238	238	238		D 76
168 Inf.	VIII	417	429	442	248	248	248	248	248	248		D 77
169 Inf.	IX	378	379	392	230	230	230		230	230		D 77

* Possibly disbanded, but may be replaced by an unknown reg.
† May be Schnelle Abt.
‡ Reserve (Ausbildungs) units.
§ Schnelle Abt.
‖ Res. Geb. Jäg. Regt.
†† Depot Divisional staff.
** Includes also Res. Pz. Abt. 7? and 18?

(*f*) DIVISIONS NUMBERED IN THE MAIN INFANTRY SERIES—*continued*

Div.	Wkr.	Component Units.									Home Stations.	*See* Page.
		G.R.	G.R.	G.R.	A.R.	Pi.Btl.	Pz. Jäg.Abt.	A.A.	N.A.	Services.		
170 Inf.	X	391	399	401	240	240	240	240	240	240	Bremen	D 77
171 Res.	XI	‡71	‡31?	‡216?							Hannover	D 122
172*	XII	Depot units only.									Mainz.	D 127
173 Res.	XIII	‡17	‡73				‡17				Nürnberg	D 122
174 Res.	IV	‡24?	‡209?	‡256?							Leipzig	D 122
. .												
176*	VI	Depot units only.									Bielefeld	D 127
177*	XVII	Depot units only.									Wien.	D 127
178*	VIII	Depot units only.									Liegnitz	D 127
179 Res. Pz. §	IX	‡29 (mot.).	‡81 (Pz. Gr.).								Weimar	D 123
180*	X	Depot units only.									Verden	D 127
181 Inf.	XI	334	349	359	222	222	222	222	222	222		D 78
182 Res.	XII	‡34	‡79	‡112							Nancy	D 123
183 Inf.	XIII	330	343	351	219	219	219	219	219	219		D 78
. .												
. .												
. .												
187 Res.	XVII	‡45	‡130	‡462			‡48?				Linz	D 123
188 Res.Geb.	XVIII	†136?	†137?	†138?	†139?						Salzburg	D 123
189 Res.	IX	‡28	‡52	‡214	‡28						Kassel ?	D 124
190*	X	Depot units only.									Neumünster	D 127
191 Res.Pz.	XI	‡20 (mot.).	‡13 (Pz. Gr.).	‡267?							Braunschweig	D 124
192*	II	Depot units only.									Rostock	D 128
193*	Prot.	Depot units only.									Pilsen ?	D 128
. .												
. .												
196 Inf.	VI	340	345	362	233	233	233	233	233	233	Bielefeld ?	D 78
197 Inf.	XII	321	332	347	229	229	229	229	229	229	Speyer	D 79
198 Inf.	V	305	308	326	235	235	235	235	235	235		D 79
199 Inf.	VI	341	357	410	199		‖199		199	199	Düsseldorf	D 79
. .												
201 Sich.	IX ?											D 115
. .												

203 Sich.	III ?												D 115
..													
205 Inf.	V	335	353	358	205	205		‖205		205	205	Ulm	D 80
206 Inf.	I	301	312	413	206	206		‖206		206	206	Gumbinnen	D 80
207 Sich.	II											Stargard	D 115
208 Inf.	III	309	337	338	208	208		‖208		208	208	Cottbus	D 80
(209 Inf.	IV	Disbanded in summer, 1940).											D 81
210 Inf.		193?		—	210								D 81
211 Inf.	VI	306	317	365	211	211	211		211	211	211	Köln	D 81
212 Inf.	VII	316	320	423	212	212		‖212		212	212	München	D 81
213 Sich.	VIII											Glogau	D 115
214 Inf.	IX	355	367	—	214	214		‖214		214	214	Hanau	D 82
215 Inf.	V	380	390	435	215	215	215		215	215	215	Heilbronn	D 82
216 Inf.	XI	348	396	398	216	216	216		216	216	216	Hameln ?	D 82
217 Inf.	I	311	346	389	217	217	217		217	217	217	Allenstein	D 83
218 Inf.	III	323	386	397	218	218		‖218		218	218	Spandau	D 83
..													
..													
221 Sich.	VIII											Breslau	D 116
..													
223 Inf.	IV	344	385	425	223	223		‖223		223	223	Dresden	D 83
..													
225 Inf.	X	333	376	377	225	225		‖225		225	225	Hamburg	D 84
..													
227 Inf.	VI	328	366	412	227	227	227		227	227	227	Düsseldorf	D 84
(228 Inf.	I	Disbanded in summer, 1940).											D 84
..													
230 Inf.¶													D 85
(231 Inf.	XIII	Disbanded in summer, 1940).											D 85
..													
233 Res. Pz.**	III	‡3? (mot.).	‡83? (Pz. Gr.).		‡3?	‡68?						Frankfurt/Oder ?	D 124
..													
..													
..													
..													
..													
(239 Inf.	VIII	Disbanded in winter, 1941).											D 85
240 Inf.¶													D 85
..													

* Depot Divisional staff.
† Reserve Geb. Jäg. Regts.
‡ Reserve (Ausbildungs) units.
§ Also includes Res. Pz. Abt. 1 ?
‖ Schnelle Abt.
¶ Coastal Division.
** Also includes Res. Pz. Abt. 5 ?

(*f*) DIVISIONS NUMBERED IN THE MAIN INFANTRY SERIES—*continued*

Div.	Wkr.	Component Units.									Home Stations.	*See* Page.
		G.R.	G.R.	G.R.	A.R.	Pi.Btl.	Pz. Jäg.Abt.	A.A.	N.A.	Services.		
242 Inf.	II			**917**	**242**							D 85
..												
246 Inf.	XII	**352**	**404**	**689**	246	**246**	*246		246	246	Trier (Treves)	D 86
..												
(250 Inf.		Disbanded autumn, 1943 Spanish Blue Division.)										
251 Inf.	IX	451	459	471	251	251	251	251	251	251	Frankfurt/Main ?	D 86
252 Inf.	VIII	452	461	472	252	252	252	252	252	252	Neisse	D 87
253 Inf.	VI	453	464	473	253	253	253	253	253	253	Aachen	D 87
254 Inf.	VI	454	474	484	254	254	254	254	254	254	Dortmund	D 87
255 Inf.	IV	455	465	475	255	255	255	255	255	255	Löbau	D 88
256 Inf.	IV	456	476	481	256	256	256	256	256?	256	Meissen ?	D 88
257 Inf.	III	457	466	477	257	257	257	257	257	257	Frankfurt/Oder	D 88
258 Inf.	II	458	478	479	258	258	258	258	258	258	Rostock	D 89
..												
260 Inf.	V	460	470	480	260	260	260	260	260	260	Karlsruhe	D 89
..												
262 Inf.	XVII	462	482	486	262	262	262	262	262	262	Wien	D 89
263 Inf.	XII	463	483	485	263	263	263	263	263	263	Idar-Oberstein	D 90
264 Inf.		891	892	893	264	264	264			264		D 90
265 Inf.	XI	894	895	896								D 90
..												
267 Inf.	XI	467	487	497§	267	267	267	267	267	267	Hannover ?	D 91
268 Inf.	VII	468	488	499	268	268	*268		268	268	München	D 91
269 Inf.	X	469	489	490	269	269	*269		269	269	Delmenhorst	D 91
270 Inf.‡	X											D 92
(271 Inf.	V	Disbanded summer, 1940).										D 92
(272 Inf.	II	Disbanded summer, 1940).									Neustrelitz.	D 92
(273 Inf.	III	Disbanded summer, 1940).										D 92
274 Inf.	II											D 92
..												
(276 Inf.	VI ?	Disbanded summer, 1940).										D 92

(277 Inf.	VIII	Disbanded summer 1940).									Augsburg ?	D 92
..												
280 Inf.‡		223?	224?									D 93
281 Sich.	II ?											D 116
282 Inf.	XII	848	849	850	282					282		D 93
..												
284 Sich.												D 116
285 Sich.												D 117
286 Sich.												D 117
..												
290 Inf.	X	501	502	503	290	290	*290			290		D 93
291 Inf.	I	504	505	506	291	291	*291		291	291	Insterburg	D 93
292 Inf.	II	507	508	509	292	292	292		292	292		D 94
293 Inf.	III	510	511	512	293	293	293	293	293	293		D 94
294 Inf.	IV	513	514	515	294	294	294	294	294	294		D 94
295 Inf.	XI	516	517	518	295	295	295		295	295		D 95
296 Inf.	XIII	519	520	521	296	296	296	296	296	296	Nürnberg ?	D 95
297 Inf.	XVII	522	523	524	297	297	297	297	297	297	Wien	D 95
298 Inf.§	VIII	525	526	527	298	298	298	298	298	298		D 96
299 Inf.	IX	528	529	530	299	299	299	299		299	Weimar	D 96
..												
302 Inf.	II	570	571	572	302	302	*302		302	302	Schwerin	D 96
..												
304 Inf.	IV	573	574	575	304	304	304		304	304		D 97
305 Inf.	V	576	577	578	305	305		305	305	305	Konstanz	D 97
306 Inf.	VI	579	580	581	306	306	*306		306	306		D 97
(307 Inf.		Probably disbanded 1940).										D 97
..												
(310 Inf.		Probably disbanded 1940).										D 97
(311‖	I	Probably disbanded 1940).										D 98
..												
..												
..												
..												
..												

* Schnelle Abt.
‡ Coastal Division.
§ Possibly disbanded.
‖ Classification uncertain.

(*f*) DIVISIONS NUMBERED IN THE MAIN INFANTRY SERIES—*continued*

Div.	Wkr.	Component Units.									Home Stations.	*See* Page.
		G.R.	G.R.	G.R.	A.R.	Pi.Btl.	Pz. Jäg.Abt.	A.A.	N.A.	Services.		
(317 Inf.		Probably	disband	ed 1940).								D 98
. .												
319 Inf.	IX	582	583	584	319	319	*319			319		D 98
320 Inf.	VIII	585	586	587	320	320	320		320	320		D 98
321 Inf.	XI	588	589	590	321	321			321	321		D 98
. .												
323 Inf.	V	591	592	593	323	323	*323		323	323		D 99
. .												
326 Inf.	VI	751	752	753	326	326	326		326	326		D 99
327 Inf.	XVII	595	596	597	327	327	327		327	327		D 99
328 Inf.	IX	547	548	549	328	328		328	†328	328		D 100
329 Inf.	VI	551?	552?	553	329	329	*329		329	329		D 100
330 Inf.	V	554	555	556	330	330		330	330	330		D 100
331 Inf.	XVII	557	558	559	331	331	331	331?	331	331		D 100
332 Inf.	VIII	676	677	678	332	332	332		†332	332		D 101
333 Inf.	III	679	680	681	333	333	*333		†333	333	Berlin	D 101
334 Inf.	XIII	754	755	756	334	334	*334		334	334		D 101
335 Inf.	V	682	683	684	335	335	335		†335	335		D 102
336 Inf.	VI	685	686	687	336	336	336		336	336	Rheine	D 102
337 Inf.	VII	313	688	690	337	337	337		†337	337		D 102
338 Inf.		757	758	759	338	338	338		338	338		D 103
339 Inf.	IX	691	692	693	339‡	339	*339		†339	339	Jena	D 103
340 Inf.	I	694	695	696	340	340	340		340	340		D 103
(341 Inf.		Probably	disband	ed, 1940)								D 103
342 Inf.	XII	697	698	699	342	342	342	342	342	342	Kaiserslautern	D 103
343 Inf.	XIII	851	852	853		343				343		D 104
344 Inf.§		854	855	856	344					344		D 104
345 Mot.		Convert	ed to 29	Pz. Gren	. Div.							D 104
346 Inf.			858									D 105
347 Inf.	II		861							347		D 105
348 Inf.		863	864	865?								D 105
. .												
(351 Inf.		Probably	disband	ed,1940).								D 105

. .												
. .												
355 Inf.		866	867	868								D 105
356 Inf.	IX	869	870	871	356					356		D 106
. .												
(358	III	Probably disbanded, 1940.)										D 106
. .												
. .												
. .												
. .												
(365 Inf.‖	V	Disbanded, 1940.)										D 106
. .												
. .												
369 Inf.**	XVII	369	370		369					369	Stockerau	D 106
370 Inf.	IV ?	666	667	668	370	370	370		370	370		D 106
371 Inf.	VI	669	670	671	371	371	371			371		D 107
(372 Inf.‖	IV	Disbanded autumn, 1940.)										D 107
373 Inf.**	XVII	383	384		373	373	373			373		D 107
. .												
376 Inf.	VII	672	673	767	376		376			376		D 107
377 Inf.	IX	768	769	770	377	377	377	377	377	377		D 108
(379 Inf.‖	IX	Disbanded autumn, 1940.)										D 108
(380 Inf.		Probably disbanded autumn, 1940.)										D 108
381††				‡‡616								D 124
382††		‡‡617	‡‡618	‡‡619								D 125
383 Inf.	III	531	532	533	383	383	383*		383	383		E 108
384 Inf.	IV	534	535	536	384		384		384	384		D 108
385 Inf.§§		537	538	539	385	385	385		385	385		D 109
386 Mot.¶	VI	Converted to 3 Pz. Gren. Div.										D 109

* Schnelle Abt.
† Coy. only.
‡ Abteilung only.
§ Static.
‖ An O.F.K. has taken on the number.

¶ 386 Inf. Div. formed Wkr. VI 1939. Disbanded 1940.
** Croation.
†† Field Training Division.
‡‡ Field Training Regts.
§§ Now possibly disbanded.

(*f*) DIVISIONS NUMBERED IN THE MAIN INFANTRY SERIES—*continued*

Div.	Wkr.	Component Units.									Home Stations.	See Page.
		G.R.	G.R.	G.R.	A.R.	Pi.Btl.	Pz. Jäg.Abt.	A.A.	N.A.	Services.		
387 Inf.	VII	541	542	543..	387	387	387		387	387		D 109
388*												D 125
389 Inf.	IX	544	545	546	389		389			389		D 110
390*												D 125
391*	XII	§718	§719	§720							Koblenz	D 125
392 Inf.												D ?
(393 Inf.†	X	Disband	ed autu	mn, 1940	).							D 110
(395 Inf.†		Disband	ed autu	mn, 1940	).							D 110
(399 Inf.†	I	Disband	ed autu	mn, 1940	).							D 110
..												
401 Depot‡	I	Varying	attached	units.							Königsberg	D 130
402 z.b.V.‡	II	Varying	attached	units.							Stettin	D 130
403 Sich.	III										Berlin	D 117
404 z.b.V.‡	IV	Varying	arrached	units.							Dresden	D 130
405 z.b.V.‡	V	Varying	attached	units.							Stuttgart	D 130
406 z.b.V.‡	VI	Varying	attached	units.							Münster	D 130
407 z.b.V.‡	VII	Varying	attached	units.							München	D 131
408 z.b.V.‡	VIII	Varying	attached	units.							Breslau	D 131
409 Depot‡	IX	Varying	attached	units.							Kassel	D 128
410 z.b.V.‖	X	Varying	attached	units.							Hamburg	D 131
411 z.b.V.‖	XI	Varying	attached	units.							Hannover	D 131
412 z.b.V.‖	XII	Varying	attached	units.							Wiesbaden	D 131
413 z.b.V.‖	XIII	Varying	attached	units.							Nürnberg	D 132
..												
..												
416 Inf.	X ?	930	931	—						466?		D 110
417 z.b.V.‖	XVII	Varying	attached	units.							Wien	D 132
..												
..												
..												
421 z.b.V.‖	I	Varying	attached	units.								D 132

..												
..												
..												
..												
..												
..												
428 z.b.V.‖	XX	Varying	attached	units.							Graudenz	D 132
429 z.b.V.‖	XXI	Varying	attached	units.							Posen (Posnan)	D 132
430 z.b.V.‖	XXI	Varying	attached	units.							Gnesen (Gniezno)	D 133
431 z.b.V.‖	XXI	Varying	attached	units.							Litzmannstadt (Lodz)	D 133
432 z.b.V.	VIII	Varying	attached	units.							Kattowitz	D 133
433‡ ..	III	Depot u	nits only								Berlin	D 128
..												
..												
..												
..												
..												
..												
..												
(441 z.b.V.¶		Disband	ed.)									D 117
442 Sich.												
..												
444 Sich.	XII											
(445 z.b.V.‡		Disband	ed.)									D 118
..												
..												
..												
..												
..												
..												
..												
..												
454 Sich.												D 118
(455 Sich.		Disband	ed.)									D 118
..												
..												
..												
..												
..												

* Field Training Division.
† An O.F.K. has taken on the number.
‡ Depot Divisional staff only.
§ Field Training Regts.
‖ Divisional staff only.
¶ Disbanded.

(*f*) DIVISIONS NUMBERED IN THE MAIN INFANTRY SERIES—*continued*

Div.	Wkr.	Component Units.									Home Stations.	*See* Page.
		G.R.	G.R.	G.R.	A.R.	Pi.Btl.	Pz. Jäg.Abt.	A.A.	N.A.	Services.		
461‡	I	Depot units only.									Bialystok	D 128
462‡	XII										Nancy	D 128
..												
464‡	IV	Depot units only.									Leipzig	D 129
465‡	V	Depot units only.									Stuttgart	D 129
..												
467‡	VII	Depot units only.									München	D 129
..												
..												
..												
..												
..												
473‡	XIII	Depot units only.									Regensburg	D 129
..												
..												
..												
487‡	XVII	Depot units only.									Wien	D 129
..												
..												
..												
526‡	VI	Depot units only.									Wuppertal	D 130
..												
..												
..												
..												
..												
..												
..												
..												
..												
..												
537 Grenz-wacht.	XVIII	Frontier guard units only.									Innsbruck	D 125
..												
..												

538 Grenz-wacht.	XVIII	Frontier guard units only.									Klagenfurt	D 126
539 Grenz-wacht.	Prot.	Frontier guard units only.									Prag	D 126
540 Grenz-wacht.	Prot.	Frontier guard units only.									Brünn	D 126
(554 Inf.	V	Disbanded late in 1940).										D 110
(555 Inf.	VI	Disbanded late in 1940).										D 110
(556 Inf.	XII	Disbanded late in 1940).										D 111
(557 Inf.	IV	Disbanded late in 1940).										D 111
702 Inf.	II	722	742	—	662				702	702		D 111
(704 Inf.	IV	Converted to 104 Jäg. Div.).										

‡ Depot Divisional staff only.

(*f*) DIVISIONS NUMBERED IN THE MAIN INFANTRY SERIES—*continued*

Div.	Wkr.	Component Units.									Home Stations.	*See* Page.
		G.R.	G.R.	G.R.	A.R.	Pi.Btl.	Pz. Jäg.Abt.	A.A.	N.A.	Services.		
707 Inf.	VII	727	747	—	657	707			707	707		D 111
708 Inf.	VIII	728	748	—		708			708	708		D 111
709 Inf.	IX	729	739	—		709			709	709		D 112
710 Inf.	X	730	740	—		710			710	710		D 112
711 Inf.	XI	731	744	—	651?	711			711	711		D 112
712 Inf.	XII	732	745		652	712			712	712		D 112
713 Inf.‡	XIII	733	746§		653?	713			713	713		D 113
(714 Inf.		Converted to 114 Jäg. Div.).										
715 Inf.	V	725	735	—		715			715	715		D 113
716 Inf.	VI	726	736	—	656	716			716	716		D 113
(717 Inf.	XVII	Converted to 117 Jäg. Div.).										
(718 Inf.	XVIII	Converted to 118 Jäg. Div.).										
719 Inf.	III	723	743	—	663	719			719	719		D 114
999 Inf.		†961	†962	†963	†999				†999	†999		D 114
Sturmdiv. Rhodos.												D 114

† Div. disbanded in 1943, some units may still **exist**.
‡ Possibly disbanded.
§ Now under Festungs-Brigade Kreta.

(*g*) INFANTRY REGIMENTS (ALL TYPES)

Grenadier-Regimenter = G.R.,
Panzer-Grenadier-Regimenter = Pz.G.R.
Jäger-Regimenter = Jäg.R.
Gebirgsjäger-Regimenter = Geb.J.R.
Fusilier-Regimenter = Fus.R.
Festungs-Bataillon = F.B.
Festungs-Regiment-Stab = F.R.St.

Identification : White, grass-green or light green piping.

	G.R.*	In Div.		G.R.	In Div.
	1	1 Inf.		17	31 Inf.
Pz.	1 mot.	1 Pz.		18	6 Inf.
	2	11 Inf.		19	7 Inf.
Pz.	2 mot.	2 Pz.		20 mot.	10 Pz. Gr.
	3	21 Inf.		21	17 Inf.
Pz.	3 mot.	3 Pz.	Pz.	21 mot.	24 Pz.
	4	32 Inf.	Füs.	22	1 Inf.
Pz.	4 mot.	6 Pz.		23	11 Inf.
Pz.	5 mot.	12 Pz.		24	21 Inf.
	6	30 Inf.	Pz.	25 mot.	12 Pz.
Pz.	6 mot.	7 Pz.		26	30 Inf.
	7†		Pz.	26 mot.	24 Pz.
Pz.	7 mot.	7 Pz.	Füs.	27	12 Inf.
			Pz.	28 mot.	8 Pz.
	8 mot.	3 Pz.Gr.	Jäg.	28	8 Jäg.
Pz.	8 mot.	8 Pz.		29 mot.	3 Pz.Gr.
Pz.	9 mot.	26 Pz.		30 mot.	18 Pz.Gr.
	10†			31	24 Inf.
Pz.	10 mot.	9 Pz.		32	24 Inf.
	11 mot.	14 Pz.Gr.	Pz.	33 mot.	4 Pz.
Pz.	11 mot.	9 Pz.	Füs.	34	35 Inf.
	12	31 Inf.		35 mot.	25 Pz.Gr.
Pz.	12 mot.	4 Pz.		36	9 Inf.
Geb.	13	4 Mtn.		37	6 Inf.
Pz.	13 mot.	5 Pz.	Jäg.	38	8 Jäg.
	14†		Füs.	39	26 Inf.
Pz.	14 mot.	5 Pz.	Pz.	40 mot.	17 Pz.
	15 mot.	29 Pz.Gr.		41 mot.	10 Pz.Gr.
	16	22 LL (mot.)		42	46 Inf.

* Unless qualified by *Pz.*, *Jäg.* or *Geb.*
† Possibly re-formed under a new number.

G.R.		In Div.	G.R.		In Div.
	43	1 Inf.	Jäg.	83	28 Jäg.
	44	11 Inf.	Jäg.	84* ?	
	45	21 Inf.	Geb.	85	5 Mtn.
	46	30 Inf.	Pz.	86 mot.	10 Pz.
	(47 mot.)†			87 mot.	36 Pz.Gr.
	48	12 Inf.		88	15 Inf.
Jäg.	49	28 Jäg.		89	12 Inf.
	50	111 Inf.		90 mot.	20 Pz.Gr.
	51 mot.	18 Pz.Gr.	Geb.	91	4 Mtn.
Pz.	52 mot.	18 Pz.		92 mot.	
	53 mot.	14 Pz.Gr.	Pz.	93 mot.	13 Pz.
Jäg.	54	100 Jäg.		94	32 Inf.
	55	17 Inf.		95	17 Inf.
Jäg.	56	5 Jäg.		96	32 Inf.
	57	9 Inf.		97	46 Inf.
	58	6 Inf.	Geb.	98	1 Mtn.
Pz.	59 mot.	20 Pz.	Geb.	99	1 Mtn.
	60 mot.	16 Pz.Gr.	Geb.	100	5 Mtn.
	61	7 Inf.	Pz.	101 mot.	18 Pz.
	62	7 Inf.		102	24 Inf.
Pz.	63 mot.	17 Pz.	Pz.	103 mot.	14 Pz.
Pz.	64 mot.	16 Pz.	Pz.	104 mot.	15 Pz.Gr.
	65	22 LL (mot.)		105	72 Inf.
Pz.	66 mot.	13 Pz.		106	15 Inf.
Pz.	67 mot.	26 Pz.		107	34 Inf.
Füs.	68	23 Inf.		108	38 Inf.
Pz.	69 mot.	10 Pz.	Pz.	108 mot.	14 Pz.
	70	111 Inf.		109	35 Inf.
	71 mot.	29 Pz.Gr.		110	112 Inf.
	72	46 Inf.	Pz.	110 mot.	11 Pz.
Pz.	73 mot.	19 Pz.		111	35 Inf.
Pz.	74 mot.	19 Pz.	Pz.	111 mot.	11 Pz.
Jäg.	75	5 Jäg.		112	38 Inf.
	76 mot.	20 Pz.Gr.	Pz.	112 mot.	20 Pz.
	77	26 Inf.		113	39 Inf.
	78	26 Inf.	Pz.	113 mot.	1 Pz.
Pz.	79 mot.	16 Pz.		114	39 Inf.
	80	34 Inf.	Pz.	114 mot.	6 Pz.
	81	15 Inf.	Pz.	115 mot.‡	15 Pz.Gr.
	82	31 Inf.		116	9 Inf.

* Possibly disbanded.
† Detached from 22 LL (Mot.) Div. as reinforced regiment, disbanded 1943
‡ Possibly withdrawn to G.H.Q. troops.

G.R.	In Div.	G.R.	In Div.
117	111 Inf.	158	82 Inf.
118 mot.	36 Pz.Gr.	159	69 Inf.
119 mot.	25 Pz.Gr.	Pz. 160 mot.*	
120 mot.†	60 Pz.Gr.	161	81 Inf.
121	50 Inf.	162	61 Inf.
122	50 Inf.	163	52 Inf.
123	50 Inf.	164	62 Inf.
124	72 Inf.	..	
Pz. 125 mot.	164 Pz.Gr.	166	82 Inf.
Pz. 126 mot.	23 Pz.	167	86 Inf.
..		168	82 Inf.
Pz. 128 mot.	23 Pz.	169	68 Inf.
Pz. 129 mot.	15 Pz.Gr.	170	73 Inf.
130	45 Inf.	171	56 Inf.
131	44 Inf.	172	75 Inf.
132	44 Inf.	173	87 Inf.
133	45 Inf.	174	81 Inf.
134	44 Inf.	..	
135	45 Inf.	176	61 Inf.
Geb. 136	2 Mtn.	..	
Geb. 137	2 Mtn.	178	76 Inf.
Geb. 138 ?	8 Mtn. ?	179	57 Inf.
Geb. 139	3 Mtn.	..	
Pz. 140 mot. ?		181	52 Inf.
Geb. 141	6 Mtn.	..	
Geb. 142 ?	8 Mtn. ?	183	62 Inf.
Geb. 143	6 Mtn.	184	86 Inf.
Geb. 144	3 Mtn.	185	87 Inf.
145	65 Inf.	186	73 Inf.
146 ?	65 Inf.	187	87 Inf.
Pz. 146 mot.	25 Pz.	188	68 Inf.
Pz. 147 mot.	25 Pz.	189	81 Inf.
Pz. 148 mot.*		190	62 Inf.
Pz. 149 mot.*		191	71 Inf.
..		192	56 Inf.
151	61 Inf.	Pz. 192 mot. ?	21 Pz. ?
Pz. 152 mot.		193 ?	210 Inf. ?
Pz. 153 mot.*		194	71 Inf.
154	58 Inf.	195	78 Inf.
Pz. 155 mot.	90 Pz.Gr.	196	68 Inf.
156 mot.	16 Pz.Gr.	..	
..		198	

* Disbanded in 1943.
† Called " Füsilier-Regiment Feldherrnhalle."

G.R.	In Div.	G.R.	In Div.
199	57 Inf.	239	106 Inf.
Pz. 200 mot.	90 Pz.Gr.	240	106 Inf.
201*		241	106 Inf.
202	75 Inf.	242*	
203	76 Inf.	243*	
Jäg. 204	97 Jäg.	244*	
205	52 Inf.	245	88 Inf.
Geb. 206	7 Mtn.	246	88 Inf.
Jäg. 207	97 Jäg.	..	
208	79 Inf.	248	88 Inf.
209	58 Inf.	249?	
210*		..	
211	71 Inf.	251	83 Inf.
212	79 Inf.	252	110 Inf.
213	73 Inf.	253	34 Inf.
214	86 Inf.	254	110 Inf.
215	78 Inf.	255	110 Inf.
216		256	112 Inf.
217	57 Inf.	257	83 Inf.
Geb. 218	7 Mtn.	258	112 Inf.
..		..	
220	58 Inf.	260	113 Inf.
..		261	113 Inf.
222	75 Inf.	262†	
223 ?	280 Inf. ?	263†	
224 ?	280 Inf. ?	264*	
..		265*	
226	79 Inf.	266	72 Inf.
Jäg. 227	100 Jäg.	267	94 Inf.
Jäg. 228	101 Jäg.	268	113 Inf.
Jäg. 229	101 Jäg.	269†	
Füs. 230	76 Inf.	270	93 Inf.
..		271 mot.§	60 Pz.Gr.
232	102 Inf.	272	93 Inf.
233	102 Inf.	..	
234	56 Inf.	274	94 Inf.
235‡	102 Inf.	..	
236	69 Inf.	276	94 Inf.
..		277	83 Inf.
238‡	78 Inf.	278	95 Inf.

‡ Possibly disbanded.
* Disbanded late in 1940. † Spanish, disbanded autumn 1943.
§ Called " Grenadier-Regiment-Feldherrnhalle."

G.R.	In Div.	G.R.	In Div.
279	95 Inf.	(319*	231 Inf.)
280	95 Inf.	320	212 Inf.
..		321	197 Inf.
282	98 Inf.	322†	
283	96 Inf.	323	218 Inf.
284	96 Inf.	324	163 Inf.
..		(325*	)
..		326	198 Inf.
287	96 Inf.	(327‡	)
288§		328	227 Inf.
289	98 Inf.	329 ?	162 Inf.
290	98 Inf.	330	183 Inf.
..		331	167 Inf.
..		332	197 Inf.
..		333	225 Inf.
..		Füs. 334	181 Inf.
..		335	205 Inf.
..		336	161 Inf.
..		337	208 Inf.
..		338	208 Inf.
..		339	167 Inf.
..		340	196 Inf.
301	206 Inf.	341	199 Inf.
(302*	)	(342*	)
303	162 Inf.	343	183 Inf.
Pz. 304 mot.	2 Pz.	344	223 Inf.
305	198 Inf.	345	196 Inf.
306	211 Inf.	346	217 Inf.
307	163 Inf.	347	197 Inf.
308	198 Inf.	348	216 Inf.
309	208 Inf.	349	181 Inf.
310	163 Inf.	350†	
311	217 Inf.	351	183 Inf.
312	206 Inf.	352	246 Inf.
313	337 Inf.	353	205 Inf.
314	162 Inf.	354†	
315	167 Inf.	355	214 Inf.
316	212 Inf.	(356*	)
317	211 Inf.	357	199 Inf.
318†		358	205 Inf.

* Disbanded late in 1940. † Reinforced regiment.
‡ Probably disbanded late in 1941.
§ " Sonderverband 288," disbanded 1943.

	G.R.	In Div.		G.R.	In Div.
	359	181 Inf.		399	170 Inf.
	360†			(400*	)
Pz.	361 mot.	90 Pz.Gr.		401	170 Inf.
	362	196 Inf.		402?	
	. .			403?	
	364	161 Inf.		404	246 Inf.
	365	211 Inf.		405	121 Inf.
	366	227 Inf.		406†	
	367	214 Inf.		407	121 Inf.
	368†			408	121 Inf.
	369	369 Inf.		409	122 Inf.
	370	369 Inf.		410	199 Inf.
	371	161 Inf.		411	122 Inf.
	(372‡	)		412	227 Inf.
	. .			413	206 Inf.
	374†			414 ?	122 Inf.
	375†			415	123 Inf.
	376	225 Inf.		416	123 Inf.
	377	225 Inf.		417	168 Inf.
	378	169 Inf.		418	123 Inf.
	379	169 Inf.		419	125 Inf.
	380	215 Inf.		420	125 Inf.
	. .			421	125 Inf.
Pz.	382 mot. §	164 Pz.Gr.		422	126 Inf.
	383	373‖		423	212 Inf.
	384	373‖		424	126 Inf.
	385	223 Inf.		425	223 Inf.
	386	218 Inf.		426	126 Inf.
	. .			427	129 Inf.
	388			428	129 Inf.
	389	217 Inf.		429	168 Inf.
	390	215 Inf.		430	129 Inf.
	391	170 Inf.		431	131 Inf.
	392	169 Inf.		432	131 Inf.
	. .		Pz.	433 mot.?	164 Pz.Gr.
Pz.	394 mot.	3 Pz.		434	131 Inf.
	. .			435	215 Inf.
	396	216 Inf.		436	132 Inf.
	397	218 Inf.		437	132 Inf.
	398	216 Inf.		438	132 Inf.

* Disbanded late in 1940. † Reinforced regiment.
‡ Probably disbanded late in 1941. ‖ Croatian.
§ Possibly withdrawn permanently to G.H.Q. troops.

G.R.	In Div.	G.R.	In Div.
439	134 Inf.	480	260 Inf.
440		481	256 Inf.
441		482	262 Inf.
442	168 Inf.	483	263 Inf.
443		484	254 Inf.
(444§	)	485	263 Inf.
445	134 Inf.	486	262 Inf.
446	134 Inf.	487	267 Inf.
447	137 Inf.	488	268 Inf.
448	137 Inf.	489	269 Inf.
449	137 Inf.	490	269 Inf.
450†		..	
451	251 Inf.	492*	
452	252 Inf.	Pz. 492 mot. ?	21 Pz. ?
453	253 Inf.	493*	
454	254 Inf.	494*	
455	255 Inf.	..	
456	256 Inf.	496*	
457	257 Inf.	497‡	267 Inf.
458	258 Inf.	..	
459	251 Inf.	499	268 Inf.
460	260 Inf.	500*	
461	252 Inf.	501	290 Inf.
462	262 Inf.	502	290 Inf.
463	263 Inf.	503	290 Inf.
464	253 Inf.	504	291 Inf.
465	255 Inf.	505	291 Inf.
466	257 Inf.	506	291 Inf.
467	267 Inf.	507	292 Inf.
468	268 Inf.	508	292 Inf.
469	269 Inf.	509	292 Inf.
470	260 Inf.	510	293 Inf.
471	251 Inf.	511	293 Inf.
472	252 Inf.	512	293 Inf.
473	253 Inf.	513	294 Inf.
474	254 Inf.	514	294 Inf.
475	255 Inf.	515	294 Inf.
476	256 Inf.	516	295 Inf.
477	257 Inf.	517	295 Inf.
478	258 Inf.	518	295 Inf.
479	258 Inf.	519	296 Inf.

* Depôt battalion only.
‡ Possibly disbanded.
† Battalion only.
§ Probably disbanded late in 1941.

G.R.	In Div.	G.R.	In Div.
520	296 Inf.	..	
521	296 Inf.	..	
522	297 Inf.	..	
523	297 Inf.	..	
524	297 Inf.	..	
525	298 Inf.	..	
526	298 Inf.	..	
527	298 Inf.	..	
528	299 Inf.	570	302 Inf.
529	299 Inf.	571	302 Inf.
530	299 Inf.	572	302 Inf.
531	383 Inf.	573	304 Inf.
532	383 Inf.	574	304 Inf.
533	383 Inf.	575	304 Inf.
534	384 Inf.	576	305 Inf.
535	384 Inf.	577	305 Inf.
536	384 Inf.	578	305 Inf.
537	385 Inf.	579	306 Inf.
538	385 Inf.	580	306 Inf.
539	385 Inf.	581	306 Inf.
540*		582	319 Inf.
541	387 Inf.	583	319 Inf.
542	387 Inf.	584	319 Inf.
543	387 Inf.	585	320 Inf.
544	389 Inf.	586	320 Inf.
545	389 Inf.	587	320 Inf.
546	389 Inf.	588	321 Inf.
547	328 Inf.	589	321 Inf.
548	328 Inf.	590	321 Inf.
549	328 Inf.	591	323 Inf.
550*		592	323 Inf.
551 ?	329 Inf. ?	593	323 Inf.
552 ?	329 Inf. ?	594	
553	329 Inf.	595	327 Inf.
554	330 Inf.	596	327 Inf.
555	330 Inf.	597	327 Inf.
556	330 Inf.	598 ?	
557	331 Inf.	599 ?	
558	331 Inf.	..	
559	331 Inf.	601†	
..		602†	
..		603†	

* Battalion only. † Infantry training or field-training regiment.

L 33

G.R.	In Div.	G.R.	In Div.
..		644ø	
..		645ø	
606†		646ø	
607†		647ø	
608†		648ø	
609†		649ø	
610†		650ø	
611†		651ø	
612†		652ø	
613†		653ø	
614†		..	
..		655ø	
616†	381§	656ø	
617†	382§	657ø*	
618†	382§	658ø	
619†	382§	..	
..		660ø	
621ø		661ø	
622ø		662ø	
623ø		663ø	
624*		664ø	
625*		665ø	
626*		666	370 Inf.
..		667	370 Inf.
628*		668	370 Inf.
629*		669	371 Inf.
630*		670	371 Inf.
..		671	371 Inf.
632*		672	376 Inf.
633*		673	376 Inf.
634*		674‡	
..		675‡	
..		676	332 Inf.
..		677	332 Inf.
638		678	332 Inf.
639*		679	333 Inf.
640*		680	333 Inf.
641ø		681	333 Inf.
642ø		682	335 Inf.
643*		683	335 Inf.

* Probably disbanded late in 1940. ø Fortress bn. only.
† Infantry training or field-training regiment. § Field training division.
‡ Disbanded late in 1940.

G.R.	In Div.	G.R.	In Div.
684	335 Inf.	725	715 Inf.
685	336 Inf.	726	716 Inf.
686	336 Inf.	727	707 Inf.
687	336 Inf.	728	708 Inf.
688	337 Inf.	729	709 Inf.
689	246 Inf.	730	710 Inf.
690	337 Inf.	731	711 Inf.
691	339 Inf.	732	712 Inf.
692	339 Inf.	733	713 Inf.
693	339 Inf.	Jäg. 734	104 Jäg.
694	340 Inf.	735	715 Inf.
695	340 Inf.	736	716 Inf.
696	340 Inf.	Jäg. 737	117 Jäg.
697	342 Inf.	Jäg. 738	118 Jäg.
698	342 Inf.	739	709 Inf.
699	342 Inf.	740	710 Inf.
..		Jäg. 741	114 Jäg.
..		742	702 Inf.
..		743	719 Inf.
..		744	711 Inf.
..		745	712 Inf.
..		746	713 Inf.
..		747	707 Inf.
..		748	708 Inf.
..		Jäg. 749	117 Jäg.
..		Jäg. 750	118 Jäg.
..		751	326 Inf.
..		752	326 Inf.
..		753	326 Inf.
..		754	334 Inf.
..		755	334 Inf.
..		756	334 Inf.
..		757	338 Inf.
		758	338 Inf.
718*	391†	759	338 Inf.
719*	391†	..	
720*	391†	..	
Jäg. 721	114 Jäg.	..	
722	702 Inf.	..	
723	719 Inf.	..	
Jäg. 724	104 Jäg.	..	

*Field-training regiment.
†Field-training division.

L 35

G.R.	In Div.
..	
767	376 Inf.
768	377 Inf.
769	377 Inf.
770	377 Inf.
..	
..	
..	
..	
..	
..	
..	
..	
..	
..	
..	
..	
..	
..	
..	
..	
..	
..	
..	
..	
..	
..	
..	
..	
..	
..	
..	
..	
..	
..	
..	
..	
848	282 Inf.
849	282 Inf.
850	282 Inf.
851	343 Inf.
852	343 Inf.
853	343 Inf.
854	344 Inf.
855	344 Inf.
856	344 Inf.
..	
858	346 Inf.
..	
..	
861	347 Inf.
..	
863	348 Inf.
864	348 Inf.
865 ?	348 Inf. ?
866	355 Inf.
867	355 Inf.
868	355 Inf.
869	356 Inf.
870	356 Inf.
871	356 Inf.
..	
..	
..	
..	
..	
..	
878 ?	
879	
880	
..	
..	
..	
..	
..	
..	
887	
888	
..	
Verst.890 (mot.)	
891	264 Inf.
892	264 Inf.
893	264 Inf.
894	265 Inf.

G.R.	In Div.	G.R.	In Div.
895	265 Inf.	..	
896	265 Inf.	..	
..		..	
..		..	
..		..	
900		..	
Pz. 901		..	
F.B. 902		..	
F.B. 903		..	
F.B. 904		..	
F.B. 905		..	
F.B. 906		..	
F.B. 907		..	
F.B. 908		..	
F.B. 909		950	
F.B. 910		..	
..		..	
..		..	
..		..	
..		..	
..		..	
916		..	
917	242 Inf.	..	
..		..	
..		..	
..		(961*	999 Inf.)
..		(962*	999 Inf.)
..		(F.R.St. 963*	999 Inf.)
F.B. 923		..	
F.R.St.924		F.R.St. 965	
F.R.St.925		F.R.St. 966	
F.B. 926		F.R.St. 967	
..		..	
..		..	
..		..	
930	416 Inf.	..	
931	416 Inf.	..	
..		..	
..		..	
..		..	
..		..	

* Afrika-Schützen-Regiment probably disbanded, some units might still exist.

G.R.	In Div.	G.R.	In Div.
..		..	
..		..	
..		..	
..		..	
..		..	
992		999	
993		..	

Also : (1) Infanterie-Lehr-Regiment.
(2) Grenadier-Rgt.-Grossdeutschland *and*
(3) Fuselier-Regt.-Grossdeutschland *in Grossdeutschland Pz. Gren. Div.*
(4) Grenadier-Regt.-Hermann Göring 1
(5) Grenadier-Regt.-Hermann Göring 2 *and*
(6) Jäger-Regt.-Hermann Göring *in Hermann Göring Pz. Div.*

(*h*) ARTILLERY REGIMENTS, BATTERIES AND TROOPS

(*Artillerie-Regimenter* = A.R., *Artillerie-Abteilungen* and *-Batterien* = Art.Abt., Battr.)

(In addition to the units listed below, there are also G.A.F. Artillery Regiments 1–22 of the G.A.F. Field Divisions, *see* Part D, Sec. (*w*).)

Identification: Red piping.

Note.—German Abt. and. Battr. is used for British Bty. and Tp. and U.S. Bn. and Bty.

A.R.	Allotted to	A.R.	Allotted to
1	1 Inf. Div.	29 mot.	29 Pz. Gr. Div.
Pz. 2 mot.	12 Pz. Div.	30	30 Inf. Div.
3 mot.	3 Pz.Gr. Div.	31	31 Inf. Div.
Pz. 4 mot.	14 Pz. Div.	32	32 Inf. Div.
5 mot.	5 Lt. Div.	Pz. 33 mot.	15 Pz. Div.
6	6 Inf. Div.	34	34 Inf. Div.
7	7 Inf. Div.	35	35 Inf. Div.
8	8 Lt. Div.	36 mot.	36 Pz.Gr. Div.
9	9 Inf. Div.	37*	G.H.Q. tps.
10 mot.	10 Pz.Gr. Div.	38*	G.H.Q. tps.
11	11 Inf. Div.	39*	G.H.Q. tps.†
12	12 Inf. Div.	40*	G.H.Q. tps.†
Pz. 13 mot.	13 Pz. Div.	41*	G.H.Q. tps.
14 mot.	14 Pz.Gr. Div.	42*	G.H.Q. tps.†
15	15 Inf. Div.	43*	G.H.Q. tps.†
Pz. 16 mot.	16 Pz. Div.	44*	G.H.Q. tps.†
17	17 Inf. Div.	45*	G.H.Q. tps.
18 mot.	18 Pz.Gr. Div.	46*	G.H.Q. tps.†
Pz. 19 mot.	19 Pz. Div.	47*	G.H.Q. tps.
20 mot.	20 Pz.Gr. Div.	48*	G.H.Q. tps.
21	21 Inf. Div.	49*	G.H.Q. tps.
22	22 LL Div(mot.)	50*	G.H.Q. tps.
Pz. 23	23 Inf. Div.	51*	G.H.Q. tps.
24	24 Inf. Div.	52*	G.H.Q. tps.
25 mot.	25 Pz.Gr. Div.	53*	G.H.Q. tps.
26	26 Inf. Div.	54*	G.H.Q. tps.
Pz. 27 mot.	17 Pz. Div.	55*	G.H.Q. tps.
28	28 Lt. Div.	56*	G.H.Q. tps.

* H.Q. and II Abt. are mechanised G.H.Q. troops; I Abt. is usually horsed and attached to a divisional artillery regiment in place of a IV Abt.

† Destroyed, possibly re-formed.

A.R.	Allotted to	A.R.	Allotted to
57*	G.H.Q. tps.	Geb. 95	5 Mtn. Biv.
58*	G.H.Q. tps.	96	44 Inf. Div.
59*	G.H.Q. tps.†	97*	G.H.Q. tps.†
60*	G.H.Q. tps.	98	45 Inf. Div.
61*	G.H.Q. tps.†	99*	G.H.Q. tps.
62*	G.H.Q. tps.	100ø	Training Comd.
63*	G.H.Q. tps.	101 mot.	(Bty. only)
64*	G.H.Q. tps.	Pz. 102 mot.	9 Pz. Div.
65*	G.H.Q. tps.†	Pz. 103 mot.	4 Pz. Div.
66*	G.H.Q. tps.	104	102 Inf. Div.
67*	G.H.Q. tps.	105 mot.	(Abt. only)
68*	G.H.Q. tps.	106 mot.	(Abt. only)
69*	G.H.Q. tps.	107	106 Inf. Div.
70*	G.H.Q. tps.	108 mot.	G.H.Q. tps.
71*	G.H.Q. tps.	109 mot.	G.H.Q. tps.
72*	G.H.Q. tps.†	110 mot.	G.H.Q. tps.
Pz. 73 mot.	1 Pz. Div.	Geb. 111	2 Mtn. Div.
Pz. 74 mot.	2 Pz. Div.	Geb. 112	3 Mtn. Div.
Pz. 75 mot.	3 Pz. Div.†	Geb. 113	G.H.Q. tps.
Pz. 76 mot.	6 Pz. Div.	114	46 Inf. Div.
77 mot.	G.H.Q. tps. (*a*)	115*	G.H.Q. tps.†
Pz. 78 mot.	7 Pz. Div.	Pz. 116 mot.	5 Pz. Div.
Geb. 79	1 Mtn. Div.	117	111 Inf. Div.?
Pz. 80 mot.	8 Pz. Div.	Geb. 118	6 Mtn. Div.
81	97 Lt. Div.	Pz. 119 mot.	11 Pz. Div.
Geb. 82	7 Mtn. Div.	120	110 Inf. Div.
83	100 Lt. Div.	121	121 Inf. Div.§
84 mot.	G.H.Q. tps. (*b*)	122	122 Inf. Div.
85	101 Lt. Div.	123	123 Inf. Div.
86	112 Inf. Div.	Geb. 124	G.H.Q. tps.
87	113 Inf. Div.	125	125 Inf. Div.
Pz. 88 mot.	18 Pz. Div.	126	126 Inf. Div.§
Pz. 89 mot.	24 Pz. Div.	127 mot.	G.H.Q. tps.?‖
Pz. 90 mot.	10 Pz. Div.	Pz. 128 mot.	23 Pz. Div.
Pz. 91 mot.‡	25 Pz. Div.	129	129 Inf. Div.
Pz. 92 mot.	20 Pz. Div.	..	
Pz. 93 mot.	26 Pz. Div.	131	131 Inf. Div.
Geb. 94	4 Mtn. Div.	132	132 Inf. Div.

* H.Q. and II Abt. are mechanised G.H.Q. troops ; I Abt. is usually horsed and attached to a divisional artillery regiment in place of a IV Abt.

(*a*) 15-cm. hows. (*b*) 24-cm. hows. ø Rly. gun depôt bty.

‡ Possibly Abt. only. † Destroyed, possibly re-formed.

§ Also C.D. Tp. of this number. ‖ Probably disbanded.

A.R.	Allotted to	A.R.	Allotted to
133 mot.	G.H.Q. tps. ? †	171	71 Inf. Div.
134	134 Inf. Div.	172	72 Inf. Div.
135	G.H.Q. tps. ?	173	73 Inf. Div.
136	G.H.Q. tps.	..	
137	137 Inf. Div.	175	75 Inf. Div.
138 mot.	38 Inf. Div.	176	76 Inf. Div.
139	39 Inf. Div.	177 mot.	(Assault gun Abt.)
(Pz. 140 mot.	22 Pz. Div.*)	178	78 Inf. Div.
..		179	79 Inf. Div.
142	(Battr.)	..	
143	(C.D. Abt.)	181	81 Inf. Div.
144	(C.D. Abt.)	182	82 Inf. Div.
145	(C.D. Abt.)	183	83 Inf. Div.
146 mot.	16 Pz.Gr. Div.	184 mot.	(Assault gun Abt.)
147	(C.D. Abt.)	185 mot.	(Assault gun Abt.)
148	(C.D. Abt.)	186	86 Inf. Div.
149	(C.D. Abt.)	187	87 Inf. Div.
150	50 Inf. Div.	188	88 Inf. Div.
151	(Abt. only)	189 mot.	(Assault gun Abt.)
152	52 Inf. Div.	190 mot.	90 Pz.Gr. Div. ‡
153	(Abt. only)	191 mot.	(Assault gun Abt.)
154 mot.	(Abt. only) (*a*)	192 mot.	(Assault gun Abt.)
Pz. 155 mot.	21 Pz. Div.	193	93 Inf. Div.
156	56 Inf. Div.	194	94 Inf. Div.
157	57 Inf. Div.	195	95 Inf. Div.
158	58 Inf. Div.	196	96 Inf. Div.
..		197 mot.	(Assault gun Abt.)
160 mot.	60 Pz.Gr. Div.	198	98 Inf. Div.
161	61 Inf. Div.	199	199 Inf. Div.
162	62 Inf. Div.	200 mot.	(Assault gun Abt.)
..		201 mot.	(Assault gun Abt.)
..		202 mot.	(Assault gun Abt.)
165	65 Inf. Div.	203 mot.	(Assault gun Abt.)
..		204 mot.	(Assault gun Abt.)
167	(Ers. Abt.)	205	205 Inf. Div.
168	68 Inf. Div.	206	206 Inf. Div.
169	69 Inf. Div.	207	C.D. regt. staff
..		208	208 Inf. Div.

(*a*) 15-cm. hows.

* Division believed disbanded; the unit (possibly renumbered) may still exist.

† Probably disbanded.

‡ Also an assault gun Abt. of this number.

A.R.	Allotted to	A.R.	Allotted to
209 mot.	(Assault gun Abt.)	246	246 Inf. Div.
210	210 Inf. Div.*	..	
211	211 Inf. Div.	248	168 Inf. Div.
212	212 Inf. Div.	249 mot.	(Assault gun Abt.)
213†	-	250‖	
214	214 Inf. Div.	251	251 Inf. Div.
215	215 Inf. Div.	252	252 Inf. Div.
216	216 Inf. Div.	253	253 Inf. Div.
217	217 Inf. Div.	254	254 Inf. Div.
218	218 Inf. Div.	255	255 Inf. Div.
219	183 Inf. Div.	256	256 Inf. Div.
220	164 Pz. Gr. Div.	257	257 Inf. Div.
221†		258	258 Inf. Div.
222	181 Inf. Div.	..	
223	223 Inf. Div.	260	260 Inf. Div.
..		..	
225	225 Inf. Div.	262	262 Inf. Div.
226 mot.	(Assault gun Abt.)	263	263 Inf. Div.
227	227 Inf. Div.	264	264 Inf. Div.
228‡	(228 Inf. Div.)§	..	
229	197 Inf. Div.	..	
230	169 Inf. Div.	267	267 Inf. Div.
231†	(231 Inf. Div.)	268	268 Inf. Div.
..		269	269 Inf. Div.
233	196 Inf. Div.	270	(Assault gun Abt.)
234	163 Inf. Div.	271	
235	198 Inf. Div.	272	
236	162 Inf. Div.*	273	(Abt. only)
..		274	(C.D. Battr.)
238	167 Inf. Div.	..	
239‡	(239 Inf. Div.)	..	
240	170 Inf. Div.	277	
241	161 Inf. Div.	..	
242	242 Inf. Div.*	279	(Assault gun Abt.)
243	(Assault gun Abt.)	..	
244 mot.	(Assault gun Abt.)	281	
245	(Assault gun Abt.)	282	282 Inf. Div.

* Also an assault gun Abt. of this number.

† H.Q. is G.H.Q. tps., the Abteilungen are attached to reinforced inf. regts.

‡ Disbanded or transferred to G.H.Q. tps. late in 1940.

§ Probably disbanded.

‖ Spanish, probably disbanded, autumn 1943.

L 42

A.R.	Allotted to	A.R.	Allotted to
283	(C.D. Abt.)	..	
284	(C.D. Abt.)	323	323 Inf. Div.
285	(C.D. Abt.)	..	
286		325	(C.D. Rgt.) ?
287	(C.D. Abt.)	326	326 Inf. Div.
288	(C.D. Abt.)	327	327 Inf. Div.
289	(C.D. Abt.)	328	328 Inf. Div.
290	290 Inf. Div.	329	329 Inf. Div.
291	291 Inf. Div.	330	330 Inf. Div.
292	292 Inf. Div.	331	331 Inf. Div.
293	293 Inf. Div.	332	332 Inf. Div.
294	294 Inf. Div.	333	333 Inf. Div.
295	295 Inf. Div.	334	334 Inf. Div.
296	296 Inf. Div.	335	335 Inf. Div.
297	297 Inf. Div.	336	336 Inf. Div.
(298†)	298 Inf. Div.†	337	337 Inf. Div.
299	299 Inf. Div.	338	338 Inf. Div.
300 mot.	(Assault gun Abt.)	339 ‡	339 Inf. Div.
..		340	340 Inf. Div.
302	302 Inf. Div.	..	
..		342	342 Inf. Div.
304	304 Inf. Div.	..	
305	305 Inf. Div.	344	344 Inf. Div.
306	306 Inf. Div.	§345 mot.	(345 Inf. Div.)
..		..	
..		..	
309	(Ers. Abt.)*	..	
..		..	
311		..	
..		351	Abt.§
313	(Ers. Abt.)*	..	
..		353	(C.D. Battr.)
315	(Abt. only.)*	354	(C.D. Battr.)
..		355	(C.D. Battr.)
..		356	356 Inf. Div.*
318	C.D. Battr.	..	
319	319 Inf. Div.	..	
320	320 Inf. Div.*	..	
321	321 Inf. Div.	..	

* Also a C.D. Battr. or Abt. of this number.
† Division believed disbanded ; unit may still exist.
‡ Abt. only. § Believed disbanded.

A.R.	Allotted to	A.R.	Allotted to
361	(C.D. Battr.)	401	C.D. Abt.
362	(C.D. Battr.)	..	
363	(C.D. Battr.)	..	
364	(C.D. Battr.)	..	
365	G.H.Q. Tps. §	405	Rgt. §
..		..	
..		..	
..		408	Abt.
369†	369 Inf. Div. †	409	C.D. Abt. ?
370	370 Inf. Div.	..	
371	371 Inf. Div.	..	
..		412	§
373†	373 Inf. Div. †	413	Rgt. §
..		..	
375	(C.D. Battr.)	..	
376	376 Inf. Div.*	..	
377	377 Inf. Div.	..	
..		..	
..		..	
..		..	
..		..	
..		422	Abt.
383	383 Inf. Div.	423	Battr.
384	384 Inf. Div.	424	Battr.
(385‡)	385 Inf. Div. ‡	425	Battr.
..		426	Abt.
387	387 Inf. Div.	427 mot.	Abt. (*a*)
..		428	G.H.Q. Tps. §
389	389 Inf. Div.	..	
..		..	
..		431	C.D. Battr. (*a*)
392	(Abt.)§	432	C.D. Battr. (*a*)
..		433 mot.	Abt. §
..		434	C.D. Battr. (*a*)
..		..	
..		436 mot.	Abt. (*a*)
..		437	C.D. regt. staff
398	(Abt.)§	438	C.D. Abt. staff
..		439	C.D. Abt. staff
400 mot.	Assault gun Abt.	..	

* Also a C.D. battr. of this number. † Croatian.
‡ Division believed disbanded ; unit may still exist.
§ Existence doubtful. (*a*) 10·5-cm. guns.

Art.	Remarks.
441	C.D. Abt.
442	C.D. Abt.
443	Abt.†
..	
445	Abt.
446 mot.	Abt.*
447	C.D. Abt.
..	
..	
450	Abt.(*a*)
451	Abt.
452	C.D. Abt. staff.
..	
..	
..	
456	Rgt. †
457	C.D. Abt.
458	Battr.
459	Battr.
..	
..	
462	C.D. Battr.
463	C.D. Battr.
464	C.D. Battr.
465	C.D. Battr.
466	C.D. Battr.
..	
468	C.D. Battr.
..	
470	C.D. Battr.
471	C.D. Battr.
472	C.D. Battr.
..	
474	C.D. Abt.
475	C.D. Abt.
..	
477‡	Regt.
478	C.D. Abt.

Art.	Remarks.
479	C.D. Abt.
480	Abt.†
..	
482	C.D. Abt. †
..	
484	C.D. Abt.
485	C.D. Abt. staff‖
486	C.D. Abt. staff‖
487	C.D. Abt. staff
488	C.D. Abt. staff
..	
490	C.D. Abt. staff
491	C.D. Abt. staff
492	C.D. Abt. staff
493	C.D. Abt. staff
494	C.D. Abt. staff
495	C.D. Abt. staff
496	Abt.
497	C.D. Abt. staff
498	C.D. Abt.
499	C.D. Abt. staff
500	C.D. Abt.
501 mot.	Regt. staff
502	C.D. Battr.
503	C.D. Battr.
504	C.D. Abt.
505	Abt.‖
506	Abt.
507	C.D. Battr.
508	C.D. Battr.
509	C.D. regt. staff
510	C.D. Abt.
511	Abt.§
512	C.D. Battr.(*a*)
513	C.D. Battr.
514	C.D. Battr.
515	C.D. Battr.
516	C.D. Battr.

* Reorganised under a new number.

† Existence doubtful.

(*a*) 15-cm. hows.

‡ Believed to have been disbanded.

§ Also a regt. staff (mot.) of this number.

‖ Also C.D. Abt. staff of this number.

Art.	Remarks.	Art.	Remarks.
. .		. .	
. .		. .	
519	C.D. Battr. (*b*)	560	Regt.
520	C.D. Abt.	561	C.D. Battr.
521	C.D. Abt.	562	C.D. Battr.
522	C.D. Battr.	563	C.D. Abt.
523	C.D. Abt.	. .	
. .		. .	
525	C.D. Battr. †	. .	
526	Abt.	. .	
527	C.D. Abt.†	. .	
528	C.D. Abt.	569	C.D. Battr. (*c*)
529	C.D. Abt.	570	C.D. Battr. (*c*)
. .		571	C.D. Battr. (*c*)
531	C.D. Abt.	572	C.D. Battr. (*c*)
532	C.D. Abt. ?	573	C.D. Battr. (*c*)
533	C.D. Abt. (*a*)	574	C.D. Battr. (*c*)
534	C.D. Battr.	575	C.D. Battr. (*c*)
535	C.D. Abt.	576	C.D. Battr. (*c*)
536 mot.	Abt. (*b*)	577	C.D. Battr. (*c*)
537	C.D. Battr.	578	C.D. Battr. (*c*)
538	C.D. Battr.	579	C.D. Battr. (*c*)
. .		580	Abt.
540	C.D. Abt.	. .	
541	C.D. Battr.	. .	
. .		. .	
543	C.D. Battr.	584	Abt.
. .		585	C.D. Battr. (*b*)
. .		. .	
546	C.D. Battr. ?	. .	
547	C.D. Battr.	588	C.D. Battr. (*b*)
. .		589	C.D. Battr. (*b*)
549	C.D. Battr.	590	C.D. Battr.
550	C.D. Battr.	591	C.D. Battr. (*b*)
551	Regt.	592	C.D. Battr. (*c*)
. .		593	C.D. Battr. (*c*)
553	C.D. Rgt.	. .	
. .		. .	
555*	Regt.	596	C.D. Battr.
556*	Regt.	. .	
557	Abt.	. .	

* Now disbanded. (*a*) 15·5-cm. guns. (*b*) 15-cm. hows.
(*c*) 10·5-cm. guns. † Also a regt. staff (mot.) of this number.

Art.	Remarks.	Art.	Remarks.
..		637 mot.	Abt. (*d*)
600 mot.	Assault gun Abt.	638 mot.	Abt.
601 mot.	Abt.ø [staff	..	
602 mot.	Abt. (*c*)	..	
603 mot.	Regt. staff†	641 mot.	Abt. (*a*)
604 mot.	Abt.ø	642 mot.	Abt. (*a*)
605 mot.	Abt.‡	643 mot.	Abt.
606 mot.	Regt. staff	644 mot.	Abt.
607 mot.	Abt.	645 mot.	Abt.
..		646 mot.	Abt.
609 mot.	Regt. staff	647 mot.	Abt.*
610 mot.	Regt. staff	648 mot.	Abt.*
611 mot.	Abt. (*b*)	649 mot.	Abt.*
612 mot.	Regt. staff	650	Abt.
613 mot.	Regt. staff	651	Abt. (711 Div.?)
614 mot.	Regt. staff	652	Abt. (712 Div.)
615 mot.	Abt.	653	Abt. (713 Div.?)
616 mot.	Abt. (*d*)	654	Abt.
617 mot.	Regt. staff		(104 Jäg. Div.)
618 mot.	Regt. staff	655	Rly. Battr. (*e*)
619 mot.	Regt. staff	656	(716 Div.)
620 mot.	Abt. (*c*)	657	(707 Div.)
621 mot.	Abt. •	658	Abt.
622 mot.	Regt. staff	..	
623 mot.	Regt. staff	..	
624 mot.	Abt.	661	(114 Jäg. Div.)
625 mot.	Abt.	662	(702 Div.)
626 mot.	Abt.*	663	(719 Div.)
627 mot.	Regt. staff	..	
628 mot.	Battr.	665 mot.	Assault gun
629 mot.	Abt.		Battr.
630 mot.	Abt.*	666	Abt.
631 mot.	Abt. (*b*)	667 mot.	Assault gun
..			Battr.
633 mot.	Abt.	668	118 Jäg. Div.
634 mot.	Abt. (*b*)	669	
635 mot.	Abt. (*d*)	670	117 Jäg. Div.
636 mot.	Abt. (*d*)	671	Abt.

* Disbanded late in 1940.
† Believed disbanded. ø Also a regt. staff of this number.
‡ Reorganised under new number.
(*a*) 21-cm. and 30-cm. hows. (*b*) 10·5-cm. guns. (*c*) 15-cm. hows. (*d*) 21-cm. hows. (*e*) 28-cm. hows.

Art.	Remarks.	Art.	Remarks.
672	Battr.	711	Abt.
..		712	Rly. Battr.
674 mot.	Battr.	713	Battr.
..		714	Abt.
676 mot.	Abt. staff*	..	
677 mot.	Regt. staff	716 mot.	Abt.†
..		717	Rly. Battr.
679 mot.	Abt. staff	718	Rly. Battr.
680 mot.	Abt.	..	
681 mot.	Abt. staff	720 mot.	Regt. staff
..		721	
..		722	Battr.
..		..	
685	Battr.	724	
686	Abt.	725	Rly. Battr.
687	Battr.	726	Battr.
688	Battr.	727	C.D. Abt.
689	Battr.	728	C.D. Abt. staff
690	Rly. Battr. (*c*)	729	Abt.
691	Rly. Battr.	730 mot.	Abt. (*d*)
..		731 mot.	Abt. (*a*)
..		732 mot.	Abt.
694	Abt.	733 mot.	Abt. (*b*)
695	Rly. Battr.	..	
696	Rly. Battr.	735 mot.	Abt.
697	C.D. regt. staff	736 mot.	Abt. (*b*)
..		737 mot.	Abt. (*a*)
699	C.D. Abt.	738	C.D. Abt.
..		..	
701	Battr.	740	Abt.
702	Abt. staff	741	C.D. Abt.‡
..		742	C.D. Battr.‡
704	Regt. staff	..	
705	Abt.	..	
706	Abt.	745	Abt.
707 mot.	Abt.	746	C.D. Abt.
708	Abt.	..	
709 mot.	Abt.	..	
710	Rly. Battr.	749	Abt.§

* Also an Ers. Abt. of this number.
(*a*) 15-cm. hows. (*b*) 21-cm. hows. (*c*) 28-cm. rly guns.
(*d*) 10·5-cm. guns. † Probably disbanded.
‡ Assault gun battr. of this number. § Disbanded.

Art.	Remarks.	Art.	Remarks.
750	C.D. Battr.	..	
751	C.D. Battr.	..	
752	C.D. regt. staff	..	
753	Abt.	..	
754	C.D. Regt.*	..	
755	C.D. Regt.*	..	
756	Abt.	..	
757 mot.	Abt.	..	
758	C.D. Regt.*	799	C.D. Abt.
759	Abt.*	800 mot.	Abt.
..		801	Abt.
761	Abt.	802	Regt.
762	Abt.*	803 mot.	Regt. staff
..		804	Abt.
764	Abt.	805	C.D. Abt.
765	Battr.	..	
766	Regt.*	..	
767 mot.	Abt.	808	Abt.
768	Abt.	809	Abt.
769	C.D. Abt. staff	810 mot.	Battr.
770	C.D. Abt.	..	
..		812	
772	C.D. Abt.	813	C.D. Battr.
773	C.D. Abt. (*a*)	814 mot.	Regt. (*b*)
774	C.D. Abt.	815 mot.	Abt. (*c*)
..		816 mot.	Abt.
..		817 mot.	Abt.
777	Abt. (*d*)	818 mot.	Regt.
778	C.D. Abt.	..	
779 mot.	Battr.	820	Abt.
780	Rly. Battr.	..	
781 mot.	Regt. staff	822	Abt.
782 mot.	Regt. staff	823	C.D. Abt. (*e*)
783 mot.	Regt. staff	824	C.D. Abt.§
784 mot.	Battr.	825	C.D. regt. staff
785 mot.	Regt. staff	826	C.D. Abt. (*e*)
786 mot.	Abt.	827	C.D. Abt. (*e*) (269 I.D.)
787 mot.	Regt. staff		
788 mot.	Regt. staff	828	C.D. Abt.
789	C.D. Abt. (*a*)	829	C.D. Abt.
..		..	

(*a*) 10·5-cm. guns. (*b*) 24-cm. hows. (*c*) 30-cm. hows.
(*d*) 21-cm. hows. (*e*) 15-cm. guns. * Disbanded.
§ Also C.D. regt. staff of this number.

Art.	Remarks.	Art.	Remarks.
831	C.D. Abt.	..	
832	C.D. Abt.	..	
833	Abt.	..	
834	C.D. Abt.	..	
835	C.D. Abt.	..	
..	(174 I.D.)	..	
836	C.D. regt. staff	..	
837	C.D. regt. staff	877	C.D. Battr.
838	C.D. Abt.	..	
839	C.D. regt. staff	..	
840		880	C.D. Battr.
841 mot.	Regt. staff	..	
842 mot.	Abt.	..	
843 mot.	Abt.	..	
844	Abt.	884	C.D. Battr.
845 mot.	Abt.	..	
846	Abt.	..	
847	Abt.	887	C.D. Battr.
848 mot.	Abt.	888	C.D. Battr. (*a*)
849 mot.	Abt.	889	C.D. Battr. (*a*)
850	Abt.	890	C.D. Battr.
851 mot.	Abt.	..	
852	Abt.	..	
853	C.D. regt. staff	893	
854	Abt.	894	C.D. Battr. (*a*)
855	Abt.*	895	C.D. Battr. (*a*)
856	Abt.	896	C.D. Battr.
857	Abt.	897	C.D. Battr.
858 mot.	Abt.	898	C.D. Battr.
859 mot.	Abt.	..	
860 mot.	Abt.	900	Abt.
861	Abt.*	901	C.D. Abt.
862	Abt.	902	Battr. (*b*)
863	Abt.	903	C.D. Abt.
..		904	Assault gun Abt.
865 mot.	Abt.	905	Assault gun Abt.
866	Abt.	906	C.D. Abt.*
..		907	C.D. Battr.
..		..	
869	C.D. Battr.	909	Assault gun Battr.

(*a*) 12-cm. guns. (*b*) 7·5-cm. guns. (*c*) 17·5-cm. guns.

* Disbanded.

† Probably disbanded.

Art.	Remarks.	Art.	Remarks
910	C.D. Abt.	952	C.D. Battr. (*b*)
911	Bty.	953	C.D. Battr.
912	Assault gun Battr.	954	C.D. Battr. (*b*)
..		..	C.D. Battr. (*b*)
914	C.D. Abt.	956	C.D. tp. (*b*)
..		957	C.D. Battr. (*b*)
..		958	C.D. Battr. (*b*)
..		959	C.D. Battr. (*b*)
..		960	C.D. Battr. (*a*)
..		961	C.D. Battr. (*a*)
..		962	C.D. Battr. (*a*)
..		963	C.D. Battr. (*a*)
..		964	C.D. Battr.
..		..	
..		966	C.D. Battr.
..		967	C.D. Battr.
..		..	
927	C.D. Battr.	..	
928	C.D. Abt.	970	C.D. Battr. (*a*)
929	C.D. Abt.	971	C.D. Battr. (*a*)
930	C.D. Battr.	972	C.D. Battr.
931	C.D. Battr.	973	C.D. Battr. (*a*)
..		974	C.D. Battr. (*a*)
..		975	C.D. Battr. (*a*)
..		976	C.D. Battr. (*a*)
..		977	C.D. Battr. (*a*)
..		978	C.D. Battr. (*a*)
..		979	C.D. Battr. (*a*)
938	C.D.	980	C.D. Battr. (*a*)
..		981	C.D. Battr. (*a*)
940	C.D. regt. staff	982	C.D. Battr. (*a*)
941	C.D.	983	C.D. Battr. (*a*)
942	C.D. Battr.	984	C.D. Battr. (*a*)
..		..	
..		..	
..		987	C.D. Battr. (*a*)
946	C.D. Battr. (*a*)	988	C.D. Battr.
947	C.D. Battr. (*a*)	989	C.D. Battr.
948	C.D. Battr. (*a*)	990	C.D. Battr.
949	C.D. Battr. (*a*)	991	C.D. Battr.
950	C.D. Battr. (*b*)	992	C.D. Battr.
951	C.D. Battr.	993	C.D. Battr.

(*a*) 10·5-cm. guns. (*b*) 21-cm. guns.

Art.	Remarks.	Art.	Remarks.
..		998	C.D. Battr. (*a*)
995	C.D. Battr.	999	(*b*)
996	C.D. Battr. (*a*)	..	
997	C.D. Battr. (*a*)		

(*a*) 15·5-cm. guns.
(*b*) Formerly in 999 Div. ; Div. now disbanded ; unit may still exist.

Also : (1) Artillerie-Lehr-Regiment 1.
(2) Art.-Lehr-Rgt. (mot) 2.
(3) A.L.R. (mot) 3.
(4) A.R. (mot) Grossdeutschland } (J.D. Grossdeutschland.)
(5) Stu. Gesch. Abt. GD }
(6) A.R. Hermann Göring *in Hermann Göring Pz. Div.*

(j) ENGINEER UNITS

(*Pionier-Regimenter, -Bataillone* = Pi.Rgt., Pi.Btl.)

Note.—The following types of G.H.Q. unit are also included in this list, as they carry numbers in the same series besides wearing the same *Waffenfarbe* (black): bridging columns (*Brückenkolonnen* = Brüko) and assault boat units (*Sturmbootkommandos*). For bridge-building battallions (*Brückenbau-Bataillone* = Br.B.Btl.), fortress engineers (*Festungspioniere*) and railway engineers (*Eisenbahn-Pioniere*) *see* E 20, E 41, E 42.

Identification: Black piping.

	Pi.Btl.	Allotted to		Pi.Btl.	Allotted to
	1	1 Inf. Div.		26	26 Inf. Div.
	2 mot.	32 Inf. Div.	Pz.	27 mot.	17 Pz. Div.
	3 mot.	3 Pz.Gr. Div.		28	28 Jäg. Div.
Pz.	4 mot.	13 Pz. Div.		29 mot.	29 Pz.Gr. Div.
	5 mot.	5 Jäg. Div.		30	30 Inf. Div.
	6	6 Inf. Div.		31	31 Inf. Div.
	7	7 Inf. Div.	Pz.	32 mot.	12 Pz. Div.
	8	8 Jäg. Div.	Pz.	33 mot.	15 Pz.Gr. Div.
	9	9 Inf. Div.		34	34 Inf. Div.
	10 mot.	10 Pz.Gr. Div.		35	35 Inf. Div.
	11	11 Inf. Div.		36 mot.	36 Pz.Gr. Div.
	12	12 Inf. Div.	Pz.	37 mot.	1 Pz. Div.
Pz.	13 mot.	14 Pz. Div.	Pz.	38 mot.	2 Pz. Div.
	14 mot.	14 Pz.Gr. Div.	Pz.	39 mot.	3 Pz. Div.
	15	15 Inf. Div.	Pz.	40 mot.	24 Pz. Div.
Pz.	16 mot.	16 Pz. Div.		41 mot.	G.H.Q. tps.
	17	17 Inf. Div.		42 mot.	G.H.Q. tps.
	18 mot.	18 Pz.Gr. Div.		43 mot.	G.H.Q. tps.*
Pz.	19 mot.	19 Pz. Div.		44 mot.	G.H.Q. tps.
	20 mot.	20 Pz.Gr. Div.		45 mot.	G.H.Q. tps.†
	21	21 Inf. Div.		46 mot.	G.H.Q. tps.
	22 mot.	22 LL. Div. (Mot.)		47 mot.	G.H.Q. tps.
				48 mot.	G.H.Q. tps.
Pz.	23 mot.	23 Inf. Div.	Pz.	49 mot.	10 Pz. Div.
	24	24 Inf. Div.		50 mot.	G.H.Q. tps.
	25	25 Pz.Gr. Div.		51 mot.	G.H.Q. tps.

* Assault engineer (*Sturmpionier*) battalion.
† Present existence doubtful.

Pi.Btl.	Allotted to.	Pi.Btl.	Allotted to
52 mot.	G.H.Q. tps.	Geb. 95	5 Mtn. Div.
53	G.H.Q. tps.	..	
Geb. 54	1 Mtn. Div.	97	97 Jäg. Div.
..		Pz. 98 mot.	18 Pz. Div.
..		Geb. 99	7 Mtn. Div.
Pz. 57 mot.	6 Pz. Div.	100	100 Jäg. Div.
Pz. 58 mot.	7 Pz. Div.	101	101 Jäg. Div.
Pz. 59 mot.	8 Pz. Div.	102	102 Inf. Div.
60 mot.	G.H.Q. tps.	..	
..		104	104 Jäg. Div.
62 mot.	G.H.Q. tps.	..	
..		106	106 Inf. Div.
..		..	
..		..	
..		..	
..		110	110 Inf. Div.
..		111	111 Inf. Div.
..		112	112 Inf. Div.
70 mot.	G.H.Q. tps.	113	113 Inf. Div.
71		114	114 Jäg. Div.
72	72 Inf. Div.	..	
73		..	
74		117	117 Jäg. Div.
75	25 Pz. Div.	118	118 Jäg. Div.
..		..	
..		..	
..		121	121 Inf. Div.
Pz. 79 mot.	4 Pz. Div.	122	122 Inf. Div.
80	44 Inf. Div.	123	123 Inf. Div.
81	45 Inf. Div.	..	
Geb. 82	2 Mtn. Div.	125	125 Inf. Div.
Geb. 83	3 Mtn. Div.	126	126 Inf. Div.
Geb. 84		Pz. 127 mot. *	27 Pz. Div. *
Geb. 85	G.H.Q. tps.	Pz. 128 mot.	23 Pz. Div.
Pz. 86 mot.	9 Pz. Div.	129	129 Inf. Div.
Pz. 87	25 Pz. Div.	..	
88	46 Inf. Div.	131	131 Inf. Div.
Pz. 89 mot.	5 Pz. Div.	132	132 Inf. Div.
..		..	
Geb. 91	6 Mtn. Div.	134	134 Inf. Div.
Pz. 92 mot.	20 Pz. Div.	..	
Pz. 93 mot.	26 Pz. Div.	..	
Geb. 94	4 Mtn. Div.	137	137 Inf. Div.

* Possibly now disbanded.

Pi.Btl.	Allotted to
138	38 Inf. Div.
139	39 Inf. Div.
Pz. 140 mot.	22 Pz. Div.*
..	
..	
..	
144 mot.	
145	
146 mot.?	16 Pz.Gr. Div.?
..	
..	
..	
150	50 Inf. Div.
..	
152	52 Inf. Div.
..	
..	
..	
156	56 Inf. Div.
157	57 Inf. Div.
158	58 Inf. Div.
..	
160 mot.	60 Pz.Gr. Div.
161	61 Inf. Div.
162	62 Inf. Div.
..	
..	
165	65 Inf. Div.
..	
..	
168	68 Inf. Div.
169	69 Inf. Div.
..	
171	71 Inf. Div.
172 ?	
173	73 Inf. Div.
..	
175	75 Inf.Div.
176	76 Inf. Div.
..	
178	78 Inf. Div.
179	79 Inf. Div.

Pi.Btl.	Allotted to
..	
181	81 Inf. Div.
182	82 Inf. Div.
183	83 Inf. Div.
..	
..	
186	86 Inf. Div.
187	87 Inf. Div.
188	88 Inf. Div.
..	
190	90 Pz.Gr. Div.
..	
..	
193	93 Inf. Div.
194	94 Inf. Div.
195	95 Inf. Div.
196	96 Inf. Div.
..	
198	98 Inf. Div.
199	199 Inf. Div.
Pz. 200 mot.	21 Pz. Div.
..	
..	
..	
204	
205	205 Inf. Div.
206	206 Inf. Div.
207	
208	208 Inf. Div.
Pz. 209 mot.	11 Pz. Div.
..	
211	211 Inf. Div.
212	212 Inf. Div.
213	
214	214 Inf. Div.
215	215 Inf. Div.
216	216 Inf. Div.
217	217 Inf. Div.
218	218 Inf. Div.
219	183 Inf. Div.
220	164 Pz.Gr. Div.
221	

* Division possibly disbanded; unit may still exist (possibly renumbered).

Pi.Btl.	Allotted to
222	181 Inf. Div.
223	223 Inf. Div.
..	
225	225 Inf. Div.
..	
227	227 Inf. Div.
228	_228 Inf. Div._*
229	197 Inf. Div.
230	169 Inf. Div.
231	_231 Inf. Div._*
..	
233	196 Inf. Div.
234	163 Inf. Div.
235	198 Inf. Div.
236	162 Inf. Div.
..	
238	167 Inf. Div.
239	_239 Inf. Div._*
240	170 Inf. Div.
241	161 Inf. Div.
..	
..	
..	
..	
246	246 Inf. Div.
..	
248	168 Inf. Div.
..	
..	
251	251 Inf. Div.
252	252 Inf. Div.
253	253 Inf. Div.
254	254 Inf. Div.
255	255 Inf. Div.
256	256 Inf. Div.
257 mot.	257 Inf. Div.
258	258 Inf. Div.
..	
260	260 Inf. Div.
..	

Pi.Btl.	Allotted to
262	262 Inf. Div.
263	263 Inf. Div.
264	264 Inf. Div.
..	
..	
267	267 Inf. Div.
268	268 Inf. Div.
269	269 Inf. Div.
..	
..	
..	
..	
..	
..	
..	
..	
..	
..	
..	
..	
..	
..	
..	
..	
..	
..	
..	
..	
290	290 Inf. Div.
291	291 Inf. Div.
292	292 Inf. Div.
293	293 Inf. Div.
294	294 Inf. Div.
295	295 Inf. Div.
296	296 Inf. Div.
297	297 Inf. Div.
298	298 Inf. Div.
299	299 Inf. Div.
300†	
..	

* Division possibly disbanded; unit may still exist (possibly renumbered).

† Battalion staff only. Now been disbanded.

Pi.Btl.	Allotted to	Pi.Btl.	Allotted to
302	302 Inf. Div.	343	343 Inf. Div.
..		..	
304	304 Inf. Div.	..	
305	305 Inf. Div.	..	
306	306 Inf. Div.	..	
..		..	
..		..	
..		..	
..		..	
311	(311 Inf. Div.)†	..	
..		..	
..		..	
..		..	
..		..	
..		..	
..		..	
..		..	
319	319 Inf. Div.	..	
320	320 Inf. Div.	..	
321	321 Inf. Div.	..	
..		..	
323	323 Inf. Div.	..	
..		..	
..		..	
326	326 Inf. Div.	..	
327	327 Inf. Div.	..	
328	328 Inf. Div.	..	
329	329 Inf. Div.	370	370 Inf. Div.
330	330 Inf. Div.	371	371 Inf. Div.
331	331 Inf. Div.	..	
332	332 Inf Div.	373	373 Inf. Div.
333	333 Inf Div.	..	
334	334 Inf. Div.*	..	
335	335 Inf. Div.	..	
336	336 Inf. Div.	377	377 Inf. Div.
337	337 Inf. Div.	..	
338	338 Inf. Div.	..	
339	339 Inf. Div.	..	
340	340 Inf. Div.	..	
..		..	
342	342 Inf. Div.	383	383 Inf. Div.

† Division disbanded ; unit may still exist, possibly renumbered.

* Possibly disbanded.

Pi.Btl.	Allotted to
..	
385	385 Inf. Div.
..	
387	387 Inf. Div.
..	
..	
..	
..	
..	
..	
..	
..	
..	
..	
..	
..	
400 mot.	(Br. coln.)

Pi.*	Remarks.
401 mot.	Br. colns.
..	
403 mot.	Br. colns.
404 mot.	Br. colns.
405	
..	
407 mot.	Br. colns.
..	
409 mot.	Br. colns.
410 mot.	
411 mot.	Br. colns
412 mot.	Br. colns.
413 mot.	Br. colns.
..	
415 mot.	Br. colns.
..	
..	
..	
..	
..	
..	
422 mot.	Br. colns.
..	
..	
..	
..	
427 mot.	Br. colns.
..	
..	
430 mot.	Br. colns.
..	
..	
..	
..	
..	
..	
..	
..	
..	
..	
..	
442 mot.	Br. colns.
..	
..	
..	
..	
..	
..	

* For type of unit, where known, see *Remarks* column.

† Br. colns. in the block 401–450 are numbered 1/ or 2/; two colns. may therefore be assumed to exist for each number identified in this block.

Pi	Remarks.	Pi.	Remarks.
..		532	
..		533	Br. coln.
..		534	Br. coln.
..		..	
..		..	
..		..	
..		538	
..		..	
..		..	
..		541 mot.	Regt. staff
..		..	
..		..	
..		..	
501		545	
..		..	
..		..	
504 mot.	Regt. staff	..	
505	Bn. G.H.Q.	..	
..		..	
507 mot.	Regt. staff	..	
508	Bn. G.H.Q.	..	
..		..	
510		..	
511 mot.	Regt. staff	..	
512 mot.	Regt. staff	..	
..		..	
..		..	
515 mot.	Regt. staff	..	
..		..	
517 mot.	Regt. staff	..	
..		..	
..		..	
520 mot.	Regt. staff	..	
521	Park bn.	..	
..		..	
..		..	
..		..	
525		..	
..		..	
..		..	
..		..	
..		..	
..		..	
531		..	

Pi.	Remarks.
..	
..	
..	
..	
..	
..	
..	
..	
..	
..	
..	
..	
..	
..	
..	
591 mot.	Regt. staff
592	
593	Bn.
..	
..	
..	
..	
..	
..	
..	
601 mot.	Regt. staff
602 mot.	Br. coln.
603 mot.	Br. coln.
604 mot.	Regt. staff
605 mot.	Regt. staff
606 mot.	Br. coln.
..	
..	
..	
610 mot.	Br. coln.
..	
612 mot.	Br. coln.
..	
614 mot.	Regt. staff
..	
616 mot.	Br. coln.
617 mot.	Regt. staff
..	
..	
620 mot.	Regt. staff
..	
622	
..	
624 mot.	Br. coln.
..	
626 mot.	Br. coln.
627 mot.	Bn.
628 mot.	Regt. staff
..	
630 mot.	Bn.
..	
632 mot.	Bn.
633	
634	
635 mot.	Bn.
636 mot.	Br. coln.
..	
..	
639 mot.	Br. coln.
..	
..	
..	
643	
644 mot.	Br. coln.
..	
..	
..	
..	
649 mot.	Br. coln.
..	
651 mot.	Bn.
652 mot.	Bn.*
653 mot.	Bn.
654 mot.	Bn.
655 mot.	Bn.
656 mot.	Bn.
657 mot.	Bn.
658 mot.	Bn.
659 mot.	Bn.

* Present existence doubtful.

Pi.	Remarks.	Pi.	Remarks.
660 mot.	Bn.	..	
661 mot.	Br. coln.	..	
662 mot.	Bn.	(*704*	*see 104*)
663 mot.	Br. coln.	..	
664		..	
..		707	(707 Inf. Div.)
666 mot.	Bn.	708	(708 Inf. Div.)
667 mot.	Regt. staff	709	(709 Inf. Div.)
668 mot.	Br. coln.	710	(710 Inf. Div.)
..		711	(711 Inf. Div.)
..		712	(712 Inf. Div.)
671 mot.	Bn.	713	(713 Inf. Div.)
672 mot.	Bn.	(*714*	*see 114*)
673 mot.	Regt. staff	715	(715 Inf. Div.)
..		716	(716 Inf. Div.)
675 mot.	Bn.	(*717*	*see 117*)
676 mot.	Bn.	(*718*	*see 118*)
677 mot.	Regt. staff	719	(119 Inf. Div.)
678 mot.	Regt. staff	..	
..		..	
680 mot.	Regt. staff	..	
..		..	
..		..	
..		..	
..		..	
685 mot.	Regt. staff.	..	
..		..	
..		..	
688		..	
..		..	
690 mot.	Regt. staff	..	
..		..	
..		..	
..		..	
..		..	
..		..	
..		..	
..		..	
..		..	
..		741 mot.	Bn.
700 mot.	Regt. staff	742 mot.	Bn.
..		743 mot.	Bn.

L 61

Pi.	Remarks.	Pi.	Remarks.
744 mot.	Bn.	..	
745 mot.	Bn.	..	
746 mot.	Bn.	770	Regt. staff
747 mot.	Bn.	771	Bn.
..		..	
..		..	
750 mot.	Bn.	..	
751 mot.	Bn.	..	
752 mot.	Bn.	..	
753 mot.	Bn.	..	
754 mot.	Bn.	778*	Landing Coy.
..		..	
..		..	
..		..	
..		..	
..		..	
..		..	
..		Also :	
..		843 mot.	Br. coln.
..		900 mot.	(90 Lt. Div.)
..		904	Assault boat unit.
..		905	Assault boat unit.
..		906	Assault boat unit.
..			

* Company only.

(*k*) SIGNAL UNITS

(*Nachrichten-Regimenter, -Abteilungen* and *-Kompanien* = N.R., Nachr. Abt., Nachr. Kp.).

Identification : Lemon-yellow piping.

*Nachr. Abt.	Allotted to	Nachr. Abt.	Allotted to
1	1 Inf. Div.	31	31 Inf. Div.
N.R. 1 mot.	1 Pz. Army	32	32 Inf. Div.
Pz. 2 mot.	12 Pz. Div.	..	
N.R. 2 mot.	2 Pz. Army.	34	34 Inf. Div.
3 mot.	3 Pz.Gr. Div.	35	35 Inf. Div.
N.R. 3 mot.	3 Pz. Army.	36 mot.	36 Pz.Gr. Div.
Pz. 4 mot.	14 Pz. Div.	Pz. 37 mot.	1 Pz. Div.
N.R. 4 mot.	4 Pz. Army	Pz. 38 mot.	2 Pz. Div.
5 mot.	5 Jäg. Div.	Pz. 39 mot.	3 Pz. Div.
6	6 Inf. Div.	F.N.R.40 mot.	G.H.Q. tps.
7	7 Inf. Div.	41 mot.	I Corps
8	8 Jäg. Div.	42 mot.	II Corps
9	9 Inf. Div.	Pz. 43 mot.	III Corps
10 mot.	10 Pz.Gr. Div.	44 mot.	IV Corps
N.R. 10 mot.	§	45 mot.	V Corps
11	11 Inf. Div.	46 mot.	VI Corps
12	12 Inf. Div.	47 mot.	VII Corps
Pz. 13 mot.	13 Pz. Div.	48 mot.	VIII Corps
14 mot.	14 Pz.Gr. Div.	49 mot.	IX Corps
15	15 Inf. Div.	50 mot.	X Corps
Pz. 16 mot.	16 Pz. Div.	51 mot.	XI Corps
17	17 Inf. Div.	52 mot.	XII Corps
18 mot.	18 Pz.Gr. Div.	53 mot.	XIII Corps
Pz. 19 mot.	19 Pz. Div.	Geb. 54	1 Mtn. Div.
20 mot.	20 Pz.Gr. Div.	..	
21	21 Inf. Div.	..	
22	22 Inf. Div.	56 mot.	G.H.Q. tps.
Pz. 23 mot.	23 Inf. Div.	57 mot.	G.H.Q. tps.
24	24 Inf. Div.	..	
25 mot.	25 Pz.Gr. Div.	Pz. 59 mot.	8 Pz. Div.
26	26 Inf. Div.	Pz. 60 mot.	XIV Corps
Pz. 27 mot.	17 Pz. Div.	(*61 mot.*	*now Pz.A.N.R.3*)
28	28 Jäg. Div.	(*62 mot.*	*now Pz.A.N.R.4*)
29 mot.	29 Pz.Gr. Div.	63 mot.	
30	30 Inf. Div.	64	44 Inf. Div.

* Except where preceded by N.R.
§ Present existence doubtful.

Nachr. Abt.	Allotted to
65	45 Inf. Div.
66 mot.	XVII Corps
Geb. 67	2 Mtn. Div.
Geb. 68	3 Mtn. Div.
..	
Geb. 70	XVIII Corps
(*71*	*now N.A.*150 ?)
..	
(*73*	*now N.A.* 172 ?)
74	
..	
76	46 Inf. Div.
77 mot.	
Pz. 78 mot.	15 Pz.Gr. Div.
Pz. 79 mot.	4 Pz. Div.
(*80 mot.*	*now Pz.A.N.R.2*)
Pz. 81 mot.	9 Pz. Div.
Pz. 82 mot.	6 Pz. Div.
Pz. 83 mot.	7 Pz. Div.
Pz. 84 mot.	
Pz. 85 mot.	5 Pz. Div. ?
86	
Pz. 87mot.(?)	25 Pz. Div. (?)
Pz. 88 mot.	18 Pz. Div.
..	
Pz. 90 mot.	10 Pz. Div.
Geb. 91	6 Mtn. Div.
Pz. 92 mot.	20 Pz. Div.
Pz. 93 mot.	26 Pz. Div.
Geb. 94	4 Mtn. Div.
Geb. 95	5 Mtn. Div.
..	
97	97 Jäg. Div.
..	
Geb. 99	7 Mtn. Div.
100	100 Jäg. Div.
101	101 Jäg. Div.
102	102 Inf. Div.
..	
104	104 Jäg. Div.
..	

Nachr. Abt.	Allotted to
106	106 Inf. Div.
..	
..	
..	
110	110 Inf. Div.
111	111 Inf. Div.
112	112 Inf. Div.
113	113 Inf. Div.
114	114 Jäg. Div.
..	
..	
117	117 Jäg. Div.
118	118 Jäg. Div.
..	
..	
121	121 Inf. Div.
122	122 Inf. Div.
123	123 Inf. Div.
..	
125	125 Inf. Div.
126	126 Inf. Div.
..	
Pz. 128 mot.	23 Pz. Div.
129	129 Inf. Div.
..	
131	131 Inf. Div.
132	132 Inf. Div.
..	
134	134 Inf. Div.
126	
..	
137	137 Inf. Div.
..	
..	
(Pz. 140 mot.	22 Pz. Div.)*
..	
..	
..	
..	
..	
..	

* Division now believed disbanded ; the unit (possibly renumbered) may still exist.

Nachr. Abt.	Allotted to	Nachr. Abt.	Allotted to
..		187	87 Inf. Div.
..		188	88 Inf. Div.
..		..	
150	50 Inf. Div.	190 mot.	90 Pz.Gr. Div.
..		..	
152	52 Inf. Div.	..	
..		193	93 Inf. Div.
..		194	94 Inf. Div.
..		..	
156	56 Inf. Div.	196	96 Inf. Div.
157	57 Inf. Div.	..	
158	58 Inf. Div.	198	98 Inf. Div.
..		199	199 Inf. Div.
160 mot.	60 Pz.Gr. Div.	Pz. 200 mot.	21 Pz. Div.
161	61 Inf. Div.	..	
162	62 Inf. Div.	..	
..		..	
..		..	
165	65 Inf. Div.	205	205 Inf. Div.
..		206	206 Inf. Div.
..		..	
168	68 Inf. Div.	208	208 Inf. Div.
169	69 Inf. Div.	(*209*	209 Inf. Div.)*
..		..	
171	71 Inf. Div.	211	211 Inf. Div.
172?	72 Inf. Div.	212	212 Inf. Div.
173	73 Inf. Div.	213†	
..		214	214 Inf. Div.
175	75 Inf. Div.	215	215 Inf. Div.
176	76 Inf. Div.	216	216 Inf. Div.
..		217	217 Inf. Div.
178	78 Inf. Div.	218	218 Inf. Div.
179	79 Inf. Div.	219	183 Inf. Div.
..		220	164 Pz.Gr. Div.
181	81 Inf. Div.	221	221 Sich. Div.
182	82 Inf. Div.	222	181 Inf. Div.
183	83 Inf. Div.	223	223 Inf. Div.
..		..	
..		225	225 Inf. Div.
186	86 Inf. Div.	..	

* Division now disbanded; the unit (possibly renumbered) may still exist.

† Coy. only.

Nacht Abt.	Allotted to	Nachr. Abt.	Allotted to
227	227 Inf. Div.	269	269 Inf. Div.
228 mot.	16 Pz.Gr. Div.	(*270*)	
229	197 Inf. Div.	(*271*)	
230	169 Inf. Div.	..	
(*231*	231 Inf. Div.)†	..	
..		..	
233	196 Inf. Div.	..	
234	163 Inf. Div.	..	
235	198 Inf. Div.	..	
236	162 Inf. Div.	..	
..		..	
..		..	
(*239*	239 Inf. Div.)†	..	
240	170 Inf. Div.	..	
241	161 Inf. Div.	..	
..		..	
..		..	
..		..	
..		..	
246	246 Inf. Div.	..	
..		..	
248	168 Inf. Div.	..	
..		291	291 Inf. Div.
..		292	292 Inf. Div.
251	251 Inf. Div.	293	293 Inf. Div.
252	252 Inf. Div.	294	294 Inf. Div.
253	253 Inf. Div.	295	295 Inf. Div.
254	254 Inf. Div.	296	296 Inf. Div.
255	255 Inf. Div.	297	297 Inf. Div.
256?	256 Inf. Div. ?	298	298 Inf. Div.
257	257 Inf. Div.	..	
258	258 Inf. Div.	300	
..		301	
260	260 Inf. Div.	302*	302 Inf. Div.
..		Eisb. 303	G.H.Q. tps.
262	262 Inf. Div.	304*	304 Inf. Div.
263	263 Inf. Div.	305	305 Inf. Div.
..		306	306 Inf. Div.
..		..	
..		..	
267	267 Inf. Div.	309	
268	268 Inf. Div.	..	

* Company only. † Division now disbanded.

Nachr. Abt.	Allotted to	Nachr. Abt.	Allotted to
..		..	
312		..	
Eisb. 313 mot.	G.H.Q. tps.	..	
Eisb. 314	G.H.Q. tps.	..	
..		..	
..		..	
..		..	
..		..	
..		..	
320*	320 Inf. Div.	..	
321	321 Inf. Div.	..	
..		..	
323	323 Inf. Div.	..	
..		..	
..		..	
326	326 Inf. Div.	..	
327	327 Inf. Div.	369†	
328*	328 Inf. Div.	370	370 Inf. Div.
329	329 Inf. Div.	..	
330	330 Inf. Div.	..	
331	331 Inf. Div.	..	
332*	332 Inf. Div.	..	
333*	333 Inf. Div.	..	
334	334 Inf. Div.	..	
335*	335 Inf. Div.	377	377 Inf. Div.
336	336 Inf. Div.	..	
337*	337 Inf. Div.	..	
338	338 Inf. Div.	380	
339*	339 Inf. Div.	..	
340	340 Inf. Div.	..	
Pz. 341 mot.	11 Pz. Div.	383	383 Inf. Div.
342	342 Inf. Div.	384	384 Inf. Div.
..		385	385 Inf. Div.
..		..	
..		387	387 Inf. Div.
..		..	
..		..	
..		..	
..		..	
..		..	
..		..	
..		..	

* Company only. † Telephone construction unit.

Nachr. Abt.	Allotted to	Nachr. Abt.	Allotted to
..		..	
..		..	
..		..	
..		..	
..		..	
400			

Nachr. Abt.	In Corps†	Nachr. Abt.	In Corps
420 mot.	XX	449 mot.	XXXXIX
..		..	
..		451 mot.	LI
423 mot.	XXIII	452 mot.	LII
Pz. 424 mot.	XXIV	453 mot.	LIII
425 mot.	XXV	454 mot.	LIV
426 mot.	XXVI	455 mot.	LV
427 mot.	XXVII	Pz. 456 mot.	LVI
428 mot.	XXVIII	Pz. 457 mot.	LVII
429 mot.	XXIX	458	
430 mot.	XXX	459 mot.	LIX
431 mot.	XXXI	460 mot.	LX
432 mot.	XXXII	..	
433 mot.	XXXIII	..	
434 mot.*	XXXIV	463 mot.	(Norway Army)
435 mot.	XXXV	464 mot.	LXIV?
436 mot.	XXXVI	..	
437 mot.*	XXXVII	..	
438 mot.	XXXVIII	467 mot.	LXVII?
Pz. 439 mot.	XXXIX	468	LXVIII
Pz. 440 mot.	XXXX	..	
Pz. 441 mot.	XXXXI	470 mot.	
442 mot.	XXXXII	..	
443 mot.	XXXXIII	..	
444 mot.	XXXXIV	..	
445 mot.	XXXXV	..	
Pz. 446 mot.	XXXXVI	Pz. 475 mot.	Afrika
Pz. 447 mot.	XXXXVII	..	
Pz. 448 mot.	XXXXVIII	..	

† For type of corps *see* pp. L 3–L 5 above. * Company only.

Nachr. Abt.	In Corps†	Nachr. Abt.	In Corps
..		..	
..		..	
480 mot.	LXX	..	
..		..	
..		..	
..		..	

† For type of corps *see* p. L 3 above.

Nachr. Abt.*	Allotted to	Nachr. Abt.	Allotted to
..		N.R. 517 mot.	Railway tps.
..		..	
..		..	
..		N.R. 520 mot.	9 Army ?
..		N.R. 521 mot.	12 Army
..		N.R. 522 mot.	
..		..	
..		..	
...		525	
..		526	
..		527	
N.R. 501 mot.	16 Army ?	..	
..		..	
N.R. 503 mot.	Army ?	530	
N.R. 504	Army Group	531 mot.	7 Army ?
..		..	
..		..	
..		..	
..		..	
509 mot.	15 Army	536	
..		N.R. 537 mot.	Army Group
N.R. 511 mot.	Army ?	..	
512 mot.	Army ?	..	
513†		(*540*‡)	
N.R. 514 mot.	Railway tps.	..	
..		542	
..		543†	

* *Except where preceded by* N.R. † Company only. ‡ Now disbanded.

Nachr. Abt.*	Allotted to‡
..	
..	
..	
..	
..	
N.R. 549 mot.	6 Army
N.R. 550 mot.	20 Army
..	
..	
..	
..	
..	
..	
557§	
N.R. 558 mot.	11 Army ?
..	
..	
..	
..	
N.R. 563 mot.	2 Army ?
N.R. 564 mot.	
..	
..	
..	
..	
..	
N.R. 570 mot.	Army Group B
..	
..	
..	
..	
..	
..	
..	
..	
..	
..	
..	
..	
..	
..	

Nachr. Abt.	Allotted to
..	
..	
..	
..	
N.R. 589 mot.	4 Army
..	
..	
592	
..	
594	
..	
N.R. 596 mot.	17 Army
N.R. 597 mot.	
N.R. 598	G.H.Q. tps.
..	
..	
F.N.R. 601 mot.	G.H.Q. tps.
N.R. 602 mot.	G.H.Q. tps.
603 mot.	Army Group
N.R. 604 mot.	
605 mot.†	
..	
..	
..	
..	
610 mot.†	
..	
612 mot.†	G.H.Q. tps.
613 mot.†	G.H.Q. tps.
614 mot.†	G.H.Q. tps.
..	
N.R. 616 mot.	G.H.Q. tps.
617 mot.†	G.H.Q. tps.
N.R. 618 mot.	G.H.Q. tps.
619	G.H.Q. tps.
620 mot.†	
621 mot.†	G.H.Q. tps.
622 mot.†	G.H.Q. tps.
623 mot.†	G.H.Q. tps.
..	
..	

* Except where qualified otherwise. † Company only.

‡ Probably G.H.Q. tps. where no allotment is specified. § Now disbanded.

Nachr. Abt.*	Allotted to§
..	
627	
..	
..	
..	
..	
N.E. 632	
633 mot.‡	G.H.Q. tps.
..	
635 mot.	
..	
..	
638 mot.‡	
N.R. 639 mot.	Army Group D ?
..	
..	
N.R. 642 mot.	G.H.Q. tps.
N.R. 643 mot.	G.H.Q. tps.‖
N.R. 644 mot.	G.H.Q. tps.‖
N.R. 645 mot.	G.H.Q. tps.‖
646	
647†	
..	
N.R. 649 mot.	
..	
N.R. 651 mot.	G.H.Q. tps.
..	
..	
..	
..	
..	
..	
..	
..	
660 mot.‡	G.H.Q. tps.
..	
..	
..	
..	

Nachr. Abt.	Allotted to
665	
666 mot.†	G.H.Q. tps.
..	
668†	
..	
670†	G.H.Q. tps.
671†	G.H.Q. tps.
672†	
673	
..	
..	
..	
..	
..	
..	
..	
..	
682 mot.‡	G.H.Q. tps.
..	
..	
685 mot.‡	G.H.Q. tps.
..	
..	
..	
..	
..	
..	
..	
693 mot.‡	G.H.Q. tps.
694 mot.‡	G.H.Q. tps.
..	
696 mot.‡	G.H.Q. tps.
697 mot.‡	G.H.Q. tps.
698 mot. ‡	G.H.Q. tps.
699‡	G.H.Q. tps.
..	
..	
702†	702 Inf. Div.
..	

* Except where qualified otherwise. † Company only.
‡ Battalion staff only.
§ Probably G.H.Q. tps. where no allotment is specified.
‖ Telephone operating regt.

Nachr. Abt.	Allotted to§	Nachr. Abt.	Allotted to
(*704*	*See 104.*)	..	
..		..	
..		..	
707	707 Inf. Div.	..	
708	708 Inf. Div.	..	
709	709 Inf. Div.	..	
710	710 Inf. Div.	..	
711	711 Inf. Div.	751	
712	712 Inf. Div.	..	
713	713 Inf. Div.	..	
(*714*	*See 114.*)	..	
715	715 Inf. Div.	..	
716	716 Inf. Div.	756	
(*717*	*See 117.*)	..	
(*718*	*See 118.*)	..	
719	719 Inf. Div.	..	
..		..	
721	Crete comd.	761	
722	Crete comd.	762	
..		..	
..		..	
..		..	
..		..	
..		..	
..		..	
..		..	
..		..	
..		..	
..		..	
..		..	
..		..	
..		..	
..		..	
..		..	
..		..	
..		..	
..		..	
..		..	
..		..	
..			

§ Probably G.H.Q. tps. where no allotment is specified.

Nachr. Abt.*	Allotted to§	Nachr. Abt.	Allotted to
..		..	
..		..	
..		824	
..		825	
..		826	
..		827‡	
..		..	
..		..	
..		..	
..		..	
..		..	
..		..	
..		..	
..		..	
..		..	
..		..	
..		..	
..		..	
..		..	
..		..	
..		..	
..		..	
..		..	
..		..	
806†		..	
..		..	
..		..	
..		..	
810†		..	
811†		..	
..		..	
..		..	
..		..	
..		..	
..		..	
..		902†	
..		..	
..		904†	
..		..	
821 mot. ‡		906†	

* Except where qualified otherwise. † Company only.
‡ Battalion staff only.
§ Probably G.H.Q. tps. where no allotment is specified.

Nachr. Abt.*	Allotted to‡	Nachr. Abt.	Allotted to
907†		..	
..		..	
..		..	
..		930†	
..		..	
912†		..	
..		..	
..		..	
..		..	
..		..	
..		937†	
..		..	
..		..	
920†		..	
921†			
922†			
..			
..			
..			
..		999§	(999 Int. Div.)

* Except where qualified otherwise.
† Telephone operating platoon only.
‡ G.H.Q. tps. where no allotment is specified.
§ Div. now disbanded ; unit may exist as G.H.Q. troops or may have been renumbered.

(*l*) ANTI-TANK UNITS

(*Panzerjager-Abteilungen* = Pz.Jg.Abt.)

Identification : Pink piping, gothic " P " on shoulder strap.

Pz.Jg.Abt.	In. Div.	Pz.Jg.Abt.	In Div.
1	1 Inf.	39	21 Pz.
2	12 Pz.	40	24 Pz.
3	3 Pz.Gr.	41	6 Pz.
4	14 Pz.	42	7 Pz.
5	5 Jäg.	43	8 Pz.
6	6 Inf.	Geb. 44	1 Mtn.
7	7 Inf.	45	45 Inf.
8	8 Jäg.	46	44 Inf.
9	9 Inf.	Geb. 47	2 Mtn.
10	10 Pz.Gr.	Geb. 48	3 Mtn.
11	11 Inf.	49	4 Pz.
12	12 Inf.	50	9 Pz.
13	13 Pz.	..	
14	14 Pz.Gr.	52	46 Inf.
15	15 Inf.	53	5 Pz.
16	16 Pz.	..	
17	17 Inf.	Geb. 55	6 Mtn.
18	18 Pz.Gr.	56	
19	19 Pz.	..	
20	20 Pz.Gr.	..	
21	21 Inf.	..	
22	22 L.L. (mot.)	..	
23	23 Inf.	..	
24	24 Inf.	..	
25	25 Pz.Gr.	..	
26	26 Inf.	..	
27	17 Pz.	..	
28	28 Jäg.	..	
29	29 Pz.Gr.	67	
30	30 Inf.	..	
31	31 Inf.	..	
32	32 Inf.	..	
33	15 Pz.Gr.	..	
34	34 Inf.	72	
35	35 Inf.	..	
36	36 Pz.Gr.	..	
37	1 Pz.	..	
38	2 Pz.	..	

Pz.Jg.Abt.	In Div.	Pz.Jg.Abt.	In Div.
..		..	
..		..	
..		..	
..		..	
..		121	121 Inf.
..		122	122 Inf.
..		123	123 Inf.
..		..	
..		125	125 Inf.
..		126	126 Inf.
..		..	
88	18 Pz.	128	23 Pz.
..		129	129 Inf.
90	10 Pz.	..	
..		131	131 Inf.
92	20 Pz.	132*	132 Inf.
93	G.H.Q. Tps.	..	
Geb. 94	4 Mtn.	134	134 Inf.
Geb. 95	5 Mtn.	..	
..		..	
97	97 Jäg.	137	137 Inf.
..		Schn. Abt. 138	38 Inf.
Geb. 99	7 Mtn.	Schn. Abt. 139	39 Inf.
100	100 Jäg.	†(140	22 Pz.†)
101	101 Jäg.	..	
102	102 Inf.	..	
..		..	
..		..	
..		..	
106	106 Inf.	..	
..		..	
..		..	
..		..	
110	110 Inf.	150	50 Inf.
111	111 Inf.	..	
112	112 Inf.	152	52 Inf.
113	113 Inf.	..	
..		..	
..		..	
..		156	56 Inf.

* Possibly is combined Pz. Jäg. Abt. and Aufkl. Abt.

† Division possibly disbanded ; the unit (possibly renumbered) may still exist.

Pz.Jg.Abt.	In Div.
157	57 Inf.
158	58 Inf.
..	
160	60 Pz. Gr.
161	61 Inf.
162	62 Inf.
..	
164	
Schn. Abt. 165	65 Inf.
..	
..	
168	68 Inf
Schn. Abt. 169	69 Inf.
..	
171	71 Inf.
172?	72 Inf.
173	73 Inf.
..	
175	75 Inf.
176	76 Inf.
..	
178	78 Inf.
179	79 Inf.
..	
181	81 Inf.
Schn. Abt. 182	82 Inf.
Schn. Abt. 183	83 Inf.
..	
..	
186	86 Inf.
Schn. Abt. 187	87 Inf.
Schn. Abt. 188	88 Inf.
..	
190	90 Pz.Gr.
..	
..	
193	93 Inf.
Schn. Abt. 194	94 Inf.
195	95 Inf.
Schn. Abt. 196	96 Inf.
..	

Pz.Jg.Abt.	In Div.
Schn. Abt. 198	98 Inf.
Schn. Abt. 199	199 Inf.
..	
..	
..	
..	
..	
Schn. Abt. 205	205 Inf.
Schn. Abt. 206	206 Inf.
207?	
Schn. Abt. 208	208 Inf.
..	
..	
211	211 Inf.
Schn. Abt. 212	212 Inf.
213*?	
Schn. Abt. 214	214 Inf.
215	215 Inf.
216	216 Inf.
217	217 Inf.
Schn. Abt. 218	218 Inf.
219	183 Inf.
220	164 Lt.
221?	
222	181 Inf.
Schn. Abt. 223	223 Inf.
..	
Schn. Abt. 225	225 Inf.
..	
227	227 Inf.
(*228*	*228 Inf.*†)
229	197 Inf.
230	169 Inf.
..	
..	
233	196 Inf.
Schn. Abt. 234	163 Inf.
235	198 Inf.
236	162 Inf.
..	
238	167 Inf.

*** Company only.**

† Division disbanded ; the unit (possibly renumbered) may still exist.

Pz.Jg.Abt.	In Div.	Pz.Jg.Abt.	In Div.
(*239*	*239 Inf.**)	..	
Schn. Abt. 240	170 Inf.	..	
241	161 Inf.	..	
..		..	
..		..	
..		..	
..		..	
Schn. Abt. 246	246 Inf.	..	
..		..	
248	168 Inf.	Schn. Abt. 290	290 Inf.
..		Schn. Abt. 291	291 Inf.
..		292	292 Inf.
251	251 Inf.	293	293 Inf.
252	252 Inf.	294	294 Inf.
253	253 Inf.	295	295 Inf.
254	254 Inf.	296	296 Inf.
255	255 Inf.	297	297 Inf.
256	256 Inf.	298	298 Inf.
257	257 Inf.	299	299 Inf.
258	258 Inf.	..	
..		..	
260	260 Inf.	Schn. Abt. 302	302 Inf.
..		..	
262	262 Inf.	304	304 Inf.
263	263 Inf.	..	
264?	264 Inf.	Schn. Abt. 306	306 Inf.
..		..	
..		..	
267	267 Inf.	..	
Schn. Abt. 268	268 Inf.	..	
Schn. Abt. 269	269 Inf.	..	
..		..	
..		..	
..		..	
..		..	
..		..	
..		..	
..		..	
..		Schn. Abt. 319	319 Inf.
..		320	320 Int.
..		..	
..		..	

* Division disbanded ; the unit (possibly renumbered) may still exist.

Pz.Jg.Abt.	In Div.*	Pz.Jg.Abt.	In Div.
323	323 Inf.	..	
..		..	
..		..	
326	326 Inf.	370	370 Inf.
327	327 Inf.	371	371 Inf.
..		..	
Schn. Abt. 329	329 Inf.	373	373 Inf.
..		..	
331	331 Inf.	..	
332	332 Inf.	376	376 Inf.
Schn. Abt. 333	333 Inf.	377	377 Inf.
Schn. Abt. 334	334 Inf.	..	
335	335 Inf.	..	
336	336 Inf.	..	
337	337 Inf.	..	
338	338 Inf.	..	
339	339 Inf.	383	383 Inf.
340	340 Inf.	384	384 Inf.
..		385	385 Inf.
342	342 Inf.	..	
..		387	387 Inf.
..		..	
..		389	389 Inf.
..		..	
..		..	
..		..	
..		..	
..		..	
..			
..			
..			
354			
..		463	(Norway Army)
..			
..			
..			
..		..	
360		..	
..		..	
..		..	
..		..	
..		..	
..		..	
..		..	

* *Where no allotment is shown it is probable that G.H.Q. tps. should be understood.*

Pz.Jg.Abt.	Allotted to*	Pz.Jg.Abt.	Allotted to
..		543	G.H.Q. tps.
..		..	
..		545	G.H.Q. tps.
..		..	
..		..	
..		..	
..		..	
..		..	
511	G.H.Q. tps.	..	
..		552	
..		..	
..		..	
..		..	
..		..	
..		..	
..		..	
..		559	G.H.Q. tps.(*a*)
..		560	G.H.Q. tps.
521	G.H.Q. tps.	561	G.H.Q. tps.
522	G.H.Q. tps.	..	
..		563	G.H.Q. tps.
..		..	
525	G.H.Q. tps.	..	
..		..	
..		..	
..		..	
529		..	
..		..	
..		..	
..		..	
..		..	
..		..	
..		..	
..		..	
..		..	
..		..	
539		..	
..		..	
541		..	
..		590	G.H.Q. tps.

* *Where no allotment is shown it is probable that* G.H.Q. tps. *should be understood.*

(*a*) S.P. mountings.

Pz.Jg.Abt.	Allotted to	Pz.Jg.Abt.	Allotted to
605	§	..	
606	§	..	
607	§	..	
..		..	
..		643	G.H.Q. tps.(*a*)
..		..	
611	G.H.Q. tps.	645	G.H.Q. tps.
..		..	
..		..	
..		..	
..		..	
616	G.H.Q. tps.	..	
..		..	
..		652	G.H.Q. tps.
..		..	
..		654	G.H.Q. tps.
..		..	
..		..	
..		..	
624	§	..	
625	G.H.Q. tps.	..	
..		..	
..		..	
..		..	
629	§	..	
..		..	
..		..	
..		..	
..		..	
..		..	
635	Pz.A.O.K.2	..	
..		670	G.H.Q. tps.
..		..	
..		672	G.H.Q. tps.

Also : (1) Pz.Jg.Abt.900 (Lehr-Brig.900).
(2) Pz.Jg.Lehr-Abt. (Pz.Lehr-Rgt.).
(3) Pz.Jg.Abt. Grossdeutschland.

(*a*) 4·7-cm. S.P.

§ Present existence doubtful.

(*m*) RECONNAISSANCE UNITS

(*Panzer-Aufklärungsabteilung* = Pz. A.A. in panzer and motorised divisions ;

(*Aufklärungsabteilung* = A.A. in other divisions.)

A.A.	Allotted to	A.A.	Allotted to
1	1 Inf. Div.	26	26 Inf. Div.
Pz. 1	1 Pz. Div.	Pz. 26	26 Pz. Div.
Pz. 2	2 Pz. Div.	..	
Pz. 3	3 Pz. Div.	28	28 Jäg. Div.
Pz. 4	4 Pz. Div.	..	
5	5 Jäg. Div.	30	30 Inf. Div.
Pz. 5	5 Pz. Div.	31	31 Inf. Div.
6	6 Inf. Div.	32	32 Inf. Div.
Pz. 6	6 Pz. Div.	..	
7	7 Inf. Div.	34	34 Inf. Div.
Pz. 7	7 Pz. Div.	35	35 Inf. Div.
8	8 Jäg. Div.	..	
Pz. 8	8 Pz. Div.	..	
9	9 Inf. Div.	..	
Pz. 9	9 Pz. Div.	..	
Pz. 10	10 Pz. Div.	..	
11	11 Inf. Div.	..	
Pz. 11	11 Pz. Div.	..	
12	12 Inf. Div.	..	
Pz. 12	12 Pz. Div.	44	44 Inf. Div.
Pz. 13	13 Pz. Div.	45	45 Inf. Div.
Pz. 14	14 Pz. Div.	46	46 Inf. Div.
15	15 Inf. Div.	..	
Pz. 15	15 Pz. Div.	..	
Pz. 16	16 Pz. Div.	..	
17	17 Inf. Div.	..	
Pz. 17	17 Pz. Div.	..	
Pz. 18	18 Pz. Div.	..	
Pz. 19	19 Pz. Div.	..	
Pz. 20	20 Pz. Div.	54	1 Mtn. Div.
21	21 Inf. Div.	..	
Pz. 21	21 Pz. Div.	..	
23	23 Inf. Div.	..	
Pz. 23	23 Pz. Div.	..	
24	24 Inf. Div.	..	
Pz. 24	24 Pz. Div.	..	
Pz. 25	25 Pz. Div.	..	

A.A.	Allotted to	A.A.	Allotted to
..		..	
..		..	
..		106	106 Inf. Div.
..		..	
..		..	
67	2 Mtn. Div.	..	
68	3 Mtn. Div.	Pz. 110	10 Pz.Gr. Div.
..		110	110 Inf. Div.
..		..	
..		112	6 Mtn. Div.
..		113	113 Inf. Div.
..		Pz. 114	14 Pz.Gr. Div.
..		Pz. 115 ?	15 Pz.Gr. Div. ?
..		Pz. 116	16 Pz.Gr. Div.
..		117	111 Inf. Div.
..		Pz. 118	18 Pz.Gr. Div.
..		..	
..		120	112 Inf. Div.
..		Pz. 120	20 Pz.Gr. Div.
..		121	121 Inf. Div.
..		122	122 Inf. Div.
..		Pz. 122	22 LL(Mot.)Div.
..		123	123 Inf. Div.
..		..	
..		125	125 Inf. Div.
..		Pz. 125	25 Pz.Gr. Div.
..		126	126 Inf. Div.
..		..	
..		..	
..		129	129 Inf. Div.
..		Pz. 129	29 Pz.Gr. Div.
..		..	
94	4 Mtn. Div.	131	131 Inf. Div.
95	5 Mtn. Div.	132*	132 Inf. Div.
..		..	
97	97 Jäg. Div.	134	134 Inf. Div.
..	.	..	
99	7 Mtn. Div.	Pz. 136	36 Pz.Gr. Div.
100	100 Jäg Div.	137	137 Inf. Div.
101	101 Jäg. Div.	Schn.Abt. 138	38 Inf. Div.
102	102 Inf. Div.	Schn.Abt. 139	39 Inf. Div.
Pz. 103	3 Pz.Gr. Div.	..	

* Possibly Schnelle Abt.

L 83

A.A.	Allotted to
..	
..	
..	
..	
..	
..	
..	
..	
..	
150	50 Inf. Div.
..	
152	52 Inf. Div.
..	
..	
..	
156	56 Inf. Div.
157	57 Inf. Div.
158	58 Inf. Div.
..	
Pz. 160	60 Pz.Gr. Div.
161	61 Inf. Div.
162	62 Inf. Div.
..	
Pz. 164 ?	164 Pz.Gr. Div.
Schn. Abt. 165	65 Inf. Div.
..	
..	
168	68 Inf. Div.
Schn. Abt. 169	69 Inf. Div.
..	
171	71 Inf. Div.
172	72 Inf. Div. ?
173	73 Inf. Div.
..	
175	75 Inf. Div.
176	76 Inf. Div.
177	77 Inf. Div.
178	78 Inf. Div.
179	79 Inf. Div.
..	
..	
Schn. Abt. 182	82 Inf. Div.
Schn. Abt. 183	83 Inf. Div.
..	

A.A.	Allotted to
..	
186	86 Inf. Div.
Schn. Abt. 187	87 Inf. Div.
Schn. Abt. 188	88 Inf. Div.
..	
..	
..	
..	
193	93 Inf. Div.
Schn. Abt. 194	94 Inf. Div.
195	95 Inf. Div.
Schn. Abt. 196	96 Inf. Div.
..	
Schn. Abt. 198	98 Inf. Div.
Schn. Abt. 199	199 Inf. Div.
..	
..	
..	
..	
..	
Schn. Abt. 205	205 Inf. Div.
Schn. Abt. 206	206 Inf. Div.
..	
Schn. Abt. 208	208 Inf. Div.
..	
..	
211	211 Inf. Div.
Schn. Abt. 212	212 Inf. Div.
..	
Schn. Abt. 214	214 Inf. Div.
215	215 Inf. Div.
216	216 Inf. Div.
217	217 Inf. Div.
Schn. Abt. 218	218 Inf. Div.
219	183 Inf. Div.
..	
..	
222	181 Inf. Div.
Schn. Abt. 223	223 Inf. Div.
..	
Schn. Abt. 225	225 Inf. Div.
..	
227	227 Inf. Div.
..	

A.A.	Allotted to	A.A.	Allotted to
229	197 Inf. Div.	..	
..		..	
(Pz. 231 mot.	Renumbered Pz. A.A. 11)	..	
		..	
..		..	
233	196 Inf. Div.	..	
Schn. Abt. 234	163 Inf. Div.	..	
235	198 Inf. Div.	..	
..		..	
..		..	
238	167 Inf. Div.	..	
..		..	
240?	170 Inf. Div.	..	
Schn. Abt. 241	161 Inf. Div.	..	
..		..	
..		..	
..		..	
..		..	
Schn. Abt. 246	246 Inf. Div.	Schn. Abt. 290	290 Inf. Div.
..		Schn. Abt. 291	291 Inf. Div.
248	168 Inf. Div.	..	
..		293	293 Inf. Div.
..		294	294 Inf. Div.
251	251 Inf. Div.	..	
252	252 Inf. Div.	296	296 Inf. Div.
253	253 Inf. Div.	297	297 Inf. Div.
254	254 Inf. Div.	298	298 Inf. Div.
255	255 Inf. Div.	299	299 Inf. Div.
256	256 Inf. Div.	..	
257	257 Inf. Div.	..	
258	258 Inf. Div.	Schn. Abt. 302	302 Inf. Div.
..		..	
260	260 Inf. Div.	..	
..		305	305 Inf. Div.
262	262 Inf. Div.	Schn. Abt. 306	306 Inf. Div.
263	263 Inf. Div.	..	
264	264 Inf. Div.	..	
..		..	
..		..	
267	267 Inf. Div.	..	
Schn. Abt. 268	268 Inf. Div.	..	
Schn. Abt. 269	269 Inf. Div.	..	
..		..	
..		..	

A.A.	Allotted to	A.A.	Allotted to
..		377	377 Inf. Div.
..		..	
..		..	
Schn. Abt. 319	319 Inf. Div.	..	
..		..	
..		..	
..		Schn. Abt. 383	383 Inf. Div.
Schn. Abt. 323	323 Inf. Div.	..	
..		..	
..		..	
..		..	
..		..	
328	328 Inf. Div.	..	
Schn. Abt. 329	329 Inf. Div.	..	
330	330 Inf. Div.	..	
331?	331 Inf. Div.?	..	
..		..	
Schn. Abt. 333	333 Inf. Div.	..	
Schn. Abt. 334	334 Inf. Div.	..	
..		..	
..		(399	Disbanded in 1940)
..			
..		..	
Schn. Abt. 339	339 Inf. Div.	..	
..		402	(G.H.Q. tps.)
..		403	(G.H.Q. tps.)
342	342 Inf. Div.		
..			
..			
..			
..			
..		(580)?	
..			
..			
..			
..			
..			
..		670	(G.H.Q. tps.)
..			
..			
..			
..			
..			
..		776	(Norway Army)

(*n*) COMBINED ANTI-TANK AND RECONNAISSANCE UNITS

May be named Schnelle Abteilung or Panzer-Jäger und Aufklärungs Abteilung

Schn.Abt. or Pz.Jäg.A.A. No.	Allotted to Inf. Div. No.
132?	132?
138	38
139	39
165	65
169	69
182	82
183	83
187	87
188	88
194	94
196	96
198	98
199	199
205	205
206	206
208	208
212	212
214	214
218	218
223	223
225	225
234	163
241	161
246	246
268	268
269	269
290	290
291	291
302	302
306	306
319	319
323	323
329	329
333	333
334	334
339	339
383	383

(*o*) TANK REGIMENTS AND TANK BATTALIONS

(*Panzer-Regimenter* = Pz.R., and *Panzer-Abteilungen* = Pz.Abt.)

Identification : Pink piping (tank crews wear black uniforms).

Pz.R.*	Allotted to†	Pz.R.	Allotted to
1	1 Pz. Div.	35	4 Pz. Div.
2	16 Pz. Div.	36	14 Pz. Div.
3	2 Pz. Div.	37	
4	13 Pz. Div.	..	
5	21 Pz. Div.	39	17 Pz. Div.
6	3 Pz. Div.	..	
7	10 Pz. Div.	..	
8‡		..	
9	25 Pz. Div.	..	
10	8 Pz. Div.	44	
11	6 Pz. Div.	..	
..		..	
..		..	
14		..	
15	11 Pz. Div.	..	
16		..	
17		..	
18	18 Pz. Div.	..	
..		..	
..		..	
21	20 Pz. Div.	..	
..		..	
23		..	
24	24 Pz. Div.	..	
25	7 Pz. Div.	..	
26	26 Pz. Div.	60*	
27	19 Pz. Div.	..	
..		..	
29	12 Pz. Div.	..	
..		..	
31	5 Pz. Div.	..	
32		..	
33	9 Pz. Div.	..	
..		..	

* Except where marked with asterisk (in such cases Pz. Abt.).
† Unallotted units probably belong to the G.H.Q. pool.
‡ Possibly disbanded or renumbered.

Pz.R.	Allotted to†	*Pz.R.	Allotted to
100*	(Flame-thrower	190*	
	tks.)	..	
101*	(Flame-thrower	..	
	tks.)	..	
102*	(Flame-thrower	..	
	tks.)	..	
103*	3 Pz.Gr. Div.	..	
..		..	
..		..	
..		..	
..		..	
..		201	23 Pz. Div.
..		202	
..		203	
..		204	
..		..	
..		..	
..		..	
115*	15 Pz. Gr. Div.	..	
116	16 Pz. Gr. Div.	..	
..		..	
..		211*	
..		212*	22 LL (mot.) Div.?
..			
..		..	
..		..	
..			
		300*	
		301	

* Pz.Abt. only. † Unalloted units probably belong to G.H.Q. pool.

Also : (1) Panzer-Lehr-Regiment.

(2) Panzer-Regiment Grossdeutschland and in *Grossdeutschland Pz.Div.*

(3) Panzer-Regiment Hermann Goering in *Hermann Goering Pz.Div.*

(p) ANTI-AIRCRAFT REGIMENTS AND BATTERIES

(*Flak-Regimenter* and *-Abteilungen* are G.A.F. personnel; *Heeresflakabteilungen* are German Army personnel; and *Marineflakabteilungen* are German Navy personnel.)

Identification: Air Force uniform (except Army and Naval A.A.), red piping.

Note.—The German word Abt. (Abteilung) has been substituted for the British Bty. (Battery) and American Bn. (Battalion).

Flak	Remarks*	Flak	Remarks
1	Regt.	20	Regt.
	S/L regt.		Naval regt.
		21	Regt.
2	Regt.	22	Regt.
	S/L regt.		Naval regt.
	Balloon Abt.	23	Regt.
3	Regt.	24	Regt.
4	Regt.		Naval regt.
	S/L regt.	25	Regt.
5	Regt.	26	Regt.
	S/L regt.	27	Regt.
6	Regt.	28	Regt.
7	Regt.	29	Regt.
8	Regt.	30	Regt.
9	Regt.		Rly. regt.
10	Regt.	31	Regt.
	Balloon Abt.	32	Regt. (10·5 cm.)
11	Regt.	33	Regt.
12	Regt. (10·5 cm.)	34	Regt.
	Rly. regt.	35	Regt.
13	Regt.	36	Regt.
14	Regt.	37	Regt.
15	Regt.	38	Regt.
16	Regt.	39	Regt.
17	Regt.	40	Regt. staff
18	Regt.	41	Regt. staff
19	Regt.	42	Regt.

* Light batteries are normally equipped with 3·7-cm. and 2-cm. guns, heavy batteries with 8·8-cm. guns, and all other batteries are "mixed" with 8·8-cm., 3·7-cm. and 2-cm. guns. Where a unit is known to be equipped with other calibres, such as 4-cm. or 10·5-cm. a reference is given in this column.

Flak.	Remarks.	Flak.	Remarks.
43	Regt.	82	Lt. Abt.
44	Regt. (10·5 cm.)	83	Lt. Abt.
45	Regt.		Regt. staff
46	Regt.	84	Lt. Abt.
47	Regt.	85	Lt. (mot.) Abt.
48	Regt. (10·5 cm.)		Regt. staff
49	Regt. (4 cm.)	86	Lt. Abt.
50	Regt.		Regt. staff
51	Regt.	87 (?)	Lt. Abt.
52	Regt.	88	Lt. Abt.
53	Regt.	89	Lt. (mot.) Abt.
54	Regt.		Regt. staff
55	Regt.	90	Lt. Abt.
..			Regt. staff
57	Regt. staff	91	Lt. Abt.
58	Regt. staff		Regt. staff
59	Regt.	92	Lt. Abt.
60	Regt.		Regt. staff
61	Regt.	93	Lt. Abt.
62	Regt.		Regt. staff
63	Regt. staff	94	Lt. (mot.) Abt.
64	Regt.	95	Lt. Abt.
65	Regt. staff		Regt. staff
66	Regt.	96	Lt. Abt.
67	Regt.	97	Lt. Abt.
68	Regt.	98	Lt. (mot.) Abt.
69	Regt.		Regt. staff
..		99	Lt. (mot.) Abt.
71	Lt. Abt.		Regt. staff
72	Lt. (mot.) Abt.	100	Regt. staff
	Rly. regt.	101	Regt.
73	Lt. (mot.) Abt.	102	Regt. staff
74	Lt. Abt.		Balloon Abt.
	Regt. staff	103	Regt.
	S/L regt. staff	104	Regt. staff
75	Lt. Abt.	105	Regt. staff
76	Lt. (mot.) Abt.	106	Regt. staff
77	Lt. Abt.	..	
	Regt. staff	108	Regt. staff
78	Lt. Abt.	109	Regt. staff
	Regt. staff		S/L regt. staff
79	Regt.	110	Rly regt.
..		111	Hy. Abt.
81	Lt. (mot.) Abt.		Regt.

Flak.	Remarks.	Flak.	Remarks.
112	Abt.	142	Abt.
	Rly. regt.		Regt. staff
113	Regt.	143	Hy. Abt.
114	Abt. (Bttr.)	144	Lt. Abt.
115	Abt.	145	Abt.
116	Hy. Abt.	146	Abt.
117	Hy. Abt.	147	Abt.
118	Abt.	148	S/L Abt.
	Regt. staff	149	Regt. staff
..		..	
120	S/L Abt.	151	Abt.
	Regt. staff		Regt. staff
121	Abt.	152	Abt.
	Regt.		Regt. staff
122	Abt.	153	Abt.
	Rly. regt.		Regt. staff
123	Abt.	154	Abt.
	Regt. staff	155	Abt.
124	Abt.		Regt.
125	Abt.	156	Abt.
	Regt. staff	157	Hy. Abt.
126	Abt.	158	S/L Abt.
	Regt. staff	159	Rly. regt.
	Naval Abt.	160	S/L Abt.
127	Abt.		S/L regt.
..		161	Abt. (?)
129	Regt. staff		S/L regt.
130	S/L Abt.	162	Regt. staff
131	Abt. (mot.)	163	Hy. Abt.
132	Abt.		S/L Abt.
	Regt. staff	164	Abt.
133	Abt.		Regt. staff
	Regt. staff		Naval Abt.
134	Abt.	..	
	Regt. staff	166	Hy. Abt.
135	Regt. staff (Bttr.)	167	Hy. Abt.
136	Abt.	168	S/L Abt.
	Regt. staff	169	Abt.
137	Regt. staff	..	
138	S/L Abt.	..	
	Regt.	172	Abt.
..		..	
140	S/L Abt.	..	
141	Regt. (mot.)	..	

Flak	Remarks
..	
..	
..	
..	
180	Regt.
181	Abt.
	Regt. staff
182	Hy. Abt.
	Regt. staff
183	Abt.
..	
185	Abt. (7·5-cm.)
186	Abt. (7·5-cm.)
187	Abt.
..	
..	
190	Abt.
191	Abt.
192	Abt.
193	Abt.
194	Abt.
..	
196	Hy. Abt.
197	Hy. Abt.
..	
199	Abt.
200	Naval Abt.
201	Regt. staff
	Balloon Abt.
202	Abt.
	S/L regt.
	Balloon Abt.
203	Balloon Abt.
204	Naval Abt.
	Balloon Abt.
205	Balloon Abt.
206	Abt.
	Balloon Abt.
207	Abt.
208	Naval Abt.
209	Balloon Abt.
210	Balloon Abt.
211	Abt.
	Naval Abt.
212	Hy. Abt.
	Naval Abt.
..	
214	Naval Abt.
..	
216	Naval Abt.
..	
..	
219	Naval Abt.
220	S/L Abt.
221	Abt.
222	Abt.
	Naval Abt.
223	Abt.
224	Abt.
	Rly. Abt.
	Naval Abt.
225	Hy. Abt.
226	Abt.
	Naval Abt.
227	Rly. Abt.
..	
229	Regt. staff
230	Hy. Abt.
231	Regt. (mot.)
	Naval Abt.
232	Abt.
	Naval Abt.
233	Naval Abt.
234	Abt.
	Naval Abt.
235	Abt.
236	Abt.
	Naval Abt.
237	Abt.
..	
239	Naval Abt.
240	Naval Abt.
241	Regt.
	Naval Abt.
242	Abt.
	Naval Abt.
243	Hy. Abt.
244	Hy. Abt.

Flak	Remarks
245	Abt.
246	Abt.
	Naval Abt.
..	
..	
249	Abt.
..	
251	Abt.
252	Abt.
	S/L Abt.
	Naval Abt.
253	Abt.
254	Abt.
	Naval Abt.
255	Abt.
256	Abt.
257	Hy. Abt.
258	Abt.
259	S/L Abt.
260	S/L Abt.
261	Abt.
	Naval Abt.
262	Abt.
	Naval Abt.
263	Abt.
	Rly. Abt.
264	Hy. Abt.
	Naval Abt.
265	Hy. Abt.
266	Abt.
	Naval Abt.
267	Abt.
..	
269	S/L Abt.
..	
271	Hy. Abt.
	Army Abt.
272	Hy. Abt.
	Army Abt.
	Naval Abt.
273	Army Abt.
274	Army Abt.
	Naval Abt.
275	Army Abt.
276	Army (mot.) Abt.
277	Army (mot.) Abt.
278	Army Abt.
279	Army (mot.) Abt.
280	Abt.
	Army Abt.
	Naval Abt.
281	Hy. Abt.
	Army Abt.
282	Abt.
283	Abt.
	Army Abt.
284	Army Abt.
285	Abt.
286	Hy. Abt.
287	Hy. Abt.
288	Hy. Abt.
	Army Abt.
289	Army Abt.
290	Army Abt.
291	Regt. (mot.)
	Army Abt.
292	Abt.
	Army Abt.
293	Hy. Abt.
294	Abt.
	Naval Abt.
295	Hy. Abt.
296	Abt.
297	Abt.
298	S/L Abt.
299	S/L Abt.
	Army Abt.
300	S/L Abt.
301	Hy. Abt.
302	Abt.
	Army Abt.
303	Hy. Abt.
	Army Abt.
304	Hy. Abt.
	Army Abt.
305	Abt.
306	Abt.
..	

Flak.	Remarks.	Flak.	Remarks.
308	S/L Abt.	..	
	Regt.	..	
309	S/L Abt.	..	
310	S/L Abt.	351	Hy. Abt.
	Naval Abt.	352	Hy. Abt.
311	Hy. Abt.	353	Abt.
312	Army (mot.) Abt.	354	Abt.
313	Army (mot.) Abt.	355	Abt.
..		356	Hy. Abt.
315	Army Abt.	357	Hy. Abt. (9·4-cm.)
316	Abt.	..	
..		..	
..		360	Abt.
..		361	Abt.
..		362	Hy. Abt.
321	Hy. Abt.	363	Hy. Abt.
	Rly. Abt.	364	Abt.
322	Abt.	365	Hy. Abt.
323	Abt.	..	
..		..	
325	Abt.	368	S/L Abt.
..		369	S/L Abt.
327	Hy. Abt.	370	S/L Abt.
..		371	Abt.
329	S/L Abt.	372	Hy. Abt.
330	Abt.	373	Rly. Abt.
331	Abt.	374	Abt.
332	Hy. Abt.	375	Hy. Abt.
333	Abt.	376	Hy. Abt.
334	Hy. Abt.	..	
335	Regt.	..	
..		..	
..		..	
..		381	Abt.
..		382	Abt.
340	Abt.		Regt. staff
	S/L Abt.	383	Abt.
341	Abt.	384	Hy. Abt.
342	Abt.	385	Hy. Abt.
343	Hy. Abt.	386	Abt.
344	Abt.	387	Abt.
345	Abt.	..	
346	Hy. Abt.	..	
347	Abt.	..	

Flak.	Remarks.	Flak.	Remarks.
391	Abt.	431	Abt.
..			Regt.
393	Hy. Abt.	432	Abt.
394	Abt.	433	Hy. Abt.
395	Abt.	434	Abt.
396	Abt.	435	Hy. Abt.
397	Hy. Abt.	436	Abt.
..		..	
..		438	S/L Abt.
..		..	
401	Abt.	440	S/L Abt.
402	Abt.	441	Abt.
403	Hy. Abt.		Regt.
404	Abt.	442	Abt.
	Regt. staff	443	Hy. Abt.
405	Abt.	444	Abt.
406	Abt.	445	Abt.
407	Abt.	(446)	(Hy. Abt.)*
408	S/L Abt.	447	Abt.
409	S/L Abt.	448	S/L Abt.
410	S/L Abt.	449	S/L Abt.
411	Regt. (mot.)	450	S/L Abt. ?
412	Hy. Abt.	(451)	(Hy. Abt.)†
..		452	Hy. Abt.
414	Hy. Abt.	453	Hy. Abt.
415	Lt. Abt.	454	Abt.
416	Rly. Abt.	455	Abt.
..		456	Abt.
..		457	Abt.
419	Abt. (?)	458	S/L Abt.
..		..	
421	Hy. Abt.	..	
422	Abt.	461	Abt.
423	Abt.	462	Hy. Abt.
424	Rly. Abt.		Rly. Abt.
425	Hy. Abt.	463	Abt.
426	Hy. Abt.	464	Abt.
427	Hy. Abt.	465	Hy. Abt.
428	Hy. Abt.	466	Abt.
..		467	Hy. Abt.
..		..	

* Renumbered II/Regt. 37.
† Renumbered 945 (Lt. Abt.).

Flak.	Remarks.
469	S/L Abt.
..	
471	Hy. Abt.
..	
473	Rly. Abt.
..	
475	Hy. Abt.
..	
..	
..	
..	
..	
481	Abt.
..	
..	
..	
..	
..	
487	Abt.
..	
..	
..	
491	Regt.
..	
493	Abt.
494	Abt.
495	Abt.
496	Hy. Abt.
497	Hy. Abt.
..	
..	
..	
501	Regt. (mot.)
502	Hy. Abt.
503	Hy. Abt.
504	Abt.
	Regt. staff
505	Abt. (ferries)
506	Lt. Abt.
507	Lt. Abt.
..	
509	S/L Abt.
..	
511	Abt.
	Naval Abt.
512	Abt.
513	Hy. Abt.
(514)	(Abt.)*
515	Hy. Abt.
516	Abt.
517	Abt.
..	
519	S/L Abt.
520	S/L Abt.
	Naval Abt.
521	Abt.
522	Hy. Abt.
	Regt. staff
523	Hy. Abt.
524	Abt.
(525)	(Hy. Abt.)†
526	Abt.
527	Hy. Abt.
528	Abt. ?
529	S/L Abt.
530	Naval Abt.
..	
532	Abt.
..	
534	Hy. Abt.
..	
..	
..	
538	Abt.
	Rly. Abt.
..	
..	
541	Abt.
542	Abt.
543	Abt.
544	Hy. Abt.
545	Hy. Abt.

* Renumbered I Regt. 8 (mot.).
† Renumbered II Regt. 52.

Flak.	Remarks.
546	Hy. Abt.
547	Hy. Abt.
548	Hy. Abt.
..	
550	Hy. Abt.
..	
..	
..	
..	
..	
..	
..	
..	
..	
..	
..	
..	
563	Abt.
..	
..	
..	
567	Abt.
..	
569	Abt.
..	
..	
..	
573	Hy. Abt.
574	Hy. Abt.
575	Hy. Abt.
..	
..	
..	
..	
..	
..	
582	Abt. S/L Abt.
..	
..	
585	S/L Abt.
..	
..	
..	
..	
..	
591	Abt.
592	Hy. Abt.
593	Hy. Abt.
594	Abt.
..	
596	Abt.
597	Abt.
..	
..	
..	
601	Hy. Abt. (10·5 cm.)
602	Abt.
603	Hy. Abt.
604	Regt.
605	Abt.
606	Abt.
607	Abt.
608	S/L Abt.
609	S/L Abt.
..	
611	Regt. (mot.)
612	Abt.
613	Abt.
614	Abt.
615	Hy. Abt.
616	Hy. Abt.
617	Hy. Abt.
618	S/L Abt.
..	
620	S/L Abt.
..	
622	Abt. ?
..	
..	
..	
..	
..	
628	Hy. Abt.
629	Regt.
..	
..	

Flak.	Remarks.
632	Hy. Abt.
..	
634	Hy. Abt.
..	
..	
..	
638	Hy. Abt.
..	
..	
641	Hy. Abt.
642	Hy. Abt.
643	Abt.
644	Hy. Abt.
645	Abt.
646	Hy. Abt.
..	
648	S/L Abt.
649	S/L Abt.
650	Abt.
..	
652	Regt. staff
653	Regt. staff
654	Regt. staff
655	Regt. staff
656	Regt. staff
657	Regt. staff
..	
..	
660	Hy. Abt.
661	Hy. Abt.
662	Hy. Abt.
..	
..	
665	Abt.
..	
667	Lt. Abt.
668	Lt. Abt. S/L Abt.
..	
670	Abt.
671	Abt.
672	Abt.
673	Lt. Abt.
674	Abt.
675	Abt.
676	Abt.
677	Hy. Abt.
678	Abt.
679	Lt. Abt.
680	Lt. Abt.
681	Abt.
682	Abt.
683	Abt.
684	Abt.
685	Abt.
686	S/L Abt.
687	Lt. Abt.
688	Hy. Abt.
689	Lt. Abt.
690	Abt.
691	Lt. Abt. Rly. Abt.
692	Abt.
693	Hy. Abt.
694	Abt.
695	Abt.
696	Naval Abt.
..	
..	
..	
..	
701	Regt. Naval Abt.
702	Abt. Naval Abt.
703	(Hy. Abt.)* Naval Abt.
704	Regt. Naval Abt.
705	Hy. Abt. Naval Abt.
706	Hy. Abt.
707	Hy. Abt.
708	S/L Abt. Naval Abt.

* Renumbered 372 (Hy. Abt.).

Flak.	Remarks.	Flak.	Remarks.
..		..	
710	Naval Abt.	750	Lt. Abt.
711	Abt.	751	Lt. Abt.
	Naval Abt.	752	Lt. Abt. (5 cm.)
712	Abt.	753	Lt. Abt.
713	Lt. Abt.	754	Lt. Abt.
..		755	Abt.
715	Lt. Abt.	756	Lt. Abt.
..		757	Abt.
717	Lt Abt.	758	Lt. Abt.
..		..	
..		..	
720	Lt. Abt.	761	Lt. Abt. (mot.)
	Naval Abt.	762	Lt. Abt.
..		763	Lt. Abt.
(722)	(Lt. Abt.)*	764	Lt. Abt.
723	Lt. Abt.	765	Abt.
724	Lt. Abt.	..	
725	Lt. Abt.	767	Lt. Abt.
726	Lt. Abt.	768	Lt. Abt.
727	Lt. Abt.	769	Lt. Abt.
..		..	
729	Lt. Abt.	..	
730	Abt.	772	Lt. Abt.
731	Lt. (5-cm.) Abt.	773	Lt. Abt.
732	Lt. Abt.	774	Lt. Abt.
733	Lt. Abt. ?	775	Lt. Abt.
734	Lt. Abt.	..	
735	Lt. Abt.	777	Lt. Abt.
736	Lt. Abt.	..	
737	Lt. Abt.	..	
738	Lt. Abt.	..	
739	Lt. Abt.	781	Lt. Abt.
740	Lt. Abt.	782	Hy. Abt.
741	Lt. Abt. (mot.)	..	
742	Lt. Abt.	..	
..		785	Lt. Abt.
744	Lt. Abt.	..	
745	Lt. Abt.	..	
746	Abt.	..	
747	Lt. Abt.	..	
748	Abt.	..	

* Disbanded.

Flak	Remarks	Flak	Remarks
..		824	Lt. Abt.
..		825	Rly. lt. Abt.
793	Abt.	826	Lt. Abt.
..		..	
..		828	Lt. Abt.
..		829	Lt. Abt.
797	Abt.	830	Lt. Abt.
..		831	Lt. Abt.
..		832	Abt.
..		833	Abt.
801	Abt.	..	
802	Abt.	835	Lt. Abt.
	Naval Abt.	..	
803	Naval Abt.	837	Lt. Abt.
804	Abt. (9·4 cm.	838	Lt. Abt.
	4 cm.)	839	Lt. Abt.
	Naval Abt.	..	
805	Hy. Abt.	841	Lt. Abt. (mot.,
	Naval Abt.		Bttr.)
806	Hy. Abt.	842	Lt. Abt.
	Naval Abt.	..	
807	Naval Abt.	844	Lt. Abt.
808	S/L Abt.	845	Lt. Abt.
	Naval Abt.	846	Lt. Abt.
809	S/L Abt.	847	Lt. Abt.
	Naval Abt.	(848	(Hy. Abt.)*
810	Naval Abt.	849	Lt. Abt.
811	Naval Abt.	850	Lt. Abt.
812	Naval Abt.	851	Lt. (mot.) Abt.
813	Abt.	852	Lt. Abt.
	Naval Abt.	853	Lt. Abt.
..		854	Abt.
815	Abt.	..	
..		856	Lt. Abt.
817	Naval Abt.	..	
..		858	Abt.
..		..	
820	Naval Abt.?	860	Lt. Abt.
..			Rly. lt. Abt.
822	Lt. Abt.	861	Lt. (mot.) Abt.
	Rly. Abt.	862	Lt. Abt.
823	Lt. Abt.	863	Lt. Abt.

* Renumbered 534 (Hy. bty.).

Flak	Remarks
864	Rly. lt. Abt.
865	Rly. lt. Abt.
..	
..	
..	
..	
..	
871	Lt. Abt.
872	Lt. Abt.
873	Lt. Abt.
874	Lt. Abt.
875	Lt. Abt.
876	Lt. Abt.
..	
878	Abt.
879	Lt. Abt.
..	
..	
..	
..	
..	
885	Lt. Abt.
..	
..	
..	
889	Lt. Abt.
..	
891	Lt. Abt.
..	
..	
..	
..	
..	
..	
..	
..	
..	
901	Abt.
902	Abt.
	Rly hy. Abt. (10·5 cm.)
903	Abt.
904	Abt.
905	Abt.
..	
..	
..	
909	S/L Abt.
..	
911	Lt. Abt.
	Regt. staff
912	Lt. Abt.
913	Lt. Abt.
914	Lt. Abt.
..	
..	
..	
..	
..	
..	
921	Lt. Abt.
922	Lt. Abt.
923	Lt. Abt.
..	
925	Lt. Abt.
..	
..	
928	Abt.
..	
..	
931	Lt. Abt.
932	Lt. Abt.
933	Lt. Abt.
..	
..	
..	
..	
..	
..	
..	
941	Lt. Abt.
942	Lt. Abt.
..	
..	
945	Lt. Abt.
..	
..	
..	

Flak.	Remarks.	Flak.	Remarks.
..		..	
..		..	
951	Lt. Abt.	..	
952	Lt. Abt.	978	Lt. Abt.
953	Lt. Abt.	979	Lt. Abt.
954	Lt. Abt.	980	Lt. Abt.
..		..	
956	Lt. Abt.	982	Lt. Abt.
..		983	Lt. Abt.
..		984	Lt. Abt.
959	Abt.	985	Lt. (4 cm.) Abt.
..		..	
..		..	
..		988	Lt. Abt.
..		..	
..		990	Lt. Abt.
..		991	Lt. Abt.
..		992	Lt. Abt.
..		993	Lt. Abt.
..		994	Lt. Abt.
..		995	Lt. Abt.
..		996	Lt. Abt.
..		997	Lt. Abt.
..		998	Lt. Abt.
..		999	Lt. Abt.
..		..	

Also Heeresflak-Lehrabteilung and Flak-Lehrregiment (Batteries I–III).

(*g*) ARTILLERY OBSERVATION ABTEILUNGEN AND BATTERIEN

(*Beobachtungsabteilungen, Panzerbeobachtungsbatterien*)

B.Abt.	Allotted to	B.Abt.	Allotted to
1	G.H.Q. Tps.	28	G.H.Q. Tps.
2	G.H.Q. Tps.	29	G.H.Q. Tps.
3	G.H.Q. Tps.	30	G.H.Q. Tps.
4	G.H.Q. Tps.	31	G.H.Q. Tps.
5	G.H.Q. Tps.	32	G.H.Q. Tps.
6	G.H.Q. Tps.	33	G.H.Q. Tps.
7	G.H.Q. Tps.	34	G.H.Q. Tps.
8	G.H.Q. Tps.	35	G.H.Q. Tps.
9	G.H.Q. Tps.	36	G.H.Q. Tps.
10	G.H.Q. Tps.	37	G.H.Q. Tps.
11	G.H.Q. Tps.	Geb. 38	G.H.Q. Tps.
12	G.H.Q. Tps.	40	G.H.Q. Tps.
13	G.H.Q. Tps.	41	G.H.Q. Tps.
14	G.H.Q. Tps.	44	G.H.Q. Tps.
15	G.H.Q. Tps.	54	G.H.Q. Tps.
Pz. ? 16	G.H.Q. Tps.	59	G.H.Q. Tps.
17	G.H.Q. Tps.	70	G.H.Q. Tps.
18	G.H.Q. Tps.	71	G.H.Q. Tps.
19	G.H.Q. Tps.	501	G.H.Q. Tps.
Pz. ? 20	G.H.Q. Tps.	531	G.H.Q. Tps.
21	G.H.Q. Tps.	532	G.H.Q. Tps.
22	G.H.Q. Tps.	555	G.H.Q. Tps.
23	G.H.Q. Tps.	556	G.H.Q. Tps.
24	G.H.Q. Tps.	616	G.H.Q. Tps.
25	G.H.Q. Tps.	617	G.H.Q. Tps.
26	G.H.Q. Tps.	625	G.H.Q. Tps.
27	G.H.Q. Tps.	642	G.H.Q. Tps.

Pz.Bb.*	Allotted to	Pz.Bb.*	Allotted to
320	2 Pz. Div.		
321			
322	10 Pz. Div.	333	
323			
324	4 Pz. Div.	335	20 Pz. Div.
325	7 Pz. Div.		
326*	15 Pz. Div.	337	
327	3 Pz. Div.		
328		339	

* Some, if not all, *Panzer Beobachtungsbatterien* have been incorporated in Artillery regiments of the Panzer divisions, *e.g.*, *Panzer Beobachtungsbatterie* 326 renumbered *Panzer Beobachtungsbatterie* 33, now found in Artillery Regiment 33.

(*r*) MINOR DIVISIONAL UNITS

(Divisional services, first line reinforcement battalion, field post office, medical and military police units all carry the same number; *see* pp. C 13–15 above.)

No.	In Div.	No.	In Div.	No.	In Div.	No.	In Div.
1	1 Inf.	..		..		114	114 Jäg.
2	12 Pz.	..		..		..	
3	3 Pz.Gr.	40	24 Pz.	..		..	
4	14 Pz.	..		..		117	117 Jäg.
5	5 Jäg.	..		..		118	118 Jäg.
6	6 Inf.	..		81	1 Pz.	..	
7	7 Inf.	44	44 Inf.	82	2 Pz.	..	
8	8 Jäg.	45	45 Inf.	83	3 Pz.	121	121 Inf.
9	9 Inf.	46	46 Inf.	84	4 Pz.	122	122 Inf.
10	10 Pz.Gr.	..		85	5 Pz.	123	123 Inf.
11	11 Inf.	..		..		..	
12	12 Inf.	..		87?	25 Pz.?	125	125 Inf.
13	13 Pz.	..		88	18 Pz.	126	126 Inf.
14	14 Pz.Gr.	..		..		..	
15	15 Inf.	..		90	10 Pz.	128	23 Pz.
16	16 Pz.	..		91	6 Mtn.	129	129 Inf.
17	17 Inf.	54	1 Mtn.	92	20 Pz.	..	
18	18 Pz.Gr.	..		93	26 Pz.	131	131 Inf.
19	19 Pz.	..		94	4 Mtn.	132	132 Inf.
20	20 Pz.Gr.	57	6 Pz.	95	5 Mtn.	..	
21	21 Inf.	58	7 Pz.	..		134	134 Inf.
22	22 L.L.	59	8 Pz.	97	97 Jäg.	..	
	mot.	60	9 Pz.	..		..	
23	23 Inf.	61	11 Pz.	99	7 Mtn.	137	137 Inf.
24	24 Inf.	..		100	100 Jäg.	138	38 Inf.
25	25 Pz.Gr.	..		101	101 Jäg.	139	39 Inf.
26	26 Inf.	..		102	102 Inf.	140	22 Pz.
27	17 Pz.	..		..		..	
28	28 Jäg.	66	16 Pz.Gr.	104	104 Jäg.	..	
29	29 Pz.Gr.	67	2 Mtn.	..		..	
30	30 Inf.	68	3 Mtn.	106	106 Inf.	..	
31	31 Inf.	..		..		..	
32	32 Inf.	..		..		..	
33	15 Pz.Gr.	..		..		..	
34	34 Inf.	..		110	110 Inf.	..	
35	35 Inf.	..		111	111 Inf.	..	
36	36 Pz.Gr.	..		112	112 Inf.	150	50 Inf.
..		..		113	113 Inf.	..	

No.	In Div.	No.	In Div.	No.	In Div.	No.	In Div.
152	52 Inf.	..		..		*(272)*	
..		193	93 Inf.	233	196 Inf.	*(273)*	
154	154 Res.	194	94 Inf.	234	163 Inf.	..	
..		195	95 Inf.	235	198 Inf.	..	
156	56 Inf.	196	96 Inf.	236	162 Inf.	*(276*	*276 Inf.*)*
157	57 Inf.	..		..		*(277*	*277 Inf.*)*
158	58 Inf.	198	98 Inf.	238	167 Inf.	..	
..		199	199 Inf.	*(239*	*239 Inf.*)*	..	
160	60 Pz.Gr.	200	21 Pz.	240	170 Inf.	..	
161	61 Inf.	..		241	161 Inf.	..	
162	62 Inf.	..		..		282	282 Inf.
..		..		..		..	
..		..		..		..	
165	65 Inf.	205	205 Inf.	..		..	
..		206	206 Inf.	246	246 Inf.	..	
..		207	207 Sich.	..		..	
168	68 Inf.	208	208 Inf.	248	168 Inf.	..	
169	69 Inf.	*(209*	*209 Inf.*)*	..		..	
..		..		..		290	290 Inf.
171	71 Inf.	211	211 Inf.	251	251 Inf.	291	291 Inf.
172	72 Inf.	212	212 Inf.	252	252 Inf.	292	292 Inf.
173	73 Inf.	213	213 Sich.	253	253 Inf.	293	293 Inf.
..		214	214 Inf.	254	254 Inf.	294	294 Inf.
175	75 Inf.	215	215 Inf.	255	255 Inf.	295	295 Inf.
176	76 Inf.	216	216 Inf.	256	256 Inf.	296	296 Inf.
..		217	217 Inf.	257	257 Inf.	297	297 Inf.
178	78 Inf.	218	218 Inf.	258	258 Inf.	298	298 Inf.
179	79 Inf.	219	183 Inf.	..		299	299 Inf.
..		220	164 Pz.Gr.	260	260 Inf.	300	S.S. Polizei†
181	81 Inf.	221	221 Sich.	..		..	
182	82 Inf.	222	181 Inf.	262	262 Inf.	302	302 Inf.
183	83 Inf.	223	223 Inf.	263	263 Inf.	..	
..		..		264	264 Inf.	304	304 Inf.
..		225	225 Inf.	..		305	305 Inf.
186	86 Inf.	..		..		306	306 Inf.
187	87 Inf.	227	227 Inf.	267	267 Inf.	*(307*	*307 Inf.*)*
188	88 Inf.	*(228*	*228 Inf.*)*	268	268 Inf.	..	
..		229	197 Inf.	269	269 Inf.	..	
190	90 Pz.Gr.	230	169 Inf.	270	270 Inf.	*(310*	*310 Inf.*)*
..		*(231*	*231 Inf.*)*	*(271)*			

* Division now disbanded ; some units may still exist, under the same number (*e.g.*, as G.H.Q. tps., *Heerestruppen*).

† Services only carry this number.

No.	In Div.
(*311*	*311 Inf.**)
..	
..	
..	
..	
..	
(*317*	*317 Inf.**)
..	
319	319 Inf.
320	320 Inf.
321	321 Inf.
..	
323	323 Inf.
..	
..	
326	326 Inf.
327	327 Inf.
328	328 Inf.
329	329 Inf.
330	330 Inf.
331	331 Inf.
332	332 Inf.
333	333 Inf.
334	334 Inf.
335	335 Inf.
336	336 Inf.
337	337 Inf.
338	338 Inf.
339	339 Inf.
340	340 Inf.
(*341*	*341 Inf.**)
342	342 Inf.
343	343 Inf.
344	344 Inf.
..	
..	
347	347 Inf.
..	
..	
..	

No.	In Div.
(*351*	*351 Inf.**)
..	
..	
..	
..	
356	356 Inf.
..	
(*358*	*358 Inf.**)
..	
..	
..	
..	
..	
..	
(*365*	*365 Inf.*†)
..	
..	
..	
369	369 Inf. †
370	370 Inf.
371	371 Inf.
(*372*	*372 Inf.**)
373	373 Inf†.
..	
..	
376	376 Inf.
377	377 Inf.
..	
(*379*	*379 Inf.**)
..	
..	
..	
383	383 Inf.
384	384 Inf.
385	385 Inf.
..	
387	387 Inf.
..	
389	389 Inf.
..	

No.	In Div.
..	
..	
(*393*	*393 Inf.**)
..	
(*395*	*395 Inf.**)
..	
..	
..	
(*399*	*399 Inf.**)
400	Gross-deutsch-land
466?	416 Inf. Div.?
..	
..	
..	
..	
..	
..	
..	
..	
..	
..	
..	
..	
..	
..	
..	
..	
..	
..	
..	
..	
..	
..	
..	
(*554*	*554 Inf.**)
(*555*	*555 Inf.**)
(*556*	*556 Inf.**)

No.	In Div.
(*557*	*557 Inf.**)
..	
..	
..	
..	
..	
..	
..	
..	
..	
..	
..	
..	
..	
..	
702	702 Inf.
..	
..	
..	
..	
707	707 Inf.
708	708 Inf.
709	709 Inf.
710	710 Inf.
711	711 Inf.
712	712 Inf.
713	713 Inf.
..	
715	715 Inf.
716	716 Inf.
..	
..	
719	719 Inf.
..	
..	
..	
..	
..	
(*999*	*999 Jäg.**)

* Division now disbanded ; some units may still exist, under the same number (*e.g.*, as G.H.Q. tps., *Heerestruppen*).

† Croatian.

PART M—VOCABULARY AND ABBREVIATIONS

(*a*) VOCABULARY AND ABBREVIATIONS

The German practice of forming abbreviations is extremely flexible, and uniformity in abbreviation is not considered of importance so long as the meaning is readily intelligible from the context. In consequence, the same term may be abbreviated differently under various circumstances, often in the same document. Thus, for example, Abteilung may appear as A., Abt., or Abtlg.; Artillerie as A., Art., or Artl., etc.

The following list includes the abbreviations used in this book plus a number of others commonly encountered in order of battle material. For a complete list of abbreviations, see *Vocabulary of German Military Terms and Abbreviations* (April, 1943).

Abbreviation.	*German.*	*English Equivalent.*
A.	Abteilung	Unit, battery, battalion, department.
A.A.	Aufklärungs-Abteilung	Reconnaissance unit.
A.Bekl.Amt.	Armee-Bekleidungs-Amt	Army clothing depot.
A.Briefstelle	Armee-Briefstelle	Army postal station.
Abt., Abtl.	Abteilung	Unit, battery, battalion, department.
Abw.	Abwehr	Intelligence.
A.E.R.	Artillerie-Ersatz-Regiment	Artillery depot regiment.
A.Feldlaz.	Armee-Feldlazarett	Army field hospital
A.H.A.	Allgemeines Heeresamt	General Army Directorate.
A.H.M.	Allgemeine Heeresmitteilungen.	General army orders (A.C.Is.)
A.K.	Armeekorps	Infantry corps.
A.Kartenstelle	Armee-Kartenstelle	Army map depot.
A.K.P.	Armee-Kraftfahr-Park	Army M.T. park.
A.N.Pk.	Armee-Nachrichten-Park	Army signals equipment park.
A.N.R.	Armee-Nachrichten-Regiment.	Army signals regiment.
A.O.K.	Armee-Oberkommando	Army (H.Q.).
A.Pf.Laz.	Armee-Pferde-Lazarett	Army veterinary hospital.
A.Pf.Pk.	Armee-Pferde-Park	Army horse park.
A.R.	Artillerie-Regiment	Artillery regiment.
Arfü	Artillerie-Führer	O.C. divisional artillery regiment.
Arko	Artillerie-Kommandeur	Artillery commander from G.H.Q. pool.

Abbreviation.	*German.*	*English Equivalent.*
Art.Lehr-Rgt. ..	Artillerie-Lehr-Regiment	Artillery demonstration regiment.
Art.Pk.	Artillerie-Park	Artillery equipment park.
A.San.Abt. ..	Armee-Sanitäts-Abteilung	Army medical unit.
A.San.Pk. ..	Armee-Sanitäts-Park ..	Army medical stores park.
Astr.Mess-Zug ..	Astronomischer-Mess-Zug	Astronomical survey section.
Aufkl.Abt. ..	Aufklärungs-Abteilung ..	Reconnaissance unit.
Aufkl.u.Kav Abt.	Aufklärungs- und Kavallerie Abteilung.	Reconnaissance and cavalry demonstration unit.
Ausb.Btl. ..	Ausbildungs-Bataillon ..	Training battalion.
Ausb.Div. ..	Ausbildungs-Division ..	Training division.
A.V.A.	Armee-Verwaltungs-Amt	Army administration office.
A.Verpfl.A. ..	Armee-Verpflegungs-Amt	Army rations office.
A.Vet.Pk. ..	Armee-Veterinär-Park ..	Army veterinary stores park.
Bäck.Kp. ..	Bäckerei-Kompanie ..	Bakery company.
Bahnhofs-Kdtr.	Bahnhofs-Kommandantur	Railway station command.
Batl.	Bataillon	Battalion.
Batt(r).	Batterie	Troop (artillery).
Bau-Btl. ..	Bau-Bataillon	Construction battalion.
B.Battr. ..	Beobachtungs-Batterie ..	Survey troop.
B.d.E.	Befehlshaber des Ersatzheeres.	C.-in-C., Training Command.
Beob.	Beobachtungs-	Observation; survey (artillery).
Betr.St.Kol. ..	Betriebsstoff-Kolonne ..	P.O.L. column.
Betr.St.Verw.Kp.	Betriebsstoff-Verwaltungs-Kompanie.	P.O.L. administration company.
Bewährungs-Btl.	Bewährungs-Bataillon ..	Rehabilitation battalion.
Bfh.	Befehlshaber	Commander.
Brandenburg z.b.V.800.	Brandenburg zur besonderen Verwendung 800.	Brandenburg formation of divisional status.
Br.Baubtl. ..	Brücken-Baubataillon ..	Bridge building battalion.
Brig.	Brigade	Brigade.
Brü.B.Btl. ..	Brücken-Baubataillon ..	Bridge building battalion.
Brüko	Brückenkolonne	Bridging column.
Btl.	Bataillon.	Battalion.

Abbreviation.	*German.*	*English Equivalent.*
Ch.H.Rü.u.B.d.E.	Chef der Heeresrüstung und Befehlshaber des Ersatzheeres.	Chief of Army Equipment and Commander of the Replacement Training Army (C.-in-C., Training Command).
Dulag	Durchgangslager ..	P.W. transit camp.
Eisb.Art. ..	Eisenbahn-Artillerie ..	Railway artillery.
Eisb.Baubtl. ..	Eisenbahn-Baubataillon..	Railway construction battalion.
Eisb.Baukp. ..	Eisenbahn-Baukompanie	Railway construction company.
Eisb.Betr.Kp. ..	Eisenbahn-Betriebs-Kompanie.	Railway operating company.
Eisb.Fsp.Kp. ..	Eisenbahn - Fernsprech - Kompanie.	Railway telephone company.
Eisb.Küchenwg. Abt.	Eisenbahn-Küchenwagen-Abteilung.	Railway kitchen car unit.
Eisb.Nachr.Abt.	Eisenbahn - Nachrichten - Abteilung.	Railway signals battalion.
Eisb.Pi.Baubtl.	Eisenbahn - Pionier - Bau - kompanie.	Railway engineer construction company.
Eisb.Pi.Pk. ..	Eisenbahn-Pionier-Park..	Railway engineer equipment park.
Eisb.Pi.Rgt. ..	Eisenbahn - Pionier - Regiment.	Railway engineer regiment.
Eisb.Pi.St.z.b.V.	Eisenbahn - Pionier - Stab zur besonderen Verwendung.	Special railway engineer staff.
Eisb.Pz.Zug. ..	Eisenbahn-Panzer-Zug ..	Armoured train.
Entg.Abt. ..	Entgiftungs-Abteilung ..	Decontamination battalion.
Entl.St. ..	Entlade-Stab	Unloading staff.
Erg.	Ergänzungs-	Reserve, supplementary.
Ers.	Ersatz	Training, depot, reinforcement.
Ers.Teillag. ..	Ersatz-Teillager	Spare parts depot.
Feldbahnkp. ..	Feldbahn-Kompanie ..	Field railway company.
Feldeisb.Betr.Abt.	Feldeisenbahn-Betriebs-Abteilung.	Field railway operating unit.
Feldeisb.Dir. ..	Feldeisenbahn-Direktion	(*see* Feldeisb.Kdo.)
Feldeisb.Masch. Abt.	Feldeisenbahn-Maschinen-Abteilung.	Field railway machine unit.

Abbreviation.	*German.*	*English Equivalent.*
Feldeisb.Nachsch. Lag.	Feldeisenbahn-Nachschub-Lager.	Field railway supply depot.
Feldeisb.Kdo. ..	Feldeisenbahn-Kommando	Field railway command.
Feldeisb.Werkst. Abt.	Feldeisenbahn-Werkstatt-Abteilung.	Field railway workshop unit.
Feldgend.Tr. ..	Feldgendarmerie-Trupp	Military police detachment.
Feldlaz	Feldlazarett	Field hospital.
Feldnachr.Kdtr.	Feldnachrichten - Kommandantur.	Field signals command.
Feldschalt-Abt. z.b.V.	Feldschalt-Abteilung ..	Special signals relay unit.
Feld-Sd.Btl. ..	Feld-Sonder-Bataillon ..	Special penal battalion.
Feld-Wasser-Str. R.Abt.	Feld - Wasser - Strassen - Räum Abteilung.	Waterways clearing battalion.
Feldwerkst. ..	Feldwerkstatt	Field workshop (ordnance).
Fernkab.Bau-Abt.	Fernkabel - Bau - Abteilung	Trunk-line telegraph construction company.
Fernschreibkp. ..	Fernschreibkompanie ..	Teleprint company
Fest.-	Festungs-	(*See* Fstgs.)
Feste-Nachr.Stelle	Feste-Nachrichten-Stelle	Static signals station
F.G.A.	Feldgendarmerie-Abteilung	Military police battalion.
Filmtr.	Filmtrupp	Film section.
Filterkol. ..	Filterkolonne	(*See* Wass.Vers.Kp.)
F.K.	Feldkommandantur ..	Administrative H.Q. in occupied countries (regimental status).
F.Kol.	Fahrkolonne	Horse-drawn supply column.
Fla-Btl. ..	Flugabwehr-Bataillon ..	A.A. battalion (army) (20 and 37-mm. guns).
Fla-Kp. ..	Flugabwehr-Kompanie ..	A.A. company (army)
Flak-Abt. ..	Flak-Abteilung	G.A.F. A.A. battalion.
Flak-Battr.z.b.V.	Flak-Batterie zur besonderen Verwendung.	Independent G.A.F. A.A. troops.
Flak-Div. ..	Flak-Division	G.A.F. A.A. division.
Flak-Korps ..	Flak-Korps	G.A.F. A.A. corps.
Flak-Rgt. ..	Flak-Regiment	G.A.F. A.A. regiment.

Abbreviation.	*German.*	*English Equivalent.*
Flieger Div. ..	Flieger Division	G.A.F. division H.Q.
Flieger Korps ..	Flieger Korps	G.A.F. corps H.Q.
Flivo.	Fliegerverbindungsoffizier	Air liaison officer with army.
F.N.K.	Feldnachrichtenkommandantur.	Field signals H.Q.
F.P.A.	Feldpostamt	Field post office.
F.P.N.	Feldpostnummer ..	Field post number.
Frontstalag ..	Frontstammlager ..	Forward P.W. camp
F.S.(Art.Rgt.) (Nachr.Kp.). etc.	Fallschirm - (Artillerie-Regiment) -(Nachrichten-Kompanie), etc.	Parachute (artillery regiment) (signals company), etc.
Fsp.Baukp. ..	Fernsprech-Baukompanie	Telephone construction company.
Fsp.Betr.Kp. ..	Fernsprech-Betriebs-Kompanie.	Telephone operating company.
F.Staffel ..	Flieger-Staffel	Flying unit of about nine aircraft.
Fstgs.Baubtl. ..	Festungs-Baubataillon ..	Fortress construction battalion.
Fstgs.Btl. ..	Festungs-Bataillon ..	Fortress battalion.
Fstgs.Nachr.Kdtr.	Festungs-Nachrichten-Kommandantur.	Fortress signals command.
Fstgs.Pi.Abschn. Gr.	Festungs - Pionier-Abschnitt-Gruppe.	Fortress engineer sector group.
Fstgs.Pi.Kdr. ..	Festungs - Pionier-Kommandeur.	Fortress engineer commander.
Fstgs.Pi.Pk. ..	Festungs-Pionier Park ..	Fortress engineer park.
Fstgs.Pi.St. ..	Festungs-Pionier-Stab ..	Fortress engineer staff.
Fstgs.Rgt. ..	Festungs-Regiment ..	Fortress regiment.
Fü	Führer	Leader, commander
Fu.Eins.Tr. ..	Funk-Einsatz-Trupp ..	W/T demolition platoon.
Fu.Kp.(O.K.H.)	Funk-Kompanie (O.K.H.)	W/T company (O.K.H.).
Fu.(Tr.) ..	Funk (trupp)	W/T (section).
Führ.Begl.Btl. ..	Führer - Begleit - Bataillon	Führer's escort battalion.
Führ.Nachr.Rgt.	Führungs - Nachrichten Regiment.	Operational signals regiment.
Fu.Überw.Kp. ..	Funk - Überwachungs-Kompanie.	W/T control company
Fz.Btl.	Feldzeug-Bataillon ..	Ordnance battalion
Fz.Kdo. ..	Feldzeug-Kommando ..	Ordnance H.Q.
Fz.St.	Feldzeug-Stab	Ordnance staff.

Abbreviation.	*German.*	*English Equivalent.*
Gassch.Ger.Pk. . .	Gasschutz-Gërate-Park . .	Anti-gas equipment park.
Geb.(J.R.) . .	Gebirgs-Jäger-Regiment. .	Mountain rifle regiment.
Geb.Werf.Abt. . .	Gebirgs-Werfer-Abteilung	Mountain projector battalion.
Gen.Kdo. . .	Generalkommando . .	Army corps (H.Q.)
G.F.P.	Geheime Feldpolizei . .	Field Security Police
Gr.	Gruppe	Section, group, G.A.F. operational unit.
Gr., Gren. . .	Grenadier	Infantryman.
G.R.	Grenadier-Regiment . .	Infantry regiment.
gr.H.Bau-Dienststelle.	grosse Heeres-Bau-Dienststelle.	Main army works office.
gr.(Kw.Kol) . .	grosse (Kraftwagen-Kolonne).	Heavy (M.T. column).
gr.Kw.Kol.f. Wass.Trsp.	grosse Kraftwagenkolonne für Wasser-Transport.	(*See* Wass.Vers.Kp.)
Gr.W.	Granatwerfer	Mortar.
Grz.Sch.Abschn. Kdo.	Grenz-Schutz-Abschnitt-Kommando.	Frontier sector defence command.
Grz.Wa. . .	Grenzwacht	Frontier guards.
Haupt-Verb. (or Verb.) Stab.	Haupt-Verbinde (or Verbinde) Stab.	Signals (?) liaison staff.
H.Betreungsabt.	Heeres-Betreungs-Abteilung.	Army welfare battalion.
H.Flak.Abt. . .	Heeres-Flak-Abteilung . .	Army anti-aircraft battalion.
H.Flak-Lehr-Abt.	Heeres-Flak-Lehr-Abteilung.	Army A.A. demonstration battalion.
H.Fz.Pk. . .	Heeres-Feldzeug-Park . .	Army ordnance park.
H.Ger.Pk. . .	Heergeräte-Park	H.T. equipment park.
H.Gr.	Heeresgruppe	Army group.
H.J.G.Kp. . .	Heeres-Infanterie-Geschütz-Kompanie.	Army infantry gun company.
H.K.A.	Heeresküstenartillerie . .	Army C.D. artillery.
H.Kf.Bez. . .	Heeres-Kraftfahr-Bezirk	Military M.T. area.
H.K.P.	Heeres-Kraftfahrpark . .	Army M.T. park.
H.Nachr.Rgt. . .	Heeres-Nachrichten-Regiment.	Army signal regiment.
H.Nachsch.Tr. Sch.	Heeres - Nachschubtruppen-Schule.	Army supply troops school.
Höh.Kdo. z.b.V.	Höheres Kommando zur besonderen Verwendung.	Corps H.Q., lower establishment.
Horchkp. . .	Horch-Kompanie . .	Intercept company.
H.Stelle . .	Horch-Stelle	Listening station.
H.Verpfl.Amt . .	Heeres-Verpflegungs-Amt	Army rations office.

Abbreviation.	*German.*	*English Equivalent.*
I.D. (J.D.) ..	Infanterie-Division ..	Infantry division.
I.E. (J.E.) (B.) (R.)	Infanterie Ersatz (Bataillon) (Regiment)	Infantry depôt (battalion) (regiment).
I.G. (J.G.) (Kp.)	Infanterie-Geschütz (Kompanie).	Infantry gun (company).
Inf.Btl. z.b.V. ..	Infanterie-Bataillon zur besonderen Verwendung	(*See* Bewährungs-Btl.)
Inf.Lehr-Rgt. ..	Infanterie-Lehr-Regiment	Infantry demonstration regiment.
Inf.Pk.	Infanterie-Park	Infantry equipment park.
I.R. (J.R.) ..	Infanterie-Regiment (now Grenadier-Regiment).	Infantry regiment.
Jäg.Btl. ..	Jäger-Bataillon	Raiding battalion.
Jagd-Btl. ..	Jagd-Bataillon	(*See* Jäger-Bataillon.)
Jäg.Rgt. ..	Jäger-Regiment	Rifle regiment in a light (Jäger) division.
K.	Kanone, Kanonier ..	Gun, gunner.
Kav.Lehr.Abt. ..	Kavallerie-Lehr-Abteilung	Cavalry demonstration battalion.
Kav.Rgt. ..	Kavallerie-Regiment ..	Cavalry regiment.
K.d.N.	Kommandeur der Nachschubtruppen.	O.C. supply troops.
Kdo.	Kommando	H.Q., command, detachment.
Kdr. der Bau-Tr.	Kommandeur der Bautruppen.	O.C. construction troops.
Kdr. der Kf.Pk. Tr.	Kommandeur der Kraftfahrparktruppen.	O.C. M.T. park troops.
Kdr. der Nachr. Tr.	Kommandeur der Nachrichtentruppen.	O.C. signals.
Kdt.	Kommandant	Commandant.
Kdtr.	Kommandantur	Administrative H.Q. Garrison H.Q.
Kesselwg.Kol. f.Betr.St.	Kesselwagenkolonne für Betriebstoff.	(*See* Betr.St.Kol.).
Kf.Pk.(Eisb.) ..	Kraftfahr Park (Eisenbahn)	M.T. Park (Railway).
Kfz.Abschlepp-Zug.	Kraftfahrzeug-Abschlepp-Zug.	M.T. recovery platoon.
Kfz.Inst.(Abt.) (Rgt.)	Kraftfahrzeug-Instandsetzungs- (Abteilung) (Regiment).	M.T. repair (unit) (regiment).
Kfz.Inst.Kp. ..	Kraftfahrzeug-Instandsetzungs-Kompanie.	M.T. repair company.
kl.Kw.Kol. ..	kleine Kraftwagenkolonne	Small M.T. column.
K.K.	Kreiskommandantur ..	Administrative H.Q. in occupied countries (battalion status).

Abbreviation.	*German.*	*English Equivalent.*
Kodina	Kommandeur der Divisions-Nachschubtruppen.	O.C. division supplies.
Kol.	Kolonne	Column.
Korück	Kommandant des rückwärtigen Armeegebiets.	O.C., army L. of C. area.
Kp.	Kompanie	Company.
K.R.	Kavallerie-Regiment ..	Cavalry regiment.
Krad	Kraftfahrrad	Motorcycle.
Kreiskdtr. ..	Kreiskommandantur ..	(*See* K.K.)
Krgf.Arb.Kdo. ..	Kriegsgefangene-Arbeits-Kommando.	Prisoner of war labour unit.
Krgf.Bau-u.Arb. Btl.	Kriegsgefangene-Bau- und Arbeits-Bataillon.	Prisoner of war labour and construction battalion.
Krgf.Hafen-Arb. Btl.	Kriegsgefangene-Hafen-Arbeiter Abteilung.	Prisoner of war dock labour battalion.
Krgs.Laz. ..	Kriegs-Lazarett	War hospital.
Krgs.Laz.Abt. ..	Kriegs-Lazarett-Abteilung	War hospital unit.
Krgs.Laz.Abt.(R)	Kriegs-Lazarett-Abteilung (Reserve).	War hospital unit (reserve).
Kr.Kw.Zug. ..	Krankenkraftwagen-Zug	Motor ambulance platoon.
Kr.Trsp.Abt. ..	Kranken-Transport-Abteilung.	Ambulance battalion
Kw.Trsp.Abt. ..	Kraftwagen-Transport-Abteilung.	M.T. battalion.
Kw.Trsp.Kol. ..	Kraftwagen-Transport-Kolonne.	M.T. column.
Kw.Trsp.Kp. z.b.V.	Kraftwagen-Transport-Kompanie zur besonderen Verwendung.	Special M.T. company.
Kw.Trsp.Rgt. ..	Kraftwagen-Transport-Regiment.	M.T. Regiment.
Landesbau-Btl.	Landesbau-Bataillon ..	Agricultural battalion.
Landw.	Landwehr	"Landwehr" (*i.e.*, men aged **35–45**).
Laz.Zg.	Lazarett-Zug	Hospital train.
Ldsch.Btl. ..	Landesschützen-Bataillon	Local defence battalion.
Ldsch.Rgt. ..	Landesschützen-Regiment	Local defence regiment.
Lehr Rgt. ..	Lehr-Regiment	Demonstration regiment.
Leichtkr.Krgs. Laz.	Leichtkranken-Kriegs-Lazarett.	War hospital for minor cases.
Leichtkr.Zg. ..	Leichtkranken-Zug ..	Hospital train for minor cases.

Abbreviation.	*German.*	*English Equivalent.*
L.E.	—	Low establishment.
le.(Pi.Kp.) . .	leichte (Pionier-Kompanie)	Light (engineer company).
l.F.H.	leichte Feldhaubitze . .	Light (10·5 cm.) gun-howitzer.
L.G.St.	Luftgau-Stab	Air District Staff (G.A.F.)
Luftsp	Luftsperre	Balloon barrage.
Ln.(Abt.) (Rgt.)	Luftnachrichten-(Abteilung) (Regiment).	G.A.F. signals (battalion) (regiment).
L.S.	Landesschützen	(*see* Ldsch.).
Lw.	Luftwaffe	German Air Force.
Lw.Felddiv. . .	Luftwaffe-Feld-Divisionen	G.A.F. field divisions.
Mar.Baubtl. . .	Marine-Baubataillon . .	Naval construction battalion.
M.G.Btl. . .	Maschinen-Gewehr-Bataillon.	Machine gun battalion.
Mors.	Mörser	Mortar, howitzer.
mot.	motorisiert	mechanised, motorised.
Mun. Verw.Kp. . .	Munitions-Verwaltungs-Kompanie.	Ammunition administration company.
N. / Na. / Nachr. } (Abt.) . .	Nachrichten (Abteilung) . .	Signals (battalion).
Nachr.Abt.St. z.b.V. . .	Nachrichten-Abteilung-Stab zur besonderen Verwendung.	Special signals battalion staff.
Nachr.Aufkl.Kp.	Nachrichten-Aufklärungs-Kompanie.	Signals reconnaissance company.
Nachr.Fern-Aufkl.Kp.	Nachrichten Fern Aufklärungs-Kompanie.	Long-range signals reconnaissance Company.
Nachr.Fü.z.b.V.	Nachrichten-Führer zur besonderen Verwendung	Special signals commander.
Nachr.Helf.(Abt.) (Tr.)	Nachrichten - Helferinnen-(Abteilung) (Trupp).	Signals female assistant (battalion) (detachment).
Nachr.Lehr-Regt.	Nachrichten-Lehr-Regiment.	Signals demonstration regiment.
Nachr.Nah Aufkl. Kp.	Nachrichten Nah-Aufklärungs-Kompanie.	Short-range signals reconnaissance company.
Nachr.Rgt.Stab. z.b.V.	Nachrichten-Regiment-Stab zur besonderen Verwendung.	Special signals regiment staff.

Abbreviation.	*German.*	*English Equivalent.*
Nachsch.Btl. ..	Nachschub-Bataillon ..	Supply battalion.
Nachsch.Kol.Abt.	Nachschub-Kolonnen-Abteilung.	Supply column battalion.
Nachsch.Kol.Abt. z.b.V.	Nachschub - Kolonnen - Abteilung zur besonderen Verwendung.	Supply column battalion staff.
Nachsch.Stab. z.b.V.	Nachschub-Stab zur besonderen Verwendung.	Special supply staff.
Nachsch.Tr.Sch.	Nachschub-Truppen-Schule.	Supply troops school.
Nbl.W.	Nebelwerfer	(*see* Werf.).
N.K.A.	Nachschub-Kolonnen-Abteilung.	Supply column battalion.
Nsch. (Kp.) ..	Nachschub (Kompanie) ..	Supply company.
Ob.Baustb. ..	Ober-Baustab	Higher construction staff.
ObFz.St. ..	Oberfeldzeug-Stab ..	Higher ordnance staff.
O.F.K.	Oberfeldkommandantur ..	Administrative headquarters in occupied country (divisional status).
Oflag	Offizierslager	Officer P.W. camp.
O.K.H.	Oberkommando des Heeres	Army High Command, War Ministry.
O.K.L.	Oberkommando der Luftwaffe.	Air Force High Command, Air Ministry.
O.K.M.	Oberkommando der Kriegsmarine.	Navy High Command.
O.K.W.	Oberkommando der Wehrmacht.	Armed Forces Supreme Command, Inter-service Ministry.
Ortskdtr. ..	Ortskommandantur ..	Administrative H.Q. in occupied countries (battalion status).
O.T.	Organisation Todt ..	Semi-military construction organisation (named after Dr. Fritz Todt).
Pfd.Trsp.Kol. (mot).	Pferde-Transport-Kolonne (motorisiert).	Motorised horse-transport column.
Pi.Btl.	Pionier-Bataillon	Engineer battalion.
Pi.Btl.z.b.V. ..	Pionier-Bataillon zur besonderen Verwendung ..	Engineer battalion staff.

Abbreviation.	*German.*	*English Equivalent.*
Pi.Landungs-Btl.	Pionier-Landungs-Bataillon.	Engineer landing battalion.
Pi.Landungs-K	Pionier-Landungs-Kompanie.	Engineer landing company.
Pi.Landungs-Rgt.	Pionier-Landungs-Regiment.	Engineer landing regiment.
Pi.Landungsboot-Kp.	Pionier-Landungsboot-Kompanie.	Engineer landing craft company.
Pi.Lehr-Btl. ..	Pionier-Lehr-Bataillon ..	Engineer demonstration battalion.
Pi.Lehr-Btl. für schw.Br.Bau.	Pionier-Lehr-Bataillon für schweren Brückenbau.	Engineer heavy bridging demonstration battalion.
Pi.Lehr-Btl.z.b.V.	Pionier-Lehr-Bataillon zur besonderen Verwendung.	Special engineer demonstration battalion.
Pi.Masch.Zg. ..	Pionier-Maschinen-Zug ..	Engineer machine platoon.
Pi.Pk.	Pionier-Park	Engineer equipment park.
Pi.Pk.Kp. ..	Pionier-Park-Kompanie ..	Engineer equipment park company.
Pi.Rgts.St. ..	Pionier-Regiments-Stab ..	Engineer regiment staff.
Pi.Rgt.z.b.V. ..	Pionier Regiment zur besonderen Verwendung	Special engineer regiment staff.
P.K.	Propagandakompanie ..	Propaganda company.
Pz.Abt.	Panzer-Abteilung ..	Tank battalion.
Pz.Abt.(F) ..	Panzer-Abteilung (Flammenwerfer).	Flame thrower tank battalion.
Pz.Bg.Zg. ..	Panzer-Bergezug	Tank salvage platoon
Pz.Gr., P.G. ..	Panzer-Grenadier ..	Infantry of an armoured division, or, in some cases of a Panzer-Grenadierdivision.
Pz.E.L.	Panzer-Ersatzteil-Lager ..	Tank spare parts depot.
Pz.Fz.Kdo. ..	Panzer-Feldzeug-Kommando.	Tank ordnance H.Q.
Pz.Inst.Abt. ..	Panzer-Instandsetzungs-Abteilung.	Tank repair unit.
Pz.Jäg.	Panzerjäger	Anti-tank (" tank hunter ").
Pz.Lehr.Rgt. ..	Panzer-Lehr-Regiment ..	Tank demonstration regiment.

Abbreviation.	*German.*	*English Equivalent.*
Pz.Werf.Abt. ..	Panzer-Werfer-Abteilung	Armoured projector battalion.
Pz.Werkst.Kp...	Panzer-Werkstatt-Kompanie.	Tank workshop company.
R.	Regiment	Regiment.
R.A.D.	Reichsarbeitsdienst ..	State Labour Service
Radf.Abt. ..	Radfahr-Abteilung ..	Bicycle battalion (*see* Aufklärungs).
r.Ag.	rückwärtiges Armeegebiet	L. of C.
Reif.Staff. ..	Reifen-Staffel	Tyre detachment.
Res.K.	Reserve-Korps	Reserve corps (controlling training divisions).
Res.Krgs.Laz. Abt.	Reserve-Kriegs-Lazarett-Abteilung.	(*see* Krgs. Laz. Abt. (R)).
R.R.	Reiter-Regiment ..	Cavalry regiment (horsed).
San.(Kp.) ..	Sanitäts(kompanie) ..	Medical (company).
Schlächt.Einh. ..	Schlächterei-Einheiten ..	Butcher units.
Schnee-R. (Rgt.) (Btl.)	Schnee-Räume-(Regiment) (Batallion).	Snow-removal (regiment) (battalion).
Scheinw.-Einh...	Scheinwerfer-Einheiten ..	Searchlight units.
schw.Werf.Rgt.	schwere Werfer Regiment	Heavy projector regiment.
sd. Funk-Überwa. Stelle.	sonder Funk-Überwachungs-Stelle.	Special W/T control station.
sd.Verbd. ..	Sonderverband	Special unit.
s.F.H.	schwere Feldhaubitze ..	15 cm. medium howitzer.
Sich.Btl. ..	Sicherungs-Bataillon ..	L. of C. battalion.
Sich.Rgt. ..	Sicherungs-Regiment ..	L. of C. regiment.
s.Pz.Jäg.Abt. ..	schwere Panzer-Jäger Abteilung.	Heavy anti-tank battalion.
S.S.	Schutzstaffel	"S.S." Nazi party troops.
St.	Stab	Staff, H.Q.
St., Staff. ..	Staffel	Echelon, detachment, G.A.F. operational unit.
Stalag.	Stammlager	P.W. camp for O.R.s
Stoart	Stabsoffizier, Artillerie ..	Artillery staff officer
Str.Baubtl. ..	Strassen-Baubataillon ..	Road construction battalion.
Str.Entg.Abt. ..	Strassen-Entgiftungs-Abteilung.	Road decontamination battalion.
Str.Dienst ..	Streifen-Dienst	Patrol service.
Stromsich.(Rgt.) (Btl.)	Stromsicherungs-(Regiment) (Bataillon).	Waterways guard (regiment) (battalion).

Abbreviation.	*German.*	*English Equivalent.*
Stubo.Kdo. ..	Sturmboot-Kommando ..	Assault boat detachment.
Stu.Gesch.Abt...	Sturmgeschütz-Abteilung	Assault gun battalion.
Stu.Rgt. ..	Sturm-Regiment ..	Assault regiment.
stv.	stellvertretend	Deputy.
Techn.Btl. ..	Technisches-Bataillon ..	Technical battalion.
tmot	teilmotorisiert	Partly mechanised.
Tr.	Trupp, Truppe	Detachment, troops, unit.
Tr.Entg.Kp. ..	Truppen-Entgiftungs-Kompanie.	Personnel decontamination company.
Trspt.Begl.(Rgt.) (Btl.)	Transport-Begleit-(Regiment) (Bataillon).	Transport escort (regiment) (battalion).
Tr.T.	Truppenteil	Unit.
Trspt.Kdtr. ..	Transport-Kommandantur	Transport office.
V.	Verwaltung	Administration.
Verk.Regl.Btl. ..	Verkehrsreglungs-Bataillon	Traffic control battalion.
Verl.St.	Verlade-Stab	(*see* Nachsch.St. z.b V.)
Verm. u.Kart. Abt.	Vermessungs- und Karten-Abteilung.	Survey and mapping battalion.
Verpfl.(A.) ..	Verpflegungs-(Amt) ..	Rations (office).
Vers.Btl. ..	Versuchs-Bataillon ..	Experimental battalion.
verst.(G.R.) ..	verstärktes (Grenadier-Regiment).	Reinforced (infantry regiment) (*i.e.* brigade group).
Vet.Kp. ..	Veterinär-Kompanie ..	Veterinary company.
V°.Messzug ..	Velocitäts-Messzug ..	Calibration troop.
Wa.Btl. ..	Wach-Bataillon	Guard battalion.
Wa.Rgt. ..	Wach-Regiment	Guard regiment.
Wass.Vers.Kp...	Wasser-Versorgungs-Kompanie.	Water purification company.
Werf.Abt. ..	Werfer-Abteilung ..	Projector battalion
Werf.Battr. ..	Werfer-Batterie	Projector troop.
Werf.Lehr-Rgt.	Werfer-Lehr-Regiment ..	Projector demonstration regiment.
Werf.Rgt. ..	Werfer-Regiment ..	Projector regiment.
Werf.Rgt.z.b.V.	Werfer-Regiment zur besonderen Verwendung.	Projector regimental staff.
Werkst. ..	Werkstatt	Workshop.
Werkst.Kp. ..	Werkstatt-Kompanie ..	Workshop company.

Abbreviation.	*German.*	*English Equivalent.*
Wett.Peilzg. ..	Wetter-Peil-Zug	Meteorological platoon.
W.F.St. ..	Wehrmachtführungsstab	Armed Forces operational staff.
Wi.Trspt.Ber. und Bz.	Wirtschaft-Transport-Bereich und Bezirk	Agricultural and industrial transport area.
Wi.Trspt.Brig. (z.b. V.)	Wirtschafts-Transport-Brigade (z.b. V.)	(Special) Agricultural and industrial transport brigade.
Wi.Trspt.Rgt. ..	Wirtschafts-Transport-Regiment.	Agricultural and industrial transport regiment.
Wi.Trspt.Abt. ..	Wirtschafts-Transport-Abteilung.	Agricultural and industrial transport battalion.
Wkr., W.K. ..	Wehrkreis	Military district.
Z.	Zugkraftwagen	Tractor (often used to indicate tractor-drawn).
z.b. V.	zur besonderen Verwendung	For special employment.
Z.E.L.	Zentral-Ersatzteil-Lager..	Central spare parts depot.
Zg.	Zug	Platoon, troop, section.
Zg.Wa.(Abt.) (Kp.)	Zugwach- (Abteilung) (Kompanie).	Train guards (battalion) (company).

(C51316) 5,000 4/44 (B.44/3)